WILLIAM III

WILLIAM III

and the Defense of European Liberty

1650-1702

By STEPHEN B. BAXTER

HARCOURT, BRACE & WORLD, INC.
NEW YORK

CONTENTS

LIST OF ILLUSTRATIONS

(Between pages 224 and 225)

William Henry in the arms of the Princess Royal

William Henry as a youth

William III

Mary II

Contemporary sketch of the Battle of Landen

William III at Torbay, 1688

Het Loo

The Funeral of William III, 1690

MAPS

PREFACE

AFTER the Treaties of Westphalia of 1648, and even more so after the conclusion of the Treaty of the Pyrenees in 1659, France stood without a rival in Europe. She made the most of her opportunities in the years of peace after 1659. Her rapidly growing prosperity provided a solid base for a flourishing cultural life; nor were her rulers idle. The efficiency of the central government increased and with it the size and quality of the French army and navy. French diplomats were as active and as successful as were Colbert, Le Tellier, and his son Louvois, the leaders of the administrative team at home. A system of alliances and understandings was built up which made resistance to French expansion seem hopeless. Then in 1667 there began a period of military aggression. If her first efforts were not particularly successful, the French did much better in the great war that broke out in 1672. It seemed that France was determined to achieve the domination of Europe, perhaps even a 'universal monarchy', and that nothing stood in her way. As success followed success what had originally been a commercial and territorial expansion was coupled with a revival of religious warfare. First in Utrecht in 1672 and then more systematically in the 1680s, French progress became identified with the interests of the Catholic cause. Protestantism was under attack as well as the political and economic liberty of Europe.

It was William III who was to oppose and eventually to contain French aggression. Although he secured the political and religious freedom of Europe, he was never an enemy of France or of the Catholic church so long as they stayed within their proper boundaries. There is something pathetic in the King's long struggle with the threat of a universal monarchy. William III admired and copied the French all his life. His ballet, his clothes, his bed, his palaces, all were French. One of his greatest ambitions was to earn the personal respect of Louis XIV. Yet he was forced to combat the ambitions of his cousin for the entire course of his public career. Nor was William III an enemy of Catholicism as such; the Mass was said daily in the chapel of his château at Orange, his personal attorneys in the Dutch Republic were Catholics, his most important ally was Leopold of Austria, and when he went to England in 1688 he saw to it that effective toleration was extended to the Catholic minority there. It is much more accurate to think of William III as the leader of a struggle for liberty and toleration than as a man fighting against France or the Catholic church.

Although William III was to be victorious, although in the course of the struggle he was to make England a great power, he has not had a very good press. We continue to refer to the Age of Louis XIV, not to the Age of William III. There are several reasons for this. In many ways the Prince was an anachronism, a dynastic figure in an age of nationalism. Louis XIV, Leopold I, and Frederick William of Brandenburg were also dynastic figures, but their positions had a compact territorial foundation. William's did not; he was at the same time a Dutch politician, an English prince, a German territorial magnate, and a French Huguenot hero. And he was more than this, he was a European. Had William III been content with any one of his tasks, it would be possible to praise him for party regularity; but since he was riding at least four horses he could not hope to win the approval of the fanatics of his own day, or of ours. Moderation and a devotion to the interests of Europe as a whole are not popular virtues.

William III has also suffered from the historians. It is difficult if not impossible to fit him into the history of any single nation. Dutch historians have held their Prince in high regard, but they have not felt him to be a very good Dutchman. English historians have been content to think of him as a foreigner, as Dutch William. No one cares to be placed in competition with Lord Macaulay, whose majestic *History of England* will continue to be a classic so long as any interest in English prose survives. Much new material, however, has come to light since Lord Macaulay wrote his masterpiece. The publication of the bulk of William's correspondence has made the task of a biographer far less difficult than it would have been even thirty years ago. This new material, and the present decline of nationalistic prejudice, may make it useful to take another look at one of the greatest men of modern times.

All of us depend to a very large extent on the work of those who went before us. My primary obligation is to the historians of past generations, and this book is essentially a footnote to their great labours. Among the living, I owe the greatest obligation to the kindness of the owners of private archives and to the custodians of manuscripts and printed books. The Queen of the Netherlands gave her gracious permission for the use of the manuscripts in the Koninklijk Huisarchief at The Hague. I am grateful to the Duke of Portland for the use of manuscripts on loan to the British Museum and to the University of Nottingham. The Duke of Marlborough, K.G., gave access to his family's papers at Blenheim Palace. I read the manuscripts of Sir William Trumbull, now at Reading, with permission of the Marquess of Downshire. The Earl Spencer allowed me to work through his manuscripts at Althorp and made my trip a delightful one by his kind hospitality. Count Aldenburg Bentinck did the same when I visited the lovely Kasteel Amerongen. Ihr. P. F.

O. R. Sickinghe, the Director of the Koninklijk Huisarchief, went out of his way to make my studies in Holland pleasant and fruitful. Everyone who uses this collection and those at the Algemeen Rijksarchief and the Koninklijk Bibliotheek must be grateful for the kindness and efficiency of their staffs; but I must make special mention of the helpfulness of Meester B. van 't Hoff of the Algemeen Rijksarchief. My gratitude to the staffs of the British Museum, the Public Record Office, the National Registry of Archives, the Bodleian Library, the Widener Library, the Folger Shakespeare Library, and the L. R. Wilson Library at Chapel Hill is of longer standing and is not dimmed by experience. Every foreign historian working in London owes much to Dr A. Taylor Milne of the Institute of Historical Research. Professor Pieter Geyl, Dr S. J. Fockema Andreae, and Professor Mark Thomson placed their great knowledge of the period at my disposal.

I am deeply grateful to Dr J. H. Plumb not only for guiding my first steps in the field of history but also for reading the proofs of this book at a time when he was very busy with his own work. His care has saved me from many errors. This book could not have been completed without a Guggenheim Fellowship and a leave of absence from the University of North Carolina. I received also two grants from the University Research Council, as well as a sum of money from the Trustees to supplement the Guggenheim Fellowship. The example and the kindness of my father and of my father-in-law, Mr James Johnson Sweeney, are always in my mind. My colleagues at Chapel Hill have been unfailing in their thoughtfulness. My greatest debt, as always, is to my wife.

Chapel Hill
November 1964

A NOTE ON DATES

By 1582 the Julian calendar was in error to an awkward extent, and Pope Gregory XIII ordered the suppression of ten days to bring things to rights. England, however, adhered to the Julian calendar until the middle of the eighteenth century, as did some continental states. In 1700 the discrepancy increased to eleven days. Thus the English 1 July 1699 (O.S. or Old Style) was the same day as the Gregorian 11 July 1699 (N.S. or New Style), while 1 July 1700 O.S. was the same day as 12 July 1700 N.S. The Julian calendar had the further peculiarity that the new year began on 25 March, so that 12 March 1677 O.S. was the same day as 22 March 1678 N.S. In this book, following modern practice, English dates are given in Old Style, but with the new year beginning on 1 January. Continental dates are given in the New Style, and both dates are given where there might be confusion.

WILLIAM III

Chapter 1

ORANGE PHOENIX

ALTHOUGH October of 1650 marked the second anniversary of the treaties of Westphalia, the world was still far from a real peace. France and Spain, of course, were still at war. Louis XIV, the child King of France, was also at war with his own people. During the summer the boy was taken to watch his armies besiege the town of Bordeaux. His presence gave courage to the royalist soldiers while it disheartened the rebellious citizens, and before the month was over Bordeaux had surrendered. Elsewhere the turmoil was just as great. On 3 September Oliver Cromwell had smashed the Scottish army at Dunbar at a cost of less than thirty English lives. Though Charles II was not present at Dunbar, the defeat made his position more precarious than ever before. His enemies were in full control in England, while his Scottish subjects gave him little respect and less freedom of action. If he still had an army, his prospects were gloomy indeed in every other way. Even in Germany the second anniversary of the treaties had little meaning. Commissioners were now sitting at Nuremberg to settle the many problems that had not been solved at Münster or at Osnabrück. In June they had given themselves a fine dinner to celebrate their progress; but the festivities were premature, for the last troops would not evacuate Pomerania until 1653.

There might have been more reason for celebration in the United Provinces, since the Dutch had formally secured their independence by the treaties. Willem II, Prince of Orange and Stadhouder of the United Provinces, had however opposed the peace and saw little reason to celebrate its anniversary. During almost the whole of the month of October he stayed at his country house at Dieren, spending his time in hunting. The weather was remarkably bad – cold and windy, with almost continual rain. Even so, the Prince insisted on hunting every day. On the 27th he varied his programme by playing a spirited game of billiards. By the time the game was over Willem II was sweating freely. Yet without stopping to dry himself or to change his clothes, he set out immediately afterwards and hunted for seven hours. When he returned he went to bed early, complaining of a pain in his groin.[1]

Next morning the Prince was still unwell. He had some fever and refused to eat anything. The Prince's sickness, and the bad weather, ruined the hunting party. Sometime during the day the decision was taken to return to

The Hague, where the Princess would be waiting. She was eight months pregnant with her first child and would be happy to have company. Perhaps also there would be news from Scotland about the success of her brother, Charles II, in his attempts to bring his subjects to reason. It would not disturb the Prince to travel by yacht down the Rhine and the Leck to Rotterdam, and from there to The Hague by canal, because he could stay in bed all the way. The party reached the Binnenhof at four o'clock Saturday morning.[2]

On Sunday the Prince was a little worse. His headache and fever continued to bother him. He was very thirsty; his urine was troubled; there was a tightness in the chest and some difficulty in breathing. In the morning the Prince agreed to an enema, which he had refused the day before, and in the afternoon he was let blood. He ate a little and drank some beer and some lemonade. Then as now the local water had an unpleasant taste and was improved by syrups. The next morning van der Straten, the Prince's doctor, noticed small pustules on the arms and chest, and over the whole body. This confirmed his tentative diagnosis of smallpox. Count Schomberg, the Prince's First Gentleman of the Chamber, was sent to inform the Princess's household and to arrange for a quarantine inside the Palace. The servants of the Princess, who had never had smallpox, were forbidden to cross over to the Prince's side. A halbardier was stationed at the connecting door to see that these orders were carried out.[3]

Now there was some cause for alarm and van der Straten could no longer bear the responsibility for the Prince's condition by himself. On Tuesday 1 November Doctors Reeck and Hayes were called in for consultation. During the course of the day William's mother, the Princess Dowager of Orange, came to see him. She had had smallpox, and since she lived in a separate palace of her own in the Noordeynde she did not need to observe the quarantine. We know that she asked the Prince to write a letter to his wife and that he did not write it; we do not know what he was supposed to say or why he refused. It was said at the time that the effort of writing might have given him a chill. In the end the Princess Dowager sent a message of her own, to the effect that all was going well and that there was no reason to worry.[4]

Her picture of the situation was too optimistic. The pox were not opening as they should, and smallpox was a most dangerous disease, often a fatal one. On Wednesday Lord Percy[5] came to dine with the Heer van Heenvliet, who was Superintendent of the Princess's household. Percy insisted that care must be taken to provide for a will.[6] To this Heenvliet and his wife, Lady Stanhope, could only agree. The Princess was not yet nineteen and was generally supposed to be completely under the influence of her Superintendent and her former Governess. Should she become a widow, the Heenvliets would be in a position of great power, but if there were no will and the Princess Dowager had her way, the Heenvliets might very well be dismissed, for the Princess Dowager was a dangerous enemy. Meanwhile, the Prince of Orange submitted to another enema and ate a very little chicken hash. His pulse and urine were better than they had been, and he had a good night. For the next few days he seemed to be on the mend. The whole Court relaxed, and there was no more talk of wills.

On Sunday morning, 6 November, the pox broke through on the Prince's back and also on his face. At five that evening his fever was higher than ever, but the medicines prescribed brought immediate relief. They did so much good that two of the attending physicians felt able to go home for four hours' rest; but in half an hour the fever was as high as before and they had to be called back. The Princess Dowager was sent for. Everyone in the sickroom knelt while a minister said prayers. When Heenvliet came back on duty in the Princess's quarters, a little after eight o'clock, he was told the bad news. The Superintendent went to find the Princess Royal, who was sitting at a table talking quietly with a few people. He said, simply, 'The Prince is very ill', and she had enough presence of mind to go to her own chamber before she burst into tears. After delivering his message Heenvliet went downstairs and saw the surgeon. When he asked how things went, the surgeon whispered in his ear 'Dead, or as good as dead.'[7] It was true. At about nine there were a few quiet gasps, and then the Prince was gone. Heenvliet needed a drink before he could face his employer, who was weeping in her chamber with Lady Stanhope. It was not until much later that anyone dared tell her that her husband had died.

The night was not yet over. Until two in the morning messages passed back and forth between Heenvliet and the Princess Dowager, who was sitting in Schomberg's room in the Prince's quarter. Gradually it became clear that the death of William II had done nothing to end the quarrels which divided the House of Orange. These quarrels were old ones, going back at least as far as 1646, perhaps even to 1641 and the marriage of the Prince with Mary of England. The Princess Royal had never been on good terms with her mother-in-law. Her husband was not fond of the Princess Amalia either; she was not, indeed, an amiable woman. Amalia von Solms-Braunfels had grown up at Heidelberg, where her father was an official at the Court of the Elector Palatine. She herself became a lady-in-waiting to the Princess Elizabeth, daughter of James I of England, who was then Electress Palatine and later, briefly, Queen of Bohemia. With the failure of the Bohemian venture the entire Court took refuge at The Hague, where Amalia caught the eye of the aging Stadhouder, Prince Maurice. In 1624 Maurice persuaded his brother Frederick Henry to marry her, and secured for him the succession to all his places in the Dutch government. The marriage was generally considered a *mésalliance*.[8]

As Princess of Orange, Amalia von Solms performed her first duty well, bearing her husband nine children, of whom five lived to maturity. Unfortunately she was very badly educated and almost completely without culture.[9] Physical purity was almost her only virtue. Naturally she was too busy with her children, too much younger than her husband, to have much influence on the Court. Husband and wife did at least share a passion for display coupled with intense social ambition. Their boy must marry one of the daughters of Charles I and Henrietta Maria. That was the plan in 1638.[10] By 1640, however, Charles I in his troubles was willing to go further and to offer his eldest daughter; the wedding took place next year when the bride was ten. Later an equally brilliant match was arranged for Louise Henriette, the eldest daughter, with the Elector of Brandenburg. Amalia was the most successful social climber of her day[11] and her efforts were warmly supported by her equally ambitious husband.

For the people of the Dutch Republic the dynastic policies of the Prince and Princess of Orange posed a serious problem. These marriages were not negotiated in the national interest, but solely in the interests of the family.[12] The United Provinces were then in the last stages of their Eighty Years War for independence from Spain. An English marriage might actually harm the war effort, because Henrietta Maria hated her brother's chief minister, Richelieu, and the French were the chief ally of the Dutch. An English marriage might even bring about the end of the Republic; it gave clear evidence that Frederick Henry was thinking along monarchical lines. His office was not hereditary. Its title, Stadhouder, translates most easily into Viceroy, and his position resembled that of a Lord-Lieutenant of Ireland. Since the House of Orange had held the position for generations, and since the reversion had already been voted to Frederick Henry's son, there was the obvious danger that the hereditary principle would be established. It would not take much more to turn the Republic into a kingdom. Frederick Henry himself had originally been content with 'Excellency' as a form of address. Now the French gave him 'Altesse', and a princely coronet into the bargain. Every Dutch republican could see how things were shaping.

The English marriage was so obvious a step towards monarchy that it united all parties in the Republic against the Prince.[13] Each of the seven Provinces had its own legislature, or States, and its own Stadhouder as well. Frederick Henry, as it happened, was Stadhouder in only six of the provinces, but he was Captain-General and Admiral-General of the Union. Of these States the most important and independent and the leader of the fight against the Prince was the States of Holland. Holland alone paid over half the taxes of the entire Republic, which gave it the strength to fight for its wishes in the legislature of the Union, the States General, and to force through a policy of neutrality in the English Civil Wars.[14] The Prince, naturally, wanted to give active support to the Stuarts. On this issue he was even deserted by his usual supporters, the orthodox Calvinist clergy. The *predikanten* hated any connection with bishops, and so opposed Charles I, supporting instead the English and Scottish Presbyterians. The Prince could not prevent the adoption of the policy of neutrality, but he did manage to evade it, using his personal resources and those of the state to assist the Royalists. His assistance was enough to annoy Parliament and to disorder the finances of the House of Orange. It was not enough to save Charles I.

Frederick Henry was finally brought to book in 1646. In the spring of that year there appeared in Dutch translation a version of the secret papers of Charles I[15] which disclosed, among other things, the misuse of state resources by the Prince. It meant the virtual end of his career. By now his health was declining rapidly, and he died in 1647.[16]

By the spring of 1646, when Frederick Henry's help to the Royalists was exposed, his mind was in full decay. His wife could now make him do whatever she wanted, and she wanted peace with Spain. The malicious noted that she was to receive two estates in the Spanish Netherlands from Spain on the conclusion of the peace. They felt that she had been bribed yet again, as she had been once before by the French when Richelieu sent her an enormous pair of diamond earrings. While the Cardinal lived, the jewels prevented any word hostile to France from entering the Princess's ear. His death seemed to have robbed them of their magic powers.[17] At this time the Princess was supposed to be so pro-Spanish that the French ambassador, d'Estrades, hoped for the early death of Frederick Henry, since the Princess would have little influence over her son. William wanted the war to continue until he should gain a military reputation. He was also a warm admirer of d'Estrades and of his preceptor Count Schomberg, both of whom were eventually to become Marshals of France. Either one of them had much greater influence with him than did his mother.[18]

In many ways William II was a rather grubby young man. He had grown up pudgy and spoiled, the victim of what would now be called 'permissive education'. By the age of fifteen he was apparently a man of experience. When he married a girl of ten it was not the plan that they should actually live together for some time. There must be a public bedding after the wedding ceremony, however, and the English took the precaution of sewing the hem of the bride's nightdress together to protect her. From the Prince's boasting to his gentlemen the next day, one would gather that the precaution was not unwise. In any case, he soon entered on a dissolute course of life, becoming at eighteen the protector of a mevrouw d'Alonne [19] and perhaps the father of her son. There were other ladies. William gambled heavily; even worse, from the point of view of the clergy, was his support of a band of French players. This irregular way of life was accompanied by laziness in the performance of business. As early as the time of his marriage, William refused to be bothered with second drafts of his French letters, though his spelling was wretched. [20] Pieter Geyl sums up the general opinion when he argues that the Prince was not really fit to be Stadhouder: that he played too much Dutch tennis, drank too much, hunted too much, and at first worked too little. When he did work, his youth, his inexperience, his immorality robbed him of the respect and cooperation of the leaders of the Republic. [21]

In 1646 it had been easy for Amalia to arouse the jealousy of the old Prince against the son who seemed to want to bury him before his time. A year later, when Frederick Henry was dead, William II automatically succeeded to all his places. But now his ignorance of foreign affairs proved to be a fatal handicap. Again and again the young man had to go to his mother or the States of Holland for advice. Naturally enough the advice was slanted. Amalia, furthermore, used the so-called Orange Party against her son in the States General. Many of his father's partisans, many even in William's own pay, treated him as a little boy and obeyed the orders of the Dowager. One of the most prominent of these was Johan Knuyt, who represented the Prince as First Noble of Zeeland in the States of that province and in the States General. Knuyt played a major part in the treaty negotiations and was actually a signatory. When the Prince lost patience and asked his mother to leave The Hague until the end of the negotiations, she simply refused to go. [22] The Princess had her way in 1648. By the Treaties of Westphalia, Spain finally recognized the independence of the United Provinces. Amalia received her two Belgian estates. The Prince of Orange was humiliated, the French abandoned and left to fight on alone for another eleven years.

From this point onward the Orange party was breaking up. Bitter memories of the struggle over the Treaties did not fade, because William kept trying to resume the war, and the Dowager, with Holland, kept emphasizing the necessity of peace. This party split demoralized the Court; and there was now a further quarrel in the family. Amalia was especially fond of her eldest daughter, Louise Henriette, whom she had forced to marry the Elector of Brandenburg. The settlements provided that if William should die without issue, Louise Henriette would be the heir to the entire Orange fortune. This alone would have made her brother jealous, as the years passed and he had no legitimate children. Louise Henriette made things worse by her tactless fondness for her husband's station. She claimed that she, as an Electress, should take precedence over the Princess Royal; the latter, she argued, was merely the wife of an official and not of a reigning prince. The Princess Royal, in turn, claimed precedence as a king's daughter. The two sisters-in-law refused to meet. William supported his wife, as he was always very careful to do in public; her position was also kinder to his own dignity. William was so angry with his sister that he conceived the plan of outwilling her. As early as November 1647 he discussed provisions for a will of his own with Laurens Buysero, the Recorder of the Nassausche Domeinraad or Prince's Council.[23] One of the most important of these provisions was the substitution of the second sister, Albertine Agnes, as his heir presumptive.[24] At the time of his death, the will was unsigned.

On that Sunday night in November 1650 the question of the Orange succession was in complete confusion. The Princess Royal was in the last stages of pregnancy. She was a thin woman, in some of her portraits a scrawny one; under such great strain she might easily miscarry. Even if a child should be born, its chances of survival were not very good. Amalia had raised only five of her nine children, and many royal and noble families of the day did not do so well. In any case, the world could not wait for a month to see whether there was to be a child. Some arrangements must be made at once. First, the business papers and jewels of the Prince must be sealed in their chests and cabinets to make sure that the estate remained intact. There were, next, three business matters to settle. With the death of the Prince, the authority of his commissions lapsed at once. A new commission must be sent to the Governor of the Principality of Orange, that small independent state completely surrounded by French territory which lay on the banks of the Rhone. Then Knuyt must have a fresh appointment as representative of the First Noble of Zeeland. Finally, a Spanish agent was now in The Hague for the signing of the private treaty between the House of Orange and Spain covering the Orange holdings in the Spanish Empire. This private treaty must be signed at once. Knuyt and Buysero came from the Dowager to the Princess Royal and insisted that she give her immediate assent to the three points. At this time, however, Mary did not yet know of the death of her husband. She was weeping, in great distress, begging to be allowed to see him. It was all the preachers could do to tell her she was too late. Heenvliet saw to it that she was not troubled with business that night.[25]

In the coming struggle Heenvliet was to prove an invaluable ally of the Princess Royal. A Dutchman, the son of a distinguished professor of theology at Leyden, Johan van Kerckhoven, heer van Heenvliet had been employed by the States General as ambassador to Charles I in the negotiations relating to the marriage in 1641. He had made such an impression on Charles that he returned to Holland with an English appointment to a place in the bride's household. Heenvliet had consolidated this position by marrying the

Governess of the Princess Royal, Lady Stanhope.[26] The couple acted to bridge the gap between local society and the English at The Hague, many of whom prided themselves on their inability to speak Dutch. Around them and the acknowledged bastards of Frederick Henry and Maurice grew up a so-called English faction, consisting of Dutch nobles who had either married Englishwomen or who for other reasons supported the Stuart cause. The Dowager, on her part, tended to attract those who disliked the bastards and the English socially, as well as those who wanted peace. She had slightly simpler manners than her daughter-in-law, a much greater knowledge of Dutch politics, and a command of the language. She had, as well, the support of the ablest of the servants of the family, Constantijn Huygens.

There can be little doubt of the existence of a bitter personal feud between Constanter, as he signed his poems, and Heenvliet. For many reasons Constanter's side of the story has had a better press. Huygens was an able poet in a land which reveres its poets; he was a first class diplomat; he built the road which connects The Hague with the magnificent beach at Scheveningen and so earned the gratitude of a people who worship the combination of sun and sand; and he was the father of Christiaan Huygens the great mathematician, whose portrait decorates a modern Dutch banknote. He is, in short, something of a national hero. When we learn that his flower garden was trampled down by the feet of the Princess Royal's toughs, it is only natural that we should sympathize. It is undoubtedly true that Huygens chose the side of the Princess Dowager reluctantly, and that he did so in the sincere conviction that Amalia represented the best interests of the House of Orange and of the Republic. But it must be remembered that Constanter made a very good thing out of his choice, for himself and his children; that he was a dirty fighter, concealing material evidence and trying to exercise undue influence on the judiciary; and that on the broad issue of the Princess Dowager he was probably wrong. Amalia was never a Dutch patriot, and at this time her hatred of her daughter-in-law blinded her even to the best interests of her House.[27]

With Huygens taking the side of the Princess Dowager, Mary was especially lucky to have the support of Heenvliet. Possibly his personality made the struggle a little more bitter than it might have been. But he did good work, and Mary had great need of a native Dutchman of real talent. Still almost a child, reading perhaps but certainly not speaking Dutch, Mary would have been hopelessly lost without Heenvliet.

Heenvliet's first goal was to keep the Princess Royal from having a miscarriage; his second was to keep her from committing herself to anything before her baby was born. It was well that he did so, for two of the three demands of the Dowager were traps. The Governor of Orange, Frederick von Dohna, was a nephew of Amalia. His estates all lay in territories of the Elector of Brandenburg. He was, therefore, utterly dependent on the faction of Louise Henriette. William II had given von Dohna a sealed letter, ordering him in the event of his death to open it and obey its contents. The letter instructed him to hold the Principality of Orange for Mary against all others, if William had no children.[28] When von Dohna learned of the contents of the letter he refused to obey his instructions, and it was to take ten years and a siege in form by Louis XIV to get him out of the Principality. At this time the Princess Royal apparently did not know of the letter, and of course her husband's papers which contained a copy were now sealed up. A confirmation of von Dohna's appointment might, at this time, have been an irreparable mistake. In the matter of Knuyt's reappointment as representative of the First Noble of Zeeland, Mary was herself aware of the trap. Her husband had never forgiven Knuyt's disloyalty of 1647 and 1648. One of the last things William had told her was that he had actually dismissed Knuyt and appointed another Zeelander, Thibaut, as his representative.[29] The dismissal must have been a private one, or Knuyt would never have dared to try to bluff his way through.

The treatment of Mary in the week after 6 November might almost have been devised on purpose to ensure a miscarriage. Constantijn Huygens began the hostilities by refusing to write the letters informing the princes of Europe of William's death.[30] The Princess might draft them herself, if she wished to; there was to be no cooperation from the Domeinraad. At this, van Heenvliet retained counsel to protect the Princess Royal until she came to term.[31] They advised her not to act at all and to agree to no action taken by anyone else. There were daily battles with the Domeinraad, with the Dutch courts, and with the Princess Dowager over the administration of the estates. Mary and her advisers remained firm in refusing to act prematurely. On the 10th the Princess Royal had to begin receiving visits of condolence. Those of the representatives of Holland, the States General, and of the city of Amsterdam involved speeches to which she must listen and make a gracious reply. Monday the 14th was her nineteenth birthday, but this was no time for rejoicing. By now her chamber was hung in black and her women, according to the contemporary prints, were in full mourning. At half-past two in the afternoon she fell into labour. Amalia was summoned to the bedside. We do not know what they said as the hours passed. Finally, at half-past eight, a boy was born. A healthy boy.

Chapter 2

THE REVOLUTION OF 1651

THE special couriers who carried the news of Prince William's death rode hard, reaching Amsterdam in six hours. The common people there could not conceal their joy [1] while the richer sort increased their almsgiving in gratitude for such an unexpected boon. One of them put several gold pieces in the poorbox, wrapped up in a piece of paper which bore the words

> De Prins is doot
> Myn Gaef vergroot
> Noyt blyder Maer
> In tachtigh Jaer

'The Prince is dead, my gift the more; never so happy in years fourscore.' [2]

In other cities of the province, though the feeling was expressed less openly, it was certainly shared. Holland and the Prince had carried their quarrel to such lengths that, although the formalities were to be observed, partisan hatreds could not be hidden. And there was no hope that the Holland party would neglect this wonderful opportunity to assert, unopposed, its interpretation of the Dutch constitution. For behind the personalities which gave the fighting much of its bitterness lay a fundamental question: was sovereignty to reside in the States General, representing the Republic as a whole, or in the States of each individual province? As a practical matter, sovereignty in the hands of the States General meant sovereignty exercised by the Orange Party; sovereignty of the seven individual provinces meant the rule of Holland over the other six, justified by the ability of her politicians and by the fact that Holland alone paid more than half the taxes of the Republic.

It is always a difficult, indeed it is probably an impossible task to sympathize with the position of a minority party in another country. Few Englishmen during the last great war understood the widespread American hatred of Franklin Roosevelt, as few Americans understood the feelings of the Labour Party towards Sir Winston Churchill. The foreigner tends to be impatient, to say 'You are trying to swim against the tide of history. You will undoubtedly lose, and lose ingloriously. Why not drown now?' Such impatience is the result of ignorance of the other country's domestic issues, coupled with disregard of the basic conservative premise that since defeat is inevitable in the long run, delay is the best one can hope for. Most partisans, of course, refuse even to admit that defeat is inevitable. The aristocratic party in the province of Holland probably thought it could win, using the slogan 'Liberty' and the claims of provincial rights to screen a plutocracy. But it was bound to lose in the end, because the commercial advantages it sought meant war, while its supremacy inside the Republic could only be achieved by the destruction of the Dutch Army as a fighting force. And even the destruction of the army, necessary as that was to weaken the Orange party, could not destroy the Orange party if it had good leadership. From 1646 to 1668 there was no Orange leader worth the name, and in these years the Hollanders governed with little difficulty. When in 1668 it began to appear that one day the Orangists might have a leader, and when it became clear in 1672 that they did have one, the party of 'Liberty' melted away like morning mist.

In modern times the cry for 'Liberty' has found almost as little sympathy among Dutch historians as it has among foreign observers of Dutch history. Provincial sovereignty was not a success; in the Netherlands as elsewhere the trend has been toward national unity. The great bulk of Dutch historical writing, therefore, has been Orangist in sentiment; possibly unfairly so. Pieter Geyl has done his best to redress the balance, reminding us that the dynastic policies of Frederick Henry and of William II were opposed to the national interest.[3] He goes further and argues that the States General did not deserve obedience and respect, since it was a thoroughly corrupt body and really nothing more than a tool of the Orange party.[4] Here, it seems to me, the argument becomes irrelevant. If the States General was corrupt, so too were the municipal governments controlled by the Holland party. Elections to municipal office were as irregular and the profits of office as large – in the shape of lower tax assessments on the property of the victors and increased assessments on loser's property – as in the golden days a hundred years ago in England and the United States. All politics in the seventeenth century was corrupt by any modern standard. The real charge against the Orange party is that it did not provide leadership for a generation after 1646. Someone, somehow, must provide that leadership if the Republic were to survive. Holland did provide it, corruptly, unconstitutionally, and at first brilliantly. Given the fatal and continuing split within the Orange party there was no alternative.

Seventeenth-century politics was a corrupt game; it was also a rough one. In England Charles I had cropped the ears of his opponents and they ended by cropping his head. In France there was the Fronde. In Germany, as we shall see, the Emperor Leopold was to make rather a habit of kidnapping the opposition. For a time it seemed as if the Dutch would play the game as roughly as their neighbours, as roughly as they had once played it themselves when another anti-Orange movement had cost Jan van Oldenbarnevelt his head in 1619. The main issue between the Dutch parties was the cost of government, especially of the army. Even in Frederick Henry's time the majority in Holland, led by the government of Amsterdam, had tried several times to reduce the cost of the war by decreasing the size of the army. Holland, furthermore, was largely in favour of Parliament in the English Civil Wars and opposed to the Stuart inclinations of Frederick Henry and his son. The main issue, though, was the cost and size of the army, and with the peace it would now be possible to effect a major reduction. At the same time peace meant that it would be possible to tax certain newly acquired territories, notably the Prince's barony of Breda, as highly as Holland was taxed. The economy campaign was a general attack on the Orange party.

The Council of State, controlled by William II, originally proposed a reduction in the size of the armed forces which would save fl.2,544,197 per annum. Holland felt that this saving was inadequate, and when she discovered that she could not carry the other provinces with her she simply wrote letters to the commanders of troops paid from Holland taxes that they were to expect no more pay after 20 July 1648. This threat was undoubtedly unconstitutional, a violation of the Union of Utrecht; but it was partially successful. By the end of 1649 the Prince was offering further cuts which would amount to fl.1,350,700 per annum. Even this was not enough, and when the Prince made a third proposal in May 1650, it too failed to give satisfaction. Orders were given to send out letters to the infantry captains and cavalry majors affected, that Holland thanked them for their services and that they were to expect no further payment.

On Whitsunday 5 June the Prince appeared at a special session of the States General and obtained by majority vote a notable victory. The States General decided to write to the officers involved reminding them that their oath bound them to the service of the whole Republic and that they could not disband without its authorization. Secondly, a special mission would be sent to the individual cities in the province of Holland to persuade them to change their minds about the separate disbanding. Thirdly, the Prince was authorized to take all necessary steps for the preservation of peace and quiet, and especially for the maintainance and protection of the Union. The vote was only four provinces to three, and the attendance was so low that Holland could deny the validity of the proceedings; but it was enough for the Prince. He decided to lead the mission himself.

William left The Hague with a large suite on 8 June and went first to Dordrecht, where his representative Aartsbergen[5] harangued the town fathers. When he received a dusty answer, Aartsbergen lost his temper and threatened them with the loss of life and property for their attacks on the Union. Instead of being frightened by this, Jacob de Witt promised to report

Aartsbergen and his language to the next meeting of the States of Holland, refusing to have anything further to do with the missionaries. From Dordrecht the Prince and his party wandered unhappily through the rest of Holland, obtaining at best general responses that promised nothing. At Amsterdam the town council refused at first to give a hearing to the Prince as a representative of the States General, but only as Stadhouder of Holland. When he agreed to appear in that capacity he was refused again. Haarlem, Delft and Medemblik also refused to receive the mission, which met with real success only at the notoriously Orangist Leyden. The whole manoeuvre was a pitiable failure, lowering still further the already shaky prestige of William II. Its only possible justification would be that it was meant to fail, as some said it was.

There followed a war of pamphlets and sermons, while negotiations were carried on between the States of Holland and the States General over the size of the army. Holland came close to the Prince's third and most moderate proposal, but not close enough; and there was every reason to believe that if Holland were satisfied this year she would soon be back for more. The Prince came to the conclusion that he must resort to force. On the morning of 30 July, between eight and nine o'clock, he invited six unsuspecting members of the States of Holland to his quarters in the Binnenhof where they were arrested and taken, the next evening, to the castle of Loevestein. The most prominent of the six was Jacob de Witt; all the others had also distinguished themselves by their opposition to the special mission. Meanwhile, on the afternoon of the 29th, Count William of Nassau had left The Hague with orders to occupy Amsterdam with cavalry. The plan was for various dispersed forces to gather during the night, so as to reach the city before dawn. But the night was exceptionally dark and rainy; one troop, lacking a guide, was late at the rendezvous; the Hamburg postboy was allowed to ride through the army to Amsterdam, where he gave the alarm. When Count William reached the banks of the Amstel late the next morning, his chance was gone. Amsterdam was in arms. Not only had the plan misfired, but Count William and his men were in some danger, because the burghers could cut the seawall and drown the lot of them without endangering the city.

It was at this point, faced by disaster, that William II showed for the first time in his life some signs of ability. Had the attack against Amsterdam succeeded, he might have been able to cover his success with the authority of the vote of 5 June, to claim that this was a necessary step for the maintenance and protection of the Union. But no suspect vote could justify failure. Now there would have to be a compromise, and it must be reached quickly: there are few timebombs so dangerous as a spoiled *coup d'état*. For three days, after the Prince had hurried to the camp before Amsterdam, the issue was in doubt. Then on 3 August the Prince and the city came to terms which were a triumph for William II. His leading enemy in Amsterdam, Cornelis Bicker, would resign from the city government. The army would receive its arrears and its peacetime strength would be that of William's third proposal. For the future no single province was to cashier troops by its own act. It was almost miraculous; but it was not victory. Had Count William succeeded, an entirely new and pliant administration would have been imposed on the city. Now Bicker was gone, yes; but the others remained, furious at the attempted *coup* and contemptuous of its failure. They would fortify the city to make sure that nothing of the kind could happen again, raising the height of the walls, palisading the canals, hiring a special engineer from Antwerp, turning the civic guard into what was virtually a private army.[6] Safe behind their new walls they would continue to oppose the Orange party with new prudence because of the prisoners still at Loevestein, but with new bitterness. And they would oppose with the old success, for the Prince lost a major vote in the States General in September. William II had done very well not to be ruined in the collapse of his plans in July. He had retrieved a lost battle; he had not won a war.

The cheering of the Amsterdammers at the news of the death of the Prince was the voice of revolution. It was to be an exceptionally mild one, bloodless and almost without victims of any kind, but a revolution nonetheless. The prisoners left Loevestein and resumed their former honours as if they had never lost them. Holland took the lead in offering to most of her towns control of their own municipal elections; hitherto the Stadhouder had chosen the aldermen and in some cases the burgomasters as well. With this step the merchant oligarchy escaped all control. The bulk of the population was totally unrepresented, and even the larger part of the middle class lacked the vote. In exceptional cases, the lower middle class could make its wishes felt through its membership in the civic guard, or *schutterij*. No regent would care to alienate the *schutterij* and so risk exposing his house and family to the mob. With this one limitation, however, the great merchants were now supreme.[7] The States of Holland assumed the gift of military offices, certain appointments at the University of Leyden, the right of pardon: in short, the attributes of the sovereignty it claimed.[8] Most of the other provinces followed the example of Holland, and even in faithful Zeeland the post of First Noble was suppressed. Count William of Nassau remained, of course, Stadhouder of Friesland. He succeeded in having himself elected Stadhouder of Groningen as well, which aroused violent suspicions on the part of true Orangists. But five provinces remained without a head, as did the army and navy. And the Republic, without a head, was at the mercy of the party of 'Liberty'.

In 1651 the Loevesteiners were not vindictive. Perhaps they were not strong enough to attempt a policy of revenge, perhaps they acted from nobler motives. Whatever the reason, the Orange party escaped remarkably lightly. A general amnesty protected even the ringleaders of the assault on Amsterdam, though of course the vote of 5 June 1650 was declared illegal and the city reimbursed for the money spent on its new fortifications. The House of Orange was now to be relatively poor, since the salaries of all his offices disappeared with William II.[9] The family did retain a remarkable series of tax privileges, which extended so far that they covered the lands of the sister of the Princess Dowager. The Princess Royal and her son continued to occupy their quarters in the Binnenhof, once the palace of the ancient Counts of Holland and now state property. Perhaps, in theory, the House of Orange was now no more than a private family. In fact, its privileges during this 'First Stadhouder-less Period' remained substantial down to 1667; and if they were curtailed then, it was at a time when the family was, most reasonably, suspected of treason.

From the very beginning the little baby in the special suite of delivery chambers was a person of international importance. From the very beginning the people of the Netherlands took him to their hearts. At his birth the bells of the capital were rung and the people rejoiced as for the birth of a king. On 15 January 1651 the baby was baptized in the Great Church, sponsored by his great-aunt the Queen of Bohemia, the Princess Dowager, the States General, the States of Holland and of Zeeland, and the towns of Delft, Leyden, and Amsterdam. Though the Groote Kerk was hung with black baize in mourning for William II it was a festive occasion. Some people had to climb the organ to get a good view. So many others crowded the benches that many of these broke, while the size of the crowds disconcerted the choir, which sang out of tune. The preacher had no chance to get the attention of such a congregation, even by clapping his hands for order, and finally had to abandon his sermon. In the midst of this hearty if muddled enthusiasm the boy was somehow christened William Henry. The names were popular, but the ceremonial was too stately for the Republicans. The baby's carriage had been accompanied by halbardiers as if he were Stadhouder. Worse, he wore an ermine train; no Orange had ever worn ermine before, and the claim to royal status was a little too obvious. The people did not care what the baby wore, and the startled godparents had to pretend that they did not notice. After the ceremony each of them called on the Princess Royal, presenting her with their compliments, generous presents for the Prince,[10] and smaller sums in cash to cover the expenses of the lying-in.[11] This confused, popular, splendid, semi-royal beginning was a remarkably accurate prediction of William Henry's later life. Unfortunately there were also less

happy portents; for among the godparents, as at the christening of Sleeping
Beauty, was a wicked fairy.

Princess Amalia had no intention of abandoning her fight to control her
children and the Orange party. A strong, active woman of forty-eight, she
was not nearly ready to retire from her position at the centre of Dutch
political and social life. She had nothing to do with her time but fight;
and she had, indeed, some real grievances. The Princess Royal took precedence over her. The Princess Royal, by her marriage settlements, would have
a dower of fl.100,000; if the project testament of William II should take
effect, Mary would receive a further fl.50,000 a year. Amalia, on the other
hand, though she still had three unmarried daughters on her hands, received
only fl.39,000 a year in dowry payments. If Mary should have control of the
estates of her son during his minority, as well as such a disproportionate
income, then Amalia would lose all hope of political influence and could
look forward to a long widowhood of nothing but humiliation. The Princess
Dowager was in the same predicament as Catherine de Medici a century
earlier; it would have taken a woman of unusual tact and forbearance to
accept the secondary role with which she was threatened. Instead she chose
war, and war on two fronts. She would fight the Republicans in an attempt
to maintain the position of the Orange party, and thus her position at the
head of it; and she would fight her daughter-in-law for control of the little
boy and his estates, even if it meant taking William Henry away from his
mother. The two fronts were, of course, closely connected, because control
of the estates meant control of appointments in their administration, and it
was this patronage which kept the Orange party together.

Amalia's first claim to lead the party came five days after the birth of the
young Prince, when she wrote a letter to the provinces[12] asking them to
remember this new sprout of the Orange tree when they came to choose
new Stadhouders and a Captain-General of the Republic. To this the
Princess Royal replied that she would not meddle with affairs of state, but
limit herself to educating her son and administering his lands (and thus the
patronage) for his profit, leaving all else to God and trusting that the provinces would remember the merits and services of the House of Orange.[13]
Mary's position was much the cleverer of the two, and Amalia's letter fell
flat. Then the Princess Dowager tried to intervene in the question of the
guardianship of the baby Prince. She asked the Grand Pensionary of Holland
to consider the House of Orange as an *Illustre Huys*, that is one above the
rules of ordinary Dutch law, and to name tutors and curators for her
grandson.[14] Under ordinary Dutch law an infant came of age by the act
of marriage and so the Princess Royal was competent at nineteen, though
she would not have come of age under Roman law until she was twenty-

five. Mary felt, or came to feel under Heenvliet's guidance,[15] that this was an attempt to take her son from her. Her defence was to claim that her husband's will must be accepted as a valid testament, even though it was unsigned and undated, and to rely on Dutch law to prove her competence. In any case, why invent a new kind of law, unknown to the Roman-Dutch system, for the control of an English princess? If Mary was in fact above the processes of Dutch law, why should she not be treated in accordance with the law of her own country as an English subject? Did she not carry English law with her wherever she went?[16]

The question of the guardianship was not to be decided by the rules of English or Dutch law, but by the respective power of the two ladies. Under Dutch law, as under English, the mother's position was far stronger than that of the grandmother. Certainly Charles II, if asked, would have given the wardship of his nephew to his sister rather than to Amalia. But none of this really mattered. So long as Charles was in Scotland, and there was any hope that he would conquer his three kingdoms, the Princess Royal's claims would seem overwhelmingly strong. If Charles should fail in Scotland, Amalia would do better than she had any right to expect; not because of any justice in her claims, but because of the army of her son-in-law and ally the Elector of Brandenburg. Frederick William was not a great power in Europe; his voice was not so strong as that of a reigning King of England. It was a good deal stronger than that of a fugitive 'King of Scots'. Frederick William was the husband of the heiress presumptive of the House of Orange. His own interest in the case was greater than that of his mother-in-law; and his troops were in his Duchy of Cleves, along the eastern borders of the Republic. In the end, his position was recognized as being second only to that of the Princess Royal.

In the early days of the quarrel, Mary almost succeeded in obtaining the sole guardianship of her son. In law her position was very strong, and thanks to Heenvliet she made very few mistakes. Not only did she promise to abstain from any political activity; she even guaranteed that she would employ only native Dutchmen in the administration of her son's estates. When in January Heenvliet was threatened with violence by the Princess Dowager,[17] this naturally aroused general sympathy for him and Mary too; when the threat was repeated in June by the Elector[18] it aroused national indignation. Heenvliet was taken under the protection of the States of Holland. A law was hurriedly passed forbidding the Elector or any great personage to enter Holland without the permission of the States. By that time, however, the Princess Royal had lost her chance of victory. Her brother was clearly not succeeding in Scotland. She herself had alienated the Dutch by appointing local officials while the guardianship issue was still unsettled, by her stubbornness in refusing any compromise, and by her most unwise action in breaking the seals of her husband's cabinets. Heenvliet claimed that she did nothing but open, inventory, and reseal all the papers in the presence of her own officers and two or three members of the late Prince's Council.[19] Naturally this story was not believed, and rumours were put about that money and jewels were missing – taken either by the Princess Royal herself or by Schomberg.[20] There can be no question as to what she was after, or as to what she found: it was the letter to von Dohna ordering him to hold the Principality for Mary should William II die without a son. This order, unlike William's projected testament, would stand up in court. The Principality was not a feudal tenure; it could be given away, and in fact it had come into the hands of the Prince's ancestors, as a gift, as recently as 1544. Should the baby Prince die, therefore, Louise Henriette of Brandenburg would inherit most of the family lands, and the Orange title. The Principality itself would go to Mary and, when she remarried as everyone expected she would, pass out of the family forever. It was a mistake to look for the paper, a mistake to find it. The uninformed thought that Mary was a common thief. Those who knew about the paper felt that the gift should never have been made, and that Mary was far too greedy in trying to deprive the Electress of the reversion to Orange. By her hasty action in opening her husband's cabinets without securing proper authority or proper witnesses, the Princess Royal forfeited for ever the respect and sympathy of the Dutch people.

It was not until August 1651 that a working compromise was reached over the guardianship. By its terms, the Princess Royal was named Guardian and received a 50 per cent vote in making decisions. The Elector and the Princess Dowager, in that order, were named co-Guardians and shared a 50 per cent voice. The two parties were to name officials equally except in the case of Mary's dower lands; finally, in 1653, Mary was given absolute control of appointments of this type, in accordance with the terms of her marriage settlements.[21] Special arrangements were made concerning appointments in Zeeland, and a committee was set up to resolve disputes which might arise between the two Princesses in future.[22] The committee did not meet with much success, and there were several lawsuits later; but the settlement of 13 August did make it possible to begin to pay some attention to the Prince and to the administration of his estates.

Chapter 3

STUART RESTORATION

IT was a blasted inheritance. In October 1651 an arrangement was made with the Spanish to replace the treaty that William II had not lived to sign. It promised an annual payment of fl.80,000 until the Spanish should repay the principal of the debt; yet payment was never made, either of principal or interest, and the debt was still outstanding a generation later.[1] The portion of the Princess Royal had never been paid by Charles I, nor of course any of the debts contracted by him and his son during the Civil Wars. All the salaries of William II had ceased. Neither of the Princesses received a pension, though the Princess Dowager at least had reasonable claims to one. Meanwhile the two widows took their dowries, together fl.189,000, while much of the rest of the income went to pay the interest on debts contracted for the benefit of the Stuarts.[2] It seemed as if the Stuart connection had destroyed the House of Orange, first by alienating the hearts of the people of Holland and then by bankrupting it. Careful management might have enabled the entire House to live within its reduced income. But careful management was impossible while the two Princesses cared only to score points against each other. Each of them refused to surrender a particle of her dowry moneys, or to take other saving measures, for fear the other might benefit. There could be only one result. With an average income of fl.505,000 for the years 1650–55, there was an average annual deficit of fl.48,000.[3] Food bills remained unpaid for years at a time. The debt mounted regularly, and as the family's credit fell it could no longer borrow at 4 per cent but must pay first 5 per cent and then 6¼ per cent. By 1659 it had come to the point of selling land.

None of this made any difference to Prince William Henry at the time. At first he lived with his mother in the Binnenhof without a separate establishment. In May of 1653, however, he was given a separate train. Now and later the Prince was to be criticized by the English for excessive simplicity and by the Dutch for the unnecessary pompousness of his surroundings. The double criticism was inevitable. There were no other families in the Republic which lived at anything approaching the rate of the House of Orange, which even in its poverty was far richer than any bourgeois family in Amsterdam or noble house in the countryside. Yet what seemed splendid to the Dutch seemed mean to the English, accustomed not only to the extravagances of the court of Charles I but to the magnificence of their higher nobility. Even when he grew up, and had no dowry payments to make, the Prince lived little better than a Duke of Buckingham and not nearly as well as the Duke of York after 1660 or Princess Anne after 1688. The Dutch, who had nothing with which to compare the Prince's scale of living, have accused him of extravagance from that day to this; but the charge does not stand up. William Henry and his mother lived simply by English or continental standards for persons of their rank. And what little display the Princess Royal did make was essential to keep up the morale of the English Royalists. She was the only Stuart who had a reasonable income, at a time when her mother had to stay in bed all day to keep warm. Her brother the King, particularly after 1654, was never very far ahead of the bailiff, while his brothers were quite penniless. The Princess Royal, like that Duchess of Burgundy who had sheltered Edward IV in 1470, was the only one left who could uphold the family honour. Any money spent in this cause also did as much good to the morale of the Orange as of the Stuart party. It reminded the Orangists that some day this little boy would grow up; and it kept a considerable number of them employed, since the overwhelming majority of those serving at the Binnenhof were Dutch.

The Prince's household of 1653 was not large. In addition to a physician, two gentlemen, two halbardiers, two pages, four lackeys, and a Controller who managed the eight male domestics, there were three women and three maids indoors and a coachman, postilion, and palfrenier outdoors. By contrast the chapel at Althorp, the seat of a not unusually rich English earl, made provision for some fifty house servants. The entire establishment of 1653, including provisions, cost a little less than fl.31,000 a year. Mrs Howard, who was appointed Governess of the Prince from the beginning of 1653, received a further fl.1,000 a year for herself, and expenses when she was away from Court. All this was less than a quarter in money terms of the establishment of the Duke of Gloucester in 1698, though of course the cost of living was far lower in the Republic than it was in England.[4] Most, if not all, of the people employed in 1653 had been in the household of William II and had continued to work without pay after his death. Eventually they were given their arrears, and somehow pensions continued to be paid to older servants who were no longer able to perform their duties. In 1654 it was possible to place an architect, a map and instrument keeper, a fountain and grotto builder, and a picture keeper on the establishment; these too, as far as is known, were former servants of William II.[5] What looked like extravagance to outsiders was merely the fulfilment of a real duty to these old retainers.

By now, of course, William Henry had solid food. His daily ration was a chicken, four loaves of white bread, a can of milk, a piece of fresh butter, two fresh eggs, two cans of beer, a quarter of a pound of sugar, and apples or pears.[6] It was not until he was six that he received any pocket money, and then only fl.50 a month.[7] He was now expected to help his own cause by appearing in public. It would be fatal to allow the Dutch to forget that there was a Prince of Orange. In July 1654, when she was temporarily absent from The Hague, Mary wrote to her son's governess giving instructions for the Prince's day. In good weather, he was to go for walks or to call on his grandmother. Twice a day, at eleven in the morning and three in the afternoon, he was to be shown to callers. The governess and the women were to be present in the room during these visits, with the two gentlemen. The lackeys were to stand before the door, or in the gallery; the halbardiers were to be in their usual places, and at least one of them was to be on duty all day long.[8]

It was not until 1656 that William Henry began his schooling, which was at first confined to religion. Dr Cornelis Trigland, a noted Hague divine, was appointed to instruct the Prince in the Dutch Reformed faith.[9] He continued to work with the Prince on a part-time basis for many years, with good results. Twenty years later William III might spend an evening during the heat of a campaign arguing Predestination with his English friends. During the war of 1672 he was a frequent communicant and regularly attended Sunday sermon, though it was sometimes necessary to hold the service in the afternoon if the army marched that day. If he conformed to the Church of England in 1688, if he had Mass sung daily in his chapel at Orange in obedience to the terms of Prince Philip William's will, it was for political reasons. William III never became a theologian, like his great-grandfather James I; but there can be no question about his deep Calvinist religious beliefs.

In 1656, also, there was an increase in the Prince's establishment. His clothes were now to cost fl.3,500 a year.[10] He was to have more expensive and adult food,[11] and there were to be eleven horses in the stables.[12] It is probable that these gains more than outweighed the loss of his mother, who left him to spend almost a year in Paris at this time. The Princess Royal has often been accused of heartless neglect of her son, particularly by Dutch historians who have no idea of English practice. Even simple gentlemen like John Evelyn left home very early, for the diarist was taken away from his parents at the age of five, and many people now alive on both sides of the Atlantic have survived despatch to boarding school at eight. In later years there were even to be complaints that William III had been left with his women too long. Whether or not that is true, it is a simple fact that his childhood was far more orderly and settled than that of his Stuart uncles, of Louis XIV, or of great numbers of English and French nobles and gentlemen of his own age, whose training was thoroughly disrupted by civil war. It was not the cosy home life of the lower middle class; no one should expect that it could have been that or anything like that.

The charge of heartlessness rests largely on a letter from Mary to the King, written probably in March 1655:

.. My lady Hide desired my sone to be anothere godfathere, with assuring me, you would not thinke it to much presumption, if he were without your leave, because it 'twould be to long to stay for it, that I was glad not to deny her. Besides you are so partially kind to him, that I feare at last my desiring your kindness to him will turne to jealousie hee may take some from me; for I must assure you, that I shall obay all your commands, except that of loving him (though he is my ownly child) above all things in this world, as long as you are in it, which I beseech you beleeve, that their is nothing truer . . .13

Any healthy adult would prefer the company of a handsome charming man of twenty-five to that of a child of five, especially if the man happened to be Charles II, the best dancer of his race and one of the best conversationalists of his age. But are we really to believe that the passage is to be taken seriously? Is it not a piece of friendly banter, designed to cheer the exile at one of the most hopeless moments of his life? Two months later the Princess Royal wrote another letter to her brother:

Your wife is resolving whither she will writ or no: therefore I am to say nothing to you from her; but will keepe open my letter as long as the post will permitte, to expect what good-nature will work, which I find now dos not at all; for 'tis now eleven of the clock, and noe letter come.14

Let us all take this letter as solemnly as we take the first one, and search for a mysterious wife whose children are the lawful kings of England; or let us take the playful letters of Charles and his other sister, Henriette, in this ponderous serious way and accuse them of incest. It is, in fact, all nonsense. The young Prince received the best of care, a sign that his mother took her duties seriously; and he received far more mother love than his mother had, who was sold into a foreign country at ten and delivered over at twelve.

It was not until the end of 1659 that William Henry escaped entirely from the apron-strings of his women and began his formal education. His Governor was to be Frederick of Nassau, Heer van Zuylestein, a bastard son of Prince Frederick Henry and a most unsuitable choice. Zuylestein seems to have been appointed because he was heavily in debt and needed the money, and because he was almost the only person whom both Princesses could tolerate. He was suspect to the Dutch government on the ground that he was too much in favour of the English, but his real defect was laziness. There are admirable instructions for Zuylestein, covering every hour of the day. We have no idea whether they were carried out, or if so how vigorously they were carried out. Certainly the Prince grew up with a very defective command of French and even of English, the language which he had spoken first. In part, William Henry's difficulties with French have been exaggerated; he wrote it quickly, using a private slang which is most unhandsome; there are many errors in it, and at times it conveys no meaning. Yet it was at least far better French than his grandmother ever wrote, or many other Germans who had to use it because French was the international military language of the day. How good is the English of many European NATO high-ups today? In part, also, any failure was the fault of an incompetent French instructor.[15] Zuylestein must certainly bear some part of the blame for William Henry's language problems, and more for allowing him to associate with people who were bad influences. The Prince was to prove exceptionally loyal to his childhood friends, however unsuitable they might be; and this loyalty was to make a great deal of trouble for him in later years. In any case, William Henry was to have a far better education than his father.

On paper, every minute was well accounted for. The household was to be established at Leyden, near the University, and the Director of Studies was to be Dr Henry Bornius, the University Professor of Philosophy.[16] Special attention was to be paid to religious instruction. The Prince was to be given 'incessament des vives impressions de l'amour et de la crainte de Dieu'.[17] He was to read a chapter of scripture a day, and to learn some psalms and the catechism by heart. A prayer was to be recited over the Prince before he rose in the morning, at seven, and there were to be regular morning and evening prayers as well. He was to go to church twice on Sunday, alternating weekly between the Dutch and French sermons so as to acquire a facility in both tongues. On his return from the sermon, the Prince was to be given an oral examination on its contents in the presence of his household, for their benefit as well as his own.

Every attempt was to be made to give the Prince civil manners to people of all ranks. His teachers were to emphasize the popularity of the House of Orange; to preserve this, William Henry must learn to live with 'grands et petits pour conserver et gaigner leur affections de plus en plus'. He and his household were to take great care to speak of the government with respect, whatever their real feelings might be. The Prince must receive according to their rank the calls of all who came to see him, and return those of the most important; and he must learn to speak with his visitors without asking his tutors what he ought to say. From this time onward the Prince ate with the four chief members of his household, and the table was always set for eight in case there were guests.[18] His preceptors were to see to it that no bad language was allowed in his presence, and that none of the young men gave him dirty books in secret. Zuylestein or Chapuiseau, the incompetent Frenchman, must always sleep in the Prince's chamber. In disciplining the Prince, his Governor was not to make him blush in public, but to correct him softly and in private. Already there is mention of the later ill-treatment of servants. If William Henry loses his temper with them, the Governor is to wait; later, when the boy has calmed down, he is to impress on him the stupidity of such weakness and the inconveniences which may arise if the servants are not treated gently. William never learned this lesson, and all his life long he would kick his valets when he was in a bad mood.

One reason why the Prince's studies were not more vigorous was his ill health. Apparently a healthy baby, he grew into a thin, pale, asthmatic boy with a weak appetite and a visibly humped back. When he grew up he always wore a cuirass into battle, by then almost an anachronism. It covered his back and made it appear straight. It was not so easy to conceal the poor appetite which continued to bother him all his life. Whenever he was tired or ill he would eat almost nothing, thus weakening himself still further. Zuylestein's orders required him to eat with the Prince to make sure that the boy ate, and ate the right things; that he should put his charge to bed at nine every evening; and that his exercises should be strictly limited. A dancing lesson before dinner, a promenade in the afternoon, or in really bad weather a game of billiards, were all that could be allowed. There could be no fencing, manège, or tennis until there was more strength. The limitations on horseback riding applied only to military exercises. Very early in life William Henry developed a passionate fondness for hunting in almost all its forms, so that nothing could keep him from the field. Hunting gave him relief from asthma. It also gave him almost the only moments of privacy he was ever to know.

The placid course of nursery and schoolroom life suffered very few interruptions. In May 1653 the little boy had been invested with the insignia of the Garter.[19] In the summer of 1659, before the Prince went to Leyden, there were many parties before and after the marriage of his young aunt, Henriette of Orange, to the Prince of Anhalt.[20] The trip to Leyden itself involved speeches and deputations, while as we have seen the entertainment of visitors was a part of the daily schedule there. Food was prepared for three guests at dinner and three at supper as part of the contract with the caterers, who might charge extra for larger parties. At nine, then, William Henry was expected to face the public alone, to inspire them with happy memories of his ancestors and regret for the new Republican ways. He seems to have done a wonderful job at it. From the moment of his birth he was wildly popular with the crowd, causing riots when he appeared in public that any modern singer might envy. His hold over the hearts of the people never weakened, and to the day of his death they cheered him wherever he went, in England as well as in the United Provinces.

This early training stood the Prince in good stead in 1660, during the public celebrations for the Restoration of Charles II. In May the King came by yacht from Breda to Delft. William Henry joined the party there and returned to The Hague in his mother's carriage. She was next to the King in the rear seat, facing her brothers the Dukes of York and Gloucester, while the Prince had to sit in a window seat. A great noise of bell-ringing and the sound of cannon and muskets firing salutes greeted them as they left Delft, led by trumpeters in scarlet velvet bordered with gold and silver. After the trumpeters came a great crowd of officers and gentlemen on unusually fine horses; then the officials of the various households; then the carriage of the Master of Ceremonies, followed by that of the Royal Family; after them, two carriages representing the States General and six representing the States of Holland were followed by seventy-two carriages belonging to English and Dutch nobles. It was a splendid sight. The procession took almost an hour to reach The Hague. When it arrived at the Mauritshuis, which had been placed at the King's disposal by the government, the party was greeted by the Queen of Bohemia, the Princess Dowager, and other notabilities. It was observed that, now and later during the visit, the King took special care to pay his respects to the Princess Dowager. Next day, 26 May, there occurred the dinner which is the subject of a famous print, with the entire Royal Family seated at a raised table in the Mauritshuis, in a great room which no longer exists. A large crowd is depicted sharing the feast below the dais. We are told that the same arrangements were followed at all meals during the visit, except when William Henry was not present. The English undoubtedly enjoyed feasting at the expense of the Dutch government, which they disliked; their enjoyment was increased by the music of a band during dinner and the firing of cannon outside as an accompaniment to every toast.

Next day the Regiment of Guards did exercises in battle formation at Zorgvliet, the villa of Cats, the retired Grand Pensionary of Holland. The Prince attended the exercises, and also a very rich supper given by the Spanish ambassador, at which the King was so well entertained that he stayed until one in the morning. Perhaps, that week, William saw his uncle touch the sick to cure them of the King's Evil, tuberculosis of the skin. Charles II had touched 260 people at Breda, and the ceremonies were repeated for three days running at The Hague. It would have made a deep impression on a boy of ten. In later years, at any rate, William detested the ceremony and would never participate in it.

Finally, on 2 June, the King and his brothers went to Scheveningen to set

sail for England. On the beach they made their farewells to the Princess
Dowager and the rest of the Nassaus, government officials, and foreign
ambassadors. Then the Royal Family went on board at about eleven o'clock
and had an early dinner. Afterwards the King, who appears to have had a
real fondness for his nephew, embraced him as a son and gave him his blessing
before saying goodbye to the Queen of Bohemia and the Princess Royal.
Brother and sister burst into tears at parting.

The year's ceremonies were not yet over for any of the participants. The
Princess Royal planned to join her brother in England, but before she could
do so she must pawn some of her jewels in Amsterdam to pay for the trip.
On 15 June, therefore, Mary and the Prince paid a state visit to the city. The
loan was easily arranged, and for the most part the pair were well received.
Amsterdam, however, was not happy at the Restoration; its memories of
1650 and of the Stuarts were still green and unpleasant. On the 17th, therefore, the city first treated the Princess Royal and her son at the Stadhuis.
Afterwards, at six o'clock, there was a parade of *tableaux* in wagons on the
Dam. As the third car came in sight the Princess turned pale with horror and
disgust. That scene was a portrayal of her father's execution. The rest
of the visit went off well, though it was noted that their pew at the New
Church on Sunday was hung with festoons of orange blossoms only. It
would have been more tactful to mix the mother's colours with the son's.[21]
They were probably happy to leave Amsterdam the next day. On the return
journey to Leyden they were much better treated at Haarlem, where the
magistrates had taken care to entwine the roses of England and the lilies of
France with their orange blossoms.

At the end of September Mary left the Republic for England. It was not a
happy excursion, for pleasure at the King's Restoration was marred by the
news of the death of her brother Gloucester of smallpox. Nor was her stay
particularly happy, even after Gloucester's funeral. Both the King and the
Duke of York seemed intent on disastrous marriages, the King with the last
unmarried daughter of the Princess Amalia and the Duke with one of Mary's
own ladies-in-waiting, whom he had gotten with child. The Princess had
been able to persuade Charles earlier in the summer that since he had been
rejected years before as a suitor for the eldest daughter, it would be too
humiliating to marry the youngest. Besides, everyone knew that the
Spanish, who had promised to make up the portion, would never be able to
pay it. Thus she saved her precedence over the hated Amalia's brood. But
with the Duke of York she had no success. Miss Hyde might be a simple
gentlewoman, without name, fortune, rank, or beauty; James had made her
pregnant, and he was determined to make an honest woman of her. He
did so. That incredible stubbornness, that almost insane persistence in fatuity

which was so characteristic of James in later life, was a part of his make-up from the very beginning.

In the midst of these quarrels, which of course made the bitterest of enemies out of Amalia and the Hydes, the Princess Royal collapsed and died of smallpox after a very short illness. She just had time to make a will of her own the day she died. To her son, besides the fl.150,000 a year in dowry payments which her death would save him, she left all the jewels given her by her husband. Presumably many of these were heirlooms in which she had only a life interest. Everything else, and there was not much after the payment of her debts, she left to her mother. It was a deeply human thing to do. Henrietta Maria was no more popular with her children than she was with the people of England. The Princess Royal, however, had shared many of the tragedies of the Queen's life. She, too, had been hated by her husband's people; she, too, had experienced the torments of early widowhood, the insults of a revolution, the bitter quarrels of a divided family. If Mary's sufferings were far less severe than her mother's, they were severe enough to give her an understanding of what Henrietta Maria had lived through. She left to her mother the memory of one dutiful child; the Queen's other children did not do so well.

For three centuries a stream of raucous abuse has been poured on the memory of the Princess Royal by Dutch writers, who have every reason to conceal their country's harsh treatment of a lonely foreigner. Mary, doubtless, had no charm. Her struggles with her terrible mother-in-law were carried too far, to the point where they damaged her son's interests. But did not the Solms family do more damage to the House of Orange than Mary Stuart? Amalia, as the older of the two women, must bear the greater blame for their quarrels. Amalia, with her husband, conceived the policy of dynastic marriages. Mary represented the fruits of that policy; she had nothing to do with its inception. She did demand, as a widow, the position which her husband had meant her to have. Here as elsewhere she was being loyal to her husband's memory, a memory which Amalia did everything she could to obliterate. What husband can complain of a widow's loyalty? Mary's husband happened to be a stupid and immature fool, and an unlucky one; that was not Mary's fault. As regards her son the Princess Royal's conduct, by the standards of her class and nation, was not only correct but intelligent. She knew, what Amalia never learned, that a waiting game promised the best results with the Loevesteiners. Nothing much could be done for the Prince until he was old enough to act for himself. What could be done was to keep the Prince well, to give him as good an education as possible, and to protect him from scandal. Mary did all this, responsibly; responsibly, she preserved her reputation and also refused to remarry, which might have done her son infinite harm. All this was far more important than the warm, romantic, emotional mother love which very few seventeenth-century princes ever received, but on which every nineteenth-century historian apparently doted.[22]

The death of his mother, and the Restoration of Charles II, mark an important turning point in the life of the Prince. It must have been a hard wrench for the young boy to lose her and her English courtiers, many of whom now settled in England. The young, however, are pretty resilient; and in any case the busy schedule at Leyden provided many distractions and very little time for sorrow. The real turning point of 1660 was not so much personal as political. So long as his mother lived, the Prince was assured of the sympathy of the French government. So long as the Protectorate endured, the French had no reason to fear William's English blood. From 1660 on, however, Louis XIV seems to have felt that William and the Orange party would inevitably support the Stuarts and the Hohenzollerns against the Bourbons. By his own efforts, largely, he made the prediction come true. From the beginning of his personal rule the French King supported the Loevesteiners, in the hope of preventing the Dutch from falling under English influence. But there was also an element of revenge in this policy. In 1645, when Louis XIV was an orphan of eight, Amalia's Spanish policy had robbed him of the fruits of victory. Why should he now be kind to her orphan grandson? William Henry could learn how unpleasant a friendless minority might be.

1660 was a turning point for William Henry in another sense. During the exile of Charles II the Stuart connection was not too important in Dutch domestic politics. With the Restoration the risk returned that the House of Orange would use its position in the United Provinces to further English rather than Dutch national interests: in other words, that it would commit treason. It was a real risk. Many sincere persons felt then, as many sincere persons feel today, that the dynastic policies of Frederick Henry and of William II were treasonable. From now on, their successor was never to be free from the same suspicion. His was indeed a blasted inheritance.

Chapter 4

THE WAR OF 1665

ONE of the chief problems of the entire seventeenth century was the question of sovereignty. Where did sovereignty lie in England? It took a century and much bloodshed to determine the answer to that question. Where did it lie in Germany after 1648? One of the reasons why diplomatic history in this time was so complicated was that no one agreed where it did lie, so that the problem of the proper ranking of ambassadors at conferences became a major nuisance. The Emperor refused to admit, for example, that the Dutch Republic was an independent state, and showed it by his treatment of the Republic's envoys; the Republic, and the rest of Europe as well, could not decide whether the German Electors were to be treated as crowned heads or not. An awkward compromise was reached, whereby the first member of a team of Brandenburg ambassadors would be given the honours due to a king's representative, but not the second and third. When the full team of three ambassadors called on anyone, the host was obliged to sail down on this diplomatic line of battle, cutting off the first and leaving the others in disgrace on his left hand.

William of Orange had the misfortune to be involved in two separate squabbles about sovereignty, one with the Loevesteiners and one with the French Court. De Witt and his cabal maintained firmly that sovereignty in the United Provinces lay with the individual province. The States General was a body of delegates, with only delegated powers. William himself was, according to this theory, no more than the richest citizen of the Province of Holland. When the *predikanten* mentioned him by name in their prayers, as they had prayed for the Stadhouders, they were ordered to stop. The people, of course, rejected this theory. As far as the crowd was concerned, the House of Orange had founded and maintained the Republic, and its safety and prosperity could not be assured without the continued association of the Family with the state. During the English War of 1652–54 the rabble forced recruiters to drum up men in the Prince's name;[1] Orange flags had a habit of appearing on holidays, and there were sometimes riots of consequence, particularly on the day of the *Kermesse*. At the Kermesse of 15 May 1654 the Government felt itself lucky when the soldiers, against express orders, shot off many volleys to salute the Prince and the Stadhouder of Friesland, without doing anything else.[2] Much more serious disorders had taken place the previous summer, when the mob had risen in The Hague on the 7 and 8 August, smashing the windows of the young Grand Pensionary Johan de Witt, of his father Jacob, and of several other unpopular republicans. When the civic guard refused to put down the rioting, the Government had to call in cavalry and later some companies of infantry to overawe the people of the capital.[3] The troubles at The Hague involved nothing more than broken glass; but at Enckhuysen there was a rebellion in form, which was put down finally by nine infantry companies.[4]

The oligarchy could maintain its view of the constitution, during the minority of the Prince, only with the support of the army. As we have seen, the civic guard could not be trusted to fight the mob, and the mob could easily be manipulated by the Orangists whenever, as in wartime, there was economic distress. What would happen when the Prince grew up? The only possible solution for the long term was to secure the agreement of the Orange faction to the concept of provincial sovereignty. The pill would have to be sweetened by the grant of a salary to the Prince and by his virtual adoption as a 'Child of State'. Holland would undertake his education and manage his estates, in order to make him worthy to exercise the high charges and employments filled by his ancestors who had acted *with commissions from the States of Holland*.[5] In this way the cabal hoped to settle the question of sovereignty. It hoped to do so even without promising anything for the future, without 'designating' the Prince as Captain-General from his eighteenth birthday. All during the summer of 1660 there were negotiations with the Princess Royal, who would agree that her son become a 'Child of State' but hoped for his designation in return.[6] For years the Princess Royal had followed a policy of compromise with Holland, on the ground that her son had nothing to hope for without Holland's agreement. She finally abandoned the question of 'designation' and agreed to the appointment of an education commission whose members were all republicans and included de Witt himself.

At this point, the Princess Dowager intervened. She felt slighted by her treatment during the ceremonies for Charles II at The Hague in May, although the King had gone out of his way to be polite to her. She demanded the right to name an equal number of representatives to the education commission, and chose Orangists, both Hollanders and Zeelanders. The Princess Royal, in choosing republicans, had abandoned the Orange party; the Zeelanders felt especially annoyed, because they had actually carried a 'designation' through the States of their province, by which the Prince would become First Noble of Zeeland at eighteen. Amalia's interference was typical, and typically disastrous for her grandson. De Witt knew the weakness of the Orange party. He knew also that Charles II would be far weaker than

Oliver had been. Cromwell had been strong enough in 1654 to force the Dutch to accept peace on terms involving the exclusion of the Prince from the offices of his ancestors.[7] In 1660 Holland might cancel the Act of Exclusion as a grace. It could not be forced by Charles II to do *for* the Prince what it had done *against* him in 1654. Charles II was no Cromwell. Holland would do what it wished for the Prince, or do nothing at all.

The Princess Royal came to realize the facts of the case. The King and the Princess Amalia overplayed their hands badly. In part at least they were the victims of the Brandenburg agent at The Hague, Weyman, who felt that the Orange party could dictate any terms it wished.[8] Mary was much more sensible. The education commission was to some degree her own idea, and it was a compromise based on a realistic assessment of the relative strengths of the two parties. Until the day of her death she was working with the commissioners, though she was arguing with them on questions of detail.[9]

On the day of her death, however, the Princess Royal made her will. By it she left the care of her son, not to the 'sovereign' States of Holland, not to the education commission, but to her brother. De Witt was furious.[10] He accused her of not leaving her son a penny, but what really angered him was the fact that her will was a denial of provincial sovereignty. She had recommended the interests of the Prince to her brother, and to the Queen her mother; she made no mention of the States, 'not even of those of Holland, to whom as high guardian (*oppervoochden*) she had turned over her son in her lifetime'.[11] The education commission tried to function for a few months longer, but it was in an impossible position. The Princess Dowager, still under the influence of Weyman, and the Elector met at Cleves and decided to send an embassy to Charles II to settle the question of the guardianship.[12] When this embassy reached London, it found that the King had already been 'tricked' into sending a letter which seemed to recognize the claims of Holland as guardians with rights superior to those of the family.[13] The ambassadors soon changed the King's mind. By the end of March Charles II was insulting even in public the people who had induced him to write the letter.[14] He made a treaty with the Princess Dowager and the Elector, by which the Princess Dowager was given in effect complete control over the Orange party and estates for the future.[15] In exchange, the former servants of the Princess Royal were not to be victimized, and by the seventh article 'all acts performed or done by her late Royal Highness in her life time, and which were lawfull for her to do, shall be confirmed and made good'.

The King appears to have known so little of Dutch politics that he thought he could rule the Netherlands through the Princess Dowager and her party.[16] He could have made no greater mistake. As early as the end of March 1661 de Witt was writing to his friend and relative Cornelis de Graeff van Zuidpolsbroek, that if the 'subaltern' guardians refused to recognize the higher authority of Holland it would be better to abandon the entire project of caring for the Prince's education.[17] Zuidpolsbroek agreed, Holland agreed, and the Prince was abandoned to his relations. Holland refused to take any further interest in his education or to grant him a pension. This was serious enough, considering the state of the Prince's finances. But the episode had greater consequences than that. It contributed substantially to the growing estrangement between England and the Netherlands which resulted in the Second Dutch War.[18] Charles II came to have a personal hatred for de Witt. We are told often enough – too often – that the Second Dutch War was purely commercial in character, and that the Third grew out of the Treaty of Dover. Neither war need have taken place, and perhaps neither would have taken place, without this element of personal hatred. De Witt had proved to Charles that he was not the man Oliver had been, and it hurt. The failure of the negotiations, furthermore, had a similarly bad effect on de Witt's mind. De Witt was driven into the arms of the French, as the only resource available against a combination of England, Brandenburg, and the Orange party against him. Provincial sovereignty had been saved, but only at the cost of clientage to Louis XIV.

The failure of the education commission scheme was a hardship for William of Orange in financial terms, but not in personal ones. He continued to live at Leyden with Zuylestein and his other friends, receiving a reasonably good education. Perhaps de Witt would have done better; we do not know. Certainly he would have tried to make a good republican out of the Prince, who was then young enough to be moulded. William was probably happier with Zuylestein, though he resented being merely the richest private citizen in Holland.

One reason why this position was so humiliating was that, at Orange, William III was himself a sovereign prince. The principality, which would not be considered an unusually large ranch in Texas, was chiefly remarkable for its Roman remains. The revenue was extremely small, even with the aid of a toll on the Rhone and the income of some nearby farms. A regular subsidy had to be sent for the support of the administration. Orange, however, was well worth whatever it might cost the Nassaus to maintain, and for two reasons. In the first place it was their only sovereignty. As reigning Princes the Nassaus could fight off the social pretensions of Electors of the Empire; without Orange they would revert to the status of German counts. The Principality, furthermore, was in some ways the key to southern France. If it were in Protestant hands, and most of the Nassau Princes of Orange were Protestants, then it would be very difficult for the French government to control the Huguenots in Dauphiné, Provence, and Langue-doc, or to prevent them from communicating with their brethren in Switzerland and Savoy.[19]

William the Silent did not introduce Protestantism into his new estates. When he acquired the Principality in 1544 he was only eleven. He did give more support to the Protestants at Orange than the Catholics, who were at that time the overwhelming majority, would tolerate; for most of the rest of the century there was civil war. Orange, furthermore, was a welcome ground for adventurers, since the Nassaus could rarely go there, and since the population seems to have been unusually turbulent. Any ambitious official could neglect his instructions and set himself up as a petty tyrant. A pattern seemed to be set in which undutiful governors would make themselves independent and become so strong that the Prince would either have to acknowledge their position or call on the French for help to turn the usurpers out. Naturally this tended to compromise the princely claim to have sovereign rights. Even William the Silent had needed a decree of the Parle-ment of Dauphiné and letters patent from Henri II before he could enjoy his own. At the time of his assassination in 1584 the situation was even more dangerous. The heir, Philip William, was a prisoner of the Spanish and was being educated as a Roman Catholic at Madrid. His imprisonment con-tinued until 1596, but the Principality of Orange was not recovered until 1607 from a family of renegades named Blacons, who had converted it into a den of Protestants and thieves. Prince Philip William needed French help to liberate Orange, and to get it he had to marry a French Princess, Eleanore de Bourbon. On his death Orange passed into the hands of his Protestant brothers, Maurits and then Frederick Henry. In his will, which Maurits honoured and Frederick Henry did not, Philip William had stipulated that the Governor of Orange should always be a Roman Catholic.

During the minority of William III the history of Orange seemed to be repeating itself. The Governor, Frederick von Dohna, like Blacons three generations earlier refused to obey the orders he received from The Hague and actually ruled as he pleased, though he defended himself by pretending to follow the orders of Amalia and the Elector of Brandenburg. Dohna's personal estates were all at the mercy of the Elector, and so in large matters he was obliged to obey him. Neither the Elector nor Amalia, however, was responsible for the disorderly government of Orange. Dohna went out of his way to assist the most irresponsible Protestants in their squabbles with the rest of the community, Protestant or Catholic. He kidnapped the emissaries sent by the Princess Royal to put affairs into better order. He tried to inter-fere with the composition of the Parlement of Orange so as to obtain a majority favourable to himself, with the result that the Parlement fled to

France. He imprisoned consuls, priests, and preachers; by 1659 he was trying to force the judges at Orange to sentence his enemies to death. He also, as he boasts in his *Mémoires*, gave aid and comfort to almost any discontented noble in the south of France so as to create a treasury of merit for himself in case of future need.

The situation at Orange got completely out of hand. Both the Princess Royal and her mother-in-law appealed at different times to the French Regency for assistance. In doing so they both compromised the 'sovereignty' of the principality, such as it was. The independence of a tiny state,completely enclaved in French soil, could hardly be more than a polite fiction even in the seventeenth century. When France had had a strong ruler, like Henri IV, it had taken the then Prince of Orange eleven years to obtain possession; the French may be forgiven for thinking of the principality as a dependency.[20] They may also, on the basis of the record, be forgiven for thinking that the south of France needed to be put into order, and that the only way to do this was to crush the two greatest dens of iniquity: Marseille and Orange. It was impossible to do anything while the Regency's own position was in danger. But in 1658, when the Fronde had been put down and the young King crowned at Reims, the French Court turned south with an army not only to negotiate the Treaty of the Pyrenees and the marriage of Louis XIV with Maria Theresa of Spain, but to bring good government to a region sore in need of it. At first the King acted at the request of the Princess Royal, who felt that the Dutch courts had no right to interfere with the affairs of the principality and who had obtained a declaration of the Parlement of Orange to the effect that she was sole regent. His interests, however, were not the same as hers. There was always the risk that he would confiscate the principality, as he confiscated a 'sovereignty' belonging to the Prince's cousin Turenne. And since the Nassau claim to Orange was by no means overwhelmingly strong, there was a further risk that Orange, even if it remained a sovereignty, might be given back to a Frenchman.

There was a further risk. The heir of William III was the wife of Frederick William of Brandenburg. In 1656 the Elector had made a treaty with France and then another with her ally, Sweden. On the death of the Emperor, the French had made Frederick William a handsome offer for his vote in the Electoral College. Brandenburg's vote went instead to Leopold of Hungary, who offered twice as much; and when war then broke out between Denmark and Sweden, Brandenburg took the side of the Dane. The French suspected that Frederick William was following the wishes of his mother-in-law in all this. It was obviously necessary to discipline the Elector and the Princess Amalia if the French were to retain any influence at all in the Empire. And disciplined they were. In 1659 a Brandenburg agent in France[21] was arrested and ill treated despite his diplomatic character. A year later, the French Government was contemplating the seizure of the Elector's duchies of Cleves and Mark as a suitable reprisal.[22] In the circumstances it is probable that Orange would have been seized whatever the Princess Royal had done; no one really believed that her frail son would live to maturity, so that Orange was substantially nothing other than a more easily accessible Cleves. By sequestering the principality, the French King would frighten his enemies and bring peace to three provinces at a single blow.

Louis XIV, or really the Cardinal in his name, proceeded with great care. At first he did nothing but put up placards in Languedoc and Dauphiné, proclaiming himself the protector of the Prince of Orange and recognizing the Princess Royal as sole *tutrice* of her son. The Governor and garrison of Orange were denounced as rebels against their prince, and those of them who were French were denounced as rebels against their king.[23] Dohna replied with his own placards, which claimed that the first set were forged. Then in August 1659 matters went a step further. Orange was blockaded. A royal frigate appeared on the Rhone to prevent the rentmeesters of the principality from collecting the toll. The rentmeesters were ordered to pay their rents on French soil, and to the account of the Princess Royal.[24] In February 1660 the Court arrived at Aix-en-Provence, only fifteen leagues from Orange. The King, who had a wry sense of humour, sent one of his most insubordinate nobles, the Duc de Mercoeur, to reduce Marseille to obedience. Mercoeur carried out his instructions, slighting the walls of the city so that it would never again be tempted to rebel. Even now the French did not choose to attack the principality or its chateau, Crevecoeur, whose normal garrison had been swollen to some four hundred men by Dohna's employment of French mercenaries. When these were threatened with the penalties of treason most of them fled and Dohna with the remainder of the garrison was in an impossible position. He held out as long as he could and obtained remarkably generous terms by a treaty of 20 March. Under its provisions, the Governor was compensated for the money he had spent in defence of the principality, given a safe conduct, and was to retain both the title of Governor and its salary until William Henry came of age. His party inside Orange was to be protected by a general amnesty, while those of his enemies whom he chose to denounce would be proceeded against. The French also promised to govern the principality in the name of William III until he should come of age, when it would be returned to him intact; if he should not live, it would be given to the Electress of Brandenburg. Dohna's officers, finally, would be dismissed with a year's wages.[25] It was the gesture of a grandee pensioning off superfluous housemaids, not an act of war.

The treaty was remarkably gracious. Louis XIV did break it, by slighting the walls of Orange as he had slighted those of Marseille. What treaty did he ever keep? But by his own standards he acted very well. After the death of the Princess Royal, when there was no longer such great disunity among the guardians, he even offered to return Orange without waiting for William to come of age.[26] There was one condition: the Governor of Orange must be a Roman Catholic, as required by the terms of the testament of Prince Philip William.[27] The choice of Governor would be left to the Guardians.[28] In the circumstances this was even more generous than the treaty. The King of France had a right to know that Orange would not be used as a base of operations against him; he had a right to demand that its administration be more efficient than in the past. Under Frederick von Dohna's devoutly Protestant but impartial parents Orange had enjoyed a golden age of peace and order. Their son had proved unworthy in every way; and Louis was justified in feeling that any other Protestant, at least any other appointed by Amalia, would be as bad. He might even have been willing to permit the appointment of a Protestant if he had been treated with respect. But this was something of which the Princess Dowager was incapable. Her loyalty to the Solms family went far beyond her affection for the House of Orange, far beyond the limits of prudence. She must find her nephew a post of distinction; she was even mad enough to consider him a proper Governor of the Prince her grandson, if she could get rid of Zuylestein.[29] When the Guardians sent an embassy to Paris in the autumn of 1661 to ask for the return of the principality, she insisted that Frederick von Dohna himself should be a member of it and that he should ask to return to Orange as if nothing had happened. Perhaps she felt that the King of France would enjoy the expense of blockading Orange and bribing her nephew once a year. The King refused to receive Dohna, though he was very kind to the other ambassador, Constantijn Huygens. Finally, early in 1665, the Princess Dowager agreed to the French terms and Orange was liberated.[30]

The Prince, meanwhile, survived – to the surprise of Europe. As he grew up and his personality developed, he showed himself to be almost a caricature of his family pattern. The Nassaus were an unhealthy lot, given to mysterious fevers which were almost certainly tubercular. Often they died young; if not, their powers failed in middle age. They did have two advantages. Many of them were able, and they matured early. Both the father and grandfather of William Henry took the field at sixteen. The boy was the extreme example of this pattern: weaker, braver, abler, more precocious than any of his ancestors, he was to prove both a first-class soldier and a first-class politician. He was, of course, born with many gifts: a great name; potentially, a great position in Europe; potentially, the wealth needed to support that position. One vital advantage, which William II had missed, was that the Prince must fight to recover every portion of his inheritance. William II had been spoiled; his son escaped spoiling, to become almost a political and military machine, ideally fitted for his particular career. His education contributed substantially to this. Zuylestein might be too easy with the boy, but he did give him a sense of the greatness that was open to him, and much of the equipment he needed to become a great man. William's education might well have been more disciplined than it was if he had been strong enough to bear discipline. As it was, he learned to express himself in Dutch, French, German, Latin, and Spanish as well as in his English mother tongue. He grew to have a real fondness for architecture and especially for landscape gardening. He collected paintings and objects with a sure taste, knowing how to distinguish original marbles as well as paintings from their copies. If he often let experts buy and arrange his pictures and objects for him, this was nothing more than an example of his ability to delegate details. It was certainly not a sign of indifference. William III grew into a real connoisseur, not merely a man who had to talk art because it was the fashion.

While Zuylestein and his colleagues were producing a truly civilized man, they did not neglect to make a professional soldier. They had to work slowly, since the boy was too weak to handle a sword or a warhorse until he was almost fully grown. In the meantime they told him stories of his family's past, so that he would 'glory' in war when the time came. They could give him a good deal of military theory in his reading and not much more until his strength and the political position allowed him some practical experience. And they cultivated what little strength the boy had with great care, teaching him to love the outdoors and the outdoor life. The Prince took up one field sport after another and continued to practise them until his final illness. At the same time he was taught how to husband what strength he had. Even as a young man he took remarkably good care of himself, eating simply, drinking very little, going to bed early. This dull regimen kept him alive, when carelessness had undoubtedly contributed to his father's early death.

Only by exercising the skill of a politician, however, could the Prince ever achieve the privilege of being a soldier. Here his family and his tutors could not help him; there can rarely have been a more uniformly inept political party than the Orangists of this generation. The only service they could do the Prince was to die off, leaving him free to act as he wished, without any obligations to the men of 1650. William was lucky in this respect, at least; he would have been even luckier if the Orangists had died sooner and left him alone to make his own mistakes. As it was, he made some natural errors as he learned to be a politician, and the surviving leaders of his party made others for which there was much less excuse. One of these came in May 1664 when the Prince was induced to insult the French ambassador.

William had returned to The Hague in 1662 from Leyden and was now living in the Stadhouder's quarter of the Binnenhof with his little Court. This gave him a new opportunity to learn about the great world, and the world a new opportunity to see his progress, while his studies were not interrupted. Dr Bornius followed the Prince to the capital and taught him for four hours a day, after the daily hour of religious instruction from the *predikant* Triglandius.[31] Three hours were allowed for dinner in the middle of the day, and in addition the Prince was free after four o'clock to hunt with his new falcons[32] or to promenade in the Voorhout in his carriage in case of heavy weather. It was here, in the centre of The Hague, that William chose to insult d'Estrades. Hurdles had been set up in the Voorhout to outline a rough oval, and the fashionable were supposed to promenade in one direction. Although d'Estrades insisted on his right to drive against the stream of traffic, there had never been any difficulties. On the afternoon of 7 May, however, the Prince's carriage was manoeuvred so as to block that of the ambassador. Neither carriage would give way. The crowd took the Prince's side, and d'Estrades was in some danger of being mobbed. De Witt happened to see what was going on. He hurried to the palace of the Princess Dowager and persuaded her to come to the rescue. She came to the Voorhout and called her grandson to her. William obeyed, on foot. His coachman took the empty carriage away, leaving the ambassador in possession of the field.[33]

Such an incident was not likely to help the Prince regain the affection of the most sensitive monarch in Europe. Louis XIV gloried in winning battles over protocol. He took them very seriously. In Dutch terms, furthermore, the Prince was clearly in the wrong. Even Stadhouders had not taken precedence over a French ambassador until the 1640s;[34] and William was no Stadhouder. His claim was made as an English prince, a 'grandson of England.'[35] He was, of course, the only legitimate grandson of Charles I; but 1664 was not a good year to remind the Dutch of this fact, when England and the Republic were slipping into war. In such circumstances the English connection might well be dangerous to the Prince, exposing him to charges of unpatriotic feeling or even, in an extreme case, to banishment. The course of the war was to prove what a threat his family connections could be to the Prince.

From the beginning of 1665, Dutch political struggles became more and more intense. The time was fast approaching when the Prince would represent, for the first time, a real alternative to the cabal. Johan de Witt and his friends had never been popular outside the regent class. Inside that class many regents were jealous of the cabal's monopoly of the best places; since de Witt was still a young man the unfortunate might well be excluded from office for another generation if the Grand Pensioner remained in office. There was, then, even among the regents a large group which hoped for his fall, and it increased day by day. The main sources of the Prince's strength were still the orthodox clergy, his relatives, and his employees. These would never be strong enough to restore their leader by themselves. But if enough disappointed office seekers joined them, and if public opinion could be manipulated well enough, the Orangists might eventually win. Unfortunately for the Prince his grandmother's health was failing at this time, and she was unable to coordinate the efforts of the party.[36] Even so, 1665 saw a great attack on the cabal's position.

The clergy were among the first to take the field. In January a preacher at Rotterdam argued strongly for the Prince, going so far as to justify the execution of Oldenbarnevelt in 1619. He was suspended and imprisoned, but the attack continued.[37] By July the dislike of de Witt had spread to Amsterdam, whose opinion was far more important than that of Rotterdam. D'Estrades reported that when an attempt was made at Leyden to drum up volunteers for the fleet in the name of the States, the citizens threw the drummer into the river, demanding that he enlist men in the name of the Prince and not in the name of traitors.[38] At the same time, sea captains and crowds of their men were saying openly that they would fight only under the Prince's banner. The situation became so serious that Louis XIV ordered d'Estrades to inform the States that his alliance was conditional on the maintenance of de Witt's authority.[39] This did nothing to stop the uproar. Toward the end of October the Orangists, having gained control of five of the seven provinces, were demanding that the Prince be made General and also that he be sent to England on an extraordinary embassy to demand peace from his uncle on easy terms.[40] Wicquefort pointed out drily that 'Kings have no relatives' and that Charles II had not said one word during the war about the advancement of his nephew. This was true, but only because Clarendon was convinced that English intervention would ruin the Prince for ever.[41] D'Estrades was able to prevent the embassy to England with the help of van Gent, a Gelderlander in French pay, and by the judicious disposal of 25,000 livres.[42] He was not able to prevent the resignation of Hieronymus van Beverningk from his post at the head of the Dutch financial administration. Van Beverningk was a man of great importance; his loss was the first real crack in de Witt's political system.

For a few months it looked as if the Orangists might win. At the beginning of February 1666 de Witt was driven to ask the French for the loan of the great Maréchal Turenne. His plan was that Turenne should command the forces of the Republic for one or two campaigns, while the Prince of Orange would learn his trade in the subordinate position of cavalry general.[43] It was a good plan; had it been carried through it would have been an excellent training for William Henry. There was, however, strong opposition to it from two sides. Louis XIV would not part with Turenne, nor did he think that the Prince of Orange would ever be anything but English in his heart.[44] The Orangists, on the other hand, demanded the Prince's immediate establishment at the head of the Dutch armed forces. This was sufficiently ridiculous, considering the Prince's age, and the fact that he had not even begun to learn how to ride a warhorse.[45] The Orange party, scenting victory, could not be bothered by mere details. By the end of February they had a clear majority of the towns of Holland on their side, and it seemed as if de Witt would have to give way. He was disheartened at the opposition of thirteen out of the nineteen votes of the province. For a moment his courage failed him. But d'Estrades was able to cheer him up, and early in March the French ambassador made a tour of Holland to make the towns change their votes.[46] He was successful. In the end, only Enckhuyzen and Edam voted even to make the Prince general of the cavalry.[47] Meanwhile the Orange party had made a fatal step which ruined their campaign at the moment of victory.

The Elector of Brandenburg, who was then at Cleves, strongly supported the elevation of William of Orange. He was under constant pressure from his family and from the English to do something for his nephew. In March he asked Louis XIV for his help.[48] He also wrote twice to the States General recommending the Prince's cause.[49] The effect was electric. Holland threatened to withhold the subsidies due to the Elector for his alliance. The Brandenburg ministers at The Hague were menaced with the possible loss of their diplomatic immunity. The Prince was reminded that all those who tried to obtain promotion by the recommendation of a foreign power were incapable of any place.[50] The intervention of the Elector destroyed any hope that the Prince might obtain a military charge.

It did more. De Witt now took up the old plan of 1660 to make William a Child of State. He wanted a complete change in the Prince's Court, so as to remove all traces of English influence. He wanted also an end to the political intrigue which was having such a bad effect on the conduct of the war. To get his way, he was willing to make vague promises to the Princess Dowager of a substantial pension for the Prince if she would ask the States of Holland to undertake the boy's education. The Dowager fell into the trap. She abandoned her supporters and her grandson, who was bitterly opposed to the idea of parting with his closest friends, and begged Holland in 'most respectful and submissive terms' to take on the task of educating the Prince.[51] Holland accepted, excluding the Province of Zeeland which had earlier been promised a share in any such arrangement. The Court was broken up. English servants of the Prince were sent home at once, the Dutch retired on full pay. Van Gent, an old friend of de Witt who happened to be in French pay, was named Governor. He had the grace to refuse the continuance of his pension, which Louis XIV offered to raise to 4,000 livres a year, but he did ask in exchange a post in the French army for his son.[52] This may have satisfied the new Governor's honour, but it did not satisfy the Prince; their relations were never to be close.

William Henry reacted strongly to the change in his circumstances. He made a pathetic call on d'Estrades and begged, with tears in his eyes, that Zuylestein be allowed to remain his Governor. It was true that Zuylestein's wife was English; but he would send her away until the end of the war. The Prince promised that Zuylestein would never do anything against the wishes of Holland; as for himself, he would look on de Witt as a father and place himself entirely in his hands.[53] It was no use. Van Gent was installed in the bedroom next to the Prince's own. And now, after this momentary weakness, William rose above the situation. He made a strong speech to his new tutors. They had taken away his domestics and wished to take care of his education. He begged them also to take care of his business affairs. His lands were being sold daily at a vile price. No one bothered to pay his debts. Though he spent very little, considering his rank, he knew that he owed his butcher and other merchants for years together. After this speech, William made it clear to de Witt that he actually was going to look on him as a father and to follow his advice. They had frequent secret conferences, in addition to the formal weekly meetings in which de Witt examined him on his lessons. The Dowager was angry at this new friendship and furious at her grandson's reflections on her stewardship. When she complained, she was told sharply that it was all her own fault.[54] The Princess never again had any influence with her grandson, who rarely took the trouble to write to her in her last years. She lived on until 1675, in increasingly bad health and stripped of all political power. Her folly had cost her what she wanted most in life, and for nothing. The promised pension, of course, was never heard of again.

With the Orangist threat out of the way, de Witt could give undivided attention to the course of the war with England which had broken out in 1665. It had not been going well. Before the formal declaration of war, the English had captured some stations on the coast of Africa and also New Netherland, which was renamed New York. An attempt had been made on the Dutch merchant fleet returning from Smyrna. This failed, but the English trounced the Dutch off Lowestoft, taking or sinking twenty-five ships and killing the Dutch admiral and two thousand of his men. They also made a subsidy treaty with the Bishop of Münster, Bernard van Galen, who invaded the Republic from the east and overran part of the Province of Overijssel. By a treaty of 1662 the French were obliged to come to the aid of the Dutch. At first, however, the French did nothing; and although Louis

XIV did eventually and most reluctantly declare war on the English, he fought as little as he could. His fleet never joined that of the Dutch. On land his assistance was more extensive. A small French army and some diplomatic pressure were enough to force the Bishop to make a separate peace. The Dutch, however, could take little pleasure in the conduct of their ally and none at all in the work of their own land forces. At sea, though they did better after the defeat of Lowestoft, they were not winning any decisive victories. It was fortunate for the Republic that the English were being crippled by domestic catastrophe. There had been an outbreak of plague in the Netherlands but it had not been too serious. When it spread to England, however, the plague soon got out of hand. The weekly bills of mortality rose to gigantic heights. Then in September of 1666 the greater part of the City of London was burned to ashes; the result, many said, of a papist plot. It was not, but the fire certainly seemed to show that God, if not the papists, was working against the English. The two disasters made it almost impossible to continue the war.

The Prince of Orange supported the efforts of his fellow-countrymen in their struggle against the English. In May of 1666 he went on a visit to the Dutch fleet. He was received warmly, all the sailors crying out 'Vivat de Prins van Oranje!', while his presence was enough to secure the enlistment of more than a thousand sailors.[55] His new governors were trying to secure the friendship of their charge. Not only did they let him make this trip; they allowed him to make another in the summer to Cleves for the marriage of one of his aunts to the Paltsgrave of Zimmern. They doubled his pocket money allowance to fl.400 a month and allowed him to spend unlimited amounts on clothes.[56] These courtesies may have softened the Prince's attitude to his new Court. They were not enough to pacify the Orange party. Some of its less responsible members were still trying to give the English an easy peace in return for help in establishing the fortunes of their master. In August, while William was at Cleves, they were caught.

One of the Prince's domestics, who had shared his table until the old Court was broken up in April, had been the French soldier Buat. He was a man of considerable courage, but a drunkard.[57] His fidelity to his 'little master' was undoubted; there can be equally little doubt of his lack of intelligence. Buat entered into negotiations with Lord Arlington through Gabriel Sylvius, who had been the secretary of the Prince's mother and was now living in England. He obtained permission from de Witt to carry on this correspondence and showed him some of the letters which came in. But there were other, secret letters, in which Buat tried to persuade the English to demand as a condition of peace the establishment of the Prince. One day, by mistake, he gave one of these secret letters to de Witt. The Pensioner refused to return the fatal letter when Buat demanded it; but he delayed for nine-and-a-half hours before having the traitor arrested. Buat was such a fool that he did not use the opportunity to flee, or even to burn his papers. He was arrested, tried, convicted, and executed before the Prince returned to The Hague at the end of September. The scandal involved a number of Orangists more prominent than the unfortunate victim. The great admiral, Cornelis Tromp, was one of them. Tromp was a bitter rival of a greater admiral, de Ruyter, who was a supporter of de Witt. Probably this was one cause of the disaffection in the fleet which was such an ugly aspect of the war. Tromp's brother-in-law, Kievit, and the Rotterdam politician van der Horst were also involved. They fled to England and remained there until the political situation changed in 1672.

William Henry was lucky throughout the Buat affair. He was known to be a friend of Buat. He had been entertained by van der Horst at Rotterdam. The conspiracy was undertaken in his name. As it happens he was perfectly innocent, but men have died for less. The Dutch, even those of de Witt's party, refused to blame William personally for the sins of his friends. They might and did use every opportunity to attack the Orange party; but the Prince was treated as being still a child, not a responsible person. It was an honourable and generous approach to a difficult problem. Yet with every year it became a more untenable position. William Henry was reaching maturity. Some place would have to be found for him within the constitution of the Republic, or else he would destroy that constitution. This was the problem that Johan de Witt had to face in the years after the conclusion of the Treaty of Breda.

Chapter 5

FIRST NOBLE OF ZEELAND

On the morrow of the Treaty of Breda Johan de Witt seemed at the peak of his power. He had trounced the English; and the victory was a family one, since his brother Cornelis had led the Dutch fleet to Chatham. His diplomacy had been as clever as his warfare. The French, however reluctantly, had been obliged in the end to make good their obligations under the treaty of 1662 and to join the Dutch side in the war. At home, the Prince of Orange and the Orange party were safely under lock and key. Under de Witt's leadership the Dutch Republic was flourishing. The tiny state was the leading commercial power of Europe and the owner of one of the greatest empires of the day. Her military strength was weak, but what did that matter if the French army could be employed in defence of the eastern frontier? At sea the Dutch had now no rivals. In the history of the world, only Venice and Athens at the height of their glory had approached the present position of the United Provinces.

It took just five years to shatter the Republic and the party of freedom, to bring the state low and the de Witts to the gallows. A good part of the explanation for this rapid collapse lies in the blindness and inflexibility of de Witt himself. In his later years, though he was still relatively a young man, there is clear evidence of a decline of ability. But there were other, more fundamental causes of the events of 1672. The Dutch had become a great power in a vacuum. Spain was in full decay, Germany still prostrate from the effects of the Thirty Years War. France was reduced to weakness during the minority of Louis XIV. At the same time the English were also beset by political troubles. The Dutch, therefore, looked very strong because their neighbours were so badly off. But this weakness was only temporary. In the years after 1659 the French demonstrated their amazing capacity for rapid recovery. Eight years of great prosperity made it possible for a vigorous government to lay the foundations of a new army and a new navy. As France quickly became the strongest power in Europe the Dutch became more and more nervous. They had a proverb to the effect that the French make a good ally but a bad neighbour. Soon, if French strength continued to increase, they might experience the meaning of that proverb. Between France and the Republic lay only the Spanish Netherlands, and Spain was now in no position to defend them.

In 1635 the French and Dutch had made plans to partition the Spanish Netherlands. This treaty had fallen to the ground when the Dutch abandoned their ally to make a separate peace with Spain. A generation later de Witt proposed the 'cantonment' of these provinces, that is, their erection into a buffer state which would be independent of any great power. The French toyed with de Witt's idea but refused to accept it. They had other plans. The Queen of France, Marie-Thérèse, was a daughter of Philip IV of Spain by his first marriage. By Article V of the Treaty of the Pyrenees she had renounced all her rights to inherit any of her father's sovereignties. By Article IV she had also renounced, on condition that her dowry be paid, any rights she might have to the private property of her House.[1] The dowry had never been paid. On the death of Philip IV in 1665, therefore, the French considered that their Queen was entitled to a share in the private property of the estate. In some parts of the Spanish Netherlands daughters of the first marriage took precedence by the so-called right of devolution over sons of a later marriage. Turenne invaded the Spanish Netherlands in May of 1667 to secure the rights of the Queen of France. Eight months later Condé invaded and soon occupied all Franche-Comté.

Now the Dutch were faced with the neighbourhood as well as the alliance of France. De Witt opposed the plans of Louis XIV on strategic, legal, and personal grounds. He did not want the French as a neighbour. Neither he nor anyone else took the Queen's claims seriously or thought that the right of devolution extended to cover such a case. He was angry on personal grounds because the French had moved without consulting him. When they demanded Dutch assistance, de Witt refused it. He did more. Early in 1668 he concluded a treaty with England, which Sweden later joined and which was named the Triple Alliance. The Triple Alliance, indirectly but obviously, was directed against the French; in certain circumstances the allies would fight to reduce France to the limits of 1659. When Louis XIV made peace at Aix-la-Chapelle in May it appeared that he had been forced to do so by the allies. Actually, the King had made a secret treaty with the Emperor Leopold, as husband of Marie-Thérèse's sister, for the eventual partition of the Spanish monarchy in January. This secret treaty gave Louis what he wanted, including the prospect of eventually acquiring all of the Spanish Netherlands. He was, therefore, willing to make peace on generous terms. But he was angry at the Dutch for abandoning him and for making him appear timid. From now on, Louis XIV considered his alliance with the Dutch a dead letter. He felt that de Witt had cheated him. In good time he would take his revenge by attacking the Dutch. In August 1668 Colbert de Croissy was sent to London to propose an alliance whose eventual purpose was an attack on the Republic.[2]

The War of Devolution cost de Witt the support of France. It showed, if further proof were needed, that the Republic must strengthen its land forces. But this could not be done by the Louvestein party. The bulk of the army was favourable to the Prince of Orange. Any increase in its strength was a gift of power to the opposition. A strong army might well involve the fall of de Witt and his friends. And so, although de Witt himself tried to strengthen the army in the years after 1667, he could not bring his followers to support him, and the land forces of the United Provinces became a laughing-stock. Meanwhile the party of freedom began to break up. De Witt had now been in power for almost fifteen years. In that time he had antagonized many people, and there were several others who hoped to replace him if he fell. His chief support in Amsterdam had come from his wife's relatives. These had died by 1665 and the city was now controlled by two men, Gillis Valkenier and Coenraad van Beuninghen, whose opposition to the Grand Pensionary was a serious blow to him. Another threat to his position came from the ambitions of the Pensionary of Haarlem, Gaspar Fagel. Fagel's talent was so great that he had succeeded in politics without family connections. Even in the Dutch Republic this was a most unusual feat. After the end of the war with England Valkenier, van Beuninghen, and Fagel emerged as the leaders of a 'middle party' which soon took the initiative away from the older de Witt and Orangist groups. On some issues they would support one side, on some the other. But their capture of the initiative was ominous for the future. If in 1667 de Witt was unchallenged in his glory, within a year he was in serious difficulties abroad and at home.

The first political success of the new middle group was the passage of the Perpetual Edict. By this measure Holland, and later Utrecht, abolished the position of Stadhouder for their respective provinces. The military position of Captain-General of the United Provinces was declared to be incompatible with that of Stadhouder of any of the five remaining provinces. Thus if William III should become Stadhouder of any one province he would be incapable of ever gaining the military authority of his forefathers. On the surface the Perpetual Edict appeared to be an attack on the Prince of Orange. In reality, however, it was his first important step on the road to power. The Edict practically assured him of becoming Captain-General one day. He was not to be permitted to hold the office until he had completed his twenty-second year. Everyone knew that this was almost a promise of the place on the following day.

De Witt had made two significant errors in attempting to handle the problems of 1667 and 1668. In the first place he continued to rely on French support even after the conclusion of the Triple Alliance. Van Beuninghen, who was ambassador to France during the critical months, realized that

French support was gone forever. This made it essential to turn towards the English and towards the Prince; de Witt, on the other hand, never understood the consequences of the Triple League. He refused to believe that Louis XIV bore a grudge against him. At the same time, he continued to do everything he could to prevent the Orange party from gaining any share of authority. This had been an easy matter while William had been a child. Now that the Prince was reaching maturity, however, de Witt could not exclude him from all power. A graceful retreat on certain issues might have made it possible to reach some kind of workable compromise. The Grand Pensionary refused to retreat. When he was forced to give way, as he was again and again after 1667, he did so as gracelessly as possible. His stubborn attitude contained some elements of grandeur; but it involved revolution, not compromise, in the end.

It is probably true that all paper constitutions are unworkable in practice. A strong leader must know how to circumvent the letter of the law so as to achieve its intent. The constitution of the Republic was an unusually bad one. This made it necessary for every Dutch leader of the seventeenth century to act roughly and often illegally to achieve the welfare of his country. De Witt was no exception. Perhaps his methods were even rougher than they had to be. Certainly they were rougher than those of the Prince in later years. D'Estrades, the French ambassador, felt that the Pensionary was afraid of a day of reckoning; that he might be brought to trial 'for many things he has done, perhaps with good intentions, but contrary to the forms of the government'.[3] For some of de Witt's actions, however, he did not have the excuse of good intentions. In March 1667 the States of Holland forcibly repurchased the feudal dues of Gertruydenberg from the Prince of Orange, which he held as security for a loan. The revenues were of no importance; it was simply an act of spite. When the Prince's Council refused to accept the payment, the States took possession of Gertruydenberg with the aid of armed men – de Witt's supporters said that he sent a single hussar, his enemies that he sent eight hundred men. The Princess Dowager's sister, the Countess of Brederode, was in possession of another estate called Viane. It had never been taxed because of the Countess's relationship with the House of Orange. In 1667 another hussar assisted by ten or twelve soldiers was sent to Viane to establish the tax rights of the States of Holland. When the Countess refused to pay, four regiments of infantry and two of cavalry were quartered on her until she gave way.[4] The brutality of these pinpricks was not conducive to any compromise between parties. In the spring of 1668 there was even a rumour that the Prince would be evicted from his quarters in the Binnenhof. When Sir William Temple complained about this, de Witt denied the rumour. There had been a plan, he wrote, to evict the Prince's falcons but not their owner.[5]

It was in 1668 that William Henry began to take an active part in his own affairs. He had a keen admiration of the French court all his life. In 1672 he was to buy his clothes in Paris; in 1698 he commissioned Lord Portland to buy him a bed there. Now, in February, he gave a *ballet de la paix* in imitation of the performances in which Louis XIV himself took part. The *ballet de la paix* had clear political overtones. At the beginning, war appeared to stir up discord between England and Holland. The Prince, appearing in the guise of Mercury, brings them together again so that between them they can maintain the balance of Europe:

> Qu'il est beau de vous voir dans cette intelligence,
> Ne vous en départez jamais;
> Quand vous serez Unis, vous tiendrez la balance,
> Et maintiendrez par tout le repos & la paix.

Later he returned as a Swiss and the following promises were made about his political conduct:

> Regardez de quel air ce Suisse se comporte,
> Son vin n'est il pas fort discret?
> Il n'entre point dans son secret
> Dont il sçait bien garder la porte:
> Il est soigneux, il est prudent
> Dans son devoir ferme & constant
> On n'y remarque aucune impatience,
> Il sçait regler tous ses desirs;
> Et par sa propre Experience,
> Il trouve le secret d'allonger ses plaisirs.

The whole consisted of an overture, twenty-two short scenes, and a Grand Ballet, all acted by young men. In addition to appearing as Mercury and as a Swiss, the Prince came on stage dressed once as a shepherd and again in the costume of a North Holland peasant woman.[6]

All this was not calculated to win the approval of the Dutch. They remembered the godless play-acting of the Prince's father. Almost any play-acting was godless to the Calvinist clergy. There had also been confusion in sending out invitations; some of the guests invited to the second performance refused to come, feeling that they ought to have been asked to the *première*. The creditors of the Prince would have preferred to be paid rather than to see a new extravagance.[7] William learned his lesson, and although he attended the theatre throughout his life he never again provided such an entertainment for his countrymen. Drunken dinner parties proved more effective in gaining votes.

In May the Prince went to Bergen-op-Zoom to see a review of the army.

The field deputies of the States of Holland seemed determined to remind him that he was no more than a private citizen. Officers were ordered not to salute him as he passed down the line, and when he went to dine with the Grand Master of the Artillery he was placed below the deputies, who of course represented the sovereign.[8] Nothing, however, could disguise the popularity of the Prince both with the army and with the people. There were actually some disorders in Friesland and in Groningen in his favour this year.[9]

The visit to Bergen-op-Zoom had meant the postponement of a more ambitious plan, which was actually carried out in the autumn. This was the installation of the Prince as First Noble of Zeeland, a place which had been promised him in 1660 and which was not in conflict with the terms of the Perpetual Edict. In March, Constantijn Huygens visited the province and presumably made plans for the *coup* with the Zeeland Pensionary de Huybert. By May d'Estrades knew about the affair.[10] But it was not until September that the Prince, telling his tutors that he was going to Breda, left The Hague. At Breda his grandmother's yacht was waiting for him; a 'chance' meeting with his cousin Prince Maurice had also been arranged. William Henry arrived at Middelburg before anyone knew that he had left Breda and was installed as First Noble by the States of Zeeland on 19 September, being introduced by the Pensionaries of Middelburg and Zierickzee. He was placed in a velvet armchair at the head of the table and made a polite speech of thanks.[11] The *coup* was important for two reasons. As First Noble the Prince gained effective control of the province. He owned two of the six towns which had votes in the States of Zeeland. As First and only Noble he gained a third vote. Unless all four of the remaining towns opposed his wishes unanimously, Zeeland was now at his disposal. As his deputy William appointed his cousin Odijk, who would not only represent him at Middelburg but also have a permanent place in the States General. Now it would be impossible to maintain the fiction that the Prince of Orange was simply the richest private citizen of the Republic.

His installation, therefore, gave the Prince a small place in the constitution. It also laid the grounds for a more important claim. This was that he would come of age at eighteen. Under Roman law William would not come of age until his twenty-fifth birthday, and perhaps de Witt intended the education commission to continue until that time. But English princes were considered competent at eighteen, and it would be ridiculous for the First Noble of Zeeland to have guardians in Holland. Having obtained the agreement of Charles II and Frederick William of Brandenburg, the Princess Dowager turned over the management of the estate to her grandson on 25 October. At the same time she sent announcements to the States of Holland, the States

General, and Louis XIV.[12] This step, following on the Zeeland affair, caused a great outcry. In her memorial, the Princess had been most provocative. Not only had she turned the management of the estate over to William Henry without asking Holland's advice; she stated that she had done so not only because of the Prince's talent but in order that he should gain experience by working with his Domein Council. She hoped that this would give her grandson an inclination to maintain and preserve his fortune. And she also hoped that the state would be given proofs of his ability to execute public affairs, which always had begun to be entrusted to his forefathers at about this age.

Holland wanted nothing less than proofs of such ability. De Witt took into consideration the possibility of ending the education commission[13] but decided against it. When some members of the States General wished to congratulate the Prince on the occasion, the delegation of Holland prevented it and announced that they would warn all the tradesmen in Holland not to do business with him, on the ground that he was not really of age. They forced the Princess Dowager to promise that she would not permit the Prince to sell any of his lands for another two years.[14] There was also an outburst of pamphlets, some of them at least inspired, against the House of Orange. *Den haestigen Zeeuw* was fairly moderate in tone.[15] It blamed the Prince for going to Zeeland without consulting his tutors and suggested that he surrender the place of First Noble into the hands of the States General in order to calm the discontent that his action had caused. The pamphlet argued that all republics save the Dutch had eventually fallen under the control of a great family. The Dutch must take care to protect themselves from a similar fate. This was much more judicious in tone than the famous *Praatje in 't ronde* of the next year.[16] This was simply a scream of abuse against Charles II, Willem II – 'traitor', the Orange Party – 'Zeelander Buatist traitors', and William Henry. The author considered that the latter, as the son of a traitor, was forever ineligible for public office. This kind of attack did the party of de Witt no good and merely assured that its eventual fall would be a hard one. By the end of 1668 that fall was simply a matter of time.

By now the Prince's character and disposition had become of international interest. The reports of foreign ambassadors were strongly favourable. Sir William Temple wrote home to Lord Arlington:

I find him in earnest a most extreme hopeful Prince, and to speak more plainly, something much better than I expected, and a young man of more parts than ordinary, and of the better sort; that is, not lying in that kind of wit which is neither of use to one's self nor to any body else, but in good plain sense, with show of application if he had business that deserved it, and that with extreme good agreeable humour and dispositions; and thus far of his way without any vice. Besides, being sleepy always by ten o'clock at night, and loving hunting as much as he hates swearing, and preferring Cock ale before any sort of wine.[17]

Already, of course, there was a serious possibility that the Prince would one day become King of England. Charles II had no legitimate children and those of his brother James were all sickly. Temple was putting the case with an eye to the future. Yet the dispatches of the new French ambassador, the Marquis de Pomponne, also spoke highly of the Prince. His first impressions were that William was growing up 'avec beaucoup d'esprit et d'application'.[18] When he later gave a fuller description of the Prince's character, he came very close to what Temple had written:

Le prince estoit dans sa dixneuvième année. Il estoit né avec de l'esprit, le jugement paroissoit pas moindre que l'esprit, et il sçavoit cacher ses sentiments sous une dissimulation qui luy estoit naturelle. Excepté la chasse, il n'avoit nulle des passions qui sont ordinaires à la jeunesse. Il estoit extrêmement réglé dans ses moeurs. Son naturel estoit sage, doux et civil. Il avoit une application et une intelligence dans les affaires au-dessus de son aage. Il connoissoit bien ses intérests et sçavoit les ménager avec addresse.[19]

Both men spoke of his intellect, his good sense, his application to business, and his good manners as well as of his high standards of personal conduct. Pomponne noted, as Gourville had done earlier, William's powers of dissimulation.[20] The Prince was almost never to show his personal feelings. He had a bad temper and could lose it in private. In public, however, he kept his temper better than most of the men of his day. Sometimes, on large issues, he remembered grievances and took his revenge at the appropriate time. Often he simply forgot them.

Pomponne, in his *Relation de mon ambassade en Hollande*, noted two other prominent characteristics of the Prince which were less attractive. The first was his frugality. 'Son inclination, ou peut estre le désordre dans lequel il avoit trouvé ses affaires, paroissoient le porter un peu trop au ménage et à l'oeconomie, et il est estonnant avec combien d'intelligence et de capacité il travailloit à liquider les debtes de sa maison, à regler ses despenses, et à restablir ses revenus.'[21] The charge was perfectly true. Six months after he took over the administration of his affairs, William was able to reduce his interest payments to the level of 4 per cent. The credit of the House of Orange had not been so good for years.[22] He took pains to attend the meetings of his Domein Council every Tuesday.[23] In the spring of 1669 he instructed his agents in Brussels and Madrid to push his claims for payment of the Spanish debt, and Huygens to write a dunning letter in May to Arlington about what the English owed him. 'It is true, My Lord, that the sum for which you detain the warrants is not small, but in a word it is all

ours, and might at least be furnished in convenient terms'.[24] In the circum-
stances it was essential for the Prince to be economical. The interest on the
Spanish and English debts had never been paid or even, in the case of the
Spanish debt, been added to capital. During the course of Condé's seizure of
Franche-Comté in 1668 six of William's châteaux had been destroyed, and
Louis XIV would not listen to any claims for damages. While these debts
were outstanding, the Prince himself must pay interest on the fl.2,000,000
borrowed from Amsterdam and on many smaller debts, including the
dowries of all his aunts. And, of course, he had no salary. He had to be
careful, no matter how unattractive it was.

Pomponne also noted that the Prince was shy and retiring. He held himself
aloof from members of his own class and made very little effort to be
popular. He was not easy of access. In particular, Pomponne noted, he paid
very little attention to women and avoided public festivals.[25] This too was
true. Perhaps William resented the schedule of his childhood, when he had
been forced to hold court while still a baby. He had excellent manners when
he wanted to use them. But he did not care for society. He devoted himself
to business, to hunting, and later to war with great enthusiasm. This gave
him an opportunity to claim that he was too busy for ordinary social contacts,
and in later life he avoided The Hague almost as much as he was to avoid
London. His enemies attributed this aloofness to pride in his royal blood. It is
much more likely that William Henry was aware of the limits of his strength
and of his remarkable ugliness. Even now his asthma made crowded rooms
heated by human bodies and by the many candles very uncomfortable for
him. And a tiny man, hunchbacked, hooknosed, with a continual hacking
cough, could scarcely have paid very much attention to women. He would
have been afraid of being laughed at. Ambitious mothers like the Princess of
Taranto and the Electress Palatine might dream of making their daughters
Princess of Orange. The daughters had taken one look and fled.[26] No wonder
that the Prince was shy. Although this did him harm with members of his
own class, William did not suffer in his relations with the general public. To
the people he was, and would always remain, 'Our Prince'.

One of the provisions of the Perpetual Edict gave the Prince a place in the
Council of State. This body had had great authority in the sixteenth century.
After their unhappy experience with Leicester, however, the Dutch had
reduced the powers of the Raad van State so that it was now little more than
an advisory group. Even so, it would be to William's advantage to become a
member. At this point the Edict had been approved by four of the seven
provinces. Zeeland, Friesland, and Groningen still stood out. Until these
three provinces agreed to adopt the Edict, de Witt and his friends could
reasonably maintain that it was the Prince's own party which in its stubborn-

ness was keeping him from office. By the spring of 1670 the Orangists had come to the conclusion that it would be to their advantage to accede to the Perpetual Edict. Though it excluded the Prince from some of the offices held by his ancestors, it granted him others. And once the Prince was a member of the Council, once he was installed as Captain-General, it would be impossible to maintain the Edict. The stadhouderships would then fall into the Prince's lap, whatever the law said.

De Witt and his party felt precisely the same way. Though they had been forced to agree to the Edict in 1667 they now tried to prevent it from going into effect. First, de Witt argued that the Prince would represent Zeeland's particular interests as a member of the Council. Zeeland already had two places there. With the Prince she would have three, a number wholly dispro-portionate to her strength and importance. Second, the Orangists were arguing that William needed to be on the Council to gain experience. If this were true he ought not have a vote until he had gained enough experience to use that vote wisely. If de Witt were driven to agree to the Prince's membership, he wanted him to have only an 'advisory' and not a 'con-cluding' voice.[27] Left to themselves the Orangists would probably have lost their case. Wicquefort noted that when the matter was brought up in the States of Holland in April, only a single town was in favour of giving William a 'concluding' voice.[28] But that town was Haarlem. Its Pensionary, Gaspar Fagel, was one of the leaders of the middle party. Amsterdam, con-trolled by Valkenier and van Beuninghen, joined Haarlem on 19 April. With the middle party fully committed to the Orange cause, the Prince had a much better chance of success. It was a bitter fight. The town of Haarlem voted that if the Prince were not given a concluding voice it would no longer be bound by the Perpetual Edict.[29] This was an open threat to revive the Stadhoudership of Holland. On the other side de Witt tried desperately to persuade William to visit England at once so as to get him out of the way.[30] William was planning to go, but not until his position at home was assured. He was working very hard and very well in his own interest.[31]

When the dominant faction saw that things were going against them they tried to bring up two new points. The first was that when and if William was appointed Captain-General it should only be for a single campaign unless the appointment was voted unanimously by all the members of the States of Holland. This would have placed the Prince in an intolerable position. A single campaign might go badly. At the end of an unfavourable campaign he might lose his post, and with it his reputation. The second point was that if William were to be appointed Captain-General for life, the question of his place on the Council of State should then be reopened.[32] These conditions were not accepted. Some minor restrictions were, however, placed on the Prince's position as a member of the Council. He was not to be present at deliberations concerning his relations 'to the fourth degree'. Did this refer to France, England and Brandenburg, or did it also include Spain, Denmark, Savoy, and several minor German states? No one knew. The Prince was also to be absent during debates on raising or lowering impositions on the Generality lands, that is, areas of the Republic not part of any of the seven voting provinces.[33] This was demanded on the ground that the Prince was the largest single proprietor of those territories. With the acceptance of these restrictions William's victory was assured. He was granted membership with a concluding voice at the end of May and installed on the 31st. Now even Holland had to admit that he was of age. In July the work of van Gent and of the education commission was formally brought to an end. When William tried to maintain from the obsolete wording of his commission that his place on the Council also gave him regular session in the States General he failed.[34] Yet even without this he had gained a substantial victory. And a large part of that victory is to be ascribed to his own political skill.

Now that he had achieved his place on the Council of State the Prince could once more turn his attention to his financial problems. The most promising of his debtors was Charles II of England. The King had never been able to pay his father's debts or his own to the House of Orange. He had, however, spoken many kind words. Further, he had agreed to compound the interest of the debt, so that the whole now amounted to fl.1,800,000 or £180,000. The payment of this enormous sum would enable the Prince to force his own creditors to accept 3½ per cent rather than 4 per cent interest. It might also persuade the Kings of France and Spain to remember their own debts to William Henry. Thus the trip to England was for the Prince little more than a collection process. But the timing must be right if he were to preserve his reputation. This always meant much more to him than money. He turned down an invitation to go over in the spring of 1670, because he had not yet won his struggle with de Witt. In June he sent his physician, Dr P. A. Rumpf, on a secret trip to London to arrange details of the visit. Rumpf was forbidden to see anyone except Lord Arlington. Their meeting took place at eight in the evening in Arlington's garden, and for greater security the doctor disguised himself with a black wig.[35] The Prince would not go at all without the permission of the States. Nor would he go without some advance assurance of receiving payment. If he failed to receive his money he would lose too much prestige at home. Finally, the Prince was still worried about the best time for the voyage. Van Beuninghen was now in London on behalf of the Republic. Should he be going to succeed in his negotiations, William wanted to be present so as to gain a share of the glory. But if van Beuninghen was going to fail he preferred to wait until after the ambassador's departure. Arlington gave Rumpf every assurance that the Prince would be satisfied in his own affairs. But since there was very little prospect of success for van Beuninghen it would be better for the Prince to postpone his visit until October.

It was not until the beginning of November that the Prince and his party left the Republic in two of the King's yachts. These were under the command of Thomas Butler, Lord Ossory, who was to guide William during the coming months and to become one of his closest friends. In 1659 Ossory had married Emilia van Beverweert, the daughter of an illegitimate branch of the House of Orange, and he was thus considered a member of the family. Outwardly at least the whole trip was a splendid affair. The Prince was attended by a group of Dutch nobles as well as by members of his own household. On 8 November N.S. he reached Rochester. The next day he went to Gravesend, where he was met by the royal barges and the Master of the Ceremonies. From Gravesend the Prince was taken up the Thames to Whitehall, where he was greeted on the water by the Lord Chamberlain, who took him ashore and presented him to the King and Queen. William Henry received an unusually warm welcome. Later he was presented to the Duke and Duchess of York, whose welcome was less warm, and perhaps also to their three children. The little Duke of Cambridge was three or four; his sister Mary was eight and his sister Anne five at this time. On the fourteenth, William's birthday, he was entertained with a comedy. And for the next few months there was to be a round of parties.[36]

The Prince received partial satisfaction from his uncle about the debt owed him. £40,000 was paid down, and order was taken about the remainder, which would have to be provided by Parliament since the King was virtually bankrupt. But the visit also had a larger meaning. As Lord Arlington had told Dr Rumpf in June, the children of the Duke of York were all in poor health and there was not much reason to suppose that any of them would live to maturity.[37] The court and the people were eager to examine the young man who might very well become their King. They saw a serious, devout, possibly prudish prince who wore his own hair rather than a wig and who dressed with extreme simplicity. All this formed a startling and welcome contrast to the debauchery of the English court.[38] William did his best to be a complacent guest, though he found it impossible to drink as deeply as his uncles. He attended the King from time to time at sessions of the House of Lords.[39] Magnificent parties were given for the whole court by the French and later by the Spanish Ambassador. With the rest of the Royal Family William attended the revels at the Temple on 27 January and those at Lincoln's Inn the next day. He went alone to dine with the Lord Mayor and Aldermen, where he made an excellent impression.

The visit was not confined to the capital. William and his suite went to Newmarket and from there to visit Cambridge. On another short trip he went to Oxford after being installed as a Knight of the Garter at Windsor. At both universities he was handsomely treated. Prince Rupert, on the other hand, gave him a cold welcome at Windsor because William had been granted precedence over the older man. Both were 'grandsons of England' but the Prince of Orange stood closer to the throne. Rupert may also have been jealous of William's instant popularity with the English people, which visibly eclipsed that of all the Stuarts. In later years both the King and the Duke of York were to show their pique at the Prince's power over the crowd.

The Prince of Orange stayed in England for almost four months. Although he succeeded in getting some of his money and though he achieved something of a popular triumph, he had had very little to do with larger political questions. Both the Dutch government and the English preferred to leave him out of such things.[40] Many years later the Prince told Bishop Burnet that the King had confided one great secret to him: that he was a papist.[41] This is doubtful. Charles had promised the French that he would not confide in his nephew. Burnet was an untrustworthy witness, and William's famous memory was a curious thing. Over short periods of time he could recall conversations *verbatim*. His recollections were not nearly so precise as to events of several years' standing. Certainly the Prince did not seem to shape his conduct after 1671 on the assumption that Charles II was a papist. He may well have suspected something of the sort, and it is always possible that the King was really guilty of an indiscretion. In any case this was the only important issue that could possibly have reached his ears. For the rest the voyage to England was a pleasant and profitable interlude. After waiting to see the Duchess of York delivered of a daughter,[42] William returned to the United Provinces. When he landed in Zeeland on 27 February there was to be a sudden change in his life. For the first time he was to find himself personally involved in great affairs.

Chapter 6

CAPTAIN-GENERAL

EVER since the conclusion of the Treaty of Aix-la-Chapelle in 1668, war clouds had been gathering over the Republic. France, furious at the insolence of the Dutch in signing the Triple Alliance, was determined on revenge. Already in 1667 a new French tariff had begun a commercial war between the two states. The burden of this tariff fell most heavily on Amsterdam, which explains in part the support given by that city to an anti-French policy. Meanwhile the Triple Alliance was becoming more of a 'scrap of paper' daily. Sweden, failing to receive the Spanish subsidies promised by the Treaty, was easily detached from the Dutch. Charles II, protesting in public his fidelity to the Triple Alliance, agreed by the Treaty of Dover of 1 June 1670 to a joint Anglo-French attack on the United Provinces. In Germany the Elector of Cologne and the Bishop of Münster joined the French. The attitude of Brandenburg was suspicious, while the Emperor Leopold had never admitted that the Dutch people had achieved their independence. For diplomatic purposes he still insisted they formed a portion of the Circle of Westphalia within the Empire. By 1670, therefore, the isolation of the Republic was almost complete.

At home the government of de Witt found it very difficult to prepare for war. The navy was in fairly good shape, but the people were bitterly divided, and the army existed in name only. During the war of 1665 many Dutch soldiers had deserted to the forces of the Bishop of Münster, England's ally.[1] The Bishop knew perfectly well that his enemy suffered from internal discord. When he invaded the Republic his troops were instructed to spare the estates of the House of Orange and the men advanced to the strains of the *Wilhelmus*, the family anthem.[2] After 1667 there was no improvement in the thoroughly demoralized condition of the Dutch army. The highest military office, that of Captain-General, was of course vacant. Those generals who were on active service were either aged or foreigners and, in either case, unable to maintain discipline. Captains were allowed to live where they chose, so their men were often scarcely able to recognize them when ordered out.[3] Every sixth military vacancy could be filled by 'persons of birth and of exceptional merit', that is, sons of politically influential burghers.[4] This meant the appointment of large numbers of officers who were civilians at heart and were almost totally without training. Perhaps the worst feature of the Dutch army was its want of arms and ammunition. When field exercises were held in June 1668 a musketeer could fire, at most, only seven rounds. Every hundred pounds of powder furnished to the army was subject to a traditional deduction of 12 per cent.[5] The powder that actually reached the men was less useful than it could have been, since heavy, obsolete *lontslot* muskets were still being furnished instead of the superior *snaphaan* or flintlock.[6] The condition of the artillery was even worse. Guns were provided for on the military budget, but none were purchased. Gunners, on the other hand, were not even entered on the 'state of the war' and so received no pay. In 1670 the Council of State was unable to determine how many artillery officers were alive. At Maastricht there were eight gunners, and only two others along the entire Rhine frontier.[7]

Sweeping military reforms were thus essential for the safety and preservation of the state. In 1665 the Dutch had found themselves unable to defend their frontiers against the Bishop of Münster. They had been forced to call for the assistance of the French. What would happen if they were now to be attacked by France itself? Each day brought new evidence that a French assault must be expected. As early as January 1668 de Witt was receiving letters of warning.[8] These warnings multiplied during the next two years. By August of 1670 de Witt was at least partially convinced of their truth. He spoke as if he was assured of the existence of an agreement between France and England, by which France would furnish four millions in subsidies to help the English prepare for the conquest of the Netherlands by land and sea.[9] Yet even though he received these repeated warnings, even though he accepted them intellectually, de Witt was unable to bring himself to act on them with vigour. What was the reason for this blindness?

The Grand Pensionary had a very low opinion of English strength. He was, furthermore, a man who observed foreign affairs with his head rather than his heart. He expected others to think as he did. Convinced that it was against English national interests to see the Netherlands fall under French control, he supposed that Charles II must agree with him. De Witt could not believe that Charles might have other views or be able to put them into effect. Convinced that the preservation of the Low Countries was also of vital interest to the Germans, de Witt believed that he could always buy the alliance and support of several German princes at his own price. He was wrong on both issues. No one was going to defend the Dutch unless they showed themselves able and willing to fight in their own cause. And the King of England felt that his own interests and those of his people could best be served by a new Dutch war. De Witt's excessively intellectual approach to foreign affairs made him underestimate the facts. Pomponne was startled at the narrowness of the Grand Pensionary's vision. He knew so much of the truth and yet he refused to act on it.[10]

Pieter de Groot, one of the most extreme members of the de Witt faction, was now in Paris as Dutch ambassador. De Groot understood the necessity of rearmament. In his letters to Wicquefort he wrote again and again that the Dutch could not rely on foreign assistance. The French were counting on an easy victory because of the internal discord of the people, because of the incompetence of the army officers, and because of the decay of their fortifications.[11] But de Groot was afraid that the war would be a means not for the conquest of the United Provinces but for the reestablishment of the Prince of Orange.[12] De Witt refused to consider any military reforms that would involve giving new powers to William Henry. It would mean a complete change in the form of government. Once the Prince was made Captain-General he would be able to acquire the other places held by his ancestors. And the worst thing about such a revolution was that it would be undertaken at the dictation of a foreign power, since England was recommending the Prince's appointment to supreme military office.[13] All through the year 1671 rearmament was delayed because of de Witt's stubbornness and because of his suspicions that the Prince was acting with the Kings of England and France to overthrow the Republic in his own personal interests.[14]

Superficially these suspicions seemed well justified. While the Prince was visiting the English court Charles II recommended to the Dutch ambassador Boreel William's appointment as Captain-General. At the same time the Province of Zeeland was refusing to adopt the 'state of the war' or military budget for the year 1671. If Odijk, William's deputy as First Noble of Zeeland, was acting under the Prince's instructions, it would be quite obvious that the Prince preferred his own advantage to the safety of the state. But Odijk was not acting in accordance with the Prince's orders. His reason for opposing the budget was a personal one. The state of the war for 1671 made more provision for naval than for military rearmament. If greater emphasis had been placed on strengthening the army, Odijk hoped that his brother might obtain a regiment.[15] The first news the Prince had of affairs in Zeeland came on his return from the English visit. He arrived at The Hague on 28 February, a Saturday, and only then discovered what Odijk had been trying to do. On Sunday he sent an express to Odijk ordering him to approve the state of the war as it stood. This may have done a little, if only a little, to allay suspicions of the Prince's conduct. As it happened he had not been told during his trip about the French and English plans.[16] Charles had been tempted to confide in his nephew, though Louis XIV objected to the idea. Charles, however, had discovered the Prince to be 'so passionately Dutch and Protestant' that the plan had been dropped.

In a larger sense the Prince's orders to support the state of the war for 1671 were important, because it was generally expected that the attack would come during the course of the year. This had been the original plan, and this was what many Dutch people expected.[17] The newly expanded French army had been given an easy training exercise during the summer of 1670 when it was sent to occupy Lorraine.[18] It might be ready for larger game the next year. Luckily for the Dutch, it proved less easy than Louis XIV had expected to win the support of the princes of Germany. He found that he would not be able to begin the war until August or September of 1671. It would be cheaper to postpone the attack for a year than to start a campaign so late in the season.[19] An added advantage of the delay would be that the Dutch would be put to the expense of maintaining their army for a year to no purpose.[20] To a certain extent the postponement of the war did work to the advantage of the French. They were able to complete their fortifications and the arrangements they were making to enlist foreign troops. It was possible for them to buy up large quantities of grain for their magazines and to execute a daring plan for the purchase of gunpowder and lead from the Dutch themselves. An Amsterdam banker named Sadoc bought up and exported very large quantities of gunpowder, saltpetre, fuses, lead and bullets. In theory he was acting for the account of certain German cities such as Frankfort and Mainz. Actually Sadoc was working for the French, and by the time his activities were discovered he had exported some 400,000 pounds of powder and proportionate quantities of other material.[21]

If the delay gave the French more time to prepare, it proved to be the salvation of the Dutch people. When war finally came, she had allies; and some steps had been taken for the reorganization of the army. Negotiations were undertaken in 1671 with the Spanish for joint action against the expected aggressor.[22] In December the Dutch and the Spanish signed a reciprocal territorial guarantee covering the entire Low Countries. If the French attacked either the United Provinces or the Spanish Netherlands, the state not subject to invasion would come to the aid of the victim. The Queen-Regent of Spain approved the action of her Ambassador, Don Manuel de Lira, in negotiating this agreement and the ratifications were exchanged at The Hague on 22 February 1672.[23] This was to prove of vital importance to the Dutch, because the Governor of the Spanish Netherlands at that moment was the Count of Monterey, one of the few able men to hold that post in the second half of the seventeenth century. While he was in command, the government at Brussels was much stronger than it usually was.

De Witt must be given the credit for obtaining Spanish help. In so far as this aid saved the independence of the United Provinces, and it was to be of great importance, the Pensionary is to be praised. De Witt did much less, however, to bring the army on to a sound footing. On 2 December 1671 the Raad van State came in a body to the States General to complain about the military situation. Army, magazines, fortifications, all were weak. The purchase of fl.50,000 worth of cannon a year had been recommended by the Raad van State as long ago as 1665, but nothing had been done. Gun-carriages were not available, although their acquisition had been authorized in May 1666. Powder, shot, fuses, victuals, and other necessities were all badly needed. The individual provinces were not paying their quotas towards the fortification of the frontiers. It was a gloomy picture.[24]

The chief defect of the army, in the eyes of the Orange party, was that their Prince was not yet at the head of it. All through the year there had been attempts to secure some kind of salary for William Henry. In the course of these debates the deputies of Gelderland in the States General had referred to William Henry as 'Captain-General designate'. This was not quite true. The Perpetual Edict prevented the Prince from becoming Captain-General before the end of his twenty-second year. It did not promise in so many words that he would be given the appointment after he had reached that age. The deputies of Holland forced their brethren of Gelderland to withdraw the paper containing the offending words from the registers. Gelderland, how-ever, was not to be put off and proposed that the Prince should now be declared Captain-General by land and sea.[25] Early in December a similar proposal was made in the States of Holland by the town of Enckhuysen. De Witt was determined to oppose the appointment with all his strength. For the moment he was able to obtain a delay, on the ground that William would not complete his twenty-second year until November 1672.[26] A compromise was proposed, by which the Prince should be given a salary of fl.25,000 and go into the field in a political capacity; that is, that he should become a field deputy rather than a general. This would not infringe the agreements previously reached, and of course the Prince might later be appointed Captain-General when he had attained the proper age.[27] The Pensionary was bitter about the weak conduct of the other Provinces, especially Zeeland. He was even more bitter about the conduct of some people in the Province of Holland itself, who were driving with great zeal to lay the foundations of their own slavery.[28] De Groot was also hostile to the promotion of the Prince, which he considered to be simply throwing oil on the fire. The goal of the English and French was precisely the advance-ment of the Prince and the overthrow of the republican system, because the Prince would be much easier to deal with than the present government.[29] Of course the Orangists were dissatisfied at the idea of sending the Prince to the war as a civilian. And so, more importantly, were the leaders of the middle party, including van Beuninghen and Hieronymus van Beverningk.[30] The lines were drawn for one of the most important political battles since 1651.

The goal of the Louvestein party in the coming struggle was clear, even though it may seem bizarre.[31] William must, apparently, be named Captain-General. Since the French were not going to wait for him to complete twenty-two full years he must be appointed now. But the party demanded two important concessions. His Instructions must be so limited that the Prince could not use the army to overthrow the constitution. Secondly, his appointment must be for a single campaign. This would salve the consciences of those who had approved the so-called Harmony of 1670, when all seven provinces had finally accepted the concept of the Perpetual Edict. Basically, William's opponents remembered the sins of the father and suspected the patriotism of the son. Might he not remember the hardships of his youth and use the army to revenge himself, as his father had tried to attack Amsterdam in 1650? Might he not, at a fitting moment, accept enemy aid to make himself sovereign? These fears were to be proved vain by the Prince's later conduct. They were by no means unrealistic at the time. Unfortunately, no one bothered to consider that the limitations placed on the Captain-General would prevent him from defending the Republic. His Instructions were so drawn that he could do little more than observe the coming war.

Abraham van Wicquefort wrote sneeringly about the projected Instructions drawn up by the Holland leaders in the latter half of December.[32] They were harsh enough to satisfy anyone else and did satisfy such an extremist as Pieter de Groot.[33] William must not become Stadhouder of any single province. He must not issue *patenten* – that is, marching orders – within the provinces. He must not meddle with affairs of state, religion, finance, or justice, or even arbitrate between quarrelling provinces unless invited to do so. He was to have no authority within a province except at the special request of its legislature. He was, finally, subject to the decisions of the civilian field deputies. These officials were, it is true, bound to listen to his advice. Once they had heard him, however, they were to take their own resolutions, which the Captain-General must obey. No project could be better devised to prevent a repetition of the events of 1650. But that was no longer the question.

Although de Groot approved the projected Instructions, he was still trying his utmost to sow disunion between the French and the English. He pointed out to the ministers at St Germain how the advancement of the Prince would tie the Republic forever to England. 'But I found to my sorrow that the great animosity here has absorbed all other considerations and that people wish for nothing but the ruin of our State by any means . . .' De Groot could only console himself with the idea that the Prince's advancement might secure the neutrality of England. And, he philosophized, who knows whether God has not kept the Prince alive so long in order to be a bulwark now against France? The Lord will easily provide some means or other to rid us of England later.[34]

After a brief recess for the holidays, the fight over the Prince's appointment was resumed in January. Six whole provinces, and a group within the States of Holland itself, wished to appoint the Prince for life or at the very least without any specific limit of time. In the latter case his commission could be withdrawn if, for example, he married an enemy of the state. But the extreme republicans stood firm. They would only appoint him for a single campaign. Now William made a serious political error. He refused flatly to accept the place on those terms.[35] His conduct irritated some of his supporters and for a moment there was a chance that he might be abandoned. He was not, but his stubbornness postponed the final decision for a month. It was not until 24 February that the States General drew up Instructions, which were similar to those projected by Holland. On the next day the Prince accepted the places of Captain- and Admiral-General for a single campaign and took the necessary oaths. As Admiral-General he was not to issue any instructions whatever to fleet commanders. This was reasonable enough since William knew little or nothing about the sea. The post gave him a title, a 10 per cent share in prizes, and very little more. Immediately afterwards Holland, having satisfied its duties to the Harmony of 1670, voted to make his place permanent as soon as he should attain the necessary age. The Prince had therefore won a great deal more than had been expected. He had won the substance of what he wanted, though not the form. He had the grace to give the States of Holland a good dinner a few days later for their pains.[36]

To the general public the appointment of the Prince was a cause for wild rejoicing. On the night of 25 February hundreds of people roamed the streets of The Hague, some singing, some beating drums, others blowing trumpets.[37] William Henry, more reserved, gave no sign of emotion. Later, however, when some courtiers were speaking of the preparations of the enemy, he burst out: 'And to oppose to all that a Captain-General who has no experience and very few advisers! God must come to our aid!'[38]

It was not necessary to rely entirely on divine assistance. During the spring the Republic did all it could to improve the quality and size of the army, and by the middle of June it had a paper strength of 107,000 men.[39] But the Dutch army had even more trouble with 'dead pays' than other armies of the day. Officers would put their valets into uniform on the day of a muster, or borrow men from companies which were to be mustered at another time. A modern expert has calculated that the real strength of a unit which the States General calculated at 10,000 men was actually between 5,000 and

6,000.[40] And if we take the strength of the land forces in June 1672 at something between 50,000 and 60,000 in all, it must be remembered that a great many of these soldiers were dispersed in remote garrisons where they could do little good. The men were very soft after twenty-four years of relative inaction, and most of the good officers of Frederick Henry's time had left Dutch service to find employment elsewhere. Some of these could be rehired. Karel Rabenhaupt, who had been a Lieutenant under William's grandfather, was now a Lieutenant-General in Hessian service. The Heer van Amerongen, who was then on a diplomatic mission in Germany, wrote to the Prince suggesting that Rabenhaupt, whom he described as 'a man of general reputation and one who knows artillery and infantry from the ground up' be secured, as well as several experienced officers of lower rank who offered to bring with them whole regiments of horse and foot.[41] The general was actually taken into service by the province of Groningen and lived up to his reputation by his defence of the northern provinces. Others were also brought in at the last moment, but it was too late to hire enough of them. Even after their appointment, good officers needed time to train their men. That time was not available. The Prince, furthermore, had so little influence over the army that he could not even give a place to Amerongen's son, the Heer van Ginckel, later famous as Earl of Athlone. Under the terms of his Instructions, the Captain-General could appoint to vacancies. But the original appointments were in the hands of the individual provinces, and van Ginckel must get his commission from the States of Utrecht.

It was also possible to do something to strengthen the frontier. Entrenchments were dug along the IJssel river, in the extreme east, to make a first line of defence. This IJssel Line, when completed, was twenty-six hours long. The whole army of the Republic could not defend such an enormous distance, and there was a strong chance that sections of the line could be taken without the defenders being aware of it. The strength of the line, furthermore, depended very largely on the depth of the river. Should there be a drought, the enemy would be able to cross the river on foot. The entrenchments by themselves afforded no protection. And what if the enemy were not kind enough to attack the IJssel Line? It would be perfectly easy for them to cross the Rhine, below the southern end of the entrenchments. Dutch troops were in occupation of a group of towns further up the Rhine in the Duchy of Cleves. If the French took these towns there would be nothing to prevent them from breaking into open country and the heart of the Republic.

There was some question of establishing a second line of defence. Between January and May negotiations proceeded between the provinces of Holland and Utrecht about what to do if Gelderland should be lost. These negotiations broke down because of the enormous costs involved.[42] Holland would not let the matter rest here. She determined to fortify her eastern border and began to do so at her own expense. This second line of fortifications was by no means complete when the war began, but a good start had been made. Such as it was it would mean the salvation of the Republic. And here too, as in the case of the Spanish mutual defence agreement and a treaty with the Elector of Brandenburg for an army of 20,000 men, credit must be given to the republican administration and not to the Prince of Orange. Defence measures were begun far too late, and much too little was done. But something was done, and it was on this foundation that William was able to defend his country. He could not have succeeded without having at his disposal the forces prepared by the rival faction.[43]

The Prince of Orange took leave of the States General on 19 April and took command of the army at Doesburg. To their dismay the field deputies found less than 8,000 men where they had expected 18,000.[44] And not all the 8,000 were worth having. The English government had received word that 'For their land Army they are in a miserable condition, with sickness & want of pay, those in ye Briel have had none these 14 weekes & from all quarters they desert in great numbers, & they are inforced to keep strong guards to prevent them . . .'[45] Confidential letters reached Paris bringing word that the preparations by land were not being made with nearly as much zeal as those by sea.[46] There were serious shortages of grenades, grenade casings, larger guns, powder, and particularly of gun carriages. A shipload of guns reached Zutphen towards the end of April without any papers, so no one knew where they were to be placed. The heavier calibres were missing from the shipment, both 18- and 24-pounders. Most of the guns which did arrive were without carriages, and there was no money with which to buy mountings on the spot.[47] What was particularly alarming was the continued fall in the level of the IJssel. It was one of the driest spring seasons of the century. By the beginning of May flat-bottomed boats, drawing only three feet of water, were trapped at IJsseloort. The level of the Rhine was not so dangerous. But that too was falling, and since the Dutch depended very largely on the river system for their transportation, a continued spell of dry weather could mean disaster.[48] The drought continued. By the end of May the troops at the front were without straw for making huts and were thus obliged to sleep in the open.[49] Since there was no rain this was not too much of a handicap. The continued shortages of gunpowder and cannon mountings were more serious.[50] And the lack of rain meant a steady and continuing fall in the level of the rivers. By the beginning of June there were perhaps a hundred places along the IJssel where cavalry could cross without difficulty, and at Nijmegen cows waded through the

Waal daily to feed on the far bank. Where water was to be had, sluices could be opened so as to flood the farmland. This gave a great measure of protection. The Prince himself went on short trips to see that the sluices were opened. Peasants, who did not want to lose their crops, returned at night to shut them.[51]

Early in May the high command decided that the line of the IJssel could not be defended without more men. The field deputies, together with Field-Marshal Wirtz and the Prince, recommended that the garrisons of fortified towns should be removed and sent to man the retrenchments.[52] In one way this would have been for the best. The garrisons were strung out along the Rhine, some of them in Cleves where the people could not be counted on to support them, and the fortifications they occupied were in such poor shape as to be untenable.[53] The recommendations were not followed. Hastily armed peasants were sent up to the line from Holland and elsewhere, but they had no training and were almost useless even for digging. Since their term of service was for a single month, it was not worthwhile to give them any instruction. The soldiers themselves were not much better. On 24 April actual hostilities began when Count Walraven van Nassau took an army corps out of the Rhine towns, from Rees through Rijnberk to Huls. His goal was to reach Meurs, a county belonging to the Prince of Orange. He never reached it. The men were completely out of control and would go off in groups of fifteen or sixteen to shoot hens and geese. Their officers made little effort to control the men, even when they approached Meurs, and the hens and geese they were plundering belonged to the Captain-General.[54] On this sour note the war began.

On 17 May the Prince held a general review of his little army on the heath between Zutphen and Deventer. William felt the quality of the men under his own command to be fairly good, but their number was much too small—some 9,200 foot and 4,800 horse.[55] The review caused considerable trouble with the local authorities. The deputies of the Veluwe quarter felt that no encampment could be made without their permission. Some of the deputies were personally interested in the land taken for the encampment and suffered a little damage. This led them to claim that the Captain-General was acting in violation of his Instructions by camping within the territories of a voting Province without its consent.[56] De Witt denied this outburst of particularism on curious grounds. Holland, Friesland, and Zeeland might be able to make such a claim, he felt, because they paid for their defence out of their own pockets. The other four Provinces were defended at the expense of the States General and therefore must do what they were told. No effective defence could be made against attack by people who held such narrow views. Even if de Witt's premises were accepted, the three Provinces that were paying their own defence costs would reserve a right of independent action. And at this time Zeeland was doing just that, by withdrawing her troops out of Bergen-op-Zoom in the 'generality lands' for her own protection.[57] Utrecht and Friesland had sent authorizations to the field deputies, though not to the Prince, to punish delinquent officers. Holland had not done even as much as that. The Prince lacked any real disciplinary authority over his men. If they were sentenced, he lacked any power to pardon them.[58] The field deputies reported during these months that he was full of energy, keeping his headquarters at his house at Dieren, going out all day and often at night as well to supervise the preparations. But one man, even with the aid of the hard-working field deputies, could not build an army out of such materials and on such conditions. The task was hopeless.

By the beginning of June the field deputies were driven to recommend the abandonment of the IJssel Line without a fight. It seemed clear that the French might pass to the south of the line. In this case the army would be cut off and easily trapped. If the French did come far enough north to attack the line, the water-level was so low that they would have no difficulty. De Witt reacted strongly against the proposal, which the deputies themselves had only made with great reluctance.[59] De Witt estimated that there were now 30,000 men at the line, which was by no means true. He felt that 30,000 men, with the help of God, could defend the IJssel and that it must be held. Van Beverningk had already commented that the Lord usually chooses to employ human tools, and that in this case there were not enough tools for Him to use. While de Witt remained at The Hague, a delegation from the States General went to examine the army at Arnhem on 5 June to see if things were really as bad as they had been told. They found the army much smaller even than they had imagined. The officers were inexperienced, the men undisciplined, and the whole force was 'frightened and jumpy'. The armed householders and *waardgelders* who had been sent up to reinforce the trained soldiers were worthless.[60] Nevertheless the delegation did not dare to take the responsibility of authorizing the abandonment of the line. Two days later they returned to The Hague, leaving behind them full powers for the field deputies to do what they thought best. They knew, however, that the line could not be held.

Meanwhile the enemy had completed their preparations and taken the field. French military planning for the war, and also a good share of the diplomatic work, had been undertaken by a young genius of thirty-one, the Marquis de Louvois. At the beginning of the year he had made a hasty trip to Cologne to sign a final agreement with the Elector. After the treaty was signed on 2 January he had been obliged to join the Elector in a toast to the success of their design; the toast was so hearty that discussions could not be resumed for two days.[61] Although Louvois did not enjoy German drinking habits, better things were in store for him on his return to Paris. On 4 February he presented to Louis XIV a report which he and his father, Michel le Tellier, had prepared, on the state of the army. The élite troops numbered almost 8,000 men. There were in addition 25,000 horse and 86,000 foot in the regular army, including the foreign troops which had been engaged. In all, then, the French land forces came to about 120,000 men; and they were real men not 'dead pays', well armed, well trained, and brilliantly led.[62] Pieter de Groot reported that the King had been so pleased by this appraisal that he made Louvois a minister of state on the spot. The French promised themselves that their opponents were so ill-prepared that half their country would be taken in the coming campaign: a prediction which we might do well to remember.[63] They declared war on 6 April. The original declaration was so worded as to make it appear lawful for French civilians to kill Dutch merchants in their country at will. After some delay the Dutch Secretary at Paris was able to secure a protection for them. He was so happy at this concession that he sent wine to the printers to speed their work in printing the protection and to the police for their share in distributing it.[64] On 28 April Louis XIV left St Germain and on 5 May he reached his army at Charleroi. There he found Turenne and 80,000 men. From Charleroi the King marched towards Maastricht, where he was joined by Condé with 40,000 men on 22 May. Maastricht had been heavily fortified and garrisoned by the Dutch. If only the King stopped and laid siege to the city he might lose an entire campaign. But the French were not to waste their time in this manner. Leaving a covering force behind them they marched down the Rhine. Condé was on the right bank and Turenne, with the King, on the left. The King decided that it would be more effective to attack the Dutch Rhine garrisons four at a time. In the first days of June Wesel, Buderich, Orsoy and Rijnberk were summoned to surrender.

Now the real fighting would begin. Except for Spanish aid the Dutch faced the world alone. Their treaty with Brandenburg for the supply of 20,000 men was of no use to them, because it was not signed until 6 May nor ratified for another month.[65] Even if the Elector should be able to raise 20,000 men so late in the year, they would not be available for months. Nor could the extent of Spanish assistance be estimated precisely. The Queen-Regent refused to declare war on France or to enlarge her commitments.[66] Her aid as an auxiliary must be small, since the resources of the Spanish Empire were exhausted. Count Monterey, the Governor of the Netherlands, might be enthusiastic but he had little to offer. The Dutch, therefore, would have to fight alone until they could secure more allies. And they must fight at sea as well as on land. The Prince's appointment as Captain-General had not changed the plans of the King of England. Wicquefort had been right when he wrote that 'Kings have no relatives'. Charles II might be fighting against the wishes of the English people and without Parliamentary support, yet even so he could wage one campaign or perhaps even two with his own resources. By that time the Republic might well be forced to sue for peace.

William Henry had done his best to avert the English threat. In January he had sent Gabriel Sylvius to England on a personal mission. Sylvius was to offer on the Prince's behalf everything that the King might desire which was not directly contrary to the foundations of the Republic.[67] This was risky business. In 1672 no one knew how 'passionately Dutch and Protestant' the Prince was. If the negotiations became known his position might be irretrievably compromised. It was perhaps fortunate for William that his uncle refused to take the offer seriously. The Prince's intentions were undoubtedly sincere. He hated de Witt and his party and would not consider their fall to be the end of the state. But there were limits beyond which he would not go. He would never agree to abandon a foot of Dutch soil, nor to do anything which would be contrary to his own honour. In our own day William has been the object of a savage attack by the greatest of Dutch historians for his conduct in these negotiations.[68] De Witt would have been justified in feeling as Pieter Geyl does, because de Witt never knew how the story came out. He could not know what the Prince meant when he refused to do anything contrary to his own honour or contrary to the foundations of the Republic. Geyl does not have this excuse.

The republicans themselves had been doing their best to placate the English. They were willing to give in on the sore point of the flag. Dutch fleets would strike their flags not only to English squadrons but to single English men-of-war. Neither de Witt nor the Prince had any success. In March Admiral Holmes tried to attack the Dutch Smyrna fleet. A few days later the English declared war. It was not too important. De Ruyter could protect the coasts, though his forces were inferior to those of the enemy. The real theatre of the war was to be on land. Everything depended on the courage and ability, completely unproven, of a young man with no experience and few advisers. A young man who must fight with his hands tied by ridiculous instructions and by the narrow particularism of a people who had been softened by a generation of peace.

Chapter 7

THE REVOLUTION OF 1672

AT the first sight of the French army the United Provinces collapsed like a bad *soufflé*. There was virtually no resistance. On 1 June the invaders came before Wesel and took a small outlying fort which no one had even bothered to protect with palissades. Two companies of men in the fort were shot up. At this the inhabitants of the town, who had at first prepared to defend themselves, put down their arms and forced the Governor to open the gates. They sent emissaries to treat with the Prince de Condé, who promised to spare Wesel if the garrison was brought to surrender in the space of four hours. The citizens obeyed, and the town was occupied on Sunday 5 June. The garrison, without any capitulation, was locked up in the church.[1] It was much the same at other places. Fortified towns surrendered without firing a shot. Sometimes the troops resisted long enough to obtain the honours of war. Often, they simply surrendered to the first party of the enemy they could find. By 8 June it was clear that the main army would not do any better than had the outlying garrisons. Van Beveringk wrote that day to de Witt: 'There is a panic terror and so great a fright among the officers of our army that I am terrified myself when I consider what the consequences of it will be. ...'[2] He felt that there was no hope of holding the frontier and recommended withdrawing on Utrecht.

In the next few days confusion, terror, and ignorance of the whereabouts of the enemy turned defeat into disaster. Although some Spanish regiments of good quality arrived at the front they were too exhausted by their march to be of immediate service.[3] On the tenth, van Beveringk wrote of formal revolts of the civilian population at Nijmegen and Arnhem. Zutphen was in panic and was only kept in some semblance of order by the presence of the field deputies. Although the Prince worked night and day – his health was always to be at its best during a campaign – he found no support from his officers. Beveringk was afraid that William might, in despair, undertake some reckless deed.[4] Cowardice among the officers made their defeat, certain as it was, more shameful than it need have been. When the people of Nijmegen refused to accept the Comte de Montbas, a French officer in Dutch service, as commander in their city he was ordered to take command of some posts in the Overbetuwe. Perhaps the orders given him were confusing. Everything was confused during those terrible days. Whatever his excuse, Montbas abandoned his posts on the 10th, sending no word of his action to the Prince. He sent some of his men off to Nijmegen and appeared himself at headquarters at Dieren the next morning, where he was arrested.[5] Field-Marshal Wirtz was hastily sent to reoccupy the abandoned posts, but it was too late. On the 12th Louis XIV and the army of Condé crossed the Rhine with little difficulty, though the Prince de Condé himself received a slight wound.

This easy crossing of the Rhine made the whole frontier untenable. Now the question was whether the Dutch army would have time to retreat, or whether it would be surrounded. If it retreated north to Campen on the Zuider Zee, the enemy might get there first. Utrecht was nearer than Campen and there was less danger of surprise on the way. And so, having left some of the men to their fate, seven regiments of foot and fourteen of horse were dispatched westwards towards Utrecht.[6] These men, perhaps 9,000 of them, were all that remained for the defence of Holland. To the north the troops of the Bishop of Münster were attacking Overijssel, Groningen, and Friesland and meeting little resistance. From now on the provinces would be separated by the enemy. If they fought on, two small pockets of resistance would be separated by the Zuider Zee.

If they fought on. Was further resistance possible? Could the army fight, and would the people let them fight? This was to be the question during June and July. When the army reached Utrecht on 15 June the people would not let them enter the city. For two days the Prince and the field deputies debated with the town fathers. They finally agreed to open their gates to the Prince's troops; but they would not agree to destroy the suburbs. Unless these were razed the city itself could not be defended. On the 16th the States General impatiently sent out orders to abandon the province which seemed so unwilling to take part in its own defence. Late the next day the army broke up a second time and retreated on the half-finished fortifications of Holland. The disaster had been almost complete, and frighteningly rapid. As early as the 13th captured Dutch flags had been seen in the forecourt of the Arsenal in Paris, and they were displayed the next day in the Tuileries gardens.[7] Not until 1940 would the pace of war move so swiftly again. The Republic had lost three provinces in little more than a fortnight. To most of the Dutch, and to almost every Frenchman, the war seemed over.

For months there had been warnings of coming disorder and tumult among the people. The republican administration had never been popular with the labouring classes, which were strongly Orangist in sentiment. De Witt's friends were a narrow oligarchy of the wealthiest men in the country. They were disliked and distrusted by the less wealthy burgers, whom they kept out of office. Thus even a large portion, perhaps a majority, of the middle classes were disaffected. As new tax followed new tax – there were three successive military budgets in the spring of 1672 – the situation became more serious. Levied taxes were very slow in coming in. Capitalists proved unwilling to lend their money even when the safety of the fatherland was at stake. The poor were as unwilling to offer themselves as the rich to offer their money. There had been an attempt to conscript one out of every ten men in good health in the generality lands for military duty.[8] When a similar attempt was made in May in Holland there were riots. At one place the peasants refused to cast lots even if they were to be hanged for it. At another they threatened to shoot the colonel through the head.[9] Even before the invasion, therefore, the situation was slipping out of control. But when the régime proved unable to defend the frontier there was an explosion. The government had placed arms in the hands of the burgers and peasants: now it was at their mercy. With almost all regular troops either captured or at the front, there were too few left to do police duty at home. The way was open for revolution.

At first the common people could not believe what was happening. Margaretha Turner fled with her household from Amerongen Castle at two in the morning of 13 June. She was not insulted on her way, and when she reached Amsterdam later that day she wrote to her husband: '. . . There is such dismay everywhere that it is unspeakable . . . men and women walk along the road weeping like children.'[10] This mood of bewilderment soon changed to one of hatred for those rich enough to flee. The people felt that the Regent class had betrayed them and was now trying to escape. Samuel Tucker, an English agent at Rotterdam, wrote on the 17th:

> The near approach of the French doth so much amaze us, and put us into confusion here that we are all in an uproar, the common people tumult, & will permit no goods to go out, pretending the great ones send away their money & best things to Amsterdam, Antwerp, Zeeland, and Hamburgh and intend to follow after, & leave the people to the mercy of the French. . . . I was last Tuesday at the Hague when the people threw stones at the house of mynheer Momba [Montbas] & broke the glass windows of the house & had gone farther but a troop of horse & the burgers in arms made all quiet and prevented the like mischief threatened to others. There were then several boats loaden with trunks and costly goods for Amsterdam which the people stopt, which the borgomaster confirmed by shutting of the boom & charging the boatmen not to depart. . . . We have had a troop of horse this day from the Hague to quiet the people . . .[11]

In his letters to his brother Cornelis, Johan de Witt described the same mutiny of the people, who in almost all the towns of Holland were arresting suspicious travellers against the orders of the magistrates. Yet more serious was the conduct of the peasants. The new line of defence, the Holland Water

Line, was well named. Five army posts were themselves covered and connected by inundations which would form a barrier of water that the enemy
could not pass. But the inundations were not yet connected with each other,
and when dikes were cut the peasants resisted by force. When the army
reached the line on the 18th, coming from Utrecht, things went a little
better. The troops could force the peasants to open the sluices and to cut
dikes. But even then things went slowly.[12] The domestic situation grew
worse, not better, and the Pensionary felt that it was more serious even than
the progress of the enemy. On the 21st he referred to a general revolt of the
inhabitants of the towns and peasants, by which the strength of the
government was enervated.[13]

It was in this atmosphere that the government had to work for the next
few months. The first task seemed to be to make peace at almost any price.
If the people refused to fight or pay taxes, if they opposed the government
with arms in their hands, there was no choice. In fact, of course, the people
merely refused to support the present government, which was completely
discredited. They would willingly support the Prince. But his time had not
yet come. On the 14th the States of Holland agreed to apply to the enemy for
terms, and on the next day the States General followed suit. Pieter de Groot,
Odijk, and van Gent, the Prince's former tutor, were sent to Louis XIV.
Another embassy was dispatched to Charles II. De Groot and his colleagues
reached Keppel, where they found no beds, at midnight on the 22nd and
saw the French ministers the next morning. Pomponne and Louvois asked
them what terms they brought. They replied that they had more respect for
the King to offer conditions of their own. At this the French ministers
retired to confer with their master. They returned before noon, bringing word
that Louis XIV insisted on terms being proposed to him by plenipotentiaries.
It was always a disadvantage to speak first. Pomponne and Louvois did give
some indication of what was expected. The Dutch must consider how things
now stood. What the French had taken was 'their own property' and they
seemed likely to take much more if fighting continued. They expected
equivalent territory for all they had won, if the conquered Provinces were to
be returned. In addition, the Dutch must pay for France's war expenses and
give satisfaction to her allies. De Groot was sent back to The Hague to
demand the necessary full powers, while Odijk and van Gent remained at
the French camp.[14]

On the 25th the States of Holland discussed the problem of whether to
make peace. De Groot indicated that the French would probably be willing
to leave the seven voting Provinces intact in return for the cession of all their
other lands and a sum of money. He added that it was no time to bargain.
The more they offered, the kinder Louis XIV would be to them. If they tried

to chaffer they would be ruined.[15] Almost all the towns of Holland, following the lead of the nobility, agreed with him. Amsterdam was virtually the only town to stand out. The Amsterdam representatives felt that the terms were impossible, that the state could not afford to indemnify the French and their allies, and that if they did accept these terms they would still have an English war on their hands. The debate was long and bitter. Many towns noted the fact that Amsterdam was farthest from danger. She was virtually an island fortress, as safe as or safer than Copenhagen. The other towns would be as brave as Amsterdam if they had her security. They tried to bully the Amsterdammers into giving full powers to de Groot on the spot. He was called back into the meeting and spoke of the plans of the French King, if the war continued and he was opposed by the great merchant city, to stay until winter when the dikes would freeze and then leave not one stone of Amsterdam standing on another. None of this had any effect. The deputies for the city insisted on their right to return home for consultations before giving their final decision, as they had a right to do. Some towns spoke of going ahead without them, although a unanimous decision was necessary on such an important matter. In the end the States agreed to give Amsterdam twenty-four hours to make up its mind.[16]

Representatives of Zeeland reached The Hague on the morning of the 26th. They too were opposed to making peace. But they had no hearing. In the evening, despite the fact that the representatives of Amsterdam and four other towns had not yet returned, the States of Holland voted to give de Groot full powers to treat. When the matter was brought up in the States General no one was in attendance from Overijssel or Groningen. Friesland and Zeeland were opposed, Utrecht refused to vote since it was now occupied by the enemy. None the less, in a completely irregular manner, Holland forced the matter through. When it came to the point of signing the decision to grant powers, there occurred a remarkable scene. Gaspar Fagel, since 1670 the Secretary or Griffier of the States General, refused to put his name to the document. According to Abraham van Wicquefort, he told de Groot that he might be able to sell his country, but that he would have trouble in putting the buyer into possession. De Groot replied that he would prefer to save something than to lose all. Fagel retorted that de Groot need have no hope for his own estates. Fagel would have them sown with salt so as to make them worthless unto the third generation.[17]

De Groot left The Hague the next morning. His way led him to the Prince's camp at Bodegrave, where he told William the news. Apparently all was lost, the war over. The Prince wrote a letter to Fagel saying that the news 'had surprised him not a little', a phrase which he used fairly frequently to indicate rage. He now asked for authority to treat directly with Louis XIV for his own interests.[18] No one should blame the Prince for making such a request at this time. For all he knew, the war was over and he would now become a great French landowner. His position was unique; he would have to secure it by special arrangements, as his father had secured his own position by special arrangements with the Spanish. William did undertake private negotiations in 1678 and again in 1697. So far as is known the permission requested by the Prince in June of 1672 was not granted and nothing more was heard of it.

When de Groot caught up with his colleagues Odijk and van Gent, and started negotiating with the French on the 29th, he began by offering Maastricht and six millions. This found no acceptance. Then he offered ten millions and all the generality lands. This would have cut the Republic off from the Spanish Netherlands. At his pleasure, the French King could have devoured either the remainder of the Republic or the Spanish provinces. So long as he permitted them to endure he would be in complete control of their trade and their policy. It was all and more than he could reasonably demand. Pomponne recommended that the proposals be accepted. Louvois wanted more; and Louvois won. When they returned to the negotiations, the French demanded everything outside the seven voting Provinces, and substantial portions of Gelderland as well; the Dutch to return to the low tariff of 1662 while the French would retain their present high rates; 'most-favoured-nation' status and other commercial privileges for France; free public exercise of the Catholic faith throughout the Republic, with political rights for Catholics; satisfaction for Denmark; and an immense indemnity. Finally, the Dutch must send an embassy to Louis XIV to thank him for his generosity once every year and present him with a commemorative medal suitably inscribed.[19] Could Louvois or de Groot have believed that these terms would be accepted? It seems incredible. But de Groot was back at The Hague on 1 July, and it is on record that the town of Leyden wanted to accept the conditions. By that time, however, much had happened. With every day the strength of the Holland Water Line increased. Soldiers appeared from nowhere to join the Prince's little army. His own resolute attitude and that of Amsterdam and Fagel gave heart to the rest, or at least shamed them into silence. The terms were to be rejected. What an opportunity the French had missed! It was never to return.

Meanwhile the roar of the mob grew louder. Confused by the military catastrophe, terrified at the horrors of a possible occupation, suspicious of the conduct of the Regent class, the common people could find only one explanation for the events of June: treason. They were, as usual, stirred up by the clergy. Orthodox Calvinists suspected the ruling oligarchy of heresy or at the least of toleration. The bulk of the clergy supported the House of

Orange, which they knew to be orthodox despite its fondness for the theatre. It must be noted, also, that the House of Orange was accustomed to give retirement pensions to aged preachers in The Hague and elsewhere. In 1672 this proved to have been an excellent investment. Sermons in the capital, at Rotterdam, and at Haarlem became openly provocative. De Groot was attacked as a traitor, 'a rotten egg hatched at Louvestein'.[20] These sermons were so effective in stirring up the mob that the Regent class was driven to seek protection behind the coat-tails of the Prince. They might not want to increase his power; but their lives were in danger, if they did not cover themselves with his popularity. As early as 20 June voices were raised in the States of Holland in favour of giving the Captain-General increased authority. The next day those voices became more fervent, for late in the evening of the 21st, as he walked home from work, Johan de Witt was attacked and wounded by four assassins. His wounds were not fatal, though they were serious enough to put him out of action for several weeks. If this could happen to the chief official of the state on the main street of the capital, who could consider himself safe?

The attack on de Witt was greeted by the more extreme partisans of the Prince as an act of piety. Now as later William was to suffer more at the hands of his friends than from his enemies. The guilty men had been recognized and one of them, a mere boy, was caught and quickly beheaded. It was a serious political error. Guilty as he was, the young van der Graaf should not have died. Now the mob was out for blood. The execution of this boy, like the execution of Buat, may have been justifiable in law. It was not justifiable at all in terms of prudence. The peaceful transfer of power had been made impossible. Again and again the oligarchy had brought its enemies to the block. All too soon it was to suffer the same fate. A few days later an attempt was made on the life of the Pensionary's brother Cornelis at his house at Dordrecht. A group of armed men came to the door and asked that he should come out. He had enough sense not to go, and for the moment he was protected by the municipal guard. But the town was completely out of control. The burgers sent a deputation to the Prince's camp asking him to visit Dordrecht and to help restore order. At first William refused to go. He was much too busy strengthening the army to pay much attention to civilian troubles. Finally, however, he accepted and came to the town on the 29th. The Regents provided a guard of honour and dinner at an inn. They showed him around the town and had him inspect its defences, which the common people felt were too weak. But they did not say a word to him about promising to make him Stadhouder. As the Prince was leaving, some of the citizens stopped his coach and asked him whether he had been given such a promise. He replied that he was perfectly satisfied with his visit. We are not, they said, until we see your Highness Stadhouder. William was led back to the inn where he had eaten, and its doors were blocked by the mob until the Regents signed a document offering him the places of his fathers so much as in them lay. After the signatures were secured the Prince was permitted to return to the camp at Bodegrave. On the same day mobs forced the Regents of Rotterdam and of Gouda to make out similar documents. At Haarlem much the same thing happened despite the fact that the town had been occupied by a regular company of horse.[21]

By 1 July eleven of the nineteen voices in the States of Holland were in favour of elevating the Prince. On that day one of William's supporters wrote to him predicting that the others would follow suit in three days, an estimate which turned out to be precisely accurate.[22] This was the day on which de Groot returned to The Hague and tried to get support for the French terms. They were received with indignation, and their severity contributed not a little to the Prince's elevation. All through his life William was to benefit time after time from the brutality of Louis XIV. Fagel, an ardent supporter of resistance and of the Prince, wrote him that he would prefer to die ten times over than to become such a miserable slave of the French. Amsterdam felt the same way. Leyden was almost the only town in the province which would have agreed to the terms.[23] Her administration seems to have been exceptionally timid. There was, however, some justification for this in her location; the town lies on the Rhine. Up river, William's camp at Nieuwerbrug was the weakest point of the Water Line. It was here, in all likelihood, that the French would break through the Dutch defence lines. Leyden was thus the most exposed of all the towns of the province, and many people felt that Nieuwerbrug could not be held against attack.

In the debates of the States of Holland there is clear evidence that the Regents who proposed abolishing the Perpetual Edict were constrained to do so by the popular uproar.[24] It was decided that the delegates should return to their towns for further instructions and then resume the discussion on the evening of Sunday 3 July. At that time Amsterdam suggested sending a deputation to the Prince to invite him to become Stadhouder with the powers held by his fathers. This caused some discussion. Among the rights of previous Stadhouders had been that of selecting the magistrates of certain towns from a short list. Haarlem, Leyden, and Gouda did not wish to surrender the right which they had secured in 1651 to name their own magistrates. Some other towns followed these three. But it was finally decided to give William the same authority that his ancestors had enjoyed in political affairs. He was also appointed Captain- and Admiral-General of the province, and given the right of issuing marching orders 'until further notice'. This last restriction was of no real importance. The final vote was taken at about four in the morning of 4 July, and afterwards a delegation was sent to inform William of what had happened.[25]

When the deputation reached the Prince his first question was whether he had been given a dispensation from his own oath not to seek or accept the place. When he was assured of this, he accepted the offer with hearty thanks. The deputies then asked him whether the Water Line could be held. He replied that he hoped to do so, with God's help, though he could use some more infantry. He said that he was also short of powder and shot.[26] This was the real meaning of his elevation. William could only maintain his new position if he beat the French. If he could not do so, it would do him no good to have been chosen Stadhouder. It might even do him much harm, for the people might blame him for failure and treat him as they had begun to treat Johan and Cornelis de Witt. His fight was just beginning.

The promotion of the Prince did nothing to calm the political situation. William had been elevated to the offices of his ancestors, true; but he was surrounded by men who had opposed him every step of the way. Nothing had been done for the Orange party, very little for the middle group. In effect the Louvesteiners, frightened by the actions of the mob, had promoted the Prince in the hope of retaining as much as they could of their old political authority. Their wishes were to be frustrated. There was a significant number of citizens and even of Regents in each town who hoped to use the Prince's name to achieve power for themselves. The mob could always be stirred up by stories that the Prince's life was in danger, that the Louvesteiners were traitors who had sold out to the French, that the French would impose the Roman faith by force, and so on. Both sides in the political struggle tried to use the magic of William's name for their own ends. Both sides succeeded in discrediting that name by dragging it into politics. What were William's own attitudes to the struggle?

Now, as throughout his life, the details of politics were not of great interest to William III. He could not defend his country while it was so bitterly divided. There must, then, be internal peace. Beyond that the Prince did favour orthodoxy in religious affairs and hoped to find places for the inner ring of the Orangists – members of his family and the most loyal of his retainers. All of this could be achieved without the displacement of de Witt and his friends from office. A few would have to go, perhaps, to make room for the more deserving. But in June and early July it is clear that William expected to work with and through the present oligarchy. His own rightful place in the state had been taken from him while he was a baby. Once he had recovered that, he did not care to deprive others of their own rights. They were aristocrats, as was he. Their position depended on heredity and wealth, as did his own. The party of 'freedom', moreover, happened to be made up of the richest men in the country. They had the most to lose. In the seventeenth century the state was viewed as we view the modern corporation. The largest stockholders, those with the greatest stake in the business, had a natural right to be on the board of directors. All that the Prince wanted was to obtain his own seat there. With these views it was only natural that he would oppose mob rule. In June and July he considered his task to be purely a military one. Certainly the army needed his full attention. When he was invited to intervene in the political wrangles of the towns of Holland, he refused to do so. At Dordrecht on the famous 29th of June, as they were together inside the inn facing the mob at the doors, William turned to the Regents and said, 'Gentlemen, I am sorry for you.'[27] He meant it. He and the magistrates of Dordrecht were members of the 'political nation'. They might have their own battles among themselves, but class warfare was a different matter. The Prince was never to be a demagogue.

One of his first actions after becoming Stadhouder was to try to put an end to the disorders in the towns. On 8 July he wrote a circular letter to the inhabitants of the cities of Holland.[28] In this letter the Prince put the blame for the progress of the French on the army commanders who had deserted their posts. He noted that the people had received the impression, which he described as false, that the Regents had not done their best. This impression had led to disobedience and disrespect on the part of the community for their lawful superiors. For his part he had no evidence and, indeed, no idea that any Regent had done anything contrary to his duty. William disavowed the 'licentious conspiracies' undertaken in his name and stated that he considered the actors in them to be 'perturbators of the common peace'. He recommended that any further disorders be suppressed by the issuance of stern decrees against the rioters. They should be made subject to severe fines and physical punishment. Finally, he promised to use his own authority to the same ends. A day later he wrote a shorter letter in similar terms to the men of Rotterdam, where the situation was particularly serious.[29]

By these letters the Prince seemed to come down firmly on the side of the Louvestein party. Were they actually written by van Beverningk, who had remained much closer to de Witt than had Fagel? It seems likely. In any case, the letters were ineffective. Provincial disorder continued to mount. The common people were convinced that the letters were forgeries. They believed as articles of faith that the Regents had engaged in treasonable activities. De Witt was accused of delaying treaties with Denmark and Brandenburg for his own ends. He was supposed to have sent his own fortune out of the country.[30] This fortune had been acquired by stealing the fl.24,000 put into his hands every year for foreign intelligence. In their sermons, the clergy actually complained against the Prince for not supporting the tumults. After all, he owed his elevation to them.[31] A similar attitude, incidentally, was taken by Charles II, who claimed that William would not have become Stadhouder except for the English attack. The Prince could have done without such friends. But he was impressed by the failure of his letters of 8 and 9 July to have any effect. Quite clearly he could not use his own popularity to protect the Regents. The mob would not obey him. It was stirred up by the clergy and by persons of position whom no edict would frighten. These men, in the hysterical conditions of 1672, could use the Prince's name and popularity, if necessary against him. William would have to ride before the storm. He was the prisoner of his own supporters.

During July and August the storm grew worse. The vermin who exist in every political party were for the moment in full control. Their hatred was directed primarily against the de Witts and Pieter de Groot, though there were other victims. De Groot was the easiest to attack and the first to fall. His negotiations with France, his support of the outrageous French terms, his haughty and repellent personality had served to make him generally detested. Long before 1672 he had been expelled from the magistracy of Amsterdam and had found a refuge at Rotterdam. There, in July, arrived the notorious Kievit who had been one of Buat's accomplices. Kievit had escaped execution by fleeing to England in 1666. Now he hoped to re-establish his old position in Rotterdam and to obtain revenge for his banishment. On 9 July he issued a pamphlet in his own defence and was promptly admitted to the city in triumph. The Prince's letter of the same day had no such friendly audience. Within a few days de Groot, openly insulted in the streets and unable to move without guards, found it wiser to remove himself to The Hague.[32] Here he found no safety. The Prince blamed de Groot for undertaking his second trip to the French camp. His personal dislike of the ambassador may well have been of longer standing, and the two families had of course been enemies for more than half a century. Pieter's father, the famous Hugo Grotius, had been sentenced to life imprisonment at Louvestein in 1619, during the administration of Prince Maurice. He escaped in 1621 concealed in a trunk and spent years in exile. Whatever his personal feeling may have been, William had come to de Groot's defence at the beginning of the month. When he wrote that no single Regent had done less than his duty or had had underhand dealings with the enemy, he clearly meant to include the man who was most deeply suspected of such dealings. But in the ten days after 8 July something happened to change the Prince's mind. On the 20th, when he entered the States General to give his opinion of the English peace terms, he refused to do so in the presence of certain persons. After some dispute, he was asked to name those he suspected, who would be removed.

He named de Groot. Thus the Prince, for the first time and, so far as the evidence shows, unwillingly, joined the party of Fagel and van Beuninghen. Shortly afterwards the unfortunate ambassador fled the country.

There remained Cornelis and Johan de Witt. Of the two, Cornelis was the more deeply hated by the people. During July there were several attempts to murder him and even his servants, while the Pensionary's servants at least were safe and he was recovering from the attack of 21 June. But the Pensionary was being hit in pamphlet after pamphlet, and his skin was apparently wearing thin. The accusation that he had profited from the secret service moneys seems to have irritated him more than almost anything else. It was, of course, false. The charge that he had not prepared the army sufficiently was true, but only in one sense. The whole party had neglected the army; the whole Regent class had neglected it. Among his party de Witt was one of the stronger advocates of military readiness; and on some issues he had been opposed and beaten by Amsterdam, which was now pretending to have a monopoly of virtue. Thus the Pensionary had reason to think that he was less guilty than most for the condition of the army. He would have been wiser had he kept silent about the attacks on his conduct. Instead, he wrote a letter to the Prince complaining about these two accusations. For some days the letter received no reply. Then, on 22 July, William wrote back to say that he knew nothing whatever about the secret service moneys. As for the army, William's praise was so faint as to be really damning. Here again the Prince demonstrated his change of plan. Two weeks earlier he would have written a much warmer letter. His reply of 22 July, which was immediately published, did de Witt a good deal of harm.

Meanwhile Cornelis was in serious trouble. Some years before he had as a magistrate sentenced one William Tichelaar, a surgeon, for rape. Tichelaar now saw an opportunity for revenge. He managed to obtain an interview with his enemy, who no longer recognized him. Then he claimed that during the meeting, which lasted some fifteen minutes, Cornelis de Witt had tried to persuade him to assassinate the Prince. He was supposed to have said that William would obviously now marry 'a certain lady', – that is, Princess Mary of York – who would re-establish the Roman faith in the Republic. Therefore it was important that the Prince should die before he could carry out his plans. Tichelaar took his cock-and-bull story to the Prince's camp and obtained a hearing from two courtiers, one of whom was William's old tutor Zuylestein. The accusation was turned over to the courts, and Cornelis arrested. There was, and could be, nothing to substantiate the charge. The court did everything it could to find a shred of proof, even torturing de Witt. But there was nothing to find. The charge was successful in one respect. On 4 August the Pensionary resigned his office, perhaps frightened at the general hatred for his family; perhaps simply realizing that he could no longer be of any use in the present state of affairs.

On 20 August the Hof van Holland gave sentence against Cornelis de Witt. It could not and did not find him guilty. It simply sentenced him to perpetual banishment from the province, and awarded costs against him. As a judicial process the trial was completely irregular. The evidence of a single witness, a felon, should not have been taken. Although torture was permitted under Dutch law, it might not be applied, as it was in this case, in the absence of the judges. The sentence was less ridiculous than the trial. De Witt was not found guilty; and his only safety lay in leaving the country as rapidly as possible. As it happened, it was the least severe sentence possible in the circumstances – The Hague was now dominated by the mob. The judges even ran some personal danger in not sentencing de Witt to death. Their failure to do so, though it must be put to their credit, meant that both brothers would die and not just one.

At the news of the sentence, so much less severe than the people hoped for, crowds began to collect around the door of the Gevangenpoort where Cornelis de Witt lay. They were not at first large, and it is just possible there might not have been too much trouble if he had been moved at once. But he was safer in the Gevangenpoort than he would be in his brother's or his father's house; and even if he had been strong enough after his torture to be moved further, the family would not have had time to make plans. In any case there was no reason to expect violence. The delay was fatal. Tichelaar and others stirred up the crowd, which was already excited by the distribution of notices inviting them to gather at the prison. It was all well organized. The turnkey's servant was sent to the former Pensionary with a message from his brother asking him to come to the prison. On his arrival, Johan de Witt found the message to have been false: his brother had sent no word. Now they were both trapped in the Gevangenpoort, which had no rear door. There was no escape. As it happened, the States of Holland were in session that day. When they heard what was going on they ordered out three companies of regular cavalry and the town guard to protect the prison. The cavalry could be trusted to do its duty, but the attitude of the town guard was less certain. When it arrived, it took the side of the mob.

The crowds grew all through the day. In the afternoon a rumour spread that the peasants of surrounding villages were up in arms and were marching towards The Hague. At this the cavalry was ordered to leave its post and defend the approaches of the town. Count Tilly refused to obey unless the order was given him in writing. When it was written down he had to obey, and now nothing could save the brothers. The doors of the prison were

THE REVOLUTION OF 1672

forced, and the two men driven out into the street where they soon perished. Their bodies were dragged to the scaffold, hanged upside down, and horribly mutilated. Fingers, toes, and eyes were sold at various prices. The hearts were removed and pickled for later display. Finally, when the mob had been satisfied, it melted away. About midnight some courageous friends of the dead men came and took their bodies away for a secret burial.[33]

This was the monstrous revenge exacted by the Dutch people for the executions of Buat and the young van der Graaf. In one sense there can be no excuse for the murder of the de Witts. Both men had served their country, with narrow vision perhaps but certainly with great devotion and exceptional talent. The Grand Pensionary holds a secure place in history as one of the great men of his century. Cromwell, Louis XIV, William III himself are all better known to the English-speaking peoples than Johan de Witt.[34] His memory deserves a better fate. Personally honest, talented beyond measure in not one but several fields, he was at the head of one of the great powers of Europe for a generation. His brother Cornelis is not such an impressive figure. Even so, Cornelis did lead the Dutch fleet to Chatham and the greatest naval victory of his time. He worked hard and ably in 1671 and 1672 to secure the Spanish assistance which was to make the survival of the Republic possible. But if in one sense the murder can have no justification, in another it was a fair comment on the roughness of de Witt's methods and the complete failure of his policy. Was it prudent to attack and sink elements of the French navy in peace time during the minority of Louis XIV? Was it prudent to attack Chatham in 1667? What justification could there be for the brutal way in which the Pensionary treated his allies Denmark and Brandenburg? His arrogance was splendid, it was breath-taking, but it left the Republic without a friend. And since the United Provinces had ceased to be a land power, she needed friends. De Witt's administration coincided with the greatest period of prosperity and the greatest cultural and artistic achievements of Dutch history. Later, looking back in less prosperous times to this golden age, men tended to blame William III for beginning the decline of the Republic. But William did not inherit a golden age. He inherited the Water Line, a defeated army, a country half occupied and more than half beaten. That William's age was less prosperous than de Witt's is at least partially the Pensionary's fault. That the Republic survived at all, that time was given for it to have a silver age if not another golden one, is due very largely to the Prince. De Witt spent capital. In terms of prestige and grandeur, he made his country live far beyond its income. And, as is usual in such cases, the heirs had a thin time of it. In domestic affairs, the greatest error of de Witt lay in failing to provide for the peaceful transfer of power. As late as 1660, perhaps as late as 1667, he might have achieved some kind of compromise with the House of Orange and its followers. After 1667 the situation became far more difficult and by the spring of 1672 it was hopeless. In this respect the Pensionary and his party prepared their own doom.

A great deal has been written to prove the complicity of William III and his followers in the events of 20 August. There can be no doubt at all of the guilt of the Orange party. The Hague mob was organized and led that day, led by men who called themselves Orangists. Zuylestein and Tromp are known to have been present. Among less important members of the party, there were clergymen near the scaffold who in their sermons the next day exulted in the just vengeance of God on two sinners. Attempts to link the Prince with the murder and to prove that he was present while it was carried out have been made, but without success.[35] On that day the Prince was at Woerden, a town between the French and Dutch lines, to see whether it could be fortified and held against the enemy. At that time it could not be held and William was forced to abandon it.[36] He did not reach The Hague until late the next afternoon, and the comment of Gaspar Fagel will find agreement among all just men: '. . . at the time when the execrable deed occurred to the Ruwaart van Putten and the former Pensionary de Witt, it was given out that the Prince was too good and that the work must be finished before his arrival in The Hague; . . .'[37]

The Prince's complicity before the fact cannot be proven. Nothing in his entire life would lead one to suspect that he would countenance murder. At times when his own life was in constant danger from fanatics inspired by France, he took the trouble to warn Louis XIV when that King was threatened by similar plots. The Prince must be held innocent of the murder itself. But his actions afterwards are by no means pleasant to read about. Tichelaar and his fellows were never punished. Several of them were given government posts, and when Tichelaar was fired from the job with which he had been rewarded he took a pension from William III that ended only in 1702. At the time, it is probable that any punishment of the 'heroes' of 20 August would merely have given rise to more rioting. The de Witts served as scapegoats, and after their deaths the lives and property of the remaining members of the Regent class were secure. The mob could not be put down without regular troops, which were all needed at the front. Since repression was impossible, the mob had to be allowed to have its own way. Doubtless, Tichelaar's pension is disgusting. So is the pension which William III was later to give Titus Oates. Tichelaar secured the death of two innocent men, Oates of some thirty-five. In both cases, bribes were given to silence men who would otherwise have caused even more trouble. In both cases, the bribes did their work. It is undoubtedly disappointing that a man who had such high personal standards of conduct made so small an effort to raise the standards of his day regarding the game of politics. It would have been delightful had he tried to do more; but it would have meant failure for his cause.

The murder of the brothers brought the political disorders in the towns of Holland to an end for the moment. The unpopular Regents, thoroughly frightened, decided that it would be better to save their skins than their places. On 23 August Gaspar Fagel became Grand Pensionary. On 27 August the Prince was authorized, for this one time only, to change the magistracies of the towns of the province of Holland so as to satisfy the people. The precise nature of the changes made is rather obscure. On the whole the new men put into office were supporters of the middle party. At Fagel's town of Haarlem, for example, only one man had to be displaced; presumably the old magistrates were his friends and he saw no need of a change. The new men as a group were less wealthy than those they replaced, and some of them were unable to retain the respect of their fellow citizens. Those who were removed from office in 1672 did not lose their other privileges. Once the war was over several of them returned to public life. The revolution was as moderate as such things can be. There was perhaps a slight infusion of new blood into the Regent class; its total composition was scarcely affected, at least in the long run. What the revolution did achieve was the unification of the Dutch people, previously so bitterly divided. Now they could concentrate for the first time on fighting the war.

Chapter 8

BODEGRAVE AND ZWAMMERDAM

THE English had had high hopes of success in the war. By the terms of the Treaty of Dover they were to make amphibious landings on the Dutch coasts and so divert the attention of the defenders from the progress of the French. It was planned to take Walcheren Island on one side of the mouth of the Scheldt, and Sluys and Kadzand commanding the other. Thus the English would regain their foothold on the continent, lost at the time of the sale of Dunkirk ten years before. These new holdings, furthermore, would be of the greatest commercial importance. But the first task was to take them. The failure of the English attack on the Smyrna fleet before war was declared proved to be a depressingly accurate omen for the Royal Navy. On 7 June de Ruyter attacked a combined Anglo-French fleet near Southwold Bay. Although the engagement was indecisive, it was a Dutch victory in that it forced the postponement of the English plans. Thus the early efforts of the English were disappointing. But the collapse of the Dutch land forces gave Charles II hopes of easy gains. When four deputies of the States General reached London on 10/20 June to sue for peace, the King's ambitions quickly passed all bounds. Many Dutchmen would probably prefer to flee to a Protestant country rather than suffer a French occupation. A proclamation was therefore quickly drawn up offering such refugees asylum and also protection for their property.[1] The prospect of new territories and a money indemnity was even more attractive. Reports reaching England indicated that they could have anything they wanted.[2] Charles II decided to send Lord Arlington and the Duke of Buckingham over to secure his share of the spoils.

Their instructions reflected the King's optimistic view of the state of affairs. They were to demand the right of the flag, which the Dutch had already conceded. They were to insist on Charles's 'Dominion in the British seas': the Dutch must pay an annual fee for the right to fish. The Republic must also pay the King's costs in the war, preferably by October. Vlissingen, Sluys, the Briel, or other towns must be turned over as cautions for the due performance of the terms. Not only were these towns to remain in English hands forever, but the surrounding territories must pay for the costs of the occupying garrisons. Trade in the East Indies must be adjusted to English satisfaction, and justice must be obtained in the matter of Surinam. In addition, the Prince of Orange should be made sovereign or at least hereditary Stadhouder.[3] These were large demands. But when the ministers actually reached the Republic, 'what we saw when we arrived exceeded all we could imagine. Our first salutation at Maeslandsluys was God bless the King of England and the Prince of Orange and the Devil take the States.'[4] At this their hopes naturally rose higher than ever before. Buckingham even thought that William might give the Dutch fleet to the Duke of York, while turning a few towns over to the English ambassadors.[5] Such wild ideas were as fantastic as those of Louvois. On the very day that Buckingham wrote, the States of Holland authorized the Prince to treat with the English. William was to be assisted, and perhaps supervised, by men of greater experience. He was to try to obtain a separate peace. But he might not surrender any province or town, or even any ships of war. Nor was he to offer any annual sum for the right to fish. On these points the whole nation was adamant.[6] The Dutch would be willing to pay a moderate sum towards the King's war expenses, and also to bribe the ambassadors themselves.

With the two parties as far apart as this, a quick peace was out of the question. Both sides had to get rid of their illusions. The ambassadors hoped that the Prince would prefer his personal ambitions to the security of his people. William, for his part, hoped that Charles might be kinder to him than he would have been to de Witt. Both were wrong, and the misunderstanding was to endure for a generation, embittering the personal relations of the Royal Family. There were other causes of misunderstanding. Arlington, like others in the years to come, felt that William III owed him support in the English party struggle. Arlington was married to one of the Prince's relations. He represented a policy which was at least less French than that of his rival Buckingham. Therefore the Prince must obediently trundle out on to the English political scene as a *deus ex machina* whenever Arlington needed him. Now and later, the Prince refused to be used in this manner. It would be fatal for him to become the prisoner of any single English faction. And woe betide any man who presumed on his connections with William III! For all his simplicity of manner the Prince was remarkably careful to preserve the respect due to his station. Impertinence and cowardice were two sins he never forgave. Ossory, who had married Lady Arlington's sister, had enough breeding not to presume on the connection and became one of William's closest friends. Arlington, a far more arrogant man, tried to patronize the Prince and lost him for ever.

When the ambassadors reached the Prince's camp they soon found that he was not to be patronized. William refused to admit that the war was lost. The forces of Brandenburg and Spain would create a diversion, forcing the French to turn their attention away from the Dutch. William, furthermore, refused to believe that it was in the interests of his uncle to see the Republic wholly overrun by the French. He would treat with England in the hope of securing her assistance against the greater enemy. As to Charles's demands for cautionary towns, the States would never give them nor would the Prince advise them to do so. The ambassadors replied that it would be better for him to establish a sovereignty supported by the Kings of England and France, which would secure him from all danger at home and abroad. William rejected this. 'He replied he liked better the condition of Stadhouder which they had given him & that he believed himself obliged in conscience & honour not to prefer his interest before his obligation.'[7] Again and again the ambassadors tried to make the Prince accept their proposals. They were encouraged by the attitude of the young officers surrounding the Prince, who wished aloud that a dozen men might be hanged so that the country might have peace and the Prince become sovereign. William did not listen to such people about political affairs. Late in the evening, no doubt as surprised as they were disappointed, the ambassadors went on to Utrecht and the camp of Louis XIV.

They found the French still hoping that their peace proposals would be accepted. De Groot had now been gone for ten days. The French thought he would soon be back to conclude a peace. One of the great mysteries of history is why the French did not complete the conquest of the United Provinces in the summer of 1672. The King had insisted on besieging town after town and then on leaving a garrison in each conquered place. His forces were therefore much smaller in July than they had been a month earlier. But the Holland Line was still very weak and could probably have been broken at this time. Yet the French simply sat down in Utrecht and waited until their opportunity was gone. Apparently they had run off their maps. In January, de Groot had written from Paris that they expected to conquer half the country in the coming campaign. The French had done just that and felt that no more was necessary. With so much of their country lost, the Dutch must make peace on any terms. Hitler made a similar delay, with similarly fatal results, in June 1940. Had he attacked England immediately after the French armistice he might have won the war at once. But he waited for a surrender which never came. Arlington and Buckingham felt that the French terms would be rejected. They had seen a little of the change which came over the Dutch in the last days of June. They did not, however, think that the Dutch could do much to defend themselves. Lord Halifax, who had come by way of Zeeland, now caught up with them and described the attitude of the Zeelanders, who were determined in the last resort to surrender themselves to the English rather than to the French.[8] This encouraged Arlington and Buckingham, but they realized that the new courage of the enemy could only be broken by a major defeat. If the Dutch navy could be beaten, or if the fleet coming from the East Indies could be captured, then the Zeelanders might put themselves in English hands.

While the leading English ministers remained at the French camp, Gabriel Sylvius, Henry Jermyn, and Henry Seymour were sent back to the Prince to get him to change his mind. They had no more success than had the others. Arlington and Buckingham accompanied Louis XIV on his march. At Heeswijk, on 16 July, the English and French agreed that they would make no separate peace with the enemy. For the first time the demands of the two Kings were put together in a single paper.[9] These terms did not differ significantly from those presented earlier as separate claims. There was now, however, far less reason to hope that the two Kings could be divided. It was the Heeswijk demands which William III refused to discuss in the States General in de Groot's presence. In commenting on the terms, the Prince said that there was not a single one of them he would accept. We ought rather to be cut in pieces than to accept them. The English proposals did not come from the King, but from his ministers; what concerned his own person was the work of his enemies and not of his friends.[10] It may have been correct constitutionally and wise diplomatically to dissociate Charles II from his advisers. It seems hardly likely that the Prince still thought that there could be any division in their points of view. Finally, after a vain attempt to bully the government at Brussels, the English mission returned home. It had gained nothing except the knowledge that the English would have to fight for what they wanted.

When Sylvius returned to England he brought with him Dr Rumpf and a new set of secret proposals from William. In addition to the flag and Surinam, about which there was no difficulty, the Prince offered an annual fee for the right to fish, an indemnity for the English war expenses, and the single town of Sluys as a caution. One of the terms was that the Prince should have the sovereignty of the United Provinces. This would give Charles II an assurance that the Louvestein party would never recover. It would also, of course, be for the Prince's personal advantage. Despite his disclaimers, William certainly wanted to become sovereign. He would only have accepted sovereignty from the Dutch people, and only then if their safety had first been taken care of. But if the English demanded sovereignty for him as part of their peace terms, and if these terms were accepted by the Dutch, the Prince would have been only too happy. In 1675 and again after peace came in 1678 he was to try for the magical title of duke. Naturally this ambition was to trouble the Dutch and also make trouble for the Prince himself. His motives lay open to attack and they have been attacked bitterly. It should not be surprising that William III was ambitious. What is surprising is that he was always, even as a very young man, willing to subordinate these ambitions to the welfare of his people. Such patriotism was not often seen in that generation.

It was the last proposal of the Prince which displeased them most. William made his offer on condition that England make a separate peace with the Republic and that it give no further assistance whatever to France.[11] The cabinet council met to discuss the offer on 29 July/9 August and found it 'very mean'.[12] Two days later at another meeting there was an argument as to whether the English should accept cautionary towns for a period of years only. Dr Rumpf had told them flatly that there was no chance of a perpetual caution. The King, Prince Rupert, and Lord Arlington would agree to moderate terms. Buckingham insisted that the cautionary towns be granted for ever. In the end it was decided to demand the Briel, Hellevoetsluys, Vlissingen, and the island of Goeree for ten years. At the same time the English would continue their plans for landings in Zeeland.[13] Their clergymen in that province were of use as agents, and the English also had a regular correspondent in one Baron de Witt.[14] The Zeelanders would certainly prefer to be united to England than to be subjected to the French. As late as March and April of 1673 the cabinet council was discussing the terms of Zeeland's union with the British crown. The people were to be offered union, with seats in the House of Commons if they wished it. Otherwise they might keep their own form of government. In either case they would retain their own form of worship.[15] But the chicken would have to be caught before it could be eaten. One of the most important obstacles in the way was the attitude of Spain.

When Arlington and Buckingham had been at the French camp they had discovered that their ally was not particularly worried about the activities of Brandenburg or of the Emperor Leopold. What bothered the French was the possibility that the Queen-Regent of Spain might declare war. If she did, and the Dutch were doing everything they could to persuade her to do so, then the princes of Germany might take heart and do some real fighting. 'In the discourse we have had here with his Majesty & the ministers here we find them fear less the Elector of Brandenburg & the Emperor than they do Spain's declaring themselves in an open war against them which will give countenance & courage to those princes to stir against them who now lie still. . . .'[16] So long as Spain remained neutral an anti-French alliance probably could not be formed. For her own part, the Queen-Regent was most reluctant to declare war. Her position in Spain was not too strong, the resources of her son's empire were visibly declining. She was willing to give the Dutch all aid short of war. Military and diplomatic assistance, even money, would not be spared. But if she made a formal declaration, the Dutch might then abandon her by a separate treaty and leave her to face the French alone. The Queen had a low opinion of the Dutch Republic even after the Revolution of July and August. She felt that it was guided only by commercial interests, and that even if the Prince of Orange held other opinions he might not be strong enough to impose his will.[17] She hoped to be able to detach England from the French, and to secure German aid for the Dutch, without formally committing herself. Her diplomacy was cautious and in many respects intelligent. Ostend privateers must not be allowed to sail against English merchant vessels. No public demonstrations in celebration of Dutch victories at sea were to be permitted. The Spanish ambassador in London must be circumspect in his dealings with the opposition so as to avoid giving offence to Charles II.[18]

At the same time, the Queen-Regent did what she could to encourage the Germans. In July she sent 120,000 reals to Vienna as a subsidy for the Brandenburg forces.[19] Later in the year, when the plate fleet had come in and the court of Madrid was for the moment near solvency, she sent 180,000 thalers to her brother the Emperor Leopold, and another 40,000 reals to Frederick William of Brandenburg. She even included a present for his minister, the Prince of Anhalt.[20] But she would not declare war. Diplomatic activity was one thing. Sending troops to help the Dutch as auxiliaries was permitted by seventeenth-century practice. After all, the French had been at peace with Spain when French help was winning independence for the Portuguese. Open war, however, would be too much. Anything less, unfortunately, would be too little. The French were correct in thinking that they had nothing to fear from the Germans while Spain remained neutral. The Germans would make treaties. They would raise armies if the Dutch and Spanish would pay for them. But these armies would do no more than promenade through western Germany without firing a shot. Leopold and Frederick William were frightened by the French victories and suspicious of the Dutch, as was the Queen of Spain. No one wanted to be committed irrevocably to a cause which had so little prospect of success.

It must be admitted that the Spanish did a great deal, and that even the Germans did something. The Elector of Brandenburg sent his brother-in-law, the Prince of Anhalt, to Vienna to obtain imperial aid. Anhalt succeeded, with the help from the Spanish ambassador there. On 25 July a treaty was signed at The Hague covering the subsidies to be paid to Leopold for his assistance. Although the treaty was not ratified for some months the imperial forces moved westward from Egra, in Bohemia, during August and joined those of the Elector in September. The very existence of this force was enough to cause a diversion. A large part of the French army, under Turenne, was removed from the occupied provinces of the Republic to face the new threat. Beyond this, however, the German army did virtually nothing. The imperial general, Montecuculi, was a man of note. Unfortunately he did not happen to want to fight at this time. He had been described by the Dutch agent in Vienna as a crafty, able, and very secretive man, like most Italians, and more given to excess of caution and to slowness than to rapid decisions.[21] The Elector, who was leading his own forces in person, found it very difficult to argue with Montecuculi. In the first place, the imperial troops might abandon him if he went too far. In the second, many of the Elector's officers were terrified at the prospect of fighting Turenne. They were only too eager to follow Montecuculi's advice. The Elector was encouraged by the Dutch Ambassador, van Reede van Amerongen, who accompanied him on the march, and by the courageous Duke of Lorraine. The majority of his ministers, however, wanted him to make a separate peace with France. Louis XIV was simply too strong to be opposed by a Brandenburg fighting virtually alone. Amerongen reported even in October that the Duke of Lorraine shared his own gloom. Neither the Imperialists nor the Brandenburg forces would do anything.[22]

For some time it was possible to believe that Frederick William would act, even if he had to act alone. Instead of crossing the lower Rhine and attacking Cologne, which would have forced France's allies out of the war, Monte-cuculi preferred to go further and further up the river – always safe on the east bank. At times the Elector protested and spoke brave words.[23] But he was always persuaded to do nothing. By the beginning of December Amerongen's suspicions had reached great heights. Not only would the Germans do nothing for the Republic, their goal was to force the United Provinces to accept a disadvantageous peace. They kept on very good terms with the French, with whom they were continually negotiating. French prisoners were released without paying ransom, while everyone was rude to the Duke of Lorraine, whose only fault was that he wanted to fight.[24] Obviously, if anything was to be done it must be done by the Dutch themselves.

During the summer months, whenever he had time to spare from the Holland Water Line, political affairs, and diplomatic negotiations, William III had been rebuilding the Dutch army. He spoke well when he said that he worked day and night this year. The Prince's most important single step was to take into his service George Frederick, Count van Waldeck. Waldeck was one of the most experienced commanders of the day and had been in the service of Brandenburg and of the Dukes of Brunswick. His wife was one of the Prince's many Nassau cousins. The two men soon became very close, though Waldeck was thirty years older than William, and the relationship endured for a generation. Waldeck taught the Prince most of what he ever learned about warfare. In many ways he did an excellent job. He knew a great deal about training an army, about caring for troops, about planning a campaign. He also knew a great deal about German political problems, and William was to consult him on many diplomatic issues. On the whole the two men worked well together. Waldeck was not, however, a perfect choice. There was a far greater man in Schomberg, who had been the preceptor of William II. If Schomberg had been available it is most doubtful that he would have forgotten to teach William III the importance of scouting, for example. Schomberg also had that very important quality in a general, good luck on the day of battle. Waldeck had consistently bad luck. But Schomberg was now in French service and there was no alternative. The Prince wrote to Waldeck in July, and asked the States to make him a field-marshal after he had actually reached the army.

It is impossible to say what share of the credit for rebuilding the land forces of the Republic should go to the Prince and what to the general. William had very little experience. He had some theoretical knowledge of war, two years' training as a member of the Council of State, and whatever he had been able to learn in actual fighting since the beginning of June. Even at twenty-one, however, the Prince knew how to be obeyed. He was more than a brave recruit. He was separated from Waldeck for much of the time and had to act on his own or on the advice of van Beverningk. Yet it is clear that Waldeck must have answered many questions, that he must have made many suggestions, and that one of his tasks was to train his master. On one subject, the necessity of strict discipline, the two men were in complete agreement. Before Waldeck entered Dutch service, a court-martial sat to consider the fate of the unfortunate Montbas who had deserted his post. On 22 July the court sentenced him to fifteen years' imprisonment. The Prince, outraged, held up the sentence. Montbas was fortunate enough to escape, and when he was finally sentenced to hang, the execution had to be carried out on an effigy of painted wood. Rigid discipline was to mark the Prince's entire career. In army affairs his severity was extreme, quite unlike the patient and compromising attitude he generally adopted towards civilians. With it he was eventually to build the best infantry in Europe. Perhaps Martinet, who had been using the same methods with some success in the French army, could have done more than he actually did had he lived longer. But he was only a brigadier, not a commander-in-chief; his influence was limited. And, as it happened, he fell in this very summer of 1672.

The need for discipline was very great. Colonels must be taught, by demonstration, that they had more to fear from the Prince than from the enemy. Many of the higher officers relied on the friendship of their colleagues to protect them. This was why the Prince had to reverse the sentences of so many court-martials in 1672 and 1673. He could not permit slovenly officers to protect each other. It was not merely a question of cowardice. Many of the officers chose to sleep in houses rather than with their men. This was completely inexcusable at the front. One morning the aged Prince Maurits made the rounds at four, only to find a sentry asleep on watch and all the officers of that company absent from their quarters. Maurits had the inferior officers put in irons and asked permission to cashier the captain involved.[25] It is important to realize that this kind of severity saved many lives and operated for the benefit of the common soldiers. On the other hand William III saw to it that his men were paid promptly, at least by the standards of the day. They were provided with free field-hospitals. In the English army, by contrast, such medical care as there was came out of the soldier's pay. Pensions were provided for over-age and crippled soldiers throughout the entire period 1672–1702.[26] In 1698 the system broke down because there were too many men eligible for pensions. They were protected by orders to captains forbidding such men to be discharged until pensions were available. Whatever this did to the efficiency of certain companies, it was clearly the correct thing to do.[27] No wonder that the common soldier loved his Captain-General.

The army needed discipline in 1672. Courage it needed even more. The men must learn that they could face the enemy on even terms. Here the Prince operated by giving a personal example. In battle he was always in the thick of the fight, to the horror of the States General which spent thirty vain years begging him to take care of his person. His Garter star made him very easy to identify, but the Prince would never take it off or disguise himself in any other way. William III relied on armour and on his faith in predestination. He had been granted complete physical bravery. This is common enough. He had also what is less common, intellectual courage. Throughout his public life the Prince was constantly threatened by assassination. Many brave men would not have been able to face, day after day after year after year, a continuous stream of murder plots and threats. William III despised them. When Arlington threatened him with the fate of the de Witts, he replied with biting contempt: 'Ne croiez pas aussi que vos menaces de me faire déchirer en pièce par les peuples, me fasse grand peur; je ne suis pas fort craintif de mon naturel.'[28] Of course it is true that the Prince's habit of fighting with his own sword created serious problems. He could not properly direct a large action while engaged in fighting one small portion of it himself. On the other hand his men would not do their best for anyone else. And most actions were on a scale small enough for the Prince to control. To a large extent the Prince was a talisman for his people. They never fought so well under another commander as they did for him. Louis XIV was a thorough nuisance to his generals whenever he entered the field. So many men had to be detached to protect their king and his train that the fighting strength of his armies was seriously diminished. William III gave strength to his armies where Louis XIV drained the strength of his. He was a professional soldier, the King of France a well-informed amateur of war.

When the remnant of the Dutch army retired on the Water Line in June it had numbered some 9,000 men. Fortunately, if the inundations had created a *Festung Holland*, the fortress was not under regular siege. The French armies controlled the towns but not all the countryside of the occupied provinces. During the summer large numbers of men made their way past the French positions. Many of these, of course, were prisoners taken by the French in June. There were too many of them to keep, their conduct had been so shameful that it inspired neither respect nor fear. Thousands of these prisoners were ransomed at nominal rates or even set free for nothing. But these were not William's only recruits. Deserters from the enemy were numerous, and although the generals did not like them they could not entirely prevent the colonels from enlisting them. Some adventurous officers managed to bring men through from Germany. Perhaps the men of highest quality were sailors, who were sent to the Water Line in batches as their ships came in. The sailors were tough, well-trained, and cheerful. They had already beaten the English, and the French could not be so bad. They were also accustomed to handling guns. It would have been a good thing if more of these brave men had been kept with the army throughout the war. The Prince was to be seriously hampered by shortages of artillery and of good gunners and engineers. In 1672, but unfortunately not sufficiently later, the seamen provided a *cadre* of experienced fighting men around whom the new army could be built.

By September the army numbered at least 30,000 effectives, in tolerably good order and discipline. It was not yet a trained fighting force: only time could turn it into one. But it would fight now, as it had not fought in June. And on a good day this army might even win. It was time to begin, first with small field exercises and then with larger ones, so that the men could learn their trade. The first attack was planned on Naarden at the end of September. A portion of the attacking force, coming on Naarden from the sea, was becalmed and the whole attempt had to be abandoned. A fortnight later, on the night of 10 October, the Prince suddenly attacked and surrounded the town of Woerden. At first it seemed possible that the place might be taken. The men were green but they fought pretty well. Unfortunately Zuylestein neglected to cut one small way by which the French could approach him. The Duke of Luxembourg was not to be treated with such neglect. He attacked with great speed, Zuylestein and many of his men were killed, and

Woerden in its turn had to be abandoned. Naturally the Dutch, who expected easy and immediate victories from their hero, were disappointed at this second failure. But it was not all loss. The men had fought. They had gained experience and confidence. With better planning and a little more luck the French might be beaten.

Almost immediately after the attempt on Woerden, William began a much more ambitious design. If he could swing south of the French army it might be possible to reach the large Dutch garrison of Maastricht. From there a junction with the armies of the Elector and Montecuculi would be possible. If the junction were made, the Germans might be persuaded to do some real fighting; and the French line of communications, tremendously long and thin, would be so threatened that the enemy might well have to withdraw from the occupied provinces. A frontal attack on one town after another held by the French would require years before the soil of the Republic was liberated. But a sweeping march around the French positions promised much more rapid results. It is remarkable that the Dutch high command had enough courage even to conceive such a plan when they were in so desperate a position. It is more remarkable that they were willing to try it with such inexperienced forces.

The pace of seventeenth-century war was, on the whole, rather slow. In the Netherlands it was possible to transport men and horses by canal and river, so things could move much more quickly there than elsewhere. William held a council of war at which the plan for a break-through was adopted on 17 October. The expeditionary force was ready, and passed in review, on 7 November; 5,000 foot and more than 10,000 horse were included. By the 13th the Prince had reached the neighbourhood of Maastricht with the cavalry. He had sent his infantry and his guns back, because they slowed him down and because he had heard of enemy activity near Utrecht.[30] On his way, apparently rather to his disappointment, the Prince had fallen in with only small parties of the French and had lost just one officer prisoner.[31] He was able to take some infantry and a few guns from the garrison of Maastricht, and his little force was augmented by a Spanish one of perhaps the same size provided by Count Monterey. But what was he to do? The two German armies refused to join him. Indeed, they began to march in an opposite direction. The Brandenburg and Imperial forces were for show, not for real business. They wanted Dutch subsidies. They were willing to create a diversion. They did not dare to come to actual blows with the French. After some delay the Prince decided to adopt a plan of Monterey's for an attack on Charleroi, an important French *dépôt* a considerable distance south-west of Maastricht.

William and his men reached the neighbourhood of Charleroi only on

16 December. By that time winter had set in. If the weather had still been mild the attack might have succeeded. The garrison was small for such an important place, and its commander Montal absent. But Montal succeeded in riding through the Spanish lines to his post. His arrival gave his men the spirit to defend themselves. The cold was now intense: the ground froze a foot and a half deep, which made it impossible to dig trenches. The Prince held a council of war with the Spanish generals who accompanied him. All of the Spanish felt that it was impossible to continue the siege, and on the 20th William wrote to the States General announcing that it would be abandoned. All that he could report was the capture of the small town of Binch by a detachment of 9,000 men.[32] The army broke up and made its way back towards Holland. Although the campaign had been without large results, it was still at least partially successful. The Prince had demonstrated that he had an army and that it could break out into open country. The French had been impressed by the march and momentarily frightened by the threat to Charleroi. It had been an expensive training exercise, for the men a harsh one. There were many sick from the cold and the fatigue of the long marches. On the whole it was worthwhile in terms of experience and valuable in terms of prestige. But when the Prince of Orange reached Gornichem on the 30th he discovered that in his absence the Dutch garrisons had returned to their old ways. In Holland, too, there had been a hard freeze. The inundations had become covered with ice so thick that it would bear cavalry. And over that ice Luxembourg had led a large force to invade Holland. His goal was to burn The Hague.

For several weeks the troop movements of the enemy around Utrecht had been quite obvious. On 16 November Prince Maurits wrote to William that all his intelligence was of an attack to be made while he was absent.[33] William had left behind him some 18,000 men to defend the Water Line. But he had taken Waldeck, who was probably the only man who could have kept the officers under control. Lacking both the Prince and Waldeck, and for that matter a clear chain of command as well, the men in charge of the five chief posts of the Water Line did not all rise to the situation. This was particularly true of the Count van Königsmarck, who had been given William's own post at Bodegrave. It was the weakest part of the line. Königsmarck complained that he had only 1,800 men and that the place would become untenable in case the waters froze.[34] By early December the States of Holland were so disturbed that they sent three field deputies to Bodegrave to observe the situation.[35] They did what they could, but their efforts were frustrated when commanders at other places simply refused to send reinforcements.[36] None the less the force at Bodegrave was increased to some 3,000 men by 22 December.

It is clear that Königsmarck wanted to retire from his exposed position to safety behind the walls of Leyden. Unfortunately his instructions authorized him to do so in case of need. This would mean abandoning the open country-side of Holland to the enemy. Unwalled villages including The Hague, which was the most important of them all, would be left completely defence-less. William had made a serious error in leaving Königsmarck at Bodegrave and another in granting him permission to retire. The Prince felt that the post ought not to be abandoned save in the 'last extremity'.[37] His own view of the meaning of the phrase did not correspond with that of the timid general. As the field deputies wrote on the 23rd, 'It is unbelievable with what prudence the army seeks to protect itself.'[38] Discipline was now poor at Bodegrave and both officers and men were mutinous and disorderly. Everything was preparing for disaster. On the 24th Königsmarck sent off his guns and baggage. The States of Holland met on Christmas day, a Sunday, to discuss whether he should be relieved of his command. This was the obvious thing to do. They did not quite dare to replace Königsmarck until it was too late.

Luxembourg marched with a considerable force on the 27th. Just as he did so the wind changed. A great thaw set in. The ice would no longer support the men and soon began to break up. But Luxembourg would not yet turn back. With great difficulty, he and his men managed to get through to Bodegrave and Zwammerdam. They found virtually no opposition. Königsmarck had retired on Leyden, though without success; the citizens refused to open their gates to him. The two villages of Bodegrave and Zwammerdam were burned, as were many farms and country houses in the neighbourhood. Luxembourg was rapidly becoming a great general, but his career was to be stained by the licence he permitted his men. His own dispatches show that in several cases the doors of houses were locked by his men, who then burned them over the heads of the inhabitants. In other cases prisoners were stripped naked and left to make their way to Leyden or Gouda as best they could. According to the Dutch, who were to base a great propaganda campaign on Luxembourg's atrocities, women were raped and then mutilated repeatedly until they died.[39] Even if the atrocities are taken at the French estimate rather than the Dutch, they were something which William III would never have permitted. When he allowed his men to plunder a town, as they had been permitted to plunder Binch, the Prince gave strict orders against the molestation of women and saw to it that they were obeyed. Houses and churches were not burned when they contained civilians. It must be said that Luxembourg's standards were well below those of his fellow French generals.[40]

A great opportunity for revenge was now at hand. As the thaw continued,

Luxembourg's position became more and more uncomfortable. He gave up the idea of going on to burn The Hague. But how to get back to Utrecht? Many of his men were drowning in the dikes and canals. Many others were wet through and would soon die of exposure. If the Dutch fort at Nieuwerbrug was held, the French were in real danger. There was, in fact, a force at Nieuwerbrug under Colonel Pain-et-Vin. Königsmarck's orders gave him some latitude: Pain-et-Vin had none. He was to stay at the fort and defend it at all costs. Despite these written orders, Pain-et-Vin and his men abandoned their position in the most shameful manner and fled towards Gouda. The raiders were enabled to make their way back to the French lines opposed only by the weather. Luxembourg himself got wet and many of his men perished. All that the Dutch could now do was to arrest Pain-et-Vin and to make an example of him. A court-martial sat and sentenced him to perpetual imprisonment. The Prince refused to accept the sentence. A second court-martial sat and sentenced him to the infamy of having his sword broken over his head by the public executioner. The Prince refused to accept this sentence too. He reviewed the charges personally and had Pain-et-Vin beheaded.[41] In some ways his action may appear harsh, especially since he bore some responsibility himself for the weakness of the Holland Line. But at a time when the army was again becoming disorderly and beginning to refuse to obey his commands,[42] severity was essential. The Prince did not act out of spite. He had to re-establish his authority, he had to root cowardice out of the army. He was successful. The raid, which could have destroyed all his efforts towards greater discipline and set the army back six months, had no permanent effects. It undoubtedly slowed the development of the Dutch land forces, and it was also a blow to William's prestige. But none of the damage done by the raid was beyond repair.

This was in many ways true of all the events of 1672. The Dutch were in a serious position. They had lost a great deal of reputation and much territory. Nothing essential was gone, however; and if the Spanish would only declare war, things might yet turn out for the best. A Spanish declaration might well force the English to make peace. It would certainly give heart to the princes of Germany. Soon the Dutch army would become a trained fighting force, able to make its own contribution. All turned on the Habsburgs and on William III.

Chapter 9

REDEEMER OF THE FATHERLAND

In many ways the early months of 1673 were the worst of the war. The Water Line had not proved a complete barrier against the French. Where they had pierced it once they could pierce it again. As the Spanish ambassador wrote to his Queen, ice covered the countryside and exposed it to the insults of the French. The Dutch government, he continued ominously, sighs for peace.[1] De Lira's letter made it clear that he did not include the Prince in his charge; but he was still uncertain about the extent of William's influence, and probably he underestimated that of Fagel. It would have been difficult for a Catholic like de Lira to appreciate Fagel's motive passion, extreme protestantism.[2] As it happened, Fagel knew perfectly well that protestantism was now threatened, not by the Habsburgs, but by the Bourbons. But van Beverningk and others who had formerly been friends of de Witt were still in the administration. The Spanish distrusted van Beverningk and tried later in the year to have him replaced.[3] No one knew how widely de Groot's attitudes were shared nor what strength they might have. In January de Groot was writing bitterly that the Prince's friends who had been placed in the town governments were 'canaille' who had nothing to lose, while those who had been expelled from the administration of Rotterdam alone were worth more than three millions. If a quick peace were not obtained from the French all the rich would emigrate, leaving Holland only a sand dune and a marsh as it had been originally.[4] The party of de Witt might be down, but it was certainly not eliminated. It might well make great concessions to the French in return for a limitation on William's authority.[5] This attitude was not generally held. But many felt that the military budget for 1673 was greater than the people could bear. It ought to have been passed by the first of the year. Yet it was so high that the debates on it continued into January, and in order to get it passed the Prince had to offer to go without his salary for the time being.[6]

The courage of the Dutch and the influence of the Prince were greater than the Spanish believed. Nothing, however, seemed to be going well. In William's absence the conduct of the army had been shameful. On their return to their posts the French commented that God was doing more fighting for the Dutch than their own soldiers.[7] The Prince had not yet won a single engagement. The fatigues of the tour to Charleroi and the discouragement caused by Luxembourg's raid had actually set back the training of the army. Time, greater discipline, and a general shifting of posts within the high command would be needed if the soldiers were to be brought to the point where they could face the enemy with hope of success. Even if this were achieved, the war could not be won without allies against so strong a foe. Here, too, things were not going well. One of William's greatest assets, supposedly, was his relationship to the English Royal Family. This relationship had not done the Dutch any good. Despite all that they could do, Charles II refused to make a separate peace and continued to plan an invasion of Zeeland. Negotiations with other powers – Denmark, the Dukes of Brunswick, Austria, Spain itself – were not bearing fruit. Worst of all, Brandenburg was now visibly leaning toward the French. His failure to join the Prince's army and his later retirement into Westphalia had embittered the Dutch, who retaliated by allowing their subsidy payments to him to fall behind. This gave the Elector a new excuse for inactivity. By the middle of February the situation had become serious. Van Reede van Amerongen wrote on the 20th that the Elector's ministers were talking of making a truce, while others in the court were speaking openly of peace within two or three weeks. In cipher, Amerongen commented that the French party had gained the upper hand at the court. Frederick William was to be pitied, because not only the imperialists but the majority of his own ministers opposed his wishes.[8] Amerongen's sympathies were with the Elector.

William III did not agree. 'I could wish', he wrote four days later, 'that the Elector had done half as much as I have; the affairs of the state would be in better posture. ...'[9] Even Amerongen could not defend Brandenburg's conduct in the next two weeks. Without consulting the Dutch or the Habsburgs, he concluded a provisional truce in the first days of March. William could not contain his anger. In a conversation with Kramprich, the imperial resident at The Hague, he described his uncle's conduct as 'foul'. The Elector had dishonoured himself and shamefully broken his treaty obligations.[11] But words could not hold Frederick William back now. He continued to negotiate with the French, and made peace with them at Vossem in June. He justified himself on the ground that the Dutch had not paid him what they owed; that they had not brought enough men into the field; and that they had not secured the alliance of Denmark and the Dukes of Brunswick.[12] His desertion was so great a blow that even William III thought for a moment of seeking an armistice. It would be very dangerous, for the French would continue to occupy what they had taken and would be able to improve their position. The Dutch, on the other hand, would not be able to save any money during an armistice. They would probably not be able to secure any allies unless they were actually fighting, and their own courage might evaporate during a truce. Even so, the Prince was considering at the end of March a truce which would last until the beginning of June. He was very tired and depressed. He spoke to the States of Holland of working night and day without help and without success.[13] Under these pressures the Dutch agreed to send negotiators to Cologne, although they felt strongly that the Swedes, who presented themselves as mediators, were dangerously partial to the French. The conferences, which were delayed because the French feared that Cologne was subject to imperial influence, began in the early days of June.

The Prince's depression may well have been caused by overwork rather than by the international situation. In May the Dutch resident at Paris was complaining about interference with the posts. Louvois was in charge of the posts, and for these and other reasons was threatening the resident with arrest. When he wrote asking for a speedy reply Constantijn Huygens had to tell him that there was hardly time to discuss such matters. 'His Highness does nothing but come and go. Yesterday morning he arrived after spending the night in the yacht to save time, and before dinner he mounted horseback to spend the night at Alphen and from there to go wherever his presence shall be necessary. It is always needed here (The Hague), but he must keep watch everywhere since our enemies threaten us on all sides.'[14] The resident had to be satisfied with this very cold comfort. But it was the darkness before the dawn. The army was finally gaining strength. In March the officers were forbidden to choose their own regimental agents, which would henceforth be chosen by the state. This meant that the agents could supply equipment without paying fees to the officers, a notable economy. A general shift of the high command took place in April. At the same time brutal regulations were put in force to require officers to be present during musters and to forbid the use of 'dead-pays'. These were valets or men from other regiments who appeared on muster days to fill out a regiment and then disappeared, so that the captains received pay for men who did not exist. In April decrees were issued threatening delinquent officers with death. One colonel, Louis-François de Grijsperre, did not take his orders seriously. He continued to introduce dead-pays into his muster rolls. On 13 November he was beheaded, and after that this particular problem did not arise.[15]

While the Prince was introducing discipline into the army, his diplomatic negotiations were also going more successfully. The cowardice of Brandenburg could have given the Emperor an opportunity to abandon the Dutch. In May William and Fagel were lying like troopers to the imperialists to prevent such a step. They said that the English were coming down in their claims, while the French would be willing to restore all they had taken if only the Dutch would renew the treaty of 1662. Even so, the Republic was unwilling to abandon its allies. It placed its faith in the Emperor and would not treat with the French unless the Emperor refused to lend his support.[16] At the time, of course, the French peace demands were almost as high as they had been at Heeswijk the year before. The French might be contented with a more modest indemnity, but their territorial claims were still enormous.[17] Luckily the Emperor was more interested in the Dutch will to fight than in their truthfulness. At the end of May he decided to join the war. He would need subsidies, since the defection of Brandenburg would make it necessary for him to supply 30,000 men rather than 15,000 and also to pay all the cost of his army's artillery. If his needs were met, however, Leopold was determined to fight.[18]

The Emperor's decision was of the utmost importance but it marked the beginning, not the end, of a long negotiation. It was not until 30 August that the Dutch signed three separate treaties with the Spanish, the imperialists, and the Duke of Lorraine. Leopold did not declare war until the middle of September and the Spanish delayed for another month. Even so, the mere prospect of such allies gave the Dutch courage and kept them from making a shameful peace at Cologne. At the same time, the campaign of 1673 did not turn out too badly. To all appearances the French and English strength was overwhelming. In May the French army paraded through the still neutral Spanish Netherlands. Where would it go? It might well besiege Breda. Then the French would be in a position to support the English if they succeeded in making landings on the coast. This was the greatest danger, and as late as the beginning of June the Prince thought that this was what Louis XIV would do.[19] The King, however, suddenly turned his march eastwards and on 16 June laid siege to Maastricht. It was one of Vauban's greatest triumphs. The siege progressed like clockwork, and although the garrison defended itself bravely the place was surrendered on 30 June. And then? Louis XIV and his court returned to St Germain. Condé did nothing but raise contributions for the rest of the summer. The campaign, which might well have involved the completion of the conquest of the Republic, ended with this one siege almost as soon as it had begun. And the conquest of Maastricht was almost worse than useless. It did give the French one more great fortress; but it did not terrify the Dutch or the Habsburgs, and it released the former garrison to join William's army. Even after the losses of the siege the garrison's strength was more than 3,100 men,[20] a very useful addition to the Dutch field army.

There are several explanations for the odd character of the summer campaign of 1673. The French apparently believed firmly, until the end of August and perhaps even later, that the negotiations still continuing at Cologne would succeed. If they did, there was no point in making expensive conquests which would eventually have to be returned. Secondly, on 7 June de Ruyter fought the combined French and English fleets off Schooneveld. He was accompanied by his old rival Tromp, whom William had ordered to be cooperative. De Ruyter had been given the newly invented title of Lieutenant Admiral-General to show that William did not resent his former connections with de Witt. Tromp was promised the survivance of the title if he worked well with his superior, and he did his best to earn it. Together the two great heroes were unbeatable. Although the Anglo-French fleet was heavily superior in numbers, it was defeated on 7 June and again at a smaller engagement a week later. On 12 August the Prince visited the fleet in person to give it encouragement. He was received with great enthusiasm; and on the 21st the men showed their patriotism by winning another victory off Kijkduin.[21] These battles ended the threat of an amphibious landing and helped to drive England out of the war. She even had the humiliation of learning that another Dutch squadron had retaken New York. Although William hastened to promise that this last conquest would be returned at the peace, the capture of the colony was a threat that the English could not overlook. The Dutch were clearly masters of the sea.

There was yet another reason for English and French inactivity at this time. According to de Groot, who risked his neck by going to Cologne and meddling in the negotiations there, Sweden was deeply concerned to prevent landings on the Dutch coasts. When the English and French boasted of their plans, the Swedish mediator Count Tott threatened to intervene. Louis XIV heard of the muffled ultimatum and asked Tott whether Sweden would declare war on France. The count replied that he could say nothing on that matter; but Sweden would certainly break with England if she went any further. At this, the King promised that he would do nothing after the siege of Maastricht.[22] The story may or may not be true. But it is certain that Louis XIV did not want the Dutch to be pressed to the point of giving any of their ports to the English. On 1 July Louvois wrote to Turenne that such a transfer would be the worst single thing that could happen so far as French interests were concerned.[23] From then on the French and English were clearly not acting in concert, and during the battle of Kijkduin the French fleet did not assist their ally.

This was perhaps the turning point of the war. As late as 16 August both the Spanish and the French thought that the Dutch would make peace.[24] Had de Ruyter lost, it is possible that the Dutch might have collapsed. His victory, however, led to the rapid conclusion of the three separate alliances of 30 August. The treaty with Spain was not of too great value to the Dutch. She had been providing all the assistance she could already, as an auxiliary. In one respect, however, the Spanish treaty was vital. De Lira signed a separate article, subject to the approval of Madrid.[25] In the main treaty the Spanish were only obliged to break with France. By the separate article she was also bound to break with England three weeks after the ratification, if she failed in a last effort to make the English come to their senses. The Spanish were empowered to offer, on the part of the Dutch, the following terms: the right of the flag, reciprocal restitution of lands taken during the war, and a sum of money of between one and two hundred thousand pounds, payable over a period of time. The Dutch again refused to offer any cautionary towns or anything for the right to fish. With the help of Spanish diplomatic pressure they were to succeed in obtaining peace with England on these terms a few months later. The treaty with the Emperor was also important. It meant that Montecuculi would fight this year, as he had not fought the year before. If the Spanish could help the Dutch to get rid of the English, the Emperor and the Duke of Lorraine would help them to change the face of the war on land.

Immediately after the conclusion of the three treaties at the end of August, William III went over to the offensive. By now he had a trained fighting force at his disposal, much more experience than he had had a year earlier, and a far better organized command. There were still serious defects in the artillery and engineering departments. Even so, the Dutch could now face the French if they had equal numbers; and the enemy forces were far smaller than they had been the year before. On 6 September the Prince suddenly attacked Naarden with an overwhelming force. Luxembourg, with less than half the Prince's army of some 25,000 men, could do nothing for the relief of the garrison. On the night of the 11th the Dutch stormed a counter-scarp in a sharp action lasting three hours. The next day du Pas capitulated, and on the 13th he was permitted to lead his men to Arnhem. He still had more than 2,000 uninjured men and supplies for a month. It was William's first victory, and a most important one in terms of prestige. The French had almost forgotten what it was to lose an action. Du Pas was court-martialled and sentenced to perpetual imprisonment, but in the following year he was permitted to serve as a volunteer at Grave and died there.[26] Luxembourg was so annoyed at William's new prestige that he wanted to retake Naarden simply to wound the Prince's reputation. Propaganda was more important in the seventeenth century than we sometimes remember, and it was a weapon used with great care by both sides. The French, however, did not have the strength to recapture the town and Luxembourg was over-ruled.[27]

It was now possible to take up again the plan of 1672 for a breakthrough to the Rhine and a junction with the imperial army. Except for the loss of Maastricht, the opportunity was unchanged from the year before; and the chances of success were far greater. If the two armies could meet, Cologne and Münster might well be forced out of the war and the French forced to abandon their conquests. The preparations for the breakthrough were noticeably superior this time. William would lead the field army in person, as before; but Waldeck was left behind with very large forces for the defence of the Republic. There would be no opportunity given for a second raid on Bodegrave and Zwammerdam. The Prince was also becoming far more concerned about security. In 1672 there had been a number of embarrassing examples of indiscretion. News of the Dutch plans had reached the enemy with frightening speed. William was forced to adopt a method of secrecy which he followed for the rest of his life. Not even his generals were informed of his designs. Plans were entrusted to the smallest possible number of men in the army, men in whom the Prince had complete confidence. Even his own secretary was given no idea of what was going on and had to rely on the gossip of the camp.[28] This threw a great burden of extra work on the Prince. To keep the younger Huygens, who seems to have been something of a gossip, out of the secret meant that William had to write a great many of his letters in longhand. At the end of a campaign, when secrets no longer mattered, those minutes of letters which happened to survive were handed over to Huygens to copy. Many were lost, and the very unsatisfactory nature of the Prince's archives is one result of this curious system. It is a remarkable testimony to the patience of William III and his loyalty to old family retainers that he was willing to put up with Huygens for twenty-five years. The physical and mental strain of writing his own letters was very great. It meant that the Prince, who spent much of the night in the trenches during a siege and a good part of every day visiting his men at all times, had little sleep and less leisure for the rest of his life. Many observers who knew little of his methods of doing business were to consider him lazy and to complain of his slowness in coming to a decision. The second criticism was partially true. William was always careful not to be surprised by a sudden proposal and spent much time in discussing various possibilities before he made up his mind. The charge of laziness, however, will not hold water. The Prince's working day started fairly late, and his first appointments were at nine or even ten o'clock. Often he took time out to hunt, a necessary remedy against his ever-present asthma. Much of his work was done in the evening. It was a rare day when he got to bed before midnight.

The Prince left The Hague for the fall campaign on 29 September. Neither the States General nor its secret committee knew anything of his plans except that he was going to Bergen-op-Zoom. On the 4th and again on the 7th he had conferences with Monterey about the timing of the Spanish declaration of war, which finally took place on 16 October.[29] On the 13th he began his march. He had with him about 9,500 of his own men and hoped to be joined by 3,000 Spanish troops. The Spanish, however, were longer on promise than performance. Their contingent fell short by some 700 horse and dragoons, so that the combined army came to rather less than 12,000 men.[30] The first goal was Coblentz. By marching there the Prince would bring the war into the territory of the Elector of Cologne. His presence would keep the Elector of Trier, whose attitude was suspect, from going over to the enemy. It would also oblige Montecuculi to cross the Rhine, which he might not do otherwise.[31] Soon afterwards William determined to join Montecuculi in the more ambitious plan of besieging Bonn, the usual residence of the Elector of Cologne.[32] On the way the army summoned a small town and sacked it on 1 November when it did not surrender quickly enough. William had threatened to hang the magistrates, burn the place, and leave the women to the mercy of his men in order to obtain a quick surrender. When it was taken, however, the Prince would only allow the soldiers to plunder the town. None of his threats was carried out and strict orders were given for the protection of women. They were obeyed.[33] Such discipline was in sharp contrast to the licence which Luxembourg permitted his men. The armies of William III were already gaining their reputation of being the least burdensome to civilians of all those operating in western Europe.[34]

On 4 November, after dark, the Prince reached the neighbourhood of Bonn. Montecuculi was there before him and the Dutch had some difficulty in finding quarters. The next evening the Prince began to open the trenches. The attackers were favoured with fine weather and everything went well. On the night of the 10th William attacked and took a half-moon in person. This was the only major incident of the siege. At noon on the 12th the defenders ceased firing and capitulated later in the day. Since they had not fought very well, they were obliged to march out of Bonn on the 13th in silence and to leave behind their cannon and horses.[35] In their letter of congratulation, the States General wrote that their joy in the victory had been much reduced by the news of the carelessness with which the Prince exposed his person. His death would mean the ruin of the state, and they begged him to consider the welfare of God's church and his people and to take better care of himself.[36]

Even so, there was much to rejoice about. Soon after 20 October, that is, after William III had begun his march but before he had made his junction with the imperialists, the French government decided to abandon the whole province of Utrecht. They had to have a field army with which to oppose that of the Prince. By withdrawing their garrisons from the towns of Utrecht they would release 30,000 men for service in the field.[37] The orders to Luxembourg were sent very late. He did not leave the town of Utrecht until 16 November, and had the Prince been able to persuade Montecuculi to help him the French might have been cut off. The imperialists, however, were so unwilling to do anything further that Montecuculi actually sneaked off to Vienna without taking leave of William. The Prince and the Spanish did what they could to harass Luxembourg's retreat for the next two months. They gave the French some bad moments, but they were unable to prevent their escape. Once again the opportunity for a great victory had been missed, and missed because the imperialists refused to cooperate with their paymasters. If they were to get a decent return for their money the Dutch would have to insist that their young hero be given the supreme command of the allied armies. Young as he was, William could always be counted on to fight. Other generals might have more experience and skill, but all too often they used their skill to avoid battle. It was quite possible in this period for a whole campaign to elapse without a single engagement. William did not like this kind of campaign and much preferred a series of combats. This affected his record. In many cases his battles were indecisive and frequently they were lost. He probably lost more battles and had to raise more sieges, as the French claimed tauntingly, than any of his contemporaries. This was because he fought a great many more battles than anyone else did. And if he lost more than did any of his contemporaries, he also won more. Clearly William III was not in a class with Turenne or Condé. On a good day, however, and there were to be several, he could beat Luxembourg, and no other commander of his period could say as much. When it is remembered how little of his time William could devote to his profession of arms and how much he, unlike any of his contemporaries, had to devote to politics and diplomacy, his military career appears in a better light. Even though he was unable to destroy Luxembourg's army on its retreat he had well earned the title of Redeemer of the Fatherland.

Now that the Republic was for the most part free of enemy occupation the immediate problem was its political reorganization. Were the three provinces of Utrecht, Gelderland and Overijssel to be penalized for their conduct during the occupation, or were they to be restored to their old position? What changes would be necessary in their form of government? Even while the army was before Bonn the Prince had been bothered with such questions, and Waldeck had recommended that he should return to The Hague at once without waiting for the outcome of the siege. For the moment the Prince could do little except to prevent the reorganization of Utrecht in his absence. On 21 November he wrote to Fagel ordering him to prevent the taking of any decisions before his return to The Hague. He recommended that the old Regents be prevented from returning to power and promised that he would do his part to keep them out of office. One point on which he and the Grand Pensionary were agreed was the need to alter the constitutions of Utrecht and Gelderland.[38] William was so busy that the solution of the problem was considerably delayed. He returned to The Hague for a week in early December. While there his time was taken up with the military budget for the next year, and with negotiations with Denmark and the Dukes of Brunswick. He had no opportunity to decide what to do with the liberated provinces.[39] In January the Prince persuaded the States that Utrecht should be readmitted to the Union with its ancient rank.[40] He was, naturally enough, chosen Stadhouder of the province. On 26 April he gave it what amounted to a new constitution. The powers of the Stadhouder were increased enormously. William secured for himself the right to appoint members of the nobility and used this authority to name military men, which was an innovation. He was to elect burgomasters and sheriffs of the towns from a short list of nominees. In the countryside he could appoint officials without any previous nomination. He must approve the delegates sent by the province to The Hague.[41] With such powers, William had very little trouble with Utrecht after 1674. The situation in Gelderland and Overijssel was not regulated until the following year, when they had been fully cleared of enemy troops.

Meanwhile the course of the war had undergone a great change. The Spanish had been pressing the English as hard as they could to force them to make peace. William III had also been doing what he could. In 1672 and 1673 his agents were continually crossing to England. With the aid of an able French refugee, Pierre du Moulin, a propaganda campaign was started to make the war unpopular with Parliament. Du Moulin had once worked for Lord Arlington and knew the English scene well. At first the campaign was not particularly successful. Then, in March of 1673, du Moulin's pamphlet *England's Appeal from the Private Cabal at Whitehall to the Great Council of the Nation* . . . was distributed throughout London.[42] This work made a deep impression. Although Charles was able to continue the war for the moment, he could obtain no more supplies. His ministers became terrified and by autumn were speaking of the possibility of a rebellion. In November Arlington assured the French ambassador that the King was no longer master of the situation. He could not protect his advisers and had so lost the respect of his subjects 'que tout ce qu'il dit n'est ni cru ni craint'.[43] A month later the King still hoped to make the Dutch fishing fleets apply to him for passports, though he no longer had any expectations of an annual revenue from this source.[44] He was not even to have this satisfaction. The Dutch were too strong for him and could have forced him to accept almost any terms. Since they hoped to obtain his alliance in time, they were quite generous. They gave the English, as they had promised, the right of the flag and returned the colony of New York in exchange for Surinam. An indemnity of £200,000 was offered on the tacit understanding that the Prince would receive most of it, to complete the payment of Charles's debt to him. Charles was given one further opportunity to save face. In January the States made the Prince's places hereditary. The King treated this as a kindness to himself and as the granting of one more of his war aims.[45] Yet the Treaty of Westminister, which was signed on 19/29 February, was a bitter humiliation for him. For the rest of his life he was to be jealous of the nephew who had been too strong for him.

As we have seen, the liberation of his country resulted in a further improvement in the Prince's position. His personal authority in the three liberated provinces was overwhelming. The hereditary establishment of his offices made him, in all but name, a constitutional monarch. True, he could not sentence civilians to death nor raise taxes. These are among the most unpopular of sovereign powers and they were easy to do without. In practice the Prince could be as strong as he chose. William was also recovering from the financial burdens of his youth. Despite the war, his private income in 1673 was a little more than fl.2,000,000 of which he saved some fl.834,000.[46] His changed situation soon brought a great improvement on this. He was supposed to receive some fl.1,600,000 out of the English indemnity. As it happened the Dutch, particularly in Zeeland, were very slow in paying him and he never got all of it. What did come in, however, was a great help. In addition, the fl.2,000,000 debt to Amsterdam was assumed by the state. The East India Company voted him a $3\frac{1}{3}$ per cent interest in their enterprise as a token of gratitude. His salary as Captain-General was now established at fl.10,000 a month, which probably enabled him to make a figure on campaign without any cost to himself. He would not have been able to save anything out of the salary, since he had to keep up two tables for his staff. Even so, he was now one of the wealthiest men in Europe and was in a position to indulge himself in building and collecting, which became the great passions of his life. On the way to Bonn he had halted in Antwerp to buy statues, which would later adorn his new palaces.

Two much more important changes had also occurred. The Prince had become a professional soldier and a very hard man. There was no softness left in him after the harsh experiences of his early years. His high concept of personal honour and his deep religious faith drove him to do what he thought right. These very standards, however, kept him from having any sympathy for the weaknesses of others. He made great demands on himself; he made similar demands on those around him – complete loyalty, absolute discretion, honesty in money matters, physical courage. Those few men who measured up to the Prince's standards were rewarded handsomely. William was as loyal to his servants as he expected them to be to him. They, and their children after them, could count on the continuing support of the House of

Orange. Those who did not meet the Prince's standards, however, were treated with contempt. In many ways these standards were unrealistic. They cut the Prince off from most of the members of his family and from much of polite society. They made him a lonely man. They also made him a great one.

The second change was in the public position of William III. By saving the Republic from the French he had become a real hero. He was still very young, not yet twenty-four. Yet no one could think of treating him as his father had been treated. For the rest of his life, no matter how bitterly he became involved in party politics, no matter what mistakes he seemed to make, his enemies had to treat him with respect. He was the Redeemer of the Fatherland. He had a claim on the gratitude of his people which could never be repaid. The Prince had also become a hero to all Europe. He was undoubtedly the leading member of the English Royal Family. His uncles might be jealous of him; but by 1674 they knew that they needed him. They were so discredited by the failure of the Third Dutch War, by the irregularity of their personal lives, and by the religious beliefs of the Duke of York, that without the support of William III they might well have suffered a second exile. Since we know, today, that the Restoration survived until 1688 it is hard for us to realize that this need not have happened. In the years after 1673 the restored monarchy, again and again, was on the verge of collapse. One of its strongest props was the prospect that one day the Prince would inherit the English throne.

If the Prince had become a hero, this very fact made him a target for his enemies. William III had not yet become a personal enemy of the French King. He did not yet believe in the necessity of containing the inordinate power of France. Some of his colleagues, Waldeck and the imperial ambassador Lisola, did believe that France was now the great enemy of civilization. The Prince did not share their attitude; but the French themselves were to make him change his mind. Popes, emperors, kings, and throngs of lesser princes were bent to the will of Louis XIV. If they took his money and did what they were told, well and good. Otherwise they were broken. The Prince of Orange was almost the only person in Europe who had succeeded in opposing the will of France. He must not be allowed to get away with it. The French would try to bribe him or else to crush him. Already, in 1673, they had confiscated Orange. They attacked his military record, they spread the foulest rumours about his private life. French is an easy language and some of us are amused by gossip. Certain portions of this propaganda campaign are still heard today, accepted by those who should know better. Who would write a life of Sir Winston Churchill based on the speeches of Dr Göbbels? Much of what has been written about William III has been

based on sources of that kind and of that quality. The French have had some
posthumous success in blackening the character of the Prince. At the time
their campaign failed. It was to make him, what he had not been and need
never have been, a bitter personal enemy of the French King and of his
policies. Louis XIV created the man who was to defeat him.

Chapter 10

THE DUCHY OF GELDERLAND

ONCE the English had been forced to make peace a great change came over the face of the war. France lost her main ally in February. In May Münster and Cologne also made peace, leaving Louis XIV to face alone the united power of the Dutch and of the Habsburgs. It seemed that all Europe was against him. The Dukes of Brunswick, the Danes, even Brandenburg sent troops against the French. The allies talked of reducing them to the borders of 1659, of dictating peace at the gates of Paris. The campaign plans for 1674 reflected this high optimism. At sea the Dutch had now complete freedom of action. De Ruyter would take one squadron to capture the French Antilles. Tromp, with a second squadron, would support rebellions in the west of France. A cadet of the great Huguenot House of Rohan, aided by an Amsterdam free-thinker named van den Ende, promised that such risings would take place. They even had hopes of kidnapping the King himself as he was riding in his carriage. The Prince of Orange also entered into negotiations with an adventurer who called himself the Seigneur de Sardan. Sardan promised to raise the four southern provinces of France if he received Dutch and Spanish support. Should Sardan and Rohan succeed, the clock would be turned back a century and France torn by civil war, while the Dutch and the August House invaded from the north, the east, and the southwest.

It was all a fantasy. True, the French were discontented and heavily burdened. True, the Bordelais would revolt in 1675. But the great majority of the people, Catholic and Huguenot alike, were loyal to Louis XIV. The days of Philip II and the League would not come again. At sea, de Ruyter would have no success. When he reached the West Indies the French were ready for him, and his landing was repulsed with heavy loss. Tromp did little better. He made two insignificant landings in the west of France and had to abandon each of them in turn. There were no rebels to help. Rohan and his colleagues had been apprehended and were soon executed. Tromp's activities did create a diversion. An army of 30,000 men was needed to guard the coast. Had Tromp not attacked the cows of the island of Noirmoutiers these 30,000 men might have served elsewhere. This diversion, and a few of the cows, were the only gains of two very costly naval expeditions. On the mainland things went no better. The French were still immensely strong. They had all the advantages of greater wealth, a unified command, and interior lines of communications. Their armies, strengthened by the men who no longer had to garrison the Dutch Republic, were large, brilliantly led, and more experienced than those of the enemy. France, furthermore, was very hard to get at. Her natural frontiers, even if they had not yet been fully strengthened by the genius of Vauban, were difficult to penetrate. When the hoped-for rebellions did not take place, it became virtually impossible for the allies to invade France. The vision of the gates of Paris continued to dance before the eyes of the leaders of the coalition. It remained a vision.

The coalition suffered in many ways from a disunity which was in sharp contrast to the centralized direction of the French war effort. The allied armies must attack on three widely separated fronts. The Spanish were not strong enough to wage war simultaneously in the Pyrenees, the Low Countries, and in Burgundy. The imperialists were still reluctant to commit their forces as far west as they should have. The Dutch suffered from internal disunity as well as from the failings of their friends. Their constitution had been improved by the events of 1672; it was still far from workable. Great as the power of William III now was, he had no control over his country's pocket book. He could influence, perhaps almost dictate, the annual military budget. He could not force the provinces to pay their share of that budget. Holland paid all and more than her share. The other provinces paid little or nothing, although their quotas together made up almost half the Republic's revenues. Since Holland's quota was the only one to come in on time, payments of subsidies to foreign princes and to the army went on very slowly. This made it impossible to set up a system of magazines like that of Louvois. It also meant that the Dutch army could not take the field early enough in the year. Lacking magazines, the cavalry had to wait until there was fresh forage. It was an axiom that the Dutch could not take the field before May. By that time the French might have achieved all their goals for the year. If William could not rely on his own money supply, he found to his disgust that the resources of the Spanish were far weaker than his own. The Spanish were very good at making promises. Monterey undertook to provide a field army of 25,000 men as well as supplies and wagons for the Dutch. He could do neither the one nor the other. What troops he could bring together were needed to garrison the fortified towns of the Spanish Netherlands. And there was never enough forage for the Dutch horses or beer for the men. As a result the soldiers became disorderly, and it was some time before the Prince could restore disipline.[1]

The Prince's personal task in the campaign was to lead the allied armies in the Low Countries. He had about 30,000 men of his own. These would be supported by whatever the Spanish could supply and also by an imperial army. It was expected that this force would be under the command of the

Duc de Bournonville; but at the last moment he was sent elsewhere and replaced by the Comte de Souches. De Souches had been a famous infantry commander. By 1674, however, his memory and health were failing. He was extremely capricious and uncooperative, and his appointment was a bad omen for the success of the campaign. There were many other such omens. In February the French had attacked the Spanish in Franche-Comté, which was occupied with very little trouble. The Prince de Vaudemont, a son of Charles IV of Lorraine by Beatrix de Cusance, did his best to defend Burgundy. But the Spanish forces were too weak, and the Swiss mercenaries of which they were largely composed fought badly. For the rest of the campaign the French would remain on the defensive. Turenne with a small army would face the Duke of Lorraine and the imperialists on the upper Rhine. By burning the Palatinate with great brutality, and by the brilliance of his manoeuvres, Turenne managed to contain and then to defeat a superior force. Condé, with an army of 45,000 men, would oppose the allies in the Low Countries. Here, if anywhere, was an opportunity for decisive victory. Although the quality of Condé's men was higher than that of the confederates, the latter would have a large superiority in numbers.[2]

William took his leave of the States on 11 May and joined the army at Duffel. It was not even then ready to enter the field. Some of the troops, as well as a part of the artillery and wagon train, had not yet come up.[3] As a consequence the Prince had to watch helplessly while the French made themselves masters of Argenteau and Navagne. Almost immediately trouble began with the Spanish and particularly with the imperialists. Souches did not want to cross the Maas. He would not believe that the French force under Condé was as strong as it really was. In any circumstances he preferred to move towards the Palatinate rather than the Low Countries. By so doing he would preserve the independence of his command. Should he cross the Maas, Souches would have to place himself under the Prince of Orange and perhaps also under the Count of Monterey. This would be a serious affront to his dignity, since Monterey was a civilian. Another source of difficulty lay in the fact that Montecuculi wished to conduct the campaign from Vienna.[4] To keep up his own authority Montecuculi had given Souches obscure and confused orders. William was finally obliged to ask the Emperor Leopold, who did not share Montecuculi's views, to order Souches to cross the river.[5] Meanwhile the imperial commander kept asking the Prince to send him detachments. This would of course increase his own importance at the expense of the Dutch, but there was no reason to suppose that he would do anything useful even with reinforcements. On the other hand, Souches was so capricious that he might retire from the area altogether if his whims were not gratified. It is impossible to say how much of the blame lies with Souches in the field and how much with Montecuculi and other officials in Vienna. On 12 July secret orders were actually sent from Vienna ordering Souches to detach 8,000 men or even to take his whole force to the Palatinate.[6] The only way to stop this was for the Prince to divide his own army. Although he was very reluctant to do so, he offered to send Souches a large detachment. In this way, and after much difficulty, he was finally able to persuade the imperialists to cross the Maas and undertake joint operations. The conjunction of the allied armies took place on 25 July. Finally the campaign was ready to begin.

The united armies may have contained 60,000 men. Probably there were fewer than that, and the contingents were of very uneven quality. The goal was to force a battle on Condé, who had about 45,000 men. Condé had chosen a camp covered front and rear by a small meandering stream called the Piéton. His position was very strong. The allies considered it unassailable. They came as close to it as they could, in an attempt to lure the French out, but the enemy were not obliging enough to leave their entrenchments and give battle. When Condé would not move, the allies decided to march off towards Binch and the road to the French border. This would force a battle or else leave the north of France exposed to allied revenge. To reach Binch the confederates would have to march past the front of Condé's army, exposing their flank. This could have been dangerous. But the nature of the ground was such that a flank attack was not to be expected.

On the morning of 11 August the army began to move. The imperial forces were in the van, the Dutch in the middle, and the Spanish in the rear. Behind them, a detachment of dragoons and 4,000 horse under the Prince de Vaudemont acted as a guard. It had been agreed that the van should wait until the baggage got a head start. Souches, however, refused to wait and started off so abruptly that he became separated from the rest of the army. His own baggage was taken care of; but that of the Dutch was left with an inadequate escort. The real danger, however, lay in the separation of the armies. The portion left behind was numerically inferior to that of the French, and without cannon. If anything happened it would take hours for Souches to return. Meanwhile Condé attacked, not the flank, but the rearguard under Vaudemont. The ground at that point was so broken that Vaudemont's horse were of little use. After skirmishing had begun he sent a request to William for two infantry battalions. William hastened to send three, comprising two full regiments, and hurried to the rear to join the fight himself. It is curious that Vaudemont called on the Dutch in the centre rather than on the Spanish who were nearer him. Apparently some of them could not be counted on, and the Spanish contingent was even smaller than usual that day. Monterey had just left the camp for Brussels and had taken with him an extraordinarily large bodyguard. Although he was still within reach of the battlefield he did not return, which was to cause a great deal of gossip in the coming months.

Vaudemont, with his Dutch reinforcements, tried to hold the village of Seneffe. He seems to have placed his men badly, so that the cavalry were too crowded and could not work properly. The French attacked him head on with one body while sending another upstream to make a flank attack or, perhaps, even to cut the detachment off. At this, the detachment was ordered to abandon Seneffe and to march to the right so as to join the main army. The first three cavalry squadrons got through, with heavy losses. The other four then took to flight. Although Vaudemont and Orange tried to stop them, beating the men with the flat of their swords, there was at first nothing they could do. Finally they succeeded in rallying the men near the priory of St Nicholas, south of Seneffe. Here there was a second short engagement, a second allied defeat and flight. Had Condé been content with his first success, or even with his second near the priory of St Nicholas, he would be credited and justly so with a signal victory. But he was not satisfied with beating up the rearguard of the allied army. From what he had seen he had every reason to suppose that a general engagement might bring a decisive victory. If he could crush the whole army all threats of an invasion of France would be at an end. It was a great opportunity, and one which few men would have been able to resist. Condé decided to call up all his forces, to push on past the priory, and to attack the main body of the allied army which was posted still further to the south in the village of Fay.

It was now about two in the afternoon. The rearguard action had lasted four hours. This had given the imperialists time to return, bringing heavy guns with them. The French on the other hand had left several of their field pieces at Seneffe or at the priory and were for the first time inferior in artillery. The return of the Germans was another blessing for the allies. Souches might be verging on senility, but he still remembered how to fight in the hour of battle. His men also did well. But the real surprise of the day was the conduct of the Dutch infantry. They were still relatively inexperienced and undisciplined, though to civilians like Richard Bulstrode they seemed 'as likely men to fight as I ever saw'.[7] For once Bulstrode was right. William's two years of desperately hard and disappointing work was finally rewarded. The Dutch held their positions against assault after assault. The general engagement at Fay continued all afternoon and late into the evening. The sun set. By moonlight the fighting continued until almost eleven o'clock. The allies did not give an inch of ground. Finally the moonlight failed. At first both armies were too tired to move. Then the French retired and the confederates soon followed their example.

Such was the battle of Seneffe. The casualties were very heavy. Some 7,000 men fell on each side. As was to be expected from the course of the action, the French took more prisoners and standards than they lost, and they captured two of Souches's field pieces as well as William's baggage. Since the imperialists and the Spanish had taken care of their own baggage while abandoning that of the Dutch, William III was angry at the loss, which included his personal effects and ciphers as well as a considerable sum of money and the pontoon bridge so necessary for a campaign in the watery Netherlands. The loss was serious. But the French had little to boast about. A great number of officers of all ranks were among the dead. The first news of the battle led the government to order the singing of the *Te Deum* in celebration of a great victory. The second, more substantial reports led them to call out, for almost the last time, their militia. The French realized that their country was now open to invasion. The Spanish also celebrated Seneffe with the singing of the *Te Deum*, although their part in the battle had not been a glorious one by any means. The real hero of the day was the Prince of Orange. Souches compared his conduct to that of a Caesar. Condé, who had been careless enough of his own person, said that William had played the part of a great general except in exposing himself like a young man. William's English uncles openly gave him the credit for saving the confederate armies from the disaster with which they were faced. The first encounter had undoubtedly ended in a French victory. Part of this may be ascribed to Vaudemont's improper placement of his cavalry. But in the general battle at Fay the allies recovered their honour and held their own magnificently. Before the battle William had remarked that, even if he lost, he could only gain in reputation since his opponent was so great a captain as the Prince de Condé.[8] He had done better than that, he had fought Condé to a draw. And if it had been an expensive draw, the French with their inferior numbers could not afford equal losses. William emerged from his first major field action with the applause and respect of all men.[9]

It took some time for both sides to recover from the effects of Seneffe. On 31 August a great convoy arrived from the Republic, bringing several hundred new wagons laden with replacements for all that the Dutch had lost. There was a month's pay for the men in the Prince's army and five fresh regiments of men. It is pleasant to note that there were rewards for good conduct as well as punishments for bad. William had had one major beheaded for cowardice during the action. The Prince hoped to use his fresh men and supplies for an invasion of France, but his idea was rejected by the other generals. Souches insisted on besieging Ath. On 3 September his liaison officer was calling it 'the most important siege that one can undertake'. Four days later a large detachment of cavalry was sent off to invest the place.

Again, as so often before during the campaign, the Prince had decided to do anything Souches asked rather than risk his departure for the Palatinate. But as soon as the cavalry had gone off, Souches changed his mind. He would not besiege Ath, and nothing more was to be said about it. The detachment had to be recalled. At this William lost his temper completely. He sent blistering letters off to The Hague and to Vienna. In them he explained that the siege of Ath had been agreed on at a council of war held at Quarignon on 23 August. This decision had been confirmed at other councils held on the 3rd and, in the presence of Souches, on the 6th. Something he said at that meeting roused William's suspicions, and he spent the next day trying to overcome the general's objections. By the evening of the 7th he had apparently been successful. It was only at 4:00 a.m. on the 8th that Souches sent a message to William saying that he could not approve of the siege.[10]

Luckily all was not lost. Souches himself proposed a siege of Oudenarde, which lies a short distance to the northwest of Ath. Many of the necessary preparations for the first siege did not have to made again, because the two towns were so close. By the 15th the cavalry had reached the neighbourhood of Oudenarde and the infantry came up in the next days. Souches now refused to work on his section of the lines or to encamp himself properly. At the same time he kept demanding reinforcements. To keep him quiet the Prince lent him a brigade of horse and six infantry regiments. Even then the imperialists refused to open their trenches unless they were supplied with 3,000 pioneers to do the digging. Meanwhile Condé was bringing up his army to attempt the relief of the town. Souches made it impossible to hold councils of war by the simple expedient of feigning illness. His absence from the councils made it impossible for the allies to occupy a commanding height whose importance they realized perfectly well.

On the 20th Souches abruptly sent off all his own guns and powder. He had borrowed ten field pieces from the Dutch. Without telling anyone, he had these ten cannon brought just inside the Dutch lines and then abandoned them. His obvious purpose was to have the cannon lost and to place the blame for it on William. By chance, the guns were found. Almost by miracle enough horses were also found to pull them to safety. By this time all hope of continuing the siege was gone. Had Souches been available on the 20th the council of war could have agreed on the occupation of the commanding height. By the next day this height was occupied by the French. Fortunately for the allies there was a great fog that morning and they were able to march off without loss. Even now Souches would not cooperate. The order of march towards Ghent did not please him. Without telling the Prince, he chose to go his own way. The Germans had been assigned the task of bringing up the rear. They refused to do so, and when William noticed that there was no rearguard he had to improvise one and command it himself. Then Souches decided to send his men through the Dutch infantry, causing indescribable confusion. To keep out of the way of the imperialists the Dutch had to take to a stream and march for a considerable time waist-deep in water.

All possibility of cooperation was now at an end. The Prince wrote circumstantial accounts of what had happened to The Hague and to Brussels for transmission to Vienna,[11] inviting Monterey to join him in seeing 'that the irreparable harm which this man has done Europe does not remain unpunished'. Even in this the Prince was unsuccessful. Souches was recalled, but not disgraced. His conduct, however, had reinforced the lessons of the previous year. The allied army could not operate with a divided command. There must be a generalissimo, and if any fighting were to be done that generalissimo must be William III. The Austrian military leaders would have preferred to control the campaign from Vienna. It was not until November that they would agree to a unified command for the coming year in the Netherlands. Since this was the Emperor's wish, Montecuculi had to agree. But he was so unhappy at the decision that the Dutch ambassador did not dare tell him until later that the supreme command would be given to the Prince of Orange.[12]

William's military reputation had been seriously endangered by the ridiculous campaign of 1674. It was useless to explain that the Spanish had not brought into the field half the men they had promised, or that the imperial general was eccentric to the point of madness. The allies had had a clear numerical superiority in the Netherlands. They had nothing to show for it but the indecisive battle of Seneffe. Hopes for peace were becoming more insistent in the Republic month by month. If William were to persuade the Dutch to continue the war, he must provide victories. He could not think of ending the season on such a sour note as the siege of Oudenarde. Not very much more could be done in the south so late in the year. There was one opportunity elsewhere. When the French had evacuated the major portion of the Republic they had retained two cities on the Maas, Grave and Maastricht. In June the Prince had authorized General Rabenhaupt to besiege Grave. Very little progress had been made and the siege continued. If William could bring it to a successful conclusion he would recover much of his lost prestige. He arrived before Grave on the evening of 9 October.

'We did not find it so far advanced as we had expected', he wrote the next day.[13] In fact the siege had been botched. Rabenhaupt had done a fine job in defending Groningen two years before. Now his talent seemed to have deserted him. Although the Prince had given him his orders on 17 June, he had not begun to open his trenches until 29 July. Even then Grave was not invested. One of the most important reasons for taking the town, other than the fact that it was the last bit of Dutch soil occupied by the enemy (Maastricht had been promised to Spain by the treaty of 30 August 1673), was the fact that it contained a great prize. Before they withdrew from the occupied provinces, the French had exacted promises of heavy contributions from the Dutch in return for not burning their cities. They had demanded hostages to ensure payment, and many of them were now detained inside Grave. If the hostages could be recovered, the contributions would not have to be paid. Rabenhaupt's neglect to invest the place made it possible for the French to transfer them to Maastricht on 16 August in two wagons under a strong guard. The value of those two wagons was estimated at 800,000 livres. Rabenhaupt's carelessness in losing this enormous sum was matched by the incompetence with which he conducted the rest of his operations. His opponent, the Marquis de Chamilly, defended the town brilliantly. He had a large garrison of some 4,000 men, virtually unlimited supplies, and so much powder that he was afraid lest it blow up the town. He tried to sell some of his excess powder to the Dutch, apparently without success. Chamilly's greatest asset was his own brilliance. Again and again he led sorties from the city to disrupt the work of the besiegers. Again and again he succeeded. He devised a floating fort by tying two boats together and let them drift down on the enemy lines at night. When the men on the fort had disrupted the Dutch to their satisfaction, they were pulled back to safety by means of a tow rope.

Chamilly's ingenuity prevented Rabenhaupt from making any considerable progress. Virtually nothing had been done by the attackers in the first two months of the siege. When Rabenhaupt understood that he was to be relieved by William III it was only natural for him to try to capture Grave before the Prince could arrive. His own reputation was at stake as well as that of the Captain-General. On the night of 29 September he tried to take Grave by storm. Two days later he tried again. He was repulsed both times with heavy losses. Since the defenders also suffered, the attacks were probably not without value, although no ground was gained. Nothing more of note was done before the arrival of the Prince. As we have seen, William was dissatisfied with the progress of the siege. But he was no Vauban himself. He made very heavy use of hand grenades and saw to it that the grenadiers were paid nine guilders a day for their work. He made better use of fascines and other equipment than Rabenhaupt had, and all this must have reduced the casualty lists. But they were still very high. A siege was a very costly operation, and when it was directed by someone who was less than expert the losses quickly became prohibitive. The Prince tried to storm Grave on the night of the 11th, and again on the 13th, 15th, 16th, and 17th. His casualties were very heavy. But even if he lost two men to one, or three to one, there would come a time when the defenders had no more men to lose. Chamilly had before his eyes the example of du Pas, who had been disgraced for surrendering Naarden the year before. Du Pas served at Grave as a volunteer and died bravely during one of the sorties. Chamilly would not surrender before he had the permission of his king. It arrived on the 24th and he began to capitulate the next day. William was happy to grant him the full honours of war and twenty-four of the French cannon in the city. He marched out on the 27th, with between 1,500 and 2,000 survivors of the garrison and most of the glory of the siege. In all, the attackers may have lost almost as many men as at Seneffe. But they had won a considerable victory. Once again the Prince had demonstrated a bravery verging on recklessness, as well as considerable technical skill. Grave proved, if proof were needed, that the failures of the allies were to be attributed to the Habsburg generals and not to the Prince of Orange. He was the only allied commander on land or sea who emerged from the campaign of 1674 with his reputation intact.

In one sense the taking of Grave weakened the position of the confederates. Now that all the territories of the Republic had been recovered, many Dutchmen felt that they had nothing more to fight for. Why should they support the fantastic Spanish demands for a return to the Treaty of the Pyrenees? They owed the Spanish a great debt for their help in 1672. But if the Spanish would not defend themselves, if they would not meet their subsidy obligations to the German allies, it would be better to make peace on the best terms obtainable. As for the Germans, the Dutch did not feel that they owed them anything. The popular longing for peace had been great enough before the capture of Grave; afterwards, it became a force strong enough to threaten the position of the administration. And if the people felt this way when things were going well, when they still had confidence in the patriotism of William III, how would they feel when the war went badly and they could no longer rely on the Prince? Two events took place in the early months of 1675 which caused a general revulsion of feeling against the war. The first was the Swedish invasion of Brandenburg in January. This created a 'second front', and it meant a very considerable diversion of effort on the part of the allies. Obviously, the invaders must be turned back. But the original demands of the Elector of Brandenburg for assistance were fantastic. All his own troops would be needed to fight the Swedes. In addition he demanded the use of the entire military strength of Denmark and of the House of Brunswick. Even if he had not done so these princes would probably have moved their men north, because they all had hopes of acquiring a share of the Swedish possessions in Germany. Bremen and Verden, particularly, were apples of discord thrown to the allies by Louis XIV. But Frederick William was not satisfied with all this. He forced the Dutch to declare war on Sweden and also demanded that they should provide a contingent of 12,000 men.[14] He did not, of course, get all he asked for. He did succeed in getting a great many men who should have been sent to the Spanish Netherlands. The situation there was rapidly becoming precarious, because the Spanish now had a 'second front' of their own. A revolt of the people of Messina had begun in 1674 and it was now being encouraged by the French. Much of the Spanish war effort had now to be devoted to the fighting in Sicily. The campaign in the Pyrenees was neglected, that in the Low Countries was almost forgotten. The Swedish and Sicilian diversions meant that the Dutch would have to fight virtually alone in the Netherlands. They would have to fight on the defensive against a vastly superior enemy. A less popular kind of warfare could hardly be conceived.

The second event of January 1675 was the Prince's attempt to gain the sovereignty of the province of Gelderland. It was a concerted affair, in which the chief actors were relatives of Gaspar Fagel. Although the origins of the Fagels were obscure enough, and this was the first generation in which they had been members of the Regent class, the Pensionary had both a brother and a nephew in the magistracy of Nijmegen. Both men had made mysterious journeys to The Hague on numerous occasions. Then, in January, the Pensionary and William himself left the capital. The Prince went to Zuylestein to hunt, yes, but not to hunt animals. On the 29th, to no one's surprise, the provisional government of Gelderland unanimously voted to give him the sovereignty of their province, with the titles of Duke of Gelderland and Count of Zutphen. William did not dare to accept the offer without consent of the other provinces. While he was waiting for their advice he kept on with his hunting. The first news, from Utrecht, was favourable; that province advised that the offer be accepted. But Utrecht was not typical. Not only did its new constitution give the Prince far more authority than he had elsewhere. There was also another Fagel brother-in-law in the States of Utrecht, who had done his work well. In the other provinces, however, there was a strong reaction against the offer of sovereignty. The people of Amsterdam felt that they had better be under the subjection of the French than have an absolute sovereignty at home. There was a financial panic. A run on the Bank of Amsterdam was coupled with a collapse of the stock market.[15] When it came to a vote in the States of Holland, a majority was in favour of having the Prince accept Gelderland's offer; but the minority was too strong to be neglected. The Prince decided to reject the proffered sovereignty before he knew of the vote of Zeeland on 16 February, which had gone against him. Instead he accepted the hereditary office of Stadhouder and revised the province's constitution as he had done at Utrecht. Early in March he did the same in the province of Overijssel and the reconstruction of the Union was finally at an end.

This was undoubtedly the most unfortunate single act of the Prince's life. By it he forfeited for a decade the popularity which was the basis of his authority inside the Republic, and the confidence of his allies which was the foundation of his influence in Europe. Amsterdam, England, and Spain could now accuse him, with some apparent justice, of acting only for his own ends. The French, of course, were delighted. The old Louvestein party, which had never been completely destroyed, was now brought back to the threshhold of power by the Prince's own folly. Historically the Louvesteiners were pro-French and they would try to obtain a separate peace so as to reduce the Prince's authority. One of Johan de Witt's clerks had now become secretary of the city of Amsterdam. By this and other channels the Comte d'Estrades could negotiate with the opposition, and give it hope and strength. The influence of the affair on the Prince's relations with Spain was only less serious than it was on his relations with Amsterdam. The Spanish, or at least their ambassador de Lira, became convinced that William III would seize a sovereignty belonging to Spain in lieu of the Dutch one which had escaped him. This suspicion had military consequences, as we shall see. But de Lira also threatened to engage in political opposition to the Prince, and it is possible that he actually did so.[16] In England, too, the parliamentary leaders began to wonder whether the Prince was really a Stuart after all. William's general loss of prestige was so great that people began to question his competence and to wonder whether Fagel had proposed the sovereignty of Gelderland in order to ruin him.[17] The idea that Fagel betrayed the Prince is probably false. He had been extremely ill at the end of 1674 and it is most likely this sickness, rather than any treachery, that caused him to be so much less effective in Holland than were his relatives in the other provinces.

The central question, however, is the conduct of the Prince rather than that of Fagel. Why did he want the sovereignty of Gelderland when he had everything else? Almost certainly he felt that Orange would never be returned to him. If Orange were confiscated, as Bouillon had been taken from the family of Turenne, then he would no longer be a sovereign prince. This tenuous sovereignty was essential to the whole position of William's house. Perhaps, a century before, the Dutch people had had no right to rebel against their lawful sovereign. Bodin would have said that they did not. But Bodin argued that it was the duty of one sovereign to come to the aid of a people oppressed by another who was a tyrant. Perhaps in making this distinction the great philosopher was thinking of William the Silent. For it was on precisely those grounds that William the Silent had justified his conduct. He was a sovereign and might lawfully wage war against the King of Spain, even if Philip's subjects had no such right. For the last hundred years the House of Orange had been clinging desperately to its sovereignty. In all formal correspondence, even during the minority of William III, great care had been taken to use the first person plural although it caused great offence to the Dutch. There had been innumerable squabbles, and there would be more of them, inside the family on questions of precedence. The claim to be a sovereign prince was worth any amount of trouble. And when Orange was occupied by the French in 1673 the finding of a substitute sovereignty undoubtedly became one of the Prince's personal war aims. He had rejected supreme authority over the Republic in 1672 because the offer had come from the enemy, and he had frowned on the Amsterdam proposal of the same year to make him Count of Holland because he thought it was a trap. But a sovereignty somewhere, outside Holland but also outside the grasp of the French King, was needed to preserve the standing of the Prince. It would be no innovation, merely a replacement for Orange. William felt that he deserved such a replacement, and in this he was undoubtedly right. He had saved the Republic, he had become the leader of the reformed religion. Without him, both of them would have been crushed by France in 1672. The Dutch, on the other hand, felt that the sovereignty of Gelderland would necessarily be followed either by internal discord or else by the grant of the sovereignty of the remaining provinces. In that, they in their turn were right. It was the fundamental opposition of the two points of view, both of them justified, that was to cause much of the bitterness of the next ten years.

The Prince had undoubtedly acted with very little political sense. He was still a young man. However precocious a twenty-four-year-old may be, it is impossible for him to have the experience of someone twice that age. The seclusion of William's youth and his recent military activity had prevented him from learning very much about the people whose destiny he shared. There is, however, a great difference between the position of William III and that of his father. The Prince was now at the same age as his father had been at the time of the attack on Amsterdam. By a singular coincidence he came down with smallpox early in April and for some time his life was in danger. Luck and his extremely temperate course of life were with him. He survived, although his health was permanently impaired. Thus he obtained an opportunity, which William II never had, of retrieving his position and his reputation. It is true that the opportunity was not an attractive one. The illness of the Grand Pensionary, followed by that of the Stadhouder, meant that very little had been done in preparation for the campaign of 1675. The balance of strength had turned in favour of the French. But if he had to face a strong peace party inside the Republic, if he had to fight a superior enemy virtually alone, the fact remains that William III did continue the fight. He did not abandon the struggle because his personal ambitions had been frustrated. Instead he fought on, against ever worsening odds. And the event was to prove again that he was driven by patriotism rather than by a desire for personal gain. At the time, many Dutchmen could not see the purpose of the war in the Netherlands. They forgot that 1672 could come again. Some scholars have made the same mistake and have divided the Prince's life into two parts at 1674. Until then, they thought, he was a patriotic Dutchman; afterwards, at best, a European. The English, who were later to call him Dutch William, were nearer the truth. After 1674, as before, the goal of the Prince's life was the safety of the Republic. By now he detested the Spanish, and he had no reason to love any of the rest of his present or future allies. Only a coalition, however, could face the enemy. The danger of a French attack on the Republic remained, that of a French attack on protestantism was actually increasing. The Dutch particularly, and the independent states of Europe too, were like people who are caught out in a blizzard. As they became numb with cold they longed to sit down to rest, which would mean death. Sometimes a determined man can keep the others walking and ensure their survival. The determination of William III preserved the life of the United Provinces. But the survivors blamed him for saving Europe as well as saving themselves, and they complained of being severely frostbitten by the costs of the war.

Chapter 11

ON CAMPAIGN

In the seventeenth century, peace negotiations began almost with the start of hostilities and continued throughout every war. Such negotiations, for the most part insincere, were useful for propaganda purposes and an essential means of espionage. Most countries, furthermore, had allies or suffered from internal division. Clever diplomats, pretending to make peace, could weaken an alliance or foment domestic discord, sometimes both. Eventually, war by diplomacy would always be replaced by serious attempts to obtain peace; but it was never easy to determine just when an enemy began to mean what he said. So far as the Dutch were concerned, peace was desirable at any time after the conclusion of the 1674 campaign. Even Amsterdam, which had been staunch in its support of the first two years of the war, had changed its mind. The integrity of the Republic's soil was assured with the recapture of Grave. Further fighting would only serve to dislocate the channels of trade. England's neutrality gave her a great advantage over the Dutch in commerce, an advantage which would increase with every month that the war continued. Once they had taken over any part of the carrying trade it would be difficult if not impossible for the Dutch to get it back. It is interesting that in February of 1674, the very month in which the Treaty of Westminster was concluded, the Dutch agreed to a partial reopening of trade with the enemy. A year later, when they were forced to declare war on Sweden, they insisted on maintaining their commercial relations with her. The Republic had much to lose from a long war, particularly if it involved an embargo on trade.

The negotiations which had been going on at Cologne with little success were spoiled shortly after the conclusion of the Treaty of Westminster by two Austrian violations of diplomatic immunity. The first involved Prince William von Fürstenberg, the chief adviser of the Elector of Cologne. Fürstenberg, who had great influence over his master, was devoted to the French cause and boasted of having worked for fifteen years for the ruin of Holland. Despairing of bringing Cologne out of the war so long as the Prince was at liberty, the Emperor had Fürstenberg kidnapped and then imprisoned on a charge of treason. Since he was a prince of the Empire, such a charge had a certain plausibility. But when a sum of French money was also stolen at Cologne, Louis XIV withdrew his ambassadors and these particular negotiations collapsed. Other attempts at peace continued to be made elsewhere. The English hoped to become mediators, which might bring them some money. Direct Franco-Dutch negotiations were attempted by d'Estrades, who as Governor of Maastricht was well placed to make trouble. He tried to reach the Prince of Orange through one of his secretaries, de Lannoy, and also through Johan Pesters, a member of the government of Utrecht. At the same time, d'Estrades renewed his old contacts with the republican party to see whether he could obtain better terms from them. In 1674 the republicans were too weak to bring about peace. But their opposition, which increased in strength as time passed, might disrupt the Dutch war effort. Eventually, if the position of the Prince became weak enough, they might be able to force through a peace against his wishes.

The purpose of the French was to break the alliance. They were strong enough to destroy any single power in Europe; only a coalition could stand against them. If they could persuade the Dutch to make a separate peace they could dictate what terms they pleased to the other allies. On the other hand, if the Dutch did make a separate peace they would find it much harder to obtain allies for any subsequent war. William III realized the importance of maintaining his treaty obligations. The Republic, he knew, could not hope to withstand the power of France unassisted. He was also impressed by the reports which reached him of French internal weakness. The Prince felt that a war of attrition would be of advantage to the allies. In this he underestimated the strength of his enemy and overestimated that of the coalition. He hoped to be able to persuade the English to join him. Here he made a second miscalculation. His personal position in England was not as strong as he thought. At the same time he was wrong in thinking that English interests were fundamentally the same as the Dutch. William did not yet understand the importance of the Channel. While the loss of the whole of the Spanish Netherlands would threaten English interests, anything short of that was an indifferent matter. France could go very far, perhaps to the gates of Antwerp, before making a direct challenge to English security. Undoubtedly part of William's error was the result of his sincere religious convictions, which his uncle did not share. Even more important was the Prince's loyalty to the United Provinces. Charles II was not, and no King of England could be expected to be, a Dutch patriot.

Immediately after the battle of Seneffe, the French were willing to make peace on the basis of what they possessed: they would leave Flanders as it was by the Treaty of Aix-la-Chapelle of 1668 and retain Franche-Comté. The military situation justified such proposals. William rejected them. When he spoke with Sir William Temple at the end of the campaign, he hoped to obtain the restoration of all that Spain had lost since 1659. Only Aire and St Omer could safely be ceded to the French beyond the terms of the

Treaty of the Pyrenees.¹ Because the Prince was generally recognized not only as the leader of the war party in the United Provinces but also as the 'centre of the coalition', all proposals for peace included provisions for his personal advantage. This caused him considerable embarrassment. If he should ever seem inclined to peace, he would appear to be acting from corrupt motives. He was extremely sensitive on this point. Temple had reached The Hague during the summer, but the Prince would not allow him to come to the front for fear of arousing Spanish suspicions. The ambassador had to cool his heels for several months before finally obtaining an audience.

One reason for the Spanish distrust was the general rumour that William would marry his cousin, Princess Mary of York. This had been the general talk of London in April.² Mary was only twelve and was certain to bring a contemptible portion. Her prospects, however, were very great. It was now probable that the King her uncle would never have any legitimate children. Her father was generally believed to be diseased. Even if his second wife should bear him children, they would inherit the Duke of York's shame and die in childhood. The truth of this suspicion cannot be proved, but the fact that it was believed was of great political importance. In the circumstances, Mary became a majestic prize. A marriage between William of Orange and the Princess would consolidate the two leading claims to the English succession. Some foreign observers found it difficult to conceive that a granddaughter of Edward Hyde would ever be permitted to sit on the throne of Edward the Confessor. In that case, William was already heir presumptive to the English throne and might marry where he pleased. In 1673 the Prince himself had believed that he might brush aside the claims of Anne Hyde's daughters. He asked the Dutch ambassador in Copenhagen, the Heer van Werkendam, to examine the qualifications of a Danish princess. Others talked of the possibility of his marrying the widowed Queen of Poland, a sister of the Emperor.³ But as the Prince learned more of the realities of English politics, he came to understand that Mary's claim to the English succession was valid and that it was stronger than his own, despite the meanness of her mother's birth.

When the Prince rejected the French proposals, Charles II sent Ossory and Arlington over on a special mission to try to change his mind.⁴ Ossory was to endeavour to get the Prince to ask for the hand of Princess Mary. It would be too humiliating for the English to make the offer themselves. William was pleased by the idea, but he preferred to postpone his marriage until after the conclusion of peace. His stated reason for delay was that a wife would not like the noise of war. Unfortunately Ossory, in writing a report to the English court, was careless in his punctuation; his dispatch appeared to indicate that the English had sued for the hand of the Prince and had been rejected. The Duke of York was, of course, angry at what he thought to be an insult. But he also had other plans. The French ambassador had given him hopes that Mary might one day become the wife of the Dauphin. At the same time d'Estrades was offering the Prince Mlle de Blois, a daughter of Louis XIV by Louise de la Vallière. Although the French and English governments were working together in general, each of them preserved freedom of action in regard to relations with the United Provinces. Each was jealous of the possibility that the other might form an alliance with the Dutch. The Prince of Orange did not care to marry Mary of York at that time; he did not care to marry a French bastard at any time. Thus these marriage proposals fell through. But there was another set of marriage proposals which he did support. This was a plan to marry Mlle d'Orléans to Carlos II of Spain, with all the French conquests since 1659 as her portion.[5] If the King of England could bring this marriage about he might expect £200,000 or even £400,000 as a fee. Although Temple felt that this plan had a French origin, the French would not accept it when it was proposed to them. The only practical steps taken towards peace this winter were the acceptance of England by all sides as mediator, and of Nijmegen as the place for negotiations. The belligerents were so little interested in ending the war that it was not until the end of 1676 that all the ambassadors arrived there.

For four years William III forced the Republic to continue the war. In many ways this was against his own interests. By doing so he lost the many personal advantages which the French were willing to give him in exchange for a separate peace. The French offered again and again to give him Maastricht, the Duchy of Limburg, and perhaps also Spanish Gelderland. The Prince also lost the affection of the Dutch and a good portion of his political influence inside the Republic. From the beginning of 1675 he was unpopular with the Regent class. He was subjected to bitter personal attacks in pamphlets, the worst of them written by one J. Rothe, a Fifth Monarchy man and a brother-in-law of the old Cromwellian, Samuel Hartlib. In 1674 Rothe published a famous print of the Prince entitled 'The Idol of Holland'. It may also have circulated in the form of a medal. William was depicted on a pedestal, uttering the word 'Dissimulation' and being worshipped by the Dutch. The next year Rothe went further. He accused the Prince in a pamphlet of having been responsible for the deaths at Bodegrave and Zwammerdam in 1672; of having conspired for sovereignty from the very beginning of his administration; and of not being a true Protestant. The last charge, which is the most curious, was supported by assertions that most of William's friends were sympathetic to papists, and most of his army commanders and personal servants actually practising Catholics. He permitted Mass to be sung daily in his army, he had formed a scandalous league with the House of Austria, he was going to marry a popish wife both of whose parents were known Catholics.[6] Rothe, like everyone else in Europe, was convinced that William would marry Mary of York. In 1676 he finally pushed his attack too far. The government had already made it a capital crime to assert that the Prince was conspiring for sovereign power. Rothe repeated all his old charges and brought out some new ones. He accused the Prince of using various means to take Amsterdam by force. The troops of Groningen had been deliberately exposed to excessive danger. The Prince had kept up a secret correspondence for years with the Jesuits, Rome, and the Stuarts. He had ordered the shipment of provisions and food to the French in the spring of 1672 when war was obviously at hand. His entire administration was described as a tyranny.[7]

No one wanted Rothe's death, since he was obviously demented. As early as September 1675 Fagel authorized Sir William Temple to negotiate with the Hartlib family. If Rothe were declared insane his wife could retain his property. At the time, the family would not agree to Temple's proposals. Two years later, however, Rothe was declared incompetent at their own request and remained under lock and key until 1691.[8] By the time of his apprehension Rothe had done his work. His pamphlets had a large share in the growing unpopularity of the Prince. William's envious and spiteful cousin Sophia had noted how popular he had been in 1674. The Dutch, she said, kiss the ground on which he walks and the horse he rides; he has more power than ever Prince of Orange had, and withal it has cost him very little effort. By the autumn of the next year all this had changed. Sophia was happy to report that the people were murmuring furiously against him. They knew that William was the chief obstacle to a peace and that his army officers were saying openly that the war could continue for another thirty years before the Dutch peasant was as poor as the German. Poor Sophia! William's unpopularity was a serious matter, but it did not do him as much harm as she wished. In 1677 she had to admit: 'Quant au Prince d'Orange il est de ces gens heureux, dont tout le monde parle mal et qui sont haïs et qui ne laissent pas de faire tout qu'ils veulent, et sont plus heureux que ceux qu'on aplaudit.'[9]

The Prince's obstinacy hurt him in other ways. We have seen that his income for 1673, apart from any salary payments, was over fl.2,000,000. This was much higher than usual. The next year, however, his accounts began to reflect William's personal share in the costs of the war. Many of his estates were in the hands of the enemy or in the path of the armies. In 1674 his landed income was down to fl.289,000, in 1675 it fell to fl.245,000, and for the rest of the war it did not again reach fl.300,000. This was perhaps one-third of what could be expected in peacetime. When the Prince remarked that his losses from the war were greater than those of any other person in the Republic, he had forgotten the special presents he received in 1674 and 1675. In terms of his rent rolls, however, he was quite right. The account for 1677, for example, lists one hundred and two separate potential sources of revenue. Seventy-eight of them produced nothing whatever.[10] The death of his grandmother in 1675 brought the Prince some relief, in that he was no longer obliged to pay her dowry of fl.39,000 a year. Amalia, however, died heavily in debt. Even though the States General gave her estate fl.500,000 in lieu of the pension she had never received, the Prince had to contribute a further fl.100,000 out of his pocket to pay the rest of her debts. Amalia had made a splendid impression with her 1818 ounces of solid gold plate and her magnificent jewels, including a great necklace of thirty-seven matched pearls each of which weighed seven-and-a-quarter carats. The impression was false. She left her grandson a final burden rather than the 'great addition of fortune' which Sir William Temple anticipated.[11] It is a remarkable tribute to the Prince's financial talent that he managed to live within his income during the war and to use all his special receipts for paying off debt. Such a course of conduct displeased some observers. In 1676 Charles Davenant, who was to be a determined opponent of William III a generation later, was disgusted by the simplicity of the prince's court. 'We were presented to the Prince of Orange January the 5th; the Court was that night pretty great, the Prince and our two Ambassadors were some time privately together. I admired to see with what little splendour the Prince lives and indeed at the meanness of great men's equipage there; why should any with such jealousy preserve, and such eagerness thirst after power, which affords them neither pomp nor pleasure?'[12]

If the continuation of the war cost the Prince his popularity and between two-thirds and three-fourths of his income, that was not all. His military reputation suffered considerably from the misconduct of his allies. At the end of the campaign of 1674 the Count of Monterey lost the governorship of the Spanish Netherlands, probably to the delight of the Prince although he wrote a formal request to Madrid asking that Monterey be permitted to remain at Brussels.[13] It would have been better had he stayed. His replacement, the Duke of Villa Hermosa, was a soldier and found it very humiliating to be placed under the Prince's command. William insisted, on the basis of past experience, that there must be a single commander in the Netherlands. Since the imperial forces were inferior to the Dutch and since the Spanish had 'no' army there, the generalissimo could only be the Prince of Orange. There were Spanish forces but they were all needed to garrison the towns. When the Spanish and Dutch spoke of there being no Spanish army, they meant that there was no field army. William's insistence on having the supreme command, though it was perfectly reasonable on military grounds, caused a great deal of resentment. Villa Hermosa himself took it pretty well. After one complaint when the issue was first raised, he accepted his subordination to the Prince and did not make any trouble about it for a year. There were even complaints from Madrid that Villa Hermosa was being too complacent in his difficult position. The man who was most annoyed about the question of the command was Don Manuel de Lira, the Spanish envoy at The Hague. De Lira argued with William to the point of making himself almost *persona non grata*. By May 1675 they were hardly on speaking terms and de Lira asked to be recalled. He was not, and for the rest of the war his dispatches were filled with personal abuse.[14] Villa Hermosa did not quite play the part he had set for himself. In the spring of 1675 he was promising to sacrifice his life in the service of his master and of the allies even if he had to fight as a common soldier with a pike. Unfortunately his patience finally snapped, and in the winter of 1676–77 he gave expression to his woes in writing to Vienna. This led to a further estrangement between the allies which became serious during the 1677 campaign.

The remaining campaigns of the war in the Spanish Netherlands are not of outstanding interest. They were holding operations, in which the Dutch did their best to keep French gains to a minimum. These gains were inevitable for the simple reason that the French had a large and continuing superiority in men, artillery, and supplies. Although the Dutch paid heavy subsidies to their allies they were unable to get any help in return. Denmark, the Dukes of Brunswick, and the Elector of Brandenburg were fascinated by the possibility of evicting the Swedes from the soil of Germany. Each of them was determined to obtain as large a share of the Swedish possessions as possible. Thus they had two good reasons for keeping their troops to themselves: they must beat the Swedes and also prevent each other from gaining too much of the spoils. The Austrians were primarily concerned with the war on the Rhine. The Low Countries meant as little to Vienna as Hungary did to The Hague. Even the Spanish seemed to care little for the defence of the Netherlands. Their war effort, such as it was, was limited to the campaigns in Sicily and the Pyrenees. If the Netherlands were to be saved the Dutch would have to do it almost alone.

It was a hopeless task. We may think of the Spanish Netherlands as a spider web whose centre was Brussels. The spider, William III, could not enter the field until May because he did not have enough money to prepare magazines. Often the French had eaten away what they wanted for the year, before the Prince appeared. With their superior organization they were able to begin fighting by the middle of February or early March. If they had not finished their campaign for the year by the time the Dutch were ready to enter the field, it did not matter. They could continue their gains by attacking, or threatening to attack, two portions of the web at once. Since there was only one spider, successful defence was impossible. In 1675 the French concentrated on the eastern side of the web, taking Dinant, Huy, and Limburg. For the remainder of the war they operated chiefly on the western side. In 1676 they took Condé, Bouchain, Aire, and Linck. The next year it was the turn of Valenciennes, Cambrai, St Omer, and St Ghislain. In the spring of 1678 the French took Ghent and Ypres, which so terrified the Dutch that they were forced to make a separate peace. Ghent, north-west of Brussels, not only threatened all that was left of the web but the territories of the Republic as well.

It is not particularly meaningful to say that William III was a poor or an unlucky general. He rarely had a chance because he never after 1674 had an equality of forces or a unified command. In theory the Spanish were supposed to obey him. In practice they resented the fact that he was generalissimo, and they were beginning to suspect that his interests differed from their own. Of course they did. The Dutch would have preferred to have a Spanish Netherlands with the borders of 1659, large enough to be capable of self-defence. If they could not get that, and it was clearly unattainable, they wanted a barrier strong enough to prevent a repetition of 1672. For the purposes of a barrier, some of the Spanish holdings were more important than others. Franche-Comté, for example, was worthless. Even in the Netherlands there were areas of only secondary value. The Spanish felt that the Dutch were not interested in the preservation of Hainault, Artois, Cambrai or the Duchy of Luxembourg. For the barrier only the four provinces of Brabant, Flanders, Spanish Gelderland and Limburg were essential, together with Mons, Maastricht, and the city of Luxembourg.[15] If the Spanish were suspicious of the aims of the Dutch government, they were also uncertain of the Prince of Orange. As it happened, the Prince had very large estates in Franche-Comté as well as in the Duchy of Luxembourg. If he had greater concern for his personal welfare than for the security of the Republic, he would have tried to keep these two provinces at the expense of the barrier. The Spanish were too stupid to see this. Instead, they suspected him either of using his military authority to take certain towns in Flanders for himself, or else of listening to the offers, made by the French, of Maastricht and the Duchy of Limburg. They did their best, therefore, to prevent the Prince from enjoying his theoretical position of generalissimo. In the campaign of 1676 they tried to persuade the Dutch to give the Duke of Villa Hermosa enough men so that he could have a field army of his own, and in this they were successful. In 1677 they went further and attempted to prevent William from taking the field. At the same time the Spanish stirred up opposition to the Prince inside the Republic.[16] William, neglected by some of his allies and betrayed by the Spanish, was in an impossible position. He is not to be criticized for failing to save all of the Netherlands; it is, rather, surprising that he managed to save anything. Of his loyalty to his allies it is unnecessary to speak. He had built the alliance, and without his continued support it would have collapsed long before 1678.

Although the general military picture was continuously gloomy from the end of 1674 onward, there were enjoyable parts of any campaign. Often the Prince went hunting. It was his custom to lodge in houses, unless the harbingers had picked such filthy ones that he was forced to use his tent. Frequently William stayed in convents, which were clean and large enough to hold his suite. The nuns, of course, would have fled long before to Brussels or some other safe place. At other times, headquarters were in private houses. William III was particularly interested in fountains, and a house with a fountain in its courtyard was always noted in his secretary's diary. Whenever possible the Prince tried to pass by Enghien, where he could visit the magnificent gardens of the Duke of Arschot. The house was in the middle of a pond which opened on to a handsome *étoile*, each of whose alleys was lined by a different kind of tree. The upkeep of these gardens alone was supposed to cost between six and seven thousand livres a year. At considerable personal inconvenience, the Prince never stayed at the house itself, presumably to protect the gardens from any damage by his men. Wherever he went he was interested in pictures and marbles for Soestdijk, which was being rebuilt and furnished at this time. Most of the Prince's purchases were made at Antwerp, but he also bought wherever he could.[17]

His chief delight, however, was in fighting. As Temple wrote of him, 'He is pleased with the life he has led this Summer, and loves the trade, and thinks himself better in health and humour, the less he is at rest: ...'[18] William's profession was arms. He made himself into an effective diplomat and a moderately good politician; but these were not his callings. Both the Prince and his closest friends were professional soldiers. William III had many of the virtues and many of the defects of a military man. He was straightforward, direct, and honourable, and he expected these qualities in others. As a result he found it extremely difficult to do business with civilian diplomats who tried to satisfy him with what he called whipped cream. When Sir Joseph Williamson tried to use some of this whipped cream, the Prince simply lost his temper: 'Why such dealing with so plain a man as he was?' Temple wrote that William 'has a way of falling downright into the bottom of a business, and is to be dealt with no other way that ever I could find; ...'[19] Purveyors of whipped cream found themselves treated with contempt and, naturally, became hostile to the Prince. Simple direct men found it easier to become his friends. Although the Prince was in many superficial ways a complex personality, he was basically a Christian soldier and basically a simple man.

The fighting that William of Orange enjoyed most was a field action, an open battle. Sieges depended for their success on many complicated factors which he could not control. They required a heavy superiority in numbers, which he rarely had, together with a patience and command of technical skills which he was slow to achieve. Gradually he learned patience. But he was always to depend on his engineers for the mathematical aspects of a siege – where to place guns and mines, how much firepower was needed to breach a wall, and so on – and in this war his engineers were remarkably bad. It was not until much later that he was able to find in Coehoorn an engineer who was a match for Vauban. Coehoorn fought in the war of 1672, but in a subordinate capacity where he was unable to be of much use. Critics of William III have over-emphasized his lack of formal training.[20] It is of course true that the Prince was largely self-taught. He soon acquired, however, a great fund of experience and used it to correct many of his early errors. What the Prince's military critics choose to forget is the fact that he had to fight so often with inferior forces, and with allies whose cooperation could not be assumed. Where he had equal or superior numbers and artillery he won, no matter how defective his education might be. And it is fitting that his last great victory was to be the capture of one of Vauban's 'impregnable' fortresses. The self-taught man does not always have a bad teacher.

Although the 1675 campaign in the Netherlands was almost completely without incident – William took Binch but decided not to keep it – that of the following year was more eventful. The Prince had made great efforts to prepare magazines, so that he could take the field as early as the French. In this he was hindered by the refusal of the smaller provinces to pay their taxes. Even so, the allied forces were ready to fight much earlier than in previous years. Or, to be precise, the Dutch were. Of 25,000 men promised by the Spanish, only 5,000 horse appeared. The German contingents could not be expected to arrive before midsummer. When the Prince reached the army on 8 April he was a fortnight ahead of Louis XIV. But if the Prince was ahead of the King, the French army was ahead of the Prince, and in over-whelming strength. On 17 April it besieged the town of Condé. Four days later, when the King arrived, the trenches were opened. The rest of the siege took five days. From Condé the French proceeded to Bouchain. One army, under the Duc d'Orléans, attacked the town, while another under Louis XIV protected the besiegers from any relieving force. Despite his inferiority in numbers, William decided to try to break up the siege. On the morning of 10 May his army met that of the King at Valenciennes. Would there be a battle? Each side expected the other to attack. For ten days the two forces faced each other. 'It is the prettiest sight in the world', William wrote to the Grand Pensionary, 'to see two such mighty armies so close to each other.'[21] Although the French were considerably stronger than the Dutch, each side considered the other too well posted for an attack to be profitable. Besides, anything might happen in a battle; and the King's reputation would be hopelessly compromised if he were to lose. The reluctance of Louis XIV to risk his reputation shows how far he was from being a real soldier. He might play at being one as much as he liked. At Valenciennes, however, his bluff was called. He never forgot it, and never forgave Louvois for exposing him to such a public humiliation. On the 20th the French retired on Bouchain, which had fallen a week earlier to Monsieur.

Meanwhile the eastern borders of the Republic had been bothered by enemy raiding parties. The raiders demanded contributions, threatening to burn villages and towns that refused payment. The only effective way to stop the raids was to take Maastricht, the French base of operations. It would be a very dangerous operation. The enemy's superiority in the Netherlands was such that it would be possible for him to relieve the siege. And while the capture of Maastricht would be a boon to the Prince's reputation, failure would involve a serious blow to his authority. As late as the middle of June, William considered the siege an impossibility. He soon changed his mind, probably for political rather than military reasons. French raiding parties could not be permitted on the soil of the Republic. The preparations for the siege went on quickly, and the Prince arrived before Maastricht as the sun set on 7 July. From the beginning, everything went wrong. It had been a very hot dry summer. The heavy guns, too large to be transported by land, were held up because the water-level in the Maas was too low to support the vessels which carried them. The Prince's engineer, Yvoy, demonstrated an ignorance of mathematics which would have shamed a schoolboy and was soon disabled by illness and wounds. There were simply not enough men to carry on the siege. Maastricht lay as now on the west bank of the river and was connected by bridges with the fortified suburb of Wijk on the east. The walls were so long that, as the Prince admitted, it would have been possible for 2,000 cavaliers to ride into the city between the Dutch posts. He had expected assistance from the forces of Brandenburg, Celle, Münster, whose Bishop had turned his coat, and Osnabrück. Of them all, only a contingent of Osnabrückers appeared, led by their Prince-Bishop.[22] Ernst August was enthusiastic for the cause. His men, however, were in poor condition; and the absence of the other forces was a serious blow.[23]

'I do what I can, but I am very badly assisted, and Ivoy's illness is a serious inconvenience.'[24] Maastricht was much stronger than when it had been taken by the French three years before. They had strengthened the walls and added seven detached bastions so as to make it a great fortress. The engineers recommended attacking one of these bastions, the 'Dauphin', in broad daylight. On 30 July a gallant group of English soldiers managed to lodge themselves in the Dauphin. When they were not reinforced they became discouraged and were soon driven out again. The Prince then resorted to sapping, but his engineers were no match for those of the enemy, who frustrated the sappers with counter-mines. Finally, the Dauphin was retaken on 4 August and it became possible to attack the main walls of the city. A general storm could not be attempted, because the Prince had so few men at his disposal. But on the night of 11 August the Dutch managed to occupy a corner of the counterscarp and to dig themselves in. For the next fortnight the attack continued, but no further progress was made. The casualties were extremely heavy, not only from enemy action but also from an epidemic of dysentery which caused many deaths. Meanwhile the French army in the southern Netherlands, which had been placed under the command of Schomberg when the King left the field, had captured Aire and the small fort of Linck. It was now decided that Schomberg should relieve Maastricht. Waldeck and Villa Hermosa, with their men, managed to reach William's army on 26 August. The French were expected the next day. The allied generals held a council of war and decided, prudently, to raise the siege. But to William's intense disgust, they also refused to fight Schomberg in the field. On the 27th the siege was abandoned in confusion. The boats carrying away the guns and the wounded were attacked by French dragoons. Luckily the wounded escaped, but a few of the more heavily laden gun-boats went aground and were captured.

The Prince was so angry at the disgraceful failure of the siege that for over a week he did not trust himself to write a letter to Fagel about it. He had attacked Waldeck personally for refusing to fight the French. Relations between the two commanders had been strained all the summer. But to judge from the surviving correspondence the Prince must have lost his temper completely at the Council of War and treated his Field-marshal as he sometimes treated his servants.[25] Even a month later William was petulant enough to complain because a salvo had been fired to celebrate the imperial capture of Philippsburg.[26] He had, indeed, suffered a major defeat and the imperialist victory rubbed salt in his wounds. For the first time the Prince's military record was laughed to scorn. His political position was so much weaker after Maastricht that there was now a chance of his losing control at home. Even Fagel was convinced that the war could not be carried on. Fagel was not abandoning the Prince; but he knew that the republicans had gained so much strength that they might both be beaten if they proved too obstinate.

Very little progress had been made towards peace in the winter of 1675–76, partly because the French refused to recognize the Duke of Lorraine. They would call him 'our dear cousin Prince Charles of Lorraine', and no more. By the time they consented to use the styles of 'duke' and 'brother', the fighting had resumed.[27] The disgrace of Maastricht and the severe shortage of money made the Dutch more eager for peace by the summer. They obliged their allies to send plenipotentiaries to the congress at Nijmegen by threatening to begin negotiating on 1 November whether the allies were there or not. At the same time, even the Prince of Orange now took a slightly more realistic view of the general position. He had been reluctant for several reasons to marry Princess Mary before the end of the war. The marriage would weaken his position inside the Republic and his relations with the allies. Because the Princess was so close to the throne of England he would be suspected of having adopted Stuart ideas of foreign policy and Stuart maxims of government. The marriage would also weaken the Prince's position in English politics. Partly as a result of the intrigues of du Moulin and his friends, William held a strong position with the English opposition. The Court was now desperately unpopular. On Good Friday 1676 its position became still weaker. Until then the Duke of York, though well known to be a Catholic, had at least attended Anglican services. Now he refused to continue the pretence. The King was worried about the consequences of this step for the whole Royal Family. Charles believed that if he died his brother would not be in England a week afterwards.[28] By marrying Mary, therefore, William III would be lending his uncles his popularity. He would incur the suspicion of the English parliamentary leaders, of the Dutch republicans, and of the Spanish. It would be a great concession. But in April 1676 he made it, in the hope of drawing the English into the alliance.

At the time the French were able to secure the rejection of the marriage proposal. James, whose divorce from reality was almost complete, still had hopes of placing his daughter on the road to the throne of France. He was also persuaded to be frightened of his nephew. Courtin, the French ambassador at the English court, was instructed to point out that William might well exclude James from the succession after the marriage.[29] Thus the French were able to gain some time. But William's more realistic attitude towards the Stuarts would bear fruit later. The Prince was also approximating to a more accurate appraisal of the possible terms of a general peace. He had abandoned the idea of achieving the frontiers of 1659. The best that could be hoped for now would be, in general, the terms of the Treaty of Aix-la-Chapelle of 1668. If the French wanted Aire and St Omer in addition to what they had gained in 1668, they could exchange them for Ath and Charleroi. Even Franche-Comté might be ceded to the French for a suitable equivalent.[30] On the possibility of a separate peace, the Prince remained firm: '. . . let the Pensioner or any one else tell me (Temple) what they pleased, they should never do it while he was alive, and he would say one thing further to me, which was that he had it in his power to hinder it, That if he died he knew very well it would be made the next day, but he did not concern himself how the world was like to go after he was gone himself. . . .' Actually these words were stronger than William's real feelings. He was so angry at the conduct of the allies that he was now willing to consider a separate peace, but only if his honour were secured. The French were offering him Maastricht and the Duchy of Limburg, as so often before, in return for a separate peace. During January 1677 William was ready to accept them. They would amount to payment of the ancient Spanish debt. In addition, they would provide him with the title of Duke; but his Duchy of Limburg would be outside the Republic and thus would not cause jealousy to any reasonable person. Limburg and Maastricht, furthermore, would be a barrier against the French, because they controlled the whole course of the Maas. Even so, the Prince demanded that the French offer fair terms to the Spanish and to the German allies. Only when these terms had been rejected would he feel free to undertake a separate peace. For the Spanish, he proposed the exchange of Aire, St Omer, and perhaps Cambrai in return for Charleroi, Ath, Oudenarde, Bouchain, and Condé. Similarly, he proposed that the French should offer to return Franche-Comté in exchange for what the Swedes had lost in Germany. He was sure that the allies would turn down these offers. Once they had, William could make a separate peace with a clear conscience.[31]

D'Estrades thought that the Prince was sincere in these negotiations. It may be doubted whether the French government would have staked Franche-Comté on their estimate of William's sincerity. They never had to take the risk. At the end of January 1677 the Prince went to Dieren and nearly entered into direct conversation with d'Estrades. For a fortnight d'Estrades thought that a meeting would take place to discuss his counter-proposals. William, however, rejected them and returned to The Hague without seeing the Maréchal. It was Pesters who carried the message. While he had been trying to use d'Estrades, the Prince had simultaneously been attempting to make a peace by means of the English. It disappointed him to find that the terms proposed by the English were at least as hard as those which he could obtain directly from the French.[32] Luckily, the Spanish chose this moment to pay some of their debt to the allies. This made it possible for the war to go on for another year, particularly because the Dutch were no longer burdened with subsidies. They refused to pay subsidies to any of their allies except Münster beyond those voted in 1676. With their war expenses reduced by perhaps a third, the Republic would be patient a little longer.

Chapter 12

THE WAR IS LOST

WILLIAM III entered on the campaign of 1677 with few illusions. Temple reported that the Prince 'expected a very ill beginning of the campaign and to make an ill figure in it himself, at least till the Germans took the field, but he was in it and must go through with it, and the best was that few campaigns end as they begin.'[1] Holland was the single province in the Union which was paying its taxes. Indeed, Holland paid more than its quota. But the others did little or nothing. In Zeeland the religious struggle between Voetians and Cocceians was at its height. William supported the orthodox Voetians against their rivals and was eventually successful in establishing their authority as well as his own. The problem in Groningen was more difficult. The rural areas of the province were furious at the men of Groningen town for keeping one of the country leaders in prison for five years on a charge of collaborating with the enemy in 1672. The Prince visited the province in the hope of securing peace, but the matter was not finally settled until the following year. His cousin Henry Casimir took the side of urban Groningen in the squabble. Even worse, he refused to permit the regiments of his provinces of Groningen and Friesland to obey the marching orders of their Captain-General. All these domestic disorders, serious in themselves, made it impossible to set up Dutch magazines in the Spanish Netherlands. The Spanish could do nothing, and the other allies were far more interested in the Swedish and German campaigns than in the defence of Flanders. The French would find little opposition in that quarter.

The campaign opened with the disgraceful loss of Valenciennes, which was taken by storm on 17 March. Flushed with their easy success, which had not been expected, the French then decided to undertake two major sieges at once. Louis XIV with one army sat down before Cambrai while his brother was placed in command of the operations against St Omer. The Dutch army had not yet assembled. William reached Breda on 20 March and had to spend almost a fortnight playing tennis and boar-hunting while waiting for his men to reach the rendezvous. It was not until 3 April that he had enough men to be able to set off in the direction of St Omer. The roads were in terrible condition at that time of year. Moving the guns was very difficult, and the men suffered greatly on their march. By the 10th the army had advanced beyond Ypres to the neighbourhood of Mont Cassel, a short distance from St Omer. The Dutch force numbered some 30,000 men, the total French force some 63,000. The larger portion of these, however, were with the King. His brother's army was reported to be quite small, although it would be easy to send reinforcements from the main army before Cambrai.

When he reached Mont Cassel William found the ground before him flat and low-lying, cut up by hedgerows and a stream called the Peene. Here and there small hills rose above the plain, on many of which were placed wind-mills. The Prince ordered bridges to be placed across the Peene and, having dined in the open field, made his dispositions for the next day with his generals.

Early on the morning of Sunday 11th April the Dutch crossed the Peene on their bridges and put themselves in battle order in full view of the enemy. The Prince commanded the centre, the Count van Hornes the right wing, and the Count van Nassau-Saarbrück the left. In the French army, called out from its trenches before St Omer, the Duc d'Orléans was theoretically in charge of the centre. He had, however, a good deal of expert assistance. The French King, if he was not a professional soldier, did at least possess a considerable measure of courage and a great fund of experience. His brother lacked both qualities. When the possibility of a Dutch attempt to relieve the siege of St Omer had first arisen, Monsieur's first idea had been to withdraw without a fight. Louis XIV had heartened the coward with cheerful words and heavy reinforcements. The last of these, nine battalions according to one account and 14,000 men according to another, had reached the Duke's camp on the night of the 10th. Thus the French had a considerable superiority in numbers and they were ably led. The left wing was under the command of Luxembourg and the right led by the Maréchal d'Humières.

After crossing the Peene, William III discovered to his chagrin that there was a second small stream still lying between him and the enemy. There was no time in which to bring up another set of bridges, and the presence of the unreported stream might make a retreat dangerous. On this occasion the Dutch scouting had obviously not been thorough enough. Another embarrassment came when the Prince and Waldeck viewed the enemy and guessed the size of the reinforcement of the previous night. This reinforcement was what might make a retreat necessary at the end of the day. Even so, the Prince of Orange does not appear to have made full use of the resources available to him. The Count van Nassau-Saarbrück with eight or ten cavalry regiments remained behind the Peene and, according to Huygens, did no more than view the battle.[2] Had he spent less time providing drinks and food for Huygens and more in fighting, the outcome of the battle might have been different. But William never sent him orders, and the cavalry regiments stayed aloof from the battle. They were to be sorely missed.

The combat began with an attack by Luxembourg on a cloister in front of the Dutch right wing. The Dutch occupied the buildings and defended them bravely for some time. After having repulsed the attack, the Dutch burned the cloister and then withdrew to their lines. There followed a lull for perhaps an hour and the battle seemed to be over. Then the enemy under Humières attacked the Dutch left wing and, after meeting with some resistance, pushed them back from hedge to hedge. Two regiments, those of Walenburg and La Verne, broke shamefully. They fled in such haste that they disordered three other regiments sent to their aid. With the left wing of his army driven in, William was forced to abandon his fight in the centre, which had gone well. He withdrew in good order and reached the town of Poperinghen about ten o'clock that evening, having abandoned all his baggage and artillery. The French, who could have followed up their victory, spent themselves in plundering the baggage and so failed to take advantage of their great opportunity. Their conduct had of course secured them Cambrai and St Omer, which soon fell. They did not grasp the larger prize, the complete destruction of the Dutch army, when it lay in their hands.[3]

After the defeat of Mont Cassel the Prince re-established discipline and order among the troops and replaced the equipment which had been lost. Nine men, chosen by lot, were hanged in expiation of the cowardice of Walenburg's regiment. The remainder were then ceremonially rehabilitated by having their standards waved over their heads. Since the enemy had such an enormous preponderance in numbers, little more could be done in the field. All eyes turned towards England, the only possible source of new strength which might redress the balance of forces. Parliament, which was now sitting, showed itself eager to enter the war on the allied side. Spanish agents in London did their best to encourage this attitude. They went too far. In trying to repeat their success of 1673, when they had forced Charles II to withdraw from the French alliance by threatening him with war, they failed completely. The King need no longer fear anything the feeble Spanish might do. Nor was he willing to be bullied by a combination of Spanish and parliamentary pressure. William of Orange disapproved of the Spanish tactics, which could only irritate his uncles and ruin his own plans for obtaining English assistance. In May he went to The Hague for a week of consultations with Fagel, and shortly afterwards his confidant, Willem Bentinck, was dispatched to London to interview the King and the Duke of York.

The timing of Bentinck's visit was fortunate. The chief minister, Danby, was at the height of success. In foreign affairs, about which he knew very little, Danby took the advice of William's great friend Sir William Temple.

Thus the Lord Treasurer would have liked to establish an anti-French policy, and for the moment he was so strong that he might be able to overcome the prejudices of his master. It was also fortunate that Bentinck arrived after the King, in his irritation, had prorogued Parliament. There could be no question this time as to the Prince's innocence in the game of parliamentary intrigue. The Spanish were guilty, and perhaps also the Dutch ambassador van Beuninghen; but the latter was thought to represent the city of Amsterdam rather than the Prince. A third factor in Bentinck's success was his curious step in addressing himself to the Duke of York before he went to the King. This was of course flattering to James, but it would have been an impertinence to Charles II in the ordinary course of events. Bentinck's instructions were largely taken up with general matters, attempts to get decent peace terms or even to lure England into the war on the side of the allies.[4] With these matters James had no particular connection. The ninth article of the instructions, however, concerned the Duke more than the King. 'Son Altesse suplie tres humblement Sa Majeste de lui permettre qu'aprez la campagne, soit paix ou guerre, Son Altesse puisse faire un petit tour en Angleterre.'[5] William III could have only one reason for a visit to England: marriage with Princess Mary. For this very reason, his request for an invitation had been turned down in the previous year, on the ground that it would not be suitable for a marriage to take place before the end of the war.

Bentinck's tact brought success. He returned with the news that the Prince would be welcome in the autumn, *soit paix ou guerre*, provided that he came at a time when Parliament was not in session. The gossips at Dutch army headquarters, guessing the real meaning of the invitation, began to discuss the charms of the Princess of Orange to be.[6] Nothing could be made public, for fear of opposition by Amsterdam and the Spanish no less than by the French. Even so, the Prince could not keep his mind entirely averted from the coming change in his life. While Bentinck was in London he scoured the art markets of Antwerp and Brussels, seeking some new ornaments for his palaces. William went to visit the ancient Jordaens, who had decorated the Huis ten Bosch thirty years before. The interview was unsatisfactory. The painter was now senile and confined to a chair, while the works remaining in his studio were of low quality. The Prince had better luck elsewhere and bought works by Rubens and Breughel, though he rejected some poor marbles and a set of very suspicious tapestries that were supposed to have been woven from Raphael cartoons. If the marriage should take place, the Princess would not be able to complain about the quality of her surroundings.

These new paintings were almost the only pleasant aspect of the approaching marriage. Although Mary was supposed to be a striking beauty, the Prince could not know whether her character would match her face and figure. Financially the match would be disastrous. His mother, the Princess Royal, had brought only £40,000. In social terms things would be even worse. In William's eyes Mary was the next thing to a housemaid, since her mother had been not only a commoner but one of the Princess Royal's servants. There would be something gained in keeping Mary from any other match, either with the Dauphin or the King of Sweden. The two strongest claims to the English succession would be consolidated. This was of course important, but there was a large element of risk in banking on the future. The Duchess of York was now pregnant. If she did not produce a son this time she might do so later; and there was always the possibility that Charles II might live to remarry. In 1677, therefore, the prospect of the English succession was remote. The only immediate advantage that the Prince could hope to gain from his marriage would be a share in the control of English foreign policy. For this, and he could not hope to gain more than a share in its control, he would have to abandon his position with the English opposition. Amsterdam and the French could be counted on as enemies of the match, and their influence at The Hague was becoming ominously strong. Even more irritating was the conduct of the Spanish, for whom William had worked so hard. At a time when they should have realized that he was their only friend in Europe, they were doing everything they could to compromise his position.

The worst example of Spanish misconduct took place in July and August. After the capture of Valenciennes, Cambrai and St Omer the French King had left Flanders and a portion of his soldiers were sent off to other theatres of war. During the summer the German contingents of the allied forces gradually made their appearance, and the balance of military strength in the Low Countries was thus substantially redressed. Louvignies, commander of the Spanish cavalry, went so far as to argue that the allies had an actual preponderance in the area. He proposed the siege of some important place, favouring the selection of Charleroi.[7] The Prince of Orange could not refuse to act, though he preferred a combat to a siege. Although he was in unusually poor health this year, he could not remain idle for the remainder of the campaign. His enemies were posting rewards for information about the whereabouts of the Dutch army and its leader. William would have to fight, or the politicians would make peace behind his back. He consented to a sham siege of Charleroi in the hope that this would force Luxembourg to leave his positions near Ath and come out to do battle. If Luxembourg refused to fight, the siege of Charleroi could then be undertaken in earnest.[8]

The Prince, accompanied by the Duke of Villa Hermosa and the Bishop of Osnabrück, appeared before the town on 5 August with a substantial army. Imperial forces under the Duke of Lorraine were at Mouzon, not far away, and might reasonably be counted on in case of need. Although Charleroi was invested, the trenches were never to be opened. William hoped that his manoeuvre would lead to a field action. If so, work on the trenches would be superfluous. Secondly, a real siege would require a vast quantity of *matériel* which was being sent down from Brussels in two great convoys. The first of these arrived on the 7th, but it contained only a portion of the needed artillery. Meanwhile Luxembourg had done just what was expected of him, leading his army eastward from Ath in order to break up the siege. His forces, despite the optimistic estimates of Louvignies, were substantially stronger than those of the allies. By the 11th he had reached Gerpinnes, thus placing himself between the allied army and possible assistance from Namur, while also threatening their lines of communication with Brussels. The siege could not proceed until the French field army had been dislodged. On the 11th itself William would have been happy to attack Luxembourg. Once the French had settled in at Gerpinnes the opportunity was lost, and the whole situation became much less favourable. The enemy positions at Gerpinnes were so strong that an attack would have been the height of folly. Every single Dutch general officer, the field deputies, and several colonels whose opinions had also been asked advised the Prince against a battle.[9] The Spanish and Germans were unable to offer any hope of victory. They felt that a battle, even a battle certain to end in failure, was essential for political reasons. For himself, William agreed with them. He could not, however, override the unanimous opinion of his own officers when the allied generals – except the Prince de Vaudemont – admitted that there was no way in which to get at the enemy. Luxembourg's positions were simply too good, and while he remained at Gerpinnes the second convoy could not reach the Prince. On the 14th, therefore, William broke up the siege and retired without opposition from the French to Sombref. Luxembourg had to invent very curious excuses for his second failure of the year to pursue William on his retreat. Condé had not acted with such timidity at Seneffe.[10]

The Spanish generals sorely regretted their failure to secure a glorious defeat. That the defeat would probably have been catastrophic meant nothing to them. The strain of a long defensive war in which they were being crushed by the sheer weight of the French military machine had broken their nerves. If they must lose the Spanish Netherlands why not do so in a blaze of glory? A great power in decay is often highly irresponsible. It is apparently more common for a people whose day has passed to be 'trigger-happy' than for a nation whose day has just begun. Thus the Spanish had already been threatening England with war if she did not join the alliance. Now they began to attack William III personally. There had already been some of this, particularly at The Hague. Now, for the first time, the Prince was accused to his face of disloyalty to the confederacy. Since many English nobles had been visiting the camp, among them Lord Ossory who had been present during one of the councils of war, the Spanish charged that the Prince had refused to fight on the orders of the King of England. The Prince took the charge seriously. He wrote a circumstantial account of the events before Charleroi to Fagel on 29 August, emphasizing the strength of Luxembourg's positions at Gerpinnes and denying that Ossory had ever spoken to him on the subject.[11]

William was literally correct. Ossory had not given any direct warning against doing battle. He had made it indirectly through Alexander Colyear, a Scot who was the Prince's Adjutant General.[12] On the whole it is likely that the Prince was being substantially as well as literally truthful. Although Ossory gave his warning, and to this extent William lied, there is nothing to show that the warning was what held him back from fighting. The unanimous opposition of his Dutch subordinates was the decisive thing. The Prince was not the man to be influenced by an English courtier, even one of whom he was unusually fond. He himself had wanted to fight. But now and later William III was to show that he felt himself to be bound by a majority decision. This was one reason why he disliked seeing his advisers in groups, where they might vote him down. He much preferred to talk with one man at a time, where there could be no question of putting things to a vote.[13] In any case William was furious at the imputation that his military decisions were being made for him by a foreign power. Since his earliest youth he had had to defend himself from charges of being a pawn in the hands of the Stuarts. The charges were without foundation, but they were most difficult to disprove.

The remainder of the campaign was without interest. The Prince took Binch once again, but plans for the capture of Dinant never matured. Although the war against Sweden was going brilliantly, victories in the Baltic could not be placed in the scale against losses in Flanders. The French had won so much this year that further defence of the Netherlands was almost impossible. One more campaign might see the end of the Spanish presence in northern Europe, and the next a war on Dutch soil. Thus it was with relief that William welcomed Laurence Hyde to his headquarters on 17 September, since he brought with him the official invitation to England. This had been promised, of course, in June. But Danby's very victory on this issue had increased the French leanings of the King. Like every member of his family, Charles was terrified of becoming dependent on a single favourite or even of being thought to be dependent. By the late spring of 1677 Danby's position seemed to be so strong as to threaten the independence of the monarchy, and

Charles reacted by calling Buckingham back into favour. The court had then become so much less friendly to the Dutch and so hostile to the Spanish that there was real doubt as to whether William's invitation would be repeated. When it was, he left the army and proceeded to The Hague.

The Prince knew that his marriage would be unpopular at first. Therefore he kept his plans a complete secret, apparently even from the Grand Pensioner. All William asked from the States General was permission to visit England for three weeks of diplomatic negotiations. When this was granted the Prince left The Hague with a large suite on 17 October. He was careful not to take the family jewels with him, which would have given the whole game away. In the event, the jewels came a day too late for the wedding. With all these precautions William was unable to keep his plans entirely secret. The Amsterdam bourse might know nothing for certain, but it was not hard to guess the truth. The market fell heavily during the Prince's trip.[14]

On his arrival William went to Newmarket to join the court. He took immense pains to flatter James, attending the Duke's *coucher* with regularity and sometimes his *levée* as well. At first there were difficulties. The English wished to speak first of peace terms, the Prince of his marriage. He could hope to make the English more sympathetic to the allied cause after the marriage than before, and by doing so he would also escape the imputation of having sold his country for his personal advantage. But the English proved obstinate, and no progress was made at Newmarket. After the court returned to London the Prince saw Mary for the first time since 1670. The next day he made a formal demand of James for her hand. Even then no progress was made, and the dejected suitor began to prepare for his return to the continent. The next morning, however, all was smiles. William's suit was granted. At the news London and the whole country gave way to rejoicing. Bonfires were lit by the hundreds. The bride herself wept for a day-and-a-half.[15] What she saw was terrifying enough: an invalid in unusually weak health, hunchbacked, half a head shorter than herself, whose only remarkable feature was a pair of brilliant eyes. William dressed much too plainly for English tastes. He had apparently forgotten or almost forgotten how to speak his mother's tongue. He had little conversation and no knowledge of polite letters. Beauty saw her Beast. She could not yet see the great man hidden behind this forbidding exterior.

The Beast saw a great beauty indeed. At this time Mary was held to be one of the finest women in Europe. But she was only fifteen, still almost a child. Apart from religion the Princess had had almost no education. Card playing and the theatre were her chief pastimes. The content of her letters, her handwriting itself, are clear proof of a most defective training. Mary could never fully share her husband's intellectual life. It was only eight or nine years later that the Princess came to be a companion, a colleague in the defence of Europe from slavery. By that time the couple could share many memories. Husband and wife were driven together since they were both under far more severe outside pressures than at the beginning of their life together. And the Princess, who possessed a very remarkable character and much native intelligence as well, took pains to educate herself after her marriage, at the cost of severe trouble with her eyes. All this lay in the future. At the time it was undoubtedly a marriage of convenience. Yet even at the beginning of their relationship each partner could find much to admire in the other. Both had very simple personal tastes. Both were deeply religious, though their faiths were different. Both were people of the highest standards of conduct. In time to come, it was to develop into a love match.

The wedding itself was a confused affair. Neither the Queen nor the Duchess of York attended, since the latter was in the final stages of pregnancy. Nor did Princess Anne, who was suffering from smallpox. To William's fury, his attempts to have his bride isolated from all contact with the sick-room were frustrated by a foolish priest who insisted on caring for the souls of both sisters at whatever cost to their lives. The ceremony could not take place until William had received permission from the States General. This was granted, thus making it impossible for the Dutch to make public objection to his choice of a wife. Many of them were by no means pleased at a step which might lead to a union between the maritime powers, a union in which the Republic must be the junior partner. Some of the Dutch were old enough to remember the haughty manner of the Princess Royal and wondered whether this new Princess would be as rude as the last.[16] When the approval of the States arrived, the wedding was performed in the Princess's bedroom at nine in the evening of 4 November, the Prince's birthday. At eleven they were put to bed, and as the King drew the curtains he said to William: 'Now, nephew, to your worke! Hey! St George for England!'[17]

Although the jewels arrived next day for the Princess and were estimated to be worth £40,000, the exact value of her portion from the King, the first days of the marriage were as hectic and unpleasant as those which had gone before. William was now engaged in negotiations with his uncles over terms for a general peace. These did not go too well. Another irritation was the refusal of an English dukedom for the Prince. Even more annoying was the birth of a son to the Duchess of York on the 6th, who was christened Charles and promptly created Duke of Cambridge. William was obliged to stand godfather to the little boy, with the King. Finally the Prince realized that he simply must return to The Hague, if only to prepare the military budget for the following year. The Princess wept inconsolably at being parted from her stepmother, and although the winds were adverse for some days her husband flatly refused to return to court and thus risk a second scene of the same nature. The party stayed at Canterbury until the wind changed, and finally reached the mainland on 9 December.

In Holland, William discovered that the French had taken advantage of his absence to besiege St Ghislain. The political situation was even worse than the military one. Although the birth of the little Duke of Cambridge had robbed the marriage of some of its danger, it was still a very frightening thing for the Dutch people.[18] Since the Princess must be spoken to in French, a language in which many of the Dutch had little fluency, her charm could not at once penetrate the minds of her new fellow citizens. These noticed only that the Princess refused to greet the wives and daughters of members of the States General with a kiss. She would salute the nobly born, but not the wives and daughters of mere officials.[19] This caused many tears. She also insisted on her right to have her carriage driven around the oval in the Voorhout in opposition to the stream of traffic, as d'Estrades had done many years before. This led to an incident when the wife of the Danish ambassador refused to give way. These social squabbles soon ceased. Within a very short space of time the Princess became a beloved figure in Dutch life, perhaps even more popular than her husband since she remained completely aloof from politics. However great her charm, the Princess could not conceal her position in the English line of succession. And the Dutch were so afraid of her prospects that for the first time since the Revolution of 1672 William lost control of the course of domestic political affairs.

The opposition now longed for peace on almost any terms. Driven on by French agents at Maastricht and at The Hague itself, the people began to suspect the existence of a family compact for the destruction of political liberty in England and in the Republic as well. William was even accused of being a secret papist. Was his father-in-law not a Catholic? Had he not shown his own popish leanings when he had greeted the English Queen with a kiss on his recent visit? Salutes were obviously dangerous this year. Much more serious was the suspicion that the Prince would be a tool in the hands of his uncles. William's position was further compromised by the fact that two of the agents carrying messages between the two courts were known to be particularly devoted servants of the Duke of York. Laurence Hyde was actually the uncle of the Princess, while John Churchill had secured his position by less honourable means. The Prince disliked both men personally and refused to have either of them as English ambassador at The Hague. If he could not have Temple, he would prefer a cipher who would do nothing more than obey orders. William himself was the best ambassador the English could possibly have.[20] The Prince went so far as to refuse a place at his court to Hyde's wife. The personal difficulties between the three men which began at this time were to continue and to cause serious political problems a generation later. For all his tact in offering James the supreme command of the Dutch as well as the English forces if England entered the war, it was quite impossible for William to become a tool in the hands of his father-in-law.

While in England the Prince had made some progress. He had agreed with the King on a set of peace terms, and a copy of them had been sent off to Louis XIV.[21] The negotiation turned on the number of towns in the Low Countries to be surrendered by the French in order to form a barrier. Charles II and William III agreed that Maastricht must be returned to the Dutch. In addition the Spanish should be given Charleroi, Ath, Oudenarde, Tournai, Courtrai, Valenciennes, and Condé. In military terms the demands were unrealistic. A strong barrier would, however, require some such list of towns. To offset these concessions, Louis's ally Sweden would regain her lost territories, while Brandenburg would be compensated with a money payment. When the proposals were brought to him the French King gave a delaying answer and prepared for a winter campaign in Flanders. He was strong enough to take it all unless the English joined wholeheartedly in the war. Her armed strength – a toy army and a number of rotting ships – was contemptible. Even so, it was possible that Parliament might grant enough money to produce something better. And the English soldier was always a formidable enemy, if only he was properly led. But it would take time to create an effective force, and most people believed in their hearts that Charles would never fight. The Grand Pensionary Fagel was one of the most important of those who discounted the possibility of an English declaration of war.[22] He made his plans accordingly. During the next few months, while never openly opposing the Prince, he rested on his oars. At Nijmegen the Dutch plenipotentiary van Beverningk followed an independent line even when sober, and one which became more independent as well as much less sober after dinner. Valckenier and Hooft of Amsterdam, together with Paets of Rotterdam, were eager for peace on any terms. Not only would this bring an improvement to commerce. Valckenier and Paets, in particular, were enemies of the growing authority of the Stadhouder. Since Fagel would not go too far out of his way to oppose them, the three men had the States of Holland and soon the States General at their disposal. Even so they could not prevent the conclusion of an Anglo-Dutch treaty about the terms of peace. By it England and the Republic would force the Spanish and French to agree to the barrier which had been defined in November.[23]

On the day after the conclusion of this treaty, Laurence Hyde brought up another matter and one which gave the opposition full scope. This was a proposal for a mutual treaty of defence, to operate after the ending of the present hostilities. Some of its provisions, such as that for the mutual extradition of political criminals, were unpopular in themselves. The Dutch prided themselves on freely offering asylum to the persecuted. Indeed, there were few families in the province of Holland which did not have one ancestor at least who had entered the country as a refugee. The real unpopularity of the proposed treaty, however, lay in its probable effects on Dutch politics. William III seemed to threaten the constitution already. An English alliance would make him overwhelmingly strong. Was it not possible that William would use the troops now being raised in England to subjugate the Republic, and then to crush the liberties of his uncle's subjects? Hyde, partly through incompetence and partly because of his fatal relationship to the Royal Family, was unable to get the treaty through. Negotiations were transferred to London and a treaty was signed, but the Dutch and English ratified it in different versions. This could be used later, if necessary, as an argument that the treaty was a dead letter. A third proposed treaty, for a quadruple alliance between England, the Republic, and the two branches of the Habsburg family, was never even completed. Quite clearly the opposition had assumed control of the state.

The Spanish were as afraid of the new family compact as were the Dutch. They suspected that the loss of the Netherlands was at hand and were determined to prevent its falling into the clutches of the Stuarts. If the Netherlands must go, why not trade them for the return of Franche-Comté? When the English King demanded control of Ostend for the duration of the war as a magazine for his troops, the government at Brussels refused to give it. This gave Charles II an excuse for further delay. He would not even levy soldiers until Ostend had been turned over to him. Meanwhile the French were able to take advantage of the pitiable confusion that beset the allied cause. On 4 March Louis XIV appeared before Ghent. This caused a general panic. Hastily the Spanish granted England the use of Ostend. Ghent, however, fell on 9 March and Ypres on the 25th. These events changed the face of the war completely. Charles and William abandoned all hope of recovering Valenciennes, Tournai, and Condé. But the French now insisted on Ypres as well. At Nijmegen d'Estrades demanded that a peace on these terms be concluded before 10 May, a deadline that was eventually extended to the 27th.

The panic was as great at The Hague as it was at Brussels. On 13 May the States General voted to accept the French demands if their allies would agree to them. They went even further. Louis XIV, not satisfied by his territorial gains themselves, insisted that they be given him in a peculiarly humiliating fashion. He asked the Dutch to send him a personal mission to beg for peace, while his court painters prepared to record the historic moment. Dutifully the Dutch complied. They sent van Beverningk off to the French camp at

Wetteren, where he had a long audience of the King on 1 June. There he obtained a six weeks' truce, apparently at the cost of exceeding his powers. Although the point is disputed, it appears that van Beverningk promised to conclude a separate peace before the end of the truce if the allies had not agreed to end the war by that time. All the while the Prince of Orange was helpless. His marriage had cost him control of the course of Dutch political life, and seemed likely to prove the death of European freedom. After the conclusion of the truce, everyone hastened to save what he could from the wreckage. On 27 May Charles II made a new subsidy treaty with France. Villa Hermosa, on behalf of the Spanish government, agreed to the French terms on 3 June. William III himself began to pay some attention to his awkward position. Once peace was made he would become the vassal of Louis XIV for his estates in Franche-Comté. On 13 June Odijk, acting on the Prince's orders, had a rather embarrassing interview with d'Estrades in which he offered William's services to Louis XIV.[24] This was followed ten days later by a letter of compliment from the Prince to the King.[25] The war seemed over.

On 24 June, with the signing of the treaties expected to take place in three or four days, the final blow fell. D'Estrades announced that none of the French conquests in the Low Countries would be returned before the conclusion of a peace between Sweden and her enemies. No one could believe that the French would keep their pledge to return the conquests, once the Dutch and English had disarmed. This would mean the end of freedom in the Republic and in all likelihood the end of freedom in the British Isles as well. Overnight the party of Charles II and William III recovered the initiative. On 27 June the States General refused to make peace unless the towns were restored forthwith. They went further. When Sir William Temple, hurriedly dispatched from England, reached The Hague they hastily signed a momentous agreement with him. If peace should not be achieved before 11 August, a peace including the immediate return of the barrier towns, the Republic and the English government undertook to continue the war together. This treaty was signed on 25 July.

The first half of 1678 was one of the most unhappy periods in the life of William III. His wife suffered the first of a series of miscarriages. His own health was still shaky. The military position was desperate, the political one scarcely better. A majority of the Dutch now opposed his plans for the continuation of the war or for the attainment of a secure peace. By their open eagerness for peace at any price, the Dutch were giving the whole game away. There were always lighter moments. William and his generals could be distracted for a short time by the newly invented magic lantern.

The Prince could obtain a few hours of exercise and release by playing billiards, or tennis, or by going heron hunting. Yet even in these hours of relaxation, William could not keep his mind completely anaesthetized. How was he to preserve his country, his inheritance, or even his reputation when Madrid, Vienna and The Hague were as hostile to him as the French? When the Stuart alliance had proved a major liability rather than an asset? The Prince of Orange knew that he had no desire to destroy the liberties of the Dutch or the English people. He knew that he was not a secret papist, that he had no intention of stealing the Spanish Netherlands. Groundless charges of this nature, however, had robbed him for the moment of all authority. And here the Prince showed for the first time the patience that set him so far apart from his father. William II had lost his temper and had ruined himself by the assault on Amsterdam. His son was the better man, flexible enough to play a waiting game. He was not abandoning the struggle. That he would never do. His confidence in God, his conviction of the probity of his own conduct and motives, gave him the strength to go on. The Spanish had given way to despair at Charleroi, in demanding a battle which they knew would lead to complete disaster. William III would never give way to such petulance. By acquiescing in what he could not prevent, he saved himself to fight another day. This is what separates the amateur from the professional in public affairs. The amateur may gain a few cheap successes, but he has no staying power. William III was a professional.

For this reason he was able to take immediate advantage of the revulsion in popular opinion that followed the outrageous French demands of 24 June. He did what he could to help Temple conclude the treaty of 25 July. He also resumed his activities in the military sphere. Mons, known to the Dutch as Bergen in Henegouwen, was the fortress next threatened by the enemy. It was under blockade rather than siege, and the French hoped to starve the inhabitants into submission. According to an important despatch of van Beverningk dated 10 July they planned to keep Mons, should it fall into their hands at any time before the *ratification* of the peace treaties.[26] Thus the mere signature of the peace treaties would not secure Mons. William III knew that there was enough food in the town to last until the end of July, but he doubted how long the inhabitants could hold out after that. When the Spanish first asked him for help in the relief of the place he had to refuse. The state of public opinion was such that he dared not undertake another battle capriciously. But when the Dutch recovered their courage in July the whole situation changed. Temple's treaty was signed on 25 July. On the next morning the Prince left Honselaarsdijk for the army.

William stayed at the camp at Vilvoorden, north of Brussels, for a week while he made his preparations. Although Luxembourg with his field army had drawn back on the blockading force under Montal before Mons, the Prince was informed that his forces would be roughly equal to the united French armies. This did not give him too much to hope for, since even if the information were correct his cavalry and artillery were distinctly inferior in quality to those of the enemy. His infantry, however, was far better than it had been at the beginning of the war. The quality of the German contingents was also high. On 2 August an army of perhaps 45,000 men set out. It reached Enghien on the 8th and Soignies on the 13th. It will be remembered that the English treaty was scheduled to go into effect on the 11th should peace not have been made by then. The French negotiators at Nijmegen waited until the last possible moment. Then on the morning of 10 August they gave in. They agreed to make peace without obtaining satisfaction for the Swedes. During the day van Beverningk, in flat rebellion against the instructions which forbade him to make a peace without the inclusion of the Spanish, worked like a slave to finish the separate treaties of peace and commerce between the United Provinces and France. They were signed just before midnight. Since Spain did not make peace that day, the States General might disavow van Beverningk's signature of the treaties. And since Mons was not mentioned in the documents or in the conversations of 10 August, no one knew what would become of the place. Curiously, van Beverningk's letter of the next day to the Prince never reached its destination. Even more curiously, the Government at The Hague sent no word at all. Perhaps the politicians at the capital dared not tell William that peace had been concluded behind his back. Perhaps van Beverningk, Valckenier and Paets wanted to trap the Prince into delivering a battle after the conclusion of the peace, so as to damage his reputation. Perhaps some of the opposition leaders hoped that their Captain-General might suffer a fatal accident. Possibly the Spanish held up the mails. Any or all of these alternatives is a possibility. What is certain is that the French had threatened to keep Mons if they should get it at any time before the ratification of the treaties. The blockade was still in progress, the inhabitants of the place still starving. Since Mons was the last great fortress in allied hands covering Brussels from the south-west, its military importance was extremely high. The most likely explanation for what happened, therefore, is that the Dutch and Spanish deliberately refrained from sending any word to the Prince that might bring him to a halt.

The Prince was of course eager for a battle for his own sake as well as for the public interest. A final victory would help his reputation. It might even lower the insane pride of the French for a few moments. On the morning of Sunday 14 August he advanced towards the enemy. At ten o'clock he reached Roeux and saw from the heights the French army spread out beneath him. Luxembourg's dispositions were remarkable. The army of

Montal was before the blockaded town. Between this force and that of Luxembourg ran the Haisne river, but a series of bridges had been erected so as to maintain communications. The main French force was on this side of the Haisne in excellent positions, so strong that Luxembourg believed an attack to be out of the question. He had taken up his own headquarters outside his own lines, at the Abbey of St Denis. Although the Abbey was a strong position itself, and was defended by a considerable number of men, its detached condition made it unsatisfactory. This was the first of Luxembourg's errors. The second is more shocking. As it happened, d'Estrades had reached the Abbey with official word of the conclusion of the peace. Luxembourg considered, and his generals voted for, sending word to the Prince de Vaude-mont. Vaudemont was a personal friend of the Duke. At the last moment the herald was called back. Was Luxembourg too proud to send word, or did he refuse to abandon Mons just as it was about to fall into his hands? It did not matter to the four or five thousand men who would fall that day what the reason was. Their fate was sealed in any case. It is kinder to believe that Luxembourg fought for Mons than simply because of his hatred of William.

The ground on which the battle was to be fought was very broken. In some places the ravines were so steep that steps had been cut in the rock, and elsewhere the French flanks were covered by woods. Luxembourg was so sure of the strength of his positions that he had a good dinner at the Abbey. Meanwhile the Prince of Orange was also having dinner, but, while he ate, his men were occupying a height commanding the Abbey and were moving forward from there towards St Denis itself. Shortly afterwards the battle began and the Abbey was soon captured. Luxembourg withdrew to his main lines, apparently in some confusion of mind. His conduct for the rest of the day indicates that he was not at his best. Obsessed with the idea that the Dutch must attack his right, he kept sending reinforcements thither while William really did attack the French left. This cost the French some of the advantage of their positions, and they suffered also from the nature of the battlefield, which was so steep that their cavalry could be of little use. Since this was the arm in which the French had a decisive superiority, they lost most of the benefit which usually accrued to the defensive in seventeenth century warfare. The Dutch and Germans for their part fought above themselves, and when he went to visit the Abbey the next day William was still surprised that his men had been able to take it.

The main battle, which lasted from about two o'clock until ten in the evening, was located along a deep ravine. Both armies engaged in an artillery duel on the heights, while the infantry and some elements of horse engaged in hand-to-hand fighting up and down the sides of the ravine itself. The opposing heights changed hands several times. At about six o'clock William mounted a fresh and sustained attack on the French left wing and made considerable progress for a while. The enemy, however, fought back with great bravery. At one point a French captain rode up and presented his pistol at the Prince of Orange. Just as he was about to shoot, Henry van Nassau-Ouwerkerck noticed what was happening and saved his cousin's life by shooting the captain dead. The Prince rewarded him later with a pair of gold-mounted pistols. By ten the French had recovered almost all the ground they had lost except the Abbey, and the battle came to an end. When it was broken off, the battle of St Denis seemed to the allies to have been almost a failure. They had captured the Abbey, Luxembourg's headquarters, but they had not been able to complete their penetration of his lines. There would in all probability have to be another battle, and if Luxembourg were to use his men better than he had this day he could in all probability prevent the relief of Mons. It was a gloomy moment. But then the exhausted soldiers heard something that they could hardly believe. The French were withdrawing from their 'impregnable' positions! During the hours of darkness the allies could only guess what was going on. But on the morning of the 15th they saw that Luxembourg had withdrawn his entire army across the Haisne so as to join Montal. Even more shameful than this flight from the field of battle was the fact that the French had left behind not only the stripped corpses of their dead but their wounded and their supplies as well. This was a full admission that the victory had gone to William III.

It was not, of course, the relief of Mons. For that there might have to be another battle. But towards noon the Prince received an informal note of four lines from Fagel telling him that peace had been signed. His Spanish colleague Grana also received a more official communication from the Marquis of los Balbases to the same effect. William maintained firmly that this note from Fagel was the first word he had had, apart from camp rumours which no commander-in-chief has any right to listen to, about the conclusion of peace. His truthfulness on this matter has been attacked by many historians, particularly those who do not care to trust the diary of the Prince's Secretary Huygens. For long the diary stood alone and it was treated slightingly by many scholars. Now it has been joined by the Prince's own letters, which bear out Huygens on hundreds, indeed thousands, of minor details. Its authority as an historical document, therefore, stands far higher than it did half a century ago. In this particular case it does not matter whether the Prince and Huygens were truthful or not, whether Fagel's note arrived on the 15th or before the battle. I happen to believe that it arrived at noon on the 15th. The real point, however, is that Fagel's note was not enough. Even after receiving it the Prince was still left completely in the dark. He had not been sent any official notice. He had no copy of the treaty, and thus no idea of the day on which hostilities were to come to an end. He had no word about Mons either from Nijmegen or from The Hague, and he could see with his own eyes that the blockade continued. He was, of course, very upset at the possible reaction of Dutch opinion to the battle; but until he should receive something in the nature of an official communication, some order to cease hostilities, it was his duty to continue in the relief of the town. If Luxembourg would not end the blockade there would have to be a second battle.

This was not to be necessary. Dijkvelt was sent to negotiate with Luxembourg on the 16th for the provisioning of Mons. The French commander insisted on referring the matter to his king, but a truce was arranged to cover the period until a messenger should return. On the 18th the courier brought word that the blockade was to be lifted, but the next day there was further argument as to which army should march away first. If the allies did, then the fact of the French defeat would be concealed from public notice. Finally an arrangement was made whereby the opposing forces left the neighbourhood simultaneously on the 21st.

There is a very large literature covering the Battle of St Denis.[27] Even from the French sources alone it is clear that Luxembourg knew of the conclusion of the peace before the action began and that he overruled a council of war which voted to send word of this to the allied army. Thus it was Luxembourg and not William III who fought with the peace in his pocket, and he did so deliberately. In the second place these same sources make it clear that the Maréchal was driven from his headquarters at the beginning of the action and that he withdrew from the field at the end of it, abandoning his wounded, his tents, and his provisions. There is no possible way to twist these uncontested facts into a French victory. In the third place van Beverningk's letter of 10 July explains why the battle was fought. The Dutch were given the impression that the French would keep Mons if it fell between the conclusion of the treaties and the exchange of the ratifications. This impression was fortified by the conduct of the French commander in the field. If the Dutch were mistaken in their impression, they had every right to be. If they were correct, if in fact Louis XIV intended the blockade to continue at any cost during the interval between the signing of the treaties and the exchange of ratifications, then of course he is personally responsible and Luxembourg was merely obeying orders.

It must be remembered that the French were barbaric in their general conduct, and not merely in this particular case. Their whole diplomacy and method of warfare was of a piece with this shabby business of Mons. The events of 1672 had not been forgotten by anyone. And as van Beverningk quickly discovered, nothing had changed in the interval. The first thing the

French did after making peace with the Dutch was to try to twist and turn their way out of their own previous undertakings in regard to Spain. To keep the French to their word the Dutch had to refuse to ratify their own treaty until they saw the final terms of the Spanish one, and the Dutch did not ratify the Peace of Nijmegen until 17 September. In one sense the blame for the gross misconduct of the French, at Nijmegen and at Mons, may lie at the door of d'Estrades and Luxembourg. But in a larger sense the responsibility must be borne by their King. He had now been in power for seventeen years. On what single occasion in this time had he kept his word? Not one. The diplomacy of Louis XIV deserves a great measure of respect entirely apart from the question of its success. On many occasions the King had right on his side. On many occasions he was more moderate than his enemies would admit. But on no occasion between the beginning of his personal government in 1661 and his death fifty-four years later did he ever feel bound by the letter of his treaties.

The war was not yet over. Ratifications of peace between Spain and France were not exchanged until December, and peace was not made in the north until the following year. Undoubtedly the war of 1672 ended in a great victory for France. Alone, except for the Swedish distraction, she had fought off the united forces of Europe. Her gains were splendid, and so too was the manner in which she had been able to dictate peace to a prostrate Christendom. In one sense, however, she had missed her goal. The Dutch Republic still stood. With all her superiority in men and resources, with all the advantages of a centralized and authoritarian government, France had lost that war. The United Provinces were still free. Poorer certainly, uncertain of the future and divided by domestic strife, but proud of their successful resistance to the tyrant's sword. And they could be proud, too, of the dour little man who had led their armies into battle and preserved their independence.

Chapter 13

THE EXCLUSION CRISIS

THE lesson of the war of 1672 seemed clear: an alliance could not fight on equal terms with a single great power. There seemed to be no answer to the problems posed by a grouping of weak states, fighting without money, leadership, or clear war aims, in a struggle against France. This lesson was reinforced by the fact that the allies had been able to beat Sweden and to drive Münster and England from the war. Without assistance from her own confederates, France had then won hands down. In the years after the conclusion of the treaties of Nijmegen, alliances, or 'social war' as it was called at the time, were at a deep discount. Social war had failed. Almost every individual state in Europe would find it advantageous to make its own terms with the enemy and to hope for the best. There were only two groups that could never hope to make a private arrangement with Louis XIV. The Habsburg lands lay directly in the path of French ambition; and there were even rumours that Louis XIV hoped to depose Leopold and make himself Emperor. Even if he did not go so far as that, Louis XIV could not expand his territories except at Habsburg expense. The Netherlands, Spain, Italy, the Empire, all were under Habsburg control. Ultimately, then, the August House had no choice. Sooner or later it would have to fight, for its very existence.

Fundamentally the maritime powers were in the same position. French commercial expansion could only take place at the expense of the English and Dutch. French political expansion in the Spanish Netherlands or in the Indies was a more direct threat to the maritime powers than to anyone else, even to the Spanish who had long since ceased to hope for any profit from their northern possessions. There were, however, in both countries men who refused to see the facts as they were. In the short run England and Holland might hope to profit from peace. It was difficult for men to keep their minds always focused on the great strategic issues. How much easier to forget such unpleasant things and to concentrate on making money while it was still possible. It is always very difficult to persuade a trading nation of the long range economies of preparedness or of the advantages to be gained from resisting an aggressor early in his career. So it was now.

William III was not to be allowed to forget the great strategic issues even if he wished to do so. Long before 1672 the French had decided that the House of Orange was an enemy. The Prince's conduct since then had seemed to provide ample confirmation of this theory. Therefore he must be punished, humiliated, if possible destroyed. It made no difference that William did not feel himself to be an irreconcilable enemy of the French or of their King, that he kept trying to reach personal accommodation for some years after Nijmegen. The French did him the honour to believe that he could neither be bribed nor fooled. With him they would never make peace. The new French ambassador to The Hague, the Comte d'Avaux, was ordered to have no relations with the Prince or with his cousins. When d'Avaux ventured to disobey these orders he was rebuked.[1] He continued to make his court to the Princess until the end of 1682, but from then on he was not even permitted to do so much.[2] In 1678 the Prince's estates of Meurs and Breda were subjected to heavy military contributions after the conclusion of peace, which at least in the case of Breda were completely unjustified. This was merely a foretaste of what was to come. Step by step, the Prince's revenues from those of his estates which were under French control were taken from him in the 1680s. It was fortunate that William knew how to live well within his income. Even with the new burden of Mary's court, the Prince needed only some fl.450,000 beyond his salary to live and to pay the interest on his debts. The remainder, some fl.700,000 in a good year, was available for building or for the repayment of loans.[3] Thus the Prince was not affected immediately by any financial pressure the French could bring to bear, however irritating that pressure might be. And in case of need he could offer to do without his salary if that would be to his political advantage. William's financial independence was in sharp contrast to the poverty of his uncles Charles II and Frederick William, and this no doubt contributed to his political independence. His uncles needed French money, William did not even need his own. Even so, he was as deeply angered by each new French theft as he was by each new French insult. They will learn, he said in 1682, what it is to outrage a Prince of Orange. And learn they did.

William knew the defects of social war better than anyone else in Europe. But he had no intention of abandoning the system of alliances. Quite simply, the Dutch could not defend themselves alone. They must have the diversion provided by a second front. The problem was therefore how to improve the alliance so that it would work better next time. The Habsburgs would have to join him, whether they would or no. Spain might be angry at the Dutch retention of Maastricht, technically as a caution for the money due to William himself. The Emperor might delay acceding to the request of the Dutch government that his Highness be given the style of Serene Highness, by analogy with the Duke of Mantua.[4] The delay, however, was over the question of whether William should receive the style Serene Highness as a grace, or whether he had a right to it as the first person in the Republic. There was no dispute about the title itself, or about the relations between the Emperor and the Prince of Orange. On the great issue of the defence of the west the Habsburgs and the House of Orange were at one.

A number of German states could also be counted on to remain firm to the alliance. One of William's longest and most important political friendships was that with George William of Celle. The House of Brunswick was the richest of all German families outside the Electoral College. To preserve itself from the fate of the House of Saxony, whose position had been destroyed by the grant of appanages to younger sons, the Dukes of Brunswick in this generation had agreed on a method of holding the family estates together. George William promised not to marry, so that eventually his lands would fall to the children of his younger brother Ernst August, Bishop of Osnabrück. Once the promise had been made, George William's resolution failed him and he not only married, as it happened a lady of obscure origins, but actually fathered a daughter. The Duchess of Celle was roundly snubbed by her in-laws and took refuge, as is often the case in such situations, behind a heavy shield of diamonds. William of Orange, who was extremely fond of her husband, was almost the only member of the family who was kind to the glittering Duchess. During the war he had come to like the Bishop of Osnabrück, whose fighting qualities he had admired during the miserable siege of Maastricht in 1676. Ernst August, unlike his older brother, was not a trustworthy or an admirable man. In general, however, he could now be counted on to follow the lead of the Prince and of the Duke of Celle, particularly if it was to his financial advantage to do so. Between them the two Dukes could put a respectable army into the field. In 1680 their position became even more important when a third brother, the Catholic John Frederick of Hanover, died without sons and Ernst August succeeded to that Duchy. Thenceforward the House of Brunswick was united in the Protestant cause. After Sweden and Brandenburg it was the leading power in the north of Germany.

Another constant supporter of William of Orange was the Landgrave of Hesse at Cassel, who could control the policies of his relative the Landgravin-Regent of Hesse Darmstadt. The Landgrave was, like the Princes of Brunswick, extremely wealthy and, like them, was closely related both to the House of Orange and to the Danish Royal Family. Down until the end of the war of 1672 there was something very like a family compact between all these cousins against the French and the Swedes. After the conclusion of peace, however, Denmark drifted towards the French interest, while Charles XI of Sweden became the friend of William and of the Princes of Brunswick. This gave rise to some danger. Brandenburg and Denmark might league themselves against Charles XI and the Brunswick Princes. On the whole, however, William hoped to be able to keep the Elector from going too far towards an alliance with Denmark. Frederick William was his uncle, a sincere Protestant, and directly interested in the prosperity of the House of Orange since his son had the best claim to the Orange estates on William's death. In August of 1678 and again in the spring of 1679 the Princess of Orange had been quite ill. Some of the symptoms resembled those of pregnancy, and naturally enough Mary hoped that she was to become a mother. Her hopes were vain.[5] By June it was being reported throughout Europe that William III could never have children.[6] This prospect, though it caused the Prince and Princess great personal distress, increased William's diplomatic influence. In 1673 he had caused his attorneys to remove the feudal restriction on his estates, converting them into free allods. At the time he probably wanted to punish the Elector of Brandenburg for concluding the peace of Vossem with the French. His freedom in testamentary affairs became a matter of some importance now that it was guessed that he would have no children of his own. From 1679 the Prince, with complete ruthlessness, used the prospect of his inheritance as a carrot to encourage two very difficult donkeys, the Brandenburgers and his cousins the Stadhouders of Friesland. The latter would be deprived of their hopes if they did not conform to the Prince's wishes in domestic affairs; the House of Brandenburg might lose its chance if it did not fall in line with William's foreign policy. At first, since William was still a young man who just might become a father after all, it was not a very effective weapon. Gradually, however, its usefulness increased. William's sterility was not without its value in other spheres. Whenever he was at his most exasperating the Dutch, and later the English, could console themselves with the thought that there would never be another William III. And the same thought had an undoubted effect on the Prince's own mind. Since he knew himself to be the last of his race, he had no need to be cautious. He had no children to provide for. It was not in his nature to enjoy himself by spending money; but he could, without regret, spend his political authority freely. This kind of capital, political capital, could be used in the greater cause of the European balance of power and the defence of the Republic.

This freedom of action is seen most clearly in William's relations with England. Ever since 1670 he had been the only member of the English Royal Family to enjoy personal popularity with the public. Charles II, in permitting the marriage of his niece to the Prince, had admitted his need for William's support. For the moment, the marriage satisfied the people and gave them hope of a change of policy. But in the long run the marriage compromised William's position without helping that of Charles and James. When it became clear that Charles had captured William rather than the reverse, there was an explosion of rage. In the crisis of the Popish Plot and the Exclusion Bills, England fell into disorder, Scotland into open revolt. For three years it seemed likely that James would be driven from the succession. There was more than a chance that his brother would be driven from the throne. In public the Prince remained loyal to his uncles and shared their unpopularity. In private, however, he continued to urge the King to come to terms with Parliament. There seemed to be a clear choice between preservation of the royal power and a strong foreign policy. The latter required parliamentary support, since it would cost great sums of money. But Parliament's terms would be high. They might include the elimination of James from the succession and parliamentary control of the executive. Charles, with his brother to think of, refused to accept such terms. William wanted above all things to obtain English support of the alliance, and he knew that no English treaty would be worth anything without parliamentary confirmation. Such a confirmation would in itself be a diminution of the royal prerogative, since the treaty-making power was vested in the King alone. Fundamentally William cared very much less for the preservation of the prerogative than did his uncles. He was not interested in the problems to be faced by his heirs. What he wanted was the real exercise of power, not a shadowy right which could never be used.

The Popish Plot scare broke out in August 1678. It was a complete fabrication on the part of Israel Tonge and Titus Oates, who claimed to have evidence that the Jesuits planned to assassinate the King so as to place James on the throne for the advantage of the Roman Church. James was supposed to be an accomplice and the Queen herself was implicated. Through bad handling on the part of the ministers the story had a chance to gain a hold on the people. The English were even more credulous then than now, and there were some coincidences which lent support to the tale. When Parliament met in October Shaftesbury and his followers saw in it an opportunity to break the ministry. By the end of the year the Lord Treasurer had been impeached, and a month later the Parliament was dissolved.

Luckily for William it was not generally known that he had met Oates some years before, when he had been working with du Moulin to stir up the English opposition.[7] Even as it was, the Prince's position was difficult enough. He felt obliged to write a sympathetic letter to the fallen Treasurer and was apparently ready to offer him a refuge in Holland, though he hoped that Danby would not embarrass him by coming to The Hague itself.[8] In the end, Danby was packed off to the Tower, where he remained for five years. But the Prince was to have even more compromising visitors. The Duke and Duchess of York, together with the Princess Anne, had come to

The Hague in October of 1678 on a pleasure trip. The Duke was back in the following March as a fugitive. Charles had not dared to let the new Parliament sit while his brother remained in England. The Prince treated his father-in-law with great courtesy and at his own expense, apparently to the Duke's satisfaction.[9] He and his wife were so pleased that there was another visit in April, though the exiles refused the offer of Breda for the summer. Later, in embittered old age, James dated William's conspiracy for the English throne to this month of April. At the time, however, he was so certain of William's loyalty that he asked him to go to England to look after his interests. His contemporary opinion is of weight, his later sniping valueless.[10] What happened in England in the spring of 1679 was not the Prince's fault. When the new Parliament sat in March it became clear that a great many members were in favour of the exclusion of the Duke. At first Charles tried to compromise, remodelling his Council so as to make Shaftesbury Lord President and to give that lord's followers a clear majority. Then he agreed to a scheme of limitations on the power of a Roman Catholic successor. His attempts failed, and the first Exclusion Bill was introduced into the Commons. The King was obliged to prorogue Parliament to prevent its passage.

The whole attempt to bar James from the succession had a fatal flaw. The opposition disliked him quite as much for his political views as for his religion, yet the Exclusion Bill was framed against him solely because of his religious beliefs. James could thwart Shaftesbury's men at any time by feigning Protestantism, as his brother wished him to do. All the possible alternatives to James were unattractive. There were only two root-and-branch solutions to the problem. The dynasty might be deposed, or Charles II might be persuaded to divorce Catherine of Braganza and remarry. Neither solution seemed at all practicable. Short of these, there were a number of far less satisfactory possibilities. The King might legitimate his son Monmouth, or the Princess of Orange might be called to the throne in her father's lifetime. In either case civil war was certain. The pressure for the exclusion of James was largely confined to the capital. Outside London his position was stronger, and he was supported by the wealthiest and most responsible elements in the kingdom. Although Monmouth had acquired a great measure of popularity in London itself and in some parts of Scotland, where he put down the rising of 1679 with moderation and intelligence, he was never an acceptable candidate to the nation as a whole. Mary would be much more suitable. She might, however, refuse to act. Even if she did agree to assume power in her father's lifetime, her Dutch connections made her suspect. Despite their common Protestantism, England and Holland had been divided by commercial rivalry throughout the seventeenth century, a rivalry that had been expressed in three wars in the past twenty-five years. Her husband, who would obviously rule the roost whatever his official position might be, was certainly a hero. He was also an autocrat, according to the accounts reaching Shaftesbury from the Dutch. His Presbyterianism made him suspect to Anglicans, while the fact that he violated the sabbath by hunting on Sundays made him suspect to the stricter Presbyterians. Thus both his political and his religious views were generally unpopular.[11] In the autumn of 1679, therefore, the opposition began to come out far more positively than ever before in favour of the candidacy of Monmouth. Whatever his other shortcomings, Monmouth was certainly ambitious for the throne and was weak enough to make a suitable tool.

Late that summer the importance of the succession was underlined when the King became seriously ill. James took the chance of coming back from Brussels and was well received by his brother, who was convalescing by the time York arrived at Windsor. The court, too, gave James a surprisingly friendly welcome. Parliament had been dissolved in July over the objections of Shaftesbury and the Council, a step which gave heart to the timid. Although the new elections were almost as unfavourable to the court as those of the spring had been, any firmness on the part of Charles rallied to him large numbers of people who were basically loyal but who feared that he might be persuaded eventually to come to terms with the Whigs. By dissolving Parliament, and by conniving at the return of James, the King indicated that he might fight and this was all that the more conservative elements needed to know. James made the most of his opportunities at Windsor. He insisted that Monmouth be dismissed from all his places and sent into exile if James must leave the country again. As to the place of his exile, York would go to Scotland rather than to the continent. After a short visit to Brussels to fetch his belongings, James returned to London with the Duchess and two weeks later set out for Edinburgh to take over the government there. Before he left England the second time he had the satisfaction of seeing Shaftesbury dismissed from the Council. He wrote the news to William in the form of a warning telling him that there was a correspondence between Shaftesbury's party in England and the Dutch opposition to the Prince in the Republic. 'I hope the little man's being out of employment here may help to breake those measurs; however, you would do well to looke a little after it where you are, for beleve me the Presbiterians and other Republicans here have as little kindness for you as the rest of our family; . . .'[12]

During James's exile in Brussels the French had done what they could to make him suspicious of the Prince. James had used a certain Fitzpatrick as a messenger to his son-in-law, and the man was secretly a French agent taking his orders from d'Avaux. Fitzpatrick's task was to colour the messages he carried in such a way as to irritate both men against each other. He tried to prevent William from placing any confidence in the new English ambassador, Henry Sydney, on the ground that Sydney was closely attached to Monmouth.[13] Then Fitzpatrick discovered that the Prince had sent one Freeman to England to keep up a secret correspondence with the Presbyterians. Freeman had been used before for the same purpose and had first come to the Prince's attention, with Oates, through du Moulin.[14] Soon Fitzpatrick had more important news to report. The Prince, he said, had come to the conclusion that Charles II would be forced to abdicate. Since the Protestants would never tolerate the Duke of York as king, William had no doubt but that he would soon be summoned to the throne by Parliament. The very words of the Exclusion Bill favoured such a view, since it spoke of the King's quitting the crown by death or abdication. William had told Fitzpatrick some time before that he would always have all the respect for the King and the Duke that he ought, and that he would never take the least step that might displease them; but that if Parliament called for him he could not refuse to go.[15]

Though the source was hostile, Fitzpatrick's report is the key to the Prince's conduct throughout the exclusion crisis and indeed for the rest of his life. William would not now or ever take the initiative against his uncles, however foolish or pigheaded their conduct, so long as they could preserve themselves on the throne. Quite naturally, for the protection of his wife's interests, the Prince would have to keep in touch with all parties. But there is a wide difference between keeping contact with the opposition and taking direction of it. Once the brothers had dug their own graves, however, it would be the duty of the Prince to intervene for the protection of his wife and for that of his country. One of the saddest duties a man can have to his family is the responsibility of placing legal restraint on a demented or senile parent. Whatever the world may say, and however much it may be to his financial advantage, it is none the less a clear moral obligation. But the Prince was not merely a private person with private obligations; he had responsibilities to the United Provinces as well as to his wife. The worst of all English governments, from the Dutch point of view, would be a republic. The history of the Commonwealth and Protectorate made that all too clear. Under a republic commercial interests would predominate to a far greater degree than under a monarchy, and the Dutch would be the first to suffer. Both in his private and in his public capacity, therefore, the Prince of Orange would have to intervene in England to prevent the Royal Family as a whole from paying for the sins of its two leading members.

The position which William III took up in the autumn of 1679 was difficult to maintain. For one thing, he was imperfectly informed about the realities of English political life. It would be hard, therefore, to be able to judge on the basis of incomplete and inaccurate information just when the Stuarts had destroyed the monarchy and it was time to intervene. In the second place, Charles and James construed family loyalty as a personal obligation to themselves and viewed the Prince's attitude as undutiful. Already they were jealous of their nephew for being so much more distinguished and popular than themselves. They had, too, the common resentment and fear of the old for the young. In private families these feelings are usually tempered by natural affection; but, as we have seen, kings have no relatives. It would be very easy for the French to play on these feelings and to create a breach within the Royal Family. Thirdly, the English parties were not going to play the political game by the rules. There was virtually no support for William as such from the party leaders. He was an admirable young man, and popular with the common people. Therefore they would try to make use of him, but for their own ends, not for his. In the spring of 1679 James had tried to get William to go to England; in the summer Sunderland, Temple and Sydney had the same idea.[16] Arlington had been the first English politician to try to manipulate William III for his own purposes, and there would be many others in the years to come. The Prince was not the man to be pushed around by politicians. But his contacts with them were open to sinister interpretations, and he could be blamed for what they did in his name. It was all too easy to suspect that the Prince's correspondence with the English factions, which was in fact limited to a desire for information and for assistance in his continental designs, was a conspiracy against the throne.[17] And when he entertained the exiled Monmouth in the autumn of 1679 with the same politeness that he had used towards the exiled James, it became difficult not to be suspicious. William denied the truth of these ideas, but he was to find it increasingly difficult to make his position clear.[18]

The Prince's situation became acutely embarrassing when Monmouth returned to England without permission. It was felt that he had come on the Prince's advice and that William might soon follow him. When the Prince did not come, and when he managed to prevent the States General from concluding a French alliance in January, these fears were laid to rest. In the early months of 1680 the Royal Family seemed united against Monmouth and against the French, and even the Duke of York was satisfied with William's conduct.[19] Proposals for the exclusion of James continued to be made, as did others for the divorce and remarriage of the King. William was supposedly to be satisfied with the position of Regent for a son of Charles in the event of a long minority.[20] But these propositions were clearly not being made by William. What he was after was a general alliance against France, which both he and the English considered at this time as a means of restoring James's position, of obtaining money from Parliament, and of unifying the King with his people.[21] As part of this plan, Princess Anne must be married off to a supporter of the good cause. During 1679 the name of the King of Sweden had been mentioned more often than any other, but William was felt to be unfavourable to the possibility of a brother-in-law of higher rank than his own. His candidate was Prince George of Hanover, one of the few German princes rich enough to afford an English marriage and, like William, a great grandson of James I. Anne's position in the line of succession could supply the defects of her dowry, and the greed of the House of Brunswick could be satisfied by a match between Prince George's younger brother and the vastly rich Princess of Celle. The double marriage would solve many problems. It would cement the new Duke of Hanover to the good cause, it would end the social isolation of the upstart Duchess of Celle, and it would – by no means the smallest of the anticipated advantages – keep the Celle fortunes out of the hands of the Stadhouder of Friesland. Prince Henry Casimir of Nassau, at the moment a near bankrupt, was, even so, a serious obstacle to William's domestic policies. His provinces of Friesland and Groningen voted consistently against the Orangists in the States General. If he could make a great deal of trouble while poor, there was no limit to the damage he might do with the Princess Sophia Dorothea as his wife. But the greatest advantage of all would be that the Stuarts would be irrevocably committed to the alliance against France. And Prince George could do what William perhaps could not, that is provide Protestant heirs.

The whole programme was a complete failure. After the fiasco of 1678, when Charles had been unable to bring Parliament into the war, every ruler in Christendom had concluded that he was a worthless ally. No one was willing to make an engagement with him alone. In the eyes of Europe, Parliament must be a party to any treaty, and Parliament was not sitting. William of Orange knew this, and he had warned in the previous autumn that even the Dutch would reject any treaty which was concluded without parliamentary sanction.[22] Now, unfortunately for himself, he had changed his mind in the hope that Parliament would ratify the treaties once they were made. In this he misjudged the temper of the continental powers and also that of the House of Commons. Of all the treaties proposed by the English ministry in the spring of 1680 the only one concluded was with Spain, and even the Spanish were reluctant to commit themselves. Their ambassador was remarkably slow in reaching London, and when he came he was without powers.[23] Despite this defect, an Anglo-Spanish treaty was signed in June. But the Emperor, the Elector of Brandenburg, the House of Brunswick, and the rest refused to be drawn, and in the end William did not even have enough influence to persuade the Dutch to accede to the treaty. By the autumn of 1680 he was back where he had been a year before, forced to rely on Parliament rather than on the Royal Family. But he was much weaker than he had been then. His closer relations with Charles and James had compromised him with the English nation and he was now positively unpopular. The advantage had all gone to Monmouth.

In the hope of saving something out of the wreck, William now turned against his uncles. As far as he was concerned his policies were completely consistent: support the Stuarts as long as they could control the course of events, and Parliament when they could not; do nothing dishonourable, but at all costs commit England to the alliance against France. By the autumn of 1680 that meant the exclusion of the Duke of York. It is clear that William at this time viewed an Exclusion Bill as *ultra vires*, something that Parliament might pass but a nullity no matter how many times it was enrolled in the statute book.[24] Henry VII, Mary, Elizabeth, and James I had all come to the throne either bastards or in defiance of statute law: four out of the last eight English sovereigns. William himself had come to power despite the most solemn enactments of which the Dutch legislature had been capable. But it was not to be expected that James should approach the subject with equal sophistication. They had been friends as recently as June. But by the end of October, when the Parliament elected a year earlier was finally allowed to sit and James banished again to Scotland in the hope of a favourable session, the Duke's confidence had broken down completely. He now believed that he had been betrayed by a conspiracy whose members included Temple, Sunderland, Henry Sydney and the Prince. The Spanish treaty had been the first step in the plot and all the rest had followed as a matter of course. Even though William was polite enough not to attend the session himself, he was sending van Leyden van Leeuwen over as a special representative so as to ensure that he rather than Monmouth would profit from James's ruin.[25]

Again James misjudged the Prince. William would never take the initiative, and he did not do so now. Again and again the English ministers begged him to come over during the session.[26] He would not come. In his absence, the Commons pushed through a second Exclusion Bill, which this time contained a definite stipulation that the succession should pass to the next heir (Mary); but the opposition of the King and a magnificent speech by Halifax secured its rejection in the Lords. Luckily for Barillon, the French ambassador did not have to carry out his instructions to support William against Monmouth: 'Votre Majesté m'a donné ordre de favoriser plustost la pretention de Mr le Prince d'Orange que celle de Mr le Duc de Montmouth. Je ne le pourrois faire dans le Parlement sans me decrediter entierement, et perdre le fruit de tout les liaisons que j'y ay faites.'[27] What the French wanted was a weak England, and they did not consider that William would be able to unite the country. If Louis XIV was guilty of bad timing when he gave instructions from a distance, the Prince did even worse. When the news of the defeat of the Exclusion Bill reached The Hague, Fagel and Sydney concocted a memorial from the States General urging Charles II to come to terms with Parliament. Although the memorial did not ask for the passage of the Bill in so many words, its intent was obvious and so was its impertinence. So too were the letters of William to Sir Leoline Jenkins and to van Leyden van Leeuwen, arguing against the alternative policy of placing limitations on the powers of a popish successor. The Prince wrote that if considerable powers were once surrendered they would be lost forever, even if a Protestant should eventually succeed.[28] Charles was outraged. With some emotion he told the Dutch envoy that no one could have more care of the prerogative than he. If he might dispose of the crown he would give it to one of his own children; but he knew that it was not in his gift and that he must leave it to those to whom it belonged. Furthermore, he assured the Dutchman, the men who were misinforming the Prince wished to take away the royal power of appointment and had even dared to propose that the governors of Portsmouth, Plymouth, Hull, and the Tower be changed, on the ground that they were James's creatures; whereas in fact they were his own servants and not the Duke's.[29] After sustaining this blast, van Leyden van Leeuwen made the rounds of the ministers and discovered that Halifax favoured limitations, while Sunderland and Godolphin were still in favour of exclusion. The two last were eager for William to come over, and William was by now so alarmed that he agreed to come if he obtained permission. But it was too late. The Parliament had so infuriated the King that on 10/20 January he prorogued it. Dissolution followed a few days later, together with a summons for the meeting of a new Parliament at Oxford in March. At the same time Lord Sunderland, who for two years had been the most vocal supporter of William III in England, was dismissed. His replacement as Secretary of State was Lord Conway, a cipher of complete incompetence and only one significant connection. It was an ominous one; he was a cousin of Edward Seymour, the former Speaker, who was soon to distinguish himself as William's leading enemy.

Although the Parliament did meet at Oxford, the real decisions had been made in January. Charles offered a new plan, a Regency scheme. Mary was to be the Regent. The plan had no chance of success, if only because its author was Halifax. After his speech against the Exclusion Bill Halifax was one of the most unpopular men in the country. The Commons would have nothing but exclusion, pure and simple, and Charles abruptly dissolved them. As long as he could hope to rule through Parliament with Dutch support he had tried, and tried hard. Now he could do nothing but fall back on James. Ever since October James had been convinced that the only possible policy was one of high prerogative rule backed by a French alliance. The fate of Europe was as nothing compared to his personal future. 'And pray let us not mind Flanders so much as to hazard the certain mine [*sic* for ruine] of the monarchy' he wrote to Laurence Hyde.[30] Before the Oxford Parliament met he sent his servant John Churchill down from Edinburgh to try to prevent the session. If Churchill could not do that, he was to urge the Duke's views:

> an Allyance with France was the only means to support the King and preserve the Monarchie and even the Church of England itself, by affording a supply without a Parliament, which aim's manifestly at the ruin of them all; that matters were come to such a head that the Monarchy must be either more absolute or quite abolished, that France would be Sorry to see England a Commonwealth, that Spain desired it, and Holland would not be displeas'd at it, and that since his Majesty was so kind as to resolve not to abandon him (York), nothing but an Allyance with France could support him in that resolution, considering how he had been used by others even the Prince of Orange himself; . . .[31]

Such a policy required a change of ministers. Halifax retired to the country in disgust, though he did not quit. The new men were Laurence Hyde, who did just what his brother-in-law James told him to, and Edward Seymour. Third-raters like Seymour's cousin Conway and Sir Leoline Jenkins filled out the government, some of them utter incompetents and the rest able administrators who did not aspire to become statesmen. Halifax's presence in the ministry was intended to blind the eyes of the Dutch and Spanish to what was going on, and probably also to give the King an opportunity to change his policies when times were better. James was able to put his brother in the way of securing from France the fruits of this policy.[32] The subsidy was to last for three years and was conditional on there being no new Parliament. Hyde, now a Viscount and First Lord of the Treasury, was to be the one to receive the money from Barillon.

In July William made a visit to England to see if things were as black as they looked. Sydney, with whom both Prince and Princess had struck up a great friendship, had been recalled from The Hague in June, and his description of the English court was really alarming.[33]

> It is very plain, that you have had very ill offices done you to the King; they make him believe that your Highness is of the party that is most against him; that you have a constant correspondence with those [they call] his enemies; that you drive a contrary interest; in short, I believe there are some in the cabinet council that are desirous enough to see a breach between the King and your Highness . . . nobody hath any credit but the Duke's creatures, and they study what is good for the Duke and

themselves, but do not consider what is good for the King or the nation, and the affairs abroad never enter into their heads.

Sydney felt that Halifax and Hyde were not really malicious, but that Sir Edward Seymour was doing all he could to create a breach between the King and the Prince. Of the three, only Hyde and a few of the lesser ministers felt that they would be physically safe in the event of another Parliament. James, of course, knew from experience what he had to expect from one. Since William would obviously ask for a Parliament and for aid to Spain against French aggression in the Low Countries, the ministers as well as the Duke of York felt almost as if William were trying to kill them. The Prince, therefore, who disliked Hyde personally and had called him a liar in April [34] though he did not know that Hyde was the channel for the French subsidies, had to do business chiefly with him rather than with the others. He also saw much of Halifax whom he liked much better, but Halifax had little power.

The Prince reached Whitehall on 23 July O.S. and went on to Windsor. His major goal was to get a Parliament summoned, and he still felt that one could be productive if the court abandoned the Duke of York 'de bonne foy'. [35] The French were now attacking the County of Chiny, which William hoped to save with joint Anglo-Dutch assistance. If the English would agree to put a token force of 2,000 men into the Spanish Netherlands, which would be matched by 2,000 new Dutch troops, the French might draw back. Although such a small force would have no military value, it would act as a trip-wire and the French robber might well hesitate to set off the alarm bell. William and the Spanish hoped also to persuade the English to send a mediator to the Franco-Spanish conversations at Courtrai. [36] One of his minor aims was to obtain for Henry Sydney the command of the English and Scottish troops in Dutch service now that he was no longer ambassador. The military post was vacant by the death of Lord Ossory in the previous August. In order to get his way the Prince was even ready to speak to the Duchess of Portsmouth, whom he loathed. But even this condescension proved fruitless. The King himself was pretty reasonable. If Parliament, he now said, would have given him money without demanding control of the military fortifications and of the fleet, he would have been willing the previous December to give his assent to the Exclusion Bill. Charles shared William's opinion that such a measure was 'une chose entièrement nulle et qui ne peut jamais avoir son effet'. [37] There was a chance that he still felt the same way; enough of a chance so that the French cut off their subsidies to the court for the duration of the Prince's visit and reopened their negotiations with Ralph Montagu and his sister Mrs Hervey of the opposition. But if the

King was reasonable, the Whigs were not. Their favourite slogan at this time was that they would not give a penny for the defence of the country even if the French were in the middle of Kent. This not very patriotic attitude gave rise to another idea. William III was far more likely to cooperate with Whig plans than Louis XIV. Why should he not send a fleet to blockade the mouth of the Thames and so force Charles to summon Parliament and to join the Dutch?[38] This was Mrs Hervey's contribution to statesmanship in the summer of 1681; but the rest of the Whigs were scarcely more responsible, and the idea of a naval demonstration was to be heard again later.

At first the Prince could not believe that the Whigs were such wild men. The King knew them better. He permitted William to return to London and to hold conferences with Essex, Sunderland, Russell, and Sir William Jones at Arlington House.[39] The Whigs were just as unreasonable as the King had said they would be. But William's visit to London posed a risk for the court. He was so much more popular than the King that his presence might well cause disorders. When the Lord Mayor invited William to a dinner the court commanded him to refuse. The Prince, furious, returned to Windsor and took out his anger by complaining of the quality of the food there. Seymour, who seems to have gone out of his way to be rude, retorted that the Prince had no right to complain of the food since he had brought over with him a low grade of champagne.[40] On this sour note the Prince settled down to serious conferences with the ministers on the problem of defending the Spanish Netherlands. The Spanish ambassador had made up a chart of all the French conquests and claims there. The chart, and the subsidiary documentation, was discussed at special meetings of the cabinet council in the presence of the King, the Prince, the Dutch and Spanish ambassadors, and Halifax, Hyde, Seymour, Conway, and Jenkins. Charles refused to send any troops, or a mediator. He did agree to join with the Dutch in using his good offices to dissuade the French from using force, and in urging them to refer all the matters in dispute to the conferences at Courtrai. That was all he could be brought to do, and it was little enough. But it was too much for Barillon, who complained in reply that Charles had had no right to permit William's visit without the authorization of Louis XIV.[41] This was apparently not an impertinence but a statement of fact. Certainly Charles was ordered by the French to withdraw his ambassadors from northern Europe, and if he later refused to recall his ambassador at The Hague on their instructions he did obey a similar command relating to his ambassador at Lisbon. The Stuarts paid a high price for their pensions.

William got nowhere with his requests. While the conferences were going on there came the news of the fall of Chiny. Charles would not permit Sydney to take command of the six British regiments, although he could not prevent William from appointing him colonel of one of them. And the Prince's argument that the King, by agreeing to the exclusion, would so strengthen the position of the Royal Family that James would eventually be in a position to defend himself, fell on deaf ears. William and Charles parted in a very bad mood, each regretting the visit had taken place.[42]

From the summer of 1681 William had to reckon on the hostility of the Stuarts. If he could not persuade them by kindness he was stubborn enough to hope to persuade them by force. Therefore he kept up his contacts with the Whigs and sent Coenraad van Beuninghen of Amsterdam over in the autumn to strengthen the weak backbone of the regular ambassador Arnout van Citters. Charles in his turn accepted the maxims of his brother, who was permitted to return from Scotland in 1682, and determined to become an autocrat. The Presbyterians were punished for their support of the Whigs by a renewal of religious persecution. The recall of the Duke of York from exile was in itself a provocative act, and so was the campaign to remodel the English municipal corporations by forcing the surrender of their charters which began soon after. Since the King was bound by his promise to the French not to summon a Parliament for three years, there was no need to worry about the political consequences of such vigour. Whig intransigence was responsible for a good deal of the trouble, and Charles had apparently been sincere in his conduct between 1678 and 1681. In any case he now took a bloody revenge. The discovery of the Rye House plot of 1683 gave the King an opportunity to execute his brother's enemies or to drive them into exile. After Essex committed suicide in the Tower and Lord Russell was beheaded, the prudent took the hint and removed themselves to The Hague or else went to watch a campaign in Hungary. The leadership of the Whigs was scattered to the four winds; but the bulk of the party remained, per-force, in England watching the court with sullen hatred. William continued to consider the broken party a more valuable ally than his uncles. In the short run he was wrong; but one day the period of reaction would come to an end, and probably a violent one. The Prince, by acting as patron of the Whigs, cut the ground from under the feet of Monmouth and kept the party from going over completely to republicanism. It was a great and truly conserva-tive service to the monarchy; but not one that Charles and James could appreciate.

During these years William's relations with Brandenburg were almost as unpleasant as his contacts with the Stuarts. The Elector was by now a gouty and querulous old man, all the more ill-tempered because he was driven by the French leanings of his second wife and the logic of his situation to play a role he did not care for. The triumph of Frederick William's life had been his eviction of the Swedes from the soil of Germany and his capture of Stettin. Although the Swedes had attacked him unprovoked, although he had beaten them in a fair fight, he had been forced by the French to restore most of what he had taken in Pomerania and in particular the city of Stettin. He was now a poor and a very angry man. It seemed obvious that the only way to improve his finances and, perhaps, one day to get Stettin was to accept a French subsidy treaty. Frederick William did so, and he stuck by it until 1685, but he hated his position and worked off his humiliations by making life miserable for everyone around him. The special victims of his rage were the Dutch, who had abandoned him in 1678. He claimed that they owed him subsidies right up to the time he had concluded his own peace with the French in 1679, plus compensation for damages to his Duchy of Cleves. The Dutch refused to admit any liability for subsidies after the end of the year 1676, nor were the individual provinces any too eager to pay what they owed for the time before that. The Elector retaliated by sending a series of insolent memorials to the States General and similar letters to William III, who tried to calm the passion of his uncle as best he might. The Elector also withheld until 1681 the fort of Schenckenschans, which the French had returned to him rather than to the Dutch on the conclusion of hostilities. At times, especially in 1683, it looked as if Brandenburg and Denmark might unite to make war on Holland, Sweden, and the Princes of Brunswick. And if the Elector never went quite that far on land, he did more at sea.

In 1675 an obscure Zeeland politician named Benjamin Raule had been evicted from the magistracy of Middelburg by William III. He felt that he had a personal grievance against the Stadhouder, and it is certainly true that his brother sat in prison for several years. Raule transferred himself to the court of Berlin, where he became far more important than he had ever been before, and persuaded the Elector to build a fleet of twenty ships. He himself seems to have provided much of the requisite technical skill. He received the title of *Oberdirektor* of the little navy. Raule, with his own scores to settle, was able to persuade the Elector to take reprisals on Zeeland shipping if that province did not pay off its share of the subsidy arrears.[43] Zeeland made an acceptable compromise, just in time; but the Spanish were not so wise. In September 1680 a squadron of eight Brandenburgers surprised a richly laden Spanish vessel, the *Charles II*, in the road of Ostend and took her. Since the bulk of the cargo belonged to Dutch citizens,[44] the Republic was as angry as the Spanish could be. The matter was all the more serious because a new Governor of the Spanish Netherlands, the Prince of Parma, was at sea on his way to take up his post. There was a chance that the Prince might be kidnapped and held to ransom. Luckily, or not, Alexander Farnese, who was contemptuously known as the Italian ox, reached Brussels in safety. But this was not the end of the Brandenburg navy. In 1683 the Elector set up an African Company at Embden in East Friesland. All the other colonial powers opposed it vehemently, and after the French had captured one of its vessels and the Dutch two others, the company gradually subsided into obscurity. Unfortunately the raw sore of the subsidy question would not disappear so conveniently. In 1683 the Prince, with great effort, persuaded the Republic to offer 300,000 dollars in satisfaction of all the Elector's claims. Frederick William demanded four, and when he did not get them he made a great deal of trouble for the Prince both in Germany and in Holland. Finally, in 1685, the Dutch were forced to pay the Elector's price and to add another 40,000 dollars as a bribe to the Electress.

In these circumstances, with both his English and his German uncles in French pay and in the French interest, it might have been well for William III to abandon the struggle. Had he been willing to stand aside and to allow France to devour western Europe, he could have received many personal advantages; and the Republic would have been one of the last courses in the meal. The Prince was not that kind of man. He was a fighter, and he knew what it was to fight against heavy odds. He would never agree that the odds were hopeless. Always there was the chance that something might turn up. And, as Fagel once remarked bitterly, the same God who had protected the Dutch a century before was still alive. He in His mercy would save them now, as He had saved them then. It required some effort, and a strong faith, to believe that even the Divine Will could save the United Provinces in the decade after the Treaty of Nijmegen. Abroad, the nation and its allies seemed impossibly weak against the power of France. At home the people were divided, suspicious of the Prince's motives, restless under his authority, doubtful of the wisdom of his policies. It seemed unlikely that the Prince could maintain the separate existence of the Republic, much less the security of the Barrier. Could he even maintain himself? Valkenier and van Beverningk had carried through the peace of 1678 despite everything the Prince could do. Now that peace had been achieved, his authority was automatically reduced even further. No one is less popular in a trading nation than an army man – when there is no fighting to do.

Chapter 14

THE TWENTY YEARS TRUCE

In the autumn of 1678 Dutch political life was in turmoil. No one knew who would exercise power in time of peace. There was the normal post-war reaction against the wartime leadership, all the more intense because of the idolatry with which the Prince had been worshipped in 1674. William's refusal to court popularity, his attempts to become Duke of Gelderland in 1675, the roughness of his political methods, were all resented. The fact that the war had been lost made the general bitterness greater. So did the fact that the Dutch, though they had not lost an inch of ground, now found themselves comparatively poor for the first time in generations. Entirely apart from the burden of war taxes and the heavy losses incurred during the French occupation, there had been a serious decay in the level of foreign trade. The English had made the most of their opportune neutrality in the years between 1674 and 1678, and they had picked up the great bulk of the Mediterranean trade. It is never easy to turn commerce back into a channel which has once been blocked. Although the merchants of the United Provinces still held a firm grip on the trade of France and of the Baltic, the fisheries and the African coast, although they were still supreme in the East Indies, their relative position was in decline. *Colbertisme* in France and the Navigation Laws in England were taking their toll. It was all too easy to blame the Prince and Fagel, the men in power, for long-term economic changes and for a post-war depression over which they had not the slightest control.

There was, then, a *milieu* of unrest and dissatisfaction in which the immediate questions of the day had to be solved. One of these was the fate of the men who had been secluded from political life during the revolution of 1672. Were they now to be restored to office, or were they to be left to cultivate their gardens for the rest of their days? The Prince's answer seems to have been to keep them in their gardens. He controlled Utrecht, Overijssel and Gelderland absolutely. Most of the towns of Holland itself were subject to his influence, since they sent him every year short lists from which he elected the magistrates. Amsterdam was the most important exception. It chose its own four burgomasters, though the *schepens* were elected by William. Zeeland was less responsive to the Prince's will, since its constitution had not been changed during the war; but he had three of the seven votes there. The real weakness in the Prince's position was that he had no control over Friesland or Groningen. Not only did these provinces preserve, like Zeeland, antique constitutions; they had in Henry Casimir of Nassau a Stadhouder of their own. In former times the two branches of the House of Nassau had worked together. In this generation there was to be no friendship. Henry Casimir wanted to be made a field-marshal, which William III would not permit. And so the latter-day Achilles sulked in his tent at Leeuwarden, welcoming those Calvinist ministers whom William had deprived of their appointments in the course of the struggle between Cocceians and Voetians. These refugees embittered still further the relations between the two cousins. Gradually, in 1679 and 1680, there emerged an alliance between Groningen, Friesland, the city of Amsterdam and the French ambassador d'Avaux, committed to the diminution of William's authority in internal affairs and the support of French interests abroad. Since the two provinces had old-fashioned constitutions, and since Henry Casimir was both young and impoverished, one may doubt how far he could have swung them towards support of the Prince of Orange even had he wished to do so. D'Avaux describes the opposition as formed by the Friesland leaders, who first united with those of Groningen and then tried to obtain the support of Amsterdam. The ambassador's own role was largely that of a cheer-leader.[1]

It was to William's advantage that most of the men of 1672, and also most of his opponents eligible for office, were old men. Many of them died off in the 1670's and most of the rest in the next decade. Thus Valkenier, the leading figure in Amsterdam, died in 1680 and as a result the Prince momentarily regained control of the city. The survivors of the party are described again and again in the pages of d'Avaux's *Négociations* as timid people of little capacity, men who would speak bravely enough in their cups but who were unable to carry out their boasts in the cold light of morning.[2] They were, furthermore, liable to succumb to William's charm whenever he chose to exercise it. Urged on by Sir William Temple and his other advisers, the Prince made a real effort in the autumn of 1678:

... nothing can be more changed than his manner of living is here since the peace, before which time he could not fall into a new *plis*. He is in perpetual consultation with the most popular of them here (and that were thought his enemies) upon all matters before they are brought into the States, or sent to the towns; and during the assembly of the States of Holland dines every day with the deputies of one town or other, all which, joined to the sense they have what a rascally peace they have made, and how true advices from the Prince they refused, has very sensibly increased his authority here, ...[3]

An open table was not the Prince's only political weapon. During the winter of 1678-79 he proposed the fortification of Naarden. It was a touchy subject, as de Witt had found in his day when he had unsuccessfully urged the same thing. Naarden was strategically important in two ways. Not only was it vital for the defence of Holland; it could, if fortified, be used to overawe Amsterdam. The city, swayed by self interest and memories of the attempted *coup d'état* of William II in 1650, opposed the plan. In the States of Holland, Coenraad van Heemskerck said that, while it might cost only fl.300,000 to build the fortifications, the day might come when Amsterdam would gladly give ten times as much not to have had them. Heemskerk soon found himself appointed ambassador to Madrid. This got him out of the way. It also served as a course of instruction. The particularism of the Dutch was notorious. Much of it was the result of ignorance. Although the Republic had very little censorship and much the best journalism of the day, it was almost impossible to form an accurate opinion of the course of events if one was not 'in the secret'. Knowledge of foreign affairs was confined to a very small group, consisting almost entirely of heads of state and their ambassadors. By sending the abler and more responsible members of the opposition off on a foreign mission, William had the immediate advantage of depriving his enemies of their leadership. And, very often, the men who went out disliking him came back his warmest supporters. The tactic was almost foolproof, since the Prince could if necessary conduct his negotiations by letter or through personal representatives. The damage that an uninformed or hostile ambassador could do to his plans was thus reduced to a minimum.

This was necessarily a long-range technique. In the short run the Prince had fewer advantages. His enemies could always point to the cost of the army and try to reduce its size. In 1679 they were blaming him for having been absent in December of 1672 when Luxembourg attacked Bodegrave and Zwammerdam. To cover up his error they claimed that William had sent an innocent Pain-et-Vin to his death as a scapegoat. They raked up the ancient story of 1619, when Prince Maurits had executed the Grand Pensionary Oldenbarnevelt, to prove the bloody methods of the House of Orange. 1650 was not forgotten, either. William was blamed particularly for the fact that in reducing the size of the army, he had let the Hollanders go and had kept the foreigners. The cost of the Prince's establishment was criticized as an extravagance for which the citizens paid.[4] This kind of whispering campaign was more dangerous in the Republic than elsewhere, since William III was very largely dependent on the support of public opinion for his authority. The Stuarts were much less so, and the remaining princes of Europe were virtually independent of the need for popular support. In the spring of 1679 some observers were so impressed by the whispering campaign that they predicted the Prince's fall. At Vienna there were even people who anticipated this event with pleasure, thinking that the Republic could not survive without the Prince and that once he was gone it must become again a dependency of Spain.[5]

It was of course true that the Republic could not survive without William III; but his position was far stronger than most of his enemies knew. In some ways his position after 1678 approximated that of his father thirty years earlier. In 1648 William II had been a young man, unable to exercise much influence after the conclusion of peace. Thirty years later William III was still a young man and he seemed to be meeting many of the same problems. But how different the positions really were! The son was a real soldier, a real hero, the Redeemer of the Fatherland. The Dutch might be tired of hearing the phrase, but they knew it was true. William III was also far more attractive to the clergy than his father had been. There were now no grubby liaisons with actresses, and if the Princess chose to go to the comedy four times a week her husband did not. Both of them gambled and the Prince sometimes drank more than he could hold; but these are venial sins. On the whole the court of William III was as pure and Christian as such things can be, and the strict lives of the Prince and Princess commanded the respect of everyone with whom they came in contact. There would be attempts to break William's hold on the affection of the *predicanten*; he was attacked for hunting on Sundays and, fantastically, for being a secret papist. None of these attempts would ever be successful. And in politics the Prince held two trump cards which his father had never possessed. The first was his place in the English succession. In 1678 this was a fairly remote prospect, but it was one which could never be forgotten. The second was the warm-hearted support of Gaspar Fagel. Historically the powers of the Grand Pensionary had been increased as a counter to those of the Stadhouder. If the two men worked together, as they did now, opposition could scarcely hope for success. A cabal of the leaders of Groningen, Friesland, and Amsterdam could, at most, block the plans of the Prince; not very often, and only with great difficulty. But the Prince could almost always veto the plans of the cabal, and he could very often get his own ideas put into practice. His political methods have been called infamous. It would be more correct to use the word to describe the Dutch constitution and particularly its unworkable requirement of a unanimous vote on the great questions of war and taxation. The Republic, like Poland, had a *liberum veto*; any town could block a decision of one province, any one province that of the States General. Like Poland, it would pay a terrible price for its liberty.

The first round of the struggle between William III and the malcontents took place in 1679. The Prince hoped to obtain an Anglo-Dutch treaty guaranteeing the peace of Nijmegen. D'Avaux opposed this and worked in his turn for a Franco-Dutch defensive alliance. His memoirs indicate that the French court felt the cabal to be strong enough to push through such a league over the opposition of the Prince.[6] This was one reason for the spiteful treatment of William by the French. The more they damaged his prestige, the easier it would be for the cabal to defeat him. Thus, when the Dutch ambassadors Odijk, Boreel, and Dijkvelt presented their credentials to Louis XIV in March 1679 their spokesman assured the King 'of the deep respect of his Highness, and that he would esteem nothing so precious as the honour of being in the good graces of your Majesty, since he is your most humble and obedient servant'.[7] Louis in his response spoke of his and his ancestors' friendship for the Republic, but he did not refer to the Prince. He showed his displeasure more sharply in June. During the war the Roman Catholic Bishop of Orange had erected a crucifix on the ruins of the castle there. In February 1679 the crucifix was thrown down by unknown hands. Without any attempt to settle the matter amicably through the Prince, Louis XIV sent orders to the intendant of Provence to have the first crucifix restored by force and a second erected in the town as a punishment.[8] Despite this, William continued to assure the King by messages to the effect that he 'had always passionately desired and still did to come into the honour of your Majesty's good graces again', and that he planned to demonstrate the sincerity of his goodwill in the next session of the States.[9] The Prince would agree to the renewal of the Franco-Dutch alliance of 1662 and help to put it through, once the Anglo-Dutch treaty of guarantee had been signed. Both Fagel and Odijk wanted the French alliance, and they were the only people to whom William listened other than Bentinck.[10] But the French did not want this. They wanted their treaty, and they wanted to prevent the signature of the English one. The struggle went on for months. In the end, d'Avaux and his friends were able to prevent the conclusion of the treaty with England, while the Prince and his friends were able to prevent the conclusion of the French treaty without the other.[11] This first round, therefore, was a draw. In the light of the relative strengths of Louis XIV and the Prince of Orange, such an outcome was by no means dishonourable to William.

In 1680, as we have seen, the diplomatic initiative passed for some months out of the hands of the French. If the Republic, England, and Spain acted together they might hope to build up a new and formidable web of alliances. But any such hope was vain. When the English agent Sir Robert Southwell reached Berlin with an offer of a defensive alliance, Frederick William's ministers gave him a flat refusal.[12] Not even the Emperor would join in, and although William himself made a tour to Celle, Hanover, and Potsdam in the autumn, he had no more success than Southwell.[13] The German courts felt that the English, and the Dutch too, were so divided that no one could count on them. They were proved right by the outcome of the parliamentary sessions of the winter and early spring. When the Whigs remained stubborn and Charles II was forced to return to the shameful policy of taking French subsidies, Louis XIV was the only beneficiary of the Whig blindness, and now he could do what he wanted.

Already the French had been making incursions into Spanish and German territory; but now there was a rapid increase in the pace of their aggressions. They moved forward in the Spanish Netherlands and occupied many areas belonging to the Duchy of Luxembourg. It was in an attempt to save one of these, the County of Chiny where he had large estates of his own, that William made his fruitless visit to England in July. In August Chiny fell, and the French promised to refer their other demands to the conference table at Courtrai. But they had no intention of abandoning violence. In September they took Strasbourg, and when their preposterous demands at Courtrai met with resistance they proceeded to blockade the town of Luxembourg. Its capture would cut off all means of communication between the Spanish Netherlands and the Empire. The Dutch, therefore, though Luxembourg was not one of their barrier towns, became very alarmed. They concluded with the Swedes a treaty of guarantee of the borders laid down at Nijmegen and van Beuninghen was dispatched to England to try to obtain a second Triple Alliance. The French had an easy counter to this move. They offered to add a million to the subsidy for 1682 if the English acquiesced in their taking Luxembourg. The King and Hyde grumbled, but they took the money.[14] If the Dutch were less complacent, the rays of *le roi soleil* were strong enough to give them a painful sunburn. William's estates in the County of Chiny, St Vith and Vianden, were confiscated when he refused to do homage for them and were turned over to the Maréchal d'Humières. The French tariff was suddenly, and quite illegally, raised to the punitive level of 1667.[15] On 8 November d'Avaux warned the States General that the original Triple Alliance had led to the war of 1672, and that a second could only have consequences of the same nature: the present conduct of the Dutch would plunge them into a new war which might be more injurious than the last.[16] The Dutch reacted to this insolence in manly fashion. Not only was the Swedish treaty completed and ratified; the States General also agreed to increase their army by 12,000 men.

These were brave steps, but they could not be effective by themselves. Of the other powers, England was the most curious in its conduct. As he grew older, Charles II became ever more fascinated by the advantages of following two contradictory policies at once. It is always difficult and often impossible to discover which of the two had his real support. Despite the fact that he had taken French money in return for not summoning Parliament for three years, and agreed to take more in return for not opposing the seizure of Luxembourg, he now promised to join the league of guarantee provided that the 'most considerable' of the German princes did so first. This was explained as meaning Denmark, Brandenburg, Sweden, Saxony, and the House of Brunswick.[17] Since the first two were in the French camp the offer was not very impressive, but the Dutch were encouraged. The English government also agreed to the joint presentation, with the Dutch, of a memorial to Louis XIV about the blockade of Luxembourg. If the responses was unsatisfactory, Charles II undertook to summon a new Parliament.[18] The French, bewildered, did not know what to make of this change of front. Barillon continued to think that Charles was basically pro-French, but he reported that the King was so untrustworthy and his administration so deplorably weak that anything might happen.[19] Louis XIV found it prudent to make some concessions. He agreed to Charles's demand that provisions be allowed into the blockaded city.[20] The news that the King of England was taking steps to live within his income was ominous for him, as it was ominous for the English opposition; if Charles were successful, both the Whigs and the French would lose much of their power.

Eventually Charles discovered that he did not dare to summon a new Parliament. When the French offered to give up all their other pretensions against the Spanish in return for the cession of Luxembourg, the King and his brother were delighted. As James put it, 'I confess I am of those that thinke the offers made by the French better than a war, in the condition things are in. I do not know what condition your country is in, but, as for ours, to engage now into a war and to call a Parliament would endanger the Monarky and the absolute ruine of our family; ...'[21] William could not agree. He kept on urging that his uncle be driven to support the good cause if he would not do so voluntarily. He blamed van Beuninghen for not bullying Charles. Anything less than victory meant that van Beuninghen was not fighting hard enough. William himself was certainly fighting hard. For all that the French knew, he might eventually persuade the States General to send 8,000 men to aid the Spanish. He did persuade them to vote on 23 March a strong memorial against the French.[22] At the same time the Spanish prepared to deliver an ultimatum to Charles II: trade between England and Spain would be suspended and the Spanish ambassador withdrawn until a Parliament should sit.[23] This was a weaker form of the threat that had forced England out of the war in 1674. The risk that it might work a second time was too great. Louis XIV suddenly ordered that the blockade of Luxembourg be raised. His troops were withdrawn, and he offered to submit all his differences with the Spanish to English arbitration.

For the moment Luxembourg was safe. There remained the question of

Strasbourg, seized at the end of the previous September. William of Orange and his friend Waldeck held to the curiously old-fashioned idea that the treaty of Nijmegen ought to be maintained. Strasbourg, therefore, must be restored to the Empire. The Prince could not persuade the Dutch to undertake the task of liberation alone. It was one in which those most closely involved ought to take the first step. Once the Empire did so the Dutch might help them, but Leopold must act first.[24] The Emperor was so frightened at the thought of appearing the aggressor – and, perhaps, so delighted that Strasbourg was now in Catholic hands – that he would do nothing. Strasbourg and its magnificent geese remained French. The initiative passed out of the hands of the allies, and the French now had leisure to return to their favourite game of tormenting the Prince of Orange. His efforts to secure peace on decent terms were pictured as warmongering. Any French aggression was, to their way of thinking, peaceful; any resistance, an act of war. When William was accused of being a warmonger, he replied that both he and the Spanish wanted nothing but peace; but it must not be a peace dictated by a conqueror with his foot on the neck of the vanquished.[25] Mere words could not hurt the Prince. The French next turned to a campaign of public humiliations. William's estates under their control were attached for the payment of a baseless claim of the Prince of Isenghien. In August d'Avaux was instructed to demand the same honours as ambassador that were given to William III as Stadhouder and Captain-General. Whenever d'Avaux came to require an audience of the States General he must go through the Stadhouder's Gate and be greeted, with beating of drums, by a guard of honour presenting arms. Naturally enough this preposterous request was refused.[26] But at that very moment the French were making more progress at Orange. On 15 August the Principality was occupied by dragoons under the command of M. de Montanegues, Lieutenant-General of Languedoc. While they were supervising the destruction of the walls of the town, the French troops had plenty of time in which to loot the houses of the old and to rape the young.[27]

It was this final insult to his position as a sovereign prince that converted William III from an intellectual to an emotional enemy of French expansion. He had been resisting that expansion for a decade; but from now on his opposition was inflamed by a personal hatred of the leaders of the French government. Though he lived very simply, the Prince was always careful to secure the respect due to his station. By attacking him at his most sensitive point, on the issue of his right to be considered a sovereign prince, the French made a mistake which was to cost them the domination of Europe. But it would be neither fair nor accurate to picture the course of William's later career as a mere vendetta or as the result of a boundless ambition. The Prince cared simply nothing about money. He cared more about status, but here he was merely attempting to defend his inheritance. No one could expect him to surrender the rank which was his birthright. And on the wider issues, it must be remembered that the policies of Louis XIV underwent a fundamental change in 1681 and 1682. It was by an edict of 14 June, 1681 that the period of religious persecution was begun in earnest. The taking of the Protestant city of Strasbourg in September was an act of religious as well as of political aggression. So too was the *dragonnade* of Orange. Huguenot children had been crossing the border to attend the Calvinist academy there, and one of the French demands was that their subjects should not be allowed to attend the school. The occupation of Orange came when the Consuls agreed, but not in a sufficiently submissive form, to the expulsion of the French scholars from their territories. It is therefore in 1681 and 1682 that the career of Louis XIV ceased to be merely one of political expansion and became a crime against the moral order, a sin. As it happened, William was not only a devout Protestant but also one of the few men of his age who had a real grasp of the principles of toleration. His lawyers were Catholics, his *maitre-d'hotel* a Jew. So too were Machado and Pereira, the Dutch army bread contractors and, more embarrassingly, Franciscus van Schoonenburg, the Prince's personal agent at Madrid. The Prince's resistance to the designs of France had a firm moral basis as well as a personal one.

However disastrous the French occupation of Orange was to be for them in the long run, it had one immediate advantage in the diplomatic sphere. The Stuarts acquiesced in the seizure; indeed, they were secretly pleased that the Prince had been so humiliated. William's relations with his uncles became very strained. It might not be possible to explain to them that family loyalty made demands on the King and the Duke as well as on the Prince; but at least he could take out his anger on Lord Hyde, the chief minister. When Hyde's nephew Cornbury, a youth of twenty, visited William's court in October, he was refused a room and had to stay at an inn. And though he was asked to sit next to the Prince at dinner, William did not speak to him once during the entire meal. The unfortunate youth was so wounded that he could not keep the tears out of his eyes.[28] The Grand Pensionary's letters to van Beuninghen at London were equally savage.

I know well that the English ministers ... would sacrifice both us and the welfare of all Christendom, if they might only remain in repose; and if only our own welfare were not endangered, I would not blame them. But I shall never advise that we should abandon everything we hold dear for the benefit of the English ministers. They have not deserved it of us, and if Europe falls into disorder ... they and no one else will have been responsible.[29]

William persisted in advising the Spanish to reject English arbitration, and to demand instead a general congress at which all the problems of Europe could be solved at once. Obviously such a congress had a better chance of obtaining decent terms from the French than did separate negotiations. If the French aggressions in the Spanish Netherlands were settled by arbitration, those against Germany at the Imperial diet, and those against Italy politely tolerated, France would win too much.

By the end of 1682 van Beuninghen, hitherto one of the Prince's chief allies, had come to the conclusion that Charles would never call a Parliament. The King, he wrote, had recently told the Spanish ambassador Don Pedro Ronquillo that he would not dare summon one even if the French were about to invade the British Isles. In such a case he would have to defend himself with the means that were available without summoning the legislature.[30] In the circumstances, van Beuninghen concluded that the only thing to do was to submit to the French terms. The attitude of Brandenburg was hostile, the conduct of the imperialists weaker than ever because of the threatening attitude of the Turk. For some time to come the Habsburgs would be fully occupied in the east. Since the four Rhenish electorates were also too weak and too frightened to do anything, the Dutch must make the best of a bad bargain and hope for better days to come. The Prince of Orange was more stubborn. He was morally committed to support the Spanish because he had advised them to reject English arbitration. He was also far more sensitive than van Beuninghen to the religious persecutions of the French, and of course he was outraged by their personal attacks on himself. Finally, he was encouraged by the appointment of a new and congenial Governor of the Spanish Netherlands. His relations with Parma had been so strained that Mary's long-desired visit to Brussels had to be postponed until after Parma's recall. With the appointment of the new Governor, the Marquis of Grana, she was at last able to make the trip.

Her husband continued the struggle for a decent peace for a year-and-a-half after he was abandoned by van Beuninghen. The odds became steadily worse. In March 1683 the French proposed a marriage between Princess Anne and Prince George of Denmark.[31] George was a Protestant, and a King's brother, but these were his only advantages. He was very poor, so the English would have to provide an establishment for the couple. Worse, his country was notoriously pro-French and it was obvious that the match was made no nearer to heaven than Versailles. There could hardly have been found a more obnoxious brother-in-law for William III. Presumably William did not know that the Danes tried to have him excluded from the succession as part of the marriage settlement.[32] But he could not be ignorant of the French cast of the marriage, and there were some aspects of it which were peculiarly irritating. There was a risk that George might set himself up as the leader of the Protestant party, in competition with William of Orange. It took some time before the Dane could demonstrate his complete insignificance in the world of politics. Even when he had done so, there remained two personal matters that were most annoying. The Prince of Denmark deserved and was given precedence over William III at the English court. Secondly, Anne was given a generous establishment at a time when the English would not even make a real effort to obtain the restoration of the Principality of Orange. Beyond her contemptible dowry, Mary did not receive a penny from English sources until 1689. Even though she did not need the money, the slight rankled.

Possibly in an attempt to break the marriage, or more probably because of the threatening European situation, William asked permission to visit England.[33] When this was refused, he sent Bentinck over as a substitute. Though d'Avaux claimed that Bentinck went over to offer the Electoral Prince of Brandenburg as a substitute for George of Denmark, his real task was to present a compliment to the bridegroom.[34] He was also to congratulate the King and the Duke on their escape from the Rye House assassins, and to sound them on public issues as well. The response was discouraging. The Stuarts were convinced that Strasbourg and Luxembourg must both be sacrificed to obtain peace, particularly because the Turkish army had now undertaken the siege of Vienna. It was not until September that the siege was raised, and although the Christians were to win victory after victory over the infidel in the years to come, these very successes meant that there were no armies to spare for the defence of the western frontier.

Since Habsburg assistance could not be expected, William had practically forced the Governor of the Spanish Netherlands to hire Hanoverian troops. There were also hopes of a Swedish contingent. But a Swedish army on German soil meant war in the north, and in the summer of 1683 such a war seemed quite likely. In the end William did not obtain assistance from Sweden, and he was actually obliged to send a fleet to the Baltic to protect that crown from attack by Denmark and Brandenburg. The squadron was successful on the main point, that of preventing the outbreak of hostilities. Unluckily it had to stay in the Baltic too late in the year for safety and was severely damaged by an early winter storm. There were many casualties, and William was considered responsible.

Meanwhile the Prince was also being attacked inside the Republic on other grounds. Ever since October 1682 he had been asking for 16,000 more men for the army. He had failed to get authorization for them, although he had offered to do without his salary in order to help with the expense.[35] His eagerness seemed to prove the charge that he was a warmonger, while his dispatch of the fleet to the Baltic without proper authorization was felt to be unconstitutional. Then in September the situation in the Spanish Netherlands became critical. At the beginning of the month the Spanish demanded the 8,000 men which, in certain circumstances, should be sent to their aid under the terms of the treaty of 1673. Amsterdam and one or two other towns in the States of Holland refused to agree to their dispatch; but Fagel by a majority vote persuaded the States General to send them anyway. Here was a second violation of the constitution. And when the Prince raised the question of the 16,000 men once more at the end of the month, he was simply throwing kerosene on an open fire. At the beginning of November Amsterdam decided that she would not support the recruitment of the men, and also that the Dutch ought to advise the Spanish to make peace with the French on the best terms that could be got.[36] They could hardly be good ones. French troops had occupied most of the open country of the Spanish Netherlands and, in addition, taken Courtrai and then Dixmude. On 5 November d'Avaux presented a memorial to the States General outlining five alternative solutions to the problem. The French had finally given up the idea of English arbitration. By the terms of the memorial the Spanish could have peace by the surrender of Luxembourg or, if she wished, by the cession of Courtrai, Dixmude, Beaumont, Bouvines and the chatellany of Ath. The three other alternatives, which concerned the soil of Spain itself and were therefore totally unacceptable, need not detain us. One of the five must be selected by the Spanish by the end of the year.

Amsterdam still refused to agree to the expansion of the army, and she was clearly in favour of the cession of Luxembourg. In the States of Holland only Delft stood with her. Constitutionally there must be a unanimous vote, constitutionally there was only one possible way to obtain it. This was to send to the recalcitrant town a deputation which would remain, eating and drinking at the town's expense, as long as necessary. Obviously a constitution as grotesque as this cannot deserve much respect from the men who have to run the country from day to day. But William III had to go through the motions and on 15 November he and twenty-two others took on their solemn obligation of swilling their way through the fortunes of the richest city in the world. The farce lasted for six days before the Prince, perhaps to the disappointment of those of his colleagues who were still hungry, rode away without saying goodbye to the burgomasters. The deputation had solved nothing. It merely served to make both sides angrier than before. During the deputation Fagel made the mistake of threatening the ruling oligarchy with a repetition of the class warfare of 1578. At that time William the Silent and the common people of the city had overthrown the leaders of the town and put in others.[37] William III had of course done precisely the same himself in 1672 when he came to power on the shoulders of the mob. But threats and dates were weapons which two could use. If Fagel recalled 1578 the Amsterdammers could recall 1619, 1650, and their own version of what had happened in 1672. They doubled the town watch and gave van Beuninghen a bodyguard. The first step had reference to William II's attempt on the city in 1650, the second to the Prince's own supposed complicity in the murder of the de Witts. This was an article of faith with the anti-Williamite party, and it received embarrassing corroboration in March 1684 when one of the accomplices in the atrocity, Joan van Banckem, escaped from prison in The Hague and made his way to Amsterdam, where he tried to speak to van Beuninghen or, perhaps, to kill him. He was speedily recaptured and returned to prison. There is no certainty that he intended to attack van Beuninghen, and no evidence whatever to connect his escape with William or any of his followers.[38] William III was not the kind of man his father had been, but it was to the advantage of the Amsterdam leaders to pretend that he was.

In December the Spanish in their agony declared war on France, in the hope of forcing the English and Dutch to come to their aid. It did them no good. Amsterdam was more determined than ever to avoid becoming involved, and she rallied to her side some of the towns of Holland, which did not like William's lack of respect for the rule of unanimity. The Prince in his turn accused the city of being in secret communication with d'Avaux, which was in its turn a constitutional irregularity. To prove it, William had the courier carrying d'Avaux's dispatch of 9 January 1684 robbed; or, according to the Prince's account, the Governor of the Spanish Netherlands stole the letter and then turned it over to him. One may prefer to believe that Grana was the actual thief, but it does not make very much difference. On 16 February, when the dispatch had been deciphered the Prince entered the States of Holland and demanded that two deputies of Amsterdam, Hooft and Hop, be sent from the room. Fagel then read the incriminating letter. Although the two deputies managed to force their way into the chamber, they could not prevent the States from voting to seal up their city's papers. Each town maintained a building in The Hague to house its deputies and papers, among which would be secret correspondence between the deputies and the town fathers. In this case a search would have indicated the exact extent of Amsterdam's negotiations with d'Avaux. Violence did William no good. Already he had outraged his opponents by forcing the authorization for the 16,000 men through the States of Holland on 31 January by a majority vote, not a unanimous one. The sealing of the papers simply made Amsterdam more angry rather than frightened. It is, however, somewhat harsh to say, as certain critics have said, that he would have been more prudent to have murdered Hooft and Hop.[39] William's enemies would like to make him out an assassin in the case of the de Witts and of van Beuninghen; yet they accuse him of stupidity in not murdering Hooft and Hop. They can hardly have it both ways. Certainly the Prince was unwise to fight so hard in 1683 and 1684. It is quite clear that he considered the allies to be a row of skittles; if only he could knock one of them over the whole row, including England and even perhaps Brandenburg, would go down too. He was wrong, or at least beaten, in 1684. But the Prince had clear ideas of the limits of party strife. He never sent his opponents to Louvestein, nor did he have the 'wisdom' to assassinate them.

Meanwhile the Prince had assembled a Congress of the allies at The Hague, consisting of men representing the Emperor, the Kings of Spain and Sweden, the Electors of Bavaria and Saxony, the Princes of Brunswick and the circles of Franconia and the Upper Rhine. In military terms the group was not very impressive, and the Congress was accused of trying to usurp the functions of the Imperial diet. The representatives met in secret with delegates from the States General, but Friesland and Groningen did not participate. This made the Congress rather a hollow reed, since anything done by the Dutch – the only strong party – would be illegal if approved in the States General by five votes to two. It was strong enough to persuade Louis XIV to offer, as he did through d'Avaux's memorial of 17 February, a truce for twenty years. The French would of course keep most of their territorial gains made since 1678 for the duration of the truce. Their offer was welcome to Amsterdam and also to England and Brandenburg, which felt that nothing better could be achieved without a general war. At the same time the French made their offer of a truce more attractive by undertaking the siege of Luxembourg, and by threatening the Dutch with the confiscation of their merchant vessels and immediate war if they came to the aid of the Spanish. Luxembourg fell in the early days of June, and the Dutch, despite all that William could do, signed the awkwardly named Treaty of Truce with the French on 29 June. The Empire and Spain signed on 20 August. If William had the satisfaction of seeing that both in the States of Holland and in the States General the Treaty was irregularly carried through by a majority vote, that was almost the only consolation available in the greatest defeat of his political career. He had been beaten, as in 1678, by a combination of Amsterdam with the French. Once again he had been forced to watch the Republic abandon its allies, which was dangerous for the future, and accept a peace dictated by the French, which was wicked. True, it was a truce and not a definitive peace; but that was only a technicality. The system of alliances had failed again. Repeated defeats, and the Spanish could not stand many more of them, would make the states of Europe wary of joining an alliance. And in 1684, unlike 1678, William's personal position was in some danger. Amsterdam might be bent on revenge; the French certainly were. And the Stuarts, who had supported him in 1678, were now among his worst enemies. After the suppression of the Rye House plot the English court had become stronger and more autocratic than ever. William's earlier friendship with the Whigs made him suspect, and the refuge which some of the conspirators found in the Republic after 1683 made him appear an accomplice. Just before the Treaty of Truce was signed, the Prince had gone to take command of the army. The English court was horrified at the prospect that he might force on a war all by himself. But the court was more than horrified at the news that the Prince had received Lord Brandon and the Duke of Monmouth while he was in the field, and that he had forced the English regiments against their will to give Monmouth military honours. Both were members of the conspiracy. By flaunting his hospitality to them, William was giving aid and comfort to the Whigs, denying that there had been a conspiracy at all. If Amsterdam and the French undertook to revenge themselves on William, they might now expect the Stuarts to be passive spectators.

Chapter 15

HEIR PRESUMPTIVE

THE long struggle was over. Luxembourg was gone, the alliance disrupted. Could it ever be rebuilt? Once again the Dutch had abandoned their allies to make a separate peace. Their diplomatic isolation was now almost complete; and who could trust them again? How could anyone join the Dutch after they had betrayed their friends once at Nijmegen and again by the Treaty of Truce? Such was the attitude of the Prince of Orange, who referred to the Treaty in public and in his letters as 'infamous'. The term did not increase his popularity.[1] But it was justified, and so were the Prince's fears for the safety of the Republic in its isolation. The French glutton was sated for the moment. No one could tell when he would demand another meal; but sooner or later he would assuredly become hungry. If he chose to consume the Dutch Republic, as he had tried to do in 1672, Louis XIV might now find no one to oppose him. Never since the days of de Witt had the Republic had so few friends.

Rarely, indeed, had the Prince himself had so few friends. Immediately after the news of the signing of the Treaty reached him, he left the army and retired to Dieren with the Duke of Monmouth. His enemies were jubilant over their victory. Not only had they carried through the Treaty itself, despite all that the Prince had been able to do to them. They had been able to exclude from the Treaty any reference to the protection of the interests of the Prince of Orange. Their success had been great, but it made them over-confident. They spoke of removing Fagel from his place as Grand Pensionary. They would make the Prince account for the contributions taken by the army in the last war. He had never submitted a formal accounting, and his enemies hoped that it would be embarrassing for him to do so. The Prince's great authority in the three provinces of Utrecht, Gelderland, and Overijssel was to be reduced by restoring their ancient constitutions. His military authority was to be limited by cutting down the size of the army and by demanding for the States the right to name officers. With this power, his enemies might be able to remove from the Court both Waldeck, who was especially hated by the people of Amsterdam, and perhaps Bentinck as well.[2] Another way of limiting the Prince's power over the army would be to secure the withdrawal of the six British regiments, a plan which was proposed slightly later. These were brave ideas. They excited the burghers of Amsterdam and the French ambassador the whole summer. Nothing was to come of these ambitious plans. In making them, the Amsterdammers forgot that William was far greater in defeat than in victory. Often, in politics as in war, the Prince was at his most dangerous just after having lost a battle.

Not everyone in Amsterdam wished to continue the struggle with William III. Van Beuninghen, particularly, felt that further discord would benefit only the French. The other Amsterdam leaders might be more pugnacious, but they were in a weak position. On the peace issue the city could be sure of general support. But on any other topic Amsterdam might well be opposed by the other towns of Holland. Only with the help of the Prince could the city get its way on a commercial issue. At this time, as it happened, Amsterdam wanted to increase the strength of the navy, which had been allowed to fall into disrepair. One way to pay for it was by an increase of one-third in the rates of the tariff. Amsterdam felt that the present tariff was unfair in its incidence. If the unfair rates were raised by a third, the city would suffer real damage. And so, in order to get some relief on the tariff, the city fathers decided to forego the pleasure of crushing the Prince of Orange. Soon after the Prince arrived at Dieren, van Beuninghen sent one Dr Marechal to him with proposals for a reconciliation.³ The Prince seemed pleased and sent Marechal back with an encouraging message. After this exchange detailed negotiations were begun between Witsen, one of the Amsterdam burgomasters, and Fagel. The first question to be solved was that of the size of the army. If the new recruits could be kept on until the end of the year the Austrians might be able to hire them for the year 1685. Actually it proved impossible to keep recruits in Dutch pay beyond the end of October, or for the Imperialists to engage them afterwards. The real issue, however, was not what to do with the recruits but what to do about the strength of the main Dutch army. Was it to return to the level of 1681, as William wished, or was it to be reduced to the still smaller level of 1650? The Prince refused to consider any reduction below the strength of 1681, or to agree to the dismissal of Waldeck from his place. In the end, he was to have his way.

Although the initiative for the reconciliation came from van Beuninghen the burgomaster himself was to have no share in the new harmony. His actions had been too independent for him ever to regain membership in the Orange party. By now the Prince hated him personally, and William was to exult in a thoroughly unpleasant way as one tragedy after another darkened the last years of van Beuninghen's life. By 1684 he was already eccentric. In the next few years he married a woman of poor reputation and lost first his fortune and then his mind. It is, however, nonsense to insinuate that the Prince drove van Beuninghen mad. Yet even if there had not been this personal element between the two men, it would not have been possible to readmit the lost sheep to the fold. Despite his great powers and his undoubted patriotism, by 1684 van Beuninghen was so eccentric that no one could trust him, no one could know what he might do next. He was, therefore, soon abandoned by all men. At the conclusion of the Truce he was reigning burgomaster of Amsterdam and one of the most important men in Europe. Within two years he had lost all his offices and was reduced to the level of a private citizen. A similar fate awaited other renegades from the Orange Party. The Prince treated his political supporters as he treated his soldiers in the field. He wanted obedience and no questions. While he could recognize merit in an open enemy, William loathed desertion as he loathed cowardice. Had the Orange party stood together, the Truce would never have been voted in the States General. The Prince was determined to make examples of the renegades. In August Johan Strick and eight others were abruptly removed from the magistracy of Utrecht, with no regard for a generation of service to the Orange cause.[4] This was not a hard task, since William had exceptional powers in Utrecht. It was much more difficult to discipline Arend Muys van Holy of Dordrecht.

Muys van Holy, like Strick and van Beuninghen, was a long-time supporter of the Orange cause who had defected on the single issue of the Truce. His power in Dordrecht was very great, and it is perhaps surprising that the Prince chose to fight him at this particular time. Muys van Holy was a particular friend of Fagel, as van Beuninghen incidentally was the particular friend of Amerongen. The pressures on the Prince not to discipline either man must have been strong. But William was determined to be master in his own house, even if this meant endangering the military budget for the coming year and a renewal of the war with Amsterdam. Clearly the Prince felt that he had his back to the wall, that having lost on the question of the Truce he was not in any position to make further concessions. The corporation of Dordrecht consisted of forty persons. Each year the gilds nominated twenty-four men, from whom the Prince of Orange elected eight as new members of the corporation. These eight, with their thirty-two colleagues, had the right of choosing the burgomasters of the town. Before the gilds had made their nominations they had, as it happened, been entertained and treated by Muys van Holy and urged to select men who would support him. The Prince chose to call this bribery and corruption. He refused to elect the new members of the corporation before investigating the honesty of the nominations, delegating this task to the Court of Holland.

If the nominations at Dordrecht had been procured corruptly, the means used were those common to Dutch politics of that day. Every town in Holland was the scene of similar treatment. If the Prince could call every kind of electioneering corruption, then he could change the nominations as he chose and make sure that they were always favourable to the Orange cause. On the other hand Dordrecht put itself in the wrong by denying that the Stadhouder had the right to investigate any list of candidates. No matter what irregularities had been committed, according to the men of Dordrecht, the Prince was required to accept the nomination given him and select eight from the list – apparently whether the nominees were legally qualified or not. The argument continued throughout the winter. When the Prince sent representatives of the Court of Holland to Dordrecht to investigate the irregularities, the local magistrates twice were able to prevent them from securing any testimony. The party of Muys van Holy demanded a special session of the States of Holland in which they denied the competence of the Prince and of the Court. Amsterdam and some other towns supported Muys van Holy, but in vain. The Prince was determined to establish his authority. The sheriff of Dordrecht, who had supported the magistrates against the Court of Holland, was removed from his place. Representatives of the Court went to Dordrecht once more and, with some difficulty, persuaded the gilds to proceed to a second nomination, from which the Prince chose the required eight men. These, naturally enough, were members of the Halewijn faction rather than that of Muys van Holy. For a while it seemed that there would be further trouble. But the corporation of the town contented itself with a protest and permitted the Halewijn group to be present at its sessions. There was no trouble with the nominations of the following year; and at that time, by a single vote, Muys van Holy lost his place as burgomaster. William and the two Halewijn brothers were completely victorious.[5] There was also a similar incident at Leyden, where the nominations included one candidate not of age and another who, born in the East Indies, was not even a citizen. The Leyden nominations were so clearly irregular than the Prince won his case there much more easily than at Dordrecht.

By such means William III re-established his authority over the Orange party. It was never to desert him again. The Prince, there can be no doubt, played a rough game of politics. It was no rougher than the game played by his enemies, and it was both milder and far cleverer than the game played by de Witt, William II, or Prince Maurice. There were no judicial murders, no military attacks on Amsterdam, in the lifetime of William III. Orangists believed firmly that de Witt had committed judicial murders, and men of all parties deplored the methods of the earlier Princes of Orange. Rough though he was, William III brought a new age of moderation to Dutch politics. Later he would do the same in England. But now, in 1684, he could not change the rules of the English game. They were still set by his uncles.

The Prince's stubbornness in defeat made his relations with the English court even worse than before. While at Brussels, and again later in the

Republic itself, William had entertained Monmouth and Lord Brandon with marked favour. The English regiments had been forced, against the wishes of some officers, to give Monmouth military honours at a review. This was bad enough. Brandon was even more closely implicated than Monmouth in the Rye House plot, and only a lack of evidence had saved his life.[6] Worst of all, the rumour was that the Prince had entertained the young Ireton, who was not only the son of one prominent regicide but a grandson of Oliver Cromwell. William, when reproached with this, denied that he had ever consciously seen Ireton in his life.[7] For the rest he defended his conduct and continued to treat Monmouth with exceptional regard, despite the remonstrances of the King and of the Duke of York. Neither James's letters to the Prince and to the Princess, nor Charles's complaints to the Dutch ambassador had any effect. William took Monmouth to Dieren for a hunting trip and remained there with his guest for the rest of the summer. Adding insult to injury, the Prince and his servants gave out a story that the King was not really angry with Monmouth but must pretend to be, so as to keep up appearances.

The Prince's conduct was deeply irritating to Charles in itself; and it had wide implications. During the spring Charles had recalled the Admiralty Commission and had made the Duke of York in fact, though he could not legally appoint him by name, Lord High Admiral. Rochester, the former Viscount Hyde, was known to be the Duke's creature. These two, with their allies the Duchess of Portsmouth and Sunderland, seemed to engross the monarchy. By entertaining Monmouth so deliberately, and by refusing to listen to the King's complaints, William indicated to the world that the King of England was a cipher 'governed absolutely by the faction of the Duke of York'.[8] No Stuart cared to admit that he was governed by a favourite. Yet William emphasized his point when he complained of the impertinence of Chudleigh, the English representative at The Hague. Chudleigh had delayed to deliver a message saying that the reception of Monmouth would be offensive, until after William had met the Duke at Brussels. Once the two had met, William refused to alter his treatment of Monmouth, and Chudleigh had been so unwise as to argue. The Prince complained of the ambassador's conduct. He made things worse by writing, not to his uncles or to a Secretary of State, but to his friend Halifax. This made the whole affair a party matter. To a certain extent William embarrassed the King. Charles felt obliged to demonstrate that he was still independent. He appointed two new Treasury Commissioners to fill up that board, one of them a cousin of Halifax.[9] Rochester as First Lord was so humiliated at the appointment of the two men, who could be nothing other than spies, that he considered resigning. His wife succeeded in soothing his temper for the moment. Shortly afterwards, however, he was

'kicked upstairs' to the dignified office of Lord President. This was not only
a much less powerful place than that of First Lord of the Treasury, but also a
much worse paid one. The Halifax faction seemed to be gaining favour at the
expense of James's friends.

Charles was now personally angry with the Prince for embarrassing him.
He had recalled Chudleigh for consultations after the alleged impertinence.
There were many versions of the story. According to Chudleigh, the Prince
had put himself in the wrong by locking the gates of Honselaarsdijk against
the ambassador's carriage. Another account was that William had threatened
to cane Chudleigh. For a short time the King seemed to control his temper.
But when he saw William continue to entertain Monmouth, when he was
told that Monmouth was recommending and William appointing unsuitable
persons to places in the English regiments, his anger broke out. Chudleigh
was ordered to return to The Hague and to cut the Prince of Orange. He was
neither to speak to the Prince nor to pay him any kind of respect. Van Citters
reported that the fire of the King's anger had blazed up again unbelievably,
and that almost everyone at court was busy stoking it. People went so far as
to recommend the recall of the English regiments before they became so
infected with sedition as to be worthless to the monarchy.[10] The stokers
continued to add fuel to the flame. Sunderland pretended to believe that the
Prince and Monmouth had a formed design to stir up trouble in England and
to cause a rebellion when they might.[11] Chudleigh for his part did his work
with great thoroughness. Not only did he carry out his orders to the letter,
he also communicated them to all the other diplomats accredited to The
Hague.[12] By the end of October Charles himself was professing to believe
that William had been in the secret of the Rye House plot, and that his treatment of Monmouth could only be explained on the basis that the Prince had
other projects in store regarding England.[13] William denied that Monmouth
had recommended any officers to him, or that he could in the nature of things
have any joint projects with the King's son; but his protestations were not
believed.[14] The King might accept William's statement that Monmouth had
not recommended any officers. Still, there were several of them in the English
regiments whom Charles could not trust. And no excuse or denial could be
made about the military honours afforded Monmouth. They had been given
publicly and in the face of all the world.[15] Although the Prince wrote another
submissive letter to the King in the middle of December[16] it was badly
received. Charles looked on the letter as an attempt to put him in the wrong,
rather than as an apology.[17] He refused to revoke or modify his orders to
Chudleigh. Indeed, he planned to replace the unhappy ambassador by Bevil
Skelton, largely because the appointment would be personally offensive to the
Prince. Skelton, too, would have orders not to correspond with William III.

Barillon, for one, thought that Skelton's appointment had an even more sinister motive behind it. It was, he thought, intended to make William lose his temper completely and drive him to perform some irregular deed, thus giving Charles a pretext for the recall of the regiments. Sunderland felt that their recall was an essential step towards crushing faction in England. If the regiments remained in Holland the opposition could always count on their availability for use against the King in case of civil war.[18]

While, publicly, relations between the King and his nephew remained broken, some contact was kept in private. Van Citters did all he could to mend the breach. We have seen that William himself wrote two ineffectual letters to Charles. He continued his regular correspondence with James, whose replies – though cold – were much more polite than the comments of the King.[19] James also appears to have maintained an affectionate correspondence with his daughter. The inevitable Sir Gabriel Silvius crossed the North Sea again and again during the last months of 1684, ostensibly without a commission from either party, trying to work out some kind of compromise. In England, Silvius grossly exaggerated the weakness of William's position in an attempt to gain sympathy for him. Fagel, he said, might be forced to resign. The Prince might not be able to prevent the conclusion of an offensive and defensive alliance between France and the States General.[20] D'Avaux was in fact trying to obtain such an alliance, and during August he visited Amsterdam in the attempt. His reception, though outwardly brilliant, was so unpromising that he later denied having ever proposed an alliance.[21] The activities of Silvius were mysterious and not too productive, although d'Avaux took him far more seriously than did Barillon. If d'Avaux's account is correct, Silvius while in Holland tried to persuade the Prince to bow before the storm.[22] He could not bend the Prince's will. In one respect, however, the work of Silvius, van Citters, and of van Beuninghen inside Amsterdam, was successful. If they could not effect an accommodation between Charles II and William III they did succeed in persuading the Dutch people that such an accommodation was about to take place. This was extremely important. Any rumour of this kind raised the stock of the Prince and increased his authority. The rumour seemed to have at least a small measure of truth in it because William had, at long last, parted from the Duke of Monmouth. With Monmouth gone there was a chance of a full reconciliation. The Prince, however, was extremely stubborn. In his letter of 15 December to the King, he had refused to admit that he was at fault in any way. When van Citters informed him of the ill reception of the letter, he replied stiffly:

I am very sorry that his Majesty takes my letter so ill; I shall never make any difficulty over making every submission to the King which he shall ask for, or over asking his pardon for any offence which he may have taken; but to admit guilt when I am sure I have not acted badly is a thing that cannot be asked of me or of any honourable man, and something to which I shall never be brought.[23]

All the work of the peacemakers was shattered by the obstinacy of the Prince. And worse was to come. At the beginning of January Monmouth returned uninvited to The Hague and was received, if that be possible, with more *éclat* than ever before. He dined almost daily with the Princess. Mary, who rarely went outdoors and still more rarely took any exercise, went on long walks with her cousin. Tying up her skirts, she even went skating with him. Balls and theatre parties were held for the Duke's entertainment. The Prince himself danced with his wife's ladies-in-waiting, while Monmouth danced with the Princess. On the anniversary of the death of Charles I, which all good Stuarts kept as a day of solemn fast, they were reported to have gone to a comedy. For a short time the Prince's court was as gay as it had been in his grandfather's time half a century before. But not for long. Monmouth's return infuriated the English. In December, before the exile had returned to The Hague, William's supporters had felt the accommodation to be fairly well advanced. They had even suggested that the Prince should try his luck in a secret visit to London, although they pointed out the risks involved.[24] Monmouth's reception killed the plan. Rumours were spread at The Hague of a possible visit to England, but the King became more and more determined to prevent one. Barillon wrote to his master on 2/12 February[25] that Charles had decided not to grant William permission to visit England. If he should dare to come without asking permission, the King would oblige him to leave without seeing him.

As he continued his letter, Barillon broke off to report that Charles II had had a stroke. Four days later he was dead.

The accession of James II was profoundly peaceful. After all the struggles of the past seven years, opposition might well have been expected. Monmouth and many other observers thought that the English would never accept a popish king.[26] Louis XIV shared the same notion. As soon as he heard of the illness of Charles II he assembled letters of change for half a million livres and sent them to Barillon, with instructions to make the money available to James in case of need.[27] There was no need for the money. The English accepted James II with scarcely a murmur. His going publicly to Mass two days after his accession caused some comment, but not very much. His retention of Halifax and the other ministers of his brother reassured the people. They were delighted with the adroit and moderate speech which the new King made to his Privy Council, which was soon printed and distributed throughout the country. It appeared that in England, at any rate, the death of Charles II made little difference and that it might even lead to an improvement in the general situation.

In Holland the King's passing made a greater change. The Princess of Orange was now heiress presumptive to the English throne. Her new position was reflected in greater ceremony at her court. She began to be served by kneeling pages for the first time.[28] The new ceremonies might well be intended to awe the Dutch opposition to her husband. They were a sign that one day, and probably one day very soon, the Princess would have the strength of England at her disposal. Her father's health was poor. Perhaps tomorrow, certainly the day after, Mary would be able to order an English fleet to reduce Amsterdam to its proper obedience. It was unnecessary to make any great show of the Princess's splendid prospects. The opposition knew perfectly well how greatly the political situation had changed.

In order to take advantage of the new state of affairs, it was essential for William to come to terms with the King. He could no longer afford open support of Monmouth and of the English 'republicans', if only because they were attacking what was almost his wife's property. On the very day that the news of James's accession reached The Hague, Monmouth was advised to leave the court. He went to Brussels, which would not be a safe refuge for long. William must have hoped devoutly that the Duke would follow his advice and make a campaign in Hungary. The Prince then sent Overkirk to London to make his submission. He did not dare to go himself, for fear of a rebuff. James would have received him, despite the long arguments and veiled threats of Barillon. James was determined to show no fear at the beginning of his reign. He would also have enjoyed the spectacle of his proud son-in-law humiliating himself in person.[29] His feelings for the Prince were a curious mixture of jealousy, fear, and respect. But James II outdid most of his contemporary sovereigns in family loyalty. If William would only abase himself sufficiently and grovel convincingly enough, his uncle would help him against anyone else.

Overkirk brought assurances that the Prince would submit himself entirely and without reserve to the King's pleasure. It remained to be seen what these assurances meant, although the departure of Monmouth from The Hague was a good sign. James discussed the message with his chief advisers, Rochester, Sunderland and Godolphin. Halifax had not yet retired from office, but he was by now so insignificant that the others could afford the luxury of division. Rochester, who had been made Lord Treasurer and who was, like the King, William's uncle, was most in favour of accepting his submission. Sunderland and Godolphin were less cordial. They were annoyed at having been given relatively subordinate offices. They disliked Rochester. And they could not compete with his Hyde blood. All three agreed that William's professions must be tested. The Prince must be required to change his attitude towards France, since James needed the support of that crown. He must promise to have nothing further to do with Monmouth. Finally, he must agree to cashier all those officers in the English regiments whose loyalty to James could not be trusted.[30] The French ambassador protested that no kind of submission could be sincere, that the Prince was too stubborn ever to abandon his ties to the Habsburgs. In vain. The King was enjoying himself, and he was determined to play his role of sovereign with greater dignity than had his brother. Barillon was told that he must ask for audiences in form and not expect to see the King at any hour, as he had been accustomed to do.

D'Alonne, the secretary of the Princess of Orange, had come over with Overkirk. He was sent back to Holland with the King's conditions. Although rumours of a reconciliation circulated prematurely, they were to prove correct.[31] In part, William equivocated. He had already abandoned Monmouth. He agreed to cashier those officers whom James distrusted. He promised to do nothing either in regard to English internal affairs or in those of Holland which might be opposed to his uncle's interests or wishes. But his statements concerning France were phrased in very general terms and were clearly not a complete surrender.[32] James told Barillon that he was not satisfied. On the 17th, however, he wrote William a cordial letter:

What you have written to me lately, and the assurances you have given by Mons. Overkerk, have so fully satisfied me, that I have ordered this bearer, Mr Skelton, (whom I send to succeed Mr Chudleigh) to assure it you from me, and hope for the time to come, the same confidence will be established between us, as our near relation and the good of our family requires. What else I have to say, I refer to him, to whom you may give entire belief, and have charged him also to let you know what measures I intend to take as to affairs abroad, that there may be no mistakes, and be assured I shall always be as kind to you as you can desire.[33]

The message itself was shown to the leading Dutch politicians and improved the Prince's standing substantially. Even more important was the fact that the new ambassador, Skelton, had orders to speak to the Prince. Publicly, at least, the breach between the two courts was healed. And William, who could be very distant with the ladies, made a joke of himself by his excessive politeness to Mrs Skelton.

William gained far more than did James from the *rapprochement*. The news of better relations within the Royal Family could only frighten Amsterdam, Leyden, Delft and Dordrecht, the leading centres of opposition to the Orange cause in Holland. In March, the Prince succeeded in winning over his cousin of Nassau, who had long been wavering between support of William and support of Amsterdam. In himself, the Prince of Nassau was a pitiable creature. His influence in Friesland was not great, in Groningen it was negligible. But he was worth having even if, as d'Avaux reported, William had to gain him by guaranteeing a loan of 120,000 livres and by promising a field-marshal's baton. With Nassau's help, the states of Friesland would vote for the military budget. And each defection from the ranks of the opposition would lead to others.[34] During the spring and summer of 1685 William established his claims regarding elections to the magistracy of Dordrecht and of Leyden. He was also able to push through the military budget on his own terms. Amsterdam blustered, but it gave way.

Abroad, William's new position revived hopes of a general league against France. The Elector of Brandenburg sent Paul Fuchs to Holland to clear up the long-standing differences between the two great Protestant powers. In 1684 Fuchs had worked against the Prince and in favour of the Truce. Now he sang a different song. With Amerongen, who had also returned from Berlin, he went to Amsterdam and did his best to reconcile the city with the Prince. Fuchs was at least partially successful here, and he did even better work for his master. By a treaty signed with the States General on 23 August, Frederick William was to receive 440,000 imperial dollars over a period of years in full compensation for all his demands.[35] Since most of the claims were frivolous, it was a high price. Obviously the Republic bought the Elector, as it had done so often before. But they were buying an old man. Frederick William might talk; he would never fight again. All that the Dutch received from the bargain was a benevolent neutrality. Even that was an improvement over the time when the Prince of Orange had complained that the Electress and all her court down to the washerwomen were French. What the laundresses received in 1685 we do not know. The Electress, like the later Duchess of Plaza Toro, received 10 per cent of the takings.

At the beginning of his reign, James faced two glorious but incompatible opportunities. The first was to follow the example of his ancestor Mary Queen of Scots and keep his religion a private affair, devoting his attention to the secular interests of his House and of his people. As Onslow noted, his accession

was a crisis that might have made this country as great in Europe, or greater, than it had been in any age, and put the King at the head of all foreign transactions, to have engaged in them more or less, as it suited either his interest or his honour: and had he but kept his religion to his own practice of it, and governed by parliaments, he would have been the happiest and greatest King at the same time, both at home and abroad, that this nation had almost ever seen. There never happened before such a concurrence of incidents to produce all this: ...[36]

William in Holland and Rochester in England were the leading proponents of this policy. The alternative and far more dangerous policy was for James to try to save the souls of his subjects by reconciling them to the Roman faith; or, if he could not do that, at least to improve the lot of his Catholic subjects to the point where they would be secure after his death. By that time, popery must be so firmly based in England that nothing could destroy it. James was considering this second, and fatal, policy as early as March 1685.[37]

For months James II seemed to waver between the two opportunities. Publicly he appeared to support the Prince of Orange. Rochester as Lord Treasurer seemed to be at the head of the administration at home, while his brother Clarendon was made Lord-Lieutenant of Ireland. The brothers, however, were opposed on personal as well as political grounds by a powerful and growing faction. The new Queen was an ardent Catholic, a supporter of the French interest, and at bottom like almost every stepmother the enemy of her husband's children. Sunderland and, to a lesser extent, Godolphin supported the Catholic faction as the only means of depressing their rival Rochester. James himself, as he grew older, became more regular in his private life and ever more dependent on his wife and on their shared faith. If he should follow a religious policy, the King would need French assistance. He hoped to obtain a grant of three million down and a regular pension from Louis XIV. The letters for half a million which had been sent in February but never delivered would form part of the initial three million.[38] Louis XIV would not hear of the plan. When the French refused to support him, James, probably as a form of blackmail, confirmed the old alliances between England and Holland. Yet even when he appeared to be carrying out a Protestant and anti-French policy, the King was never fully committed to it. He was the most suggestible of men. The ease with which Argyll and Monmouth were able to obtain supplies and shipping in Holland, the ease with which they slipped through the careless hands of the Dutch for their invasions of Scotland and England at the beginning of the summer, aroused James's suspicions. William III did his best to allay them. He hastened to send over first the Scottish and then the English regiments to his uncle's assistance. He sent Bentinck over in July to offer his own services or those of any of his generals for the suppression of Monmouth's rebellion.[39] The Prince sincerely deplored the rebellion and misjudged its scope. In Holland it seemed far more dangerous than it did on the spot. On the surface James was placated by the Prince's prompt assistance. Yet he could not believe the Orangist claim that Monmouth and Argyll had had French support for their plans.[40]

Although James appeared to accept the Prince's protestations of loyalty and devotion, his real attitude was far more reserved. He refused to give William any public mark of distinction that would emphasize his position as heir-presumptive by marriage. The Prince was refused the style of Royal Highness.[41]

By now almost half William's revenue was under French control and these rents were being withheld from him. James made representations about this at Versailles, though not very strong ones.[42] He refused flatly to give the Princess any allowance which would indirectly make up for her husband's losses.[43] This was the more serious because Mary's sister Anne had a large English establishment. Probably the differential treatment of the two sisters was one cause of the jealousy between them which broke out some years later. What gave James's favouritism its importance was the possibility that it might be carried to the extreme point, that Mary might be excluded from the English succession. James was particularly fond of Anne. The Catholic extremists had hopes of her conversion. If the King should follow a full Catholic policy, if he should thereby make a complete break with William III, then eventually he might be persuaded to outwill his elder daughter in favour of the younger.[44]

During the summer and autumn of 1685 the situation was complicated by a personal indiscretion. The Prince of Orange had chosen this most awkward moment to be found out in adultery – with Elizabeth Villiers, one of his wife's ladies. Elizabeth Villiers, though she came from a handsome family, was generally described by contemporaries as ugly long before she lost her figure. Her strength lay in her wit and intelligence. It was possible for the Prince to discuss politics and current affairs with her, as he did not yet discuss them fully with his wife. At first, the Princess reacted with spirit to her husband's infidelity. There was a dramatic confrontation late one night when Mary followed her husband and on his return upbraided him for his misconduct. She sent Miss Villiers packing. Men who marry above their station cannot safely betray their wives. Mary's English servants and the ambassador Skelton himself meddled in the affair, which might have had the most serious consequences. Rabid Catholics were contemplating the possibilities of an annulment. Fortunately for the Prince, James decided that he could not intervene in such a personal matter.[45] The Princess eventually became even more complacent than her father. Elizabeth Villiers returned to court and remained William's mistress, according to all the available evidence, until the spring of 1695. Those who had meddled in the affair were punished for their impertinence. Dr Covell, the Princess's chaplain, had written a foolish letter to Skelton which was intercepted.[46] Both of them lost their posts. Yet if the Prince had his way the incident contributed to the growing estrangement between him and his father-in-law.

Even before the Villiers affair broke out in October, Sunderland and Godolphin had triumphed over Rochester in the King's cabinet. The Treasurer was inescapably tied to the interests of William III. Sunderland had seen his own opportunity in this and had become the leader of a party

favouring the interests of the Queen and of the Catholics as against those of
her step-children and her subjects. Sunderland's star was now in the ascendant.
James II abandoned his early, half-hearted attempts to be King of all his people.
For the remainder of his reign he became more and more committed to the
single cause of his religion. When the dangers of such a narrow policy were
pointed out to him, he would merely reply that he wished to have a red-letter
day as his memorial. Feasts commemorating martyrs are so printed in the
Catholic calendar. James could not understand that he had made up his mind
too late. He might, just possibly, have been able to break William III and
thus have left his enemies without leadership if he had acted in February. He
did not do that. Correctly, he made a reconciliation with William. In the
spring and summer he appeared to be giving the Prince his active support.
There was nothing real in it on James's side, but the news of the reconciliation
itself enabled the Prince to recover his strength. Never again would he be as
weak as he had been in 1684. Never again could he be bullied as he had been
then. When James decided to change his plans, to spurn William and to
support the Catholics, he thought he had a real chance to obtain the repeal
of the Test Act and perhaps to go even further. There was no such chance.
James had chosen martyrdom but would not even have a red-letter day for
his pains.

Chapter 16

RELIGIOUS WARFARE

THE conclusion of the Twenty Years Truce satisfied the territorial ambitions of Louis XIV for the moment. In the years that followed he had more time to devote to matters of religion and commerce. The European balance of power, however, was most unstable. Almost every power hated him and only by frightening his enemies could he prevent the formation of a general league against France. Some of the states of Europe could be bought. Others could be terrified into an alliance. Still others would have to be disciplined. By such means the French hoped to be able to perpetuate disunity. As long as her enemies were divided, France was safe. One of the easiest and most obvious methods of dividing the opposition was to strike the chord of religion. Leopold in Vienna, Innocent in Rome, James II at Windsor could hardly join Protestant states in a struggle against the Most Christian King. As it happened, Louis XIV had at last become devout. His religious policy might be expected to pay dividends; it was, however, fundamentally sincere, and any diplomatic advantages gained in the process were so much frosting on the cake. Ever since 1679 the King had fallen more and more completely under the influence of his priests and of Mme de Maintenon, who had risen from the position of governess of the royal bastards to that of confidante and finally wife of their father. The court might sneer at their master's new piety. It might point out that Louis XIV was trying to expiate his sins on the backs of others, where Henri III had at least had the decency to submit to beatings in person. Yet the court had to cooperate. Outwardly, at least it must become moral; and if the mask sometimes slipped, Versailles certainly did become very dull. In the last thirty years of his life Louis XIV came more and more to resemble his great-grandfather Philip II. If Versailles could never quite become a second Escorial, the resemblance became marked. Advancement at court went only to the pious, and piety was measured in terms of the numbers of converts obtained from the *Religion Pretendue Reformée*.

The famous dragonnades began in Poitou in 1680. At first they were considered too brutal, and the intendant who had introduced them was dismissed. Later, men became less squeamish. The dragonnades were resumed, their author re-employed. Between 1679 and 1684 the Huguenots were successively excluded from one profession after another until none remained open to them. Their schools, their colleges, their chapels were closed or razed. Their hospitals, with their endowments, were taken over by Catholics. Where common hospitals existed their management was put entirely into Catholic hands. As the persecution increased, crimes against the person became more significant than crimes against property. Protestant boys were encouraged to conform to the Roman Church at the age of fourteen, girls at the age of twelve. Later the age was reduced to seven for both sexes. Those children who later relapsed into Protestantism were subject to the full penalties of the Church. Calvinist clergy and laymen were tortured into forced conversions. A life sentence to the galleys awaited the obdurate. Conversions obtained by impossible fines, by threat, by torment were perhaps unpleasing on high and were certainly condemned in Rome. More important were the beams of approval which emanated from the Sun King.

We need not dwell on the loathsome nature of the persecutions, which were detested at the time by the best men of all faiths, Catholic and Protestant alike, and which have been remembered in horror down to our own day. It would be useless to multiply accounts of the atrocities. What must be considered is the effect of the persecution on the balance of power and on the position of William III. In the first place the dragonnades embittered all the Protestant states of Europe and intensified beyond measure the general hatred for Louis XIV. When war came again, as it surely would, it would be for many people a war of religion. Nor did France gain any sympathy from Catholic states to counterbalance the rage of the Protestant powers. Secondly, France was seriously weakened by the attempt to unify the religious beliefs of all her people. Long before the formal revocation of the Edict of Nantes in October 1685 the richer Huguenots had begun to flee the country, sending as much of their money ahead of them as they could. Many took with them irreplaceable skills, others were able to escape with their employees and their capital as well. France had a traditional advantage in the manufacture of luxury goods of the highest quality. Now the refugees set up factories for the production of the best grades of paper, of hats, of flowered silks. For sixty years the finest silver in the world was made by Huguenot refugees and their sons, the most famous of whom was Paul de Lamerie. The new establishments were set up in the Dutch Republic, in England, and around Berlin, where Frederick William gave the refugees an especially warm welcome. It has been estimated that some 200,000 people succeeded in making their escape in 1685 and the years that followed, and that by 1715 perhaps a million had fled.[1] Possibly France, with her great wealth and her population of twenty millions, could afford to lose five per cent of her life's blood. She could by no means afford to have these people join her enemies and compete against her. She lost her monopoly of skills as well as a great amount of capital. In terms of the balance of trade the persecution were a disaster of the first order.

The dragonnades also had important effects on the army which was required to execute them. The quartering of soldiers on private houses with instructions to commit every kind of brutality destroyed, obviously enough, any semblance of discipline. The armies of Louis XIV never fought as well after 1678 as they had before. Often this decline has been ascribed to the deaths of Turenne and of the grand Condé, followed in 1691 by that of Louvois. Yet Turenne had died in 1675 and Condé was long past his prime even in 1672. The army had fought well without them. It would fight again under Luxembourg, it would fight on even after Luxembourg's death in 1695. In the later wars, however, something was missing; and that something was discipline. The reforms of Le Tellier and of his son were sacrificed to a false concept of religion, and nothing could take their place. The French army lost men as well as discipline because of the persecutions. Schomberg, despite his age one of the best marshals of France, was permitted as a special grace to resign his commission and to leave the country in peace. Hundreds of lower-ranking officers who could not obtain similar favours fled abroad. They knew that their fate if they were ever captured could at best be a life term in the galleys. They fought with the courage of despair. A number of them on the field of St Denis, had preferred death in a burning château to surrender. Others, more fortunate, fought on with equal bravery. In many ways the Nine Years War was to be a civil strife of Frenchman against Frenchman. No fewer than 796 refugee officers were reported to have accompanied the Prince of Orange on the expedition of 1688 alone.

If the persecutions aroused the loathing of Europe in general, if they added materially to the resources of the enemies of France, they were of especial importance as an influence on English and Dutch public opinion. The English had only to read their newsletters to see what might be their own fate in the very near future. In public James II deplored the revocation of the Edict of Nantes and raised money for the relief of the refugees. As well he might; for the conduct of the French government compromised his own position hopelessly. From now on James was to be faced with ever-increasing suspicion and ever-increasing opposition on the part of his subjects. Their early docility, shown by the remarkably favourable results of the elections in the spring of 1685 and the pliancy of the men then chosen for the House of Commons, was gone for good. In the United Provinces the persecutions had a similar effect. French refugees, especially men like the distinguished ministers Claude and Jurieu, became ardent Orangists. As a group, the Huguenots aroused the sympathy and support of the Dutch people, who were forcibly reminded of their own sufferings at the hands of Louis XIV during the War of 1672. In Amsterdam, as in other towns, collections were taken up for the benefit of the unfortunate, pensions were given to people of quality, and there was no envy when the Prince of Orange made up a company of Huguenot cadets and found other places for the needy. Amsterdam, however, bore a special responsibility. The city had forced through the Twenty Years Truce, which had given the French King the leisure he needed to complete the ruin of Calvinism in his dominions. Thus Amsterdam could be accused, as she was by Fagel and others, of being the cause of the disaster. There could be no defence. Worst of all was the fact that Dutch citizens, as well as Frenchmen, were among the victims.

For many years Holland had had a great and prosperous trade with France. Before the grapes were ever gathered from the vine they belonged to Dutch merchants who bought the crop in advance and then financed the various stages of the manufacture of wine, particularly of the wines of Bordeaux. When ready for shipment, the barrels were put on board Dutch vessels and shipped to the Republic itself, to the various states of Germany, or to the Baltic countries. Large quantities of other French agricultural products and manufactures were also traditionally handled by Dutch merchants. In exchange, cloth, salt herring and other goods were imported from the north. This vast trade was too large to be handled by factors who came and went on the same ship. Many Dutchmen had therefore settled in France. A good number of them, relying on the Edict of Nantes, had become naturalized. Their letters of naturalization made specific reference to the legally established toleration as a condition of their settlement. Relying on these documents, the merchants had felt safe in marrying, in buying houses, and in bringing up families. Now they were trapped.

In September 1685, a month before the Edict was revoked, Fagel pointed out in a bitter speech that Dutch citizens were being denied permission to leave French territory. What Louis XIV chose to do to his own subjects might be disgusting, but it was an internal affair. When, however, he quartered dragoons on Dutch citizens he was breaking every known concept of the law of nations. When he refused them permission to leave the country with their goods and families, he was trampling on his own treaties as well. By the terms of these treaties the traders had nine months' grace after a declaration of war in which to retire with their effects. Now, in full peace, this essential condition of commerce was denied.

The French equivocated. No mercy would be shown those who had become naturalized. They were now subjects of the King, who might do with them what he pleased. Thus the Dutch consul at Nantes, who was forced by torture to become a Catholic, had no redress because he was supposed to have taken out French papers.[2] As for those who had not become French subjects, they would be protected from the dragoons and allowed to leave the country if they wished to do so. But not at once. To permit all the

Dutch merchants to leave with their capital would cause economic chaos. They must be kept as long as possible, by fair means or foul. D'Avaux, who had to explain this policy at The Hague, was in an impossible position. He was required to delay requests for repatriation as much as he could. He must give assurances that repatriation would eventually be permitted, while trying to reassure the people that they had no reason to worry about their detained relatives or partners. But when he asked his master to grant a token repatriation of four families as a special favour to Amsterdam, he got nowhere. The four families for which the city interceded were not granted passports, and the matter dragged on and on. No wonder that the ambassador's relations with the city deteriorated! Eventually he had to report that there were only four or five men left of the once-great party of the 'well-intentioned'.

As the horrors multiplied the Republic continued to find itself involved. Dutch vessels leaving Bordeaux in 1686 laden with prunes were suspected of concealing Huguenots. The ships were fumigated in order to kill the stow-aways. In the process the prunes became poisoned, and when they were distributed in Holland several consumers died. The fumigations had to be stopped; but still Dutch traders were not allowed to leave France. Indeed, the King seemed to go out of his way to infuriate the Republic. In 1687 he suddenly forbade the importation of salt herring on the specious ground that the salt used in curing the fish was not of sufficient quality. Rarely has a health measure been more obviously an act of commercial warfare. Later in the year this warfare became more serious. In open violation of the Treaty of Nijmegen the French suddenly reimposed the punitive tariff of 1667. D'Avaux warned of the possibility of reprisals, but the King blandly concluded that they would not take place. If the Dutch were to place an embargo on the importation of French wine they would simply lose the trade to others and deprive three hundred ships of their employment.

By the summer of 1688 Dutch trade with France had been reduced by one-fourth and was actually less than it had been during the last war. This was an important point. The trading towns now had nothing further to lose. Under normal circumstances they would have been in favour of peace for the preservation of their commerce. Now, however, war could hardly make any significant difference. The last straw was the news which came at the end of September of the seizure of all Dutch vessels in French ports. When it was learned that, in addition to the confiscation, the sailors were being offered the choice between popery and the galleys, the rage of the people knew no bounds. The massive interference with trade and the forcible conversion of so many traders united the Republic as nothing else could. When the English expedition sailed it had behind it the prayers of almost every family in the country.

The kidnapping, torture and forced conversion of Dutch citizens would have been enough by themselves to outrage the people of the United Provinces and to drive them into a preventive war. But the mistreatment which they suffered was only a small portion of the French aggressions in these years. Even before the conclusion of the Twenty Years Truce Genoa had been bombarded for refusing to surrender a portion of its own fleet at the demand of the French, and afterwards the Doge was obliged to make his apologies in person at Versailles, though by law he might not leave his native city. This barbarous treatment was a lesson that was not lost on Amsterdam, which henceforth took the lead in building up the strength of the Dutch navy so as to gain protection from a similar insult. In 1686 the French touched an even more sensitive nerve. Their commercial rivalry with Spain had continued unabated and had been marked by brutalities of every kind. As early as February 1686 the Dutch became aware of a French plan to bombard the great entrepôt of Cadiz. A very great quantity of Dutch property would be exposed if the bombardment took place. Even more alarming was the rumour that the French also intended to attack the plate fleet of that year, which contained perhaps more Dutch and English property than Spanish. The United Provinces responded to this threat by dispatching a squadron to Cadiz. Significantly enough, Amsterdam sent four extra ships at its own expense to strengthen the squadron. In the end the French contented themselves with a partial blockade of Cadiz and, when the Spanish proved submissive, did not attack the *flota*. During the operations, however, a Dutch man-of-war was attacked by elements of the French fleet and her captain was killed. Again and again the Dutch were forcibly reminded that they had no choice but to follow the policies of William III. The French left them no alternative.

In his treatment of his supposed friends Louis XIV had no greater moderation than he did for the Spanish and the Dutch. His cousin the Duke of Savoy was disciplined for permitting the Duke of Carignan, heir presumptive to the Duchy of Savoy, to marry a Princess of Modena. Even after the marriage had been consummated the French government attempted to have it annulled, though the attempt failed. This was an insult not only to the House of Savoy but also to the Modenese Queen of England, though Mary Beatrice was expected to uphold French interests at her husband's court. The mistreatment of Savoy did not stop here. Despite the Duke's protests he was obliged to accept a French force under Catinat whose task was to extirpate the Savoyard Protestants known as the Vaudois. The Vaudois resisted bravely, but in vain. The majority perished. Only a small band managed to find refuge in the mountains or to make their way to safety in Switzerland.

The Pope was treated in similar fashion. Innocent XI had at first been pleased by the conversions taking place so rapidly in France. As he came to learn their true nature, however, he changed his mind and began to show open disapproval. The French retaliated by enforcing their claims to diplomatic immunity, not merely for the palace of their ambassador in Rome, but for the whole quarter in which it lay. Such a wide claim had nothing to do with any French interest. It served to irritate the Pope and made the proper government of the city impossible. Large mobs of criminals took asylum in the privileged quarter, sallying forth to sack the palace of each dead cardinal or to commit some similar outrage. In 1687 Innocent XI announced that he would refuse to receive a new French ambassador unless the claim to immunity were waived. In reply the new envoy was sent off with an escort of troops. He was excommunicated; but he continued to worship openly in Rome, and when the Pope placed the church concerned under an interdict the French threatened to sequester Avignon and to march on Rome itself. Early in the following year they went further, appealing from the authority of the papal see to that of the next General Council of the Church. Such an appeal was two centuries and more out of date; but to make it on behalf of the criminal element of Rome was doubly fatuous. The motive was completely unworthy, and Innocent XI could not be bullied. In 1688 he was to have his revenge, and posterity has rewarded his courage by enrolling him informally among the ranks of the saints. One has yet to hear of a St Louis XIV.

The roughness of the French King's policy had in it a large measure of the irrational. In so far as it had any relevance at all, it was meant to frighten Europe and so to prevent a new coalition, a resumption of war. In this it failed. What held Europe back was not the conduct of the French but the sober judgment that a new league would lose, as the old one had. By ruining his army in the dragonnades and in the construction of canals for Versailles, Louis XIV diminished the main source of his power. The flight of the Huguenots was a more serious blow, and all the bluster of the French could not conceal the fact that their strength was on the wane. The warm reception given to the refugees by Frederick William of Brandenburg was the first open sign of a coming diplomatic revolution. If the Elector, that most prudent of men, was willing to accept the Huguenots it meant that he was no longer afraid of the possible consequences. In 1685 he patched up his quarrel with the United Provinces. Early in the next year Sweden also made a treaty with the Dutch. Shortly afterwards the princes of Germany formed the famous League of Augsburg. This was a purely German affair; the Dutch did not join the League, nor as it happened did Frederick William. The Emperor, the King of Spain (representing the Circle of Burgundy), the King of Sweden for his German estates only, and a number of other princes of whom the most important was the Elector of Bavaria, united to protect German soil from any further encroachments. At the time the League was not a success. Louis was not deterred from building a fortress at Huningen on land seized from the

Markgrave of Baden. But the very formation of the League showed that much of the Empire was no longer afraid. As the Turkish threat receded, and as the disunity within the United Provinces gave way to a strong and unified support of William of Orange, their courage rose even further. None the less, the basic fact remained: no coalition could hope to hold its own against France without English participation. If James II would only die, or else follow an independent policy, all would be well. Unfortunately for himself and for Christendom, James would do neither the one nor the other.

It is against this background of the European diplomatic struggle that the domestic policies of James II must be examined. Sometimes the background is omitted, which results in the presentation of a false picture. Among the axioms of modern politics, whether accurately so or not, is the idea that foreign affairs do not swing elections. This axiom is supposed to be especially relevant in the case of the British, whose insularity is so notorious. In the seventeenth century, however, foreign relations could not yet be divorced from religion; and for religion the English would do anything. Public opinion hardened measurably with the revocation of the Edict of Nantes. If the King took some steps for the relief of Huguenot refugees, the rest of his conduct was much less satisfactory and it was now subjected to far more searching criticism than it had been in the spring. The political honeymoon of the new administration was definitely at an end.

By October 1685, as we have seen, Sunderland had outstripped Rochester in the King's favour. In that month Halifax was dismissed from office. By himself, Halifax had long been powerless. His dismissal, however, was a sign that the King had determined to follow a religious rather than a secular policy. As such the dismissal was important, and it was followed by a sharp popular reaction against the court. In the spring James had been able to do what he would with the Parliament. When it sat again in November it had ceased to be complacent. During Monmouth's rebellion James had employed Catholic officers in the army. Now he wished to retain them, despite the provisions of the Test Act. Parliament was willing to absolve the Catholic officers from any punishment for their previous violations of the statute, but it would not tolerate their continued employment. The Catholic officers must go. James, rather than give way, prorogued the Houses. This failure of the session was blamed by the court on William III and on Rochester. It had been observed that the leaders of the opposition were men known to have been previously the Prince's supporters, and it was natural enough for James to suspect that the Prince was actually directing them. As for Rochester, he had been employed in order to manage the Church party, and he had failed. From now on the King came to rely more heavily on Sunderland and on a small group of Catholics, consisting of Father Petre and the Lords Arundell, Tyrconnel and Dover. Outside this inner group his closest followers were the Chancellor, Jeffreys, and Lord Godolphin. By the early months of 1686 James had promised the Catholics that Rochester would be dismissed.[3] He was, however, still fond of his brother-in-law and still had a high opinion of Rochester's financial and administrative talents. The Earl's fall would be a slow one.

Meanwhile the court began to suspect the continued existence of a formed opposition, even though Parliament was not in session. The King's advisors claimed to see forming an association of Protestant lords for the defence of their religion.[4] In The Hague the news of the existence of such an association frightened William's friends, who were still trying to cooperate with the King as best they might. Fagel insisted that the peace of Europe depended on the maintenance of unity between the King and his people, and he hoped for the avoidance of all untimely disputes. He placed part of the blame for the persecution of the Protestants on the continent on the stubbornness of their English co-religionists, which had forced Charles II into the French camp in 1681.[5] No one, he wrote, has a greater interest in seeing England at peace than his Highness; disunity there can only serve to the unspeakable prejudice of the Republic and of the Prince himself.[6] 'If the Parliamentary leaders will only reflect', he continued, 'I believe that they must see that they can bring the religion for which they now seem so devoted into no greater danger than by falling into disputes with the King.'[7]

Had James been able to see these letters, he might have formed a more accurate opinion of William's position. But his mind was poisoned by Sunderland and Barillon and by the long record of misunderstandings of the past. Whatever he did, the Prince of Orange was suspected of fomenting trouble. He continued to be blamed for the failure of the November session of the Parliament of 1685. He was accused of corresponding secretly with the Bishop of London after that prelate's disgrace.[8] Later in the year, when a session of the Scottish Parliament had also gone badly, the Prince and Fagel were accused of a similar correspondence with the Duke of Queensberry for the purpose of wrecking the King's measures.[9] Denials were useless. Attacks on William were among the easiest ways to wound Rochester and Clarendon, the Prince's uncles, in the minds of the King and Queen. Even if Sunderland had been willing to take a more moderate attitude, he could not have done so. Moderation might ruin his hold on the Queen; and Sunderland was also being pushed on by the zealot Tyrconnel, who was willing to use any weapon to obtain control of the government of Ireland.

In July of 1686 the dispute between the King and his people became sharper. Without the slightest regard for the law James named four Catholics to his Privy Council. At the same time he established an Ecclesiastical Commission for the government of the Church of England. The latter step might be justifiable on a technicality, though many people felt that the Commission was prohibited by the Act of 1641 which had suppressed the Court of High Commission and all bodies of a similar nature. The two moves could not have been more ill-timed. By his weak conduct during the French blockade of Cadiz, which had just taken place, the King had given the general impression that he was now firmly attached to France in continental affairs. Although it was known that he was now actually in the process of concluding a French treaty, the fact that its provisions were limited to the western hemisphere was not. The treaty was, indeed, concerned only with problems beyond the line; but no one would believe that. And this is not a full catalogue of the events of that busy July. James somehow found time to recommend the appointment of a Catholic, the Earl of Carlingford, to the command of the British regiments in the United Provinces.

All this bustle pointed in one direction and to one conclusion: that 1672 was come again. James and Louis XIV must have taken up the Grand Design of 1670 for the conversion of England to the old faith and for the destruction of the Dutch Republic. In 1672 the attack had failed, by the narrowest of margins. A second attempt was to be expected in the spring of 1687. Such were the reports of the Dutch ambassador van Citters to the Prince.[10] His fears were intensified by the continuance of rumours of an approaching change in the succession, which van Citters and the Prince took seriously. As Barillon reported a little later:

... Votre Majesté aura vu dans une lettre de Mr Ziters qu'il y est fait mention de la succession, c'est une matière fort délicate à traitter. Je sçais pourtant qu'on en parle au Roy d'Angleterre, et qu'on ne désespère pas avec le temps de trouver des moyens pour faire passer la Couronne sur la teste d'un héritier Catholique. Il faut pour cela venir à bout de beaucoup de choses qui ne sont encore que commencées.[11]

On the first of August the Grand Pensionary, in the name of the Prince, issued an official warning to the States that there would be war in the spring of 1687, and he insisted that the prophecy be formally entered in the registers.[12]

Amsterdam, which thought the prediction ridiculous, refused to agree to any increase in the military budget. In England, the only men who shared van Citters's ideas were the Duke of Hamilton and his son, who were pleased to fancy themselves as candidates for the throne if the succession were ever changed. Everyone else knew that van Citters must be mistaken. And since he could not have any valid reason for thinking that there would be war next spring, were his letters not probably inspired by the Prince himself in order to stir up trouble? As it happened, the ambassador's command of French was very imperfect. He did not fully comprehend what was said to him, and this led him to exaggerate the importance of the events of July. But the conduct of Louis XIV and of James II was such that even a man with a far better understanding of the French language than van Citters had might have been excused for believing the worst. The real significance of his mistaken interpretation lay in the gap it showed between the two courts. There was now a complete failure of communication between the English and the Dutch governments. Each imputed the worst motives to the other's conduct. Perhaps it was already too late for a full explanation and a full reconciliation. None was attempted at the time, and there was not to be another opportunity.

In September Lord Mordaunt visited the Prince and urged him to invade England.[13] According to Burnet, Mordaunt

represented the matter as so easy, that this appeared too romantical to the Prince to build upon it. He only promised in general, that he should have an eye on the affairs of England; and should endeavour to put the affairs of Holland in so good a posture, as to be ready to act when it should be necessary: and he assured him, that, if the King should go about either to change the established religion, or to wrong the Princess in her right, or to raise forged plots to destroy his friends, that he would try what he could possibly do.

William's cautious view of the situation coincided with that of Barillon. When the Ecclesiastical Commission had been set up, Barillon reported a good deal of grumbling. Some said that the King went too far, and that the English people would not tolerate the overthrow of the laws or the destruction of the Church. The French ambassador admitted the general discontent; he discounted the possibility of revolt. Men of property had too much to lose.[14]

In November the Prince had a visitor of another stamp. William Penn, the great Quaker, was one of the few English dissenters to take the King's protestations of religious tolerance at face value. There were more of them in Scotland, where the dissenters had been more harshly treated; in England, Penn stood almost alone. He tried to persuade the Prince that no sinister motive lay behind the King's actions, that no more was intended by the proposal to repeal the penal laws and the Test Act than appeared on the surface. His mission failed. By this time the misunderstanding had gone too far. James II and Penn were sincere in thinking that they spoke the truth. But no man of sense could believe them, or trust the King not to be led further than he intended. How could his feeble mind withstand the pressures that were being brought to bear by the extremists? When even Innocent XI, who was violently opposed to much of the King's policy, urged him to secure the conversion of the Princess Anne, how long could James be expected to remain merely tolerant? Anne's position was at least as important in this reign as it was to be in the next. It was now highly probable that William and Mary would have no children; it was not yet suspected that Anne would outlive her own. If she did, the next two heirs were Catholics – the Queen of Spain and the Duchess of Savoy, the two daughters of 'Minette' – but their position was too remote for serious consideration. What was needed was the conversion of the Princess of Denmark. The position achieved by the court in July was inherently unstable. It had to go forward or to retreat, and James and William Penn were alone in thinking that things could remain as they were. Of course they were wrong; for in the closing days of 1686 the King took a new step.

First he asked Rochester, still Lord Treasurer, to become a convert. When this failed the Earl was dismissed, with a handsome pension, and the Treasury was placed in commission. Two of the five members of the commission were papists. At the same time steps were taken to alter the government of Ireland by increasing the authority of the Catholic Earl of Tyrconnel. As early as October William of Orange had been informed that Tyrconnel was working to turn Ireland into an independent Catholic state, whose King might be James FitzJames, the later Duke of Berwick.[15] Given the overwhelming numerical predominance of Catholics there, and the nationalism that they had displayed in the 1640s and were to display again in 1689 and 1690, this rumour did not seem so unlikely at the time as it might now. William was seriously worried. Any scheme to give FitzJames an appanage or to convert the Princess of Denmark to her father's faith would meet the conditions of his pledge to Mordaunt in the previous September. Any such scheme would both change the established religion and also deprive Mary of her rights. In January, therefore, the Prince sent Dijkvelt over to England on a special mission.

Dijkvelt's task was twofold. He was to try to persuade the King of the sincerity of William's support in every field save that of religion. He was to do what he could to secure a reconciliation on such terms if that were still possible.[16] Secondly, he was to sound out the leaders of all parties and to encourage them to stand firm against the King's romanizing policies. The mission could hardly have been more provocative, though James had earned it. The King had replaced the odious Skelton as his ambassador at The Hague by the even less attractive figure of Ignatius White, Marquis of Albeville. An Irish adventurer who had received his title from the Emperor and his income from Barillon, Albeville was not only a Catholic but also a mere spy. The French, though they paid him, distrusted him and suspected that he might also take money from the Prince of Orange. One of the most pathetic aspects of the attempts of James II to appoint Catholics to high office was that there were so few able ones available. At the moment of Dijkvelt's arrival in England, Albeville was having disputes at The Hague over points of ceremonial which delayed his formal reception. The King would not grant

Dijkvelt an audience until his own ambassador had been permitted to perform his duties. Even then, Dijkvelt did not see the King often because he had hurt his foot. This most opportune but painful injury kept him from court and gave him a better opportunity to receive calls from the leaders of the English opposition. It was perhaps as well that James and the Dutchman did not see each other more often. The King was furious at the charge that he meant to alter the succession, furious at the obvious encouragement given by Dijkvelt to the enemies of the court. [17] His rage would have been even greater had he known of Dijkvelt's instructions. The Prince had ordered him to make it clear that he would never consent to the abolition of the Test and of the penal laws. William would undertake not to punish those Catholics who had accepted office in defiance of law, when he himself should come to the throne, but no more. [18]

Luckily there was no opportunity to discuss the matter until after the publication of the First Declaration of Indulgence in April. This made the Prince's refusal far more timely than it would have been in February. But the interval gave alarm to the English, who feared that William might be bribed into supporting the King's plans. He received a remarkable warning against doing so from Lady Sunderland. [19] The Countess was as devout an Anglican as her husband was a gambler. It is probable that she wrote on her own initiative. But her letter has intrigued historians with the idea that her husband was playing a double game. The French were suspicious of this possibility at the time, but they were unable to find any proof to substantiate their fears. [20] Dijkvelt later received additional instructions to tell his friends in England what had passed between him and the King on the subject of toleration, so as to make the Prince's position perfectly clear. [21]

The most important result of the mission was the discovery that Anne was staunch. Until now her position had been far from obvious. When she had asked permission to make a trip to Holland while her husband visited Denmark in the summer, her political views were considered so innocuous that the Queen at first gave her approval. It was only later, when Mary Beatrice and James were made to realize the implications of such a tour, that the trip was forbidden. [22] Yet if Anne might not go, she could make plenty of trouble at home. Suddenly she began to attend the sermons of popular preachers, and this public display of her Protestantism became even more marked after the publication of the Declaration of Indulgence. Later in the year she retired from court to underline her alienation from her parents. [23] Of equal import-ance were her instructions to Churchill to explain her position. Anne 'was resolved, by the assistance of God, to suffer all extremities, even to death itself, rather than be brought to change her religion'. Churchill felt this to be worth putting into a letter which Dijkvelt carried back to the Prince. [24] Such a statement, and Anne's new conduct, more than justified the mission. Now the Catholics would have no reason to alter the succession.

Another result of the trip was the visit of crowds of English nobles to the Prince's court in the summer of 1687. Several observers had noted that the English court had been empty since 1686, and that the royal officials had a thin reception when they passed through the provinces. Apparently William III had decided to engage in a popularity contest as a means of humiliating his father-in-law. He let it be known that he would appreciate such attentions and promised any visitors a cordial reception. Many went; but Rochester for one did not, though he came as near as the Spa. He was never to be forgiven for his failure to complete the journey. Perhaps it was the success of this popularity contest that drove James to undertake a progress of his own through the western counties. If so, he was to be disappointed. He was for the most part poorly received.

By the summer of 1687 the Prince of Orange was being bombarded with requests for his intervention in English affairs. The Catholics threatened him, both through Dijkvelt and to his face, with stories to the effect that all was ready for the introduction of a republic on the death of James.[25] Obviously there were not enough Catholics in England and Scotland to do much of anything. They claimed, however, that the Protestant dissenters would adhere to them in the cause of religious toleration. Meanwhile the English and Scottish refugees in the Republic, of whom there were now considerable numbers, were making some threats of their own. They pointed out that James might, despite his assurances, still change the succession. They argued, further, that William would be lost if the English were forced to take matters into their own hands and free themselves without his assistance:

One thing the Prince will doe well to be persuaded of and lay to heart, and it is a note for himselfe alone: if the nations come once into extreme suffering, that their case require it, the Prince must either hazard himselfe for them and become their deliverer or els he will risk and hazard his interest in these kingdoms for ever; for if they get deliv'rance by their owne means or by any other save his, then his interest of respect breaks at least in England; the reason is, that the far greater part, even of those that like monarchy, of that Nation cary to this houre a dislike of the race and branches of the Scots family, and if they could fix elsewhere, would certainly reject it: ...[26]

During the remainder of the year the breach between James II and William III, which was now complete, became more open. It could not grow worse, but it did become a matter of public knowledge. The Prince refused to appoint any Catholic officers to commands in the British regiments in Dutch service. James responded by making plans to recall the force as soon as he could find a suitable pretext, and enough money to pay for their wages. The decision to recall the troops was taken in October and the bill was presented to Louis XIV. Would the King agree to take the six regiments into the French army?[27] He refused to do this, but he did agree to pay for the entertainment in England of such men as obeyed the recall. Before commanding the regiments to return, James at the end of the year tried one last throw of the dice. This was an attempt to persuade Mary to conform to the Catholic Church. When she remained firm, her father demanded the return of his subjects in January. The position of the men was rather anomalous. They had been raised at Dutch expense and were, of course, in Dutch pay. There was no capitulation governing their treatment. One had been drawn up between William III and Lord Ossory at the time when the latter had expected to command the six regiments. The capitulation had never been ratified and thus remained without force. This fact could not have been more opportune. The States General were in a position to argue that the King had no right to demand the return of the regiments as units, since neither he nor his predecessors had had anything to do with their formation. He might, as sovereign command his own subjects to return to their native land; but the order must be given to individuals and not to the men as a body. Although James was outraged at this response, it was technically correct. Those individuals who wished to return to England or Scotland were permitted to go. Many went. But those who stayed on could now be trusted completely. Their only hope lay in blind obedience to William III.

Meanwhile a startling rumour spread over Europe. During his progress to the west of England, the King had visited the shrine of St Winifred's Well. After making his devotions there he had joined the Queen at Bath towards the end of September. His prayers were answered with remarkable speed. By November the pregnancy of Mary Beatrice was generally known. For the moment the news did not have to be taken seriously. The Queen had had so many miscarriages, and so many children either stillborn or dead soon after, that one domestic tragedy more or less was not a matter of general importance. Most likely she would abort, as she had so often before.

Chapter 17

THE REVOLUTION OF 1688

THE summer and autumn of 1687 saw a remarkable shift in the balance of European power. The Turk stood at bay. The Russians were able to advance as far south as Perekop in the Crimea. In the Mediterranean the Venetians took Corinth and, in the course of bombarding Athens, seriously damaged the Parthenon. The imperial army under the Duke of Lorraine and the young Elector of Bavaria was even more fortunate. On 12 August, near Mohacz, the imperialists succeeded in destroying the army of the Grand Vizier. The Habsburgs had recovered the crown of St Stephen. Hungary was theirs, for the first time since the days of Charles V. Although France was not a formal ally of the Turk, the campaign of 1687 was a disaster of the first order for the King as well as for the Sultan. Even if peace were not made, the military position had so changed that it would now be possible to put an imperial army on the Rhine for the first time in years. Meanwhile, in the Baltic, French diplomatists had made the fatal error of becoming involved in the latest chapter of the interminable Schleswig-Holstein question. They did succeed in keeping the peace in the north, but at the price of losing the friendship of Denmark. In October the Danes were obliged to submit their claims to the arbitration of a congress meeting at Altona. Ultimately, in 1689, the Duke of Holstein recovered the territory in dispute. Yet the French lost more from the congress at Altona than did the Danes. Sweden and Brandenburg were already in the camp of William III. Since Denmark did not receive French support she gradually drifted in the same direction, and Louis XIV was left in the novel position of having not a single one of the three northern powers for a friend.

Having sustained such great losses, it was necessary for the King to move if he was not to lose the whole game by default. The Archbishop Elector of Cologne was his client. The Elector was also Bishop of Liège. This prince was so old than an insurance policy on his life was a matter of prudence. French agents and French money circulated among the chapter at Cologne, and in December they attained their goal. William von Fürstenberg, the Bishop of Strasbourg, was elected Coadjutor of Cologne. The election was irregular, since the Pope had the right to say whether there should be a coadjutor or not. Even so, the election was better than nothing. And in the following May when the Archbishop passed away, Fürstenberg seemed to hold most of the cards. His position was illusory. It is a dangerous thing to play ecclesiastical poker against a pope, and especially a pope so determined as Innocent XI could be when backed by Calvinist bankers. Agents of William III bought up the chapter of Liège and succeeded in obtaining the election of a friendly candidate there. This was important, not only because Liège could provide a line of communication between the Low Countries and the Empire, but because it was the centre of the hand-grenade industry at this time. Thus Fürstenberg lost one part of what he had aimed at. There remained Cologne itself, and in due course thirteen out of the twenty-four votes of the chapter were given to the French candidate. Only nine went to Joseph Clement of Bavaria, the candidate of the Habsburgs and of William III. A two-thirds majority was needed. Either candidate would need a dispensation, Fürstenberg for translation from Strasbourg, Joseph Clement because he was only seventeen years old. The Pope pronounced in favour of the Bavarian, who was enthroned on 20 September 1688. Five days later the infuriated Louis XIV invaded Germany in support of his puppet of Strasbourg. His armies laid siege to the great fortress of Philippsburg, where they would be pinned down for the next two months.

James II made a grave error when he allowed himself to become involved in the Cologne affair. His ambassador at Vienna, Lord Carlingford, was notoriously French-minded and worked far too closely with French agents there in any case. Carlingford's conduct was merely a nuisance. English support of the candidacy of Fürstenberg, however, outraged the Emperor Leopold. For the rest of the year he watched the rapid progress of events in England with a grim smile. Later the bewildered James was never able to understand why the Habsburgs, such devout Catholics, were among his worst enemies. At the time he had few moments to spare for such matters. The Queen's pregnancy, announced officially in December of 1687, continued. Although it was a difficult one, it was finally to be successful. A boy, christened James Francis Edward and created Prince of Wales, was born on 10 June. Now Mary and Anne were postponed in the line of succession. Now there was nothing to fear from the King's enemies at home and abroad. The Prince of Wales would be trained as a Catholic and, if his father had anything to do with it, as an absolutist. James was wild with joy. He did not realize that the opposition, cornered and facing absolute defeat, might choose to fight back.

It is worth examining the expectations of William III in regard to England in some detail. He expected, as he had since childhood, to inherit the throne. At first he had discounted the rights of the Princesses of York, on the ground that their mother's base origins disqualified them. Later he had been forced to realize that their claims were stronger, in English if not in continental eyes, than his own. What would have been considered a morganatic marriage at a German court was sufficient in English law for the transmission of any kind of property right, including a right to the crown. Therefore, to consolidate his claim, William had been forced to marry Princess Mary. He had also had a second motive for the marriage. It would, he hoped, give him control over English foreign policy. In this the Prince had been bitterly disappointed. Mary had brought with her a contemptible portion, in influence as well as in cash. Not until 1685 did her husband receive any tangible political benefits from his marriage. Then and only then did the beam of King James's favour, weak as a February sun though it might be, come to William's aid. The feeble signs that James might follow a Williamite policy were enough to bring Brandenburg and later Sweden to his side, and to reduce if not to eliminate domestic opposition inside the Republic. Then towards the end of 1685 it became clear that James II had changed his mind. The victory of Sunderland over Rochester, the dismissal of Halifax, and finally the dismissal of the Bishop of London from the Council early in 1686 were all indications that the King would not carry out an active Williamite policy. He might well remain neutral, favouring neither Holland nor France; but this was not enough. To redress the balance of power England must do more than remain neutral. She must become active on the side of the allies.

Ever since James's change of policy there have been attempts on the part of French propagandists and of historians of every political hue to demonstrate the existence of a conspiracy headed by William III for the dethronement of his father-in-law, dating from – when? D'Avaux, the most malicious of all, puts the date at 1679. He claims that William was a participant in the movement for the exclusion of the Duke of York. James himself sometimes thought of 1679, at others of the early months of 1685. No serious student agrees with them. A recent American professor[1] preferred to date the conspiracy from the famous conversation between the Prince and Gilbert Burnet in the summer of 1686. Other scholars, such as Ranke and Klopp, have often considered William's meeting with the Great Elector at Minden later in 1686 as the decisive moment. There are a number of arguments to be made against each of these views, although it is important to point out that not enough evidence survives for certainty. We know that a great many papers of these years were destroyed at the time; we cannot know what they contained. All that can be said with confidence is that every shred of surviving evidence corroborates the latest of all possible dates, which is that given by Gilbert Burnet: the spring of 1688. It is true that the good bishop got the story a little wrong, as he did most stories: he wrote that 'Russel coming over in May, brought the matter nearer a point. ...'[2] Both Russells came in April, with Arthur Herbert, and waited upon the Prince at het Loo where he was about to entertain the Elector

William Henry in the arms of the Princess Royal

(Ascribed to Honthorst.
Collection, Town Hall, Breda, Netherlands)

William Henry as a youth

(*Ascribed to Abraham Ragueneau.*
Copyright: Franz Hals Museum)

William III

*(After Sir Peter Lely. Reproduced by gracious permission of
Her Majesty the Queen of the Netherlands)*

Mary II

*(After Willem Wissing. Reproduced by gracious permission of
Her Majesty the Queen of the Netherlands)*

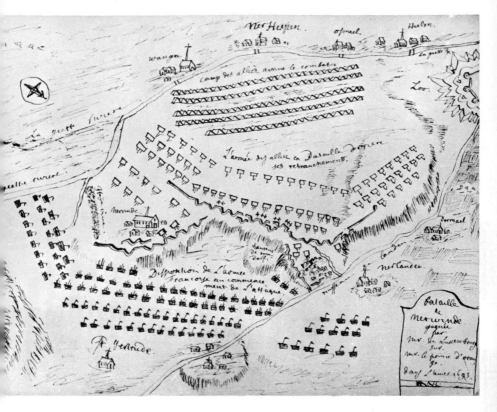

Contemporary sketch of the Battle of Landen
(*Property of the Dutch State,*
copyright reserved)

William III at Torbay, 1688

(*Allegorical print by Romeyn de Hooghe*)

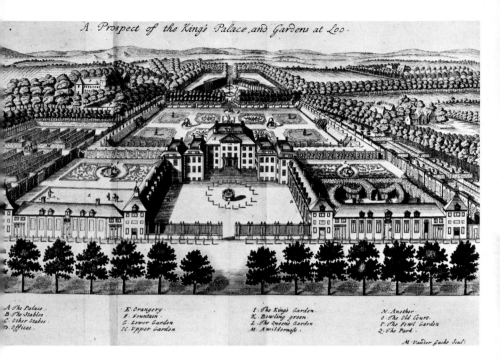

A Prospect of the King's Palace, and Gardens at Loo.

A. The Palace.
B. The Stables.
C. Other Stables.
D. Offices.

E. Orangery.
F. Fountain.
G. Lower Garden.
H. Upper Garden.

I. The King's Garden.
K. Bowling green.
L. The Queen's Garden.
M. A wilderness.

N. Another.
O. The Old Court.
P. The Fowl Garden.
Q. The Park.

M. Vander Gucht Sculp.

Het Loo

(From Walter Harris' A DESCRIPTION OF
THE KING'S ROYAL PALACE AND GARDENS AT LOO, *1699)*

The Funeral of William III after His "Death" at the Boyne

(*The original French caricature was reissued by the Dutch
to celebrate the King's survival, 1690*)

of Saxony. William refers to the departure of the Englishmen in a letter of 29 April.³ Obviously they had brought letters, among them two from Danby to which the Prince replied on the 30th.⁴ Thus we must apparently ascribe to the last days of April the conversation described by Burnet:

So Russel put the Prince to explain himself what he intended to do.

The Prince answered, that, if he was invited by some men of the best interest, and the most valued in the nation, who should both in their own name, and in the name of others who trusted them, invite him to come and rescue the nation and the religion, he believed he could be ready by the end of September to come over.⁵

It is probable that Russell returned to The Hague and saw Burnet there a day or two later, which would have been just inside the month of May. Burnet would naturally remember the date of his own interview with Russell rather than that of William's, and nothing more precise than the fact that it took place before the death of Frederick William of Brandenburg. The passage quoted above continues: 'The main confidence we had was in the Electoral Prince of Brandenburg; for the old Elector was then dying. And I told Russell at parting that, unless he died, there would be great difficulties, not easily mastered, in the design of the Prince's expedition to England.' There can be no doubt at all of William's decision having been made before he returned to The Hague, because at het Loo he tried to obtain troops from his house-guest the Elector of Saxony. The Elector was at first favourable to the idea of a treaty of mutual defence and Amerongen was sent to Aachen to conclude matters towards the end of May.⁶ Unfortunately the Elector became timid and the projected treaty was never signed, although William considered bribing not only the Electoral mistress but even the Electoral mistress's aunt in the hope of obtaining the troops. By that time, however, Saxony was no longer so important. Frederick William of Brandenburg died on 9 May. The Prince of Orange was so delighted at the news that he wrote two separate letters of condolence to the new Elector, Frederick III, on 17 May.⁷ Even though he had been obliged to eat and drink far too much while entertaining the Elector of Saxony, William was so pleased by his uncle's death that he looked better than he had for years past.⁸ He had reason. His decision had at last been made. And already the wisdom of his timing was being confirmed by accidental pieces of good luck. What is to be said for this latest of possible dates?

No sane man prefers a risk to a certainty. In human terms, William III was certain to inherit the throne of England if only he lived long enough. James II was generally known to be diseased and therefore incapable of having any further healthy children. Another child might be born, perhaps even another boy; but not one strong enough to grow up. No sane man would have taken seriously, until well into the spring of 1688, the possibility of the birth of a healthy Prince of Wales. If, on the other hand, William decided to play the role of a Monmouth, he might well share Monmouth's fate. The risk simply was not worth taking, except under one of two conditions. The first was that James could go about to defraud William and Mary of their right. He could do so by selecting Anne as his heir. This, as we have seen, had been a possibility ever since 1683. The Prince and Princess of Orange took the matter seriously. They had been encouraged to learn from Dijkvelt that Anne had no intention of becoming an apostate. This merely made the matter a little more complicated. James might not be able to pass over both his daughters and give the succession at once to the Queen of Spain or the Duchess of Savoy, who were next in line after Anne. But he could obtain the same effect a different way by foisting a supposititious child off on his people as a Prince of Wales. The idea, true or false as it may be, that the King was diseased was an article of faith. Therefore he could not have any more children. Therefore any child he did have must be supposititious. Mary at least was firmly and sincerely convinced that the pregnancy of her stepmother was a fake:

... I find that notwithstanding those great assurances your Ma.tie has been pleas'd to give their R. H.ss of the succession in the true line, yett the Prince, measuring your Ma.ties conscience by his own, has possess'd her R. H.s that there is no releying upon it, and that the Jesuits and priests will at long running prevaile with you, to act against your Ma.ties present assurances....

I do not comprehend how men and letters com from England, dare assure it is resolved allready there, that if both their Royal Highnesses your Ma.ties daughters should com to have no children, they will never admitt of the Queen of Spayne, nor of her sister the Duchess of Savoy; and this is say'd confidently at this Court methinks it looks as a kind of a tacit denunciation, they will not admitt of a Prince of Wales, if they can.[9]

The Princess of Orange did not need the warnings of her sister, contained in a letter of 14 March, to become suspicious of the Queen's great belly.[10] She had become suspicious of the whole business before the end of 1687.[11] Then while she was at het Loo with the Prince in April her suspicions were confirmed:

Dans ce temps-cy je reçeus une telle relation de la grossesse de la Reine, que cela me donna juste raison à soubçonner qu'il y avoit quelque tromperie. Je ne sçay ce qui en arrivera, mais je mets tousjours ma confiance en Dieu; c'est sa cause, et il prendra soin de son Église.[12]

It is obvious that Herbert and the two Russells had to persuade the Princess as well as the Prince. The invasion could not take place without her knowledge and consent. She, not her husband, was the heir to the throne. She, not her husband, would have to authorize the conspiracy. She, not her husband, would depose her father. For it was obvious from the very beginning that this was what was involved. It was a very great responsibility to undertake, and it seems highly unlikely that Mary would have had the strength to act as she did unless she had been sure that her father was trying to rob her and thus to destroy the true Church. Luckily her firm belief never wavered:

Les considérations de tout cecy, et de penser que mon Père soit coupable d'un crime si horrible, et que humainement parlant il n'y ait point d'autre voye pour sauver l'Église et l'État que celuy que mon Époux aille le déthroner par la force, sont des réflexions les plus affligeantes, et ne seroient pas meme supportables sans l'assistence de Dieu, et une confiance ferme et inébranlable en luy, sa grace s'etendant par dessus tout ce qu'il a fait.[13]

The Prince had his own deep religious faith; but he was educated, as his wife was not, and he approached the problem from a broader point of view. Mary could appreciate the idea of her inheritance being stolen from her and could respond to the cry of 'The Church in Danger!' Her husband could see another reason for intervention. This was that James had already destroyed the English monarchy, and that the only way of saving anything out of the wreckage was to take direct action. For two generations the Stuarts had indulged in the most fatuous misgovernment, and had done so largely at the expense of the House of Orange. Once before, Charles I had dragged the House of Orange down with him into ruin; what might not be the consequences of the fall of James II? William had every reason to intervene for the protection of his own position as Prince; and it is clear that he more than half thought of himself as the head of the Stuarts as well. One might argue that James's first marriage had been morganatic. Or one might argue that James, as a Catholic, was disqualified from being King of England. This did not become the law until 1689, but it had been the deep-felt belief of the Whig party for a decade. And whichever theory William used to justify himself, there was always the demonstrable fact that James had misgoverned and that he had destroyed the monarchy. The favourite remark of Charles II had been that his brother would not be able to govern England for four years. He repeated it again and again. Sometimes he gave James four days, sometimes four years: never longer.

In fact, James II had reigned with success for almost exactly eight months before going off the track. Even then his conduct had not become really outrageous until July 1686. The most likely consequence of his actions since that time would be that the English people would rise not only against their King but against monarchy as such. The resulting republic would in all likelihood have a Great Person at its head. Poland, the United Provinces,

Venice, and Genoa, the four chief republics of the day, all had their great persons. England herself had had one in Oliver. But William III could not expect to be chosen to head an English republic unless he could manage to control the revolution that brought it into being. And he did not want to be the great person in an English republic. In William's eyes, such a place would not be worth having. His task, therefore, was and had been for years to keep himself informed. He would have to listen to the opposition so as to know what was going on. He would have to keep friends on all sides so as to prevent the leadership from slipping into other hands. This was why he entertained Monmouth in 1684, this was why (if he did) he went to the theatre rather than fasting on the anniversary of his grandfather's murder in 1685. D'Avaux is our only evidence that William and Mary actually did go to a comedy on 30 January of that year. If they did so, it was to preserve their few remaining friends in England. There were not many of them at that time, and it was only after Monmouth's execution that the Whigs were forced, *faute de mieux*, to turn their eyes towards The Hague.

In the November session of the Parliament of 1685, when the King's plans were thwarted, it was pointed out to him that the opposition consisted of partisans of the Prince of Orange. The situation was not as simple as that. There is no evidence, none at all, that William was directing the opposition. Nor could he have bribed the parliamentary leaders, as has been charged, for the simple reason that he did not have the money. What little he had was to be spent in 1686 on the purchase of het Loo and of the Huis ten Bosch. And since his total income was of the order of that of the Princess Anne or of the Duke of Buckingham, and his expenditure higher than theirs, there was none to spare for English politicians. What William actually did do in 1685 and 1686 was merely to keep in touch with the leaders of all parties in the British Isles. And we have evidence that he actually disapproved of the conduct of the English parliamentary leaders.

The great bulk of it indicates that in his relations with the English parties William III was on the defensive. Support our plans, said the Catholic extremists, or we will divert the succession from you. In 1686 and the early months of 1687 they hoped for the conversion of the Princess Anne, to be followed by her nomination as heiress-presumptive. Later in 1687, when the illness of Prince George with pneumonia took a severe turn, they were for marrying her to a Catholic prince after a very short widowhood. Still later, after George's recovery, they threatened William III with the establishment of a republic. Antiphonally, the chant was taken up on the other side of the choir. Support OUR plans, said the English and Scottish refugees in Holland, or WE will set up a republic in England. The Prince, like Tarbaby in the Uncle Remus stories, lay low and said nothing. Why should he do anything?

Again and again for the last fifteen years he had been threatened with disaster by one English politician after another if he did not act as a puppet in that politician's hands. Arlington had warned the Prince in 1672 that he faced the same fate as the de Witts; William replied, 'Je ne suis pas fort craintif de mon naturel'. Arlington was gone, the Prince survived. During the Exclusion Crisis one Englishman after another had told him that all was lost if he did not make a visit to England. William had not come until all was over. And nothing had been lost, except Sunderland's office.

But by the end of 1687 the problem was far more serious than it had been in 1672 or in 1680. The English political situation was completely out of hand. In Dublin Tyrconnel was obviously building a Festung Ireland, which would be a Catholic refuge in case of disaster and which might well be turned over to France in case of need. To such an extent James was clearly dismembering the inheritance to which the Prince felt himself entitled. William also felt, and to all appearances he felt sincerely, that James would join with Louis XIV for a war on Holland as soon as he felt strong enough. Undoubtedly, the Prince and Fagel were hysterical. Undoubtedly they read more into the situation than was actually there. In such hysterical circumstances, the pregnancy of the Queen took on a most sinister aspect. Mary Beatrice's medical history, to say nothing of her husband's diseases, made a pregnancy most unlikely. What, then, was happening? Was it a fraud? Both Mary and Anne convinced themselves that it was, that their father was trying to rob them and that they must intervene for the protection of their property. Whether or not William thought that the pregnancy was fraudulent we do not know. Even if the Queen were truly pregnant, however, it seemed clear that the Jesuits would not allow her to have anything other than a healthy son. If a Prince of Wales were not forthcoming it would be necessary to create one; and here was one miracle that the most sceptical Protestant knew that the Catholics could bring to pass.

There has been a rather general reluctance to think of the English expedition of 1688 as a conspiracy with a short life. The Prince must, according to some authorities, have been scheming ever since 1679; according to others, ever since 1685. He may well have considered the possibility of an invasion, at any time after 1684, as one among a number of alternative plans. How else could the Prince save his inheritance from the stupidity or malice of his uncles? What else could he do if for example James were to die suddenly and the English chose Anne ahead of Mary? In some circumstances William would have to invade England at short notice, and there is no reason to think that he did not include invasion among his list of *possible* courses of action. But invasion for what? Not to usurp the right of another, but to protect his own right from theft. And there is a wide difference between considering a possible course of action, among many other possible courses, and the adoption of a definite plan of campaign. According to every scrap of surviving evidence, Englishmen and Scots of all parties were pressing William to intervene in England in 1686 and 1687. They wished to force his hand. And again, according to all the evidence we have, the Prince listened to each group politely enough but refused to take the advice. In December the situation was altered by the official announcement of the Queen's condition. Now a revolution became a distinct possibility. The people of England had been remarkably patient, at least in part because their King was in visibly poor health. Once he died Mary would step in and repair any damage which James might have been able to do. Now the very ill health of the King became the strongest threat to his dynasty. Suppose the birth of a Prince of Wales. Could anyone hope that James II would live long enough to see his son come of age? The idea was preposterous. But the alternative, a Regency in the hands of Mary Beatrice, was unthinkable. Barillon reported a very curious story at third-hand about a month before the actual birth of the Prince of Wales, of a plan to seize the boy and bring him up forcibly as a Protestant in the event of the King's death.[14] Barillon had no doubt but that such a project was 'dans la teste des premiers hommes de la nation, et qu'ils n'y trouvassent mesme une grande facilité par le nombre de gens qui seroient pour eux'.

Who these conspirators were is not made clear by the French ambassador. There can, however, be no doubt of their identity. At the time of Dijkvelt's visit he had had interviews with the leaders of the opposition at the house of Lord Shrewsbury. The English lords included, in addition to the host, Halifax, Danby, Devonshire, Mordaunt, Lumley, the Bishop of London and Admirals Herbert and Russell.[15] Burnet, who gives their names, informs us that they met often at Shrewsbury's house. Presumably they formed something of a standing committee and continued to meet, as opportunity offered, for a year-and-a-half after the visit of Dijkvelt had first brought them together. In the spring of 1687 there was no thought of rebellion or, at least on the part of William III, of armed intervention in the affairs of England. Such intervention became a possibility in December. In a contemporary account written on or before 26 December, Burnet reflected:

And if there should be a comm[otion], or if the violence of the Irish should create a disorder in that island, the Prince will be reduced to great difficulties; the ties of nature will make it hard for him to head a rising against his father in-law; but, on the other hand, if the King's ill conduct throws the nation into such a violent fermentation, that a rebellion that prospers will turn to a commonwealth; and if it is subdued it will put all things into the King's hands. So that the difficulties will be great on all hands; ... It is true there is a report, now generally believed to be true, which may change the whole scene. It is said that the Queen is with child ...[16]

Burnet was not the only one to receive intimations of what was going on in the mind of William III. At much the same time Fagel mumbled something mysteriously to the leading Dutch politicians, who inferred from the mumbling that the Prince might decide to play the role of a Monmouth.[17] From what we know it appears that Fagel was sounding these politicians to discover whether they would acquiesce in such a game or not; and the decision to intervene was not taken until later.

Burnet, who was on the spot and in a part of the secret, has the outlines of the true story. Every writer uses his work, but not every writer bothers to read it through. He says, perfectly clearly, that the Prince was being pressed to invade from 1686 on; first by Mordaunt, then by others; that he refused, again and again; that, finally, on the visit of Admiral Russell to The Hague in May 1688, he was forced to agree to participate. Why? Because Russell told him that the English would wait no longer, that if William did not support them they would rise anyway. The threats came from responsible quarters. In May 1688 William had to capture control of a conspiracy. Otherwise, as he himself put it, the English would set up a republic. This would, obviously, deprive both the Prince and the Princess of their right. Also, and more important, it would be fatal to the Dutch. Of all conceivable forms of English political structure, that of a republic would be worst for Dutch interests. A republic would concentrate on colonial expansion and commercial enterprise. The Dutch knew this from bitter experience. They remembered Cromwell. Their trade had never recovered from the Navigation Acts of 1650 and 1651. Charles II had re-enacted the Navigation Laws, but he had not been able to enforce them. Indeed, he had been obliged by the Treaty of Breda in 1667 to modify them in important respects. But a second English republic could be expected to enforce and even to extend the policy of the Navigation Acts. When, therefore, Russell threatened that if William did not join the conspirators they would go on without him, the Prince was obliged to acquiesce. By doing so he could direct the course of a revolution which was going to take place anyway. He could see to it that as much as possible of the English inheritance was salvaged. He could see to it that the revolution did not turn out to the disadvantage of his own fellow Dutchmen. In 1688 he was obliged to sell his inheritance for a mess of pottage; but he chose to sell it dearly, he was clever enough to make sure that the pottage contained as many raisins as possible.

There are usually two arguments raised against this thesis that the Prince did not make up his mind until 1688. For one, how could the Prince mount an invasion in November if he did not begin his plans until May? How could he raise the necessary forces so quickly? Would it not have been necessary to have formed plans much longer ahead of time? Obviously it would be difficult for a nobody to raise and equip 15,000 men and to provide transport for them in so short a time. But the Prince was already at the head of an excellent army and navy. It is much less difficult to expand than to create an armed force. And in fact the records show that the Prince did not enter into specific negotiations to raise his forces until 20 July. His plans were delayed by the failure of the English to invite him until 30 June O.S., and also by the illness of Bentinck's wife. This put off the invasion from September to the beginning of November; but it did not do more than cause a delay. The Prince, with an army and navy in being, and more significantly with a staff and commissariat in being, could and did mount the invasion of England in less than three months' time. Had he taken longer to do it, the secret would have leaked out and the execution of the plan become impossible. And also, had he taken longer, the expenses would have become insupportable. As it was, William had no money to spare; but if, as his critics argue, he had been making preparations for two or three years, the costs would have been wholly prohibitive.

The second argument against such a late decision to intervene in England is not often expressed in precise terms. It is based on William's character. If he decided to intervene only in the late spring of 1688, he is open to the charge of having intervened for selfish motives, of having intervened because of the Prince of Wales. To avoid charging the Prince with having deposed the Stuarts for selfish reasons, it is better to place the decision to intervene as early as possible, and at any rate earlier than the beginning of the Queen's pregnancy. William does not need such a defence. Undoubtedly his actions were not dictated by base motives; undoubtedly he was not merely taking candy from a babe. He intervened, not for himself or for his wife but for his faith and for the protection of his native land, the United Provinces. In that cause he had lost his Principality of Orange, his estates in Franche-Comté and Luxembourg – roughly half his income. In that cause he was prepared to risk the English inheritance which was by far the largest asset he had left. It was a real risk, a real sacrifice. He might well have decided not to make it had he had a son. Since he did not have one he was free to act in the public interest. The fact that the Prince's gamble succeeded is irrelevant. It was a great gamble, and only a man of the highest devotion to duty would ever have consented to make it.

There are other arguments against the idea that the Prince's plans should be dated 1686 or earlier. Until 1686 he did not have control over the Dutch navy, and until then that force was too weak to be of any use. It was only when the Customs duties were put to farm and the revenues placed under the Prince's control that the rebuilding of the navy could proceed, and even when those revenues became available the process of strengthening the fleet took years. Secondly, the diplomatic situation was impossible in 1686. William did not even dare to support the League of Augsburg in that year, and for that reason among others the League proved fruitless. The basic problem in 1686 was the age and querulousness of Frederick William of Brandenburg. The old man might lend troops to the Emperor for a campaign in Hungary, which happened to be the wrong war in the wrong place. He would not act on the Rhine or join the League of Augsburg. Luckily, the news of his death reached The Hague at much the same time as Admiral Russell's visit. The new Elector, Frederick III, was by no means of the same quality as his father; but he was young enough to act if he wished to do so, and he happened, unlike his father, to be the heir of William III. He could be persuaded to support the English enterprise by appeals to his personal interest. Should William perish in England, Frederick III would certainly inherit the Prince's estates; and he might well succeed to the Stadhouderate as well. Frederick was a hard man to deal with. He kept thinking of a voyage to Prussia, which might have ruined everything. He insisted on a most extravagant funeral for his father, which cost a sum that might better have raised four regiments. As late as 22 July, Marshal Schomberg who was now in the service of Brandenburg felt that nothing was going to happen in the West that year, and that he might as well accept Austrian offers of a command in the Turkish war. Then and only then did Schomberg receive William's instructions to prepare for a Western campaign. It was not until September that William met the Elector at Minden and secured the definite support of Brandenburg. The Elector was made to realise that his Prussian inheritance could wait, while his prospects in the United Provinces could not. William adroitly avoided a flat promise of his inheritance, which was a useful carrot to wave before the nose of that other donkey the Prince of Nassau. It was to his advantage never to choose between the two, and he delayed until 1695. Greedily and more than a little ghoulishly, the Elector hovered at The Hague during the invasion to protect his claims should William die. He was to be disappointed.

When the Prince did decide to intervene, he insisted on directing the conspiracy in his own way. The English wanted him to bring a small number of men, but a large fleet. William insisted on bringing enough soldiers so that he would be able to act independently. There was enough unrest in the army of James II so that it might well not fight. And, of course, its quality was such that even if it did try to fight it could not put up much resistance. Yet the Prince would leave nothing to chance. He would take over more than enough men to destroy the royal army in the field if that became necessary.[18] It is also very likely that the Prince foresaw the actual result of the invasion. His wife, in her *Mémoire*, spoke of William going to dethrone her father. In all probability this is precisely what the Prince intended to do. Only Parliament could make him King, and he might have to settle for less. But any compromise solution, such as a Regency for James or for the Prince of Wales, simply would not work. He had no desire for the external glories of monarchy. The pompous ceremonies of the English court bored and disgusted him, and even if he had been able to perform them, as he never was, he would have slighted the public functions of kingship as much as he could. What the Prince wanted was power, power enough to bring England into an alliance against Louis XIV and to keep her there. He could do this only as King Regnant. The position of Philip II as King Consort would not be enough. Don Felipe's own experience proved the truth of this. Any lesser position would have been much too weak. In 1686 Burnet discovered that Mary hoped that her husband would become King Regnant. The task now was to lead the English into agreeing with her wishes.

Obviously there had to be cover-plans. William could not tell the Habsburgs that he planned to usurp the throne. Nor could he tell the English parties of his goal, nor could he tell the Princess Anne. The only prudent thing to do was to announce that he was going to England to ensure the sitting of a free Parliament. This might be all that William could get. He might hope for more, but this was the least that he could reasonably expect. A free Parliament, even if it decided in favour of the legitimacy of the Prince of Wales, could be expected to declare for a French war and to provide for the education of the baby as a Protestant. There were, in addition, three different cover-plans to disguise the meaning of the military preparations. The expansion of the Dutch fleet was explained by the possibility of war in the Baltic. The congress at Altona was not going well. Thus it was plausible to hint that a Dutch naval force might be needed to keep the peace in the north. In private, negotiations were carried on with the Danes by which the Prince undertook not to do anything very unpleasant to them if they did nothing very unpleasant to him. It was not a cordial agreement, but it was an important one and it did work.

There were two cover-plans to mask the preparations on land. The more important of them was the possibility of war in the Archdiocese of Cologne. Since Louis XIV proposed to install and maintain his friend Fürstenberg by force of arms, the Dutch might well be arming themselves to oppose this design. In actual fact Brandenburg forces under Frederick III did undertake operations in the archdiocese in September. Alternatively, the Dutch might be planning a descent on the coast of France. The idea may seem strange. It was, however, taken seriously by Louvois, who at the end of August ordered that the garrisons of Calais and Boulogne be strengthened.[19] On 8 September the French court seemed to be convinced that the design was really intended for England, but that it would not take place until the following spring.

Such a delay would be useful for the French, since they could not bring their Mediterranean squadron to the assistance of James II before the 1689 campaign.[20] This was wishful thinking indeed: the Dutch must not act before the French have time to forestall them. But as late as 27 September, Louvois was still confused, thinking that William III might move towards Cologne or Bonn, which was 'en fort mauvais état', or perhaps towards Mont Royal.[21]

It was not until 4 October that Louvois had, finally and at long last, a just appreciation of the Prince's design.[22] And by that time it was too late for the French to do anything. They had pinned down their forces in the siege of Philippsburg on such a scale that they could not change their plans. Had the French sat down before Maastricht, or invaded the Spanish Netherlands, William would have had to cancel his plans. Even had he tried to sail, he said later, the common women would have pulled him back by his shirt tails. One may explain the French preoccupation with the Rhine by their own campaign plans, which naturally filled their days in September. It is not in the least necessary to think of Louis XIV cynically allowing William to invade England in the hope that he might be locked up there indefinitely. In any case, the French King here made what was undoubtedly the most important error in his long reign.

William carefully fostered the illusion that he would attack on the Rhine by mustering his army near Nijmegen. Solemnly the ammunition boats went up the river to the camp; but the stores remained on board, and the boats went downstream more quickly and far more secretly than they had gone up. The news of the French siege of Philippsburg reached The Hague on 27 September, proving that the Prince's cover-plans had successfully bemused the French. At the report, which meant that the Republic was safe for the moment, the stock market rose by 10 per cent.[23]

On 8 October the Prince told the Deputies for Foreign Affairs of his plans. He began by stating that he found the religion, freedom and prosperity of the Republic in danger. It was obvious that the French and English kings would subdue the Reformed Religion if they could; that James II was just as zealous a papist as the King of France; and that James, moreover, had long detested the United Provinces. He blamed all his troubles on the Republic, lacking only the opportunity to show his resentment. The desire of the two kings to crush the Dutch, to make 1672 come again, was proved by their attempt to subvert the House of Austria. It was obvious that the English situation, which was all that prevented James from carrying out his design, could not continue. Either James would surmount his difficulties, in which case the Republic could expect a repetition of 1672. Or else he would lose and an English republic would be set up again. In that case the Dutch could expect another 1652. The Prince could not deny that both he and his wife, as princes of the blood, were directly interested that the disputes between the King and the nation should not exclude them from the crown. He felt that there was a very good chance that intervention would be successful if undertaken now. Another opportunity would be hard to find, and if once the zeal of the English were allowed to cool and if the court gave them somewhat better treatment, they might be led into very wrong measures. The Prince could give no details of his plans. Humanly speaking, however, he could promise success; and therefore he was resolved, with God's grace, to go to the aid of the English nation. He would undertake the affair as a sovereign prince, in his own name and that of her Royal Highness. He could not undertake it without the powerful assistance of the Republic, for which he asked; but the Dutch would act only as auxiliaries and would not be committed as principals. He had no intention of dethroning James II or of making himself master of England. What he wanted was to summon a free Parliament which would secure the Protestant religion and satisfy the nation in regard to their laws and liberties; thus the King and the nation might live together in a good understanding and be of some use to their friends and allies.

The Deputies approved. If the Prince won, the Dutch would have security for their religion and welfare. If he lost, they would be no worse off than they were at present, since James could not possibly be more angry with them than he was now. The Deputies added that they thought their Highnesses to be entirely justified in what they were doing, while the Dutch owed so much to the Prince that they would be wanting in duty if they did not support them – at least, in a case where justice and right were so much on their Highness's side, and where the interest of the State so strongly concurred.[24] The States General approved the report, and thanked both the Deputies and his Highness. The die was now cast.

There is, of course, one element of truth in the Prince's statement that he did not mean to make himself master of England. Obviously he went, as he had told his wife months before, to dethrone the King: so much of his statement to the Deputies was misleading. But he did not mean to follow the example of Henry VII, to proclaim himself king first and only then to summon a Parliament. Such a Parliament would not be free. Now and later William was to insist that Parliament should invite him to assume the crown. William the Deliverer would be in a much stronger position in the long run than William the Conqueror. And William the Deliverer would be justified, not only by the Dutch Deputies for Foreign Affairs, but by a far higher authority in the world of philosophy. Did not Bodin hold that it was just for a sovereign prince to intervene for the liberation of an oppressed people, though that people might not lawfully rebel themselves? It might be necessary for those holding the complete doctrine of non-resistance to suffer a second Nero with patience, although their patience was wearing thin now that the second Nero was at hand. But Bodin, referring most probably to the conduct of the Prince's great-grandfather William the Silent, had approved the intervention of that prince as a sovereign – of Orange – even though he could say nothing for the conduct of the Dutch rebels against Philip II. Now Bodin's words seemed to have a new relevance. William's conduct in 1688 stretched the legal fiction of his sovereignty over Orange to its full limit. But it was a very useful legal fiction, justifying his own conduct and freeing the Dutch from the charge of aggressive war against England. Certainly the claim to the sovereignty of Orange was far nearer the truth, and far more specifically endorsed by every European treaty since 1544, than some of the claims of Louis XIV as brought forward in the Chambers of Reunion.

The Prince had by this time assembled an army of nearly 15,000 men and a considerable fleet as well. He went on board ship on Friday, 19/29 October, and sailed the next day. That night there was a bad storm, with high seas and lightning. On Sunday the fleet had to put back to Hellevoetsluys. At first it seemed that the storm might have caused heavy casualties. But by Tuesday almost all the ships had come in safely, and it proved that the only losses had been of some 400 horses. These were soon replaced. Repairs to the ships' damaged rigging took some time; but this delay did not matter, since the wind remained obstinately unfavourable. It was not until 1 November O.S. that the fleet was able to set out a second time. During the interval between the first and second sailing morale, naturally enough, had dropped very low. There were arguments as to whether the fleet should head for the north of England or for the west, or whether it should divide itself into two task forces. Luckily this last suggestion, which might well have resulted in the piecemeal defeat of the whole enterprise, was rejected. So too was a plan for the ships of war to go ahead and defeat or neutralize the royal navy before the transport vessels crossed over. If possible, William hoped to avoid an engagement at sea. In any case it was vital to keep the transports and their convoy together. Any questions that there may have been about the landing place were settled by the wind, which continued steadily N.E. With such a wind a landing in the north of England would be out of the question. The seamen, who had always opposed the idea of a landing on the east coast of the island, were delighted. And the landsmen, who had been terribly seasick during the first attempt, could enjoy the present fine weather. The fleet had to sail very slowly so as not to lose the heavily laden transports. On Saturday, 3/13 November, it passed Dover, and next morning it was off the Isle of Wight. There was some argument as to whether a landing should be made that day, the Prince's birthday. In the event the landing took place on Monday, the anniversary of the Gunpowder Plot. About noon the fleet put into Torbay, and Count Solms was rowed ashore with ten or twelve grenadiers. The Prince followed as soon as it was clear that the people of Brixham would put up no resistance. He had already been the subject of an assassination attempt this year, and his life was much too valuable to be risked unnecessarily.

During the afternoon of 5 November the landing of the foot proceeded smoothly, and next morning a place was found where the shore dropped off steeply so that the horses could get ashore with only a short swim. The Dutch, even those who had been in England before, were shocked at the filthiness of the country. But they were amused by the fact that the peasants, men, women and children, smoked pipes while offering the invader apples or cider or mead. Certainly it was a warm welcome. Wherever the Prince went, the people cried 'God Bless You' and gave him their best wishes. But countrywomen smoking pipes had not invited William to England, and gifts of apples could not make up for the absence of members of the gentry and nobility. Where were they? When the army marched to Newton Abbot on Wednesday the 7th they began to find the explanation for the absence of those who had anything to lose. The poor were as friendly as ever; but men of property remembered the executions which had followed the suppression of Monmouth's rebellion three years before. They were terrified by a proclamation of the King threatening those who sold or gave anything to the Dutch with the penalties of treason. As they said, 'If this thing do miscarry, we are all undone.' The Prince met with the same reception when he reached Exeter two days later. There were blessings and cheers as he rode into the city, and some of the bystanders threw their hats into the air. But the mayor refused to cooperate and the dean of the cathedral, and almost all the men of position or property, fled the town.

The little army stayed almost a fortnight at Exeter waiting for the English to come over to them. At first things seemed to go badly. The gentlemen of the countryside made themselves conspicuous by their absence from the Prince's court. But in fact things were better than they looked. As Shrewsbury told William, no one wanted to be the first to come over; but no one, for the same reason, would want to be the last. The whole country was disgusted with the misgovernment of James II. There was serious disaffection in the navy and worse in the army, which might come over to the Prince in a body. As Evelyn had noted in his diary a month earlier,

... the universal discontent, brought people to so desperate a passe as with uttmost expressions even passionately seem to long for & desire the landing of that Prince, whom they looked on as their deliverer from popish Tyrannie, praying incessantly for an easterly wind.... The apprehension was (& with reason) that his Majesties Forces, would neither at land or sea oppose them with that viggour requisite to repell Invaders.[25]

Already the navy had not fought, and this was one great step gained. And the real attitude of the English was far more favourable to the Prince than to the King. Popular feeling was so strong that the Duke of Norfolk had had to advise Lord Middleton against lighting beacon fires to give the people notice of the invasion, since these 'might as well guide them where wee would not have them go, as shew them where they should'.[26] The news reaching the government from the west was even more ominous. The Duke of Beaufort reported that nineteen people out of twenty in the city of Bristol were opposed to the King, and that the place could not be held.[27] Such news had broken the spirit of the King long before the fleet came into Torbay. As early as 16 October he had said at his levée, 'You will all find the Prince of Orange a worse man than Cromwell.'[28] These were not the words of a man who expected to win.

During the month of October the King had done what he could to make concessions. On the 5th he dissolved the Ecclesiastical Commission. On the 17th he went further, restoring the old franchises to the municipal corporations. These concessions were worse than useless because they were so badly timed. A generous line of conduct might have been effective at the time of the birth of the Prince of Wales. In October, however, concessions were so obviously the result of William's activities that the King merely made himself look as weak as he really was. When word came of the Prince's landing the King seemed dazed. He tarried in London when his only hope of rousing the nationalistic feelings of his people was to force a battle at all costs. As the imperial ambassador Hoffman remarked, James consistently chose the worse of evils. He dithered in London for almost exactly a fortnight and did not reach the army at Salisbury until the 19th.

Meanwhile the tide had turned at Exeter. On the 10th a number of the King's guard had joined the Prince, including Lord Colchester. Three days later the Dutch received word that three whole regiments were on their way. This caused great joy until Lords Cornbury and Abingdon appeared with only a fraction of their men. Although the royal army lacked training and discipline it was perhaps twice as large as that of the Prince of Orange, and if the majority of the King's troops were as loyal as the men in Cornbury's regiment there might have to be some heavy fighting. But better news was on the way. On Saturday the 17th Sir Edward Seymour rode in to Exeter with some of his neighbours. During the late 'seventies and early 'eighties he had distinguished himself by his rudeness, to the point of sneering about the poor quality of William's champagne. This past history made Seymour's adhesion to the cause all the more important. He would not have come unless he thought the Prince's ultimate success to be a certainty, and where he came today hundreds would come tomorrow. The other great man of the west, the Earl of Bath, was at Plymouth. Even before Seymour reached Exeter, Lord Bath was involved in secret negotiations for the surrender of the only important military position to the Prince's rear. Once the arrangements had been completed, and Bath appointed Governor of Plymouth in the Prince's name, the army could move forward. It left Exeter on the 21st.

When James II reached his army at Salisbury he was in no state to take command of it. His nerves were shattered. Only with the aid of drugs could he get any sleep. He was also bothered by a heavy bleeding at the nose. The defection of Lord Cornbury, his own nephew, distressed him and he wondered whom to trust. Had he been in better health he might have played a better part. As it was he was completely incapable of providing leadership. On the 23rd he held a long and, as it turned out, decisive council of war. At its end the King decided not to pursue the Prince of Orange, but to retire towards London. By doing so he admitted defeat. There had, it is true, been some sort of a conspiracy in the army against him. Yet that conspiracy had failed, and if James had been willing to lead his men against the Prince he might have saved his throne. At worst, even if he had been defeated and killed, his conduct would have aroused enough admiration to have been of some benefit to his son. The King was incapable of taking almost any decision, certainly of taking a right one. An accusation of cowardice could easily be made, but it would be irrelevant. Entirely apart from the famous nose-bleed and the insomnia, James seems to have been suffering from a nervous breakdown. His actions, and even his appearance, in the next few weeks can best be explained by assuming that the King was temporarily insane.

After the council of war was over on the night of the 23rd, Lord Churchill and the Duke of Grafton left the King's camp with about four hundred men. They reached the Prince about half-past three the next afternoon, failures. The task of Churchill, Ormonde, Trelawny, Kirke and the others had been to bring over the army. This they had not done. The bulk of the common soldiers remained loyal to the King. And Churchill even at the end had not been able to bring over the men under his immediate command. He was supposed to come with three full regiments, a whole battalion; not four hundred men. It is true that the Duke of Ormond followed him a day later with the Prince of Denmark, and it is also true that the news of Churchill's defection sent the King hastening back to London. But his services to the Revolution would appear to have been enlarged out of all proportion by his biographers. From now on, the Prince became more and more upset about the future of the English army. He had brought with him enough trained soldiers to destroy it. Since that had not proved to be necessary, he now wanted to take it over *en bloc* and to make a professional fighting force out of it. Unfortunately this was not to prove possible. James's army melted away, and a new one would have to be built to take its place.

The virtual flight of the King from Salisbury to London was public proof of the success of the invasion. At two in the afternoon of Sunday the 25th Godolphin wrote a despairing note to Lord Middleton which showed that the game was up. 'God Almighty,' he concluded, 'preserve his Majesty & putt it into his heart to doe what is best for his owne safety. I remayne in much affliction, Your Lordship's most faithfull humble servant Godolphin'.[29] From this point onward the march of the Prince ceased to be a military campaign and became a parade. Bristol offered to come over to the invaders if anyone was sent to them, and Shrewsbury went off with some dragoons to take over the city. On Tuesday the main force advanced into Dorset and reached Sherborne. As it crossed the border of the county it was met by a great body of gentlemen, including the Earl of Bristol. On Saturday 1 December the Prince reached Hindon, and on the following Tuesday he went on to Salisbury. On the way there the Prince took the time to visit Lord Pembroke's house at Wilton, where the van Dijks were so important that he sent his secretary Huygens back to get a look at them. The weather had been so cold that Huygens had at first passed by Wilton without stopping.

On Friday 7 December the Prince reached Hungerford where he stayed for some days. There he met Halifax, Nottingham, and Godolphin, who came as commissioners from the King to arrange a truce. William was now in a position to dictate his own terms. He demanded the instant dismissal of all officials, civil and military, who held their places in defiance of the Tests. All proclamations against himself and his adherents must be recalled. The Tower of London must be put into the hands of the City. Should the King remain in London while a Parliament met, the Prince must be there too with an equal number of guards; otherwise they should remain at an equal distance from the capital. The royal army and the Prince's should both remain thirty or forty miles distant from the City. Tilbury should also be placed in the hands of the men of London, and Portsmouth under control of such men as the Prince could trust. He and his army should be supported by the public funds until Parliament met.

These terms were justified by the military situation, and they still left the King hope of recovering something out of the wreckage of his defeat. But James now thought only of escape. First he sent his wife and son away to France. Then in the night of 10 December, without waiting for the report of his own commissioners, he fled himself. Before he left he wrote a very bitter letter to Lord Dartmouth, who was in command of the fleet:

My affairs are, as you know, in so desperat a condition that I have been obliged to send away the Queene and the Prince, to secure them at least, what so euer becoms of me, that am resolued to ventur all rather than consent to anything in the least prejuditial to the crowne or my concience, and hauing been basely deserted by many officers and souldiers of my troups, and finding such an infection gott amongst very many of those who still continu with me on shore, and that the same poysone is gott amongst the fleett, as you yourself owne to me in some of your letters, I could no longer resolue to expose myself to no purpose to what I might expect from the ambitious Prince of Orange and the assosiated rebellious Lords, and therefore haue resolued to withdraw till this violent storme is over.... I know not whether any of the fleett vnder your command are free to continu seruing me; if they are, their best course will be to go to Irland, where there are still some that will stick to me. If any are free to go order them thither to follow such orders as they shall receue from Lord Tyrconnel. If they will not there is no remedy, and this I may say, neuer any Prince took more care of his sea and land men as I haue done, and been so very ill repayd by them.[30]

Luckily Dartmouth did not receive these instructions until the 14th. Two days earlier the loyal but bewildered admiral had gone over to the Prince so as to preserve order.

Sadly enough, the King did not make good his escape. He fled in the company of Sir Edward Hales, who was known and hated by the men of Kent. Hales was recognized at Faversham and the party was taken. James was subjected to a number of indignities at the hands of the mob, including that of being searched to his skin. By this time he was really beside himself. He took refuge in scripture. Certain that William had had designs on his life from the very beginning of the campaign, the King remarked that though he might fall a sacrifice, as Abel did by the hand of Cain, yet he doubted not but he and his cause would be accepted of God.[31] 'For I repent', he went on, 'that I gave my daughter unto him, for he sought to slay me.'[32] At the time of his arrest one of the mob, named Moon, had cursed the King to his face. When James discovered the man's name he said 'It ought to be called Shimei, for Shimei cursed the Lord's anointed.'[33] Returning to the conduct of his son-in-law, he compared it as many others were to do later with that of Herod. 'Arise, and take the young child and his mother, and flee into Egypt, and be thou there until I bring thee word: for Herod will seek the young child to destroy him.'[34] No one could fail to be sorry for the sufferings of the pathetic old man. No one, watching the quiet dignity with which he met his misfortunes, could easily remember that the King was personally responsible for every disaster which had befallen him. Had James succeeded in making his escape on 11 December his political career would have been judged at its true value. His capture made him a martyr. It gave him a party, and it was to spoil the victory of his antagonist.

Chapter 18

THE CONVENTION

THE first news of the King's flight reached the Prince at Abingdon at about three in the afternoon of 11 December. Here was absolute victory. The flight of James II from Salisbury had marked his defeat as a military commander in the field. His flight from Whitehall was a cession of the civil government. Nothing was as yet cut and dried. There would still be many difficulties on the way to a permanent settlement. Yet the worst problems were now solved. The King and the Prince of Wales had been removed from the stage. Fortunately they were both presumably unharmed. Any remaining difficulties could hardly be considered critical. The most beautiful aspect of the victory was that the Prince owed so few political debts. The 'Immortal Seven' who had issued the invitation had done much, but they could not treat the Prince as their prisoner. If William should prefer to employ Halifax and Nottingham, two of the opposition leaders who had refused to sign the invitation, he might do so with a clear conscience. And no one else could put forward so strong a claim as the Immortal Seven. The English navy had been prevented from fighting by the Protestant wind. No seaman, therefore, could demand a reward. The army conspirators had failed, and it was the King himself who had given the order not to fight. Not even the Princess Anne could claim to have made any significant contribution. It is true that she had fled from Whitehall in the night, after learning of the defection of her husband and of Lord Churchill. Placing herself under the guidance of the Bishop of London she had moved north by easy stages to Nottingham. But neither she nor the militant Bishop Compton had anything which might be called an independent position. When William III sent orders to Compton that the Princess should join him at Oxford, there was nothing to do but obey. As for Danby, who had raised the north and captured the city of York, the Earl's position was even more humiliating than that of the Bishop. Danby, at least, had performed very considerable services of a military nature. Yet his hopes of being able to dictate a settlement were shattered by the flight of James. That event made all his work vain. The Prince of Orange sent Danby orders on 12 December to disband his irregulars and to join the court. The Earl hastened to do so. His brief career as a Chinese warlord was over, and he found himself back in the ranks of the courtiers.

One of the great myths of the Revolution of 1688 is that it was made by the nobility rather than by the people of England. It was not. The ultimate cause, of course, was the misgovernment of James II which so alienated the people that two abortive risings occurred as early as 1685. Here we mean all the people, what were known at the time as the *menu peuple*, rather than the tiny group which formed the political nation. Had the *menu peuple*, the countrywomen with their pipes and their offerings of apples, not been bitterly hostile to the Restoration government it would not have fallen at the first sight of 15,000 armed men. The fact that the militia so hated the King that he did not dare use it is a most significant fact.[1] It is undoubtedly true that the upper classes went along with the invasion once it had established a beachhead and that a few of the early arrivals at Exeter, such as Lord Colchester and Sir Edward Seymour, deserved perhaps even more from the Prince than did the Immortal Seven. Colchester and Seymour gave courage to the fainthearted. But the Prince could easily have argued that his political debts were limited to those two men and to a very few others. His debts to those Englishmen who accompanied him were of course very large. His debts to the gentlemen and nobles who had stayed in England were not.

This, perhaps, is the ultimate basis of the conquest theory of the Revolution. There was an opportunity for William III to claim that he had done in 1688 what he had done in 1672: leading the *menu peuple* in a revolution against the political nation. Such a claim would have meant that the Revolution of 1688 was a class war. It might well have led to a second supersession of the House of Lords, a return to the constitutional position of March 1649. Levellers and Diggers and the like might reappear, with demands for political and perhaps even economic equality. This is presumably what James meant when he told the peers at his *levée* of 16 October that they would all find the Prince of Orange a worse man than Cromwell. William III, however, avoided this trap in 1688 as he had avoided it in 1672. He did not want to be a traitor to his class, to overthrow the political nation. All he wanted on both occasions was what he felt to be his rightful place in the existing polity. He certainly used the *menu peuple*, and in doing so he laid the foundations for the bitter hatred of the magnates against him. They were terrified by the possible consequences of his conduct, and they were to resent as the Stuarts had the threat posed by his popularity. But William III was no Cromwell, no Napoleon, no Lenin. He had no need to be. It is possible to compare him to George Washington. It is not possible to make him into anything resembling a true revolutionary. It is equally impossible to give the English magnates much credit for the conservative nature of the Revolution of 1688. It was indeed a conservative revolution. But that happy result was the effect of an act of will on the part of William III. In December of 1688 he could have had anything he wanted. As Halifax told him, the English did not know what to do with him; but neither did they know what to do without him.

When the news came of the King's flight, the Prince changed his course and marched towards Windsor rather than Oxford. His conduct in the next few weeks was to be a model of circumspection and prudence. The same cannot be said of the English peers, who met at the Guildhall on 11 December and tried to restore order in the capital. In this they were largely successful, though the mob destroyed a number of Catholic chapels. On the larger issues, however, the peers were not yet ready to face facts. They did not ask the Prince to come at once to London. The first invitation came from the City Fathers on the 13th. And when the news came that James was a prisoner at Faversham they made the political error of treating him as a King. However generous their attitude may have been in personal terms, it made no contribution to solving the constitutional dilemma. James II, like Humpty-Dumpty, had had an irretrievable fall. The peers' despatch of his coaches and a guard might bring him personal comfort and safety. Nothing on this earth could restore his prestige. The King returned to Whitehall on the 16th, which placed the lords of the Guildhall in a strange predicament. How were they to justify their conduct if James resumed his functions? If he were still King, what had they been doing for five days? Halifax, for one, could see no logical answer to that question and retired to the Prince's court at Windsor.

The return of James II to London was a serious nuisance. William had tried to prevent it by sending orders that James should come no nearer the capital than Rochester; but these were not delivered in time. From the moment of his return James, if he could not command respect, aroused a great deal of pity. No one had wanted him to be mobbed by the rabble. His sufferings made him a sympathetic figure. He was actually cheered by the crowd on his return to Whitehall and the court that day was quite full. He was no longer a King. This made it all the easier to see him as a father, betrayed and deserted by his children. But it made the problems of government impossible. As Sir Henry Sheeres, the Surveyor of the Ordnance, reported to Lord Dartmouth:

I waited on his Majesty this morning to have directions how we are to proceed at our Board, who told me that he could not tell how to direct me. But just now we are assured the King has declared the Prince of Orange generalissimo by sea and land; the King desired a guard from his highness telling him he had more assurance of those than his own – sad state of a Prince but yesterday so great. In a word the Prince issues his orders to all the troops already.... I cannot say but that I now wish the King had not come back. We have made no application to the Prince as yet, though all other officers have, and what we shall do God knows, or what is best in prudence and honesty. ...[2]

Sheeres was later to be a prominent Jacobite. But even he would have agreed that this confusion could not be allowed to continue. On Monday the 17th what remained of the royal army was ordered by the Prince of Orange to march out of London. These forces were replaced by the six English and Scottish regiments in Dutch service, together with the famous Blue Guards of William III. Count Solms, commanding the Guards, occupied Whitehall late in the evening. When these arrangements had been made James was informed of the Prince's order that he retire to Ham. He agreed to go there the next morning, but then on second thought he asked whether he might go to Rochester. Ham House lies upstream from London, while Rochester would be halfway back to Faversham. This meant that James might try to escape once more, and of course his request was granted. On the morning of the 18th he left London for the last time, guarded by the Prince's men.

That afternoon William came to London from Sion House, where he had spent the night. On his way he passed through crowds of coaches and people on horseback, and numberless thousands of cheering men and women who had come a mile or two out of town on foot to see their hero despite the miserable weather. Many of them wore orange ribbons, and others had put oranges on sticks and waved these about in the air. The Prince reached St James's Palace at about three o'clock. He plunged almost at once into the steamy intrigue of English politics. The return of James, and the consequent shift of public opinion in favour of the broken man, meant that the Prince's victory would be less than complete. Even though James made a second escape on 23 December, and this time a successful one, he now had a party. Some of its members were merely deluded by false sentiment. Others, like Archbishop Sancroft, were men of principle. The largest and most dangerous group was made up of people like Lord Clarendon, men without principle who became Jacobites because the Revolution did not bring them personal advantage. No political leader ever has enough jobs at his disposal to satisfy all his followers. The problem was particularly acute in 1688 because William had virtually the whole political world on his side. One of the advantages of a two-party system is that the loaves and the fishes need fill the mouths of only half the crowd at any given moment. Now, however, the politicians claimed that the Revolution had been a national act. Each of them did his best to describe his own part in the struggle as the decisive factor leading to the Revolution's success. Only the Messiah could have satisfied all their demands.

The Prince himself was the only person whose contribution had been vital. He knew it, and he knew also that he was indispensable to any solution. He could, therefore, afford to play a waiting game. For the most part he stayed quietly at St James's. On the 20th he and the Lords came to an agreement whereby they took over the civil administration while William retained command of the forces. Then, to give the Lords some measure of popular support, the surviving members of the Parliaments of Charles II, together with a substantial delegation from the City, were assembled to represent a House of Commons. Together with the Lords these men could at least give the appearance of having regular authority. On the 29th William accepted the provisional exercise of the civil government from them. Elections were then held for a Convention, which was to meet on 22 January. The Prince took care not to influence the course of these elections; but he was eventually obliged to bring the Convention to heel. A very small number of its members favoured the recall of James II, on conditions. A much larger body, including a majority of the House of Lords, would have preferred a Regency. Some, chiefly Lord Danby, hoped to make Mary Queen of England in her own right.

William would have none of these solutions, all of which were hopelessly irrelevant. He let it be known that he would leave the country if the former King returned. He made it clear that he would not accept a Regency, or the position of being his wife's gentleman usher. Superficially a Regency, at least, had some attractions. Such a solution would preserve the large revenue granted to the crown in 1685 for the lifetime of James II. But what then? Who would become King when James died, as he might at any moment? He was already as old as Charles II had been at the time of his death, and his course of life had been quite as irregular and quite as damaging to his health as had been that of his brother. William, furthermore, would have been placed in an impossible position if, as Regent for James, he issued one order and the titular King issued a conflicting one. A Regency could only work if the King and the Prince of Wales were under lock and key. Even then William would have had no guarantee of maintaining his position for his own lifetime. It was only to be expected that the enthusiasm of the English people for him would wane with the passage of time. In 1672 the Prince had held the same attitude and demanded a life tenure of the post of Captain-General of the United Provinces. He had much greater reason to demand life tenure now, when he was about to govern a people who considered him a foreigner. The same problem of tenure rose in connection with the proposal to make William King Consort. Mary might die before him. He would then be left high and dry, to face in all probability an alliance between Queen Anne and the French. The only solution that made any sense was to make William King for the term of his natural life. This got rid of James, the Prince of Wales, and the Princess Anne at one blow. To sweeten the pill, the Prince agreed to a 'double-bottomed monarchy', that is, that he and his wife should rule jointly. The administration, of course, would be single-bottomed. Mary received only the title of Queen, and while her husband was in England she did not have the sword of state carried before her as she went to her chapel. A second concession was that Anne and her children should take precedence in the line of succession before William's children by a second marriage. The Prince would make no further concessions. The politicians barked, but there was nothing they could do. The Princess, whose voyage had been delayed as much by bad winds as by policy, reached Whitehall on 12 February. Next day William and Mary went to the Banqueting House where Halifax as presiding officer of the House of Lords offered them the crown. Holding his wife's hand in his own, the Prince accepted for them both.

By now the frantic activity of the past eight months was beginning to tell. William III was in worse health during the spring of 1689 then he had ever been in his life. The smoke rising from the coal fires of London was intolerable to him. So too were the crowded, malodorous rooms at court where thousands of candles and hundreds of courtiers robbed him of the air he needed. Something must be done. Before the end of February the new king moved to Hampton Court, to the great disappointment of society and of the tradesmen. There his condition grew worse rather than better and it was observed that William was coughing blood. Early in April he confided to Dijkvelt that he thought he might die. He was a little better the next week and was able to go through with the ceremonies of the coronation on 11 April. Hampton Court was not really a satisfactory solution of the problem. It was too far out of town for the King to go in every day. Wolsey's palace was also not only very old-fashioned but much too small. Windsor, which had been restored by Charles II, was more comfortable yet even more remote. Soon after the coronation the King bought Kensington House from Lord Nottingham. While his new palace was being rebuilt and the new works at Hampton Court begun, he used Holland House as a temporary residence. Kensington was still too far out of town to please the people, but it was near enough so that the administration could be carried on without great inconvenience.

These domestic arrangements isolated William III from society and contributed to his growing unpopularity with the upper classes. There were other reasons for his failure to make friends. Although the King spoke English he lacked confidence in his command of the language. He consistently refused to write in it. As we all know, speaking in an imperfectly mastered tongue makes the simplest conversation sound stilted and unfriendly. The King's manners and his great preoccupation with business gave the same impression. He refused to eat or drink as much as his courtiers wished to do, so that although he made a point of dining with individual peers these occasions were hardly convivial ones. William III, furthermore, represented a continental concept of birth and position which was completely foreign to the English way. Many, if not most, of the island peers were quite recently descended from tradespeople on one side or the other. They were often actively interested in commerce themselves and their intellectual pursuits were usually literary or musical in character. This was all to the good. The new King, however, would if asked have given quite a different definition of what a noble should be. The origins of his own family could be traced back to the barbarian invasions. He cared nothing for literature and is not known to have paid any particular attention to music. Instead he devoted his leisure hours to art, building, and gardening. Most important, it was impossible for him to conceive of a civilian noble class. To William III this was simply a contradiction in terms. Before 1689 the most recent soldier kings of England had been Henry V and Edward IV. Since their day the English had become, as they remained, one of the most stubbornly civilian societies on the face of the earth. There had been a brief revival of interest in military matters during the Civil Wars. But the men of that generation were now for the most part dead, and their soldierly attitudes had died with them.

The King and the political nation, then, soon found that they shared very little common ground. It would have been a good thing had there been time for them to become acquainted. But there was no time. Even in England the Revolution was by no means completely over. In Scotland the outcome was still doubtful, while in Ireland Tyrconnel and his crew were in almost full control. The situation on the continent was even more serious. Although the French army had decayed both in quality and in numbers during the years of peace, William III knew from experience what a dreadful threat it still represented to the civilized world. All these problems had to be faced at once. Entirely apart from the very serious condition of his lungs that spring, the King was in many ways unprepared to face them. In the Republic he had been able to delegate political details, which rather bored him, to Fagel or on local matters to Odijk and Dijkvelt. A good share of his military and diplomatic work had been handled by Waldeck. Many of these men were a generation older than the King and even a subordinate figure like Solms was his senior by seventeen years. Fagel died in December 1688 and many of the others followed him in the next few years. Thus in the midst of so many other changes in his life the King suddenly found himself to be almost the senior member of his party. It is interesting to note that the first men he turned to in England, Halifax and Danby, were both almost twenty years older than their master. Clearly the King felt the need of a Nestor's counsel and guidance.

The Marquis of Halifax, who became Lord Privy Seal, kept rough notes of his conversations with William III during the first year of the Revolution. A portion of these survive.[3] They give a far more valuable picture of the King than that of Huygens in his *Journaal*. The Marquis examined William III as if he were a laboratory specimen, while the Secretary rarely did more than record names and dates. Like almost every man who came into close working contact with William III, Lord Halifax was clearly and deeply impressed. He noted the King's reluctance to pursue political enemies, his broad sense of toleration even for Catholics, his reliance as an officer and a gentleman on the word of honour of another officer and gentleman. All these characteristics were dangerous, perhaps, but they aroused the admiration of the Marquis. He also noted the new King's ignorance of the details of English affairs. This was only to be expected, and it is remarkable that more mistakes were not made in the first two years. At The Hague the Prince of Orange had been surrounded by exiles, a class known for the peculiar haziness of its daydreams. These 'republicans' had convinced themselves and momentarily convinced the Prince that they were the strongest party in England. In making his first appointments, therefore, William went distinctly further to the left than the real political strength of the 'republicans' warranted. Mordaunt was made First Lord of the Treasury and Earl of Monmouth. Delamere was made Chancellor of the Exchequer and, in time, Earl of Warrington. John Wildman, of all people, became Postmaster while a sinecure was found for the aged Ferguson. Oates, the most infamous man in England, was given a pension though the King found it a nauseating concession.

These extremists and their friends soon ruined themselves. Their demands for vengeance on their enemies disgusted the King. Their refusal to grant him his legislative programme was fatal. The invasion of England had been, in terms of money, a victory without a margin. Of the funds which had been supplied by the States there was only fl.100,000 or £10,000 left. The pacification of Scotland and Ireland, the strengthening of the armed forces, the very expenses of the court, could not be met for more than a few days from such a ridiculous sum. Yet the Convention, which was turned into a Parliament on 23 February, seemed oblivious of the need for money. It soon decided that the life revenue of James II had fallen in. It failed to provide a new one and its grants were completely inadequate stop-gaps. Hampden was responsible for persuading the King to surrender the Hearth Money,[4] a hereditary and profitable tax though a burdensome one. William's sacrifice of the Hearth Money was not met by any corresponding generosity on the part of the Commons. Not until midsummer was £600,000 voted to repay the Dutch for the costs of the invasion, and this was some 13 per cent less than what had actually been spent. For his own affairs the King was granted little or nothing, certainly much less than what was needed to complete the Revolution. It was only after a disaffected regiment at Ipswich had mutinied on 15 March that the Convention began to think seriously of the problems of the army. The revolt of the soldiers led to the rapid passage of the Mutiny Act, a measure which made it possible for the King to begin to train the wilful and undisciplined men of the old royal army. Not many of these remained, and many new regiments were raised in 1689. The new levies were not much more raw than the men left over from the days of James II. It would take years of training under disciplinarians like Count Solms before any of them became real soldiers. The King was careful to appoint Dutchmen not only to the highest commands but also as provost-marshals and ordnance officials. This would eventually secure the development of a professional army and also serve to protect the person of their Commander-in-Chief, who was to be in great danger from assassins for the rest of his days. The most ominous of the reports coming in from France was one that was sent on from Vienna as early as 6 January. Hop's despatch of that day brought word that the French considered William's actions not as a war but as a private quarrel between the Prince and his father-in-law. It would therefore be permissable to use all such methods as were customary in such cases.[5] Thus an open season was declared on William III. Brave as he was, he did not venture to risk his life at the hands of the English army until the Mutiny Act had been in force for fifteen months.

In other respects than finance the conduct of the Convention was also obnoxious. Although a Toleration Act was passed, its provisions were narrow in the extreme and it was only by a consistent refusal to enforce the penal laws that the King was able to give the English the blessings that are so inaccurately associated with the statute. William's hopes for a Comprehension Act and for the repeal of the Tests in so far as they affected Protestant dissenters were blasted. Habeas Corpus was suspended, but not long enough to give the King any real personal safety. It was not until 7 May that war was declared on France. Worst of all, William's plans for the succession were only to be carried out in part. He had hoped to have the Duchess Sophia of Hanover, the next Protestant in the line of succession after the Princess Anne, mentioned by name. This would secure the Protestant Succession, since Sophia had several sons. It would also secure Hanover, an important piece in the diplomatic jigsaw puzzle and one that happened to have a treaty with France at that moment. But the Convention would not agree, and Sophia's claims were not to be recognized by Parliament for another twelve years.

Fortunately the King was not entirely dependent on the vagaries of the English. If he had been, the Revolution would probably have foundered during the course of the year. William's position as virtual leader of a dual monarchy made it possible for him to use Dutch channels when the English ones were clogged. Thus as early as 15 January the Prince asked the States of Holland to forward an ambitious diplomatic scheme. He wanted the Republic to declare war on France, which would entitle it to assistance from its allies Sweden and Spain. He hoped that the States would conclude treaties promptly with the Emperor and with the whole House of Lunenberg. For his own part, William promised substantial military and naval assistance.[6] Before William's suggestion for an alliance with the Emperor had time to reach Vienna, Leopold had had the same idea.[7] Negotiations proceeded quickly,

complicated only slightly by the fact that the Emperor had not yet recognized
William as King of England. The Grand Alliance was signed at The Hague
on 12 May as between the Republic and Leopold. The latter recognized
William III as King a month later and was gracious enough to give him the
style of 'Majesty', which had been refused to James II in 1685 and later. On
9 September William III acceded to the Grand Alliance, and Spain followed
in June 1690.⁸ Two other powers, Bavaria and Denmark, joined the confederacy by other routes. The young Elector of Bavaria was Leopold's son-
in-law, but his sister was married to the Dauphin. He might have joined either
side. In 1688 the Emperor captured Max-Emmanuel by giving him command
of the imperial forces. This coup was completed by a treaty of 4 May 1689
under the terms of which the Emperor promised to do his best to get his
son-in-law the government of the Spanish Netherlands.⁹ During that summer
William III drew Denmark towards the allied camp by hiring a large contingent of her soldiers. Originally they were meant to fight in Scotland.
Since that country was pacified before the arrival of the Danish troops, they
were actually used in Ireland.

A second important element in the successes of the year 1689, over and
above the diplomatic work of the King, was sheer luck. The Protestant wind
had not ceased to blow. In France, neither Louis XIV nor Louvois was prepared for a major war. Luxembourg, the best field-commander the French
had, was in disgrace. His position at the head of the army in the Low Countries
was taken by Humières, succinctly described by his countrymen as *le maréchal
sans lumière*. Even the aged Waldeck could contain such an opponent. The
Dutch did even better than contain their enemy. By buying the commander
of Rijnberk for fl.100,000 they consolidated their gains in Cologne, and
later in the year their German friends took Bonn and Keiserswerth. Thus on
the continent the campaign of 1689 went well. The King was even luckier
at home. There had been very little he could do for Scotland beyond sending
Hugh Mackay and portions of the three Scottish regiments in Dutch service
to Edinburgh by sea. This force, which arrived in March, was much too small
to achieve anything by itself. The Revolution in Scotland, therefore, took
place without any central control or direction, and for that reason it was more
violent than its English counterpart. A convention was already sitting at
Edinburgh when Mackay and his men arrived, its sessions untroubled by the
fact that the Duke of Gordon was rather languidly holding Edinburgh Castle
for King James. On 11 April the convention offered the crown of Scotland
to William and Mary.¹⁰ Before the offer was made, Viscount Dundee had
left for Stirling to take up arms. A considerable number of the clans opposed
the Revolution since it was accompanied by the return of the exiled Camp-
bells. If the proscribed Archibald Campbell were to become tenth Earl of

Argyll, many and many a man would be dispossessed as Argyll recovered his family estates. A second disaffected element in Scottish life was the Episcopalian Church. One of the clauses of the Claim of Right which the Scots attached to their offer of the crown condemned the bishops and foreshadowed the end of the episcopalian scheme. With Dundee, an experienced and talented soldier, to lead them these disaffected groups would be able to fight.

Since Mackay had nothing like an army at his disposal, the situation soon became extremely serious. Had James been able to reach Scotland with French supplies during the summer, the recurrent nightmare of the government in London, there would have been nothing to stop him until he crossed the border into England. No one could be quite sure what might happen even then. Luckily, James did not come. Luckily, Edinburgh Castle fell in June. Luckily, as Mackay advanced towards Blair Atholl in the last days of July, he met Dundee at the head of the clans. On 27 July they beat him at Killiecrankie. But the Jacobite victory was turned to ashes by the fact that Dundee perished in the fight. He was their only leader of any ability. A few weeks later they were badly defeated at Dunekeld. From now on there would be little to fear from the Scots.

In Ireland, too, William's luck held in the long run. At first the picture was as black as could be. Tyrconnel, a native Irishman, was determined to hold the island for his King. Other natives fought with equal determination for their faith and for national independence. Ireland posed a serious and perfectly obvious problem even in December 1688. At that time William had neither men nor money to spare. He would have to leave it to solve itself until Parliament should grant him money. There was the merest chance that something could be gained by negotiation. John Temple, the son of Sir William, suggested using Richard Hamilton as a go-between. Lord Devonshire did what he could by writing to his Irish friends. These attempts, and there may have been others, failed of their purpose. Irish nationalism could only support James, as English and Scottish nationalists could only oppose him. As it happened the negotiations ended in personal tragedy as well as in failure. Hamilton, a soldier, had given his parole that if he failed he would return to England. When he reached Dublin and saw that he could not persuade Tyrconnel, he broke his word and threw in his lot with the Irish. The sensitive Temple, to everyone's distress, was driven to suicide by his friend's dishonourable conduct and by the collapse of his romantically optimistic scheme.

In March James reached Ireland. He brought French arms and French advisers with him, and he found that the Irish were determined to make the most of their opportunity by breaking the English connection. Thus the poor man was doubly a marionette. Some of the strings were pulled by the French, some by the Irish. There was very little that James could do for himself and almost nothing for his cause. Apparently he used what little influence he had, and it is to his credit, to modify the brutal tone of the fighting. In particular he did manage to prevent the soldiers from burning Dublin, a meaningless atrocity. But he could not be everywhere and no one could have controlled the untrained savagery of the natives or the trained and purposeful savagery of the French soldiers, whose fellows on the continent were even now obeying the orders given them to turn the Palatinate into a desert. The Protestants were driven from one place to the next. Many of them managed to escape with their lives, if little more, to England. Others were soon crowded into Londonderry and Enniskillen. In mid-April began the famous siege of Derry.

It would make more sense to blame George II for the Black Hole of Calcutta, or Queen Anne for the Deerfield Massacre, than to blame William III for the difficulties of Ireland in 1689. The small army he had brought with him had succeeded in England and was now in the process of helping to secure Scotland. The King himself, despite his frightening cough, was busy negotiating the Grand Alliance. Somehow he found time to negotiate for the dispatch of the Danish troops. Somehow he found time to order supplies and ammunition to be sent to the relief of Londonderry. If the governor of Derry refused to accept reinforcements and sent them back, if the English supply system was almost hopelessly corrupt, William III was not to blame. He could not be everywhere at the same time. There is an armour museum at Madrid in which all kinds of suits are displayed on models, from the elaborate and costly outfit of a king to the simple pot and leather coat of the common soldier. Every one of the hundred models has the face of the Emperor Charles V. Had William III been a hundred men he could not have prevented all the treachery and corruption which were to be found in the three kingdoms. Had he been two hundred men he would still have found it difficult to persuade the Convention to grant a meaningful sum of money. The English, after thirty years of civilian sloth, had no concept of the cost of modern warfare. They demanded victory on the cheap. Since their King seemed to be a miracle worker, it must be his personal fault if the waving of a magic wand did not bring instant victory in Ireland. And in fact they were not completely in error about the magic wand. Of all the different forms of warfare, amphibious operations are among the most difficult even in our own day. In the seventeenth century the problems were almost insuperable. Yet William III had had the skill to mount one such operation against England in the autumn of 1688, and to send Mackay by sea to Edinburgh in the following March. In both cases the troops had the good fortune to land on a friendly, or at least a neutral, shore. Even so the operations were difficult enough. Now the King had the skill to overcome the treachery and corruption that surrounded him.

On 30 July the boom at Lough Foyle was broken and the English ships were at last able to relieve Londonderry. On the same day the men of Enniskillen, ably led by Colonel Wolseley, beat the Irish at Newton Butler. In the middle of August Schomberg with a scratch force landed in County Down. The bravery of the people of Derry and Enniskillen had preserved a beachhead, without which Ireland's reconquest would have been immeasurably more difficult than it was. But it cannot be said that the King did not respond to the opportunity which was presented to him. What is remarkable is that he was able to throw troops into Ireland in 1689 and to begin the long process of the reconquest. Only the most ignorant of amateurs could have asked for more.

On 20 August the King was obliged to prorogue the Convention, which had been spending its time in attacking his ministers rather than in providing him with any assistance. By this time, despite the antics of the politicians, the Revolution was visibly prospering. England was much more confident of the stability of the new régime than it had been in the spring. Scotland was well on the way to order. In Ireland things were going better, if they were not yet going well. On the continent an alliance had been formed which was gaining ground from the French. Even the Princess Anne had done her share by giving birth in July to a boy. The life of the little Duke of Gloucester, frail though he was, gave a promise of permanence to the dynasty. The King, however, had little to hope for from his present ministry or from the Convention. Halifax, able as he was, was neither an administrator nor a party leader. William wanted to forget the past; but the Commons had not passed a bill of indemnity, nor had it settled the revenue. During the parliamentary recess the King went to Newmarket and politely lost four or five thousand guineas in an attempt to court popularity with the nobles. His efforts were not very successful. As he remarked gloomily to Dijkvelt, 'I see that I am not made for this people, nor they for me'.[11]

The political advantages to be gained from an opening to the right seemed ever more attractive to the King as the year progressed. The Earl of Nottingham and the Marquis of Carmarthen, as Danby had now become, combined obvious administrative talent with a tender care of the prerogative. Their friends, furthermore, seemed willing to lend money on a considerable scale without demanding such great political concessions as did the Whigs.[12] Another advantage of an opening to the right was that it would diminish the political importance of the Princess Anne. When the Convention met for its second session in October it voted £2,000,000 for the reduction of Ireland. Its generosity did not extend to a permanent settlement of the King's revenue, which was granted for a single year. Lord Cornbury, however, introduced a clause which would have granted Anne a permanent revenue of £70,000 a year when the King himself was given provision for twelve months only. Although the clause was warmly supported by the Church interest, it had to be modified. The sum proposed was outrageous, and the contrast between the demands of the Princess and the moderation of the King and Queen all too glaring. In the end the Princess was given £50,000 for one year. Even this contributed to the growing estrangement between the two courts. Anne had been unwilling to accept her establishment from the King. She had tried, or the Countess of Marlborough had tried for her, to set up an independent political interest based on the Church party and the xenophobic feelings of the nation. The King could not disguise the fact that he was half foreign. He could at least capture some of Anne's party by showing more kindness to the Tories.

The rest of the Convention's conduct was of a piece with its refusal to grant the King a life revenue. In February the King and Queen had accepted the crown of England on conditions, those contained in the famous Declaration of Right. William III was annoyed at any reduction of the royal power and hoped that the crown would not be the worse for his wearing of it. At the time, the Declaration was explained to him as being a mere restatement of existing law. Whatever it might be, he hoped to have heard the last of it. Yet at the end of the year the Convention made the Declaration into a statute, known as the Bill of Rights. In one important respect the Bill went further than the Declaration. The suspending power had been declared illegal in February, and so too the dispensing power 'as it hath been assumed and exercised of late'. In December the dispensing power was quite taken away. At the same time that the royal powers were being whittled away, no progress was made towards a Bill of Indemnity. The Whigs also attempted to ruin their enemies by means of a Corporation Bill, put before a thin House during the Christmas festivals. The Sacheverell Clause of this Bill would have disqualified all those who had taken part in the surrender of the old charters to Charles II and his brother from holding municipal office for a period of seven years. Had the clause taken effect, a very large number of the best qualified men in the kingdom would have been proscribed. The King was warned that the Whigs would withdraw their loans if he opposed the measure. Luckily the third reading of the Bill did not take place until 10 January, and by that time many Tories had been able to return to their places. After a long debate, the Clause was rejected. Some angry men did demand their money from the Exchequer, but other lenders were soon to come forward.

All through the year William III had been eager to get away from paperwork and into the field. He had hopes of commanding a descent on France, of returning to Flanders, and even of fighting in Scotland. In December he threatened to return to the continent. Although this has frequently been interpreted as a proposed abdication, it seems more likely that William had something much less drastic in mind. He had been worried for months that the Dutch might make a separate peace if they received no more English assistance than they were getting at the moment. The political situation in the Republic was very bad. Bentinck was sent over in December to put things in order, but he might not be able to maintain the Stadhouder's authority. Waldeck was not up to the task of defending the Low Countries. Again and again time was to prove that only William himself could obtain obedience from his generals. His presence in command of his armies was essential. The English political situation could probably be left to take care of itself. William was also desperately homesick. Thus it is likely that he planned a trip, rather than an abdication. In any case Shrewsbury and Carmarthen would not hear of any such plan. They insisted that the government could not be carried on in their master's absence. William was forced to abandon his original idea. Instead, he decided to take personal command of the campaign in Ireland. During December and January his preparations were obvious. The Convention feared, or pretended to fear, for the King's welfare. An address was planned against his voyage to Ireland. To forestall the address, William prorogued the Convention on 27 January and dissolved it on 6 February. His step secured him not only his voyage to Ireland but the opening to the right as well. The new Parliament was far less radical than the Convention. There were sympathetic changes in the ministry. Monmouth and Delamere disappeared from the Treasury. Halifax resigned at once and Shrewsbury, to the King's dismay, followed him later in the spring. Carmarthen and Nottingham emerged as the leaders of the administration.

Chapter 19

THE RECONQUEST OF IRELAND

HARDLY had the expedition for England sailed when opposition began to raise its head in the Republic. For the moment, the chance that William might lose in England and return as Stadhouder – together with the presence of the Princess in The Hague – kept this opposition within bounds. But as soon as the Prince's victory was assured, and the Princess had left to become Queen of England, a new prospect opened. Fagel's death, which could not have been more inopportune, gave the malcontents more of an opening than they would have had otherwise. Provisionally, Michiel ten Hove was appointed to succeed him. Ten Hove, however, was already mortally ill. He died in March 1689. Thus during the winter of 1688–89 there was for most purposes no Dutch government worth the name. And although Anthonie Heinsius succeeded ten Hove as Grand Pensionary he was at first too new at his job to act with the needed vigour. In the long run Heinsius was to become one of the greatest of Dutch statesmen. Even in 1689 he was a man of proved experience, pensionary of Haarlem and a member of the Seventeen, the secret committee which governed the East India Company. In his early years Heinsius had not been a supporter of the Prince, but his eyes had been opened when he went on a diplomatic mission to Paris in 1683. At that time Louis XIV threatened to send him to the Bastille as punishment for an imagined impertinence. Heinsius was not the man to be bullied with impunity. He returned to Holland with a greater understanding of the Prince's policy in foreign affairs, and he learned more during a mission to England as a representative of the East India Company in 1685 and 1686. In March of 1689 he was the obvious candidate to succeed ten Hove as provisional Grand Pensionary.[1]

As a person, Heinsius was a charming host, a discreet negotiator, a sincere patriot, an immensely hard worker. As a bachelor, he had nothing to distract his attention from his country's service. But he was not a fierce partisan, as Fagel had been. Both William and his chief advisers complained at first that Heinsius was too soft, too timid. His position, in the absence of the Stadhouder, was admittedly a difficult one. In fact, Heinsius tried to refuse the place of Grand Pensionary on the ground that no one could function successfully with William in England. He was to prove himself wrong in this respect. Over the years he was able to establish an administration that worked well without a Stadhouder. The 'second Stadhouderless period' has its origins not in 1702 but in 1688.² It took time, however, for Heinsius to gain confidence in himself and the respect of others. William gave the Grand Pensionary his full confidence from the beginning. Often Heinsius was permitted to elect the magistrates of the various towns in William's name. At other times he was asked to discover from some politician the names of those who ought to be selected, a process which gave Heinsius experience as well as prestige. Gradually William found that he could withdraw from the details of Dutch political life, and the Pensionary eventually found himself being used as a mediator even in the very unpleasant personal wrangles of the Nassau family.

William's other arrangements for the government of the Republic in his absence were less fortunate. Waldeck had been left behind in charge of the army, not merely as field-marshal but as personal representative of the Captain-General. As a field-marshal he would have been subject to the instructions of the Council of State, the Raad van State. As William's substitute he was authorized to protect every one of the Prince's rights from attack from any quarter. The attacks were not long in coming. Waldeck was by now far too old and weakened by gout to be successful in the field or in the political arena at The Hague. He did not have enough influence to persuade the States of Zeeland and Friesland to vote their shares of the military budget. The province of Holland disputed his right to issue marching orders inside her borders. The Raad van State acted independently, trying to increase its own authority and sometimes issuing orders without informing Waldeck of what was going on. After William appointed Walraad, Count of Nassau-Saarbrück, as second field-marshal and Henry Casimir, Prince of Nassau and Stadhouder of Friesland and Groningen, as third field-marshal in the spring of 1689, there was more trouble. The Prince of Nassau did not like to be by-passed, and he had a place on the Raad van State itself. During the campaign of 1689 he cooperated with Waldeck fairly well. But there were others who were eager to stir up disputes between them, and to try to give these disputes a grave turn.

A month after William's departure for England, Waldeck reported the formation of a hostile political faction. It was based on the general dislike of Dijkvelt, a faithful and talented servant of William III but an arrogant and spiteful man, who created enemies wherever he went. Odijk and de Huybert controlled the states of Zeeland; by forming an alliance with the discontented in Friesland and Groningen they could hold up the conduct of the government.³ They were soon joined by Amerongen, who resented Dijkvelt's superior position in the States of Utrecht. This was an old hatred, which had been controlled for years by appointing Amerongen to one diplomatic mission to Berlin after another. Unfortunately he was now at liberty, and as a member of the Raad van State he could do a great deal of harm.⁴ The King did what he could to bolster Waldeck's position, authorizing him to give the password at The Hague and to be accompanied wherever he went by the Stadhouder's guard of honour, which was later given royal livery so as to outshine the guards of Henry Casimir. Waldeck was also given William's salary and his share of the profits from military contributions and *sauvegardes*. This would give him enough to enable him to set a good table during the campaign.[5] It was not enough to establish his position.

The malcontents disliked Waldeck personally, as they also disliked him for his friendship with Dijkvelt. They would have been pleased to have the scalps of both men. What they were after, however, was bigger game. They wanted to weaken the powers of the Captain-General to such a point that the Raad van State would be able to take over the military conduct of the war. Then Amerongen hoped, at least so Waldeck suspected, to be able to direct the Raad van State through the weak Henry Casimir of Nassau.[6] On the surface this was simply a military conspiracy, or at least one confined to the Raad van State, and it could be countered quite easily. Amerongen's son Ginckel was sent over during the winter of 1689 to calm his father's temper. When his success was only partial, Amerongen was sent into gilded exile as ambassador to Copenhagen until his death. Another of the malcontents, Slingelandt, happened to die in 1690; and William III could always bring Odijk around himself, though no one else could ever do it for him. But this was not simply a feud between two branches of the Orange party. Amsterdam had joined in the game during the summer of 1689 by trying to set up field deputies to control Waldeck's actions in the field, and behind Amsterdam lay France. Correspondence between the 'well-intentioned' of the great city and the French had been resumed.[7] If the French could re-establish their influence, they might be able to induce the Republic to leave the war. Alternatively, they might be able to replace William as Stadhouder by Henry Casimir. This would probably break the close relationship between the Republic and England and also remove Brandenburg from the alliance, since the Elector Frederick III was chiefly interested in his position as William's heir. If Frederick lost his hopes of the Orange inheritance, including the survivorship of William's offices, he might well change sides.

In January 1690 Amsterdam altered its tactics and began to deny the competence of William III in civilian rather than in military affairs. As Stadhouder, his authority over the city was more limited than it was over the other towns of Holland. He did, however, have the right to select the seven sheriffs each year from the list of fourteen names submitted to him. Often the names of the seven men the city particularly favoured were marked on the list. That for 1689 had been sent over to England, and William had chosen five of the marked men and two others. During the course of the year two of those elected had died in office, and in each case Amsterdam had sent over two names of possible replacements, of whom William had elected one. Now, however, the city claimed that the elections had to be made by a certain date; that by an ancient law they were to be made in the Stadhouder's absence by the Court of Holland; and that, since William III could not make the election from England in good time, the Court of Holland ought to do it. The King had meanwhile sent Portland to The Hague with an expedient, a signed letter of election with the names left blank. If Amsterdam agreed to send the letter of nomination to Heinsius, directed to the King, Heinsius was authorized to open the nomination and to fill in the blanks of William's 'reply' with the seven names the city had marked.[8] Thus in substance Amsterdam would get the men she preferred, in exchange for preserving William's rights. If she insisted on thwarting the King, Portland was ordered to explain, delicately, that William had quite sufficient authority to arrest all the city's ships which lay in English ports.

Amsterdam would not even permit Portland to take his seat in the States of Holland. He was now in the service of a foreign potentate and had therefore lost the exercise of his rights as a member of the nobility of Holland. The meaning of this step could not have been more plain. For if the Heer van Rhoon was now Earl of Portland, the Prince of Orange had a new title of his own and might be excluded on the same grounds. When the matter was argued in the States of Holland, all the nobility and all the other towns supported Portland. Amsterdam stood alone. The deputies of the city then left the assembly, announcing that they considered everything done in the Earl's presence null and void. Their Pensionary would attend meetings, but only as an observer; and, of course, without a unanimous vote no new treaty could be made nor taxes voted. The crisis continued for two months, during which Portland had reason to commend the patience of Heinsius in his support though he lamented the loss of Fagel's vigour.[9] The new Grand Pensionary had judgment and goodwill, but he had not yet learned to fight.[10] Finally, at the end of February, the States of Holland decreed that the sheriffs of the previous year were no longer qualified to perform their functions in Amsterdam, and that whatever they had done since their appointments came to an end on 2 February, was null and void. At the same time the States asked William III to aid them by exercising his legitimate authority. Portland hoped that the King would cross over, if only for a week, to crush the city by changing the magistrates as he had in 1672. They were hated even by the respectable people of their own city. Officers of the Amsterdam watch came to Portland to offer their assistance in opening the gates to an attacking force.[11] William would have liked to come but he could not make the trip and return before the opening session of the new Parliament. It was not until the middle of

March that Amsterdam agreed to the taxes for the year, nor until the 27th that her representatives agreed to sit in the States of Holland in Portland's presence. A compromise had been worked out under which the city sent its letter of nomination to the assembly, which sent it on to William in England to make the election. It would, perhaps, have been better if the King had been able to crush Amsterdam once for all. Even if he had been able to come over, however, his victory – though more brilliant – would probably not have been a permanent one. As it was, William maintained his authority and the leaders of the city were made to look both foolish and unpatriotic.[12]

Meanwhile the King continued his preparations for the Irish campaign. Entirely apart from his hatred of the trade of politician, he had come to the conclusion that the Irish war would drag on and on unless he went there himself. The aged Schomberg lacked the authority to make himself obeyed as well as the vigour necessary to secure a rapid victory. It was in some ways a hard decision. The frightened Queen[13] would have to undertake the government, which would be difficult for her and perhaps dangerous as well. She was totally inexperienced, and too kindly a person to control factions with the needed severity. William, however, was convinced that nothing worth while would be done in Ireland without him.[14] Having decided to go, he wished to make sure that he had an overwhelming preponderance of force. The Dutch were required to lend cannon and officers they could ill spare. The English would somehow have to provide money, though the financial situation was particularly depressing at this time. The King himself would have to provide organization and drive to overcome the 'incorrigible slowness and negligence' of the administration. He worked so hard that he damaged his health, which was always to be particularly bad during an English winter.[15] Kensington was just tolerable, as Whitehall was not; but the air at Kensington was not nearly as good as that at Hampton Court or at Richmond. William, however, did not discover Richmond until 1695. Luckily, though his condition became alarming, there was nothing seriously wrong with him.

The original plan had been to go to Ireland by way of Scotland, leaving about the beginning of March. Political problems forced a change in the schedule. The election took time. Parliament did not sit until 20 March, and when it did there were further delays. At long last the revenue was granted, the Excise for life and the Customs for four years. The grant of the Customs for a term of years was an innovation, and thus displeasing to the King. In his speech from the throne he had asked for the same revenue as that given to James II, and to have it on the same terms.[16] It is undoubtedly true that the theoretical power of the crown was limited by the terms of the grant. William III was supposed to be an authoritarian at heart, on the evidence supplied by his enemies at Amsterdam. By tying his hands, Parliament would secure itself from the dangers of tyranny and at the same time make frequent sessions necessary. But there was a more practical reason involved. The gift of the Customs for a certain term would encourage lenders. This was more important than the preservation of a shadowy portion of the royal authority. It was most unfortunate that the King did not appreciate the generosity of his subjects. His financial requests were unprecedented, and on the whole the people of England responded nobly to a sharply higher level of taxation than they had experienced since Cromwell's time. The King saw only that the amounts granted, large as they were, were still too small. His ministers did not even dare ask Parliament for what was really needed in these early years of the reign. What was asked for, however, seemed breathtaking to the Commons.

William solved the problem of the Indemnity Bills by sending down an Act of Grace, which excepted only thirty-five particularly notorious persons. Even so, Parliament did not move as quickly as he wished. Many Members did not want the King to go to Ireland. They dragged their feet as much as they dared over the Regency Bill, which granted the exercise of the administration to the Queen during her husband's absence, and some of them were brave enough to state their real reasons for doing so. They were not able to prevent the King's departure. Their delays did cost him a further two months, and he was not able to adjourn the Houses until 23 May. This forced him to abandon his trip to Scotland. William was very angry at the waste of so much good campaigning weather. The Queen, left behind to face one conspiracy in favour of her father and the suspicion of another in favour of her sister, was disconsolate.[17] But she had a Council to assist her, even if Carmarthen was the only one of its members whom she could trust.

William estimated his own force at a paper strength of 34,560 foot and 9,300 horse, and put the enemy numbers at approximately a tenth less than his own. King James's forces, however, were known to be very badly led.[18] In fact the 'late King' had only about 25,000 men in all, and he was as weak in artillery as he was in officers. William's superiority, therefore, was unusually large. Never before had he enjoyed such luxury. He had had a numerical superiority in the campaign of 1674, but his troops were not then experienced and his armies had suffered terribly from a divided command. Only twice in his life, in 1690 and in 1695, did William III have superior forces under his personal direction.

At dawn on 4/14 June the King set out from London with a large train. George of Denmark was taken along for his only campaign, probably to ensure the loyalty of his wife. William spent three nights on the road to Chester. He was cheered over the whole route by the common people, squads of women running along after his coach and demanding to kiss his hand.

Even the secretaries who went by another way were given the good wishes and prayers of the crowd.[19] At Chester there was a delay, and the crossing of the Irish Channel was a bad one. William landed at Carrickfergus at midday on the 14th and went on the next day to Belfast, to the horror of his English officers who felt the air there to be most unhealthy.[20] Bonfires lit that night soon carried the news of his arrival all over the island. Affairs were in better state than the King had expected, and he determined to force a battle on the enemy as soon as possible.[21] Only so could he end the Irish diversion and secure the release of his armies for service on the continent. The French advisers of James II knew perfectly well that this was William's intention. Their own goal was to try to persuade James to avoid a battle and to fight a delaying action for another year or two.[22] Luckily for William III, and for the Irish people, the Frenchmen were not able to make their wishes prevail. The Irish had suffered terribly from the war already. They were naked and starving. Huygens noted particularly one famished boy of seven or eight who looked more like a skeleton than a human being.[23] Two more campaigns would have meant terrible suffering.

William's personal appearance, as he had foretold, was needed if there was to be a quick victory. The prudent Schomberg had refused to push things, feeling that he was too short of men and supplies to take great risks. It was noted that the King was quite cold to him, probably for this very reason. And William had never forgiven Schomberg for being his understudy in 1688. His attitude was unfair, since he brought with him the very men and material for which the Duke had been so greedy. When these had been landed the army was able to march on the 19th. It was very hot. The countryside was picturesque, but the roads were very poor. Often a narrow stone causeway ran through the middle of a morass. So long as one pair of the wagon wheels remained on the causeway, well and good. If a wagon was forced to leave the safety of the paving, however, horses and all disappeared in the mud.[24] The path of the army led through Hillsborough towards Newry. On the way a deserter came in, saying that King James's army had gone towards Ardee so as to have more room for a battle. William therefore marched towards Ardee and reached it on the 29th, to discover that the enemy had retired over the Boyne the day before. On the 30th his men marched another six miles and camped in sight of the enemy, roughly a mile north of the river and a mile west of Drogheda.[25] The ground slopes down fairly steeply on both sides of the Boyne. This meant that the English camp was open to view and subject to the attention of some Irish six-pounders. William arrived about midday and rode along his lines, intending to inspect the river. He was so well attended that there could be no doubt of his identity. The Irish fired two of their six-pounders. There was a sudden movement among the courtiers and a great cheer went up from the Irish ranks. William had been hit. One of the two balls had grazed his right shoulder-blade, tearing away coat, waist-coat, and shirt. The wound itself was merely a contusion, about as big as the palm of one's hand. The official account said that his Majesty lost 'near half a spoonful of blood'.

When he was hit William gave no sign except to rise a little in his stirrups. After a plaster had been placed over the wound and he had put on a fresh coat he continued his tour of inspection. But he rode alone except for Schomberg, so as to be less conspicuous. At four o'clock the King dined, and afterwards he insisted on riding up and down the entire line waving his hat in his right hand to prove that he could still use that arm.[26] That night Count Meinhard Schomberg, a son of the Duke, led a detachment upstream to cross the Boyne by the bridge at Slane and so turn the enemy's flank. He succeeded in making a useful diversion, but the main action took place at three fords in front of William's camp. The Blue Guards were ordered to cross the river by the central ford. On the south side of the Boyne were two houses with walled gardens, one on each side of the road that led up the hill from the ford. In these there were some Irish foot, but their fire was silenced by the King's cannon. The Guards crossed the river through water over their knees. As they were coming out on the south bank the Irish fired once and then fled. The Guards were not yet safe. They had no cavalry support, and as they were forming up they were charged by a body of Jacobite horse. William watched, fascinated, while his Guards heroically stood their ground. 'My poor Guards, my poor Guards', he muttered. They did not give way. Firing by platoons, they beat off two cavalry attacks. A great shout of applause broke from the English army at this feat and the King, calling for his horse, rode across the river to lead them up the hill and capture the enemy's cannon.

Meanwhile, some of the Jacobites had entered the river and a few men, perhaps thirty, of whom twenty-five were soon killed, managed to get across. They killed the Duke of Schomberg before they were wiped out. At the other fords William's forces got across without much trouble, because the Irish had no pikes. The King led his men onward with complete disregard for his own safety. Resistance, however, did not continue for long. The Irish retreat soon turned into a flight. Only the French detachments fought well and retreated in good order. As for the natives, when they saw King William appear at the top of the hill and heard that King James had abandoned them, they threw away their weapons and ran across the fields faster than the English cavalry could pursue them. William chased the enemy beyond Duleek and then returned to that village to spend the night. Some of the Irish, and their King James, did not stop even at Dublin.[27]

In numbers of casualties, the Boyne was little more than a heavy skirmish.

Perhaps sixteen hundred of the enemy were killed, wounded, or captured. William's losses were less than a third as large. None the less Ginckel was correct when he wrote to his father the next day: 'This is a great victory, which will do good throughout Europe and give great satisfaction to the allies.'[28] James, when he saw how the battle was going, retired from the Boyne as hastily as he had from Salisbury. Luckily for the Irish he refused to accept the advice given him to burn Dublin and passed through the city to the protection of the French fleet. His political career was at an end. For the rest of his life he would be a pathetic exile, sometimes plotting for the recovery of his heritage but more often praying for the remission of his sins. It was not a harsher fate than he deserved.

The victory at the Boyne made the reconquest of all Ireland merely a matter of time. At first William III proceeded with deliberation and care. After a ceremonial entry into Dublin he moved against Waterford and secured that important port. Then he turned west. At first he planned only to direct the crossing of the Shannon, where difficulties were expected, and to delegate the siege of Limerick to Count Solms. Unfortunately for his reputation, William changed his mind. When the crossing of the Shannon proved easy he moved on towards Limerick in person. By this time the rains were beginning. A portion of the royal artillery was surprised by Patrick Sarsfield. Although a breach was made in the walls of the town, the attackers did not obey orders. Trying to storm the place before reinforcements could reach them, an advance party was cut off and suffered heavy losses. The rains continued and were so heavy that further progress became impossible. William reluctantly raised the siege of Limerick and returned to Kensington by way of Waterford and Bristol. If he had not completed the reconquest, he had personally made that reconquest inevitable. During the autumn Marlborough was sent to take Cork and Kinsale from the sea, a limited task which he carried out with admirable efficiency. For the rest, Ginckel was given supreme command of the army in Ireland. During the summer of 1691 he proceeded methodically, taking Athlone and then Aghrim and finally Limerick itself. Although Ireland might very easily have been reduced in 1690 except for the slowness of the English parliamentary session, which wasted so much of the year's good weather, the King was fortunate in having two such able subordinates. Ginckel was made Earl of Athlone for his work. Marlborough had already been made an Earl by William and had, at Cork and Kinsale, done something to deserve his promotion. He was ceasing to be purely the 'general of favour' and was in the process of earning his spurs. What he wanted, however, was not spurs but the moon – or at least the Garter, a Dukedom, and the lucrative post of Master-General of the Ordnance. We shall see what was his reaction when he was disappointed.

By clearing Ireland to the point where a civilian administration could be set up again in the eastern provinces William III had once again put his subjects in his debt. The Revolution was now substantially achieved, and achieved without the loss of any portion of the empire. For a while, at any rate, the people would be grateful to their deliverer. And the Boyne did more than set the seal of permanence on the Revolution. It happened to be most fortunately timed. By now the French King and his ministers had been able to set their military machine going again. Luxembourg was once more in command of the armies in the Low Countries, and on 1 July he thrashed the much smaller allied forces under Waldeck at Fleurus. The battle was bravely fought and without serious consequences. By now the Dutch infantry was so well trained that it shrugged off losses such as those at Fleurus and was ready to fight again within a few days. The cavalry, less well trained and less good, achieved the same effect by running away from the field of battle. Thus it succeeded in preserving itself as a force 'in being', but it was not a force of which the enemy need be very respectful.

Far more important than Fleurus was the loss of the naval action off Beachy Head on 30 June. Lord Torrington, as Arthur Herbert had become, was given orders to fight a much larger French force at all costs. He may have resented the orders of the cabinet council. He may have been involved in the political squabbles that were almost destroying the fighting capacity of the English navy. He may have been jealous of the Dutch. He may have played the coward or the traitor. For whatever reason or combination of them, he left the Dutch ships under his command to fight and die alone. After the battle had been lost he would not make adequate dispositions to tow away the disabled ships, several of which had to be scuttled. Many even of the English captains thought that the action, despite the odds, could have been won had Torrington performed his part. The consequences were serious enough and might have proved catastrophic. France now had command of the English and Irish Channels and could have prevented the return of William III from Ireland. Since the allied fleet had now retired into the Thames, an invasion of England could not have been forestalled at sea. On land there was little strength, since William had most of the trained soldiers and even more of the arms with him.

The Queen's advisers fell into panic. It was suggested that Mary ought to allow Parliament to meet before the King could return. Frantic letters were sent off to William asking him to come back with his army before the French could block the Irish Channel. The Queen Dowager, a focus for Jacobite intrigue, was packed off to Windsor. Mary herself kept her head and so did the mass of the people. Regiments of volunteers came forward, the militia was called out. The Queen sent William Harbord to The Hague to apologize for the cowardice of her admiral and to distribute a large sum of money to the widows of the fallen. For some time the picture was extremely serious. But the French did not know what to do with their victory. They bombarded a few fishing villages and satisfied themselves with a cheap propaganda stunt. Landing as near to Brixham as they could, they burnt Teignmouth. Presumably this was to demonstrate that William III had done nothing very exceptional in the autumn of 1688. In reality it demonstrated nothing more than the jealousy of the French for their great enemy. In July a rumour had spread across Europe to the effect that William had perished at the Boyne. The obscene joy with which this rumour was greeted in France was proof positive of the importance of the King's life. He was now the greatest man in Europe. He had achieved an immense victory by bringing the British Isles into the alliance. The progress of the French had been checked after two generations of steady success. Their victories in 1690 proved empty. All that William and the allies need do now was to hold on. The despised system of social war, after so many failures, was now proving its value.

Chapter 20

THE DUAL MONARCHY

WHEN William reached Kensington on 10 September, tanned and in excellent health after the summer's exercise, the critical stage of his affairs was over. He now had time to look around him and make plans for the years to come. Symbolically enough, the new apartments at Kensington were just finished in time for the King to move into them. Until now he had been occupying temporary and unsatisfactory housing, and his ministerial arrangements had been similarly haphazard and uncomfortable. With all three kingdoms substantially under his control, it was time to set up something more stable. The King hoped at first to be able to cross to the continent in October. Then the date was postponed for a month. Actually it was not until the middle of January that he reached The Hague. But by that time a system of administration had been set up which could function in the King's absence without causing excessive panic. The King had not dared to return to Holland during the winter of 1689. When he went a year later the administration functioned with at least some of the efficiency of Mr Tompion's new watches, in which William was much interested.

It would be futile to search for a first minister, either a medieval justiciar or an eighteenth-century prime minister, in the reign of William III. There was none. During 1689 there was scarcely even a ministry. Everything had had to be done in a hurry and it was success enough that the Revolution survived to the year's end. William had hoped to create a national administration, including representatives of all the groups which had risen against James II. He would have been happy to employ men of all faiths, political and religious, in a general war against the French. Such a policy was perhaps the only way left to preserve the royal authority. For William was now beginning to see what his invasion had done to the prerogative. In his own eyes, he had merely anticipated a dividend which was due in any event at the end of the quarter. The anticipation had been morally justified not only by the threat which the link between James II and Louis XIV represented to Christendom, but also in a more personal sense by the fact that James had been wasting his children's inheritance. The invasion itself had been mounted and brought to success by the Prince himself, and he had at first thought that he would have few debts to pay. How wrong he had been! His conduct and his election as King had destroyed the theoretical foundations of the monarchy. For the duration of the war, at least, he would have to face annual Parliaments. The Whigs, on whom he had relied heavily in 1689, seemed determined to reduce the royal authority as much as possible. They had eliminated the suspending power by the Declaration of Right and the dispensing power by the Bill of Rights. Their failure to grant the revenue for William's lifetime was an even more serious invasion of the constitution and it was obvious that there would be other entrenchments on the royal authority. By the summer of 1689 the King was complaining to Halifax about this condition: 'Said that a K. of England who will governe by Law as hee must do, if hee hath conscience, is the worst figure in Christendome. ... Hee hath power to destroy the Nation and not to protect it.'[1]

During the year the King searched for men who would obey his wishes without regard to party. Most of those he found were Tories, of whom the chief example is perhaps Nottingham. The Whigs disliked Nottingham not only for his ties with the Church, but because they suspected him of drawing up a book in which he explained the full extent of the King's lawful authority. This was not at all the kind of instruction that the Whigs planned for William III. They would have preferred to treat him as their ancestors had treated James I, and to have told him just as much about the constitution as they wanted him to know. Nottingham's primer is not known to survive. It may never have existed. But even Nottingham had some axes to grind: he wished to secure the independence of the judiciary. Technically William III, unlike his successors who were bound by the Act of Settlement of 1701, might lawfully have dismissed judges for their verdicts in just the same way as had the Stuarts. Whatever else Nottingham may have told him about the extent of the prerogative, he did not tell him the truth in this respect. Writing to the King in May 1691, he stated flatly: 'you canot remove them, ...'[2] With such men to deal with, the King would have been insane had he put himself into the hands of any single group or party. Only by balancing parties could he hope to hear both sides of any question and so to come at the truth.

Balancing was dangerous. The English politicans, who had after all been killing each other as recently as 1685, were not prepared to forego the pleasures of revenge. Halifax was bitterly attacked during the Convention and was driven to resign on its dissolution. Godolphin, a personal friend of William III for more than a decade, resigned soon afterwards, possibly because of his hatred for Carmarthen. Shrewsbury followed him just before the King set out for Ireland. While William was there the Whigs offered Mary loans of £200,000, but only if she dissolved the new Parliament which was unfavourable to them. Even more disgraceful was the conduct of Sir Thomas Lee of the Admiralty Board, who refused to allow the appointment of Sir Richard Haddock as one of three admirals who were to replace Lord Torrington after

Beachy Head. Lee actually had the insolence to tell the Queen that the appointment of Haddock, a Tory, 'could not be'. When Mary, heartily angry, replied ironically that she saw that the King had given away his own power, and could not make an admiral whom the Admiralty did not like, Lee answered 'No, no more he can't'.[3] Professional rivalries, such as the bitter warfare between Coke and Bacon, had been a feature of the legal world for centuries. However high they went they could not destroy the nation. But now they were repeated in the navy and in the army as well, where the consequences could easily have been fatal. By balancing, the King gradually accustomed his subjects to a new and milder kind of political warfare in which the losers might at least hope to escape with their lives and estates. It was to be many years before these lessons were fully absorbed. In the meantime the government suffered and the war could not be carried on with anything like full vigour. Luckily, at war as at football, it is not necessary to be good. It is only necessary to be better than the other side.

William III did not carry the system of balancing so far as to have secretaries of opposing parties. He tried this in England in 1689, matching the Whig Shrewsbury against the Tory Nottingham, and was soon tired of it. Even at the beginning he refused to have two Scottish secretaries. As he told Halifax, 'he would not have two Secretaries of Scotland to have one advise him one thing and the other to another'.[4] When Shrewsbury resigned in 1690 he was not replaced, and the King used one makeshift after another. Reasonably enough, he took the Irish Secretary Sir Robert Southwell with him on the Boyne campaign. When he began his tours to the continent, the King took Nottingham with him once. But Nottingham was too useful at home. He took Sydney once, who turned out to be the worst Secretary William ever had. Finally, the King found William Blathwayt, a smaller version of Nottingham. Blathwayt wrote and spoke French well, worked hard, and could even be used for official entertaining. Once beyond English shores, he had the salary and position of a Secretary of State, reverting to his subordinate position as Secretary at War at the end of each campaign. It was an ideal arrangement for the King, though a less happy one for the servant. He never received a peerage. William III also tended to choose efficient commoners as his regular Secretaries. Never after 1692 were both the Secretaries peers. At times both were Members of the House of Commons, and sometimes the King managed to get along quite happily with a single Secretary. Since all he expected was clerical assistance, there was no real need to employ two great politicians. Few if any Englishmen were experienced enough to assist William III in the conduct of his foreign policy. The country had not been a great power until 1688 and its need for close continental contacts or even for trained personnel had been small. The shortage of personnel was so great that during the summer of 1690 Don Pedro Ronquillo, the Spanish ambassador, helped Mary's Council of Nine on foreign affairs. Throughout his reign, William III most often conducted his diplomatic negotiations in person, or through Heinsius, or else by way of the Dutch diplomatic corps. He had no alternative.

The traditional description for William's administrative technique is the phrase 'the departmental system', by which is meant that the King saw the head of each department in private. At these meetings the sovereign gave detailed instructions on matters of policy and patronage. In return he received information and advice, generally confined to the matter in hand. In regard to Treasury business, at least, these meetings had informal agendas in the 'memorandum' which the First Lord brought with him. This was a sheet of scratch paper on which the minister had jotted down the topics which he wished to bring up. The King's answers were entered, item by item, either below or to the left of the question. This was a common method of business, used by Charles II at least as early as 1667 and by William III long before the Revolution.[5] Where, however, Charles II rarely went to the Treasury unless accompanied by Privy Councillors, William III regularly went alone, in addition to his private sessions with the First Lord. He was a financial expert in his own right, as his uncles had not been, and his intervention was often necessary if a loan was to be secured. Only the King could conduct negotiations with the lender Suasso, or the city of Amsterdam, or with the Dutch government official van Slingelandt. If he engaged his personal credit, either by pawning his Dutch jewels or by hypothecating his continental estates, there would be a lower rate of interest. William III was thus not only his own foreign minister but his own minister of finance. While he was in England he went to the Treasury for board meetings once a week. When he was abroad the First Lord corresponded directly with the King or else wrote to the Secretary in attendance. Before leaving the country the King often made a disposition of the money that was expected to come in during his absence, but even so the Treasury could not be left to run itself.

In general, it may be said that the King kept policy in his own hands and used the heads of departments as if they were clerks. He preferred to see department heads individually. There were certain groups, such as the cabinet council and the Treasury, which he had to see in a body. This was regrettable not only because of the risk of indiscretion but also because the King might be out-voted. It was a further inconvenience that certain persons claimed a right to attend board meetings. In 1689 several people demanded places at the Treasury, though the King managed to put them off. As for the cabinet council, the heir to the throne appears to have had a place as of right. Princess Anne did not exercise her right in person and was represented there by her husband. If the great officers of state also claimed entry to the cabinet council by virtue of their places, the result would be a body of doubtful composition and unmanageable size. During the summer of 1694 the King tried to do without a cabinet council, leaving behind him a small war committee or non-cabinet. This experiment was spoiled by Lord Normanby, who insisted that he had a right to attend any meeting, however small, which took place at the Secretary's office. Throughout his reign William III was uneasy with the institution of the cabinet council, and although he met it fairly regularly on Sundays and the Privy Council on Thursdays he would probably have preferred to work alone.

Such a system imposed a tremendous burden on the King. He worked late into the night with regularity, to the damage of his health. His ministers complained, accurately enough, that they had to wait for days at a time to see their master and explained this by calling him lazy. In this they were mistaken. The King did in fact spend a great deal of time in hunting and quite a considerable number of hours in discussing art or in gossiping with old friends. He would then try to catch up with his papers by signing them in batches. Such habits posed the risk that the King would be surprised. William used Portland, and later Albemarle, to protect him from surprises. None the less, a single 'minister for Scotland' or 'minister for Holland' had tremendous opportunities to abuse his position. The King was successful in attracting to his service a number of loyal and discreet persons. Yet he could not avoid all abuses, as the wretched affair of the Glencoe massacre was to show. During the summer of 1691 the chiefs of the highland clans were encouraged by bribes to make their peace with the government. They were given until 1 January 1692 to take the oaths of allegiance. Macdonald of Glencoe took them five days after the expiration of the time limit. Technically, therefore, he and his clan were subject to military execution. The King, however, wanted to spare any late-comers and the tragedy began when local officials at Edinburgh obliterated the document which proved that Macdonald had really come in on 6 January. The Master of Stair, William's Secretary of State for Scotland, was in London and did not know this. He hated the men of Glencoe, however, and on 16 January he presented William with a batch of papers including one with the severe sentence: 'If Mac Ian of Glen Co and that tribe can be separated from the rest, it will be a proper vindication of public justice to extirpate that set of thieves.'

There is no comparable act of severity in the entire career of William III. He signed the letter without reading it. But it must be said in defence of the King and of the Secretary that as late as 30 January the Master of Stair did not know that Macdonald had come in, that is that the problem had ceased to be a military one. The shameful murder of men, women, and children at

Glencoe on 13 February was the responsibility of the men on the spot and at Edinburgh, who had concealed the facts. The King's responsibility for the massacre began only in 1695, when he refused to punish the guilty after an investigation had taken place. This was William's consistent practice. He had gone so far as to pension Tichelaar in 1672 and Oates in 1689. On all three occasions his conduct was deplorable by the standards of private morality and wise by those of political life. One may at least say that the government of Scotland was far milder and more beneficial during the reign of William III than it had been during the Restoration. Unfortunately one cannot say that it was well governed. The King had to work through the men who presented themselves for his service, and their standards were not nearly so high as his own. In the same year 1692, for example, there occurred extensive disorders in the Zeeland town of Goes. Eventually one of the Regents of the town was sentenced to be beheaded and several others were allotted severe though lesser punishments. On this occasion the matter was properly brought to the attention of William. He set the original sentences aside, substituting others which were markedly less harsh. Had the King had access to the facts, there would have been no Glencoe massacre.

Although William preferred to delegate particular topics to individuals, he did his best to prevent any single one of his servants from achieving too powerful a position. The simplest way of doing this was never to allow any subordinate figure to engross a wide range of business. It is highly unlikely that the King ever told anyone his whole mind. Portland came the nearest to being a factotum. He had the essential qualities of loyalty, discretion and bravery which were shared by all of the close associates of William of Orange. Like many of them he lacked any particular talent. Thus he was not a gifted general. In this area the King relied more heavily on Waldeck and Solms, and later on Ginckel, then he did on Portland. Nor was the favourite an able diplomat. He did not achieve complete success on his mission to Holland in 1690, and he was to be even less successful in his French embassy at the end of the war. William kept secrets from Portland, as he did from everyone else. The Earl, for example, advised his master on the government of the Republic and was permitted to read the letters which were exchanged between William III and Heinsius. When some matter was to be kept secret it was difficult for the King to hold back an entire letter, since Portland knew that Heinsius had orders to write regularly twice a week. William solved this problem by telling the Grand Pensionary to write any really confidential matter on a separate sheet of paper.[6] He would then be able to hold back the single sheet, while giving Portland the body of the letter to read. Thus the very existence of a secret would be unknown. It is quite clear that Bentinck never had any of the freedom of action which had been enjoyed by earlier favourites such as

Lord Burleigh in the days of Queen Elizabeth. He carried messages and ran errands, he cared for the King's welfare and for his delicate health. In the course of his long career he accumulated a vast fortune. But his position was that of a male nurse tending a semi-invalid rather than that of a Burleigh or even a Buckingham.

If the King kept secrets from his favourite of a quarter of a century, it was not to be expected that he should trust any single Englishman. Between 1690 and 1693 Lord Carmarthen was theoretically at the head of the administration. Only he could have said how empty his position really was. William had always detested corruption among his servants. When he employed Carmarthen and his gang he had to use some of them in places where they touched money. The most notable example of this was Lord Ranelagh, a crony of the Lord President for a generation, whom the King reluctantly continued as Paymaster-general. No Osborne, however, was to have any direct contact with the revenues in this reign. Although Carmarthen had been a highly successful Treasurer in the days of Charles II, William never took him to Treasury meetings or, so far as we know, discussed Treasury business with him to any particular extent. In a rather contemptuous way the King gave Carmarthen the small change of patronage which he so enjoyed. The Marquis became Lord-Lieutenant of all three ridings of Yorkshire. He was given a substantial pension and later the title Duke of Leeds. But his influence was far smaller than it had been when he was Lord Danby or even Viscount Latimer. If he made recommendations regarding promotions in the Church or the Army his suggestions were more likely than not to be met with a snub. The King happened to dislike Henry Compton, the Bishop of London, a Tory who fancied himself as the next Archbishop of Canterbury. In 1689, since Sancroft refused to act but had not yet been deprived, Compton functioned in the primate's place. William was so displeased with him that he planned to translate him to Durham, where he might enjoy a splendid income and be completely out of things. Unfortunately Crew, the reigning Bishop of Durham, took the oaths to William and Mary, much to everyone's surprise. The King exempted Crew from pardon in his Act of Grace, but he could not deprive him of his See, and the wicked old man did not die until 1721. Compton, therefore, remained at London. Although he was one of Carmarthen's oldest political allies and one of the Queen's oldest servants, the King would never agree to promote him. Compton was passed over when the See of St Augustine was filled in 1690 and again in 1694.

Though both men must be classed as Tories and Churchmen, Carmarthen and Nottingham were by no means friends and they often found it difficult to work with each other. Their influence was far from all-pervasive. On his return from Ireland the King was determined to bring Lord Godolphin back into the Treasury. It is impossible to classify Godolphin as Whig or Tory at this period. He appeared regularly as a Tory in lists drawn up by some politicians, because of his close associations with the court during the reign of James II and because of his friendships with people like Evelyn the diarist. At the same time others, with equal justice, classed him as a Whig since he seemed to be inseparable from Marlborough and Shrewsbury. The King, who had known him for a decade, liked him personally. He also found him indispensable as a man of business. Godolphin was the only hold-over from James II's Treasury Board in the Commission of April 1689. At that time the King was not strong enough to put him into the Privy Council as well, but he intended to do so later.

During the spring and summer of 1690 the King sorely missed the services of his friend. In March Monmouth, Delamere and Sir Henry Capel were dismissed. The new First Lord, Sir John Lowther of Lowther, was an ally of Carmarthen. He was a man of good intentions though 'weack' – that is, stupid – whose chief task was to be leader of the House of Commons. It soon became obvious that Lowther was not fitted to run the Treasury, and the King set about wooing the reluctant Cornishman. Marlborough, who knew Godolphin best, advised that the only way to secure him was for William to emphasize the elements of personal friendship between them. The King had already done his best in the previous January, when he had attended a dinner party given him by Godolphin and Shrewsbury. He did not enjoy such occasions, for he knew from long experience that he needed boiled or braised meat washed down by beer. The English preferred roasts and wine, and more of both than was good for them. Marlborough and three other lords were at the feast, and all present were reported by a Jacobite spy to have lost consciousness. At two in the morning, the spy's account continued, the servants finally managed to get their sovereign into a carriage. This was a wild exaggeration. The King in fact retained his senses, returned from the dinner at six in the evening, and had enough stamina to go on to a gambling party at Kensington with the Queen and the Princess Anne. Marlborough was the only person to become completely stupified, though it must be admitted that the King had no further desire to transact business that day. Lord Selkirk, singing hymns of praise about William's prowess with the bottle, said repeatedly: 'Qu'il avoit parlé ce soir en vray Roy.'[7]

One of the first things that the King did on his return from Ireland was to attend another debauch.[8] This time he was successful in getting what he wanted. In November Godolphin became First Lord of the Treasury. Even now he was reluctant to take the post, and as time passed he became more reluctant about keeping it. Early in 1691 he was determined to resign. Since the King by that time was on the continent, it was impossible to hold a third dinner party. Instead he wrote a very warm and friendly letter.[9] The First Lord still wavered, but was ultimately to keep his place for six years.

Although Carmarthen was considered by the public to be the first minister, he was not even informed about Godolphin's appointment as First Lord of the Treasury. The two men were ancient enemies. The King saw to it that Godolphin called on the Lord President and offered his friendship, but that was the only notice taken of Carmarthen in the entire affair. His ally Sir John Lowther, who had been demoted from First Lord to Second by this transaction, could only retire to the country to indicate his disgust. In March of 1692 Lowther withdrew entirely from the Treasury Board, though he continued to act as manager in the Commons. It would seem, therefore, a misnomer to call the ministerial arrangements of 1690–93 the Carmarthen ministry. The Lord President had no influence whatever on foreign or military policy, the Treasury, or major appointments. His influence on minor appointments was substantial, and his real function was that of being minister for parliamentary affairs. Here he was in his element. He was a great counter of votes, a great persuader of men, a great manager. As a peer of some years' standing, Carmarthen could not take direct charge of the House of Commons. This task had to be delegated to Lowther and to the Speaker, Sir John Trevor, who was Carmarthen's nominee. Yet even in this limited field the Lord President was not without rivals. In 1689 William Jephson, who had acted as the Prince's personal secretary during the invasion, became Secretary of the Treasury. Jephson, a Whig who had lived in exile at The Hague since 1683, was no friend of Carmarthen. When he died, in June 1691, Carmarthen proposed the appointment of his own wife's brother, Charles Bertie, who had held the post before. Instead, the King named Henry Guy. Guy had succeeded Bertie as Secretary in 1679 and was thus also a man of experience. But his political connexions were with Lord Sunderland rather than with Carmarthen. Guy's appointment was an ominous one for the Carmarthen interest.

In September 1690 Lord Portland received a lesson in politics from Lord Sydney and Thomas Coningsby:

... it is without question impossible for a King of England to doe any considerable thing in a Hous of Comons, without a form'd management; & by that wee mean, a number of men on whome ye King may confidently relye, Joyned wth the Speaker, (whoe now is most certainly yrs) and they to meet privately every night, and there to resolve how and by w^t methods, they will oppose anything wch may obstruct his Majestyes affairs, or propose anything y^t will further his interest ye next day, amongst these there ought to be had att any rate, tow or three men whoe have fair reputations in ye Hous, such as Sacheverill Laven Gower & Sir Tho: Clerges, whoe must by noe means have any imployments during ye Sessions but be rewarded afterwards, & we look upon these three to be those y^t have ye Greatest influence over the three partyes of ye Hous y^t are not for King James; Sacheverill of ye Whiggs, Laven Gower of ye middle party and Sr Tho: Clerges of ye high Church; ye first of these is soe full of himself, y^t we believe it may be a matter difficult enoufe to secure him, but ye other two may most certainly be had ... but noe body living is better able to give you characters of men fitt to serve ye King in ye Hous of Comons and the ways of Gayning them, then ye Speaker ...[10]

There was a great measure of sense in this advice, though nothing that could by any means be called novel. The difficulty lay in finding what was called a 'scheme'. Men of different parties would find it difficult enough to meet and work together under a single, known, head. If they could not tell whether the King favoured Carmarthen or Sunderland, a coalition predominantly Tory or one predominantly Whig, the problems of parliamentary management would become immeasurably more difficult. The system of balancing between parties saved the royal authority and freedom of action, but at considerable cost. As one observer, admittedly a biased one, remarked in November of this year: 'You say you do not understand the present scheme. I don't know who does, and that which is most melancholy and discouraging is that there seems to be no scheme at all.'[11] And there would come a time when it would no longer be possible to balance between the parties. Only if they were agreed on all major issues was there any chance of avoiding a predominantly one-party government. By 1692 the parties were divided on one of the greatest issues of all, the continuance of the war on land. At that point the King had to make up his mind whether to make peace or to employ more Whigs. But that time had not yet come. For the moment, the King remained his own political manager as well as his own foreign minister and minister of finance. And if William III refused to touch for the King's Evil, or to wash the feet of the poor on Maundy Thursday, he was willing to distribute loaves and fishes with his own hands. It was not merely a question of giving employments and honours. During the course of his reign the King took, in addition to the sums handled by the Privy Purse, some £160,000 in cash from the secret service funds. Neither Charles II nor James II had taken more than trifling sums in cash. If some of this went to Betty Villiers, some of it undoubtedly went to the politicians. Today we think almost less of the man who offers a bribe than of the man who takes one. William III loathed corruption, particularly when it was practised by the French. He never took bribes himself, as Charles II had done. When he offered them he could justify himself with the thought that this was the English method, or that it was a cheap way of gaining support for the good cause. Nothing could make him like the men who took his bribes.

William III was by no means the inventor of the departmental system, and he was no by means the last King of England to make it work. What sets him off from his immediate predecessors and his four immediate successors is the superior quality and range of his talent. Charles II had been an effective politician; George I would come to England with a proved reputation in arms and diplomacy. But the life of Charles II had been a perpetual holiday interrupted by brief spasms of administration or diplomacy. If James II worked harder and with more regularity, England in his day was still a minor power and the misgovernment of his people had taken James only a few hours a day. In the years after the Revolution England abruptly became a great power. In terms of the royal authority the immediate risk was that government would become too large for the King to control. That this did not happen in the lifetime of William III was largely the result of his unique training in the Republic. He could reasonably claim to know more about several of the departments than any of his subjects. In others, such as parliamentary management, he knew much less and did less well. But he was never willing to abandon management or indeed any of the royal functions to any other single person or party.

There were, of course, many elements contributing to the success of the King's system. Luckily, his wife was not only loyal but able as well. William could delegate to her the only part of his task which he did really badly, the ceremonial and social aspects of monarchy, and get on with more important things. Rather to everyone's surprise, the Queen demonstrated in 1690 that she had the courage and talent to rule the country during the interval between parliamentary sessions. Of course this was much easier than meeting a Parliament would have been, and it is also true that the King and his armies were never more than a week's distance away from England during the periods of Mary's administration. Even so Mary did a fine job, one which permitted William III to be effectively in two places at the same time, since his wife carefully refused to follow a policy of her own. Had she done so, the arrangement would have been impossible. But the Queen carried out her instructions with such remarkable fidelity that in 1692 William was willing to let her hold a Parliament in his absence. Portland was dispatched to her aid, and one must assume that he would have done most of the detailed work of management. Luckily Russell's magnificent victory at La Hogue made it unnecessary to attempt the experiment at that time. Four years later William was willing to let Portland hold a Parliament alone, during the currency crisis, but the ministers did not dare take the risk. Mary's loyalty to her husband was so great that it is difficult to discern what her true feelings were. It is obvious that she came to hate her sister more openly than was wise, where the King's own relations with Anne and her husband remained correct. The actual steps taken, however, in disciplining the Princess were extremely moderate and must have been approved by William before they were put into effect. Apparently the Queen had a fondness for Lord Rochester and for his brand of churchmanship. It is possible that she may have assisted his return to the Council in 1692, though here again the King would have had to approve and had his own reasons for doing so. It is certain that Mary loathed Sunderland, that she resisted his return to court, and that she failed completely in her campaign to exclude him from favour. Perhaps she knew that she had no hope of success if she took an independent line. She must have known how disastrous disloyalty would have been. By consenting to act as a puppet the Queen made herself one of the most substantial parts of the new system.

By 1690, then, William III had succeeded in setting up, both in the Republic and in England, administrations which could function in his absence. It was a remarkable feat. Superficially his system worked better in the Republic. During his own lifetime he succeeded in maintaining his authority as Stadhouder, while in England one prerogative after another was lost. In a way this superficial view is inaccurate. Charles had maintained the royal authority only by not exercising it. Whenever an active person came to the throne it would have meant the diminution of the prerogative. James demonstrated what would happen to an active king who did not obtain the support of Parliament; William demonstrated what would happen to an active king who had that support. Yet William, and to this extent he must be considered a conservative, maintained the existence of the kingly office. Had he come to the throne in the ordinary way he would undoubtedly have had more freedom of action and he might have kept more of the prerogative than he actually did. Even as a usurper he maintained it to a remarkable degree. And when he died he left his English successors not only an office but a very powerful one. In the United Provinces he was less successful in the long run. Partly because the succession was disputed there, but largely as a reaction to his own conduct, the very office of Stadhouder disappeared in 1702 on the death of William III. Although it was to be restored two generations later, the tradition had by that time been effectively broken, and the Stadhouders of the eighteenth century were never to be strong. There is a case, therefore, for the point of view that William was more successful as a King than as a Stadhouder.

He was not interested in the long view. As he said again and again, he did not care how the world was like to go once he was out of it. This attitude shocked some of his contemporaries. It was, of course, comprehensible in a man who had no son. With the exception of his wife, the relations of William III were a most unpleasant group of people and few men would have cared to conserve capital for the benefit of any of them. He did much more for his people than he did for his family. The threat of a French domination of Europe was immediate and pressing. Here was a great cause. In its service the King maintained the independence of both his countries, and in the process he incidentally made England into a great power. If the Dutch bore an undue share of the burdens of the alliance, if by the end of William's life they were beginning to stagger under the load, they were in 1702 still free and still strong enough to put more troops into the field than they had ever done before. Surely this was enough of an inheritance. And even to his heirs William III left more of a position than they could maintain.

If the King succeeded in creating a dual monarchy which could function wherever he happened to be, there was one department which he had to manage on the spot. No letter, no delegate, could run the army for him. This was the weakest point in the entire system. William III had to lead his men himself, or they would not move. Waldeck had proved himself a failure on the continent, Schomberg in Ireland. Of all the military commanders he ever worked with, the King found only three or four who were ready for independent commands. Vaudemont was one, and William virtually ordered Carlos II to give him the direction of the forces in the Spanish Netherlands. Charles, second Duke of Schomberg, was another, and he was to do well in the southern campaigns before his untimely death in 1693. Ginckel was among the select number. Of them all Marlborough was by far the greatest in the field. He had done well in Flanders in 1689 and brilliantly against Cork and Kinsale in 1690. At this time, however, he lacked experience as an administrator and as a disciplinarian. In Flanders he had been unable to prevent his men from plundering the native inhabitants, or even from stripping their own wounded comrades while they were still alive. In the French army this would have not been such an important matter. Luxembourg was careless, but Luxembourg had Louvois behind him. In the Anglo-Dutch system there was no Louvois and the generals had far greater administrative responsibilities than did their French opposite numbers. Many years later, when Marlborough had demonstrated his superiority over William III as well as over the French as a field commander, there were still complaints over the tolerated indiscipline of his men.

During the Nine Years War the Dutch army was a far better instrument of war than it had been a generation earlier. Savage discipline had moulded what was generally considered the best infantry in Europe. During the campaign of 1688 in England, one of the Prince's most successful arguments with civilians had been the fact that his men did not plunder, but paid on the nail for whatever they required. If the discipline of the Dutch forces was not perfect, it was by far the best of its day – a fact which reduced the number of casualties as well as serving to keep up the friendship of the local population. Another reward of the superior training of the Dutch infantry was that the men returned to their colours after a defeat which would have smashed other armies for the rest of a campaign. A fortnight after Fleurus in 1690 and Landen three years later, both of them badly lost, the French were astonished to find themselves facing larger armies than they had before the fighting; nor had there been any decline in the equipment of the Dutch troops. This was perhaps the greatest contribution of William III as a soldier. In battle he was not the equal of Turenne or Condé; but he shone in the area of organization and discipline. Despite the fact, which he could not control, that the army's wages were always in arrear – at one time the men were twenty-three months behind in their pay – the number of desertions was relatively small. In the French army payment was more prompt, though the scale was lower. Even so, desertion was a greater problem for the French than for the allies.

The years of peace had given time for some straight thinking on military matters. In several cases William's innovations imitated the French, as in other cases he took over good ideas which had developed out of the German war against the Turk. Credit for quite a few of the changes must be given to the Dutch alone, even where they made improvements on a French invention. The idea that France was solely responsible for improvements in the art of war in this period is as foolish as the idea that she won all the battles. In the care of the sick and wounded, for example, the Dutch were the innovators and Louvois copied them; and the Dutch had had to develop field and base hospitals because the nuns of Flanders would not care for Protestant soldiers, a problem which was not relevant for the French army. The important thing to remember is that William III was an eager and active innovator, taking ideas wherever he found them and adapting them to his own purposes. As a result of his open mind, the quality of his armies improved steadily. The men he led into battle in the campaign of 1696 were the best he had ever seen. On the other hand the French army, even before the death of Louvois, was in decay. The reforms of Le Tellier had been abandoned in favour of the dragonnades and the building of aqueducts for Versailles. By 1689 the French army was a flabby giant, which could still win victories under Luxembourg from time to time, but which was fundamentally past its prime. Otherwise, given the enormous advantages of internal lines of communications and a unified command, it simply could not have lost the next two wars.

The most important change in the Dutch army was its immense increase in firepower. Although he did not become Master-General of the Artillery until the end of 1697, Menno van Coehoorn had by now achieved a rank high enough to enable him to exercise effective influence. Favoured consistently by William III although his projects were often frighteningly expensive, Coehoorn became a major-general of infantry in 1692 and was appointed Director General of Fortifications in 1695 as a reward for his brilliant work at the siege of Namur. Although he was not responsible for all the improvements in fire-power during the Nine Years War, Coehoorn and his colleague Willem Meesters were undoubtedly the guiding spirits behind the changes as a whole. In 1690 the Dutch began to cast their own howitzers and to use them in considerable numbers. In 1692 the artillery train had a dozen of them, as compared with fifty 24-pounders. Among the lighter weapons, grenades remained a favourite and were used even more heavily than they had been in the past. Some of the grenadiers were now mounted and were listed as cavalry, although they presumably dismounted before going to work. Since grenadiers were peculiarly exposed during an attack, they received high pay and also were issued sacks filled with wool, which they used as shields by pushing them along before them on a light wheeled carriage. Coehoorn developed a more effective device, the so-called Coehoorn mortar, which could throw a grenade six hundred paces. Another development made it possible to fire artillery at night as well as during the day, and the Dutch became renowned for the accuracy and rapid fire of their weapons. This was noted especially during the siege of Namur, when the fortress underwent such a terrible bombardment that there were casualties from shell-shock as well as from wounds, and the French complained of the unsporting nature of the new methods of warfare.

During the Nine Years War the flintlock began to supersede the older matchlock musket. It was difficult to find enough flints of the proper size and quality, and it was not yet the rule to supply the flintlocks with a ring bayonet. This accounted for the survival of the musket and the even less satisfactory pike, which did not disappear from use until 1713. In all these developments Coehoorn worked with Willem Meesters, Controller-General of the Dutch Artillery and of the English as well, though the English hated him. Meesters was made Commandant of the Tower of London in 1691. He was particularly interested in the development of collapsible bridges, often made of tin, for the crossing of rivers, and in this he had great success. He was less fortunate in his experiments with mortars for use at sea, and with flame-throwers, and these failures as well as his personality made him one of William's most unpopular officers. Coehoorn apparently did not share his colleague's unpopularity, nor did he deserve to. One of his more important minor innovations in this war was the establishment of the engineers on a regular salary. In the war of 1672 they were taken on and paid by the day, which may well explain William's early difficulties with siege operations. Coehoorn's fortifications cost millions. They were, however expensive, the first in Europe that could compare in quality with those of the great Vauban. And when Coehoorn proved in 1695 that a Vauban fortress could be captured, he gave the lie direct to the French claim of invincibility.[12]

It is perhaps too simple to say that there was no British army in 1689, that William III and his Dutch generals had to build one from scratch. Of course there were regiments. Some of them were made up of 'native Irish', or had Catholic officers, and these could not be used by the Protestant Deliverer. Since English Catholic officers had, as a group, far more experience in warfare than their Protestant fellows this was a severe loss. Of the Protestants, many were politically unreliable and most of the rest were amateurs with little or no experience. Marlborough himself, one of the most battle-hardened of Englishmen in the spring of 1689, had no experience by continental standards. He and his fellow 'brave and haughty society officers'[13] knew as much about war in 1689 as does the average men's chorus in an amateur performance of *Patience*. They were brave, some of them were intelligent, they would eventually learn their trade. But in 1689 they did not yet know their trade. In the Irish campaign of that year, some 6,000 out of 14,000 Englishmen perished not in battle but in camp at Dundalk because their officers could not be bothered to take the simplest health measures. They saw the Dutch and French Huguenot troops putting up huts, they saw them keeping their area of the camp clean. The English would not follow their example or the orders of Marshal Schomberg, and two out of every five of them paid for their ignorance with their lives. Among the experienced continental troops, the casualties at Dundalk were within the range of normal expectation.

The men themselves, as always, were brave. They fought hard and well, to the admiration of Waldeck in 1689 though they were still little more than raw levies. But Waldeck, though he could not praise the men too highly, noted that the officers were of different stuff. They were more interested in cheating the men of their pay than in anything else, they permitted the men to plunder, and the English casualty rates from sickness – a sure sign of ill discipline – were frighteningly high in Flanders as well as in Ireland. It would take years of hard work to make professionals out of these men, excellent though the material was. And it would be humiliating work for the officers of James II's toy army to go to school under the Dutch task-masters who, after all, had beaten them. Eventually, painfully, the English learned their lesson. By the opening of the 1696 campaign they had become the best troops their King had ever seen. And their conduct in the War of the Spanish Succession was to justify William's praise of the army he had created.

In 1689 there was, simply, no central direction of the British army. As Colonel Walton pointed out, 'although there were regiments of men, there was no army. There was no organisation, no field-administration, in fact none of that fitness for immediate service to be found even at that time in continental armies. There was no transport train, indeed scarcely any Commissariat of any sort; ...'[14] He might have added that there were no arms to speak of, for the weapons that had not disappeared when Feversham disbanded the old army in December were largely defective. They had to be replaced by imports from Holland, and eventually, as we have seen, a Dutchman had to be appointed Controller-General of the Artillery. Faced with this situation, the King tried to delegate the problem to a committee of the Privy Council.[15] The experiment was not successful. No Privy Council committee had the authority or the experience to run a campaign, in this case the reconquest of Ireland. The English subordinate officials, Henry Shales from James's camps at Blackheath and William Harbord – one of the more prominent English exiles who had returned with William – were completely inadequate. Both of them were very probably corrupt as well as being politically untrustworthy.[16] The Secretary at War, George Clarke, was little better. A young Tory, M.P. for Oxford University, he accompanied the King on the Irish campaign in 1690 and then had to be replaced. Eventually the King was forced to take over personal control of the army. For the rest of his reign he, Lord Ranelagh as Paymaster of the Forces, and Clarke's successor William Blathwayt, were an informal committee of three for the management of the army. Supply was delegated to the Dutch contractors Machado and Pereira. It was a rough solution of the problem. Ranelagh was generally thought to be corrupt and Blathwayt, though an extremely hardworking and efficient subordinate, was a civilian unused to personal danger. After the defeat at Landen in 1693 he fled all the way to Breda without stopping, which made his relations with the King difficult for some time.[17] Whatever the defects, the King's military arrangements did work after a fashion and continued to do so for a century and a half. Some of the problems of the Crimean War arose from the fact that William III had used Machado and Pereira rather than setting up a supply system of his own.

There were three specific areas in which the King's personal intervention was essential. Each winter he had to make the plan of campaign for the following year. This involved detailed negotiations with Vienna and with many German princes and might be considered almost more diplomatic than military in character. One of the trickiest aspects of this problem was the assignment of winter quarters. If the allied troops were not quartered in the right places they would be missing at the beginning of each campaign and the enemy would meet with no resistance for perhaps the first two months of the year. The German contingents hated to winter in the Netherlands. They preferred more profitable and more comfortable quarters elsewhere. Luckily for the allies, Louvois died in July 1691 and with him went much of the efficiency of the French army. His son Barbesieux filled his office but could by no means take his place. Under Barbesieux the French troops reached Flanders two months later in the spring than they had in his father's time. This delay contributed substantially to the successes of the allies in the last thirty years of the life of Louis XIV.

The difference between March and May was a vital one. Partly it depended on the location of winter quarters. Another factor was the size of magazines, since there would be no natural forage for the horses before May. The preparation of sufficient magazines depended on money, and it must be remembered that William III never had adequate control over the financial machinery of either of the maritime powers. He had far more control over the English Treasury than over the Dutch. Even in England, however, he could not make the taxes come in on time nor could he levy them at will. Parliament voted too little and what was voted came in almost a year late. In the United Provinces, the States General dutifully voted the 'state of the war' as William drew it up. Yet nothing could make the six poorer provinces pay their share. Some of them, particularly Zeeland and Friesland, would not even vote for the levy of their proportion. Even if they did the money came in late, and William had few friends in the college known as the Rekenkamer, which controlled it. Holland provided far more than its share of money, and from time to time it also lent the central government items of equipment such as cannon from its private stores. The whole situation, however, was unsatisfactory. It is apparently the case that the provinces were much further behind in their payments during the Nine Years War than they had been during the War of 1672. The King did what he could, and some magazines were prepared. He would have had to spend the whole year on the continent to make the provinces pay even a reasonable proportion of what they had promised to do.

The third and most difficult problem was the management of the general officers. All of them overrated their own services. They spent much of every day worrying about questions of rank and seniority. If A is promoted and B is not, B will resign his command. If B should be promoted, A will feel no gratitude for his own promotion; and so on. This kind of professional jealousy, often inflamed by drink, occurred in every seventeenth-century army and is presumably not quite unknown today. In an allied army, however, commanded to a large extent by mercenaries, these jealousies were ever-present. Only the King could control them, and whenever he was absent they broke out uncontrollably. Letters did no good. It was at army headquarters, therefore, that the King's presence was absolutely essential. William resented the length of parliamentary sessions, which kept him away from the army far longer than he should have been. Parliament, quite naturally, resented the fact that the King always wanted to cut short the debates. Despite their mutual irritation, William managed to get his supplies and to keep something like the schedule he set for himself. It is not to be wondered that his system of government did not work smoothly. What is really remarkable is that it worked at all. It was a very great achievement for any man, and particularly for one in such poor health.

Chapter 21

WAR ON THE CONTINENT

On his return to England in September 1690 the King found himself facing once more the problems of maintaining the alliance, a body of little cohesive strength. Fundamentally the Grand Alliance of 1689, like the alliance of 1673, was held together by the stubbornness of William III. This was a glue of quite unusual strength, but it was not enough by itself to do the job. In the terrible months before the conclusion of the Twenty Years Truce the Prince had experimented with a congress of ministers of the allies, and shortly after the Revolution he suggested the revival of this body.[1] The congress of ministers was to meet for some years at The Hague and to provide what few elements of structure the alliance ever had. It was a remarkably simple and economical body, especially by modern standards. The ordinary ministers and agents accredited to The Hague met with Heinsius – and, apparently, the Dutch Committee for Foreign Affairs – to discuss matters of common interest. This kept any single member from feeling left out while making it more difficult for him to negotiate secretly with the enemy. Geographically, the choice of The Hague was ideal; both Vienna and London were too remote. But The Hague had other advantages than its central location. Keeping the congress and eventually the peace negotiations away from Vienna minimized the harm that the Jesuits could do to the alliance. Keeping them away from London limited the trouble that foreign diplomats could stir up in Parliament, or that M.P.s could do to the war effort.

In the spring of 1690 the problems of keeping up a common front were increased by the death of the Duke of Lorraine, who was not only an able general but a man of quite remarkable ability in smoothing out the personal difficulties that were always coming up between German nobles. The adhesion of Savoy to the alliance later in the summer did little at first to make up for the loss of the Duke of Lorraine. Potentially, Savoy was of great strategic and religious importance. A new theatre of war was opened there against the French, who were now encircled save for Switzerland. Savoy, however, had little strength of its own and the loyalty of its Duke Victor Amadeus II was suspect. Any fighting in this area would have to be done by others and paid for by the English and Dutch. These were bills which the allies paid with relative cheerfulness, and not only because Savoy offered almost the only point from which an invasion of France could be mounted.

Victor Amadeus was obliged on joining the alliance to grant relief to his Protestant subjects. The Vaudois had been so cruelly mistreated at the hands of French soldiers that their physical survival had been almost despaired of. Now they were saved from complete destruction; and beyond them lay the Huguenots of France, who might possibly be raised in rebellion against their tyrant. This dream of a French rising had been an anachronism when William III had first succumbed to it in 1674, but it still held its fascination for him and for Protestants in general. It may be considered the ancestor of the concept of the soft underbelly of Europe. In 1690 at least the soft underbelly proved to be well muscled. The French beat the Savoyards and their Spanish auxiliaries at Staffarda in August and made further gains later. Although a new front had been opened, it did little at first other than provide the French with new opportunities for conquest.

In the long run the Italian and Mediterranean fighting was to return the allies a substantial profit. If there were few or no permanent territorial gains in the area, the fighting did immobilize large numbers of the French and many of these men were killed. This was really to be the story of the Nine Years War as a whole. France had no soft underbelly; she was extremely hard to get at. The only way to bring her to reason was to weaken her in a war of attrition. Already the victories of the alliance were immense. Cologne, Liège, the British Isles, and Savoy had been freed from clientage to Louis XIV and were now fighting against him. If Sweden, Denmark, Hanover, Portugal, and the Holy See remained neutral their neutrality was at least better than alliance with France, and in time the position might be changed for the better. The French sphere of influence, which between 1682 and 1684 had blanketed all Europe save the palace in which the Prince of Orange had happened to be spending the night, had now withered away almost to nothing. France stood alone, a tiger caught in the nets of Assamese villagers. Despite her enormous strength and the feeble nature of each individual native spear, the tiger would eventually bleed to death from large numbers of superficial wounds.

One of the more effective weapons in this war of attrition was the embargo placed on French trade. Such an embargo had been contemplated but never put into effect in 1678. The idea was revived eleven years later, and it seems to have been an essentially English concept. Amsterdam and Zeeland were reluctant to forbid the consumption of French wines. During the course of hostilities the vintages of Portugal gradually came into use, but at first there was no substitute for claret and both merchants and consumers suffered real hardship. So too did their governments, whose Customs revenues were sharply reduced. The burden could at least be shared, and the damage to the French economy increased, by preventing neutral commerce with the enemy. William III determined to take this course early in the war, 'though I do not know whether we can do it with much right, but it is an absolute necessity'.[2] The trade of Sweden, Denmark and Hamburg with France was forcibly interrupted by the fleets of the maritime powers. Although large quantities of the goods thus confiscated were purchased, it was not possible to allay all resentment of these violent proceedings, and at one point the Danish government seized six Dutch merchant vessels in retaliation. Eventually these six ships were released; the Baltic powers were too weak to protect themselves. The allies permitted a limited amount of licensed trading and with this consolation the Danes and Swedes had to be content. Of course the blockade could not be completely effective on these terms, and another serious leak took place through the Spanish Netherlands. Horses, of which the French cavalry was in serious want, were exported from this area with the connivance of the government at Brussels. Even with these defects the blockade would seem to have been a significant factor in bringing Louis XIV to terms. In a specie economy any government, even the most autocratic, had less freedom of action than does a modern state with a printing press for its paper currency. Coins can be raised in value, and the gold and silver of which they are made can be adulterated. But there is a point at which the business community cannot go on, and that point occurs far sooner in a specie economy than in a modern one. Thus, want of money eventually forced the French to withdraw their navy from the seas which they actually commanded in 1690 and 1691. Among the people distress became acute, and by 1693 there was actual famine in France. There was certainly not enough in the purely military history of the Nine Years War to justify the terms of the Treaty of Rijswijk, and a substantial part of the difference seems to have been made up by the economic warfare waged by William III.[3]

Since the Nine Years War was primarily a war of attrition its strategy differed greatly from that of the War of 1672. In his first campaigns William III had been fighting desperately for every inch of ground in the Spanish Netherlands, and each town lost had been an irremediable disaster for the allied cause. After 1688, however, conditions had changed. Although the King fought just as hard as he had in his youth, and in the same areas, the battles and sieges now had a very different significance. They were no longer important in themselves so much as in their effect on allied and neutral opinion. If the French took X or Y, would an ally decide to become neutral or a neutral to join the side of Louis XIV? If not, his victories had no real meaning. So long as the allies held together the French might gain ground, but they could not win the war which had already been lost by 1690. Hence the importance of propaganda directed personally against William III. If confidence in the leader of the struggle could be broken the alliance would collapse. At best, the dual monarchy might be split apart. This was not likely to happen, but the French need not go so far. If they could only secure the defection of a secondary power, a Brandenburg or Bavaria or Savoy, that would be enough. Their propaganda campaign was intense and remarkably abusive, and it was accompanied by a stream of assassination attempts. Even better than the destruction of the King's image would be the elimination of the King himself. In their attacks, the French showed their nature. Indirectly, of course, they also gave honour to the man they hated. No one bothered to attack the character of Leopold, the second leader of the alliance; no one ever called him 'New Absalom, New Herod, New Cromwell, New Nero'.[4] Leopold was not worth taking that much trouble over.

The most important threat to the unity of the Grand Alliance was the existence of what came to be called the 'third party' of neutral states in the north of Germany. In the early years of the war its potential members included Denmark, Sweden, Hanover, and Münster. Denmark's position was compromised by the presence of some of her troops in the armies of William III, which were to a certain extent hostages for their country's good behaviour. In a sense, their employment and that of certain other contingents was more diplomatic than military in character. Hanover's position might have been affected by an offer of the English succession to the Duchess Sophia, but as we have seen the Convention blindly rejected William's proposals on this score in 1689. By itself, any one member of the third party was of negligible significance. There was, however, strength in numbers and each of the neutrals had friends. Denmark might influence Brandenburg, while Hanover might seduce the courts of Celle and Wolfembüttel. There were also disputed successions in Saxe-Lauenburg and Deux-Ponts which the French might use to stir up trouble among the allies and the members of the third party. It was the task of William III and Leopold of Habsburg to smooth over these differences, to keep the third party as small as possible, and at all costs to prevent it from growing. William's personal victories between 1688 and 1690 gave him immense prestige which contributed greatly to the achievement of these goals. But the failures of his subordinates at Fleurus and at Beachy Head, together with the imperial defeat at Belgrade and that of Savoy at Staffarda, weakened the King's position. In October Sweden offered herself as the mediator of a peace.[5] If the north German states should actually unite into a third party they might be strong enough to force the acceptance of the Swedish proposals. In making them, the Swedes claimed that their sympathies were with the allies and that a peace would be 'firm and certain, not like the last one but better'.[6] This was not enough. The 'last one', presumably, was the Truce of 1684, and no one was fighting merely for improvements on that. The mediation offer was a serious threat to the allied cause.

William III was so upset that he felt the proposals to be the result of French corruption.[7] This was all too likely. Charles XI and his chief minister Oxenstierne were favourable to the allies, but the rest of the court was pro-French and the King himself was almost the only political figure in his country with clean hands. The offer of mediation came at a difficult time. At almost the same moment the government at Brussels refused to continue employing Hanoverian troops, whose demands were exorbitant, and let them go home. This step was doubly ominous. For one thing, the troops were sorely needed and their departure left the Spanish Netherlands almost naked. For another, the retirement of her men left Hanover free to join the third party and push on the mediation scheme. William knew that Sophia kept up her correspondence with James II, that she acknowledged the legitimacy of the pretensions of the Prince of Wales, and he feared that she might refuse to displace the Prince in the English succession – a step which she actually took for a short time in 1699. It was essential for William to keep Sophia from taking this fatal course of action, and the employment of the Hanoverian troops had been almost his only means of bringing pressure to bear on his difficult cousin. The King was even more angry at the conduct of the Marquis of Gastañaga, the Governor of the Netherlands, than he was with the Swedes.

For the moment there was little that he could do. So long as the parliamentary session continued the King would be unable to cross over to the continent and take personal charge of the council of ministers at The Hague. Eventually the session dragged to an end, after the grant of £4,000,000. This generosity and the suppression of a plot against his life in which Lord Preston and Lord Clarendon were involved, would give the King a strong position in his negotiations once he reached the Republic. But he still had to get there, and he was to have a miserable voyage. William set out on 6/16 January and spent the night at Sir Joseph Williamson's house at Cobham. There he discovered that a strong east wind and a sharp frost made further progress impossible, and two days later he returned to the capital in disgust. He was not much more fortunate when he set out a second time on 16/26 January. This time he boarded the royal yacht *Mary* at Gravesend and sailed, protected by a convoy; but the wind was northeast, very cold, and accompanied by snow showers. The captains, at a council held on board the *Mary* on the 18th, advised returning to England. William would hear nothing of this idea and preferred listening to his Dutch pilot who predicted a change in the weather. When the pilot proved to be correct the convoy proceeded on its way. It was soon lost in fog and thus at the mercy of French privateers, shoals, and floating ice. At about two in the afternoon on 20/30 January, the ships found themselves in only two or three fathoms of water and guessed that they were off Goeree. The King then got into a small open boat with some beer, wine, two capons and four or five small loaves of bread for what was expected to be a short journey. He was attended by courtiers in his own boat and in two others, and courtiers and rowers alike had to share the provisions. In the loose ice and fog the men rowed for sixteen hours before they reached Goeree. Here the party rested for some time before setting out on a second journey of seven hours in order to get nearer to Honselaarsdijk. Finally they landed near the farm of Jillis, an aged huntsman in the King's service who had difficulty in recognizing his master. William was so cold by now that he could hardly speak, but he managed to greet Jillis and while he waited for the carriages he walked up and down in the peasant's cowbarn. The nobles, who had asked for something to drink other than water, laughed when they were given fresh buttermilk. After an hour's wait the carriages came and the King drove to Honselaarsdijk. His dignity was marred by the presence of two days' beard on his face; but he was lucky to be alive after such a perilous and foolhardy crossing. Later on the 31st William went on to The Hague amid the cheers of his countrymen.[8]

The very warmth of his welcome made work difficult. Everyone wanted to greet the King and the court was packed from morning till night. At the beginning of the following week he made a state entry into The Hague, passing under triumphal arches, and was greeted by a splendid show of fireworks whose effect was somewhat marred by fog.[9] Now it was possible to confirm William's authority as the leader of the Republic. He was careful to take his place in each of the colleges of the government, one after the other, and to announce that he intended to act in person as Captain-General as well as Stadhouder. The King was soon joined by a large number of princes and ambassadors for a discussion of the forthcoming campaign. This congress has received a good deal of notice, but it is important to remember that the work of the council of ministers had begun long before February 1691. This particular meeting, despite its unusually distinguished membership, was not an innovation. The presence of so many sovereign princes gave the congress a fictitious air of novelty, and it was certainly a glittering affair. The Electors of Brandenburg and Bavaria, two Dukes of the House of Brunswick and the Landgrave of Hesse-Cassel were the most prominent after the King himself. The Emperor was represented by the Count of Windischgrätz, the King of Spain by Gastañaga. Under pressure from William III the allied leaders agreed to put a total of 220,000 men into the field against France.

While the allies made their plans, the enemy acted. On 15 March an army under Boufflers appeared before Mons and Gastañaga hastened to invite William to come to the city's deliverance a second time, as he had once before in 1678.[10] From the very beginning the relief of the place was hopeless. The King himself admitted that there would be 'extraordinary difficulties'.[11] Had the French not been sure of victory they would not have permitted their monarch to appear before Mons in person. If William III had taken half as much pains over his public image as Louis XIV took to preserve his own, he would have stayed hunting at het Loo and allowed Mons to fall by itself. William, however, was a real soldier. Optimistic as ever, he permitted himself to believe that Gastañaga would supply the necessary three or four thousand wagons for a relief expedition. It was, of course, much too early in the year for an army to obtain its own forage in the field. On the 21st the King left het Loo for The Hague and went from there to join the army at Hall, not far from Brussels. Instead of the promised thousands of wagons he found five hundred, many of them broken.[12] Without wagons the army could not move. It might as well have been on the moon. Meanwhile Louis XIV was enjoying himself in the trenches before Mons, while Louvois let the citizens know they would be fined 100,000 eçus for every day they resisted after the opening of the trenches.[13] Terrified by this threat, the magistrates forced the garrison which had acted bravely to capitulate on 8 April.

The siege of Mons was not a glorious affair for either side. The French King was annoyed that William had appeared at all, though he had been able to do nothing. Louvois had promised him that William would not appear, and Louvois had been wrong. As a result, the Minister of War was in difficulties with his master for some time.[14] William III was also angry and with greater reason. Once again the Spanish had exposed his reputation to no purpose by breaking their engagements. More important, the loss of Mons endangered the rest of the Netherlands and the Republic itself. Diplomatically speaking its loss was perhaps yet more important. The third party would gain strength and the Baltic powers might well become unmanageable.[15] It appears to have been the loss of Mons which made William agree, rather reluctantly, that Gastañaga must be replaced. Though he was sufficiently an enemy of France the Governor of the Netherlands spent what little money he had on his mistresses and his favourites. He took few pains over his work and lacked the influence necessary to wring money out of the home government at Madrid. Already, during the congress, the Elector of Bavaria had asked William's help in obtaining the government of the Spanish Netherlands.[16] There were several possible objections to the appointment. Now, however, it was perhaps the only way to save a barrier for the Republic or to keep Max Emmanuel among the allies. The Elector was always open to French influence though his sister the Dauphine had died a short time before. William was obliged to recommend Max Emmanuel to the Spanish, and the appointment was finally made in the following December.[17]

On 15 April the King left the army for The Hague and a week later crossed the sea, this time pleasantly enough. His three months stay had re-established his authority in the Republic and had confirmed his leadership of the alliance.

The loss of Mons was embarrassing but without consequence. There had been one other incident, unimportant at the time, which was to have a sequel. On 20 February the King had gone hunting. One of his courtiers had fallen from his horse, breaking a leg. The youth did not cry out while the bone was being set, and William now as always admired bravery. 'That is such a good lad, he withstood terrible pain', he remarked.[18] The courtier's name was Arnout Joost van Keppel, and that day he made his fortune.

It was a flying visit to England. The King hoped to be able to patch up his dilapidated ministry. Although its majority had been great enough to secure a substantial parliamentary grant in the autumn session of 1690, the funds happened to be inadequate and in every other field the King's servants did even less well. They were so divided by faction that an administration could scarcely be said to exist. Carmarthen and Nottingham were drawing apart again, while Godolphin and the other lords who disliked both chief ministers bided their time in hostile silence. As is the case with most coalitions of the centre, the opposition consisted of extremists at either end of the political spectrum who found it difficult to unite on a common plan of campaign. To this division among its enemies the ministry owed its continued existence. It was still, with its parliamentary majority, a going concern; but it was terribly weak and no one could tell how long it would survive. William did his best to steal the thunder of both opposition groups. He made advances to Rochester as the representative of the High Church party and honoured him by dining at his house.[19] At the same time the King made advances to Lord Sunderland, who now re-entered political life as a friend of the Whigs. The coalition would have been strengthened by the addition of these two men. Neither of them, however, would take office at this time and the government was left to stagger on as best it might. Sooner or later, since it was as shy of men of talent as it was powerful in voting strength, it would surely fall. But for the moment nothing better could be found. Temporarily English politics were in a stalemate. His hopes of patching disappointed, William III departed for the continent on 1/11 May.

In the Republic he found that the military situation was as much of a stalemate as English domestic politics had been. This was to be the most boring of all his campaigns, a war of manoeuvre in which neither side was able to gain an advantage. The King prevented the enemy from taking Hall. Later, a French attack on Liège was frustrated. They were able to bombard the place but not to take it. William's marches and countermarches were not skilful enough to force the enemy to a field action. Their importance lies in the fact that the barrier was held without Mons. Until the campaign of 1691 was over, no one had really believed that this was possible and the Dutch at least were pleased at this rather negative result. But it was not the kind of success which would be easy to explain to English civilians. Almost the only spectacular events of the entire summer were a series of brilliant Irish victories by Ginckel, who completed the conquest of the island early in the autumn.

The stalemate in the main theatre of the war increased the danger of attempts elsewhere. The cheapest of all victories would be the murder of William III. There were at least two attempts on his life during the campaign, though both were frustrated. The King cared very little about such things and was far more worried about the possibility of a descent on England or Scotland. If a landing took place it might possibly be coordinated with a domestic rising. By this time the conduct of the Princess Anne was extremely suspicious. She was supported by the same curious combination of 'high flier' and extreme Whig that William had tried to capture in April. The existence of a conspiracy between such disparate groups cannot be proven, and by its nature it could have very little strength. But the government had to take the possibility seriously, and the King went so far as to try to borrow £200,000 in Amsterdam on his personal credit so as to be able to pay the troops on the continent if they should be cut off by a descent on England. In the end the danger faded away. No descent took place, and whatever may have been planned there was no rising in favour of the Princess or her father by any of their friends.

Meanwhile William did what he could to improve the strength of the alliance. The fall of Mons had led the Swedes to renew their offer of mediation, and by now a third party was definitely in existence. Hanover made a treaty with Sweden during the course of the summer. Münster refused to supply troops. Brandenburg's conduct was more cooperative than before, since General Schöning had left the Elector's service. He was suspected of being a French agent and he was certainly hostile to William III. His departure from the service of Frederick III, however, did the allies positive harm. Schöning's next post was in the service of George III of Saxony. Here he was more dangerous than ever; for the old Elector died in September and his son was a very weak and impressionable young man. George IV soon made Schöning his favourite and virtually his only minister. William tried to bribe the Elector with a Garter and his minister with a pension, but without success. In the summer of 1692 the Emperor had Schöning kidnapped and imprisoned for the remainder of the war. Luckily George IV soon forgot his friend, and Leopold's brutal tactics were successful now as they had been twenty years before at Cologne.

Certainly the Emperor could be a man of resource when he tried. In many respects he was a most difficult ally. Bursts of violent activity punctuated what was for the most part a languid and ineffectual line of conduct. Leopold would not fall in with the wishes of the maritime powers on even the most minor points unless they happened to suit him, and even on such occasions he preferred his own methods. Thus he kidnapped Schöning where William III preferred the milder use of bribes. Although the two sovereigns worked so closely with each other for so many years, there could never have been much confidence between them. The difference in religion was one great barrier. Leopold was such a bigot that the Greek Orthodox Poles who saved Vienna for him in 1683 at the cost of their lives were denied burial in consecrated ground. If he could treat Orthodox dead with such contempt his feelings towards live Calvinists were equally severe. There were, it is true, many legitimate political differences between the two leaders of the alliance. Their interests were by no means identical. Thus one of William's fondest hopes in 1691 was a conclusion of the Turkish war, which would have freed large armies to fight in the west. Negotiations were undertaken and the Dutch agent Colyear, by origin a Scot, was active in pushing them forward. But they fell through, and the Turkish war did not finally come to an end until 1699.

If Leopold did not make peace in the east, he contributed substantially towards the weakening of the third party in the north of Germany. Before the end of 1691 he was deep in negotiation with the princes of the House of Brunswick. In return for the use of their men and the gift of a large sum of money, the Emperor was willing to give the House an Electorate. The family was quite rich enough to support that dignity and its inclusion in the Electoral College might even improve the Emperor's position there. As King of Bohemia he had a seat in the college, but on most occasions his Statthalter was not permitted to vote. If a ninth Electorate went to the protestant House of Brunswick, it might then be able to obtain a full vote for the representative of the catholic King of Bohemia.[20] This was a matter for the future. Immediately, a Brunswick Electorate might be expected to detach Hanover from her neutrality while providing reinforcements for the imperial armies. The negotiations were delayed by haggling over the amount to be paid and also over the recipient of the glittering prize, since George William of Celle was older than his brother Ernst August of Hanover. Eventually Ernst August received the Electorate and Leopold 6,000 men. A large part of the price, however, was paid by the English and Dutch, who were forced to hire some 8,000 other troops at an absurd rate.[21] In time, therefore, Leopold's independent conduct brought a number of advantages to William III even though they had to be paid for. By midsummer of 1692 the threat in Saxony had been parried. Hanover had been brought into the struggle, and Max Emmanuel of Bavaria was at long last installed at Brussels. These gains more than offset the military victories of the French in the Low Countries.

William had need of someone like Leopold in his dealings with English politics. When he returned from the Republic in October 1691 he discovered that the growing dissention between Carmarthen and Nottingham had now become open. The ministry was in no condition to resist attacks, which now came from inside the House of Commons and from outside as well. Inside the House a squadron of able debaters led by Musgrave, Clarges, Seymour, Harley, and Foley argued that the country could not afford to support an army of 65,000 men. In his Speech from the Throne on 22 October William had demanded this number. He also made the silly error of not thanking the Commons for their past generosity. This gave the malcontents their opportunity and no thanks were returned for the Speech. Although they were able to deliver this snub and to mortify the ministers, the opposition leaders had no further success. After long debate a vote of 65,000 men was carried. Then the government leaders explained that this figure did not include officers and a second vote was carried on their behalf. Thus despite the lacklustre appearance of the administration, it was still in control of the Commons and still able – though no one could tell for how long – to raise funds for the war. Its difficulties lay elsewhere. Apart from Nottingham and Godolphin there were very few men of real administrative talent in the government and even fewer men of distinction. Carmarthen could deliver the votes but his friends and his methods were almost equally embarrassing. Society was bored and restive, and humiliated by the contemptuous way in which it was bought.

Such a situation provided brilliant opportunities for an adventurer. The government badly needed individuals of talent, especially peers. Anyone who could debate or fight or administer might reasonably set his price very high. Hitherto Carmarthen had been able to balance extreme Whig against extreme Tory, to occupy himself the broad middle ground of politics and to exclude from office almost every potential rival. Now his system broke down. In January Lord Marlborough demanded the command of the English land forces in Flanders for the coming campaign. Although Churchill was already the highest ranking officer of English birth, he was extremely dissatisfied with his position. The denial of a dukedom, of the Garter, of the most lucrative place in the Ordnance infuriated his ambitious nature. He was particularly angry that foreigners such as Solms, Leinster, the younger Schomberg and Ginckel stood in his way. Here was a popular and a plausible issue. There were indeed too few English born in high commands. But William did not pick men on the basis of their national origin. He chose them largely on the basis of experience, and in this respect Marlborough was still only half qualified for the posts he now held. There were several English and Scottish born who were now rising to positions of responsibility. Mackay, Tollemache, Ormonde and Cutts are the most well-known members of this group, though there were many others.

When Marlborough demanded that only native born Englishmen should command English troops, his aims were purely selfish. Nothing but time stood between his colleagues and further promotion. But his own further advancement was likely to be hindered by factors which the Earl was careful not to mention. For one thing Marlborough had never served in the British regiments paid for by the Dutch in the years before the Revolution. The King had favoured officers of these regiments in making his promotions because he knew them and had trained them. Mackay was perhaps the most prominent of the generals selected from this source. Tollemache may also have been favoured because of his Dutch service, though it was much shorter than Mackay's. But Tollemache had a second advantage. He was well-born, as Churchill was not. The King was certainly not a snob in the ordinary sense of the word. He did not, however, understand or appreciate the open English social system. He felt that the Queen herself was ill-born because of her Hyde blood. And whatever William's own feelings on the matter, how would the allied generals react to Marlborough's further promotion? Would an Elector of Bavaria, an Electoral Prince of Hanover, a Duke of Württemberg even speak to such an upstart? It was later to prove impossible for the Elector of Bavaria to forget the enormous distance which separated him from Walraven of Nassau, who though a prince was not a sovereign prince. The two generals would not speak, to the confusion and dismay of the allied army. Since this was the way the world went in that generation, it was hardly likely that William III would make a man who was scarcely even a gentleman a full general. When the time came for an English native to reach that rank, the person chosen might be an officer of good family, like Tollemache. But there were others with yet higher claims. For twenty years William had appointed distant connections of his own to the highest posts. Waldeck, Solms, the Prince of Nassau, and Ouwerkerck were all cousins of the King. These were foreigners; but in the Duke of Ormonde William had an English cousin. Young, able, popular, the second Duke of Ormonde was a darling of the court for many reasons. The King remembered his father, Lord Ossory, with great affection. Ossory's sister, now the Countess of Derby, was Mistress of the Robes to the Queen and was beloved in her own right. Ormonde was still a young man, not yet thirty; but his birth and position were such that he was a likely choice for the highest military commands whenever these should be given to a native Englishman.

Marlborough's attempt to organize the officers of the army for an exercise in collective bargaining was therefore fundamentally insincere. English officers were already being promoted to positions of responsibility, and more of them would be eligible for promotion with every passing year. The insincerity of his conduct did not make it any less dangerous. Marlborough's attempt to force William's hand struck at the heart of the King's system of government. Other parts of the scheme could be delegated or abandoned if need be: but the core of the dual monarchy was control of the allied armies, exercised by William III in person. He simply could not tolerate opposition in this field. The intrigues of the Raad van State and of Henry Casimir in the Republic had to be crushed because they threatened the King's position as Captain-General. The intrigues of Marlborough with the English army threatened his position as Commander-in-Chief. Had the officers actually gone out on strike the King might have been forced to give over the personal command of his forces. Even if the malcontents should not be able to carry their campaign that far, William might well have lost the right to name his own officers. In either case his control over the English army would have been lost, and with it his chances of winning the war. Marlborough was dismissed, as he had to be.

There were of course many other threads to the incident. The Earl had been almost unbelievably offensive. According to one account he had said publicly that William 'had not virtue enough to value high ends, a corage to punnish his enemies'.[22] And behind the words themselves lay the threat of a conspiracy against the régime. Anne had made her peace with the late King in December. It was all too easy to imagine the existence of an army plot for the restoration of James, supported by the Princess, her favourites, the Church party and perhaps the 'republicans'. Alternatively and more probably, the goal of the plot might be the premature and violent placement of the Princess on the throne. Whatever the wider meaning of Marlborough's misconduct may have been, it was a great political misfortune that punishment was not restricted to his own person. The Queen made the tactical error of demanding that Anne dismiss Lady Marlborough from her service, and then the greater error of not seeing to it that her orders were obeyed. The Princess and her court were permitted to retire to Sion House. Since no one cared to state publicly that Anne was a traitor as well as a stubborn fool, she not only kept her Sarah, but, with the popularity of a martyr, became more dangerous than she had been before. Now it was absolutely necessary to capture as much of her political strength as possible. Rochester was appointed to the Council in the spring, while Sir Edward Seymour was even more richly rewarded with a place in the Cabinet Council and at the Treasury Board.

This sudden lurch to the right was fatal to the Carmarthen coalition. Although the King appointed the brilliant young Whig Charles Montagu to the Treasury, this step was offset by the almost simultaneous removal of Sydney from the post of Secretary of State for which he was so unfitted. Sydney was sent to gilded exile as Lord Lieutenant of Ireland and so made a personal profit out of the transaction. His party did not fare so well. Russell, it is true, took command of the fleet. The net effect of the changes, however, was to create an almost purely Tory ministry. If this cut the ground from under the feet of the Princess, it did precisely the same thing to the ministry. The worst aspect of the whole affair was that Rochester and Seymour could not deliver the vote. They were powerful only so long as they were in opposition. When they went over to the court they did not bring their friends with them. Mulgrave took over the task of opposition in the Lords, while Musgrave, Clarges, Foley and Harley succeeded to Seymour's position in the Commons. The Church party in the Commons was as difficult to control as was the Lower House of Convocation. Tory peers were no more successful in imposing discipline on their troops in Parliament than were the bishops in their own sphere. Such followers could not really be led. They were against every proposal, against every leader who did not have a purely negative programme. They hoped to turn back the clock, to return to the happy days of divine right monarchy and low taxes. It must be remembered that William III brought with him something in the nature of a New Deal. His government was three or four times as expensive as that of his uncles. It was paid for by the landowners and the money went for the most part into the City – to money-lenders, contractors, and so on – so that there was not only big government but a perceptible shift of wealth from one class to another. The process did not begin in 1689. Apparently rents fell rather steadily during the second half of the seventeenth century, and the new men were far richer in 1689 than they had been in 1660. Yet the process was sharply intensified after the Revolution, not only by the war but also by a series of bad harvests. Of course individual members of the opposition were often able to make money out of these changes. Some of them did very well. But they resented the greater success of the evil men who throve on the favour of that wicked foreigner, the King.

The coalition's lurch to the right in the spring of 1692 was thus foredoomed to failure. Only the Whigs had enough party discipline to add strength to the government, and it was a waste of time to negotiate with anyone else. At the time, however, the conservative threat seemed dangerous; but only briefly. In May Grandval's plot to assassinate the King at his headquarters was frustrated. Since both Louis XIV and James II seemed to be implicated, the plot's discovery caused a great revulsion of feeling against the Jacobite cause. In the same month Russell's great victory at La Hogue ended the possibility of a descent. No conspiracy came to light in the forces. If during the summer Anne's court at Bath was very well attended, so too was that of the Queen. The many disaffected elements in the country were unable to organize themselves, and slowly the danger of a counter-revolution passed away.

Meanwhile the King had crossed the sea in March and had gone to hunt at het Loo after a short visit to The Hague. William bought the estate in 1686.

It was close enough to Dieren so that he could hunt from one house to the other, spend the night, and then return the next day as he had come. In the two years before the Revolution the Prince built a great palace at het Loo, and from henceforth the original château was used as a guest house. Some 6,000 soldiers were employed on the works. Unfortunately the magnificent gardens were destroyed at the end of the eighteenth century and most of the interiors were altered during the nineteenth. All that remains today of the work of William III is the shell of the palace, which was universally condemned by contemporaries as its worst feature. During the Nine Years War improvements were constantly being made both to the house and to the gardens. The King had, of course, no other use for his private income after 1688. He gave some remarkably generous pensions in his later years, but such things could not absorb his rents and the bulk of his income was available to adorn the most personal of all his buildings. Many of his houses were inherited, while the new works at Hampton Court and Kensington were heavily influenced both by the needs of English court ceremonial and by the wishes of the Queen. But at het Loo William III could give full rein to his personal tastes in building and landscape architecture. His activities there served also as items in the propaganda war against France. The King never permitted his writers to be as rude about Louis XIV as the French were about him. The King of France was so vain that he might well prolong the war simply to avenge a pamphlet. Yet if William III must be discreet he could at least get in some sly digs. By adding to het Loo he pointed out that he was still a rich man. His works at het Loo were in sharp contrast to the suspension of all projects at Versailles for the duration of the war, and the point was not lost on any of the allies.

Early in May the King was obliged to move nearer the coast. At first he did not believe in the possibility of a descent or a rising in England, but as the reports became more circumstantial William thought it prudent to return to The Hague. Yachts were kept in readiness to take him across the sea in the event of an invasion. Portland was dispatched to assist the Queen if she should have to summon an emergency session of Parliament. Later in the month William joined his army near Brussels, but he was careful to move the yachts to Willemstad and the convoys to Goeree. There was still a possibility that he might have to return to England.[23] The French preparations near Mons were, however, even more frightening than anything that could happen in England and it was on Mons that William kept his closest watch. Enormous concentrations of heavy guns and the news of the coming of Louis XIV in person left no doubt that something serious was about to happen. Now that Louvois was dead his master was able to display his own military talents for the first time; and they were not inconsiderable. The French Monarch would likely undertake some great siege. William had been so worried about Namur that he had sent his best engineer there during the previous winter to extend the defences of the place. In May 1692 the new fortifications were only half finished, but the garrison was unusually well manned and the commander, the Duke of Aremberg, had the assistance of Coehoorn himself. For the first time in his career, the French engineer Vauban had an opponent worthy of him.

Louis XIV began the siege of Namur on 25 May. Although the new works were unfinished and the conduct of the citizens was infamous, the castle held out until 30 June. The dates themselves indicate the extent of the decay of the French army. Had Louvois still lived the siege would have begun in March and it might well have taken three weeks rather than five. But this gave little comfort to the allies. William had only one army, pinned down by a French field force under Luxembourg. Had the German contingents been in the field they could have formed a second allied army to undertake the relief of Namur. The Germans, however, were nowhere to be seen; and without them William would have to defeat Luxembourg before he could come to the rescue of the town. He tried to force on a battle. But he was prevented by some unusually heavy weather from crossing the Mehaigne which lay between the allied forces and Luxembourg's army. On 8 June it rained so hard that the level of the river rose between one and two feet. Still William drank to the success of the coming battle. But the rains continued and next day the attempt to cross the Mehaigne had to be abandoned.[24] The rains were so heavy that many tents collapsed or were blown away, and the common soldiers complained that Luxembourg controlled the weather by sorcery.

After the fall of Namur Louis XIV returned to Versailles, but the campaign was not yet over. During the latter half of June and all July William III and Luxembourg indulged themselves in an intricate series of manoeuvres, each trying by marches and countermarches to secure an advantage over the other. Ultimately the King was successful. On Sunday 3 August he surprised the French between Enghien and Steenkerk. The French were doubly unfortunate, since the ground was not suitable for their superior cavalry. Their positions were, however, covered by a wood and by a hedge, so that the allied army had to advance uphill on a very narrow front. Early in the morning the advance guard set out under the command of the Duke of Württemberg. They came in sight of the enemy about nine o'clock. An hour later, after the cannon had come up, the opposing forces began to skirmish and a general engagement was opened at about one in the afternoon. At first Württemberg's men were successful, pushing the French back and capturing some of their guns. Both sides suffered considerable losses. Towards evening Boufflers arrived with fresh men and some heavy cannon to assist the flagging efforts of the main body of the French. The cannon, particularly, did much damage and since the light was now failing William brought the action to an end. The allies retired to their camp in good order.[25]

Since some 2,000 men were killed and a thousand wounded on each side, Steenkerk may be considered a drawn battle. Each army lost one standard, so that the honours of war were shared with almost precise accuracy. If anything the allies achieved a limited success. The King forced on a battle which the French wished to avoid; he gave the French a bloody nose; and he gave them a shock sufficient to send them into winter quarters early in the year. The casualties among the French officers were unusually heavy and without the assistance brought by Boufflers Luxembourg's army would probably have suffered a decisive defeat. William's own conduct during the battle was as remarkable as ever; 'The part the King had had in all the danger had been no less than is usuall to his Majesty on the like occasions having expos'd himself both in the Action & in the Retreat, not only as a Generall but as a lesser Officer & more especially to the Canon which destroyed a great many of our men very near His Majesty, But it hath pleasd God to Preverse [sic] his Person ...'[26] The King also deserves credit for planning the battle. His chief fault, an old one, lay in the inadequate nature of his scouting, which led him to mistake the lie of the land. In its military consequences Steenkerk was a limited allied victory. It gave the King time to deal with the very serious problems arising from the loss of Namur. After taking Namur, the next obvious place for the French to attack was Liège. Should that city fall the barrier could hardly be maintained, while the procurement of grenades would become far more difficult. Liège, unlike Mons or Namur, was a position which the allies could not afford to lose. At Steenkerk William III saved Liège for a year and to this extent the drawn battle was a limited victory for him. But the real significance of the battle lay in its political consequences, and it is to these that we must now turn.

Chapter 22

MYTH AND FACT

IN England the reaction to Steenkerk was immediate and profound. It was assumed to have been a defeat for the King, whose personal authority was deeply and permanently wounded by this erroneous conclusion. On the whole, neither the battle nor the campaign in general had gone badly; but William's enemies preferred myth to fact. They forgot that a French descent had been foiled. They did not care about the Savoyard invasion of southern France which, though in itself unproductive, seemed to promise victories in the years to come. Steenkerk was the only thing that mattered. Steenkerk 'proved' that war in Flanders was a waste of time. A Dutch agent reported that the Whigs were downcast and the Tories boastful over the outcome of the campaign, while Jacobites were growing bolder day by day.[1] This particular agent was an outsider and his observations must be taken with caution; yet his analysis of the political situation is of some interest. He divided the parties into Whigs, high and low Tories, and Trimmers. The Whigs in general support the true religion, their country, their Majesties, the Republic and its interests, and the war. The high Tories, on the other hand, hate the Dutch, the Whigs, and the King and Queen. They assume the cloak of righteousness and claim to be true to the Church of England, whose interests they equate with those of the whole kingdom. In fact they hate virtue and have nothing less in mind than the service of God. The low Tories differ from the high only in that they do not drive on so hard. They wish to place the crown on Anne's head while the high Tories prefer the restoration of James. Trimmers are neither hot nor cold and join the stronger side. The very rich care only to preserve their estates, but the rabble or Captain Tam are whiggish and are inclined to William and Mary.[2]

Although the picture thus drawn was highly coloured, it contained elements of truth. Even an outsider could see that the King's general political position was weak. What could not be seen by a foreigner was that the ministers shared the doubts of the public. On 27 August Nottingham wrote that the majority of the Committee felt that it would be very difficult to obtain such grants this year as last. Even if large grants should be made, 'it was not likely the Parliament would be of opinion that so great a share of the expense should be or could be spent in Flanders'. Nottingham made this report 'to the end that His Majesty may judge whether some other measures may not be taken both abroad and at home for the carrying on the war at such a Charge as probably may be had, rather than to think of doing it still at such Expence as perhaps cannot be furnish'd'.[3] Carmarthen, Lowther, and Devonshire were absent when the Committee took this defeatist position, but this does not mean that they disagreed with the advice offered to the King. They may have disagreed. Or they may have been too prudent to give such unpalatable advice.

William ordered Blathwayt to reply that he was 'not a little surprized' at the opinion of the lords, the strongest phrase in the royal vocabulary. When William said that something was intolerable he was annoyed, perhaps even angry. When he was 'not a little surprized' he was outraged. In June 1672 he had been 'not a little surprized' at the news that de Groot had full powers to treat with the enemy.[4] Now the King ordered Blathwayt to write that the mere report of the Committee's opinion would force the allies to a separate peace and ruin the prospects for a favourable parliamentary session. Such a broadside took care of the members of the Cabinet Council. But nothing could secure obedience from the Admiralty. Plans had been maturing at least since June for the dispatch of a large squadron to the Mediterranean. Immediately after Steenkerk the King repeated his commands. The Admiralty refused to obey them, and the disaster to the Smyrna fleet of the following year was the direct consequence of this insolence. William foresaw what would happen and waited for months in an agony of despair for news of the fate of the merchant fleet and its convoy.

In the Republic, naval affairs, about which William knew very little, had been handled by subordinates throughout his public lifetime. The Secretary of the Amsterdam Admiralty, Job de Wildt, ran the navy with machinelike efficiency, though his economies were sometimes shortsighted. Given the nature of this system it was only natural that William III should attempt to duplicate it in England by delegating naval affairs to his Secretary Nottingham. The senior service, remembering the personal attention bestowed on it by the last two sovereigns, refused to cooperate and the results were chaotic. In January 1693 Russell refused to serve while Nottingham remained in office, but even before this the position of the Earl was pitiable. It must have been very humiliating to write, as it was infuriating to read, such words as these:

I have formerly told you the utmost to which the Admiralty can be brought in relation to the Mediterranean Squadron when I hear from you, that the King is satisfied I will take care that the Ships be ready by the appointed time. ...[5]

After the loss of the Smyrna fleet proved the King to have been right, as he almost always was, on the larger questions of naval strategy his personal authority had to be accepted. But that of a Secretary of State did not, and after Nottingham's removal from office William III had to take on a great portion of the detailed work of naval administration himself. This was a tremendous nuisance. Trenchard and Shrewsbury were of some use in 1694, but, from then on, the personal intervention of the King was apparently required at every level if anything was to be done.[6] Not the least awkward part of this arrangement was the fact that the King refused to write in English, while his First Lord of the Admiralty could read nothing else.

If in the long run the King established personal control over the Navy, as he had over the Treasury and Army, by becoming involved in its day to day administration, this was to be the work of years. In the autumn of 1692 the Navy was out of control. So, more ominously, were the Tories. It was at this point that the Tories developed the so-called 'blue water' strategy: that is, the idea that England should withdraw from the war in Flanders and rely entirely on fighting at sea.[7] In terms of specie there was something to be said for this idea, since the money spent in Flanders by the English never came back into the country, while most of that spent on the fleets never left it. The 'blue water' scheme, however, was hopelessly irrelevant in military terms. Even if the British conquered every French colony these gains could not have been traded for Strasbourg alone, much less a strong barrier, at the end of the war. Although seapower could do much in the Mediterranean, it could not save Savoy or Spain unless it was used in conjunction with substantial armies on land. And the allies could not win, could not reasonably be expected even to continue fighting, without the assistance of English men and English money. The true lesson of Steenkerk was that the English contribution should be increased, not that it should be cut off.

Another problem facing the King when he landed near Yarmouth on 18 October was the possible treachery of his servants. Godolphin's conduct was as imprudent as that of any. In July there had been rumours that the First Lord of the Treasury was to be seen walking with a prominent Jacobite in St James's Park at one in the morning, and dining with Marlborough and Shrewsbury at midday. Three months later there was a report that Godolphin entertained Marlborough, Shrewsbury, Lord Montague and even Lord Feversham at his house near Windsor Castle.[8] Here again was the old danger of a conjunction between disgruntled army officers, Jacobites, and Whigs for the overthrow of the present ministry. Godolphin's motives have never been satisfactorily explained. Perhaps he was actively engaged in a conspiracy; more likely he was simply taking out an insurance policy on the King's life. Even if he continued to escape assassination, the King could not live forever, and in 1692 he was visibly less well than he had been for three years. William was not in fact in any danger, but he looked as if he might die at any moment; and in the circumstances most prudent men would have agreed with the attitude of the Tory in a pamphlet of the following year: 'As long as the

Government can maintain it self, and will maintain me, it is sure of me: But I have liv'd too long at Court to die a Martyr for any Monarch, and will always behave my self so in one Court, as to be well with the next.'9

The King met these problems by an unusual display of charm. He reached Kensington on 20 October and was strikingly obliging in his greetings to the court the next morning. Admiral Russell was honoured above all the rest, a tacit apology for the fact that the Queen had neglected to order a public thanksgiving for the victory at La Hogue. William then retired to Windsor until the opening of Parliament on 4 November, both to rest and to prove that he was not attempting to influence the parties. He agreed to dine at Whitehall on Thursdays throughout the winter. Great care was taken over the Speech from the Throne. The original draft in the King's hand in French was translated by Nottingham and discussed by the Cabinet Council before the final revisions were made. As a result the Speech was one of the most tactful that William ever gave, and in sharp contrast to the peremptory tone of the previous year.[10] On the evening of 4 November, after delivering his Speech, William had to endure a great ball given in honour of his birthday. He complained that the ceremonies had exhausted him, but at least he had the satisfaction of seeing Prince George at the dance. Although Anne did not do so, her husband had called on William as soon as he returned, and he had the manners to wear a new suit to the birthday. This was the general custom of the period; and if the prince's birthday suit was very plain it was at least new. Throughout the winter both King and Queen went out of their way to be affable and to take their part in society.

Despite the King's new politeness, the session began badly. His Speech met with no applause, and affairs grew worse day by day. A fortnight after the opening of Parliament William in despair wrote to Heinsius ordering him to open peace negotiations with the French.[11] D'Avaux was now being sent as French ambassador to Sweden, and William wanted Dijkvelt to interview him on his way. Ultimately it proved impossible to arrange a meeting; but the King's gloom and his desire for peace continued throughout the winter. Although Parliament granted him among other things a land tax of four shillings in the pound he could not bring himself to express thanks for it, since he felt the supplies to be both too small and unsuitable as funds of credit.[12] One reason for the failure of the session was the bitter fight between Nottingham and Russell. The Secretary was so busy defending himself in Parliament that he had neither time nor energy to help plan for the coming campaign.[13] Nor could he do more than defend himself. The ministry was in no condition to take the initiative. It was so weak that William had to expose himself by vetoing the Triennial Bill, which any strong ministry would have disposed of at a much earlier stage in the proceedings. In these circumstances it is not surprising that the King continued to be strongly in favour of peace. Heinsius entered into informal negotiations with Lilienroth, the Swedish ambassador at The Hague, in February and Dijkvelt would seem to have found out a channel of his own before the end of the same month.[14]

In the end, the King managed to secure something of what he wanted. Although the funds granted were far too small, England remained a partner in the war on land. Neither Nottingham nor Solms, who was viciously attacked in Parliament for his supposed misdeeds at Steenkerk, was driven from the royal service. Nottingham knew what to expect from parliaments and had no intention of resigning over a few insults. Solms, less experienced, refused to speak to William III for months and it took Dijkvelt six solid hours to persuade the general to serve for the coming campaign.[15] Yet if the King kept his freedom of choice, on measures and on men as well, he kept it only in show. William III had now spent all the gratitude and a large part of the respect accorded him by the political nation in 1688. In reality he retained only the right to choose men or measures. He could have war, or he could have a predominantly Tory ministry: not both. The Tories were of course inconceivably stupid in forcing such a choice on the King. It was not merely that William preferred the Tories, 'the party he thincks alone will support the throne',[16] and disliked many individual Whigs as well as their party. By forcing the King and his three successors to choose between the employment of themselves and a forward foreign policy, the Tories destroyed their party as a national force. After 1693 their terms in office were brief and troubled, and in 1714 they disappeared from the scene.

The King and the monarchy suffered as well. William turned to Lord Sunderland, who advised a straight Whig ministry while himself remaining prudently behind the curtain. As he left for the continent at the end of March, the King complied to the extent of making Somers Lord Keeper and Sir John Trenchard Secretary of State. Other Whigs were appointed as the law officers; but William asserted his independence by refusing to dismiss Nottingham. It would have been better had he swallowed all his medicine at once. He was now the prisoner of a single party. Had he acted graciously, had he kept Russell in January and abandoned Nottingham, he might have obtained more adequate supplies and the campaign at sea would certainly have gone better than it did. By keeping Nottingham and appointing three Tory admirals to replace Russell, William kept the shadow of his prerogative. But the result was a disastrous campaign, and in the end Nottingham had to be dismissed in November. Nor was the King much more fortunate in his other attempts to preserve the royal authority. Lord Bellomont disobeyed the direct commands of the Queen to abstain from voting on the Triennial Bill. She dismissed him from her household and generously gave him a pension, since he was a poor man. Her firmness made her unpopular, while her generosity remained unnoticed. The King had more trouble with Lord Lansdowne and with the Duke of Ormonde. Lansdowne asked for the payment of an ancient debt and was so impertinent as to beg 'que s'il ne reçevoit pas des marques de sa faveur, il n'en receust pas au moin de son injustice'.[17] The King lost his temper and forbade Lansdowne the court, though he could not afford to antagonize him. With Ormonde William had better luck. There were many competitors for the place of Governor of the Isle of Wight, which was supposed to carry with it the right to name six Members of Parliament. When the place went to Lord Cutts instead of Ormonde the latter resigned all his places in a huff; but he was given three days in which to change his mind and eventually he came to his senses.[18] In general, William's attempts to discipline his courtiers did little more than emphasize the weakness of his position.

When he reached The Hague after a difficult and tedious crossing, the King found affairs there in an equally cheerless state. His ancient friend and colleague the Prince van Waldeck had died in the previous November, leaving no obvious successor to the place of first field-marshal of the armies of the Republic. Solms and the Elector of Bavaria might be able to take over some of Waldeck's diplomatic work, but the army command presented the greatest difficulties. The King left the post unfilled until the end of the campaign and eventually appointed the Duke of Holstein-Ploen. This infuriated the Stadhouder of Friesland, who left the army and was soon involved in treasonable intrigues with the French. Shortly after the King had gone on to het Loo, The Hague was rocked by the arrest of Simon van Halewijn, a former burgomaster of Dordrecht and a trusted associate of William. Shortly after Steenkerk, Halewijn had gone to Switzerland where he had entered into unauthorized private negotiations with the French ambassador there. His stated intention was to procure a peace; but he may also have wanted to use the promise of one to overthrow the Stadhouderate. Halewijn's guilt was obvious, and he was soon sentenced to life imprisonment. In itself Halewijn's treason was a sad affair. It was also an ominous one, for the war weariness of the Dutch was becoming increasingly evident.

Nor was this all the bad news. The elevation of Ernst August of Hanover to the Electoral College had infuriated the princes of the north, reviving the strength of the dreaded third party. Denmark was especially annoyed at the promotion, while d'Avaux's presence at Stockholm was a continuing threat to the allied cause. Throughout the summer of 1693 war in the north seemed likely. Several contingents of men that William needed in Flanders were withheld by their princes because of this unrest, and more would be withdrawn if hostilities should actually break out. Meanwhile the King had no money to pay the troops he had left, and there were very few of them. It was not until he reached the army in mid-May that the King realized the full extent of his difficulties, though he had predicted the general situation accurately enough. At the end of the month he reported to Heinsius that 'the enemy's superiority in numbers is incredible'.[19] Throughout most of the campaign the ratio of the French forces in the Low Countries to those of the allies was 8 to 5. These odds were hopeless, and therefore peace negotiations continued right through the summer.

The French proved willing to offer the treaties of Westphalia and Nijmegen as a basis of negotiations; but they wished to keep Strasbourg and Luxembourg as well, and to provide for the education of the Prince of Wales in England as the immediate successor of William and Mary.[20] It is to the King's credit that he would never agree to discuss the possibility of displacing the Princess Anne in the line of succession. He might say that he did not care how the world went once he was out of it, but his actions belied his words. He wanted a strong barrier, if possible one better than that of 1678. For England, he remained loyal to the Revolution Settlement and to all it implied, even though he might have gained personal advantages by the adoption of the Prince of Wales. At five, the boy could still have been trained as a Protestant; but William refused to hear of the idea. He preferred to take a thrashing from the French armies.

The King's goal in 1693, as the year before, was to keep Liège. The loss of Namur made this a much more difficult task. From Namur the French could easily follow the course of the Maas downstream in a north-easterly direction to Liège; only the small town of Huy stood between them and the city. Beyond Liège, so important in itself, lay Maastricht and the Republic. The place simply must be held. But the French need not follow the river; they could march northwards from Namur and take what they wished in Brabant. There lay Louvain and the capital city of Brussels itself, while neither Mechlin nor Antwerp was far beyond. Strategically the situation was very gloomy in the Low Countries, and the news from Germany was even worse; on 22 May a French army took Heidelberg unopposed. Meanwhile Louis XIV, having created seven new marshals of France and the military order of St Louis to encourage his generals, left Versailles and reached his army near Mons on 2 June. He found that William III had been too clever for him. The King had joined his men in mid-May. On 5 June he took up his quarters at the Norbertine abbey of Parck, near Louvain. Parck was a picturesque and delightful spot, with three ponds, charming gardens, and a stream that operated a mill. Its real importance lay in the fact that by placing his army there William covered Liège and the Duchy of Brabant as well. Louis XIV found that he could not get at Liège or indeed any other worthwhile fortress while his enemy was so well placed. On 8 June he decided to return to Versailles; he never took the field again.[21]

After the departure of the French King the situation was still most serious. If the French sent off a detachment to strengthen their forces in Germany, William had to make two detachments of his own. The first went to strengthen the garrison of Liège. The second was sent off under Wirttemburg to raise contributions, which at this point were absolutely vital. The first news of the loss of the Smyrna fleet near Cape St Vincent was grossly exaggerated. The facts were bad enough: perhaps thirty merchant vessels captured by the French and another fifty scuttled by their masters to prevent them from falling into enemy hands. But if many were lost many others made their escape to the Canaries and then slowly succeeded in getting home. The early reports, however, spoke of a complete disaster and they caused trouble in Amsterdam and panic in London. Loans could not be raised in such circumstances on either side of the North Sea. The gravity of the financial situation is well illustrated by a letter of Godolphin to the King of 14/24 July, in which he announced that the Treasury had run dry that very day. He had hoped for loans of £300,000 on the Act for the Review of the Poll;

'but the very ill news that we have received today of the destruction of a great part of the Turkey fleet, makes the consternation so great in the City at present, that it is impossible to hope for any money from thence; ... so that I do not see how it is possible to provide any longer either for the subsistance, or any other part of the expence, unless Your Majesty can furnish us with one hundred thousand pounds, at least, ...'[22]

Since there was no credit to be had on the continent as late as 27 August, the army had to raise contributions or starve.[23]

The detachment of Tilly to reinforce the garrison of Liège saved that city. The detachment of Württemburg to raise contributions provided enough money to keep the army alive. But the forces which remained under William's personal control were now too small to defend themselves or to cover the Low Countries. In mid-July Luxembourg attacked Huy, the forward bastion of Liège. This forced the King to leave Parck on 20 July and advance to the relief of the town. Had Huy put up a good defence all might have been well; but it surrendered just as William was on the point of coming to its rescue. Now the French threat was more ominous than ever before. It is no wonder that the King was noted to be in a pensive mood. On the 25th he took up his quarters at Neerhespen, on the north bank of a small stream named the Geete. The army camped in a number of small villages on the south bank. Several bridges were thrown across the Geete, the most important at Neerhespen for easy communication between headquarters and the camp. William's forlorn hope of an army had little chance to withstand a direct assault. Yet if it retired to safety across the bridges the French would have a free choice, either to attack Brussels or to attack Liège. The King, therefore, stayed where he was. Like the bird which protects her fledglings hidden in the nest by fluttering weakly in full sight of the hunters, the King proposed to distract the attention of the enemy from his two defenceless cities. On Tuesday 28 July the French approached the allied camp and prepared for battle on the morrow. The King, however, was not idle on his part. On the 28th the baggage was sent off to Louvain and such non-combatants as Huygens were also dismissed. Then in the darkness of the night the allied infantry was sent out to occupy the hedgerows and to throw up earthworks along a line between the village of Neerwinden and the heights above the village of Neerlanden. The allied right wing was covered by hedges and Neerwinden; the centre by the earthworks; and the left wing by heights and then by marshy ground, which extended to the Geete. According to all accounts the guns were unusually well placed in positions from which they would be able to fire down on the approaching French in the morning.

At dawn on Wednesday the 29th the overwhelmingly superior army of the enemy appeared. How could they possibly be stopped by a few snipers in hedgerows and by the feeble retrenchments which were all that the soldiers had been able to dig in a single night? But for long they were. The royal cannon did heavy damage to the French troops, whose own guns were not well placed. A lucky shot severed the right leg of Count Solms below the knee; the unpopular general died a few days later. But this was almost all that the enemy were able to do with their artillery. When the French advanced to the attack, their soldiers at first did even less well than their guns. At ten o'clock they began to attack the King's right wing. When they were repulsed here with heavy losses, they turned to attack the allied centre and left wing. Here the defenders did even better than before. The French were driven back again and again, and for a time it appeared that the King had actually won the battle. Eventually, however, the enormous disparity of numbers began to tell: 50,000 allied troops could not indefinitely repel an army of 80,000 without becoming tired. The French were also tiring, but fresh reinforcements were reaching them and these were finally able to drive the weary allies from their positions. A great assault was made on the Dutch right wing. The defensive line was penetrated, Neerwinden taken, and the right wing was forced to retire across the Geete. This left the allied centre without protection on its right flank and it was soon in confusion, though the left wing was still holding its own when the order was given to withdraw. During the course of the battle William III had fought with a recklessness unusual even for him and had been shot twice. Luckily one of the bullets passed through his wig and the other through his Garter sash without doing any damage. He now improvised and commanded a rearguard to cover the other troops who were crossing the river, and he had some difficulty in reaching the bridge at Neerhespen. He got across the river just in time. Most of the infantry had used the bridges too, but there were many casualties among those horsemen who tried to ford the Geete and drowned when their horses were unable to climb up the soft banks of the stream.

The bulk of the foot and a portion of the horse retired on Louvain. The remainder, led by the King in person, passed through Tienen towards the neighbourhood of Mechlin, where the whole army would rendezvous. The retreat, in darkness, must have been a terrible ordeal. No man could know whether his comrade was dead, a captive, or in the other segment of the army. Until the troops were reunited and sorted out it would be impossible to make any accurate estimate of the casualties and the first guesses were naturally very high. A few panicked at the thought that nothing now stood between them and the enemy. Blathwayt, for one, rode sixty miles in hysterics and did not feel himself safe until he was behind the walls of Breda. There he wrote a stupid letter to Heinsius referring to 'la défaite entière' of their master and ordering the ports to be closed to prevent word of the disaster from reaching England.[24]

Had Blathwayt been a soldier he might have noticed one significant fact: Luxembourg made no effort to prevent the allies from crossing the Geete, nor did he pursue them afterwards. Had he even tried to push the defeated army into the river its casualties would have been much higher than they were. It is true that this failure to pursue a victory was the greatest weakness of the Maréchal; but this time he had a good excuse. His surgeons were so busy with amputations that they measured their work not by patients but by wagonloads of severed limbs. It is highly likely that the allies were correct in claiming that the French losses exceeded their own by a wide margin. A week after the battle the King's army was larger than it had been on the day of Landen. Württemburg's detachment, rich with the contributions it had extorted from the defenceless peasantry, was of course doubly welcome on its return to camp. These were relatively fresh men. But another significant feature of the allied army was its superior discipline. Hundreds, thousands of those who survived the battle had an excellent chance of disappearing unnoticed during the retreat. They did not do so; they returned to their colours to fight again for their hero. As a soldier William III met with little of that envious hatred which was so often his fate in civilian life. His men, officers and private soldiers alike, admired and respected him; many of them, particularly the men in the ranks, loved him. They showed their feelings by fighting for him with a devotion and courage that they would never display when they were commanded by one of his subordinates.

It is a pity that the English do not remember Landen for what it was, a battle that saved both Brussels and Liège. In terms of 29 July alone it was of course a defeat. In terms of the campaign as a whole, however, it was not only a victory but an important one. It took the French six weeks to recover from the stunning blow that William III had dealt them. And the King had not fought alone. The right wing had been led by the Elector of Bavaria while George Lewis of Hanover also distinguished himself that day. Yet the greatest praise was given by all observers to the English infantry and especially to the men of Ramsay's brigade. If it is too humiliating to give any credit to William III, if the future George I must be denied praise, surely the men of Ramsay's brigade deserve a better fate. But the worshippers of the great Marlborough, who conveniently enough are as ignorant of the French and Dutch languages as they are of the English sources, will swallow any tale that redounds indirectly to their hero's credit. Marlborough was not present at Steenkerk or Landen; therefore there can have been no good in either battle. In truth Marlborough needs no such defence. And in truth William III saved Europe once in 1692 and once again in 1693, as he did throughout his public life. He was almost always on the defensive, a fact that robs his military career of the brilliance of that of a Marlborough or a Turenne. But if the very limited nature of his resources and the effective use he made of them is remembered, his record appears in a much better light.

In its consequences Landen was not nearly so important as Steenkerk. This time the English politicians did not misread the meaning of the engagement, nor did they become fainthearted even in September when the French recovered to the point of being able to take the field again. After Landen they had no hope of taking either Brussels or Liège. They were, however, in a position to work off their frustrations by besieging Charleroi. This was an important place, but by no means a vital one. After an heroic defence Charleroi fell on 11 October. Its loss was a pity, yet it had no slightest effect on the strategic position in the Low Countries. At the end of the campaign, without Namur and without Huy, the barrier still stood firm. And so did the alliance.

When the King reached London at the end of October he found the political situation to be most delicately balanced. His whiggish appointments of the spring had not satisfied the party, which demanded Nottingham's scalp. All during the summer Sunderland had been urging the King to comply, and to form a solid Whig ministry. William was reluctant for many reasons. He distrusted the party and disliked many of its younger men personally. He liked Nottingham and hoped to be able to save him as late as the time of his return from the continent. By 3 November, however, he had come to accept the inevitable.[25] When attempts to persuade Nottingham to resign were fruitless he was dismissed on 5 November, and next day Russell was reappointed admiral. These changes and the prospect of others made the Whigs cheerful. For the most part the session went quite well. The Commons voted £5 million for the coming campaign. If the new system did not work entirely smoothly, if William had to veto a Place Bill in January, it worked much better than had Carmarthen's ministry in the last two years. The King was uncomfortable and the Queen more so, but their measures went through. Their Majesties' discomfort was personal. The Queen detested Sunderland, while her husband could barely bring himself to speak to men like Russell, Wharton, and Montagu. They needed Whig votes, but they hoped to find a manager who would make it unnecessary for them actually to speak to Whigs. William would presumably have been willing to use Sunderland if the Earl could have taken office, but for the moment this was impossible. Trenchard was not important enough to act as a manager. Somers, the Lord Keeper, would just do and for the moment the King had to use him because there was no alternative. The ideal solution, of course, would be the return of Lord Shrewsbury to office. Shrewsbury hated the idea, and during the winter he withstood the pleas of the King, of Mrs Villiers, of his own mistress Mrs Lundy, of Russell and of Wharton. It was not until March that he was forced to kiss hands as Secretary. Since Shrewsbury was neither well nor pleased to be in office it was not, in the abstract, a good appointment. His charm, however, made the King easy while it kept the party happy too. Sunderland continued to do most of the work of management in his chosen place behind the curtain. Before the King returned to Holland in the spring he made another large batch of whiggish appointments.

Once the King's political gamble proved successful he had time to concentrate again on the peace negotiations. These were becoming more complicated. On paper, the French were offering the treaties of Westphalia and Nijmegen. If they had meant what they said, all would have been well. What the French really wanted to do was to keep their gains of the years 1678–88: that is, Strasbourg, Luxembourg, and the *réunions* in Germany and in the Spanish Netherlands. William III would have been willing to trade Luxembourg for a stronger barrier in the Low Countries. Deliberately he set the price very high, demanding the five towns of Tournai, Condé, Ypres, Maubeuge and Menin in addition to what the Spanish had held in 1678. This gave him room to manoeuvre; Maubeuge and Menin were not important and could be conceded graciously when the time came. For the rest, William remained firm in his demands for a return to the treaties of Westphalia and Nijmegen. His difficulties were great. There were rumours that Savoy was considering a separate peace. These proved inaccurate at the time, but there was greater difficulty with the Dutch. The Polish resident in the Republic, one Mollo, had married the daughter of a burgomaster of Amsterdam. In

1693 and again in 1694 he was sent by his father-in-law to Paris to conduct secret negotiations with the French ministers. Mollo's dispatch was told to the King and William sometimes used him, though he never trusted the man. He preferred to use Dijkvelt, who was negotiating at Brussels with two Frenchmen. Unfortunately one of these was insulted by the Spanish authorities in 1693 and so this channel became blocked. Unfortunately again, Dijkvelt came from Utrecht and this fact aroused the jealousy of the men of Amsterdam, who felt that a Hollander should be employed. This was one reason why the King had to tolerate the activities of Mollo.

Far more annoying was the activity of Henry Casimir, the Stadhouder of Friesland. During the winter of 1693–94 the Prince engaged in personal negotiations with the French agent d'Asfelt at Hamburg. Henry Casimir offered his good offices to the French in return for a fee of between two and three hundred thousand ecus and their assistance in overthrowing the position of William III in the Republic. He was so incautious as to meet d'Asfelt himself in the neighbourhood of Hamburg on 6 February. This was a remarkably silly thing to do if Henry Casimir hoped to keep his plans secret; but greater care would have been fruitless, for the Dutch were intercepting all the letters that passed between the King of France and his agent.[26] In the end, the French were only willing to pay the Prince van Nassau 30,000 ecus. This was so much less than he needed to pay this debts that the negotiations were broken off. Later in 1694 Henry Casimir came to his senses and attempted to improve his relations with the King. William had to put up with a great deal from his relatives. Even the little Duke of Gloucester was being trained to make pert remarks, at the age of four. The little boy was taken to say good-bye to the King before the opening of the campaign in Flanders, and William III playfully asked him about his two companies of musketeers. These were boys of nine or ten years of age who had been given uniforms and were learning to march at the command of Prince William. The Duke of Gloucester told the King that the two companies were going to fight the Turk and the King of France, but not grandfather – James II.[27]

There were more serious things to worry about when the King, after several delays, reached The Hague at the beginning of May. Although the French had failed in their attempt to persuade Denmark to join the war against the allies during the winter, the diplomatic position in the north was still precarious. At Stockholm, d'Avaux appeared to be making progress and the Swedes were not much more friendly than the Danes. At Liège, despite the campaigning of Dijkvelt, the election of a new Prince Bishop had gone against the King. The victor was the Elector of Cologne, Joseph Clement of Bavaria. In 1688, it had been a triumph for William III to make Joseph Clement Archbishop of Cologne. Now it was important to prevent the Wittelsbachs from improving their position any further, because Louis XIV was offering the Spanish Netherlands to the Elector of Bavaria on the death of the King of Spain instead of giving a larger number of towns for the barrier. This flattered Max Emmanuel, while French support for Joseph Clement at Liège flattered his brother. It was very embarrassing for the allies to have to oppose the personal interests of the two Electors, who might easily change sides if they were pushed too far. It was even more embarrassing to see forming a possible Wittelsbach state, comprising the Spanish Netherlands, Liège and Cologne, which could only be a client of France in the long run.

The opening of the campaign was delayed by both sides until it was clear that the negotiations of Mollo would not succeed. Indeed one might say that the campaign never opened at all. Both the Dutch and the English had made substantial additions to their armies this year, so that there was not the usual allied inequality of numbers. This led to a stalemate, since there was such an advantage in taking the defensive that few generals would dare to hazard a battle without having a crushing superiority in men. This stalemate, however dull, was a good sign for the allies. They had turned the tide. The French, under the titular command of the Dauphin though actually directed by Luxembourg, could no nothing but march back and forth across the country-side. In September the allies took Dixmude, a town of no importance near the coast. This was apparently a ruse, and it was certainly a successful one. The King remained at his camp at Rousselaere (Roulers) after the capture of Dixmude. Obviously, the French thought, they need not watch anyone except William III. They watched and waited. And then, behind their backs, an allied force under the command of the Duke of Holstein-Ploen brusquely attacked and captured Huy. By the end of the summer, therefore, the allies had recovered the initiative in Flanders. The men were visibly of better quality than they had been in the earlier years of the war, and the capture of Huy recovered all the ground lost since the siege of Namur. Next year, if things continued to go well, William might be able to undertake a great siege himself. By comparison with these gains the failure of Tollemache in his attack on Brest in June was completely insignificant. The losses, except for that of Tollemache himself, were negligible; and the general was an important man because he was English, rather than because he was an able general. By now, however, there were so many more experienced officers of English birth than there had been at the beginning of the war that the death of one of them was not a political embarrassment. At sea, the depredations of Jean Bart were more serious. But even here the allies were going over to the offensive. Russell was sent to the Mediterranean with a squadron and was ordered, over his loud protests, to remain there for the winter. Thus in 1694, for the first time since 1690, the King had reason to be pleased with his summer's work.

Chapter 23

NAMUR

WILLIAM had an ideal crossing of only twenty-two hours and landed at Margate, spending the night at Canterbury. The next day he was met by the Queen at Rochester. Together they drove straight through London on their way to Kensington. The bonfires and illuminations, the cheers of the people, were greater than ever before. The welcome of the politicians was equally warm. L'Hermitage reported that rumours of peace had been silenced by the return of the King, and that some of the most important Members of Parliament were saying 'que puis quon est a la veille de reduire la France au point ou lon la souhaite, il faut continuer la guerre, ne pouvant autrement sassurer davoir une paix ferme et durable, et tout le monde est rempli des bonnes dispositions. ....'.[1] The only cloud in the sky seemed to be William's health. He was visibly weaker than before, and when he got a slight chill while hunting the week after his arrival it was serious enough to be reported not only by L'Hermitage and Blathwayt but by the King himself. All three made light of it, but the fact that the King mentioned the matter showed its importance.[2] The chill was followed by a slight fever, which responded to a diet of apples and milk. For the next fortnight the King was busy with the Parliamentary session, which went well despite the loss of Archbishop Tillotson, and with the communication of Dijkvelt's peace negotiations to the representatives of the allies. Although the King was able to go hunting on Hounslow Heath on 11/21 December, he was so weak that he was ill again ten days later.[3]

Meanwhile the Queen's health had also been giving cause for concern. She had had a cold when she went to Rochester to greet her husband, and although this passed off quickly she was again indisposed a fortnight later. It had been a bad year for smallpox, which Mary had never had; L'Hermitage was afraid that her indisposition might develop into that disease, but happily he was mistaken.[4] A day later she was perfectly well. A week before Christmas, English style, she spent a day at Hampton Court making arrangements for the furnishing of the new wings of the palace. Four days later, on the 22nd, Mary was taken ill again, and this time it was more serious. The physicians at once assumed that she had smallpox. At this the King, who had lost both his parents from the disease, broke down completely. He had a camp bed moved into the Queen's bedroom so that he could know her condition at every moment. This was dangerous for him, as the windows of the room were shut and he got no fresh air; had he even been willing to sleep in an antechamber William would have been far better off. So would Mary, who complained that the King's continual weeping bothered her. On Christmas Day, to the annoyance of a Jacobite lady who had planned a ball to celebrate the Queen's death, she was so much better that the doctors began to hope that it was measles rather than smallpox. Her improvement was such that the King agreed to have his camp bed moved into an adjacent room. But hope was shortlived. At ten in the evening there was a marked change for the worse, and the next day the Queen was told by Tenison, the new Archbishop of Canterbury, that she must prepare for death. She replied that she was completely resigned to the will of God, who might dispose of her when he pleased. Since she was strong enough to feed herself with 'water gruel' and did not feel ill, it was hard to believe that the end was near. Even on the morning of the 27th, when she asked to be given Holy Communion, Mary said she did not feel badly and that it was astonishing that one could die without feeling ill. After she had received Communion, she took leave of her husband, and grew weaker moment by moment throughout the day. The end came at about eleven at night.[5]

Although the Queen had been much beloved and was to be mourned deeply and sincerely – the House of Commons was said to have burst into tears as one man at the news of her death – the immediate danger was for the life of the King. If he went too, and for some days there was a risk that he might, the Revolution and the war against Louis XIV would collapse immediately. No arrangements had been made for the transfer of authority in the event of the King's death, and so far as anyone could know Anne and the Duke of Gloucester were as ardent Jacobites in December as they had been in May. The King's condition was serious. On the 27th, as he watched by the Queen's bedside, he had collapsed and his cough had stopped. This was very ominious, since William needed to cough continually to clear his lungs. As soon as the Queen died Portland picked his master up in his arms and carried him to the other side of the palace, where Tenison tried in vain to console him. The Duke of Leeds was sent by the Council to beg his Majesty to take care of himself; but the King was unable to sleep, and found it impossible to bring himself to see anyone except the Archbishop, Portland, and the page la Fontaine. For the next few days he was so weak that the Archbishop stayed at Kensington day and night. On the 31st William had to admit a delegation of the two Houses of Parliament and to reply to their addresses of condolence, but he broke down and had great difficulty in speaking a few words.[6] Vernon noted that he looked thin and wasted with sorrow. When the King tried to go into the gardens for fresh air he could not walk and had to be carried in his chair. Fortunately his appetite returned. He missed only one night's sleep, and when he went

into the gardens a second time he was able to walk.[7] Even so, it was impossible
for him to talk of business, and at a brief audience to the leaders of the administration he repeatedly broke down.

Because Mary had been Queen Regnant, the seals were all broken on the
day of her death. The political situation was almost as serious as the King's
health, and it could not wait. Fortunately Anne sent a respectful and submissive letter by the hands of the Archbishop of Canterbury.[8] The King had
not permitted her to see the Queen during Mary's illness because Anne was
in the last stages of pregnancy and he was afraid of possible damage to the
child. There had been a reconciliation between the sisters, even though they
had not spoken to each other, and everyone expected that Anne's letter to the
King would mend the breach between the two courts. Sunderland is supposed to have been the one to persuade the King to be as generous as possible.
He gave Anne, not her old apartments in Whitehall, but St James's Palace as
well as her guards. Prince George was among the first to be given an audience.
As soon as Anne was able to do so she visited the King, who greeted her at the
door of his bedchamber. They talked for more than a quarter of an hour and
William then conducted her as far as her conveyance. It was noted that
William 'luy donna la main', that is gave Anne the place of honour, throughout the interview,[9] as he was to do for the rest of his life. The malicious comments of the Duchess of Marlborough half a century later are the twisted
memories of a sick harridan.[10] Perhaps Sarah did not want to remember
that, according to rumour, Anne offered at this time to part with her and did
refuse to see the Earl of Clarendon until he had made his peace with the
King.[11]

It was almost a month before William began to recover. At first he had no
idea of what to do with himself. He said to Portland 'je ne puis pas me
representer mon estat et ordre que je suis privé par toiours de la Reyne, il me
semble mesme que je dois comme a mon ordinaire aller souper ce soir avec
elle'.[12] Normanby, who had officiously gone the rounds of the foreign
ambassadors promising that the Queen's death would mean no change in
British policy, then presented himself at Kensington and demanded to see the
King. When Portland refused to let him in, Normanby threatened him.
What would happen if the King were to die while Portland was concealing
him? And how had Portland dared, he shouted, have the Queen's body
opened without the authority of the Privy Council?[13] Portland shouted
back that nothing had been done without order, and Normanby had to leave
without an audience.[14] Despite the unwelcome attentions of Normanby the
King continued to eat and sleep well, and his strength slowly returned. At
the end of January he was able to go to Richmond for three days for shooting
on horseback. He found it so pleasant that he continued to go regularly on

Saturdays. There was even talk that he would fit up the old palace as a hunting lodge.

Slowly the normal routine of life was resumed. There was only one outward change, in that William now went to prayers twice a day rather than only once. This made a small change in the King's public hours. He was now available twice a day immediately before meals, from noon till one o'clock and from eight to nine in the evening. Those who went noted that he looked well, though touchingly sad.[15] But he was a changed man. He had had long talks with Archbishop Tenison, during one of which the following conversation is said to have taken place. 'Sir, we must repent, and mend our life.' The King replied, 'Aye Sir, we must mend our life, I must mend my life, and you must mend yours'.[16] It was a spirited reply, but Tenison's emphasis on his sins struck a chord, for William's early Calvinistic training had persuaded him that the Queen's death was a visitation caused by his own sins.[17] Since his only known sin – for which Mary is supposed to have rebuked him on her deathbed – was his relationship with Betty Villiers, she was soon disgraced and in danger of banishment.[18] In the autumn of 1695 she married Lord George Hamilton, who was then created Earl of Orkney. So far as is known, the King, whose religious life became far more strict at this time, remained completely loyal to his wife's memory until he died.

When William began to turn his mind again to public affairs, his first thought was to end the war as speedily as possible. His affliction weighed heavily upon him, and the general condition of his health – despite his recovery in January – was poor. 'Molo's negotiation should be pushed on as much as possible, though I fear that France will be more difficult than before because of my great misfortune; I must tell your Excellency in confidence, what must be kept secret, that I no longer find myself well enough to carry on the war; even so I will do my duty as best I can, hoping that the good Lord will give me strength ...'[19] Soon William felt more like his former self. When Mollo's attempts at a speedy peace were fruitless, the King ordered that secret talks should be held between Dijkvelt and Callières at Utrecht; but his mind was now working on how to make one last great campaign. He might have neither health nor money for another.[20] A major victory was particularly important at this time. It would raise the King's credit with the English; it would bring the enemy to more reasonable terms; and it would end his military career on a happy note. It would be particularly fitting if this last victory took the form of a successful siege. Not only would the French be doubly humiliated at being beaten at their own game, but nothing could do more for the King's reputation than the taking of an important town. It was one form of warfare in which he had never been very successful. In his first war the Prince had usually been obstructed by the incompetence of his engineers, and in both wars he had been hamstrung for want of money. Now, however both difficulties could be overcome. By the end of February the King's plans began to take shape and care was taken to find the necessary magazines and artillery.[21]

The timing of the siege was fortunate in military as well as in political terms. Luxembourg's death in January deprived the French of their best general. Although he had been too careless about discipline, Luxembourg was a great fighter and would have been sure to risk everything in order to raise a siege. His successors, though solid and not without merit, were more cautious, more rule-bound. Then too, the war was making great inroads on the French economy and particularly on the quality of her infantry. In February a spy reported that the French cavalry was still good, but that the infantry would be much worse than the year before. Money had virtually disappeared from circulation. Conditions were so bad, particularly in the heart of France, that the army could not take the field as early in the year as it had in 1694.[22] On the other hand, the quality of the English and Dutch infantry was still improving with each campaign, as was also their relative lead in artillery. And the alliance concluded with the shifty Bishop of Münster in February would not only help to settle the condition of western Germany but would also provide 7,000 fully equipped men. The English and Dutch still had enough money to pay them, and for the siege too. What they could not do was to get the allied army into the field early enough in the year. Dissension among the generals was so great that they would do nothing in the absence of their master. 'To speak openly I do not think, whatever orders I may send, that they will be obeyed before I get there myself.'[23] But the King was pinned down in England by the politicians. He had no control whatever over the length of the session of Parliament.

Immediately after the death of the Queen, there had been attempts to prevent a reconciliation with the Princess Anne. Most of the men involved were of the extreme High Church section in the Lords; Nottingham, Halifax, and especially Rochester were the leaders. There was even a brief attempt to claim that Parliament had been dissolved by Mary's death, as it normally was on a demise of the crown. Since the administration had been vested in William for his lifetime, the claim had no merit and was recognized as factious. Then on 25 January the question arose of preventing the King from making the campaign. Apparently Devonshire was involved on this occasion with the other malcontents. Although the idea of keeping William in England did not meet with much support, it became a part of a larger and very bitter debate against the administration. Nottingham was the chief of the wreckers, but Halifax and Rochester also played important roles. The government was supported by its natural leaders, Leeds, Godolphin, and Normanby. However obnoxious Normanby might be outside the House, he was very nearly the best speaker of all the peers and this talent gave him strength. The government speakers welcomed the warm support of Marlborough during the debate. This was an indication that the accommodation between William and Anne was more than an empty form.[24] The extreme Tories had burned their bridges by trying to prevent the reconciliation, and they were now left in the political wilderness. Their isolation went so far that neither Rochester nor his wife nor his daughter paid court to the Princess after the reconciliation. At least they secured themselves from insult by staying away. When Nottingham had the temerity to speak to the King at Kensington a few days after his outburst in the Lords, William cut him.[25] The malcontents could only watch in fury while the King demonstrated his attachment both to the Church of England and to his sister-in-law. On Sundays and Wednesdays during Lent he attended service at the Chapel Royal in St James's Palace, and this gave him a perfect opportunity to call on Anne after the sermon. Thus on 6 February he went first to church and then to pay his respects to the Princess.[26] Next day, the 7th, Prince George attended a meeting of the Privy Council.[27] At the end of March Marlborough was admitted to kiss the King's hand, and in the autumn Prince George began again to attend cabinet council sessions.[28] Cleverly, the King had secured himself from attack by the Tory high fliers. But if they could do nothing else, they could at least delay the session.

The Whig split in the Commons was far more serious. On the one side were the moderates, together with Sunderland's henchmen; on the other were the most ambitious and irresponsible of the extremists, Charles Montagu and Philip Wharton. Admiral Russell belonged with them by nature, but he was now far away at Cadiz. Luckily so; Montagu and Wharton could make quite enough trouble without him. Russell and Montagu were extremely able cadets of very great families, with all the ambition of men who have inherited name and position without the wealth necessary to support them. Wharton, temporarily, was in the same boat; his father had lived far too long. In February the extremists found a magnificent opportunity. The government was already unpopular because of the long war, the heavy taxes, the corruption of what was known as the Officers' Parliament, and the standing army. In January the Commons had begun to investigate a complaint by the inhabitants of Royston, from whom the soldiers had demanded free quarter because their pay was far in arrear. This led to an attack on the conduct of the regimental agents, who had not paid the men and had, instead, given bribes to certain Treasury officials. It was a perfect issue. On 16 February the Secretary of the Treasury, Henry Guy, was sent to the Tower for taking a bribe of 200 guineas from one of the regimental agents. Guy was hated by the general public as the paymaster of the Secret Service. Those who knew enough about the administration to realize that the Secret Service payments were generally innocent disliked him as the friend of Sunderland and envied him for his extremely well-paid post.

In March the Whigs found bigger game. A Commons Committee reported that in the years since the Revolution the East India Company had paid out in cash 'for the Company's special service' just over £107,000. The trail led straight to Sir John Trevor, the Speaker, and to the Duke of Leeds. The latter had received 5,000 guineas, and when he was found out he made the double mistake of protesting his innocence and of dispatching his servant Robart, who had actually handled the money, back to the man's native Switzerland. This meant that any prosecution would fail for want of witnesses; but it ruined the Duke's reputation once for all. He was impeached for the third time, and although the matter never came to trial it was the end of Leeds's career. He had enough delicacy or prudence not to meddle in business during the King's absence in the summer of 1695; and in the autumn, when his ambition got the better of his manners and he tried to attend a Cabinet Council, the King forbade it.[29] Trevor could be given more summary treatment. After a terrible day in which, as Speaker, he had had to put the question 'That Sir John Trevor ... is guilty of a high Crime and Misdemeanor', he retired to the lucrative obscurity of his place as Master of the Rolls. William would have liked to see Sir Thomas Littleton become the new Speaker. He had been chairman of one of the committees investigating government extravagance and he was a Whig, but he was a warm supporter of the King. Wharton, perhaps on purpose, indicated that Littleton was the royal nominee. Without this he would have won; but the House was insulted and rejected him by thirty-three votes, choosing instead Paul Foley, a wealthy coal magnate. The King had never met him and had to spend an hour at a private interview getting acquainted.[30]

The King was angry at the whole business, which he knew to be an attempt by Montagu and Wharton to get office for themselves. He had hoped to be able to cross the sea by the end of March. The extremists had cost him six weeks, but he made sure that they had no other benefit. Leeds continued in office as Lord President and kept his pensions. Guy kept the profits of the Treasury Office and continued to meddle both in patronage and in higher politics. Montagu had, indeed, driven Trevor out of the House of Commons; but Trevor kept his other place, and the new Speaker disliked and distrusted the Whig wild men. Foley soon began to have regular weekly meetings with Guy, who reported gleefully 'that *Paul Foley* in all his discourses declares a wonderfull aversion to *Mr Mountagu*; & that he neither can nor will communicate with him; ...'[31] Montagu had made another serious error by opposing the King's siege plans, on the grounds that the cost was far too high.[32] He compounded his error during the summer by slighting comments on the

King's activities during the campaign.[33] It seems likely that Montagu had wanted the place of Secretary of the Treasury for his brother. In any case his baffled rage did him no good, for it bound Foley and his relative Robert Harley more and more firmly to the side of Guy and Sunderland. It disgusted Shrewsbury, the titular leader of the party, and it may possibly have contributed to the eclipse of Portland.

Almost nothing is known of Portland's loss of favour in 1695. The King, in surviving his wife, found his life shattered. Perhaps until Mary's death he had hoped that she would outlive him, re-marry, and have children. He had certainly planned for such a remarriage in 1688, and it was virtually the only way in which he could be sure that his work would be carried on. At the end of 1694 the Queen was still only thirty-two. Given her husband's bad health, it was highly likely that she would become a widow while still capable of bearing children. Any such ideas in the back of the King's mind were swept away by the pox, together with almost everything that made his private life worth living. The shock was enormous. And it led, in this as in many similar cases, to a rearrangement of William's personal friendships. In the first few weeks after Mary's death, Portland seemed to be as close to his master as ever. But as William began to emerge from his first seclusion, there came a change. The disgrace of Betty Villiers, Portland's sister-in-law, was one thread broken. The rise of the unobtrusive Blathwayt in the King's favour was another. Since Shrewsbury was always in the country and Trenchard, the other Secretary of State, was dying, the foreign ministers found themselves obliged to address themselves to Blathwayt. Technically, he was only a Secretary of State during the campaign. As soon as he reached England every autumn his salary and rank were reduced to the inferior level of Secretary at War. This was a fiction that could easily be dispensed with at a time when Shrewsbury and Trenchard were not to be seen. Blathwayt had health, the King's friendship, and the necessary languages. In February he began to give semi-official dinner parties for the foreign envoys.

Superficially, this might not seem to be a threat to Portland's position. Blathwayt was not and never became a contender for the place of favourite. What was happening was that Portland's monopoly of the King was being broken. The Queen had always been very fond of him and of his children; now she was gone. Betty Villiers was gone. Portland's great position as William's confidant in foreign affairs was eroded by the King's ever-increasing reliance on Heinsius in matters of policy and on Blathwayt and James Vernon, Shrewsbury's under-secretary, in matters of detail. Portland, furthermore, was identified as a Whig. His work as liaison man between the King and that party continued, but there would have to be a man to replace Nottingham as the King's go-between with the Tories. Blathwayt might do for this job.

So might Keppel, who since 1692 had been on roughly equal ground with Portland. Now he took the lead, and by the end of the 1695 campaign he was definitely the favourite. When William returned in the autumn to a newly arranged set of apartments at Kensington, it was noted that Keppel's suite communicated with that of the King and Portland's did not. Keppel's rise towards the position of sole favourite in 1695 may well have been simply the result of his age. William was now very sensitive about growing old himself and hated to see his age reflected in the white hair and limping gait of his servants. Keppel, at twenty-six, could make it possible for the King to pretend that he was still young. The younger man also had very much better manners than Portland and was not nearly so unpopular with the English. His lack of definite political ties with the Whigs was another advantage. Almost all the King's closer friendships after 1694 were with people who were either apolitical or else moderate Tories.

William prorogued Parliament on 3 May and crossed the sea nine days later, leaving behind a Regency consisting of Tenison, Somers, Pembroke, Devonshire, Shrewsbury, Dorset, and Godolphin.[35] He found that the French had been given time to set up a defensive line of retrenchments which prevented him from undertaking anything important near the coast. But the quality of his infantry was extremely high, and this put him in a remarkably good humour.[36] For the first time since 1674 he had a clear superiority in numbers over the enemy in the Low Countries, and thus the opportunity for some great undertaking. By the end of June he had pitched on the siege of Namur.[37] The town was far to the east of the French defensive lines. Its walls, which had been incomplete when the French took it in 1692, had since then been perfected by Vauban and this had given rise to over-confidence on the part of the defenders. Who had ever heard of the fall of one of Vauban's works? William had given orders for the place to be surrounded on 30 June. When he arrived on 4 July, however, he found that he had not been fully obeyed. On the 3rd the Maréchal de Boufflers had been able to enter Namur with a large force, increasing the number of the defenders to some 16,000. The town, which lies at the junction of the Maas and the Sambre, was difficult to get at because the rivers acted as natural moats. Just south of the city itself rises a great rock, in profile much resembling Gibraltar, on which stood the castle of Namur. Even today, when the fortress is a delightful park, the rock would be difficult to take without modern artillery. In 1695 the French might be forgiven for thinking it impregnable. At the very least, it could hold out until Villeroi with his field army of perhaps 80,000 men could come up and relieve the siege.

Because of the nature of the place, the attackers were divided into three armies. William's headquarters were to the west of the town, those of the

German auxiliaries, chiefly Brandenburgers, on the east. The Elector of
Bavaria had his headquarters between the two rivers, to the south of the castle.
Connecting the three forces were three bridges, one over the Sambre and two
over the Maas, one above and the other below Namur. The lines were so
extended that when, on 10 July, the King rode the whole circuit around the
besieged town, it took him more than six hours. A cannon ball landed in the
middle of his party without doing any damage,[38] but the courtiers were not
always to be so lucky. A few days later Lord Selkirk received a cut on the
head from a stone thrown up by a cannon ball, and Michael Godfrey, a deputy
governor of the Bank of England who had brought money over for the siege
and proved too curious in watching how it was spent, was killed in the
trenches. Despite misadventures such as these, the attack made slow but
steady progress. The heavy artillery came up on the 11th and began to fire
into the town the next day. At first the gun batteries were not well placed,
and it was not until the 23rd that their fire fulfilled expectations. Meanwhile
the trenches were opened on the night of the 11th. On the 18th the garrison
made a sortie but they were forced back inside the town with considerable
losses, since the English troops would give no quarter. On the 27th the King
in person led 400 men in a successful attack on a counterscarp, where he was
under heavy fire for an hour-and-a-half. He succeeded in making himself
master of the counterscarp, though at a cost of forty-four killed and ninety-five
wounded. At the same time the Elector of Bavaria attacked a small fortification on the other side of the St Nicholas Gate, and succeeded in driving out
its three hundred defenders. On 2 August, however, things went badly. An
attempt to storm a demi-bastion failed with heavy loss after the men had
lodged themselves there three separate times. The next morning there were
long faces at court, and the King wrote an extremely gloomy letter to Vaudemont at noon.[39] Then to their delight the allies saw a party coming from the
castle under two white flags. The town, though not the castle, wanted to
surrender. By nine that evening, the King was able to write another and far
happier letter to Vaudemont.[40]

In any siege the attackers must expect heavy casualties and the ruin of a
number of guns. But the real cost comes from the need for a second army, or
army of observation, whose task it is to prevent the enemy from coming to
the relief of the besieged place. In June William had managed to lure the
French forces under Villeroi far into Flanders before he left his own army
under the command of the Prince de Vaudemont and suddenly appeared
before Namur to strengthen the army of the Elector of Bavaria. Vaudemont
was left to defend the Netherlands. His forces were far inferior to those of
Villeroi, and he happened also to be seriously ill. On 13 July Villeroy came
up to attack Vaudemont at a point where he had entrenched himself, while

another French force under Montal marched around the entrenchments so as to be able to attack from the rear. For a few hours it looked as if Vaudemont would be trapped. But he was too clever for the French. While some of his men continued to fire and others kept on working at their entrenchments, the rest very quietly left the camp without attracting notice. Vaudemont stayed to the end to make sure that he got off with all his men and all his guns. The enemy was completely fooled. It was a glorious affair, and it was followed by another when Vaudemont prevented the French from taking Nieupoort. On the 28th, however, the garrison of Dixmude surrendered to the French after a miserable defence of thirty-six hours, and two days later the garrison of Deinse followed suit without firing a shot. Even worse, the ten battalions involved surrendered themselves as prisoners of war. Later, William had the Danish commander of Dixmude beheaded and the Scottish brigadier in charge at Deinse sentenced to life imprisonment for cowardice. The immediate task, however, was to recover the ten battalions before they were bullied into joining the enemy army. By the terms of the capitulations they should have been exchanged or ransomed; but the capitulations were not observed and the prisoners were marched off for France.

Villeroi then marched on Brussels. After delivering a manifesto in which he claimed to be taking resprisals for the allied attacks on French coastal towns, he began to bombard the city on 13 August. The bombardment lasted thirty-six hours and more than three thousand bombs were used as well as red-hot bullets. Losses, largely by fire, ran into millions and included the Hôtel de Ville and the Grand' Place. It was purely and simply an atrocity. In military terms the siege of Ath, which could not have been relieved, would have been far more important. But it failed in its main purpose of drawing the allied armies away from the citadel of Namur. The siege continued, though William himself and a large detachment went to join Vaudemont at Waterloo where he could cover Namur and be within easy reach of Brussels. His defensive arrangements, according to Villeroi, were admirable.[41] At least the Maréchal did not dare to attack, and after facing William's army for three days he withdrew to await the outcome of the fighting at Namur. Here things did not go well. A simultaneous attack on five or six different places on the 30th was not uniformly successful, even at a cost of over 2,000 men. As one of the field deputies wrote to Heinsius: 'My dear friend, things do not go well; ... yesterday's attacks turned out badly; we have lost a great many men, the generals are discontented, there is a shortage of provisions ... God be with us.'[42]

As one general put it, their ears were hanging down. Not for long; for on 1 September the castle capitulated. On the 5th the 5,000 survivors of the garrison marched out. They were permitted to take six cannon with them. As he left the castle, the Maréchal de Boufflers was asked whether he would see to it that the garrisons of Dixmude and Deinse were returned according to the capitulations. When he refused, Dijkvelt placed him under arrest. Boufflers was furious. Portland did his best to assuage the Maréchal's grief by entertaining him with every honour during his brief captivity. Louis XIV did more, by the rapid return of the captives and by promoting Boufflers to the august rank of *duc et pair*. This was really more of a compliment to William III than to Boufflers. It had in fact been a magnificent victory. Perhaps the strongest place in Europe had been taken in the face of an army of nearly 100,000 men which had not dared to come to the relief of the fortress. In the Republic and in England as well there was a day of thanksgiving. The preacher at St Martin's in the Fields chose as his text Samuel 3: 17-18 and compared William to David as the savour of Israel. The simile met with general applause, and so did the fireworks display given the next day in St James's Square by Lord Romney. As the Lords Justices ate Romney's food and watched the fireworks, they drank the King's health to the firing of salutes by the Guards.[43] Of more practical importance was the assurance that Parliament would now vote William anything he wanted for the next campaign.[44]

Chapter 24

PEACE PRELIMINARIES

THE fact that there might have to be another campaign was clear from the failure of the secret peace negotiations, which had continued off and on all through the year. William would have preferred that talks be carried on at Brussels between Dijkvelt and the French agent d'Aguerre. The French for their part would not accept Brussels, where one of their men had had the humiliation of being arrested. Nor would they use d'Aguerre, preferring Callières; and they did not much like negotiating with Dijkvelt. All this difficulty over small details made it clear that the French were not sincere in desiring peace in the spring of 1695. On the more important issues the French refused to offer a reasonable equivalent for Luxembourg. They put a great value on the cost of their fortifications at Namur since 1692: one good reason for taking the place from them. Another was that the fantastic pride of the French had to be humbled before they would listen to anything like reason. When William's agents proposed the Treaties of Westphalia and Nijmegen as a basis of negotiation, Louis XIV was supposed to have replied that he would rather see all France in flames than suffer anything of the kind. After the fall of Namur the French became a little less unreasonable, but William and Heinsius still had many problems with their allies. Should the allies actually agree that the Treaties of 1648 and 1678 ought to form the basis of the negotiations? The Spanish, who contributed nothing to the cost of the war, said No. They were perfectly happy to fight to the last pound and the last guilder, since no *patacoons* were involved. The Austrians, though they tried hard enough to shove the whole cost of the war on to the Dutch and the English, had not been quite so successful as their Spanish cousins; and, as it happened, their campaign in Hungary in 1695 had been a failure. What they wanted was to keep the war going until the King of Spain died, so that the maritime powers would be obliged to support Leopold's claim to the Spanish Succession. Though they did succeed in having the Grand Alliance renewed in August, they had to pretend to be in favour of a reasonable peace. When, however, it came to the point of where to conduct the actual negotiations, the imperialists made endless difficulties. They were embarrassed at being found in direct conversations with the French in Switzerland, and abandoned them. This made them all the more eager to prevent the English and Dutch from having talks of their own with the enemy. At no time was the government of

Leopold I an easy or accommodating ally. Now things were even worse than usual because of the bitter fight between Caunitz and Kinsky for predominance at the court of Vienna. Kinsky, in particular, pictured himself as the saviour and peacemaker of Europe. This made him prefer that negotiations should be carried on in Stockholm rather than in the Low Countries, because he would have more influence there than would the English or Dutch. Stockholm was a ridiculous choice, and not merely because it was so far away. Most of the Swedish senators were pro-French, and almost all of them were corrupt. Even the chief minister, the ageing Oxenstierne, was bribed heavily by William III with both English and Dutch money though he was a sincere friend of the allies. The others were paid less, and were worth nothing at all; but they had to be bribed, too, to offset the charms and gifts of the French ambassador d'Avaux. Fundamentally William III and Heinsius were determined to arrange terms with the French and then dictate them to the allies. They and they alone had a right to act in this manner. Not only was it true that the English and Dutch bore the cost of the war. It was also certain that William and Heinsius could get far better terms for the allies as a group than they could get for themselves. It was, however, a dangerous game to play. Some one of the minor allies, such as Brandenburg or Savoy, could always ruin things by making a separate peace; or Amsterdam might show herself too eager, and so spoil the terms. To some extent the King was able to secure the support of Amsterdam by employing one of their burgomasters, Boreel, as a negotiator.[1] He was less successful with the Duke of Savoy, who in the spring of 1696 made a mysterious pilgrimage to the shrine of Loreto which looked more politic than devout. From that moment, rumours of his approaching defection from the allies began to spread over Europe.

For the time being the capture of Namur made all such problems seem less important. The King was worried about retaining control of the Mediterranean for the coming year, but for the rest he was optimistic and he was now in much better health. In September he left the army and went to het Loo before going on to The Hague at the beginning of the following month. There he conferred with the Elector of Brandenburg and expounded the state of the war for 1696 to the States General. This posed no special difficulties since he was now on good terms with Amsterdam and also with his cousins of Friesland. Henry Casimir had been so cooperative in the past year that William now made a new will, granting his entire estate to Casimir's son Friso van Nassau.[2] William was so eager to return to England that the yachts were already waiting for him when he reached The Hague; and so impatient to have a new Parliament that he sent full powers to the Lords Justices to dissolve the old one if he were detained by contrary winds.[3] Luckily the winds were fair, for the Regents did not dare to make use of their authority.

William landed at Margate on 10/20 October after a very easy crossing and dissolved the Parliament himself as soon as he reached the capital. There was some risk in having an election so late in the year, since the session could not begin before 22 November and no one knew when it might be over. In the hope of ending the disputes of the previous year the King ordered Leeds not to come to the Council and forbade Trevor to stand for election.[4] Whether he ordered Guy to lie low, too, is not certain, but it is highly probable that he did so. At any rate Guy did not make use of his pocket borough of Hedon and stayed away from this Parliament.

While the elections were proceeding there was nothing to do in London. William decided to improve this time by making a short progress through the country, though as he apologetically assured Heinsius he took care that the foreign mails were delivered to him wherever he was. William went first to Newmarket and then to visit Sunderland at Althorp, which caused some unfavourable comment. From there he went on to visit the Dukes of Newcastle and Devonshire, returning to Windsor on 9/19 November and Kensington two days later. Though the trip tired him, it was a great success. Wherever he went he was warmly greeted by both the nobility and the common people, thus proving that his personal popularity was not confined to London. When on his return, he reached Burford after ten at night, crowds of people were waiting for him with torches outside the town, and the place itself was completely lit up by bonfires and illuminated windows.[5] Even the King was pleased by the demonstrations of affection that greeted him everywhere.[6] His birthday present, another of Romney's displays of fireworks at St James's Square, had been held over for his return. And the elections turned out to be a more lasting and solid birthday present; the new Parliament had a firm majority in favour of winning the war at any cost. In other respects the political situation was less satisfactory. The monarchy as an institution would not recover from the blow of Mary's premature death. If the nonsensical warming-pan story[7] could be credited, Mary II had either been the 'rightful and lawful' Queen of England or the next thing to it. William was nothing of the kind. James II, his son the Prince of Wales, and Anne all had better claims. With Mary in her grave, the fact of the usurpation became all too glaring. Mary had, furthermore, been a delightful and charming woman who captivated those who met her as much by her personality as by her position. Neither William nor Anne was capable of taking her place. The King was now rapidly becoming an invalid; he had never been able to make himself liked by the political classes in England; and the issues with which he was associated became less relevant hour by hour. The Parliament men preferred him to a Catholic despot, but the memory of James's reign was fading. They wanted victories, but a victory on the scale of Namur did not happen every year. As for Anne, she was unknown to most of the English and unpopular with those who knew her. An invalid herself, a recluse, seemingly a captive of the bitterly hated Sarah Churchill, Anne was by no means an acceptable substitute for her sister. Her reconciliation with the King robbed her of what little political strength she had once had, without giving him any new support. It was a situation in which politicians of every stamp saw that they could derive personal advantage from an attack on the Royal Family and the royal powers. And, except on the question of the war, the Parliament of 1695 and its successors must be considered 'republican' in tone.[8]

Every party competed in the game. Although the new Parliament cheerfully voted supplies of more than £5 million, and gave a hum of approval to the speech with which William opened the session, its first act was to push through a bill for regulating trials in cases of treason. This measure, which granted an accused the benefit of defence by counsel and insisted that any indictment must be supported by the sworn testimony of two lawful persons, may seem to be nothing more than an overdue and welcome extension of civil liberties. In part it was; and so in part was the failure of Parliament to extend the expiring censorship laws. At a time when the nation had no police force and was at war, however, both steps were 'republican' in character. Both of them exposed the King's person, one to insult and the other to murder; and the exposure was obviously a deliberate act. William already had reason to feel personally unsafe while in England, because he was unaccustomed to a judicial system in which torture played no part. The English system made it very difficult to obtain confessions.[9] Now the sport was made even easier for the hunter by the Treason Trials Bill. As Edward Southwell explained it to Huygens, 'Parliament is not particularly well intentioned for the King, and at bottom has a commonwealth in its head; one can see it from the steps they take to regulate criminal trials so that virtually no one can be convicted of high treason.'[10] Another means of attacking the King was by reflecting on his generosity to favourites. William had given Portland the honours of Denbigh, Bromfield and Yale, which would have belonged to the Prince of Wales had there been one. Elizabeth, also childless, had once granted Denbigh alone to her favourite Leicester. The result had been a Welsh rising. Now the Welsh M.P.s merely found it necessary to complain, and the House of Commons presented an address against the grant on 22 January. William was obliged to recall it. He had enough spirit to add that he would find some other way of showing his favour.

These were pin pricks. More significant was the intervention of Parliament in the conduct of the executive. Such intervention was, first of all, an insult, and as such might gain a few votes at the next election. It was also an interesting constitutional experiment, though one which no king could enjoy. The most pressing domestic issue of the year was the state of the coinage. Practically all the silver in circulation had been badly clipped, so that an ounce of silver bullion which was worth only 5s 2d in undamaged currency now passed for 6s 3d. The ratio between gold and silver was also seriously out of balance. The guinea, which should have been equal to 21s 6d or 22s in silver, now went for 25s or even 30s. This made arbitrage transactions irresistibly attractive. As L'Hermitage explained the problem to Heinsius, the normal ratio between gold and silver was 16 to 1. With silver bullion passing for 6s 2d, sixteen thousand ounces of silver was worth £4,930. By sending the silver abroad, however, it was possible to buy a thousand ounces of gold and bring the gold back into England to be coined into 3,708 guineas. At 30s apiece, these guineas had a value of about £5,562. In other words, there was a profit of about £632, less the cost of transport, on such a transaction.[11] A good deal of the increase in the value of gold and silver was the result of wartime inflation. Prices generally had risen, and in January 1696 the actions of the Bank of England stood at 110.[12] William III had taken the matter in hand as soon as he returned in October, and at the Cabinet Council meeting of 16 October he had been firm on two points: any remedy must not include a change in the standard, that is, what would now be called a devaluation; secondly, Parliament must not meddle with the problem – 'The K. sd, by no meanes any thing to come before Parlt.'[13] At the foot of the memorandum for that meeting is a notation to the effect that in the reign of Henry VII the coinage had been regulated by King and Council, and in the reign of Philip and Mary by a proclamation. The Cabinet Council was more cautious about giving offence than the King. At a committee meeting at Shrewsbury's office on 10 November, the Lords heard a long paper by Dr Davenant on the problem. Shrewsbury was the first to comment; he feared that Parliament might take it ill if the matter were settled by proclamation. Devonshire seconded him. Godolphin then said that no individual minister would advise proceeding by proclamation unless all of them were unanimous, and the others agreed with him.[14] In the end the King was obliged to concede defeat. In his speech of 22 November at the opening of the session, he remarked: 'I must likewise take notice of a great difficulty we lie under at this time, by reason of the ill state of the Coin; the redress of which may perhaps prove a further charge to the nation: but this is a matter of so general concern, and of so great importance, that I have thought fit to leave it entirely to the consideration of my parliament.' Another and much more generally known attack on the prerogative took place this same session, when the House of Commons voted to set up an independent Council of Trade whose members should be nominated by Parliament.[15] Here William was more successful. He was able to set up a Board of Trade of his own, thereby preserving his power of appointment.

All these attacks were interrupted by the discovery of an attempt on the King's life. At first it seemed to be merely another invasion scare, of which William had some vague information as early as the end of January.[16] From all sides, he wrote to the Grand Pensionary, he was receiving advice that the French intended to make a descent on one of the three kingdoms. William asked Heinsius to make enquiries about the story, but the reports could not have been very impressive. Ten days later the reports had been confirmed by Vaudemont from Brussels, and by the boasts of the Jacobites. The King knew that an invasion was impracticable. To his regret he felt that he would have to retain more of his troops in England than he wished to, just to be on the safe side.[17] It was not until 23 February that the King had to take the invasion threat seriously, when he was informed by the Duke of Württemberg of great French preparations at Dunkirk and along the coast for an invasion. The troops were already embarked; and King James had arrived at Calais accompanied by the Maréchal de Boufflers, ready to go aboard. William reacted with great vigour and equal confidence. He ordered Württemberg to send over twenty battalions of men, and Heinsius to provide transport for them. 'The enemy may very well fool themselves, not believing us to be as strong at sea as we are.'[18] The fleet was at once dispatched from Spithead to cruise in the Downs, with Russell to command it.

Meanwhile, ever since the beginning of the month, informers had been coming in with tales of an assassination plot. As ever, the King paid no attention to the first of these. Then a few days later a second informer came with the same story, and a few days later a third. All said that the King would be attacked while on his return from a Saturday's hunting at Richmond which had now become his custom. William still would not take it seriously and made plans to go out as usual on Saturday, 16 February, but Portland threatened to make the matter public if he went, so the hunt was cancelled on the ground that it was too cold and windy. Another hunt was planned for the 23rd. On the Friday, however, a fourth informer brought new details. He said that there would be some fifty men on horseback, commanded by one of King James's brigadiers, who would attack the Guards riding behind the royal carriage. The Guards, part of Lord Oxford's regiment, had been tampered with and might not put up much of a fight. Then ten or twelve men led by Sir George Barclay would come up on foot and, after killing some of the horses, fire through the windows. 'Les pauvres glaces de mon carosse auroient esté bien maltraittées' was William's dry comment when he heard about this part of the plan. At first he wanted to go out to Richmond as planned, with extra guards, but it was objected that this might tip off the conspirators. On the 23rd, therefore, he rode in the park at Kensington with a heavy guard of nobles who had no idea why they had been invited. That night the town was searched and fourteen men were seized. This prevented the execution of an alternative plan to attack the King as he returned from church at St James's on the morning of Sunday the 24th. The cabinet council met twice that day, before and after dinner, and the privy council sat in the evening until midnight. For some time the King refused to believe that James's son, the Duke of Berwick, was involved in the conspiracy; but the capture of his valet and the discovery that Berwick had been in London recruiting the gang made his guilt all too clear.[19]

In political terms, the assassination plan was a godsend for the King. When he informed Parliament on Monday the 25th of the conspiracy and the threatened invasion, both Houses were so shocked that they took an address of congratulations on his escape to Kensington that same evening. A few days later the Commons formed an association pledged to exact revenge for the blood of their 'rightful and lawful' King if it should be untimely spilt. The lords did much the same, though they would only agree that William 'hath the right by law' to the throne. The Tory Blathwayt referred, in words more reminiscent of Filmer's *Patriarcha*[20] than of anything else, to the assassins as 'parricides'.[21] Those whose patriotism was not satisfied by supporting the Association began to wear red ribbons on which were printed 'General Association for King William', and these threatened to become so fashionable that it might be unsafe not to wear one.[22] Naturally the Jacobites retorted that the whole thing was a sham, but no one believed them. For the moment the Whigs rode high, and those few Tories whose consciences would not let them sign their names to the statement that William was 'rightful and lawful' King found themselves deeply embarrassed. The non-jurors sadly misjudged the state of popular feeling. When Friend and Perkins went to their deaths at Tyburn on 3/13 April, three of them gave the conspirators public absolution of *all* their sins in a loud voice. By thus giving open approval of the plot the non-jurors forfeited all public respect, and their position became very much weaker. The three priests were imprisoned for their insolence.

William soon tired of the whole business. Apparently there had been some Irish Catholics in Oxford's regiment, and these had to be dismissed. He was not able to go hunting at Richmond again until 7/17 March, and then only under a heavy guard. Kensington, too, had its extra guards, and they were to stay. Other precautions, such as searching the carriages which came into the palace yard, had to be taken and the King was put to some personal inconvenience for the rest of his life. Debates on the Association slowed down the parliamentary session, and the Association itself gave more power to the Whigs than the King might have liked. Worst of all were the strategic results of the invasion scare. The twenty battalions which had been brought over to bolster public morale rather than for any military reason were so many men lost from the army in Flanders. The Mediterranean squadron was also brought home, and though it was needed to offset the large enemy concentrations at Brest there was nothing else to send to Cadiz in its place. This would mean the probable loss of the Duke of Savoy and of Barcelona as well, if the Spanish did no more fighting than they had in the last few campaigns. Thus, even though the assassination and the landings had been prevented, the French received a considerable military benefit from them. They were also making a last effort. At sea and on land, quite unlike the situation in the previous year, they would be at least as strong as the English and Dutch combined. Man for man the allied seamen and infantry were superior to the French. The problem now, after the dislocations caused by the invasion scare, was to deploy them properly and to pay them enough so that they would neither starve nor desert.

Most wars have been paid for by inflation. Henry VIII, and Louis XIV for that matter, adulterated the coinage. The younger Pitt and his successors used paper money and printed what they needed. In 1696 there were a number of experts, of whom the new Treasury secretary William Lowndes was probably the most important, who recommended that the inflation which had already occurred should be recognized by a devaluation. The clipped silver currency was already circulating at 6s 2d or 6s 3d the ounce. Therefore, argued Lowndes, the best thing to do was to make a new coinage in which the crown, or old 5s piece, would go at 6s 3d, the shilling for 1s 3d, and so on. The new coins would be given fancy names as a token that the inflation was merely a temporary measure to be followed by a return to the old standard after the end of the war. The King, as we have seen, felt that a devaluation should not take place. He was quite wrong in taking this stand, but he was supported not only by the magic name of Locke but by the great majority in Parliament. The matter became a party issue dividing still further the two groups which insisted on calling themselves Whig. Charles Montagu was the leader of those who wanted to keep to the old standard, Speaker Foley and his relative Harley the leaders of those who wanted inflation – either by having no recoinage at all, or by recoining according to the proposals of Lowndes. The split between court Whig and country Whig had been visible for some time. Now it became so deep that Foley's men began to be called Tories. In one sense the nomenclature was curious, since Harley had a nonconformist background and Foley the support of Sunderland. The real split on any such purely economic matter, of course, was between London moneyed men and country landlords. Montagu represented money, Foley and his friends represented land.

Montagu won on the recoinage. Not only would the silver be called in and reissued at the old standard, but also the cost, estimated at £1,200,000, would be met by a regressive Window Tax, which was merely Hearth Money all over again. The only improvement was that windows could be counted from outdoors, while Hearth Money had involved the use of search warrants so that the inspectors could enter the house and count the number of hearths within. The only concession was that deflation would proceed by stages rather than all at once. The effects were catastrophic. Many people believed that Parliament would not in the end have the courage to carry through its deflationary programme. Coin of all sorts disappeared from circulation, guineas and old silver and new. Trade virtually ceased. No one was willing to move until it became clear whether Parliament would eventually be forced to a devaluation. The country members were unwilling to concede defeat. Led by Harley, they proposed and carried a bill for a Land Bank. This would, as the name implies, lend on the security of land. It would also compete with the Bank of England, and it would secure inflation as well: there was no slightest chance that the projectors would be able to raise the anticipated £2,564,000 for the government unless they took guineas at 30s apiece.[23] The scheme might well fail anyway; but there was no hope for it at all unless there was a devaluation, which was the camouflaged essence of the whole idea.

While the struggle between land and money continued it was impossible to carry on the war. The Dutch refused to make loans or to honour English bills of exchange, since they did not know what they were worth. If this continued for any length of time the soldiers would simply starve to death. By the middle of April remittances to the continent were almost impossible unless made in specie.[24] According to Bonnet, all that the King could scrape up to take with him to Holland in May was £44,000 in gold ingots and £100,000 in letters of change on the Bank of England, and the latter would probably be protested.[25] It was not until he reached the continent that William discovered the full extent of the financial crisis. No more money was to be had in Holland than in England. The want of funds had enabled the enemy to take the field before the allies, and there was so little that William could do that he did not care to expose his reputation by joining the army merely to sit in his tent.[26] It would have been as well had he spent the summer at the Loo. The campaign was almost completely uneventful. The King's fine plans to besiege Dinant or Charleroi were frustrated, and also those to send an army to bombard Dunkirk. To prevent quarrels between his generals – the Elector of Bavaria and the new commander of the Dutch forces, Prince Walraad van Nassau, were barely on speaking terms – William did spend more than two months in camp. But he had the windows of his headquarters glazed, and everyone knew that he would not have been so extravagant had there been any chance of action.

The position was so serious that in June the King thought of having Parliament sit in his absence to enact a devaluation:

I own I was strongly of opinion to reduce the value of the guineas to 22 shillings, but I now see, too late, that I was in the wrong, and there appears to be no remedy for obtaining credit, but the acceptance of guineas by the Treasury, at 24 or 25 shillings, and giving a premium or interest, so as not directly to violate the laws. But in such extreme necessity, we should not be too scrupulous, for all will be lost, if credit be not soon found to pay the fleet and the army, especially the troops who are in these parts. As you know all the importance of this business, I flatter myself you will do every thing that is possible, to assemble the parliament in June, for the purpose of remedying this great evil.[27]

He also toyed with the idea of accepting French proposals for a general truce.[28] Eventually William rejected the idea of a truce; but this made the pressure for a solution to the money problem all the greater. The court Whigs, having won on the recoinage in Parliament, simply refused to obey the King. Let the army perish. Let the war be lost. Nothing and no one would make them surrender their party victory of the preceding winter. By the middle of July things had reached a crisis: '... his Majesty has commanded me to let Your Lordship know in one sorrow-full word that Our Condition is such that if we do not receive some Releif from England, within one week or 10 days at furthest, The English Army must be certainly dissolved to prevent their Starving; This my Lord his Majesty would have the Lords of the Treasury take into their consideration'.[29] Some of the bills of exchange were being refused, and for those on which payment was still being made the discount had now risen to 47 per cent.[30] When the ministers continued to send no money and did nothing but bleat about the necessity of peace at any price, William finally sent Portland over to shake them out of their lethargy. It was high time. When he arrived, Portland found that some of the ministers were on holiday, others at Windsor for the installation of the Duke of Gloucester as a knight of the Garter. Only one was at Whitehall, Somers: and the Lord Keeper was of little use in money matters.

The town was as startled to see Portland as it would have been to see the King.[31] He and the Lords Justices had authority to let Parliament sit. They did not dare to go as far as that, nor to meet the demands of the promoters of the Land Bank. That project now failed completely. Luckily the Jewish community was able to lend £20,000 at once, and after the Land Bank men had been completely discredited their rivals of the Bank of England were eventually persuaded to raise £200,000 more. This was enough to keep the army from actual starvation, though the terms of the loan were terrible. It was not merely a question of interest rates and promises to reimburse the Bank of England for what it claimed to have lost by sending money to Flanders in 1695. William was now, by the logic of the financial situation, delivered over to the rabid Whigs bound hand and foot. Harley and his friends had been ruined by the failure of their pet Land Bank, and Speaker Foley was furthermore known to be in correspondence with the enemy.[32] On the failure of the Land Bank scheme Sunderland had dropped these people, and now he smoothly resumed his close association with Shrewsbury and Somers. Shrewsbury was a moderate, but Somers was a member of what was coming to be known as the Junto. The others, Wharton, Montagu, and Admiral Russell were all wild men and were all more or less personally distasteful to the King. But he would have to do what they wanted, even if he might use go-betweens in order to keep them out of his sight as much as possible. There was no alternative, for Godolphin too was discredited by the crisis, and at the end of October Sunderland tricked him into making a *pro forma* resignation of his place as First Lord of the Treasury. The King jumped at it, and Godolphin remained out of office for the next five years.

Meanwhile the Duke of Savoy had made a separate peace with France on terms which had been known to Heinsius ever since April.[33] By doing so he obtained the restoration of Pignerol, and the hand of the Duc de Bourgoigne for his daughter without having to provide a dowry. His defection was a disaster for the allies. The war in Italy had been an important one, not in terms of victories but because of its cost to the French. A large army and Catinat, one of their better generals, had been pinned down in Piedmont for years. This was the only reason for the allied superiority in numbers in Flanders during 1694 and 1695, and the cost in money to the French had been just as frightful as the cost in men. At first William hoped to keep the war going in Italy by giving the Austrians the subsidies which had previously gone to the Duke of Savoy.[34] Leopold, however, agreed to a neutrality for the whole of Italy without consulting the maritime powers, and it was highly doubtful whether he would even send to the Rhine the 14,000 men he had been using in Italy for the campaign of 1697. Since the French would be able to concentrate all their forces in the north, this was a double betrayal. The King has been severely criticized for his treatment of the Austrians in the last years of his life.[35] Leopold's conduct in 1696 and 1697 was so bad, however, that he was not treated any worse than he deserved to be. The English were forced to make peace, partly because of the shortage of money and partly because of the ending of the war in Italy; and for the latter the Emperor was very largely responsible. William's reference to the conduct of the Viennese as 'the villainous step they took in agreeing to the neutrality of Italy' was by no means too strong.[36]

It was now imperative to obtain peace. The first problem was how to get peace from the French now that their bribes to Savoy had been so successful.

The second was how to persuade the Habsburgs to accept reasonable terms. In the winter of 1695–96 the court of Vienna had been tired of the costs of the war and depressed by their failures in Hungary. Now their attitude had been changed by the serious illness of Carlos II at Madrid. If the King of Spain should die while the war was still in progress, the maritime powers would be obliged to carry out the terms of the grand alliance. Once peace was made, Leopold's chance of obtaining any real military and naval support was much less. He had, furthermore, a personal reason for opposing any peace based on the treaties of Westphalia and Nijmegen. His sister Eleanora, the widowed Queen of Poland, had married the Duke of Lorraine in 1678. Her infant son, Leopold's nephew, had succeeded to the title twelve years later. The provisions of the Treaty of Nijmegen regarding Lorraine were completely unacceptable. Something better would have to be done for the young Duke or he, like his father before him, would prefer to live and die in exile. The Savoyard defection, however, had persuaded William III that the war must somehow be brought to an end. He was reluctant to force his allies.

'... I do not think we can oblige the allies to accept the offer of peace made by France, unless we force them: that is, by declaring that we can give them no farther assistance, which is a declaration hazardous, not only because the House of Austria may anticipate us, by making a separate peace, but also, because after the conclusion of a general peace, there are no hopes of continuing the grand alliance, which is, however, our only security. ...'³⁷

There was, in fact, no choice. The imperialists could and did slow down the progress of the negotiations by making a series of frivolous demands, but they could not stop them altogether. William's mind was made up. He wrote to the Queen of Spain on 20 August: 'je ne hesiteres point a vous dire, que je croi quil est de l'interest du Roy Chatolique et de toute la cause commune, de conclure promptement une paix generale avec la france. ...'³⁸

On the 26th the King left the army for het Loo. The Duke of Celle came to visit him there, and no one talked of anything but dogs, foxes, hares and horses except Matthew Prior and the young James Vernon, who preferred to read Virgil in bed.³⁹ A few days later William went to visit the Elector of Brandenburg at one of his houses in the Duchy of Cleves. There were strong rumours that the Electoral Princess would soon become Queen of England. She was certainly no great beauty: '... the young lady is not above 15. very lean & dos not seem marriageable these 2. years. ...'⁴⁰ Wooing a child one-third his age would have made the King even more ridiculous than he had been during the summer campaign, when he had had glass windows in his headquarters. In any case he came back from Cleves still a bachelor; but the note of ridicule continued to cling to him. During the crossing to England his yacht lost its way and he suddenly found himself sailing straight into the harbour of Calais. Luckily the French were not prepared to receive him and the yacht managed to escape without harm. Then, after he landed in England on 6/16 October, his carriage turned over; William and Portland were found, unhurt, in an undignified heap at the bottom of the wreck.[41] It was all a sharp contrast to the glories of the year before.

The parliamentary session was almost wholly taken up by the problem of money and the case of Sir John Fenwick. The latter, one of the conspirators in the assassination plot, could not be tried in the ordinary course of law. Friends of Fenwick had tried to suborn the two witnesses against him, Porter and Goodman, and had succeeded in persuading Goodman to leave the country. Only Porter remained, and his unsupported testimony was not enough to secure a conviction on a treason charge. Yet Sir John could not be allowed to go free. Not only was he notoriously guilty, he had made a false confession implicating the leaders of the administration. This insolence must be punished, and the government proceeded against Fenwick by bill of attainder. He was beheaded on 28 January 1697. The Fenwick case illustrated the shortcomings of the Treason Trials Act with its requirement of two witnesses. It also served to push the King more firmly into the pocket of the junto. Shrewsbury, a moderate who had exercised a restraining influence, was so embarrassed by Fenwick's charges against him that he resigned. Godolphin was cozened into doing the same thing. As a result the government lost much of its breadth and became almost purely a one-party affair. Foley, as Speaker, did what he could to embarrass the ministry, but that was not very much. For the moment the country party, or new Tories, were discredited by the failure of the Land Bank. They would have to lie low until the conclusion of peace. Meanwhile the junto had an easy time of it. Montagu was able to put through a series of financial measures confirming the decision to stick by the old standard value of the coin. In modern phraseology the country was 'put through the wringer', and however painful the process might be it was eventually successful. By 1699 the nation's credit was restored, the new coins were circulating in sufficient quantity, and the damage caused by the long crisis was beginning to be forgotten. The gentlemen of the Bank of England, Montagu's allies, were among the chief gainers. They were amply rewarded by the grant of a banking monopoly that should continue until 1710, and the government showed almost more eagerness – and certainly it had more success – in restoring the Bank's credit than in restoring its own. The junto was also successful in obtaining rewards for its members. Somers became Lord Chancellor and a baron. Admiral Russell was made Earl of Orford and Treasurer of the Navy, while retaining a place on the Admiralty Board. Though Sir Stephen Fox, the senior member of the

Treasury Board, became First Lord on Godolphin's retirement, he was replaced by Montagu a few months later. Only Wharton failed to taste the fruits of victory. The King's personal dislike of him was too strong to be overcome. In part, Wharton was compensated by the long delayed death of his father, which brought him the barony and a splendid fortune.

The imminent prospect of peace contributed largely to the smooth and fairly rapid progress of the session, which was ended by a prorogation on 16 April. But it was easier to want peace than to get it. The defection of Savoy had not broken off the conversations between Dijkvelt and Callières; but the French position was now much stronger than before and the new situation was reflected in a stiffening of their demands. Now they would only offer to return Luxembourg without its fortifications, and a razed Luxembourg could hardly be of much use as a barrier fortress. More important was the question of the return of Strasbourg, which the French might demand to keep if they offered tolerable conditions to the Duke of Lorraine. Up to the conclusion of the separate peace in Italy, the King and Heinsius hoped to obtain Strasbourg and Lorraine as well. After they were betrayed by Savoy their optimism dwindled; and their contempt for the conduct of the imperialists made them feel that they need not be too scrupulous in looking out for the interests of the Habsburgs. The manner in which the court of Vienna had agreed to a truce in Italy was as offensive as the truce itself. For Caunitz at The Hague had been ordered to say that Vienna would refuse to conclude the truce, at the very time that Prince Eugene was directed to sign it. Eugene's instructions became known to Heinsius twenty-four hours after Caunitz had assured him that the war in Italy would be carried on. His reaction was correspondingly severe.[42] William was as angry as the Pensioner.

In August the French presented their ultimatum. They would be willing to return Strasbourg, but only without its new walls, and only then if the town remained Catholic as it had become after 1682. If they were allowed to keep it, the French would give an equivalent which would include good terms for the Duke of Lorraine.[43] For some months the negotiations stood still at that point, for even now William was reluctant to force the imperialists. While the Habsburg ministers invented one reason after another for delay, without ever quite breaking off the negotiations, the King found himself in new difficulties with the city of Amsterdam. The merchants were eager for peace and let the French know it all too well. Their weak conduct brought peace no nearer. It merely made the enemy feel safe in refusing all concessions. By the middle of November the French felt strong enough to refuse to recognize William III as King of England in the preliminaries, although they had previously agreed to do so.[44]

The imperialists and the minor German princes were eager to break off the conversations on this point, since they knew that the King could never concede it. The imperialists would have preferred to keep the war going until the death of the King of Spain. If peace must be made before the opening of the question of the Spanish Succession, Kinsky hoped to control the negotiations by having them take place either in Stockholm or else in Italy. In either case the maritime powers would be left on the sidelines and might lose all the advantages they had earned. Thus William and Heinsius, however much they were provoked by the French, could not break off the Dijkvelt-Callières talks. These were their only direct channel of communications with the French; and the thread of the negotiations must, at all costs, be kept in their hands. Fundamentally the English and Dutch were negotiating from weakness, but they held one trump card. The French were as eager to make peace before the death of Carlos II as the Austrians were averse to do so. The terms which the French offered were in fact quite generous, considering the military situation. And what seems to have delayed the peace for another year was the long record of distrust, suspicion and hatred from the past. After a quarter-century of strife it was almost impossible for the enemies to place any confidence in each other's good faith. Mutual confidence would have to be restored before there could be any lasting peace. For more was involved than a simple treaty.

By this time William III was becoming more of an Englishman than a Dutchman. The change was never to be complete. He could never in his lifetime boast of being 'mere English', as he could never in his lifetime have been simply a Dutch William. What had happened since 1688 was that the English aspect of his life was taking far more of his time and interest than ever before. It was the new job, difficult, annoying, but also exciting. The Republic was home; there was never any question about that. William loved it as he could not love England. But the job there was smaller and, after 1690, routine. Amsterdam was generally cooperative after 1690. Even when it was not, Amsterdam was simply insignificant in comparison with the House of Commons. All this had its impact on the King's policy as well as on his personal life. As Prince of Orange William was perhaps fated to be the enemy of Louis XIV. Certainly Louis had driven the Prince to take up such a position. But the King of England was the natural ally of France; and what did England care about the fate of Luxembourg or Strasbourg? Crossing the Channel had made William view the problems of Europe in a different perspective. As his strength failed, he delegated more and more of his Dutch responsibilities to Heinsius, whom he could trust as he trusted no Englishman. Thus his divorce from Dutch life became ever more pronounced. In the 1680s he had boasted that he was more vitally concerned in the fate of the Republic than the entire

Amsterdam patriciate. Fifteen years later we find him writing to the Grand Pensionary: 'As to the conditions relating to the Republic, your Excellency knows their interest best; and, as to what concerns me. ...'[45] The sentence ends with a reference to English affairs. In public, and even perhaps to himself, the King would have refused to admit that anyone could know or care more about Dutch interests than he did. But the situation had changed. After eight years of concentrating on England and Europe, William found that he had delegated not only the management but the initiative to his most able servant. For the last five years of his life he was to be an observer rather than the director of the Republic's affairs. In the sphere of Dutch domestic politics this meant that the 'second stadhouderless period' was already beginning in William's lifetime.[46] In the field of diplomacy, it meant the possibility of a *rapprochement* between William III and Louis XIV. Once peace came, and with it some sort of personal confidence, France was a far more natural ally of England than was the Emperor.

In December 1696 the French, to the surprise of the allied negotiators, suddenly agreed to give satisfaction not only on the question of William's recognition but also about the fortifications of Luxembourg.[47] This was all that could be hoped for in the preliminaries, and the King was now eager to end the war. He was strongly opposed to another campaign, which could only go badly. The immediate threat of a descent on Ireland by the squadron of the French Admiral Pointis was serious. Even if Pointis should attack the West Indies rather than the British Isles, there was no hope of progress on the continent. Barcelona would probably be lost. In the Low Countries the French would have a great superiority in numbers and might do whatever they wished. It was still impossible to find any ready money in England. As the King pointed out, if he could not even find enough money to dispatch a single agent, the Comte de Frise, how was he to pay for the support of whole armies? He became more and more eager for the conclusion of peace before the opening of the campaigning season, or at least for a truce if there was not time enough to complete a treaty so soon. If the Austrians made difficulties it would be necessary to 'represent' them in the negotiations. The Habsburgs needed to have some intelligent person do just this. They could no longer fight; but they were too stubborn to admit their need for peace. Heinsius was less eager to force the Habsburgs than was William. Not only did the Republic need the Habsburg alliance far more than the English did, but Heinsius must also plan for a day when William III would no longer be on the scene. When that day came, the Dutch could not count on the continuance of English support. The Heinsius *Archief* is stuffed with the most minute accounts of William's health, sent over twice a week by agents of every degree of importance. While William was being forced by the logic of his position into a *rapprochement* with France, the Grand Pensionary was being forced by the logic of his own position to look beyond the King's lifetime. The two men worked loyally with each other for their common interests, but by 1697 they were beginning to have a number of interests beyond their partnership.

Chapter 25

THE TREATY OF RIJSWIJK

By the spring of 1697 Lord Portland had decided to leave the court. He was one of William's oldest servants, having become a page in 1664. Three years later, when the Prince's household had been dismissed by de Witt, Willem Bentinck was presumably too unimportant for anyone to worry about. Certainly he had no English ties, and it was these ties which the Grand Pensionary was determined to break. Bentinck stayed on to become the closest friend as well as the leading servant of his master. It is unlikely that William III ever confided his whole mind to any one man; but if he did so it was to Bentinck. Most of the Prince's friends shared one or two of his interests – warfare, religion, hunting, art collecting, landscape gardening, the management of Dutch politics, relations with England or with the continental powers. Bentinck saw to it that he shared them all. When the Prince married, the servant dutifully followed suit, and during the 1680s the state chambers of the Dutch palaces on the *piano nobile* were directly above those of the Bentincks on the ground floor. It was dreadfully hard work. There was almost no privacy at court, since the Prince worked late at night and might call at any hour; and there were no holidays. In the summer of 1688, when the Vrouw van Rhoon was thought to be dying, it is true that her husband was called back from his negotiations in Germany to her bedside. But when she did die, later in the year, she was alone: nothing could interfere with the English expedition, not even death.

However hard the work might be, it was very well paid. William III was an exceptionally generous man to those who were in his immediate circle. He was close, perhaps even tight with his money on most occasions. His accounts had balanced ever since he was eighteen, and the habit of reading them once a week was one which the King kept up throughout his life. His prudence deserted him when he came to consider the services of those he saw almost every day. His valets, his pages, his clerks made their modest fortunes; a greater prize awaited William's friends. Fagel, Bentinck and Keppel were all given large properties, and when Fagel died before the bequest to him could take effect, the gift was replaced by generous pensions to his sisters. Although William detested corruption, particularly in the army, he had turned a blind eye to the rapid progress of Waldeck's fortunes in his service. Perhaps he remembered that the Princess van Waldeck was a Nassau, perhaps he was taking into account the fact that Waldeck's estates had been ruined by William's own enemies. Whatever the reason, Waldeck alone among the Dutch colleagues had been permitted to make what he could from his place. In England there had been larger opportunities for generosity and the scale of reward was much higher than before. If Leeds and Rochester, Sir Stephen Fox and the lords of the Junto must be given so much when they did not deserve it, why should not more be given to those who did? Over the years the presents to favourites reached startling levels. Bentinck took care that his own nest had more feathers than any other. His was a grasping and jealous nature.

For almost thirty years he succeeded in monopolizing the interest and friendship of his master; and then the spell had been broken. Keppel was in many ways the image of what Bentinck had been a generation before: young, handsome, brave, discreet enough to use as a personal secretary. Like Bentinck, Keppel was a member of the provincial nobility. His family background was such that the King could consider him a friend rather than a servant, while his poverty was such that he would be willing to be a companion. In the struggle for favour which developed between the two men in the early 1690s, Keppel had a number of advantages beyond his youth and his quite exceptional good looks. His manners were more polished than those of his rival. He was the better soldier of the two: Portland had demanded and obtained the rank of major-general, but his military talents were quite weak. And since he was still poor, Keppel might be expected to work harder than Portland now cared to. All this more than made up for the irregularity of Keppel's private life. A dissolute young man, he was credited by rumour with a number of adventures, a case of gonorrhea, and a mistress whom he kept in Chelsea.[1] The mistress, a pretty brunette, had been the personal maid of Mlle la Pertine, the daughter of one Dr Monginot. Keppel allowed her £300 a year, but she was by no means the only woman in his life. They took a good share of the favourite's time, and the King complained that Keppel was too often absent from court. But he had a clear superiority over Portland some time before his elevation to the English peerage as Earl of Albemarle in 1697; and the news of this, together with that of his military advancement to the rank of major-general were the last straws. Portland retired from court in March of 1697. Although he went to the continent in May with his master, Portland went to Brussels instead of to the army. William hoped that the Prince de Vaudemont, an old mutual friend, would be able to talk him around; but he was wrong. Portland's jealousy was so great that on 30 May he wrote a letter to the King indicating that, for the preservation of William's reputation, Albemarle must be dismissed.[2] For some time there had been rumours in England that the King's affection for Albemarle had a homosexual basis. Portland wrote that he had been startled to find the same disgusting rumours circulating at The Hague and in the army. If the King did not agree to protect himself from these rumours, Portland would be obliged to retire from his service.

Given Albemarle's character, to say nothing of that of William III, it is hard to understand how such rumours ever arose. That they had arisen was an undoubted fact. They have continued to circulate down to our own day. The only ground for them, beyond the King's open liking for a man nineteen years younger than himself, lay in the curious arrangement of the King's secretariat. William III began his day fairly late and spent a good part of it in hunting. Unlike most of his contemporaries he worked on far into the night. After the formal ceremony of the *coucher* he would often continue writing, either in his own cabinet or in that of the person who was his chief private secretary. Until 1695 that person had been Portland. The fact that the two suites of rooms, the state apartments and those of Portland, had connecting doors had not caused any comment. After the rearrangement of the apartments at Kensington in 1695, however, it was the suite of Keppel and not that of Portland which had the connecting doors. Outsiders, who did not know what the King's working habits were and had no conception of the burdens with which he loaded himself and his staff, wondered how the two men spent their time. The malicious, who hated the King and cared nothing whatever about the truth, were happy to discover a misleading historical parallel. Robert Ker, the favourite of James I, had come to the attention of his master by displaying courage when he broke his leg. So too had Keppel. In both cases the fractures had been followed by a steep rise in favour and the place of private secretary. And in both cases, as least as far as William's enemies were concerned, the former page became a Ganymede as well.

Accusations of sexual irregularity are easy to make, quick to spread, and virtually impossible to refute. It is not necessary to argue that these particular accusations were the work of the fallen Duke of Leeds, who had a generation earlier suborned a youth to testify that he had been the victim of an attempt at seduction by the Duke of Buckingham. Certainly Leeds was capable of using the same charge a second time, and certainly the Tories used stories about Keppel to embellish their anti-Williamite myth. But Leeds was not the only man in England who knew about Ker of Ferniehurst, nor the only one to see the many parallels between the lives of James I and William III. Anyone could see the parallels, and a great many people knew about the connecting doors at Kensington. What went on behind them was not nearly so obvious at the time. But now, with the aid of the documents, it is possible to explain how William III handled his correspondence. The King had always been annoyed by job hunters and terrified that they would surprise him into making a mistake. After 1688 he had separate groups of secretaries, each with a clerical staff, to handle the affairs of the four governments over which he presided. But the secretaries were often indiscreet and were often interested in the advice that they gave. William, therefore, delegated a great deal of his correspondence to Portland and later to Keppel. He also allotted them certain areas of business in which they acted as co-ordinators of information. The King would then turn to Portland, for example, for confidential advice on the affairs of Scotland.[3] When Keppel came into the King's confidence he took over the management of the subsidiary correspondence with the army on the continent and then more and more of the business of the civil government of the Dutch Republic. Huygens was the King's Dutch Secretary, but he found himself pushed aside. During the campaign of 1694 he lost the King's favour, and he had never had his master's confidence. As Keppel took over the work, Huygens could not even get in to see the King. Documents would be sent to him to countersign and transmit. If a letter was not confidential, the minute might be sent to Huygens who would then write the letter and take to it the King. But the minutes had been written by Keppel, and Keppel was now always present on the rare occasions when Huygens was admitted to William's cabinet. After the death of the Queen the position became even worse, and Keppel gave direct orders to Huygens's clerks without bothering the sick old man. Finally, at the end of the 1696 campaign, Huygens was retired with a handsome pension.[4]

The working of the system is even more obvious in the case of Ireland. Until the end of 1697 the co-ordinator of Irish affairs was Lord Sunderland. On his retirement there was a brief period in which the King acted as his own Irish specialist, in the hope that the Duke of Shrewsbury would assume the Chamberlain's place and with it the functions which Sunderland had abandoned. When that hope vanished, the Irish themselves turned to Albemarle and asked him to take over the job:

... My Lord Shrewsbury his coming being now despaired of, ... To setle our Correspondence I spoke to the King about My Lord Albemarle having first his leave, I find the King and My Lord Albemarle both enter into the matter very warmly, that is that Mr Secretary Vernon shall be appointed for Your Lords[ps] [the Lords Justices of Ireland] to Correspond with in all things. But that in all matters of importance we shall give a private account to My Lord Albemarle from whom we shall be sure to receive the King's particular commands from Mr Vernon. I had upon this foot two hours conference this morning with My Lord Albemarle who seems very desirous to be well informed in order to render himself usefull to the King. ... Thus My Lord the matter seems well concerted, how farr it may succeed is uncertain, by reason My Lord Albemarle is abandoned much to his pleasure but I believe it can do no hurt turned any way and probably it will serve to the present extremity. ...[5]

Albemarle was later given the business of the Swiss cantons as well. It is certain that he read the very heavy correspondence between the King and Heinsius, and highly probable that he took minutes of the King's holograph letters. Copies must once have been in existence in the King's files and the letters were too confidential to be given to any clerk. Before these letters were written, the King, who was slow to make up his mind, would have discussed their contents with the favourite. He would also have discussed the contents of Albemarle's own letters to Heinsius.[6] Perhaps we should say that he dictated the letters that Albemarle wrote as if they were his own. The two series are so close that they are obviously the product of a single mind.

We can, then, reject the charges of homosexuality on the ground that the King's tremendous burden of work left no time for it. No one of the secretaries who knew the system ever paid any attention to the accusations. Those who knew Albemarle knew him to be a young rakehell, who nearly caused one international scandal by trying to seduce the mistress of the Elector of Bavaria and who did cause another by having a child by Mme de Richelieu. At almost the very moment when Portland was complaining about the King's reputation, his brother-in-law Lord Villiers was trying to arrange a match between Albemarle and a daughter of the Earl of Rochester.[7] It is in the last degree unlikely that either Villiers or Rochester would have considered the match had there been anything of truth in the accusations of vice. And we have not said anything about the character of William III. In 1695, grieving over the death of the Queen and remorseful at his adulteries, he had dismissed Betty Villiers. It is inconceivable that a man would turn his mistress away under the influence of a deep religious feeling, only to fall into a far graver sin. And if by any chance he had done so, he would never have dared to call in, as William did, a mutual friend to arbitrate between him and the dissatisfied Portland. The risk of exposure would have been far too great. The fact that William did turn to Vaudemont for help is the strongest single argument for his innocence. The next strongest is the fact that Portland, after referring to the existence of the disgusting rumours, denied that they had any validity and shortly afterwards resumed his duties.[8]

William III had a great deal to worry about as he left for the continent from Margate on the morning of 26 April/6 May. In addition to the possibility that he might lose Portland, for whom he retained a deep friendship, there were a number of serious problems awaiting him on the continent. There was almost no money for his English forces, and little chance of getting more. The Elector of Brandenburg would not permit his troops to be used as William wanted, and the Hanoverians threatened not to send theirs at all if their claims to an Electorate were not pressed. The Elector of Bavaria was not on speaking terms with the Prince of Nassau-Saarbrück, who commanded the Dutch army in the King's absence. Piteous appeals for help from the Queen of Spain were accompanied by threats to make a truce for Catalonia if an English fleet were not dispatched to the Mediterranean. Although the ships were sent they could not possibly arrive in time to save Barcelona; and if the Spaniards carried out their threats to make a truce, the alliance would be at an end. The defection of Savoy had been a serious loss for the allies; the defection of Spain as well would mean complete ruin. As it was, the closing of the Italian operations made it possible for the French to concentrate their forces in the Low Countries. They would have a large superiority there for the entire campaign, and the best that William could hope for would be to act successfully on the defensive. Not much was to be expected from the imperialists in the way of military support or diversion. But they could be expected to do anything to delay the conclusion of peace on reasonable terms.

These were some of the problems awaiting the King when he reached The Hague on the evening of 7 May. The next day, Wednesday, was spent in receiving the compliments of the diplomatic corps and of Dutch society. Such ceremonies had always tired the King, but he was allowed no rest. On Thursday the formal opening of peace negotiations took place at his palace of Rijswijk, between The Hague and Delft. The building, which no longer exists, had been one of the most successful of his grandfather's architectural efforts. Its extreme symmetry made it an ideal place for negotiations. One driveway led to the central door of the palace, which opened on to a large hall. This could be used by the Swedish mediator, Count Lilienroth. The remainder of the building consisted of two suites of rooms which were exact mirror images of each other. The French, who occupied the suite nearer their lodgings at Delft, could not complain of being less well housed than the allied ministers on The Hague side of the palace. And both sides had driveways of their own leading to the building, so that there could be no argument about the proper order in which carriages should come and go – except among the allies. The only defect in this perfect symmetry was the personality of the mediator, who was thought to lean towards the French side. In February, however, the King had ordered Heinsius to correct this bias: 'It is particularly necessary to win over Lilienroth since he is by himself and neither promises nor money are to be spared; however poor I am I shall gladly contribute my share. Your Excellency will figure out how best to do it.'[9] Heinsius does not appear to have been very successful in dealing with Lilienroth, who continued to favour the French; but it was something gained to have the negotiations begun at all.

On Friday the King had to take his place in a meeting of the Raad van State, and it proved too much for him. His health had been uncertain all the spring. At the beginning of April he had eaten a curious dinner, of codfish washed down with cider, which had made him violently ill for an hour-and-a-half. He

had been better the next morning, but the general condition of his health was
by no means good and he was much too tired for the crowds at The Hague.
He was supposed to leave for Zuylestein on Saturday morning. There was still
another group of assassins in the offing, and he would be safer in the country
than in the capital. When Saturday morning came, the King had collapsed
and was too ill to be moved. Blathwayt loyally tried to keep the secret and
wrote merely that William 'being somewhat out of order by the sudden heats
and Crowd of Business was pleased to deferr his Journey till this Morning
His Majesty has been somewhat feavorish but having been let blood and had
other favorable evacuations seems almost perfectly recovered. ...'10 It was
more serious than that. The diplomats gathered at Rijswijk were alarmed for
the King's life. Attempts were made to obtain a truce from the French, who
refused to grant one. A week later the King was still very weak and could
hardly write a letter to Vaudemont.11 Gradually his health returned, but
recovery was very slow. It was as well that this was to be the King's last
campaign.

On 16 May a French army under Catinat began the siege of Ath. William
thought that the place could be relieved without too much difficulty unless
the forces of the enemy turned out to be much greater than his own. Until
now the allied commanders had expected to be almost equal to the French in
numbers. They were surprised and discouraged to find that the two enemy
armies, one under Catinat and the other under Boufflers, exceeded their total
forces by at least one-third.12 In such circumstances the relief of Ath could
not be attempted, and the commander of the place was obliged to surrender
on 5 June. It now seemed likely that the French might move towards Brussels.
William shifted his camp to Kockelsberg and sent officers to view the old
French camp at Anderlech, from which they had bombarded the city in 1695.
Whether he was moved by curiosity or by a premonition does not matter.
Whatever the reason, he was ready to act when he heard on the 22nd from
French deserters that their armies were on the march. William and his own
troops marched the entire night, and by ten the next morning he had occupied
the camp at Anderlech. The French plans were forestalled. An attack on
Brussels was now impossible, the greatly superior enemy forces were stale-
mated for the remainder of the campaign. William's defensive tactics were
masterly, and for once they were given due recognition. As Sir Joseph
Williamson wrote bitingly of the French: 'In Flanders they lose their time and
honour, by the wise and vigilant care of the King, who has gotten himself a
most wonderful increase of reputation and love amongst all the allies, by that
great deliverance of Brussels from being besieged, and their canal ... from
being totally ruined, and laid even with the ground. ...'13 William remained
with the army until 3 August, to make sure of his success, and then went to

Dieren by way of Breda. For the rest of the summer he watched his health hunted, and supervised the peace negotiations.

These were not going too well. Despite the fact that their resources were completely exhausted, that they were unable to furnish provisions even for the army in Hungary, to say nothing of the campaign on the Rhine, the imperialists were not yet ready to make peace. The court of Madrid was more serious, but its orders were not obeyed. The Spanish representative at the Rijswijk negotiations, Don Bernardo de Quiros, wanted the fighting to continue. He ignored repeated instructions from his government to secure peace, truce, anything at all that might save Brussels and Barcelona. The admirable defensive tactics of William III had saved Brussels, and though he could not save Barcelona he eventually obtained its return. His diplomatic activities, though they were in the best interest of Spain and more successful by a wide margin than the fondest hopes of the court of Madrid, were seriously hampered by the mulish conduct of de Quiros. Luckily William had two friends at Brussels in the Elector of Bavaria and the Prince de Vaudemont. These succeeded, by bribing the secretary of de Quiros, in discovering that the ambassador had formal instructions of the most pressing nature to conclude peace. Once the existence of these instructions became known to third parties de Quiros had to obey them and one obstacle was out of the way.[14]

A far more important stumbling-block was the question of the personal relations between Louis XIV and William III. Obviously enough, the French King would have to recognize the fact of the Glorious Revolution before there could be any peace. But what was to happen to James II? The English were willing to provide his wife with the £50,000 per annum that would have been her dowry in the event of James's death. This would be enough for the exiled court to live on, if it accepted the money. William had been frightened by the Assassination Plot and was deeply angry at the fact that the Duke of Berwick had been one of the plotters. Other attempts of a similar nature must be expected so long as the Jacobites had a refuge in France. The dowry payments, therefore, would only be made if the late King and his family retired to Italy, and then only if Louis XIV agreed in set terms not to assist them. These conditions were rejected by the French negotiators at Rijswijk, who became much more difficult after the capture of Ath. In order to see whether the French at Rijswijk were obeying orders or whether they were acting independently, Portland opened direct communications with the Maréchal de Boufflers, his prisoner and then his friend after the siege of Namur. The meetings took place in the open fields outside Brussels between the two armies. Even after the first session on 8 July William had a very low opinion of these conversations; but they were in fact to bring about the end of the war.[15]

The most coherent account of the meetings is to be found in the dispatches of Boufflers to his master.[16] At the first meeting Portland gave assurances that William was satisfied with the preliminaries. If an agreement could be reached on those points which concerned him privately, he would then force the Habsburgs to make peace on those terms or else he would abandon them. There were three of these personal issues. In the first place, James II must be named in the Treaty as an enemy of William III. The French must promise not to aid him directly or indirectly, and they must oblige him to go to Rome or some other part of Italy. In the second place, William would not and could not agree to the return of the Jacobites from France as a group. He could not restore their estates, since these had been confiscated by Parliament. And he would be unsafe if he let them all back, since it was only natural to expect that they would continue to plot against his life. As a grace, William would agree to pardon individual Jacobites after the conclusion of the peace if they wished to live quietly in England. The third point was a demand that William should permit no Frenchman to settle in the Principality of Orange. Such a concession, if made in the text of the Treaty, would be a derogation of William's sovereignty.

Obviously there was only one vital point. The Jacobite exiles were soon abandoned by Louis XIV, while William III agreed to the clause about Orange orally rather than in writing. The real problem was the future of James II. At their meeting of 15 July, Boufflers reported that the French could not name James II or make him leave France. They were, however, willing to insert in the Treaty a promise by Louis XIV 'de n'assister directement ni indirectement les ennemis de Mr le Prince d'Orange, sans aucune exception'. The last three words of the formula were new and could only refer to James. According to Boufflers, Portland acceded to the formula, adding that William hoped that once the peace was made Louis would persuade James to leave France of his own accord: 'De sorte que sur ce poinct ... Mr le Prince d'Orange s'en désiste entièrement.'[17] But Portland did not think that he had given in. As he described the interview in a letter to Shrewsbury:

Of the necessity that king James should retire from France, I have spoken very urgently, even from the first interview. But the answer of marshal Boufflers was, that, as this could not be stipulated without naming him, it was not to be expected that the king of France would accede. Upon which I told him, that, in consideration of the king, his master, this stipulation should not be demanded; but I declared that the king, my master, expected the same regard should be paid to him; and that they should cause king James to depart, as soon as a peace should be concluded, without the appearance that the king of France was obliged to adopt this measure. And if this were not done, it must be concluded that he cared not for the duration of peace; since the king, my master, could never suffer king James to be so near England, as this would foment cabals, which the king of France promised, by this article, not to countenance. I even desired him to state this very positively in writing.

He has since spoken to me of it, adverting to the place whither he might be sent, and even mentioning Avignon as the fittest for his residence ... it was better to take the thing as verbally granted, when I could obtain no more ...[18]

Boufflers gave a completely different interpretation to the discussions. He reported that at the next interview, on 20 July, Portland had produced a new and more detailed formula to describe the French promise not to assist William's enemies. At this meeting, the Frenchman added, Portland did not mention his hope that James would be persuaded to leave France voluntarily – 'ainsy il n'y a point d'apparence que l'on releve d'avantage cet article'.[19] Apparently it was not brought up again in the remaining meetings and the two men parted, each thinking that he had made his point.

When the King left the army and went to het Loo he hoped that the peace would soon be made. The only remaining issue of importance, now that his personal affairs seemed to have been settled, was the question of Strasbourg. Would Leopold demand the return of the city, which would be to the advantage of the Empire and of the Protestants in Germany, or would he accept the alternative offered by the French? Strasbourg itself, as a free imperial city, would mean nothing to Leopold. The alternative included lands which would become his personal property, and better terms for his nephew the Duke of Lorraine as well. If Strasbourg remained French it would also remain Catholic, and the pious Emperor could find no objection to that. Leopold might not dare to abandon Strasbourg in any obvious way; but nothing could prevent him from allowing the time limit set by the French to elapse. If the Treaty were not signed by the end of August, the French would be able to set new terms. William suspected that the imperialists and the French delayed purposely, but there was nothing he could do. In due course the time limit did elapse, and the French announced that they would keep Strasbourg; for the rest, their offers would remain open until 20 September. William III hated the humiliation of submitting to French dictation, but he badly needed peace and the terms were better than the military situation would justify. At the last possible moment, Heinsius secured peace for the English, Dutch, and Spanish. Even now the imperialists refused to sign, and a certain further term was allowed them. Finally, reluctantly, and in the most awkward possible manner, Leopold agreed to make peace and the Nine Years War came to an end.

It is not always realized that the Treaty of Rijswijk represented a substantial victory for the allies. By it the overwhelming majority of the *réunions*, both those in the Spanish Netherlands and in the German Empire, were restored by France. By it the French admitted their loss of influence over England, which of course altered the whole balance of power against them. During the summer of 1697 the Elector of Saxony had managed to establish himself as King of Poland despite the efforts of the French candidate, the Prince de Conti: a further and obvious sign of the decline of French prestige. Far more important than this was the fact that for the first time in living memory France had lost a war. Her armies had been contained, defeated; a maréchal of France had been forced to capitulate; a fortress of Vauban had been captured. Undoubtedly the terms would have been better except for the defection of Savoy and the chaos caused by the recoinage in England. Even so, even if the French remained frighteningly strong, they had been clearly and publicly beaten. Almost all the credit belonged personally to William III. He had planned the alliance, planned the war of attrition, conducted its battles in person, shared the losses but the victories too. His position as the greatest man in Europe could not be contested in 1697 or indeed for the rest of his life. It did not matter that victory had not been absolute. No reasonable person could expect absolute victory for what had been, in terms of resources, the weaker side on land and sea. Patience and planning and limitless courage had led the weaker side to a magnificent outcome. For the moment, England and the Dutch Republic might be exhausted by their great effort. The French were more so, and in a particularly humiliating way for Louis XIV. During the Nine Years War he had been obliged to suspend his building operations at Versailles. The fact that in this same period William built and rebuilt het Loo and Kensington and began his great work at Hampton Court was not lost on any of his contemporaries. It was a deliberate and delicious piece of propaganda. Here was a man who could dominate the Republic and rule England at the same time, who had created a personal union between the maritime powers and led it successfully against the greatest power of the continent. And if it was a war to the last guinea, who had had that last guinea? Obviously, the man who could still afford to build palaces.

It is not in England or in the Netherlands that we must seek a true estimate of William's stature in his last years. In both countries his personality obscured his achievements. We must turn to the French, who for once were in the right about him. As Matthew Prior was to report a year later, William's reputation was at its highest in the neighbourhood of Versailles. 'For all the caresses this Court, in imitation of their Master, make to King James it is incredible what true respect and veneration they bear to King William (as they call him) and his merit, and how the soldiers particularly speak of him. "Le premier homme de son métier"! "Le plus beau prince du monde!" are the least things they say of him; ...'20 The poet continued to report his findings in this strain of exuberant loyalty and to heap contempt on Louis XIV: 'The Monarch himself is old, and, I think, has a good mind to be quiet; to say the truth out he is quite cowed by King William, and since the taking of Namur he has as fairly wheeled and run as ever any cock did in a pit: ...'[21] It was a measure of England's isolation and ignorance that her upper classes could not appreciate their good fortune. The people knew, and were grateful. Their leaders saw in the King a standing reproach to their physical cowardice – the number of peers and gentlemen who fought in the war is quite remarkably small. But William was also a standing reproach to their irreligion, their corruption, their lack of culture and learning, their dowdy provincialism. It was too much to bear. At the time the only retort was to accuse the King of being homosexual. Later it became possible to give all the credit to Marlborough and to forget that the first and most hard-won victories belonged to William III. And the army, and the alliance too. No self-respecting country could have admitted the true extent of its debt to William; the debt was too great to repay, and therefore its existence must be forgotten as speedily as possible.

William landed at Margate on Sunday 14/24 November and spent the night at Canterbury. The next day he moved on to Greenwich, where he was greeted by many peers and other persons of quality. On Tuesday the 16th, in brilliant weather, there was a great procession through the City to Whitehall. The Lord Mayor himself in crimson velvet carried the sword, followed by many lesser officials and then by the aldermen and sheriffs. Behind the King there was a long line of carriages of the gentry, drawn by six horses apiece in honour of the occasion. At first there had been plans to erect triumphal arches along the route. Burnet claimed that these were discarded because of the King's natural modesty. The real reason, however, was that no householder would agree to give up his chance to see the spectacle; the arches would have blocked the view from many windows. At Whitehall there was a festive supper. It had been a splendid day, and William was touched by the ceremonies. He drank a toast to all his good subjects. Later he wrote to Heinsius that he had never seen so many people of quality on a single occasion. It was a demonstration of affection and gratitude on the part of the people for their deliverer. The common people at least were devoted to their King, and everyone could be happy that the war was over. But the welcome was no sign that things would go well in Parliament. As in 1688, the people cried 'Hosanna' today; tomorrow it would be 'Crucify him! Crucify him!'[22]

Fundamentally, the conclusion of the Treaty of Rijswijk made it appear that many of the issues with which William III was associated were no longer relevant. He had come nine years before to deliver England from popery and tyranny, and to deliver Europe from the threat of French domination. All these goals seemed to have been achieved. James and his son still lived on at St Germain. When Louis XIV recognized William as King, however, the threat of a Jacobite restoration faded into the background. Even the Jacobites themselves knew that they had nothing to hope for during William's lifetime. In a sense, this increased the danger of an assassination. More meaningfully, it weakened him in his relations with his subjects. Since the prospect of a counter-revolution was now remote, the English could indulge in the luxury of division. The King was personally unpopular with a large portion of the upper classes. High taxes and bad harvests had combined to render the 1690s a time of want, especially in comparison with the prosperity of the previous decade. The money generated by the war seemed all to have gone into the hands of the army abroad or into the pockets of a few foreign favourites or war profiteers at home. With the coming of peace, many felt that they no longer needed William III. The high taxes imposed during the war would have to go on for many years; as time passed, it was becoming more and more difficult for the English to remember why they had chosen to mortgage their future so heavily. They were war-weary, and tax-weary, and most of all weary of their little Dutch master and his rapacious Dutch friends.

The ministry had foreseen this inevitable reaction in the spring. In March, James Johnstone had written to Lord Polwarth: 'My Lord Shrewsbury is now mightily in favour, and there is a verry good understanding betwixt him and my Lord Sunderland, so the secret and weight of the Administration is wholly in them two, and I am told the King will do verry popular things when the peace coms.'[23] It was hoped that the King would make an effort to be more popular by increasing the amount of his entertaining and by making himself easier of access. Unfortunately William may still have felt weakened by his collapse in May; he was certainly bothered at the end of November by a fever which left him with gout in one knee. In any case he refused to consider the idea of doing much more entertaining at this time, and it was not until two years later that he would agree to hold regular entertainments. This weakened his hold on society. His political position was undercut not only by his personal reserve and the apparent irrelevance of his policies but by a serious division among the Whigs. Had the secret and weight of the administration actually resided in Shrewsbury and Sunderland, who had at long last accepted the post of Lord Chamberlain, all might have been well. The two lords, however, were unable to control the activities of the junto. And the junto itself proved to be completely unable to exert leadership in the House of Commons. The split between court Whig and country Whig had been obvious for some time. Fundamentally there was not one split, but two: the first between nobility and gentry, the second between money and land. The court Whigs were unpopular in the Commons for their friendships with the London moneyed men; they could not defend themselves because many of them were in the Lords and the rest went there as fast as they could.

The rapid multiplication of peerages weakened the debating power of the court Whigs and eventually left them almost silent.

It is unlikely that the ministry could have managed the Commons in the years after the war even if it had been united. The country gentlemen were too angry at the Land Tax and at the profiteering of the King's favourites to be willing to listen to reason. Too many fortunes had been created in the last five years for even a strong government to have the confidence of Parliament. In fact the ministry was far from united. Tired out by the work of the long war, suspicious of each other, greedy for the last morsel of profit but terrified of the possibility of impeachment, each man was out for himself. There was no question of putting up a common front, of uniting in defence of the party and of the government. The ministers began the proceedings by devouring their own entrails and then invited the public to eat what was left over. In theory there should have been complete harmony between Shrewsbury and Sunderland on the one hand and the lords of the junto. All were 'Whigs'. Every member of the junto, however, was more or less personally distasteful to William III. He used them as tools, while Shrewsbury and Sunderland were on the much higher level of a Portland or a Heinsius. The junto lords naturally resented the fact that they were being manipulated. They felt that they deserved an even larger share of the King's favour than they were getting, and they expected the two managers to obtain it for them. In the autumn of 1697 they demanded that Wharton should become Secretary of State in case Shrewsbury was forced by ill health to retire. They demanded also that Charles Montagu be admitted to the cabinet council, and perhaps they hoped that he would be made Lord Treasurer.

Of course they failed. Montagu did obtain a present of £14,000 and admission to the cabinet council. But Wharton was out of the question and so was the recreation of the Lord Treasurer's place. When Trumbull resigned his place as Secretary, Sunderland saw to it that Shrewsbury remained and that his under secretary James Vernon succeeded Trumbull. This manoeuvre took care of Wharton. And there were wild rumours that Sunderland was working to make Rochester, not Montagu, Lord Treasurer. The junto determined to revenge itself, which was all too easy. The country gentlemen in the House of Commons thought of Sunderland as the servant of James II, not of William III. When they attacked him as the proponent of a permanent standing army, the bulk of the Whig party simply stood aside and did not defend the Lord Chamberlain. There was no need to do more. Sunderland was so terrified that he resigned at Christmas.

The King was furious at the junto for driving Sunderland into retirement, though he, like everyone else, felt that the Chamberlain might well have shown a little more courage. William was doubly angry at the fact that

Sunderland had been attacked on the issue of the standing army. The country M.P.s still felt, as they had ten and twenty years before, that a standing army was as great a threat to their liberties as it was to their pocket books. The King could not believe that anyone seriously suspected him of a design on the liberties of the English people. He wanted a considerable army and knew that the country needed one. When he returned to England in November he thought he could obtain a standing army of between 20,000 and 30,000 men, but he was unwilling to name a figure or to authorize any of his servants to name one for him.[24] None of the ministers dared name a figure which might seem too small to the King and too large to the people. As a result, although the Commons voted a generous Civil List of £700,000 a year to the King for life, it would only grant £350,000 for the army. This was enough for some 10,000 men, and it did not include a force of 12,000 for the defence of Ireland; but it was much too small. Heinsius had warned William that 10,000 men more or less made no difference in comparison with the political effect of a visibly cordial relationship with Parliament.[25] The advice was sound, but William was not the man to take it. He said openly that the House of Commons had done more in one day than the King of France had been able to do in eight years.[26]

When it became clear that the lords of the junto were not working for him but merely for themselves and against Sunderland, the King withdrew his favour. After Sunderland's retirement William refused to set up any new channels of communication with his ministers. He saw them in groups, and from time to time he had private conferences with Somers; but the bitter letters of the Lord Chancellor dispel any idea that Somers had his confidence. 'Your grace,' Somers wrote to Shrewsbury later about this period, 'knows how resolutely the king declined speaking of his business, to any in his service, all the winter, and that, in such a manner, as if he was not unwilling it should be known.'[27] What William actually did was even worse. On the Irish question, for example, he took the advice of Methuen which he liked and dictated it to the Cabinet Council. As Methuen reported,

> My Lord Chancellor alone seems not to be perswaded to govern our Affairs with the King, the rest of the Ministers seem no great Friends to us and to a great Degree Enemies to Ireland. All the hopes that Offer are that the King looks on the intentions of the Ministers toward Ireland to be very wrong, and contrary to his own Interest directly, & seems capable to take resolutions in his Closset and declare them in the Cabinet Council in such manner as to prevent contradiction. ...[28]

Soon Methuen had lost all respect for the junto. 'I confess it is not very proper to speak of the Ministers here since there are not properly any that at present ought to be so called. But when I use the word I mean My Lord

Chancellour, Mr Montague, Lord Orford, Lord Wharton who are the only persons that are at present in the management of Affairs if it may be said that anything is managed. ...'[29] Not much was being managed. The King and the public blamed Lord Wharton for Sunderland's retirement, and during January there was an attempt to reach some kind of a compromise. If the junto agreed to Sunderland's return, the King might appoint Wharton Secretary and Tankerville Lord President. The bargaining was rendered difficult by a series of accidents. On 4/14 January the palace of Whitehall burned to the ground. The King cared nothing for the buildings, since he could never live there; but he was very much upset at the loss of a collection of metal busts. Most of the furnishings had been saved, but these had been forgotten and the loss was estimated to be on the order of £80,000.[30] Another annoyance was the visit of the Tsar. Peter the Great was a difficult guest, since he did not care to be seen during one of his fits. Often he would break his appointments if he thought that there would be a crowd staring at him. When he did come, the Tsar could talk of nothing but the navy and carpentry, neither of which interested William III. William had already had his fill of the Tsar in August on the continent. The King, however, must continue to be polite and must let it be known that he considered the Tsar to be 'une Personne de jugement et de bon sens'. It was rather difficult to maintain this position after a visit to Kensington, during which Peter became so excited by the sash-weight windows that he had never seen before that he raised and lowered one window more than twenty times.[31]

In the middle of all these distractions, Mr Smith of the Treasury Board announced that he would resign in the event of Sunderland's return to public life. As Vernon wrote, 'I have spoken with Mr Smith, who I find does not disguise his sentiments, that he is so far from consenting to an accommodation with Lord Sunderland, that he declares he will have nothing to do with public business, whenever he comes to be concerned in it. I believe his firmness has made Mr Montague much cooler in the thoughts of it; so that I began to think it impracticable. ...'[32] Although rumours of a possible return of Sunderland to office continued to circulate for months, the matter was now at an end. William then turned to Shrewsbury, who had not come up to town all the winter. The reluctant Duke was well enough to come as far as Windsor, and William went to meet him there on 7 March. By now, rather to Shrewsbury's surprise, the King had abandoned all hope of obtaining Sunderland's return.[33] William clearly hoped to draw Shrewsbury into a greater share of business; but was to be disappointed once more. The Duke began to spit blood, and the King had to return alone to London to face the dragging session of Parliament. 'From here there is no news except that people in Parliament now occupy themselves with private animosities and party quarrels and think little of the national interest. God knows when this Session will end.'[34]

The new French ambassador, the Comte de Tallard, had a good deal of respect and sympathy for the King as another old soldier. He did not think so highly of the English people, and he found them to be in extreme want. It seemed unlikely that the English would have enough money to cashier the army or even to pay the interest on the national debt. Even if they were able to do as much, the effort would leave them so exhausted that 'le Roy d'Angleterre peut estre a compter pour beaucoup a cause de ses qualites personneles mais son royaume doit estre regardé comme un pays sans resource pendant plusieurs années'.[35] He soon discovered the extent of William's unpopularity with the upper classes:

Il s'en faut de beaucoup Sire que le Roy d'Angleterre ny soit le maitre: il y est haï generallement de tous les seigneurs, et de toute la noblesse, je n'oserois pas dire meprisé car en verité ce mot la ne luy convient point, mais c'est le sentiment ou ceux que je viens de nommer sont pour luy.

Il n'en est pas de mesme du peuple qui luy est tres favorable, cependant qu'il est moin que dans les commencemens.[36]

Tallard went on to explain that the English hated William for his Dutch favourites, for the immense gifts he made them, and for Albemarle's sake. The King was also becoming very lazy, dining two or three times a week at Albemarle's lodgings. On one of these occasions he stayed at the table for five hours. Undoubtedly he was slowing down physically, and this might make him seem lazy. He also liked to postpone unpleasant business, and almost all the business this year was unpleasant. Probably, like many ageing people he was becoming shy and frightened of a world he no longer felt a part of. Sunderland's retirement and Shrewsbury's relapse had left him terribly isolated. The only politician in England with whom William could talk now was Somers, and as we have seen he did not choose to do so. In any case, the Lord Chancellor had neither the time nor the inclination to be the King's confidant. Portland had returned to the King's service and was increasing in his favour; but he was away in France, and only Albemarle was left. Keppel was much more interested in Mme de Richelieu, who would bear him a child at the end of 1698, than he was in the King, and it was probably he rather than anyone else who complained if William actually did spend five hours at one meal. He became more and more difficult, and during the summer he absented himself from court. It was a very lonely, weak old man who sealed his papers one July evening at Kensington and slipped away to Holland, leaving orders behind that the papers must not be opened until ten the next morning. In that way he could hope to make himself safe from the demands of the importunate.

Chapter 26

ARMED TRUCE

THE King's goal when he reached the continent on 1 August was the conclusion of a treaty with France for the peaceful partition of the Spanish monarchy. The problem of the Spanish Succession had been part of the background of European diplomacy for almost forty years. For two generations, the elder Infanta of Spain had become Queen of France and the younger had become Empress. In each case, the elder Infanta had renounced her claims to the throne of Spain while the younger had not. Thus it was expected that Spain would eventually go to an Austrian Habsburg when the elder branch of the family died out. Carlos II had always been an invalid and there was no prospect of his having children. Indeed, it seemed unlikely that he would live nearly as long as he actually did. His surprising talent for survival made it possible to take a closer look at the tangled question of the succession. When Don Carlos died, Spain ought to go to the representative of his sister the Empress. This lady had had one daughter, the Archduchess Maria Antonia. On her marriage to the Elector of Bavaria in 1685 Maria Antonia had renounced her claim to the Spanish Succession. Before her death she did so again. Both renunciations were generally considered invalid, and the consensus of opinion was that the little Electoral Prince of Bavaria was the lawful heir to the Spanish throne. In Vienna, however, the renunciations were taken seriously. Leopold felt that he had every right to inherit Spain himself, either as the heir male of Charles V or else through his mother, the younger sister of Philip III. The Emperor was so certain of the justice of his claim that the text of the Grand Alliance of 1689 merely committed England and the Dutch Republic to the support of the lawful heir to the Spanish throne. It seemed superfluous to name that heir as Leopold. Even when the Grand Alliance was renewed in 1695 Leopold did not take the precaution of naming a particular individual. He did not propose to take up the inheritance himself, but to pass it on to his younger son by a third marriage, the Archduke Charles. Perhaps, Habsburg mortality being what it was, he did not care to name his candidate only to be obliged to renegotiate the Alliance whenever that candidate died. Whatever the reason, it was a fatal mistake. In 1698 there was a real question as to whether the Grand Alliance was still in existence. It might not be, in which case William III had no obligations. Even if it did subsist, the Grand Alliance only obliged William III to support the 'lawful heir'; and that, of course, was not the Archduke Charles but the Electoral Prince of Bavaria.

Louis XIV would have agreed that the renunciations of the Archduchess Maria Antonia were invalid. But this did not matter, because to him the renunciations of his wife were also invalid. In the eyes of the French king the Dauphin was not only 'fils unique', his normal encomium, but sole heir to Carlos II as well. It is impossible not to agree with the abstract justness of this claim. Quite unlike the claims raised on behalf of Marie Thérèse herself during the War of Devolution in 1667, or some raised in the *chambres des réunions* in later years, this one was soundly based. The Dauphin was without question the heir in blood. Whether he was also the legal heir depended on the lawfulness of his mother's renunciation. Could she renounce; if she might do so for herself could she renounce for her unborn children; had the renunciation and the will of her father the force of law even if registered with the Cortes, and had they been properly registered? All these minor details could be left to the lawyers. What mattered was the right of the blood, backed up by the strongest army in Europe. For the French, unlike the allies, had not disbanded after Rijswijk.

A change, however, had apparently come over Louis XIV. He was growing old, and his country was growing tired of war. The famines of 1693 were still remembered; financial conditions were extremely serious; and the loss of Louvois and of Luxembourg was not to be repaired. Carlos II, furthermore, just might make a will of his own even if he could not make an heir. The Queen of Spain and the current wife of Leopold were sisters. What was more likely than that the Queen, a notorious termagant, should force her husband to declare in favour of the Austrian candidate, who happened to be her nephew? The situation became serious in February 1698, when Carlos II grew seriously ill. His condition was diagnosed as dropsical – then considered not only fatal but speedily so – on 7 February. As soon as this news reached Versailles, the King acted. He had at this time a high respect for the ability of William III and an exaggerated idea of his strength. Instead of negotiating with the Austrians, who would be too slow, or with the Bavarians who were too weak, Louis XIV opened negotiations with Portland on 14 March.[1]

He soon discovered that Portland had neither the authority nor the talent for such work. Only William III could speak for himself, or for either of the maritime powers. The negotiations were therefore transferred to England. Luckily the Comte de Tallard, the new French ambassador, reached London on 29 March. Detailed conversations between Tallard and the King began in April and continued throughout the summer. When William crossed to the continent Tallard followed him and the First Partition Treaty was signed provisionally on 8 September.[2]

A full discussion of the negotiations would require another volume and will not be attempted here.[3] It is, however, possible to indicate the main out-lines of William's thought on the matter. By March of 1698, when the negotiations began, the English army had virtually ceased to exist and the King was deeply depressed. The politicians seemed completely uninterested in foreign affairs. At the same time the French were deliberately evading the commercial provisions of the Treaty of Rijswijk, so openly that they seemed to be determined on a speedy resumption of the war. Heinsius was so troubled by the situation in England that he suggested that William should keep a sum of two million guilders in cash in the Republic, ready for any emergency. The King agreed as to the wisdom of this advice, but he could not spare the interest needed to borrow the two million guilders.[4] As the negotiations began, William continued to be gloomy and Heinsius full of suggestions. The King felt that nothing could prevent the French from taking the whole of the Spanish Succession if Carlos II were to die in the near future.[5] In military terms this was perfectly true, and it is William's justification for negotiating in the first place. Every foot of ground gained from the French was pure profit. Certainly he did not forget that Louis XIV was not a man of his word; William III had suffered more than any individual in Europe from the faith-lessness of the French, and at that very moment the provisions of the Treaty of Rijswijk were being broken before his eyes. But however dishonest, how-ever much of a bully the French King might be, William had to negotiate. Otherwise the French would take everything.

Heinsius was much bolder, much more bitter against the French, and far more reluctant to abandon the traditional connection with the court of Vienna which the Partition Treaty would involve. Here again we see the divergence between William III, on the way to becoming an Englishman, and the Pensionary of Holland. At no point could it properly be called a split. The two men were ancient colleagues and close friends. They agreed on the importance of limiting French power while also preventing an Austrian take-over at Brussels, if that was possible. Fortunately both goals would be achieved if the Electoral Prince of Bavaria were selected as heir to most of the Spanish inheritance. A few morsels, as few as possible, would be thrown to the other contenders. And English commercial interests must be preserved. The King was later to be subjected to vicious attacks by his enemies in the Commons for not protecting these interests. Jack Howe, Dick Grenville, Robin Harley, and the rest, for the most part men interested in the Levant Company as shareholders or in the cloth export which the Levant Company carried on, could not have been more savage. They would not have changed their ways had they known the truth. But in fact the King did try to get what he could for the English merchants. His first, superficial thought was to demand Dunkirk.[6] As the negotiations continued his plans became more mature. He wanted a commercial treaty for the Dutch and English; but posts would have to be ceded in order to ensure that the treaties were carried out. Since the French continued to violate the commercial provisions of the Treaty of Rijswijk the necessity for these posts was obvious. A list of them is impressive, both as a sign of the King's command of commercial and strategic issues and as proof of his real attention to English affairs. The list included Havana, Gibraltar, Ceuta, Oran, and Port Mahon.[7] These places would give the English enough strength to make sure that any commercial treaty was carried out, even if a French prince should become king of Spain.

They were not so necessary if Spain should go to the Electoral Prince of Bavaria. In that case the maritime powers needed no guarantees. The negotiations proceeded in a very complex style, with the French king offering alternatives: so much of the empire to go to one side if the Electoral Prince should obtain the core of the monarchy, Spain and the Indies; so much to be parcelled out if a French prince were to go to Madrid. At his worst moment, Louis XIV offered no fewer than five separate alternatives for the disposition of the Empire in case the Electoral Prince became King of Spain.[8] He may have had five others in mind to meet the eventuality that his son or one of his grandsons inherited Spain itself. Luckily this was not a real issue. William III and Heinsius were determined to favour the Bavarian candidate if they possibly could. In the end, the bulk of Italy was sacrificed to the French.[9] The lion's share would go to the Electoral Prince, and in case of his death the boy would be succeeded by his own father. Thus William managed to do something for Maximilian Emmanuel, whom he liked. He preserved the barrier in the Netherlands, which was vital both for the Republic and for England. If he gave much of Italy to the French, Italy was far away and the last time the French had controlled it they had suffered heavy losses. In any case, Italy was less important than the whole of the Spanish Succession, even in terms of English mercantile interests. The Levant trade might be threatened by a French Italy; it would be quite ruined if France controlled Spain as well.

Nor was Leopold abandoned entirely. The Emperor was clearly unable to understand his own interests, or to pursue them if they were pointed out to him. William III had supported the Habsburg cause with loyalty and intelligence for more than a quarter of a century. He had been bitterly disappointed at the defection of Savoy in 1696 and the imperialist abandonment of the Italian front which had ensued. He was suspicious of the turn of events in 1697, when the Elector of Saxony had made himself King of Poland, and a papist, with the aid of imperialist men and money. He had been cheated a third time when Leopold had left Strasbourg to the French. All three betrayals had taken place within the space of twelve months. Even so, the Dutch and English governments did what they could to assist the court of Vienna.

Obviously there must be a peace with the Porte if the Emperor was to have any hope of intervening effectively in the west. Interestingly enough, the first reaction of Heinsius to the news of Don Carlos's illness was to push on the negotiations between the Austrian and the Turkish governments.[10] English and Dutch diplomats acted as mediators, and peace was made at Carlowicz early in 1699. On the morning of 7 February 1699, Heinsius was able to send William an express with the news of the conclusion of peace. It was, perhaps, the high point of the Anglo-Dutch alliance. Together the maritime powers had fought the French and won a favourable peace. Together they had been able to impose peace on the northern powers, to end the fighting between the Austrians and the Turk, to divide the Spanish empire so as to avoid the prospect of another great war. Despite the fact that their military resources were inferior to those of the French, the allies had been able to give the law to all Europe. It had been a splendid performance. But it had been a precarious one. William III had no true power base. He was not negotiating from strength, or even from weakness; he was negotiating from nothing at all. He was by now increasingly out of touch with Dutch public opinion. In England, on the other hand, he was almost completely isolated. His army had been destroyed by the opposition in Parliament and it seemed unlikely that the King would be able to regain control there. All of the King's diplomatic successes between 1697 and 1699 were reflections, fundamentally, of the enormous prestige he had gained from the victory at Namur. So long as he continued to be successful, it did not matter that William no longer had an army or navy, or the support of Parliament. But if he were once checked, his basic weakness would become apparent. He would no longer be William the Deliverer, the happy ruler of the united and victorious maritime powers. He would be a tired and ailing old man whose military strength was rather less than that of a middling German princeling.

There was to be no time for rejoicing over the Peace of Carlowicz, over the diplomatic triumphs of the alliance. Later on that same seventh of February Heinsius was obliged to send a second courier with a second express. This one announced that on the night of 5–6 February, the Electoral Prince of Bavaria had died. With the boy had gone the last real chance of peace. It is true that a secret clause of the Partition Treaty provided for the substitution of the Elector of Bavaria if his son died a minor. Once the prince had become King of Spain, such a substitution might possibly have been effected. It was hopeless to attempt it during the lifetime of Carlos II. Now there could only be war, unless a second treaty could be concluded. A new treaty would be very difficult to arrange, since there was no longer any attractive candidate for the Spanish throne. It must now go either to a Habsburg or to a Bourbon. However carefully the Empire was divided, one of the two families would in all likelihood become too strong for the other. Even if Habsburg and Bourbon strength could be precisely balanced in relation to each other, both families would become too strong for their remaining neighbours. The minor powers of Europe would probably lose their independence.

In the event, a second Partition Treaty was concluded; but it was a stillborn child. William's motives in negotiating the second treaty were the same as those which led him to negotiate the first: since France was strong enough to seize the entire inheritance, anything gained by an agreement was a free gift. He who sups with the devil should use a long spoon, and the King has been criticized ever since for using too short a spoon or even for eating with his fingers. Surely the fault lies with the Parliament, which would not provide the King with any cutlery. The people were war weary, and they had a right to be; they had fought their first major continental war in more than two centuries. One would be more sympathetic if this war weariness had been the mood of the entire nation, but it was not. William III was still, by every account, popular with the great bulk of the English. Both the *menu peuple* in the countryside and the middle classes in London supported him. Yet the King was desperately unpopular with the Parliament elected in 1698, which seemed determined to extinguish the last traces of the royal authority by attacks on William's person and policies.

The Parliament of 1698 was an unrepresentative and an increasingly detested body of men; but it held the reins of power, and for the moment neither the King nor the people could check it. In the winter of 1697–98 the politicians had forced through a premature and unwise demobilization. Now the new Parliament went further, reducing the army to 7,000 native-born Englishmen. This infuriated the King, who thought briefly of abdicating and had to send his Blue Guards back to the Republic; and it impoverished the Scots, since the Guards were kept in service on the continent and an equivalent number of Scots in Dutch pay were cashiered. The Parliament was no more popular in London than it was at Kensington. The supplies granted for 1699 were far too small to meet the expenses authorized for the year. William complained bitterly that not a penny had been granted towards the reduction of the debt and that credit had been ruined by the frivolous conduct of the Commons. On all counts it had been a 'miserable session'.[11] The government's creditors might have used even stronger language. Yet while they could sit down with their losses, the King had to go on. He had to get the best terms he could from the French even though he was ill, depressed by the loss of his Guards, and interrupted by such diversions as a trip to Newmarket in April.

At the end of that month the King's personal life was disrupted by a second and this time final retreat by Lord Portland. If William was able to persuade his friend to continue with his French and Scottish work, that was all. The two men rarely even met during the next three years. William's two new private secretaries, John Robéthon and Abel Tassin d'Alonne, could help him with the work that Albemarle was too lazy to do. Nothing could make up for the emptiness and loneliness of the King's life or for the almost complete absence of a ministry. In the spring of 1699 Edward Russell, now Earl of Orford, resigned the place of First Lord of the Admiralty which he had held for five years. Charles Montagu had found himself a cosy nest in the Exchequer, as Auditor of the Receipt, and resigned as First Lord of the Treasury in November. Shrewsbury had done what he could to help out at Newmarket and later continued his efforts as a peacemaker at Windsor, but he was not well enough to act as a minister. Somers remained. But Somers was a man whose importance has been overrated, and he was now suffering from a combination of ill health and bad humour himself. In short, the emperor had no clothes.

Despite his nakedness the King had been making slow progress in the French negotiations and on 11 June he concluded a protocol regarding the division of the Spanish empire. The definitive treaty would have to wait until the Dutch, the imperialists, and the Duke of Lorraine accepted the terms. That night the King left for the continent, his work apparently done. It was oppressively hot, and the night departure gave William some relief from the weather as well as from the importunity of place-seekers. He passed the summer hunting at het Loo in considerable splendour, since each of the courtiers was now required to have two laced coats. These cost £50 apiece, and if a rider was permitted to wear an old one during the hunt he must have a new one to put on afterwards. Apparently this was almost the only pleasure to be had from the summer's work. It was as hot in the Republic as it had been in England; the dogs were in poor shape; and in one week the King missed three stags.[12] William was no longer strong enough to ride a horse of any spirit:

What you said about a horse you thought might please the King for a hunter has encouraged me to acquaint you that the King has lost so many of those hunters which were fit for his own riding and is grown so difficult to be fitted, being only able to ride such nags as are very temperate and have a very easy motion in their gallop that, though he has many fine horses in his stable, he is almost quite on foot. You will do the King a very great pleasure if you can sell him such a nag as is temperate and has an easy motion and that you have already used to hunting.[13]

Apparently a visit from Sophia of Hanover, who was known at court by the not very complimentary nickname of the Old Strumpet, did little to improve anyone's spirits. It was still possible that the Old Strumpet and her son might be passed over in the English succession, in which case the crown might eventually go to the Electoral Prince of Brandenburg. This young man was Sophia's grandson by her daughter; but William III preferred the House of Brunswick to that of Hohenzollern. He had fought alongside George Lewis of Hanover as he had fought alongside his father Ernst August a generation earlier. The King was also a close friend of the aged Duke of Celle, and he seems to have been impressed by the promise of the boy who later became George II. A second house-party during the summer of 1700 convinced the Old Strumpet that she must abandon her Jacobite proclivities and permit her name to be inserted in the Act of Settlement of 1701.

Meanwhile time was passing. According to the agreements made with the French, the Dutch should sign the Second Partition Treaty by 15/25 September whether or not the court of Vienna agreed to it. At first there had been some hope that Leopold would accede to the protocol, which granted his son Charles the bulk of the inheritance. When it became clear that Leopold would not do so, the city of Amsterdam refused to cooperate any longer. Had Amsterdam agreed to the terms, the draft treaty would have been presented to the States General as the suggestion of the States of Holland. Now it must be presented as the suggestion of William III, which would place the King in an embarrassing position. And there was no question of meeting the deadline of 25 September. Actually the final version of the Treaty was not signed in London until 3 March 1700, or at The Hague until 25 March.[14] By that time the French had come to doubt the good faith of the Dutch and English and, with more reason, to doubt their capacity to observe their obligations. Was it really to be expected that the Dutch and the English would be willing to fight Leopold in order to obtain the person of the Archduke Charles, and then to fight the Spanish in order to make the Archduke king? It was not. At least, if William III had misjudged the temper of his two peoples, he had not disregarded their commercial interests. The Second Partition Treaty did make serious efforts to prevent the French from acquiring complete control of Italy. Thus the Duke of Lorraine was to exchange Lorraine for Milan; and by a secret clause the Duke of Savoy was to exchange his own homeland for Naples and the two Sicilies. As Matthew Prior commented in his private journal: '... this I take to have been an Admirable Proposal and a great Instance of the King's Wisdom Since it wou'd have taken off all Objections which Our Merchants cou'd have as to the Hazard of their Levant Trade and tho it did augment the Dominion of France that Augmentation signifyed nothing to us and Holland. ...'[15] Prior was one of the very few Englishmen who knew of the clause concerning Savoy. The Levant Company did not, and when the other terms of the Treaty were published in the summer of 1700 there was a great outcry from that quarter. The Bank of England men, and those who were interested in either of the East India Companies, were enthusiastic about the published terms; but exporters of lead, tin, and wool to Italy or Turkey, or importers of silk, could not know that their interests had been protected.[16]

As it happens, Harley, Seymour, Howe and Grenville were all interested in the Levant trade financially and one of Harley's brothers spent many years in the East in person. This may have given point to their opposition, but it was by no means the whole story. Here was a King, allied like Charles II to France; and far more dangerous than Charles II, since William III was the ruler of the Dutch Republic and the hero of the Huguenot refugees as well. In such circumstances it was essential to fight the King at every point in order to keep the monarchy in its place. During the summer of 1699 many of the Huguenots wished to leave Switzerland and to find a permanent home elsewhere. Ireland would have been an obvious place to put them. Such a step, however, would have been unpopular with the House of Commons. According to Bonnet, 'bien des Parlementaires ne consentiroient jamais que des personnes qu'ils croyent fort attachees au Souverain, s'etablissent en Irlande, ou le Parlement veut contrebalancer le pouvoir du Roy'.[17] And so the poor Huguenots found a refuge at Berlin, while the Parliament men made plans to reduce still further the excessive influence of William III in Ireland.

On the surface, the political situation in the autumn of 1699 was better than might have been expected. Shrewsbury had agreed to return to business once more, this time in the place of Chamberlain, and the Whig Lord Tankerville became First Lord of the Treasury shortly after the King's return to England. As William passed through London he was greeted by bonfires and illuminations, and it was noted that the mob smashed the windows of the houses which had not been lit up for the occasion. Albemarle was confused by this demonstration and hoped that affairs were not in such a bad way as had been thought.[18] The King was determined to do what he could to improve the situation. There was a large ball for his birthday at St James's Palace, given by the Princess Anne. On Monday 27 November there occurred the first of a series of 'apartments' or gambling parties at Kensington. Prudently enough, a series of small guardhouses was erected along the way through the Park so that the winners might hope to get home safely at the end of the party. Their Royal Highnesses reached Kensington at about seven in the evening, to find two tables set for basset and eight others at which the guests might play what they wished. The King greeted the Princess Anne, who acted as hostess, and conducted her to the central table where they played for some time. Then the King rose and went to greet those at the other tables; he refused to let anyone get up as he passed by, acting as if he were a private person. The first evening was a splendid success even though it was 'dry'. Wines were offered at the second 'apartment', when for the first time in this reign the King was at home to all the Members of the House of Commons, their wives and daughters.[19] Nor was this all. The Princess had apartments of her own, for ladies only, twice a week and Lady Jersey also did some official entertaining as the wife of a Secretary of State.

It was undoubtedly the most pleasant Season since the death of the Queen; but a pleasant Season and a pleasant Session are two different things. As early as the end of November the King had some idea of what was about to happen. 'One can as yet say little about parliamentary affairs; superficially they appear to be more moderate than they really are, and I have all too much reason to fear a very bad session.'[20] It was in fact to be the worst he ever faced. Harley's comments, though not made until the following June, are relevant for the entire winter:

The King ought long since to have been convinced, that the persons he employs are not capable of carrying on his service; ... the King's business must miscarry when blasted men had the conduct of it, whose avarice and oppressions would never be borne. ... It was now a general complaint we had no ministry, no right management of public affairs; and if the King did not mind it, a reformation would be wrought in a more disagreeable manner.[21]

Finding a ministry was more difficult than it appeared. The King clung to the Whigs, or to what was left of them, because they seemed more willing to forward his programme than any other combination that he could build up. But the Whigs were now in a minority in the House of Commons, dependent for the passage of money bills on the sufferance of Robert Harley and incapable of putting any other measure through. William for his part still felt that his ministers should attempt at least to put through his measures, an attitude which had been sound doctrine in the early years of the reign. Now, however, the Whigs had developed a new doctrine to the effect that the ministers were only responsible for trying to put through those portions of the royal programme that had a reasonable chance of success:

If they cannot do every thing that the King may think a gratification to him, yet I believe he may depend upon it they will keep the government upon its present basis, which is no small consideration; but then they must be at liberty not to meddle with things they see reason to despair of; ...[22]

Such a theory of the constitution still left the King with the right to frame policy; but he would not be in any position to carry it out. His servants felt their day's work done if they preserved the dynasty. Anything else must be left to chance. William's legislative programme had no hope of success if the game were played by such rules. He had three goals this winter beyond the conclusion of the Partition Treaty and the grant of supply. The first, and

superficially the least contentious, was the modernization of the calendar.
England was already ten days behind the continental reckoning; in 1700 she
would be eleven days behind the times. In the second place, he hoped to
secure a legislative union with Scotland. There would be more trouble over
this, and not only because the last union with Scotland had been the work of
Cromwell. One of a union's most valuable by-products would be the inclusion of a large Scottish contingent in both Houses of Parliament, which
could only add to the strength of the court party in the legislature.[23] The main
reason for a union, however, was the failure of the Scottish Darien scheme
which had led to an outburst of ill-feeling in the northern kingdom. It was
quite likely that Scotland would refuse to agree to any determination of the
succession made in England. In 1699 and 1700 it was even more likely that
the Scots would rise in rebellion, and in fact William did not dare for this
reason return to the continent until July 1700. Neither measure had any hope
of success, if only because each of them had the King's support. The reform
of the calendar had to wait for more than half a century. A legislative union
with Scotland was of more immediate importance and it was to be achieved
within a decade; but for the moment the King's fine plans were blown up by
a jest of Sir Edward Seymour. Seymour announced that he would oppose
the Bill 'for this reason: that a woman being proposed to a neighbour of his
in ye country for a wife, he said he would never marry her, for she was a
beggar, and whoever married a beggar cou'd only exspect a louse for a
portion; ...'[24]

The chief issue of the session, however, was the question of the resumption
of the Irish forfeitures. It is impossible not to connect this question with the
reluctance of the opposition to permit massive Huguenot plantations in
Ireland: they felt that the King was too powerful in that island and that his
authority there must be cut down. The generous terms granted to the
Catholic Irish by the Articles of Limerick, together with the general toleration
given to Catholics throughout his dominions, had made the King the hero of
his papist subjects as he was for other reasons the hero of his Calvinists. The
easiest way to diminish William's influence in Ireland, and to strengthen the
position of the Anglican Ascendancy, was to attack the use the King had made
of the lands forfeited to the Crown during the disorders of 1689–91. There
were also the lands there which had been the private holdings of James II as
Duke of York, to which Anne had some reasonable claim but Parliament
none whatever. A Bill was introduced into the Commons for the resumption
of the forfeitures, and this was something for which there was ample precedent. It was tacked to the Land Tax Bill for the year, although tacks were
irregular and an invasion of the rights of the Lords. When the measure was
finally passed into law the Commissioners sent out to Ireland meddled with

the private estate of the Duke of York, which was perfectly illegal. This did not really matter, since the whole business was a personal attack on the King and on his friends. No one today would argue that the King was wrong in protecting the Catholics as much as he could. His generosity to his former mistress, the Countess of Orkney, was perhaps not in good taste, but there were many more precedents in English history for it than there were for acts of resumption. The King had also given lands to the generals involved in the reconquest, which they had amply deserved. And here came the rub. When it became clear that the Irish forfeitures were to be resumed, the King ordered his servants to obtain the insertion of a clause reserving one-third of the forfeitures for his personal disposal. Though he was warned of the possible consequences, William persisted until the courtiers agreed to move for the clause in the Commons. Dutifully James Vernon proposed the clause; dutifully, Lords Ranelagh and Coningsby and Messrs Smith, Boyle, and Ned Clark came into it. But they received no support, and the only result was that the bill passed the House with a number of impertinent and seditious reflections on the King's conduct.[25] The court was also punished by the passage of a limited Place Bill excluding the Customs and Excise Commissioners from the House of Commons.

Of course there was every precedent in English history for the reservation of one-third to the King, precedents going back to a time before the Norman Conquest. And who had reconquered Ireland? Certainly not the men who were in control of the Parliament of 1698, or the people of England, or even the Parliament of 1690 which had tried to prevent William from undertaking the Boyne campaign. William himself had reconquered Ireland, with the assistance of Solms and Ginckel and Schomberg and Marlborough. Everyone had been paid for his services except the King. Even now, even after his defeat in the Commons, William kept stubbornly to his demand for the third penny which was rightfully his. Amendments were proposed in the Lords by his friends; and on one occasion the King called for his crown and set out for Westminster, presumably to prorogue the session and thus to save the Irish lands. As he went he recovered his self-control; without the Land Tax the government could not be carried on. And so he gave in once more, accepted the Bill, and prorogued Parliament on 11 April. But he was angry enough to dismiss Lord Somers for failing to support him.

On the surface it was a curious, almost a petulant thing to do. If Somers had been languid in his support of the King, Sunderland had been actively opposed to the royal wishes on the question of the Irish forfeitures. Yet Sunderland soon returned to favour. The explanation seems to be that Sunderland consistently advised William III throughout the reign to fall in with the wishes of those who could control the Commons. In 1693 he had supported the Whigs and helped to bring them into power, and he had been far more loyal to that party than the party was to him. Now, since the Whig ministry was smashed, Sunderland had accepted the inevitable and was backing the new leaders. The King's only hope, in Sunderland's opinion, was to turn towards the Tories and to try to educate them to their responsibilities once they were in office. At the time, the King would not accept the full burden of this advice. One of his personal reasons for dismissing Somers was that he wished to appoint his friend Methuen Chancellor of England. Unfortunately Methuen was not an acceptable candidate either to the Bar or to the politicians. He had to be satisfied with the position of Chancellor of Ireland, while the Tory Sir Nathan Wright was selected as Keeper of the English Seal. To balance this, William made a number of whiggish household appointments and assured the lesser Whigs still in office that they need not fear any further changes. But when he attempted to use this language to Lord Orford, who though out of office was still influential, the Earl replied bluntly that he did not know that any Whigs still remained in the King's service.[26] This was extreme, like most of Orford's conversation; but it was clear to everyone save the King that there would have to be a Tory administration. Such a ministry would be obnoxious to William III for many reasons. He had been willing to make Lonsdale, the former Sir John Lowther, Privy Seal, some time before. Lonsdale was not too much of a party figure. Sir Charles Hedges, Godolphin, and Rochester were far more partisan and were bitter medicine. For months the King refused to submit. It was not until the autumn that he agreed to make Hedges Secretary of State, and the beginning of December before Godolphin was restored to his former place at the Treasury. Even then it was another week before Rochester was appointed Lord Lieutenant of Ireland, and a further week passed before William took their advice and dissolved the Parliament of 1698. The new one did not meet until the first week of February 1701. It was a remarkably awkward and ungracious performance from first to last, and the King's obvious reluctance cost him most of the benefits to be expected from the change.

It is undoubtedly true that as he grew older William III became much harder to serve. This was a family failing. His grandmother the Princess Dowager had been extremely difficult in old age, and in the last ten years of his life the King's gruffness and ill temper grew on him apace. William and his servants had much to suffer from his poor broken body. His later portraits show him to have been thin to the point of emaciation, and during the winter of 1699–1700 his condition gave cause for general alarm. As better weather came on in the spring the royal appetite improved, and this was always a sign of relative good health. Now, however, there was a new problem. William's legs began to swell. His condition was diagnosed as dropsical, like that of

Carlos II of Spain; in both cases a speedy death was freely predicted. In the event, both Kings survived for a surprisingly long time. But it could be only half a life, and William III was a querulous and unpleasant patient.

Entirely apart from his progressive ill health, the King had legitimate political reasons for refusing to take Sunderland's advice when it was first offered him. He hoped for a national ministry such as he had had in the first years of the reign. He feared that the Tories were still wedded to the 'blue water' school and would refuse to come to the aid of the Dutch in the event of a land war. In the summer of 1700 the King ordered Rooke to make a demonstration at Copenhagen, and this sternness did succeed in bringing the Danish aggressors to heel and so limit the fighting that had broken out in the Baltic. Would the Tories have permitted the expedition to sail if they had been in office? Another reason for the King's reluctance was his personal dislike of Rochester and Seymour, which dated from the late 1670s. Godolphin was no longer William's friend; the King had lost confidence in him by 1694 and there is no evidence that their relations ever improved afterwards. Perhaps, if he had retained freedom of action, the King would never have submitted to the humiliation of forming a ministry out of such uncongenial material. When he finally managed to cross to the continent in July the Whigs were out but the Tories had by no means replaced them. All still depended on the turn of the cards.

When the deck was cut, the card turned up proved to be the queen of spades. It was not the death of either of Europe's most famous invalids, the Kings of England and Spain. Late in July the frail Duke of Gloucester, Anne's only child, died after an illness of little more than twenty-four hours. Now the whole Protestant Succession was in danger. The King succeeded in making his arrangements with Sophia of Hanover while she was his guest at het Loo. But it would be more difficult to come to an agreement with the English parties, or to form an administration which could enact a statute formally placing Sophia in the line of succession. When he returned to England in October William found that Sunderland had been correct, and that there was no choice. Slowly and as unpleasantly as possible the King admitted that he was now the prisoner of the Tories and assumed the difficult role of marriage broker between the Old Strumpet and the English Parliament. But now the queen of spades was turned a second time.

Chapter 27

THE MAN OF GOD'S RIGHT HAND

ON the evening of 11/12 November William received news that Carlos II had died, and that in his last days he had made a Will in favour of one of the sons of the Dauphin. William thought it likely that the Emperor would now agree to sign the Partition Treaty, while the French would be even more eager than before to obtain Savoy and Piedmont for themselves in exchange for Naples and the two Sicilies.[1] The English party leaders in general also thought that France would accept the Treaty. Since, however, they were not aware of the proposed exchange, many of them would have preferred that Louis XIV should accept the Will. A French Naples would ruin the Levant trade. By the next post they found that their wishes were granted. The Duc d'Anjou, who at sixteen spoke no word of Spanish, was being greeted at Versailles as Philip V. When William consulted Rochester and Godolphin individually about this startling development, each of them replied that it was the best thing that could have happened. William would now be able to escape from the embarrassing position he had put himself into by the Partition Treaty which was so unpopular with the nation. Both of them felt that Anjou, far away in Spain and surrounded by a Spanish council, would become a good Don.[2] The markets in London and Amsterdam agreed, and both rose. William, however, knew better. 'We must now admit that we have been duped', he wrote to Heinsius. '... I am convinced, that if this Will takes effect, England and the Republic are in the greatest danger of being completely lost.' He felt that war must come, but that the initiative would have to be left to the Emperor. The least that Leopold could properly do would be to seize control of Milan and try to make himself master of all Italy. William was particularly worried about the situation in the Spanish Netherlands and about the safety of the Dutch garrisons there.[3]

The French did their best to justify their conduct. The Treaty, they said, had been made to secure the peace of Europe, but it could not achieve that end because of the refusal of the Emperor to enter into it and of the Spanish people to permit the division of their monarchy. Therefore the acceptance of the Will would achieve the purpose of the Treaty, though in a different form. At first their protestations were believed by the general public. Even the Dutch, for a time, approved of the institution of Philip of Anjou. It was not

until the end of November that they began to understand what the consequences might be. The English were even slower: '... the people remain as
stupid as ever', was William's gloomy comment.⁴ At first there was some
hope that the Barrier could be preserved. The Elector of Bavaria might
demand the Spanish Netherlands as a fief, in payment of the enormous sums
of money owed him. William thought that this could hardly be obtained,
but he hoped that the Elector might be confirmed as Governor of the Netherlands for his lifetime.⁵ The real difficulty was that the barrier fortresses were
untenable, even if the Elector supported the Dutch. William and Heinsius
did not discover for some months that Maximilian Emmanuel would choose
the French side; but this made no difference. Even had he remained loyal,
the garrisons were trapped. Maximilian Emmanuel was only one man. The
rest of the government was Spanish, and they – particularly the army officers –
hated the Dutch.

For the moment there was very little that the King and Heinsius could do.
They agreed that it would be necessary to recognize the Elector of Brandenburg as King in Prussia, and that it would be good to obtain an alliance with
Denmark. But this would not be enough to protect the Republic from what
seemed to be the imminent prospect of invasion, especially since the French
had started moving their troops up towards Longwy and Thionville and
were busily raising new forces. The only useful assistance would come from
the Emperor; but it might well come too late. And it would be very difficult to
make an agreement with the Emperor, since he wanted an offensive alliance
together with the promise of all Italy and the Spanish Netherlands.⁶ Of course
the English and Dutch would be expected to pay for a good portion of his
war expenses. Meanwhile the Republic would be completely exposed if it
signed an offensive alliance. Her own army had been reduced; the English
army scarcely existed. Before the imperialists could come to her aid the
Republic might well have been overrun by the French. At the end of December both William and Heinsius were convinced that they would have to
recognize the Duc d'Anjou as King of Spain in order to gain the time needed
to rearm. But if they did, they might lose the Emperor entirely. It might be
more prudent to make an alliance with the French and Spanish, setting conditions which would ensure the continuance of the barrier. This possibility
was suggested by the Swedish ambassador at The Hague, Lilienroth. As an
alternative it presented difficulties of its own. Lilienroth was in the French
interest and could not, therefore, be trusted. Secondly, what conditions could
be required that might prove of value? Even if the Dutch were permitted to
keep their barrier fortresses, which seemed hardly likely since the French were
boasting that they would not allow the Dutch a foot of ground, not even a
windmill, the fortresses could not be defended. If the Dutch withdrew their

men from the Spanish Netherlands on condition that the French kept their own forces at home, it would only take the French two days to occupy Flanders at any time they wished to do so. The King and the Grand Pensionary did not know which way to turn.

They were helped out of their predicament by the insensate stupidity of the Spanish Regency. Without waiting for the new King to reach Madrid, the Regents asked Louis XIV to undertake the conduct of the Spanish government and ordered all their viceroys to obey his orders as if they were those of Philip V.[7] The effect was immediate. Tallard had returned to London in December. His first reports were that the English in general were for peace, and that Lord Rochester in particular was in favour of accepting the Will. A certain number of the 'Presbyterians' – that is, Whigs – were in favour of war as the only means of regaining office; but Tallard thought that even they had such a distrust of William III that they would not permit him to have an army again.[8] Within a fortnight there had been a complete change. The news of the orders sent out by the Spanish Regency persuaded people that, indeed, there were now no Pyrenees. The new King of Spain would not be independent; he would be nothing more than a viceroy for his grandfather.[9] The talk of war became much louder in England.[10] The Dutch were equally alarmed by the news. They soon had another shock. To replace the moribund Comte de Briord, Louis XIV had decided to send d'Avaux back to The Hague. No greater enemy of the welfare of the Republic could have been found. The appointment could only be taken as a threat. The Dutch became more and more convinced that they would soon be attacked. Very secretly they began to rearm.

At the beginning of the year it seemed likely that William III would not live to see the new forces. In Christmas week he had a bad spell. It was noticed that his appetite was poor, that he had to lean heavily on his cane as he walked, and that he looked ill.[11] He was soon better, but even so his doctors said publicly that he did not have long to live. He kept to his regular schedule, though on one occasion it took him three-and-a-half hours to make the trip from Hampton Court to Kensington through snow and ice for a Council meeting. He was so weak, however, that when he arrived he had to be carried up the palace stairs in a sedan chair.[12] During the spring William's health continued to fluctuate. One day it would be better, the next day worse; but the general trend was definitely frightening. His legs continued to be swollen. Most people attributed this to dropsy and felt that it would soon prove fatal. Others, including Lord Galway who suffered from the same complaint, were more optimistic and merely advised the King to change his diet, which consisted very largely of liquids. He drank beer and soup regularly and had his meat boiled and served in broth; if only he would be more English and change to roasts! Early in March he began to suffer from gout in his left hand. The doctors thought of this as a blessing which might well cure his other problems. At first William agreed with them, but he suffered greatly from the pain and was soon saying that he would rather have lost an arm or a leg. As the weather became milder and he got out more often, his health began to improve. In April he started to go to Hampton Court every week-end. Exercise helped to reduce the swelling in his legs. He also took pills to promote the evacuation of fluids.[13] No one knew whether the credit for his recovery should be given to William's exercise or to the pills. It did not matter. What was important was that he seemed to be on the mend.

The state of the King's health was immensely important, not alone for England or the Republic, but for the world at large. Would there be peace, or war? Would it be possible to maintain the alliance between England and Holland, on which the defence of European liberty depended? Who would be named heir to the throne of England, now that the little Duke of Gloucester was dead? The answers to all these questions depended on whether William could live another year. The uncertainty raised the tone of English political warfare to the highest pitch of hysteria. As the election returns came in during January it seemed likely that the Whigs had secured a narrow majority in the House of Commons. Rochester, as the leader of the Tories, was blamed for not having paid sufficient attention to the elections and began to lose credit with his own party.[14] But the situation was complicated by the fact that both the old and the new East India Company had campaigned in force, electing more than sixty 'nawobs' by means of direct bribery and displacing just so many persons of better family who were considered to have a prescriptive right to a seat in the House.[15] Even if the Whigs and Tories did not unite to oust this India interest by voting against the nawobs when the inevitable election petitions came before them, no one could really tell much about the complexion of the House until it had sat for ten or twelve days.

It was, therefore, amid great confusion that the King met Parliament on 6/17 February. He had two objects in mind, resistance to France and the settlement of the English succession. On both points his views were fixed. He felt that war was the only alternative to French mastery of Europe, and he wanted the throne one day to go to his favourite relative the Electoral Prince of Hanover.[16] But he was careful not to express his own opinion in his opening speech to the two Houses on the 11th. He wrote to Heinsius that day: 'I thought it best simply to propose the problems for their deliberation, without expressing my own opinion for the moment, thinking that this will have more effect than if I told them what I think; since, God save the mark, they have paid very little attention to it hitherto.'[17] By now the King had come to feel that the 'war party', as Tallard called it, might prevail in the Commons. For some time he had felt that it would be necessary to recognize Philip of Anjou as King of Spain in order to gain time. But the strength of the Whigs in the election, and their eagerness for immediate war, surprised him; and on 9/20 February he wrote an express to Heinsius ordering him to stop the Republic from formally recognizing Philip V.[18]

He was too late. Amsterdam, like the English Tories, feared war. The City would do almost anything to avoid giving provocation to Louis XIV. Its argument was that the Dutch could not fight or pay taxes with enthusiasm if they felt themselves to be the aggressors. If they recognized Philip V, then the French would have no legitimate grounds for attacking the United Provinces. This might keep the peace. But if the French attacked anyway, then the Dutch could make war with a clear conscience. Amsterdam backed this sophistry with guns of a larger calibre: it would not vote for rearmament until after Philip V had been recognized. By the time William's letter, delayed by bad weather, reached The Hague, Amsterdam had had its way.[19] For Dutch political purposes it was right to make the step; the country was more united by it. But in England, the recognition was disastrous in its effects. The Whigs were dismayed, the Tories exultant.[20] There was only one thing that the King could do. He and the Dutch ambassador van Geldermalsen concocted a memorial which the ambassador then solemnly presented to him as if it came from The Hague, and the King with equal solemnity passed the memorial on to the House of Commons. The House responded even more warmly than William had expected. Unanimously the Members begged the King to make all the alliances he might judge appropriate for the security of England, the maintenance of religion, and the peace of Europe, promising to support him with their lives and fortunes. The House did not even, as the King had feared, ask him to recognize Philip V. Tallard reported that some of the Church party had tried to argue but had scarcely obtained a hearing.[21]

Since the Address of the House also included an assurance of support in case the King, acting under the provisions of the Treaty of 1678, sent troops for the defence of the Dutch, William had every reason to be pleased with the success of his forged memorial. He was so delighted that when the Address was presented to him by more than 250 M.P.s he made an unusually charming reply. After the ceremony he asked them to form a large circle so that he might see each of them. Then he took one of them by the hand, asking after his health, and afterwards invited them all to stay for a collation. There were three large tables of excellent food and unlimited amounts of champagne and burgundy. It was not often that William tried to be popular. The startled M.P.s made the most of their opportunity. A few of them stayed at Kensington until four the next morning, and the great majority went home drunk.[22] Nor was this the only display of royal affability. When the Countess of Rutland attended one of William's gambling parties at Kensington a month later, she reported to her husband that the King had talked pleasantly with her twice, and that he had walked over a stool rather than make her give way when he passed on.[23]

There were some people whom the King could not charm. Rochester and Godolphin had not been consulted about Geldermalsen's memorial and thought that it would go no further than the cabinet council; they were surprised and annoyed when William sent it to the Commons.[24] Godolphin's position at this time was curious. He was thought to be in favour of the recall of the Prince of Wales, and to be using his powers of office so as to lower credit. If he succeeded, this would obviously make war impossible and might also wreck the plans for the Hanoverian Succession. In the Commons the Tories were spreading tales to the effect that the King was in favour of recognizing Philip V. In fact the state of William's health alone would have been enough to disturb credit, to say nothing of the uncertainty of the situation abroad. And the last Parliament, by refusing to make good the deficiencies on previous bills of supply, had defrauded the public and contributed substantially to the gloomy financial position of the government.[25] Tallard considered that the Address of the Commons had made war inevitable; but he thought that it could not last two years without a revolt, considering the state of England's finances. The only good thing to be said was that the French position was even worse. In March the French government had had to offer 14 per cent to obtain even four or five million francs.[26] Financial conditions were generally disturbed in 1701 and there is no real proof that Godolphin was trying to upset the market. Whigs, however, were certainly refusing to lend money unless he was dismissed.

Rochester and Godolphin were in a difficult position. The first, in particular, had been extremely outspoken in favour of accepting the Will of Carlos II and against any step that might lead towards war. He seemed in danger of losing control over his own party because of the outcome of the elections, though these had in fact turned out better for the Tories than they at first thought. They were now in a majority in the Commons on every issue but that of opposing France. Although the two men were theoretically at the head of the government, they saw the King surrounded by Whigs and feared that he preferred that party to their own. It was particularly irritating to Rochester that William continued to admit Methuen to his closet for long conferences, an apparent sign that the Earl might soon lose his place as Lord Lieutenant of Ireland. Rochester and Godolphin tried to bully Methuen into returning to Dublin, or even into going to Lisbon, in March. Methuen went to the King and told him that he was ready to go, but William would not hear of it.[27] Even more ominous was the rumour that Princess Anne was in favour of the Hanoverian Succession and bitterly irritated at the intrigues of the Tory chiefs.[28] If they had neither the favour of the setting nor the rising sun, the Tories were in real danger.

It was not, of course, a monolithic party of the modern type. Although the evidence is very obscure, it is possible to infer that Rochester and Godolphin were actually dallying with the idea of restoring the Prince of Wales at this time. Certainly they were on very bad terms with Anne and Marlborough, and even more certainly they were unable to control their friends in the House of Commons. These men were in the worst of positions. Should William live for another year or two, it would be political suicide not to support rearmament. If, however, he were to die in the immediate future there would be another election; and the next sovereign, whoever it might be, would hate the memory of William III as the public hated his taxes. The leaders in the Commons, Harley and Sir Edward Seymour, did not work well together and this added a further complication to the tangle. The best that could be done was to support William's policy, grudgingly and as little as possible, while attacking his person. Thus the Commons did vote to support the Dutch under the terms of the Treaty of March 1678, by sending them 10,000 men. And it did pass the Act of Settlement which formally named Sophia of Hanover the next heir to the crown after William and Anne. But the Settlement was so unpopular with the Commons that a number of personal insults to the King were tacked to it in the hope that the bill would fail.[29] It would be unwise to read into the clauses of that famous measure any deep insight into the nature of an ideal constitution. The clauses which restricted the powers of a future foreign-born ruler looked to the past, not the future. By forbidding such a king to leave the country without Parliament's permission, or to make war for the benefit of his foreign estates, or to make a foreigner a member of his Council, or to conduct business elsewhere than in his Privy Council, Parliament was attacking William III personally. The useful portions of the Act of Settlement, such as the provision for the independence of the judiciary, had already been put into practice at the beginning of his reign. But the useless insults, which made up the larger portion of the Act, had to be dropped in Anne's reign before they ever came into effect, simply because they could never work and no longer had any relevance. The true nature of the Act of Settlement is best seen by the tone of the rest of the session. The Commons, not content with insulting the King, determined to rob him. Although he had been granted £700,000 a year for life for his Civil List, the Commons reduced this to £600,000 in 1701. In theory the reduction could be justified by the death of the Duke of Gloucester, which saved the King £15,000 a year and by the refusal of Mary of Modena to accept the strings attached to her grant in lieu of dowry, which saved him £50,000 more. In fact the King was left without enough to live on, and arrears to his servants were still being paid at least as late as 1718. At the same time the Commons determined to impeach Somers, Portland, Orford, and Halifax (Charles Montagu) for their share in the second Treaty of Partition. The debates on the impeachments offered a splendid opportunity to carry personal abuse of the King to new heights. In the Lords, Rochester claimed that the Treaty was contrary to the laws of England and so 'impertinent' that the ministers should have refused to obey the King's commands. Godolphin was reported to have referred to it as 'aussi iniuste que sot'. Nottingham called it the most pernicious treaty since that by which John had subjugated England to the papacy. Devonshire was considered moderate when he did not insult the King, but merely demanded the heads of his ministers.[30]

In all this Rochester and Godolphin distinguished themselves by the intemperance of their language. It was so bad that they were generally suspected of a set design to rob the King of all his remaining prestige.[31] In the short run the campaign had some tactical success. Since William kept silent, his 'friends' and those who were not committed to any party joined what seemed to be the stronger side.[32] During April the Tories were saying that they were not obliged to send the 10,000 men to aid the Dutch until they were actually attacked, and not at all if they were the aggressors.[33] The Tories were so clearly in the ascendant that the King was finally obliged to recognize Philip V as the Spanish monarch. This gave the party a new advantage while it confused and outraged the Whigs. They began to speak as if there were two conspiracies, one between the King and the Tories for their destruction, and a second between the King and the French.[34] The situation became so unpleasant that William intervened by sending a second memorial of the States General to Parliament, this time an authentic one. Like its predecessor, the memorial operated with remarkable success.[35] There was now no possibility that the 10,000 men would be refused. The King himself had always felt they would be provided, but the Dutch correspondents of Heinsius in London had been far more gloomy

There was, of course, a political risk in sending the 10,000 men to Holland. In the event of William's death their commander would be able to dictate the succession, whatever the law might be. The Whigs were worried that if Marlborough were appointed to the command, he might prefer the Prince of Wales to the Princess Anne. Only if the country were actually at war would the Whigs be safe from proscription and a restoration.[36] Actually, of course, Marlborough had no intention of supporting the Prince of Wales and the Whig suspicions were nothing more than hysteria. They had been hysterical before in 1678 and would become so again in 1714. The three crises have a fundamental similarity. In 1678 a change of dynasty seemed likely, in 1701 and in 1714 it was certain. Those who were on the winning side would get the spoils, the losers would in all probability go to the block. There was, then some justification for the hysteria. But there was no alternative to Marlborough. Ormonde was compromised because he was Rochester's son-in-law. Galway was a foreigner, Cutts only a lieutenant-general. Bellasis was neither loved nor esteemed, and was considered to combine slight capacity with great avarice. Marlborough was appointed to command the 10,000 men, as he had to be.

The Tory attacks on the King seemed to work. The party managed to stay in office and even to keep his approval, at least so far as the public could tell. They needed it. Their unpopularity had been growing ever since April, when the gentlemen of Kent had publicly attacked the conduct of the House of Commons and had been arrested for their pains. The general hatred for the Commons grew as the spring progressed and was intensified by Defoe's famous Legion Memorial. Pasquinades began to appear. 'Resolved, that the arbitrary power resides in the House of Commons.' 'Resolved, that Lord Somers be hanged because he knows our laws too well. ...' 'Resolved, that the three kingdoms are for sale, Sir Edward Seymour to carry the news to the King of France.'[37] To protect themselves from the general feeling the Commons felt obliged to pass a measure limiting their privilege in actions for debt. This took away one important grievance of the people and was a far more real reform than the subsidiary clauses of the Act of Settlement. This measure and the ridiculous collapse of the impeachments when the Commons refused to appear before the Lords to press their charges were not, however, enough to restore the popularity of the Tories. They had to beg the King to come down in person to give his assent to the Act of Settlement in words that might be a fig-leaf to cover their nakedness. William did more, and gave them a whole cloak by means of a strong speech that confounded the Whigs.[38] It was apparently a concerted arrangement, and the Tories were left with a bill to pay. At Nottingham's house a group of the leaders, including Rochester, Godolphin, Abingdon, Sir Edward Seymour, Sir Christopher Musgrave, and Simon Harcourt, decided to pay their debt by addressing the King to reduce the exorbitant power of France. Sir Bartholomew Shower, in proposing the Address in the Commons, was carried away and used stronger language than had been planned. But the Tories had to go through with the Address anyway, and they were treated almost as well in June as they had been in March. After the King had replied to the Address in very warm terms, he engaged in conversation with Sir Christopher Musgrave and said that he was happy to see him in good health. Sir Christopher, forgetting the political struggles of the past thirteen years, was so overwhelmed that he asked permission to kiss William's hand. It was the first favour he had asked in this reign, and it caused a corresponding amount of attention.[39] On this insincere note of comedy the session ended.

No definite steps for the defence of Europe could be taken without the support of Parliament. During the spring of 1701 the King and Heinsius, therefore, had perforce to wait on events; and, for the moment, the French could do what they wished. Early in February French troops occupied the Spanish Netherlands and the barrier was no more. 'It is now more than twenty-eight years', William wrote bitterly, 'that I have worked without interruption to save that barrier for the Republic, sparing neither my pains nor my person, and you can easily imagine how angry I am to see it lost now in a single day without firing a shot.'[40] But nothing could be done without Parliament. For a short while it looked as if the Dutch garrisons in the Netherlands would be made prisoners of war by the French. Luckily they were released after the United Provinces recognized the new King of Spain. Louis XIV seems to have hoped that he would be allowed to take the whole of the Spanish inheritance without a war. And well he might have, if he had played his cards better. They were excellent cards. If he had been willing to offer the maritime powers some assurances as to their trade and their barrier in the Netherlands; if he had coupled this with some negligible offer of satisfaction for Leopold such as Milan, which as an escheated fief of the Empire was the portion of the inheritance to which he had most right; then it might well have been impossible for William to reform the Grand Alliance. But Louis XIV would not offer any reasonable satisfaction, to the English or the Dutch or the Emperor. Perhaps the French thought they could keep everything. More likely they felt war to be inevitable, and by their conduct they made it so.

In February d'Avaux arrived at The Hague to replace the Comte de Briord. He asked the Dutch what they felt they needed for their security, advising them underhand to set their price low. William III had already sent over his demands for a barrier: Luxembourg, Namur, Mons and Charleroi for the Dutch, Nieuwport and perhaps Ostend too for the English, and a flat promise that no French troops would be sent into any of the remainder of the Netherlands.[41] The Dutch disagreed with his advice. For local political purposes, they found it necessary to ask for one town after another so as to protect each exposed group in the Republic. Eventually they demanded for themselves, in addition to the four places mentioned by the King, Venloo, Roermond, Stevensweert, Dendermonde, Damme and St Donaes.[42] William III disapproved of this demand, which he thought to be bad tactics. There were so many towns on the list that the French would think that it was put forward only as a bargaining counter.[43] If four places had been demanded, and four only, then there might have been a better chance of getting all of them. William, however, was not in control of the negotiations or of Dutch policy. His advice was treated with respect and his support, as King of England, was essential to the Dutch government; but his position as Stadhouder had by now almost completely disappeared. It is quite clear from the correspondence that ever since the Rijswijk negotiations the Grand Pensionary had had the initiative in his relations with the King. The firm of William and Heinsius had gradually and amicably changed its name to become the firm of Heinsius and William. The Grand Pensionary remained deferential, even obsequious;but he was definitely the senior partner.

Negotiations with d'Avaux dragged on fruitlessly. All that the French would offer was a guarantee of the treaty of Rijswijk, which was both irrelevant and completely useless, since that treaty was still in force without any guarantee. The difficulty was that until England and Holland declared war they would find it hard to obtain allies.[44] Some of the smaller states would not dare to declare against France unless they were certain of protection. Others, like Denmark, demanded subsidies which they knew Parliament and the States General would refuse to pay before fighting actually began. Almost the only friend that the Dutch could be sure of in the spring of 1701 was the Elector Palatine, who could scarcely be called a great military power. The fundamental military situation had, of course, changed very sharply against the French since 1697. The Emperor's peace with the Turk had released all his energy and attention for a war in the west. At the same time, the Spanish inheritance weakened the Bourbons as it strengthened the Dutch. The mismanagement of the Spanish government under Carlos II had been so great that it would take years before French experts could wring any money out of it. For some time the French would have to defend the Spanish possessions at their own expense. In 1701, however, the immediate military situation was quite different. The Dutch were exposed to the dangers of a war in which they might be overrun before they could rearm. Their cautious diplomacy did give them the time they needed, but at the expense of some friends whom they had hoped to gain. Portugal, for example, found herself obliged to choose the French side for the moment but rejoined the allies shortly after the war began. A more permanent loss was the support of the Elector of Bavaria and his brother of Cologne. The enmity of the latter prince, who was also Bishop of Liège, was made more important by the defection of Anton Ulrich of Wolfenbüttel and the wavering of the Bishop of Münster. The Dutch were virtually under blockade. The support of Austria and Brandenburg, as in 1672, might come too late to be of use. In fact, Heinsius and the generals had to discuss the possibility of a campaign like that of 1672. The generals reported, gloomily, that the enemy could reach Utrecht as easily as he had twenty-nine years before. And Athlone, not only a general but also a leading noble of that province, predicted that if the French reached the walls of Utrecht the city would surrender now as it had then. Whatever the long-term prospects of a war might be, the immediate facts were frightening. The United Provinces were ringed by enemies on the landward side.

Fortunately the French conduct was provocative enough to irritate the English and Dutch, without being actually harmful. As in the 1680s, the French managed to obtain the worst of both worlds. Their haughtiness inspired resentment, not fear; while their territorial gains aroused the hatred of Europe without giving France real protection. They did not attack in the spring of 1701, when they would have met little resistance. Thus the French gave the allies time to rearm and regroup, and at the same time provided plenty of reasons for doing so. English and Dutch ships were excluded from the ports of the Spanish empire, and it was announced that the important Spanish wool crop would henceforth be reserved for French weavers. Nothing could have been more irritating, short of open war; but it was not backed by force. When the Austrians finally decided to do as William III asked, and make war in Italy in the hope of drawing the allies in after them, their army under Prince Eugene of Savoy met with success near Carpi and again at Chiari. Nor were French diplomatists much more successful in the north of Europe than Catinat and Villeroi in Italy. In June the English and Dutch were finally able to persuade Denmark to join them. The Elector Palatine was already a sure friend, and soon afterwards the Bishop of Münster chose the allied side.

In July the King, having prorogued Parliament, was finally able to cross to The Hague. He took Marlborough with him, not only to command the English troops but to negotiate as well. There was nothing exceptional in Marlborough's appointment. For many years William had systematically won over opponents to his side by giving them responsible diplomatic appointments. These were flattering, and at the same time educational. In this manner William had won over van Leyden van Leeuwen after 1678 and Heinsius himself in 1683. Like them, Marlborough would learn to appreciate the justice and intelligence of William's attitude, while becoming personally committed to its support. The King himself appears to have taken very little part in the negotiations of the Grand Alliance. Leaving Heinsius and Marlborough at The Hague, William insisted on going in person to review his troops. Since he had never fully recovered from his illness of the previous winter the courtiers were horrified, but there was nothing they could do except pray.[45] After a tour of the southern frontier William went on to het Loo, where he gave an audience to the imperial ambassador Wratislaw.[46] For the most part, however, the negotiations were carried on in The Hague and the King confined his role to that of giving advice by mail.[47] The Grand

Alliance, by which England and Holland joined with the Emperor for the defence of their joint interests, was perhaps too favourable to Leopold. It promised him all the Spanish islands in the Mediterranean and possessions on the Italian mainland, if only he could take them. On the other hand, the maritime powers might keep what they wished of their conquests in the West Indies, and they were assured of a barrier in the Spanish Netherlands. The Treaty was signed on 7 September, and a month later the allies entered into an arrangement with Sweden which was destined to be rendered fruitless by the progress of the Great Northern War. More useful were arrangements for the employment of the troops of Brandenburg, Hesse, Hanover, and Celle.

William's absence in the country was as calculated as his appointment of Marlborough had been. It was an old trick he had often made use of in Fagel's time, of staying away when anything really important occurred so as to shift the responsibilities for his policies away from himself. By staying away, William lowered the political temperature. No one could accuse him of using undue pressure if he was not even at hand. There was a special reason in 1701 for not exerting obvious political pressure. He was now in somewhat better health, for the simple reason that in Holland he always ate breakfast. His Dutch physician, Dr Bidloo, had found a remedy for his dropsical legs, by wrapping them in hot flannels. This and the greater exercise that he always took in summer reduced the swelling and made him feel more comfortable. William could not, however, reasonably expect to survive the coming war. It was not a subject which he discussed, and no man likes to calculate the hour of his own death. In the King's case it was of great importance that he should appear as well as he could; otherwise he would lose all influence on the course of events. But he knew he was so weak that he could not go on much longer. What would happen to his beloved Holland? The alliance might well be kept up. Anne and Marlborough would have the strongest personal reasons for following the course which William had outlined for them. If they did not, and James or his son were restored, Marlborough might expect the block and the Princess, at best, lifelong imprisonment. They would have to accept the greatness which William was thrusting upon them. But even if the alliance were maintained, the English might be expected to try to place on the shoulders of the Dutch an undue share of the costs involved. This is in fact just what Marlborough was trying to do even in the King's lifetime. Although the Dutch agreed to furnish the same proportion at sea as in the last war – that is, three ships to the English five – and were planning to have greater forces on land than ever before, Marlborough toyed with the idea of offering for the English share just half the soldiers of the Nine Years War.[48] This despite the fact that he could reasonably expect to command the English contingent himself, and despite the fact that England was believed to have gained in wealth by one-fifth in the years since the Revolution.[49] William could not possibly take a visible part in setting the proper proportions of the common burden to be carried by his native and his adopted country. He had to try to persuade the English to bear a fair share, but he would have to perform this delicate task behind a curtain.

To do so successfully, William would probably have to dissolve his present Parliament. Rochester and Godolphin could not be expected to be hearty in their support of the Dutch finances. When Godolphin heard of the possibility of a new Parliament he threatened to resign and exploded in a letter to Marlborough:

Yours of the 3/14 surprises mee extreamly, to hear that on that side of the water, the king hears no discourse but of a new parliament is an amazing thing; especially, if one considers the particulars of what this parliament has done, & how they left the publick affairs when they parted, they provided while they were in expectation only that a warr might come onn, the greatest supply's that ever were given when the kingdome was not in an actuall warr, and those supply's upon the best fonds that ever were given....[50]

Sunderland, more accurately, felt that the Tories had done nothing but what they had been forced to do and urged the advantages of a new Parliament. He felt that if the present ministry survived, the King would 'be wheedled, and complimented, and cheated, and at the latter end ruined'. If the Tories should be forced into the war, 'it will be with a design of raising money, which shall be both insufficient, and laid so as to be the most uneasy to the people that is possible'.[51] Obviously his curious flirtation with Rochester and Godolphin during the previous session had come to an end. The King listened to the advice that was given him, but for the moment he did not make up his mind. However bitterly he might resent the personal insults to which he had been subjected, it was more important to carry the whole nation into the war behind him than to bring off a party coup.

The news of the death of James II in September strengthened William's hand. He went into mourning, both as King and as Prince of Orange. Anne had already done so, so that there was little choice; but William had been outraged when James refused to go into mourning for Queen Mary in 1695, and he refused to make a similar mistake. Louis XIV was not so wise. At once he recognized the Prince of Wales as James III. This was the best thing that could have happened to strengthen William's position in England.[52] The King ordered his ambassador to withdraw from France without taking leave of the court and also sent instructions for the dismissal of Poussin, the French secretary in London.[53] The messenger De Bas (du Puy?) found Poussin at the Blew Posts in the Haymarket with a group of friends. Later, Mr Hopkins of the Secretary's office returned to the Blew Posts in the company of Lord Halifax, Lord Carbery, and Lord Edward Russell. Hopkins discovered that Poussin's party had included the Spanish consul Navarra and three Tory M.P.s, Dr Davenant, Anthony Hammond and John Tredenham.[54] This was an extra dividend, because not only the three 'Pousineers' but the whole Tory party could now be tarred with the brush of Jacobitism.

Meanwhile the King had reviewed some troops in the rain and had refused to change into dry clothes. His carelessness was followed by a cold and an upset stomach which so weakened him that, although he was able to make the journey to The Hague, he was not strong enough to cross the sea or even to see foreign ambassadors while he was convalescing.[55] Early in November his strength had recovered to the point where he was able to sail, and he reached Hampton Court on the evening of Guy Fawkes's Day. William was so tired that he went to bed at once, and even the next day could not attend to business except that of greetings.[56] Luckily the voyage had been rough and the King unusually seasick. Once he recovered from the trip William found that it had stimulated his appetite, and he felt better than he had for some time. The hot flannels which were applied to his legs daily were doing their work well. He was able to ride almost every day and to keep to his regular schedule, though it was noted that for the first time in his life he sat in a chair for the circle.[57] He entertained the Prince and Princess of Denmark to dinner at Hampton Court and then called on them at Windsor soon after his arrival.[58] And, after taking some soundings, he decided to dissolve Parliament and to gamble on a new one.

The risk was considerable. As Robéthon pointed out, the English were so angry at France that even the old Parliament would have been obliged to declare war.[59] But the old Parliament would have revived the impeachments of the last session, and no one could tell how much money it would vote, or for how long it would support the King's policy. William, at least, took the Jacobitism of the Tories seriously. Whether he should have done so or not is unclear; but the political accounts written by his servants leave no doubt of William's opinion: 'Elle connoit parfaitement les principes et les inclination des Torris, qui estoient les maitres soit dans le Parlement soit dans le ministere, comme leurs sentiments tendent et favoriser le pretendu Prince des Galles, il est tres seur que de commencer une guerre sous leus ministere auroit capable de perdre entierement les affaires du Roy.' So wrote Albemarle in a remarkable private letter which could never have been intended for campaign propaganda.[60] Though Keppel has been thought to lean towards the Tories, in so far as he was permitted to have any political opinions of his own, he was now at least a warm Whig. And, of course, he was not permitted to have any independent opinions. What he wrote was at the dictation of the King and represents the opinion of his master just as accurately as William's holograph letters. William's spelling was better than Albemarle's: that is the only difference between the letters from the two men. One of the most interesting things about this particular dispatch is the tone of pessimism: 'Il est aisé de comprendre ou en seroit le Roy si tout reussissoit mal ... Il ny a rien au monde qui n'aye son beau et son mechant costé, mais dans ceste occasion tout promet un changement tres avantageux ... il faut se soumettre a la maniere dont il plait a la providence de dispenser les evenements: ...'[61] Perhaps these sententious flourishes are nothing more than a schoolboy exercise in French, but Albemarle's letters usually mirror the King's attitude.

In any case, the early betting on the election was remarkably favourable and Albemarle himself soon cheered up. A week after his dubious first report he was writing 'on ce confirme de plus en plus que le Roy a pris le meilleur party, en appellant un autre parlement'.[62] Robéthon's dispatches were almost lyrical. The Tories claim that only fifty or sixty new men will be elected. That would be enough if they were good ones, but I am assured that there will be almost one hundred and fifty new members of whom few or none will be Tories. Hedges has been rejected at Dover. Davenant has lost his seat, Hammond may well lose Cambridge and Harcourt, Powis and Shower run the same risk. Vernon and Colt will carry Westminster and four Whigs will be chosen by the City.[63] And so on. A little later he reported that Sir Christopher Musgrave had lost a county seat and might be too proud to sit for Totnes. Hammond, one of the Pousineers, had lost at Cambridge and at Ipswich as well.[64] At the end of December he concluded that the Whigs had beaten the Tories by fifty, 'et si le Roy fait quelque demarche en leur faveur, cela les renforcera de jures de 50 autres Membres qui sont toujours devoüiez à la Cour par les charges qu'ils possedent ou par celles qu'ils esperent. De sorte que les gens de pareille etoffe qui estoient Toris l'année passée, seront Wigs cellecy, si Sa Majesté le desire'.[65]

The King himself was more prudent than the Whigs would have liked him to be. When Godolphin resigned on 10/21 November, the day before the news of the dissolution became public, William did show his intentions by appointing the Whig Lord Carlisle as his replacement. He also encouraged the Whigs privately according to Lord Roos, who wrote to his father Rutland: 'The King has been pleased to signify he hopes that those who are his friends and have interest will use it for such as are of the opinion wee were of last sessions.'[66] But the King did not show his favour publicly enough. At the New Year van Vrijbergen reported that the Whigs thought they had won, but that they complained strongly that the King had not yet declared himself enough in their favour. And if he tried to keep the Tory chiefs in office the Whigs, 'who alone can furnish money and credit, would then be in an uncertainty'.[67] Van Vrijbergen had just come over as ambassador from the

Republic, but his reports – including threats of political blackmail – seem to have been accurate enough. For years the Whigs had been demanding political concessions in return for their loans. The King, however, was not yet certain that they had really won, as they claimed. Until he was certain of their victory, his public steps in their favour would have to be tentative and modest, so that in case of need he might be able to draw back. William's caution was soon justified. When the new Parliament met at the beginning of January he indicated his preference for Littleton, the Whig candidate for Speaker, over Harley; but Harley won by four votes. William continued to favour the Whigs by dismissing Secretary Hedges for refusing to support Littleton. But he had to hold the balance fairly even, since the two parties were almost precisely equal in strength. The general election, despite Defoe's propaganda and the French recognition of James III, had resulted in another draw.

On the whole nothing could have worked better for the King's interest. When he had first become King, William had been overheard to say that the crown should not be the worse for his wearing it; on which one sour prerogative man commented that he had made it little better than a nightcap. Perhaps this is not fair comment; but the powers of the crown were certainly far more limited in 1702 than they had been in 1689. For the most part the initiative which the crown had lost passed to the parties in the House of Commons. A situation had now arisen, however, in which the parties, by their equal strength, cancelled each other out. William, as arbiter between them, resumed much of the authority which had been lost since the Revolution. His followers realized how great was the present advantage and hoped that it might endure.

Les 2 partis sont si egaux, Et se ballancent en telle sorte que si l'un des 2 agissoit d'une maniere opposée aux intentions de Sa Majesté et de la nation, l'autre party auroit un moyen seur d'abysmer ce party là, et de l'exclurre de toutes les charges. Ainsy l'unique moyen d'avoir part au gouvernement et de conserver du credit parmy la nation pour estre elu dans les Parlements qui suivront, c'est de faire à present tout ce que le Roy demande. C'est la plus heureuse situation de monde si elle pouvoit durer. Et tres constamment si l'un des 2 partis estoit beaucoup superieur, les affaires generalles iroient moins bien. ...[68]

The history of the next reign was to show how fatal to the royal power was an overwhelming majority, even when it was made up of supporters of the ministry.

Now that the elections were over it was possible to devote greater attention to preparations for the coming campaign. Up to now, the Austrians had been fighting the Spanish; but they had carefully avoided open hostilities with

France. The maritime powers, too, though they had sent a squadron to seize the plate fleet[69] had avoided war on land. Such a state of affairs could not continue for long. In November the French troops occupying the Spanish Netherlands began to build a fort on the Sas van Gent canal, within a musket-shot of the Dutch fort St Anthony. At the same time they occupied the strong places belonging to the Elector of Cologne, including Liège, Rijnberk, Keyserwerth, and Bonn. Both steps were intolerable. The French fort was insignificant, and it was soon blown away by a few cannon-balls. The threat to the Rhine frontier of the Republic was far more serious. If the French were not removed from the territories of Cologne, and that quickly, they might be able to make contact with their other important friend in west Germany, Anton Ulrich of Wolfenbüttel. If this occurred, the Dutch would be almost completely cut off from the Empire and their position would be one of extreme danger. William would have liked to take Keyserwerth during the winter, though his forces were not yet fully ready for action.[70] There were also plans for a surprise attack on Anton Ulrich, so as to force him to join the allied cause. Neither could be carried out at once, partly because of the weather and partly for want of men, and both were postponed until the summer campaign of 1702. During the winter, however, the French advantage in the Electorate of Cologne was minimized by the Elector Palatine, who closed the Rhine to French vessels and prevented them from supplying Bonn.[71] If the military delays were disappointing, William and Heinsius were more successful in the diplomatic field. Brandenburg, Hesse, and Münster were still more firmly tied to the allied cause. Sweden and Poland, at war with each other, both seemed interested in joining in the war against France. Portugal, though it had recognized Philip V as King of Spain, was otherwise well affected to the allied cause and might perhaps be persuaded first to neutrality and then to a formal juncture with England and the Dutch.[72] In February, William, becoming impatient with the slow passage of his letters and the delays in completing plans for the campaign, dispatched Albemarle to The Hague. The favourite was fully instructed, and William hoped that his coming would speed up the preparation for the war.[73]

Meanwhile things went on surprisingly cheerfully in England. The nation was united, and the King's health much better than it had been the year before. His long speech at the opening of Parliament did not tire him, and observers noted that he had not looked so well for years past.[74] The French were startled at the news which reached them. They had taken the victory of Harley over Littleton in the contest for the Speaker's place as a great advantage to themselves; but they were soon disabused. At the same time, the French were in great financial straits and did not know how to get out of them. The court was blamed for the hauteur with which it had so unjustly treated all the other courts of Europe, by which it had brought a terrible war on itself.[75] But soon the French were to have better news. On Friday 21 February O.S., the King tried out a new horse in Richmond Park. As he began to gallop, the horse stumbled and fell. An almost identical accident had occurred in November of 1700, and that time William had escaped without injury. Now he was not so lucky. He fell on his right shoulder and broke his collar-bone. The fracture was soon set, and he was able to have dinner at Hampton Court before returning to Kensington in his carriage. On the way there he suffered from the jolting of the coach and his shoulder had to be set once again at Kensington.

A broken collar-bone is not usually a serious matter, and this one was not permitted to interfere with the King's regular schedule. He continued to rise at eight in the morning and to go to bed at eleven, eating at the usual hours and working with his ministers and secretaries as if nothing had happened. He could not write or for the first week put on his coat, for which he substituted a dressing gown; otherwise there was no change. His wound might make it impossible for him to go to Parliament by coach to pass necessary Bills and to recommend a union with Scotland; but there was no reason why he could not be carried there in a chair.[76] The only real difficulty was that William's legs might swell again because of his inability to exercise. Despite Dr Bidloo's attentions this did happen, but for the rest all was well. One dutiful subject even reported that the King was 'very merry' during his convalescence.[77] After eight days, William was able to put on his coat and to appear again in public; though he stayed at Kensington, Bidloo assured everyone that the King would be able to go to Parliament in a few days.

Then, on the very day that he was 'very merry', William after walking up and down the gallery at Kensington found himself weary. He sat down in a chair and fell asleep. When he awoke he was cold and feverish. The next day he was much weaker, his digestion was disordered, and he could hardly eat. That night, 5/16 March, he slept well. But on Friday the 6th, though there was no fever, he was still worse than before. He could not even keep down soup, and the weakness of his pulse was alarming. At seven that evening the doctors reported to the Cabinet Council that his life was in danger. An hour later, very tired, the King went to bed. He seemed to have a good rest. But the doctors were convinced that he could not withstand the strain of another fever.

On Saturday the fever which the physicians had dreaded returned. There was now no hope of recovery. He was in great pain, which he had come to feel more in the last few years than he had in his youth. His suffering was the more because his senses remained perfectly clear. As the day passed, Albemarle returned from The Hague and tried to cheer his master up. William knew that there was no hope: 'Je tire vers ma fin' was his reply. He was given quinine to reduce the fever, but by now he was too weak to respond to drugs. He remained conscious during Saturday night, and at five the next morning received Holy Communion according to the English rite. His pain was so great that he turned to one of the doctors and asked whether it could continue much longer. The answer was that it could not. After giving the keys of his cabinets of papers to Albemarle, William composed himself to die. But there was to be one final meeting. Portland had been kept from the sickroom by his jealous rival. When he finally gained entry, the King could no longer speak, but he had enough strength to grasp Portland's hand and to carry it to his heart. Between eight and nine o'clock in the morning of 8 March he died.[78]

The King's personality was now no longer contentious. His policies remained, and since they were wise they were carried out. William had already prepared the campaign for the year, and it was executed with little change. His broader political views took longer to put into effect, but in time they too were implemented. The Union with Scotland took place in 1707. In 1714 the Hanoverian Succession was effected. By that time the Dutch had secured their barrier and the English had advanced to the position of a great power. Though the French did not cease to be the first power in Europe for another half-century, their strength had been brought within bounds, and their aggressions would not again strike terror into the heart of the civilized world until after the Revolution of 1789.

The place of William III in European history depends on two separate developments: his defence of the United Provinces and his creation of a modern government in England. There can be no question as to where his heart lay. He was and remained throughout his life Dutch William. Perhaps, in a super-ficial view, he was a failure on the continent. He was never a uniformly successful commander, and his wars bled the Republic white. Though she was able to put more men into the field in 1702 than in 1689, her days of greatness were passing. By the time Heinsius died in 1720 she had definitely settled into the status of a second-class power. The Dutch, looking back to the golden days of de Witt, envied their grandfathers and sighed with relief at the thought that William had carried with him to the grave the office of Stadhouder and that of Captain-General. It is, of course, unfair to compare William III with de Witt in this superficial way. Certainly the United Provinces were relatively more powerful in the 1650s than they were fifty years later – but the credit for that does not go to de Witt. The high position of the Republic in his day rested on a European power vacuum. Germany was exhausted by the results of the Thirty Years War, France weakened by the long minority of Louis XIV. England had not yet become a great trading nation. In those years Holland seemed strong because there was no competition. But as soon as Louis XIV grew up and the English Navigation Acts began to take effect, the balance of power shifted. Dutch commercial and political predominance began to decay in the 1660s, while de Witt was still in power. And if we are to make a true comparison between the administration of William III and that of the first Stadhouderless period, we must take the year 1672. The Prince did not inherit control of a great power. He inherited a country occupied by the enemy, abandoned by her friends, ready to sink beneath the waves. What he left behind him thirty years later was a nation, in danger it is true, but a nation with a mighty army and navy, at the head of a Grand Alliance, fully capable of defending herself. It is to William III that the Dutch Republic owed her survival, when the mistakes of de Witt had made survival extremely unlikely. Defence was costly, certainly. And there were those who cried 'Liever Frans als Prins', as there have been those who in more recent times cried 'Mieux Hitler que Blum' or 'Better Red than Dead'. Until now, the cause of freedom has been able to silence such cries. As long as freedom endures, it will continue to do so.

In England the task of William III was different. Here he was creating something new rather than defending the old. It was not to be expected that his work should be appreciated at its true value.

> He had their Rights and Liberties restor'd
> In Battle purchas'd, and by Peace secur'd:
> And they with *English* Gratitude began,
> To feel the Favour and despise the Man.[79]

Or, as it was put in another pamphlet a year later:

He that's fallen into a Pit, may chuse whether he will be help'd out, or no; and if he stretches out his Hands, and strains his Lungs in begging for Help, 'tis hard that all this Fatigue must pass for nothing, but that he who only lends his Hand, should set up for his sole Rescuer. Yet thus stupid were all the Parliaments in K. W's Reign, and gave him the only Honour of a Redeemer, when 'tis notorious, that the whole Kingdom was as fond of being redeem'd, as he was of coming to their Rescue.[80]

Most Englishmen, once the King was safely dead, were able to take a more balanced view of his work, even if they refused to go so far as Bishop Burnet and apply to him the words of the Psalmist, 'The man of God's right hand, whom He made strong for Himself'.[81] Obviously enough, William III was the Deliverer of England from the tyranny and arbitrary government of the Stuarts, as he was the Deliverer of Europe from the tyranny of Louis XIV. But in England he was more than this. He repaired and improved an obsolete system of government, and left it strong enough to withstand the stresses of the next century virtually unchanged. The army of Marlborough, and that of Wellington, and to a large extent that of Raglan, was the creation of William III. So too was the independence of the judiciary. In law he might, like the Stuarts, have displaced judges for decisions he did not care for. Voluntarily he refused to do what his successors were prevented from doing by the Act of Settlement. How great a portion of the success of the Revolution Settlement do we not owe to him for his refusal to accept the crown of England by the title of conquest! In 1688 almost all the lawyers would have preferred that he usurp the throne by such a claim, but William refused to make it. He may not have foreseen all the consequences of his decision, and he certainly did not enjoy all the difficulties in which that decision later placed him, but the credit for it is William's and William's alone. So too is the new moderation of political warfare after the Revolution. We should not blame him for the fact that he was the last English king to execute a man by Act of Attainder. It is, rather, to his credit that Fenwick was the single victim of such a barbarous procedure in his own reign, and that Fenwick has had no successors.

In England as in Holland, the government of the King was very expensive; at their peak, the annual expenditures of William III were four times as large as those of James II. This new scale of government was bitterly unpopular. But the new taxes, which were not in fact heavy by comparison with those borne by the Dutch, made England a great power. And they contributed to the prosperity of the country while they contributed to its strength, by the process which is now called 'pump-priming'. In building a new economy, and a new civil service to manage that economy, the King and his ministers made many mistakes in detail. But they found the answer to a problem that many later governments have missed, that of combining war and strong government with the preservation and indeed the increase of civil liberties. Perhaps they went too far. Nowadays the rights of property and of the individual are everywhere disappearing, and they are as unfashionable as they are rare. But our heritage of freedom and liberty, on both sides of the Atlantic, is a great one; and when we have finally exchanged it for the homely security of socialism we may discover, too late, that we have made Esau's bargain.

If the direct influence of William III on English constitutional practice was a great and beneficial one, his indirect influence on society was of equal importance. It is notorious that the religious revival of this period, which led to the foundation of the Society for the Promotion of Christian Knowledge and of the Society for the Propagation of the Gospel, owed much to the personal purity of the King and of his wife. Their simple manners and high sense of duty provided an example to the upper classes which had been wanting throughout the century. And as they worked to make England a more moral country, they worked too to make it a more comfortable one. In many fields, from the gift of Greenwich as a home for aged seamen to the introduction of superior stoves in the hothouses that contained his collection of tropical plants, William made England a better place in which to live. He was not an easy teacher, and his manners were most resented by the nobility. But the nobles followed his example, though they disliked his person, and William was always far more popular with the people – on both sides of the North Sea – than he was with their leaders. In 1703, the writer whose satire on English ingratitude is quoted above continued: 'I appeal to daily Experience, whether all this be not effectually forgotten, and K. W. and his Redemptions turned into a common Ridicule?' He was wrong. The upper classes might forget or ridicule; the people were more faithful to the memory of a great man. As Charles Hatton noted on the anniversary of Queen Anne's accession in 1704, 'Yesterday was generally observed here as a day of mourning, not of thanksgiving. Severall sermons for Kg William were preach'd in most churches; and, in our market, ye butchers shopps were generally shut up, and few wou'd sell any meat, tho it was market day, they postponing their gaine to faction; from ye effects of wch, good Lord, deliver us!'[82]

THE ENGLISH SUCCESSION

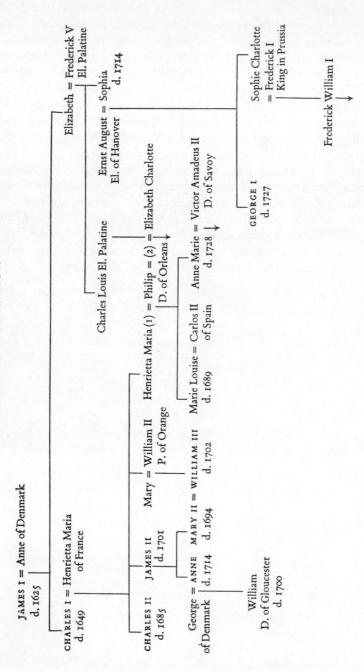

THE SPANISH SUCCESSION

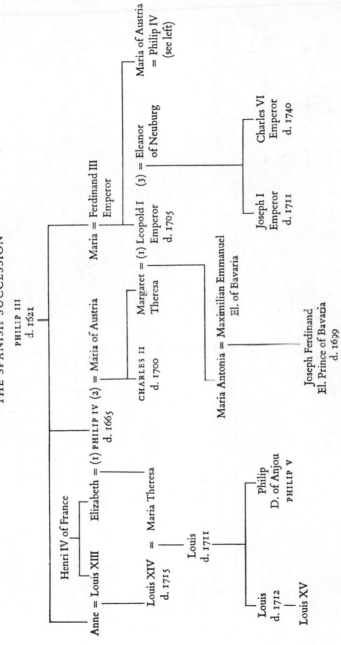

404

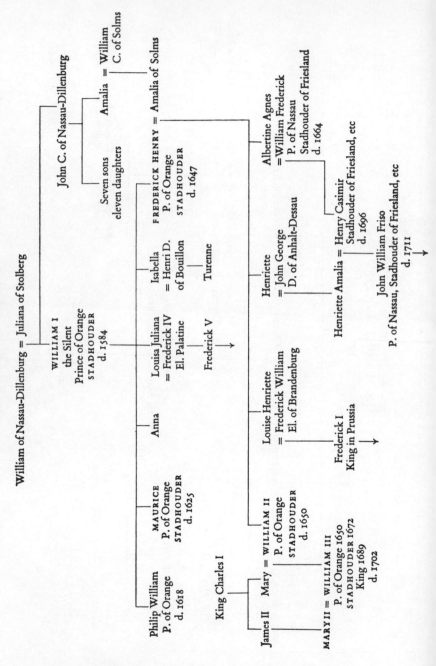

THE HOUSE OF ORANGE

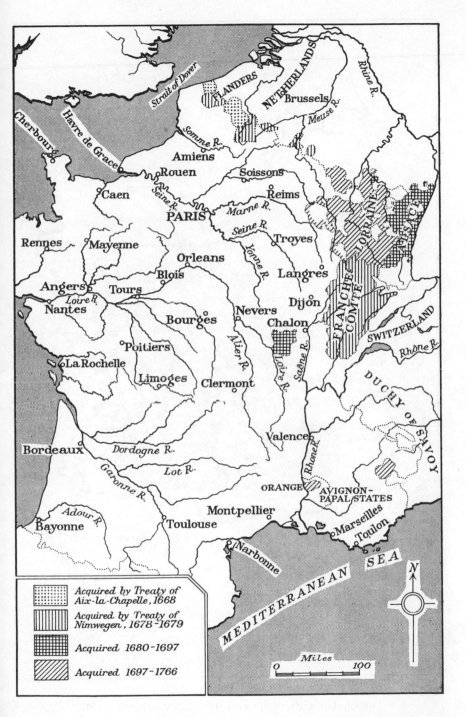

The Expansion of France

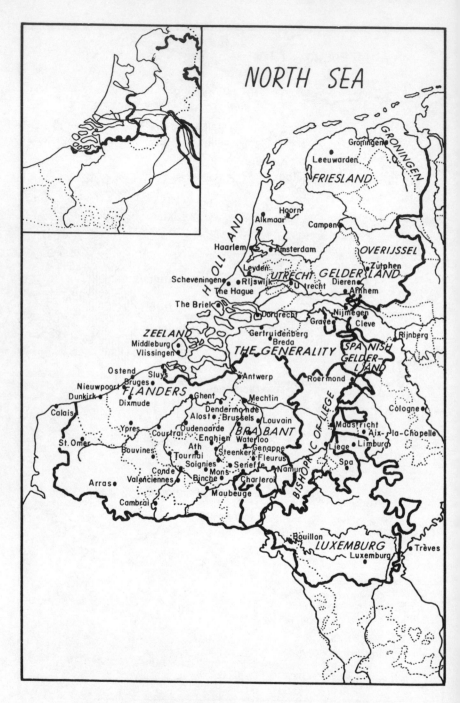

The Netherlands at the end of the Seventeenth Century

Insert: The Holland Water Line of 1672

ABBREVIATIONS TO FOOTNOTES

A.R.A.: Algemeen Rijksarchief, The Hague, followed by the name of the particular collection, e.g. A.R.A. St. Gen = Algemeen Rijksarchief, Staten Generaal...

Archives: *Archives ou correspondance inédite de la maison d'Orange-Nassau.* 2nd series 1584–1688, ed. G. Groen van Prinsterer, 5 vols., The Hague 1858–1862. 3rd series 1689–1702, ed. F. J. L. Krämer, 3 vols., Leiden, 1907–1909.

B.M.: British Museum, London, followed by the name of the particular collection, e.g. B.M. Add. Ms. = British Museum, Additional Manuscript...

Correspondance de la cour d'Espagne: *Correspondance de la cour d'Espagne sur les affaires des Pays-Bas*, ed. H. Lonchay, J. Cuvelier, et J. Lefèbvre, 6 vols., Brussels, 1923–1937.

Correspondentie: *Correspondentie van Willem III en van Hans Willem Bentinck, eersten graaf van Portland*, ed. N. Japikse, 5 vols., The Hague, 1927–1937.

D.N.B.: *Dictionary of National Biography*

Knuttel: *Catalogus van de pamfletten-verzameling berustende in de Koninklijke Bibliotheek* ed. W. P. C. Knuttel, 9 vols., The Hague, 1889–1920.

K.H.A.: Koninklijk Huisarchief, The Hague.

P.R.O.: Public Record Office, London, followed by the name of the particular collection, e.g. P.R.O.S.P. = Public Record Office, State Papers...

R.A.: *See* A.R.A.

Urkunden und Actenstücke: *Urkunden und Actenstücke zur Geschichte des Kurfürsten Friedrich Wilhelm von Brandenburg*, ed. B. Erdmannsdorffer *et al.*, 23 vols., Berlin, 1864–1930.

NOTE: The bibliography is to be found in the footnotes. For reasons of space a bibliographical note is to be published separately in a forthcoming issue of the *Journal of Modern History*.

NOTES

Chapter 1

1. L. van Aitzema, *Saken van Staet en Oorlog*, Hague 1669, xxx, 456.
2. Journaal of Johan ven Kerckhoven, heer van Heenvliet, in *Kronijk van het Historisch Genootschap te Utrecht*, Vde Serie, Vde Deel (1869), 541. Hereafter referred to as Journaal Heenvliet.
3. *Ibid.*
4. *Ibid.*, 542.
5. Henry, Lord Percy of Alnwick. See the D.N.B. article.
6. Journaal Heenvliet, 543.
7. Journaal Heenvliet, 544.
8. There are two poor biographies of Amalia von Solms; the less bad is Kleinschmidt, A., *Amalie von Oranien*, Berlin, 1905. The main facts are in Nieuw Nederlandsch Biografisch Woortenboek, i, 103. The Princess was a granddaughter of a sister of William the Silent, a poor relation rather than an upstart. J. Eysten, *Het Leven van Prins Willem II*, Amsterdam, 1916, 19.
9. R. Fruin, *Verspreide Geschriften*, Hague, 1900–05, iv, 112.
10. J. Eysten, *op. cit.*, 48.
11. R. Fruin, *op. cit.*, iv, 103.
12. P. Geyl, *Oranje en Stuart 1641–1672*, Utrecht, 1939, 9. It is to be hoped that this important work will be translated.
13. *Ibid.*, 21.
14. *Ibid.*, 22.
15. *The Lord George Digby's Cabinet.*
16. P. Geyl, *Oranje en Stuart*, 47–8.
17. Geyl, Fruin, and most of the other leading authorities are agreed that the Princess was corrupt. See *Verspreide Geschriften*, iv, 102–03.
18. J. Eysten, *op. cit.*, 93.
19. *Ibid.*, 78.
20. *Ibid.*, 61.
21. P. Geyl, *Oranje en Stuart*, 49–50.
22. J. Eysten, *op. cit.*, 104.
23. K. H. A. Archief Constantijn Huygens Sr., 7.1.
24. The draft will is printed in *Kronijk van het Historisch Genootschap te Utrecht*, IIe Serie, 1854, 500–08.
25. Journaal Heenvliet, 545.
26. Katherine Wotton married (1) the titular Lord Stanhope, d. 1628; (2) Heenvliet, d. 1660; (3) Daniel O'Neale, d. 1664. She died in 1667. Created in 1660 *suo jure* Countess of Chesterfield, her son by her first marriage became Earl of Chesterfield and her son by Heenvliet Earl of Bellomont. G.E.C., *The Complete Peerage*, iii, 160.

27. Jorissen's *Mémoires* of Constantijn Huygens, which actually rejoices at the death of Mary, is so extreme that it betrays its own case. Worp, the editor of the six-volume *Briefwisseling van Constantijn Huygens*, is more moderate. Jorissen has no reputation with the best Dutch scholars and Worp does not have a good one. See Geyl, *Oranje en Stuart*, 93.

28. The letter was dated 24 February 1649. There is a version of it in K. H. A. Archief Constantijn Huygens Sr. 7.1., and another in *Les Mémoires du Burgrave et Comte Frédéric de Dohna, 1621–1688*, ed. H. Borkowski, Königsberg, 1898, 125. The text of the K.H.A. version is as follows:

Le Prince d'Orange

Ordonne par cette au Sieur de Dona Gouverneur d'Orange, de ne rendre laditte place entre les mains de personne (apres sa mort) mais suivre les ordres que la Princesse Royale son espouse luy donnera. Et aura ledt Sieur Comte a maintenir la place pour Elle contre tous autres qui pourroit pretendre.

G. P. d'Orenge
L. Buysero

29. Journaal Heenvliet, 547–48.

30. He was the Secretary of the Prince. The Princess's Secretary, Nicholas Oudart, was in Scotland with Charles II.

31. Journaal Heenvliet, 546.

Chapter 2

1. Wagenaar, *Vaderlandsche Historie*, Amsterdam 1755, xii, 119.
2. Aitzema, xxx, 458.
3. P. Geyl, *Kernproblemen van onze geschiedenis*, Utrecht 1937, 82.
4. *Ibid.*
5. Alexander van den Kapelle, Heer van Aartsbergen.
6. Aitzema, *op. cit.*, 456.
7. Towns which had never had, or had lost, freedom of election were not given it now; they were placed under the authority of the States of Holland.
8. See on this A. de Wicquefort, *Histoire des Provinces-Unies des Païs-Bas*, ed. L. E. Lenting, Amsterdam, 1861, i, 336.
9. Together, they came to some fl.250,000 a year. His private income was about twice as large, not counting the money owed him by the Spanish and English.
10. Gold boxes, containing life pensions totalling fl.15,800 a year. The sum was later raised to fl.17,500 p.a.
11. Aitzema, *ibid.*, 551–2.
12. Printed in Aitzema, *op. cit.*, 460–1.
13. Journaal Heenvliet, 557.
14. *Ibid.*, 558.
15. *Ibid.*, 563–4.
16. According to the thoroughly untrustworthy *Mémoires de Comte Frédéric de Dohna*, 137, Mary went to the length of asking the advice of the French courts on this

point, and 'Le conseil de Paris regarda cela avec indignation', i.e. the possibility of subjecting the Prince to the mercies of English wardship.

17. Journaal Heenvliet, 574.
18. *Ibid.*, 621–6.
19. *Ibid.*, 606.
20. *Mémoires de Comte Frédéric de Dohna*, 141.
21. Aitzema, xxxiii, 823.
22. K.H.A. Prins Willem III, v, 19. See also Journaal Heenvliet, 639–44.

Chapter 3

1. Text of the agreement, Aitzema, xxxi, 558–9.
2. William II's testament, unsigned and undated, was invalid; his provision of a dowry of fl.150,000 for his wife was in a separate codicil, signed and dated, which was accepted as valid by the courts in 1653. Aitzema, xxxiii, 823.
3. K.H.A. Prins Willem III, vii, 19.
4. The same is true today. In official transactions between the Stuarts and the House of Orange the exchange was taken to be ten guilders to the pound sterling. The commercial rate fluctuated between 9.5 and 10.5. From the bitter complaints of Dutch diplomats stationed in England, and the difference in official salaries, the English cost of living must have been almost twice as high as the Dutch, which would give the £ a real value of fl.5 or even fl.4.
5. R.A. Nass. Dom. 600, ff. 251, 259 b, 260.
6. *Ibid.* f. 194.
7. R.A. Nass. Dom. 601, f. 34.
8. K.H.A. Inventaris 15, xiii, 4, 106.
9. R.A. Nass. Dom. 601, f. 28.
10. *Ibid.* ff. 22–3.
11. *Ibid.*, f. 16.
12. *Ibid.*, ff. 34–6.
13. *Thurloe State Papers*, i, 664.
14. *Ibid.*, i, 665.
15. Samuel Chapuiseau, appointed 31 October 1659; R.A. Nass. Dom. 601, f. 108 b.
16. *Ibid.*, f. 107.
17. Zuylestein's Instructions are at R.A. Nass. Dom. 601, ff. 91–100 and have also been printed in *Mémoires de Constantin Huygens*, 163.
18. *Ibid.*, ff. 115–18.
19. Aitzema, xxxiii, 824.
20. *Ibid.*, xxxix, 471.
21. On the visit, see Aitzema, xl, 633; and for the parade, *Briefwisseling tusschen de gebroeders van der Goes, Werken uitgegeven door het Historisch genootschap.* IIIe Serie, No. 10, 1899, i, 87–8.
22. Ten years of the most malicious gossip could only credit Mary with one friend, and even her enemies admit that there is no reason to believe that her friendship with Jermyn was improper.

Chapter 4

1. *Brieven aan de Witt*, i, 68, *Wicquefort*, ii, 216.
2. *Thurloe State Papers*, ii, 263–4.
3. *Wicquefort*, ii, 216.
4. *Ibid.*
5. Res. St. Holl. 28 September 1660.
6. *Brieven van de Witt*, ii, 240–2.
7. In the end this provision was accepted by a secret separate arrangement between the province of Holland and the English, since it would never have been accepted by the States General. The old story that de Witt was responsible for suggesting the exclusion is nowhere believed today. It was, of course, widely believed at the time. *Brieven van de Witt*, i, 164–5.
8. For Weyman's influence over the Princess Dowager see *Brieven van Johan de Witt*, ii, 248–51.
9. *Ibid.*, 254.
10. *Ibid.*, 277.
11. *Ibid.*, 281–3.
12. A. de Wicquefort to de Witt, *Brieven aan de Witt*, ii, 41–2. Wicquefort hated the Orangists, but he was unusually venomous about Weyman, who was sent to England with Prince John Maurice of Nassau ('The Brazilian').
13. Charles II to the Hof van Holland, 25 February 1660/1, O.S. A copy is at K.H.A. Prins Willem III, v, 13.
14. They were Beverweert, whom Charles accused of being a 'creature' of de Witt; and the Princess Royal's Secretary, Nicholas Oudart, who was named 'rascal' for his pains. Unsigned letter of 25 March 1661, *ibid.*
15. There are copies, in French and in English, of the agreement in K.H.A. Prins Willem III, v, 13.
16. D'Estrades, *Mémoires*, i, 144. To Louis XIV, 25 July 1661: 'Il croit aussi, par la liaison qu' il a faite avec Madame la Princesse d'Orange & l'Electeur de Brandebourg, & par leurs Cabales, etre le Maitre de la Hollande: . . .'
17. Letter of 30 March 1661, *Brieven van Johan de Witt*, ii, 289–90. Reply of Zuidpolsbroek, 3 April, *Brieven aan de Witt*, ii, 34–5.
18. See on this d'Estrades, *Mémoires*, i, 157 and 177–8.
19. On Orange, see A. de Pontbriant, *Histoire de la Principauté d'Orange*, Hague, 1891. A Leyden doctoral dissertation, J. M. Sernée, *Het Geschil Over Het Prinsdom Oranje in de Jaren 1650–1660*, Amsterdam, 1916, is a competent piece of work but adds little or nothing to the known sources.
20. For example de Thou, the French ambassador to The Hague; *Archives de la Maison d'Orange-Nassau*, IIe Serie, v, 190.
21. Abraham de Wicquefort, the writer.
22. *Urkunden und Actenstücke*, ii, 238.
23. Dohna, *Mémoires*, 160–1.
24. *Ibid.*, 164–5.
25. *Ibid.*, 184–92.

26. Dohna, *Mémoires*, 199–201, and J. A. Worp, ed., *De Briefwisseling van Constantijn Huygens*, v, *passim*.

27. *Briefwisseling Huygens*, v, 418, 443, and *passim*.

28. *Ibid.*, 519.

29. *Ibid.*, 385.

30. The inhabitants of Orange did not like the French occupation and accused them of frequent murder, duelling, and poisoning, as well as perversion of justice. *Ibid.*, 367. They were similarly dissatisfied with the administration of the Prince's Governor after 1665. One is almost tempted to believe that they received the government they deserved.

31. A. R.A. Nass. Dom. 601, f. 237. Bornius lost the salary of his professorship at Leyden and received a fee of fl.2,400, diet, and lodgings in compensation. *Ibid.*, f. 238 b.

32. Contract with the falconer dated 14 June 1663 : A. R.A. Nass. Dom. 601, f. 251.

33. On the incident, see d'Estrades, *Mémoires*, ii, 429–30.

34. *Ibid.*, 440.

35. *Ibid.*, 429–30.

36. *Mémoires du Comte de Guiche*, . . . London 1744, 107.

37. G. Downing to H. Coventry, Hague 21 January 1664/5 O.S., Longleat House, Coventry Papers xli, 24.

38. D'Estrades, *Mémoires*, iii, 232.

39. Louis XIV to d'Estrades, 17 August 1665, in d'Estrades' *Mémoires*, iii, 299.

40. The five were Friesland, Groningen, Overijssel, Gelderland, and Zeeland. D'Estrades, *Mémoires*, iii, 454, 476–7; *Wicquefort*, iii, 210.

41. P. Geyl, *Oranje en Stuart*, 256.

42. D'Estrades, *Mémoires*, iii, 504–05, 513.

43. D'Estrades, *Mémoires*, iv, 100–01.

44. *Ibid.*, 129–35.

45. The appointment of a Monsieur d'Orival as riding master, at fl.2,500 p.a., was made on 31 October 1666, some eight months after this episode. R.A. Nass. Dom. 602, f. 55.

46. D'Estrades, *Mémoires*, iv, 144–5, 160.

47. Wagenaar, *Vaderlandsche Historie*, xiii, 192.

48. *Urkunden und Aktenstücke*, ii, 374–5.

49. D'Estrades, *Mémoires*, iv, 184–5.

50. *Wicquefort*, iii, 285–6.

51. D'Estrades, *Mémoires*, iv, 202–03; *Brieven van Johan de Witt*, ii, 169–70.

52. D'Estrades, *Mémoires*, iv, 262, 311.

53. *Ibid.*, 223.

54. *Ibid.*, 241–2.

55. Wagenaar, xiii, 204; d'Estrades, *Mémoires*, iv, 282.

56. A. R.A. Nass. Dom. 602, f. 43. His clothing allowance had previously been fl.3,500 a year.

57. *Mémoires du Comte de Guiche* . . ., 282.

Chapter 5

1. A. Legrelle, *La Diplomatie Française et la Succession d'Espagne*, 4 vols., Gand, 1888. i, 19–20.
2. The instructions are printed in *Mignet*, iii, 28–9.
3. D'Estrades, *Mémoires*, v, 358–9.
4. *Wicquefort*, iii, 375–6.
5. *Brieven van Johan de Witt*, iii, 434.
6. Knuttel No. 9621.
7. Knuttel No. 9683.
8. *Wicquefort*, iii, 405. Wicquefort, of course, was a hostile witness and a malicious one.
9. Wagenaar, *Vaderlandsche Historie*, xiii, 351.
10. D'Estrades, *Mémoires*, vi, 438.
11. C. Huygens to William, 12 September 1668. *Worp*, vi, 235–6. An extract from the *Notulen* of the States of Zeeland describing the installation is in K.H.A. Prins Willem III, VIII, 24.
12. The original decree, with copies of the announcements, can be found in K.H.A. Prins Willem III, v, 16. A copy of the memorial to the States General was published, Knuttel No. 9685, with the date 26 October.
13. De Witt to Valkenier, 25 October 1668. *Brieven van Johan de Witt*, iii, 440.
14. Wicquefort, iii, 414–15.
15. *Den haestigen Zeeuw of Brief aen N. N. Raeckende 't Subject van 't avancement van den Heer Prins van Orangien* (1668), Knuttel No. 9683.
16. Knuttel No. 9763.
17. Temple to Arlington, 3 February 1669. Printed in Thomas Peregrine Courtenay, *Memoires of the Life, Works, and Correspondence of Sir William Temple, Bart.*, 1836, i, 285–6.
18. Pomponne to Louis XIV, 7 March 1669. *Mignet*, iii, 579.
19. *Relation de mon ambassade en Hollande*, ed. H. H. Rowen, Utrecht, 1955, 55. Werken van het Historisch Genootschap, 4ᵉ Serie, No. 2.
20. *Mémoires de Gourville*, 395.
21. *Op. cit.*, 55.
22. R.A. Nass. Dom. 602, f. 101.
23. *Worp*, vi, 256.
24. *Worp*, vi, 250–1. On the Spanish debt see *Correspondance de la Cour d'Espagne*, v, No. 153.
25. Pomponne to Louis XIV, 3 October 1669: *Mignet*, iii, 598.
26. Elizabeth Charlotte of the Palatine did take a second look and maintained in later life that she had fallen in love with William. It is doubtful how far her memory is to be trusted.
27. Johan de Witt to the Baron van Dijkveld, 30 March 1670. *Brieven van Johan de Witt*, iv, 27–9.
28. *Wicquefort*, iv, 132.
29. A. de Fouw, Jr., *Onbekende Raadpensionarissen*, The Hague, 1946, 96–7.

30. Pomponne, *Relation de mon ambassade en Hollande*, 133.
31. Pomponne to Louis XIV, 1 May 1670. *Mignet*, iii, 611.
32. Temple to Sir John Trevor, 27 May N.S. 1670. Sir William Temple, *Works*, ii, 216.
33. *Wicquefort*, iv, 137–8.
34. Cornelis to Johan de Witt, 6 June 1670. *Brieven aan Johan de Witt*, ii, 502–05; and P. J. van Boetselaer van Asperen to same, 7 June 1670. *Ibid.*, 505–07.
35. His instructions, dated 20 June: *Correspondentie*, II, i, 25–7. His report of 1 July: *ibid.*, 28–32.
36. Details of the voyage are to be found in the dispatches of the Dutch ambassadors, Boreel and van Beuninghen, R.A. St. Gen. 4290 and 4291.
37. *Correspondentie*, II, i, 30.
38. Pomponne, *Relation de mon ambassade en Hollande*, 149, gives a good summary of the English reaction to William Henry.
39. Hist. Mss. Comm. 12th Report, Appendix, *MSS. of S. H. Le Fleming*, 75. News-letter of 24 January 1670/71.
40. Johan de Witt to van Beuninghen, 3 October 1670. *Brieven van Johan de Witt*, iv, 93. Colbert de Croissy to Louis XIV, 13 November 1670. P.R.O. 31/3/125. (Baschet transcripts.)
41. G. Burnet, *History of His Own Times*, 1833 ed., Oxford, i, 502.
42. The young Princess died almost immediately and her mother also died on 31 March/10 April. The Duke of Cambridge died some two months later.

Chapter 6

1. F. J. G. ten Raa and F. de Bas, *Het Staatsche Leger 1568–1795*, Breda, 1921, v, 160
2. *Ibid.*, 164.
3. *Ibid.*, 229.
4. *Ibid.*, 233.
5. *Ibid.*, 243.
6. *Ibid.*, 241.
7. *Ibid.*
8. Jan van Zuylen to Johan de Witt, 27 January 1668. *Brieven aan Johan de Witt*, ii, 393. The writer offered to sell evidence of an Anglo-French treaty for an attack on the Republic, to be accompanied by an internal mutiny in favour of sovereignty for the Prince of Orange.
9. Pomponne, *Relation de mon Ambassade en Hollande*, 142.
10. 'Ce qui me surprit dans la suitte fut qu'ayant eu advis de nos liaisons avec ce prince qui approchoient sy fort de la vérité, il ne parut pas que l'on y fit depuis toutte la réflexion que l'on aurait deu, et l'on demeura dans un assés grand repos sur l'amitié de ce prince Jusques à ce que ses mesures avec le Roy esclattèrent par la déclaration de la guerre.' *Ibid.*
11. P. de Groot to Wicquefort, 3 October 1670. *Lettres de Pierre de Groot a Abraham de Wicquefort*, ed. F. J. L. Krämer. Werken uitgegeven door het Historisch Genoot-schap, Derde Serie, No. 5, 17. This was his regular note and there are many letters to the same effect, e.g. 23, 24, 25, etc.

12. P. de Groot to J. de Witt, 27 February 1671. *Brieven aan Johan de Witt*, ii, 545.
13. Pomponne to Louis XIV, 12 February 1671. *Mignet*, iii, 629.
14. On the neglect to rearm in 1671, see Basnage, *Annales des Provinces-Unies* (1719–26), ii, 168–9.
15. *Wicquefort*, iv, 288–9.
16. Colbert de Croissy to Louis XIV, 13 November and 4 December 1670. P.R.O. 31/3/125, Baschet transcripts.
17. Pomponne to Louis XIV, 23 October 1670. *Mignet*, iii, 625.
18. Camille Rousset, *Histoire de Louvois*, Paris, 1862–64, i, 294.
19. Louis XIV to Colbert de Croissy, 7 October 1670. *Mignet*, iii, 233.
20. Same to same, 2 November 1670. *Ibid.*, 239.
21. C. Rousset, *op. cit.*, i, 337–8.
22. For preliminary negotiations, see the Consulte of the Council of State at Brussels of 2 September 1671. *Correspondance de la Cour d'Espagne*, vi, No. 1818.
23. For the guarantee, dated 17 December 1671, see R.A. St. Gen. 2321, ff. 221–2. For the ratifications, see R.A. St. Gen. 2322, f. 85.
24. R.A. St. Gen. 2321, ff. 201–03.
25. *Wicquefort*, iv, 298–301.
26. Johan to Cornelis de Witt, 6 December 1671. *Brieven van Johan de Witt*, iv, 212–15.
27. Same to same, 10 December 1671. *Ibid.*, iv, 216.
28. Same to Adriaan Paets, 13 December 1671. *Ibid.*, iv, 219.
29. P. de Groot to Johan de Witt, 25 December 1671. *Brieven aan Johan de Witt*, ii, 551.
30. See on this *Urkunden und Actenstücke*, iii, 207.
31. On the whole matter see Wagenaar, *Vaderlandsche Historie*, xiii, 445–60 and 480–7.
32. *Wicquefort*, iv, 306.
33. P. de Groot to Johan de Witt, 1 January 1672. *Brieven aan Johan de Witt*, ii, 579.
34. P. de Groot to Johan de Witt, 8 January 1672. *Brieven aan Johan de Witt*, ii, 581–2.
35. A. de Wicquefort to G. A. van Reede van Amerongen, 26 January 1672. Huisarchief Amerongen I, Portefeuille 116.
36. Basnage, *Annales des Provinces-Unies*, ii, 198.
37. M. Turner, Baroness van Amerongen, to G. A. van Reede van Amerongen, 29 February 1672. Huisarchief Amerongen Familie-Archief No. 101 C.
38. Comte Frédéric de Dohna, *Mémoires*, 270–1.
39. 15,910 horse and 91,125 foot or a total of 107,035 at 17 June. *Het Staatsche Leger*, v, 270.
40. *Ibid.*, 237.
41. G. A. van Reede van Amerongen to William III, 29 December 1671. R.A. Leg. 369 No. 57.
42. *Het Staatsche Leger*, v, 304.
43. The same is of course true of Sir Winston Churchill in 1940 in somewhat similar circumstances.
44. *Het Staatsche Leger*, v, 320.

45. 'A Narrative of the condition of the Holland Fleet.' 22 March 1672. B.M. Add. Ms. 34339, f. 3.
46. Diary of C. C. Rumpf, R.A. Leg. 640. Entry for 25 April: 'Is my mede van ter seyden in confidentie toegeschreven geworden, dat men in Hollt. door ick weet niet wat voor onbegrypelycke maxime, den grootsten eyver en naedruck betoonde tot het uytrusten en sich in postuyr stellen ter Zee, maer te Landt soe eyverigen aenstalt niet en stelde. . . .'
47. Field Deputies to G. Fagel, 28 April 1672. R.A. St. Gen. 7153.
48. Field Deputies to the States General, 9 May 1672. R.A. St. Gen. 7153.
49. Same to the States of Holland, 28 May 1672. R.A. St. Gen. 7153.
50. Johan de Witt to William III, 15 May 1672. *Brieven van Johan de Witt*, iv, 332.
51. Field Deputies to G. Fagel, 1 May 1672. R.A. St. Gen. 7153. *Het Staatsche Leger*, v, 304.
52. Field Deputies to G. Fagel, 6 May 1672. R.A. St. Gen. 7153.
53. W. J. Knoop, *Krijgs- en Geschiedkundige Beschouwingen over Willem den Derde*, i, 96.
54. Field Deputies to G. Fagel, 28 April 1672, second letter. R.A. St. Gen. 7153. *Het Staatsche Leger*, v, 317.
55. The Prince to Johan de Witt, 16 May 1672. *Brieven aan Johan de Witt*, ii, 628-9. H. van Beverningk to same, 22 May 1672. *Ibid.*, ii, 643-4.
56. H. van Beverningk to Johan de Witt, 17 May 1672. *Ibid.*, ii, 638-41.
57. For de Witt's attitude, see Johan de Witt to H. van Beverningk, 23 May 1672. *Brieven van Johan de Witt*, iv, 342-3.
58. H. van Beverningk to Johan de Witt, 27 May 1672. *Brieven aan Johan de Witt*, ii, 645-6.
59. Johan de Witt to H. van Beverningk, 4 June 1672. *Brieven van Johan de Witt*, iv, 345-8.
60. *Het Staatsche Leger*, v, 324.
61. C. Rousset, *Histoire de Louvois*, i, 343-4.
62. *Ibid.*, i, 346-8. On the share of Le Tellier in the work of his son, Rousset is corrected by L. André, *Michel Le Tellier et Louvois*, Paris, 1942.
63. P. de Groot to Johan de Witt, 5 February 1672. *Brieven aan Johan de Witt*, ii, 585.
64. Diary of C. C. Rumpf *sub* 18 April. R.A. Leg. 640, unpaged.
65. For the negotiations leading up to the treaty, see *Urkunden und Actenstücke*, iii, 195-262.
66. On this, see the letter of the Queen of Spain to Count Monterey, 27 April 1672. *Correspondance de la Cour d'Espagne*, v, No. 328.
67. Sylvius's letters of credence, *Correspondentie*, II, i, 40-1; his instructions, *ibid.*, 41.
68. P. Geyl, *Oranje en Stuart*, 430-1. The work was written at two different times. Its original portion makes an important contribution, but the latter half of the book is not authoritative.

Chapter 7

1. Field Deputies' letter of 7 June. R.A. St. Gen. 7153.
2. *Brieven aan Johan de Witt*, ii, 649.

3. Field deputies' letter of 10 June. R.A. St. Gen. 7153.
4. H. van Beverningk to Johan de Witt, 10 June. *Brieven aan Johan de Witt*, ii, 650.
5. Field deputies' letter of 11 June. R.A. St. Gen. 7153. Montbas escaped and later published *Mémoires* (Utrecht, 1673) which are unusually untrustworthy.
6. H. van Beverningk to Johan de Witt, 12 June 1672. *Brieven aan Johan de Witt*, ii, 654.
7. Diary of C. C. Rumpf, R.A. Leg. 640.
8. *Het Staatsche Leger*, v, 286.
9. *Notulen Gehouden ter Staten-Vergadering van Holland* (1671–75), ed. N. Japikse, Werken uitgegeven door het Historisch Genootschap, Derde Serie No. 19, 84–6. A work of the first importance for the events of 1671 and 1672.
10. M. Turner to G. A. van Reede van Amerongen, 13 June 1672. Huisarchief Amerongen, Familie-Archief No. 101 C.
11. P.R.O. S.P. 84/189, f. 21. S.T. to 'J. A.'Pereira', presumably a cover name for a clerk in Lord Arlington's office. Tucker had also acted as a spy during the 1665 war.
12. Johan to Cornelis de Witt, 18 and 20 June. *Brieven van Johan de Witt*, iv, 385–7.
13. In a letter to Nicolaas Vivien. *Brieven van Johan de Witt*, iv, 389.
14. Van Gent and Odijk to the States General, 23 June 1672. R.A. St. Gen. 7153. The letter is printed in *Notulen*, 127–8.
15. *Ibid.*, 128–9.
16. For the debate, see *Notulen*, 129–35. The account given by Wagenaar, xiv, 47–53, which is taken almost verbatim from this source, is perhaps more easily available.
17. *Wicquefort*, iv, 431.
18. *Wagenaar*, xiv, 61. Mary Caroline Trevelyan, in *William The Third and the Defence of Holland*, 1930, 229–30, argued that he wrote the letter 'because he wished to remind the States of the existence of domains in the Generality which were not their property'. This is a complete misreading of the facts. Breda was not a sovereignty. On Miss Trevelyan's book the last word was written by Geyl in a devastating review which he reprinted in his *Kernproblemen van Onze Geschiedenis*, Utrecht, 1937.
19. The terms are given in full by *Wagenaar*, xiv, 99–100.
20. *Wagenaar*, xiv, 67.
21. See *Wagenaar*, xiv, 71–83, for the events of 29 and 30 June. Samuel Tucker wrote from Rotterdam on 29 June and mentioned the disorders there, but without much detail. P.R.O. S.P. 84/189, f. 58.
22. P. J. van Boetzelaer, heer van Asperen, to the Prince, 1 July 1672. *Correspondentie*, II, i, 56–7.
23. G. Fagel to the Prince, 1 July 1672. *Ibid.*, 57–8.
24. *Notulen*, 157–65, esp. 164.
25. *Ibid.*, 167–71.
26. *Ibid.*, 184.
27. *Wagenaar*, xiv, 75.
28. It appeared as a pamphlet, Knuttel No. 10144.
29. It was also published as a pamphlet. Knuttel No. 10151.

30. Though the Pensionary died in his father's lifetime, he had married well and had invested his wife's fortune with remarkable skill. He lived very simply. By the time of his death he was a wealthy man.

31. These generally held attitudes are conveniently summarized in a very moderate dialogue between a sergeant and a corporal. The sergeant supports de Witt, the corporal believes all the Orangist rumours he hears. *Onpartydige Consideratien Over de Missive van sijn Hoogheyt* . . ., Knuttel No. 10340.

32. *Wagenaar*, xiv, 116.

33. The bibliography for 20 August is enormous. See, chiefly, *Wagenaar*, xiv, 142–79; *Notulen*, 284–8; B. Costerus, *Historisch Verhaal*, 3rd. edn. Leyden 1737, 234–6; and, among later works, Fruin, R., 'De Schuld van Willem III en zijn Vrienden Aan den Moord der Gebroeders de Witt, *Verspreide Geschriften*, iv, 356–76.

34. There is real need for a good life of de Witt in English, and we are promised one by Professor H. H. Rowen.

35. The most important of them is Costerus, *op. cit.* The most widely read is of course Alexandre Dumas's *La Tulipe Noire*.

36. The bitterness of Bernard Costerus, the author of the *Historisch Verhaal*, arose from the fact that he was in 1672 Secretary of the town and had to undergo the subsequent French occupation.

37. *Notulen*, 301.

Chapter 8

1. Draft, dated 12/22 June 1672, in Dutch: P.R.O.S.P. 84/189, ff. 37–40.

2. To Mr Bond, Amsterdam, 24 June 1672. '. . . I find many would rather be under the King of England than the King of France. . . . I am fully persuaded the King may have any terms.' P.R.O.S.P. 84/189, f. 45.

3. P.R.O.S.P. 84/189, f. 68.

4. Buckingham to Lord Clifford, Hague, 25 June/5 July 1672. P.R.O.S.P. 84/189, ff. 48–50.

5. *Ibid.*

6. *Notulen*, 180.

7. Monmouth, Buckingham, and Arlington to Lord Clifford, 28 June O.S. 1672. P.R.O.S.P. 84/189, f. 144. The whole dispatch, which is very important, occupies ff. 143–51.

8. *Ibid.*, f. 148.

9. They are given in detail by *Wagenaar*, xiv, 120–4.

10. *Notulen*, 226.

11. The proposals are printed. *Correspondentie*, II, i, 80.

12. P.R.O.S.P. 104/177, f. 69.

13. P.R.O.S.P. 104/177, f. 70.

14. His relationship, if any, to the former Pensionary was negligible. His letters are to be found in P.R.O.S.P. 84/191 and 192.

15. P.R.O.S.P. 104/177, f. 151 b.

16. Monmouth, Buckingham, and Arlington to Clifford, 28 June 1672. P.R.O.S.P. 84/189, f. 148 b.

17. Queen Regent to Monterey, 7 December 1672. *Correspondance de la Cour d'Espagne*, v, No. 407.

18. Same to same, 3 July, 1672. *Ibid.*, No. 357.

19. Same to same, 20 July 1672. *Ibid.*, No. 366.

20. Frederick William and Anhalt had married sisters, both of them Princesses of Orange. When the Electress died in 1668 he married a second time. The members of the Elector's first family were largely pro-Dutch and those of his second pro-French, which was to cause a great amount of trouble, especially in the years 1678–85.

21. Hamel Bruynincx to G. A. van Reede van Amerongen, 17 November 1672. *Weensche Gezantschapsberichten*, ed. von Antal and de Pater, i, 50.

22. Amerongen to William III, from Frankfort, 3/13 October 1672. R.A. Leg. Archief 370, No. 103. Badly summarized *Urkunden und Actenstücke*, iii, 299.

23. E.g. Amerongen to H. Fagel, 27 October 1672. *Urkunden und Actenstücke*, iii, 315–16.

24. Amerongen to G. Fagel, 8 December 1672. *Ibid.*, 343.

25. Johan Maurits of Nassau to William III, 16 February 1673. *Archives de la Maison d'Orange-Nassau*, deuxième série, v, 310–11.

26. *Het Staatsche Leger*, vi, 168–9.

27. *Ibid.*, vii, 223.

28. William III to Arlington, 7 October 1672. *Correspondentie*, II, i, 115–16.

29. William III to the States General, 7 November 1672. *Correspondentie*, II, i, 139. Most of the traditional accounts, e.g. that of W. J. Knoop, *Nederland in 1672 en 1673*, 125–30, relied on sources such as *Het Ontroerde Nederlandt*, Amsterdam 1674 (ascribed to T. van Domselaar), i, 472–9, which were defective. They should be corrected by William's own letters, printed in the *Correspondentie*, and by *Het Staatsche Leger*, v.

30. William III to the States General, 11 November 1672. *Correspondentie*, loc. cit.

31. Same to same, 14 November. *Ibid.*, 140.

32. Same to same, 20 December 1672. *Ibid.*, 164–5.

33. Prince Johan Maurits van Nassau to William III, 16 November 1672. *Correspondentie*, II, i, 141.

34. Lt-Gen. Conrad van Königsmarck to William III, 18 November 1672. *Ibid.*, 144–5.

35. *Notulen*, 338.

36. *Ibid.*, 364–5.

37. William III to G. Fagel, 18 December 1672. *Correspondentie*, II, i, 162.

38. *Notulen*, 369.

39. The Knuttel pamphlets concerned with the attack are Nos. 10706–10710. They were put out in several languages and distributed all over Europe. See also *Het Ontroerde Nederlandt*, i, 484–91.

40. See on this, in addition to Rousset and André, P. de Ségur, *Le Maréchal de Luxembourg et le Prince d'Orange 1666–1678*, Paris, 1902, esp. 88–9. De Ségur's biography of Luxembourg, which eventually filled three volumes, is seriously defective.

41. *Het Ontroerde Nederlandt,* i, 494–8.
42. *Notulen,* 386.

Chapter 9

1. Don Manuel de Lira to the Queen-Regent, 7 February 1673. *Correspondance de la Cour d'Espagne,* v, No. 427.
2. Cf. the character of Fagel given by A. de Fouw, Jr. in *Onbekende Raadpensionarissen,* Hague, 1946.
3. Queen-Regent to de Lira, 16 August 1673. *Correspondance de la Cour d'Espagne,* v, No. 458.
4. *Lettres de Pierre de Groot à Abraham de Wicquefort,* 92–3. Letter of 30 January 1673
5. See an unsigned letter from Amsterdam of 26 August 1673, printed in *Mignet,* iv, 149–52.
6. *Notulen,* 386.
7. Prince Johan Maurits of Nassau to William III, 6 January 1673. *Correspondentie,* II, i, 171.
8. *Urkunden und Actenstücke,* iii, 366–70.
9. *Ibid.,* 372.
10. Amerongen to William III, 9 March 1673. *Ibid.,* 373.
11. Kramprich's dispatch of 13 March 1673. Quoted by O. Klopp, *Der Fall des Hauses Stuart,* i, 334–5.
12. *Notulen,* 391.
13. *Ibid.,* 391–3.
14. C. Huygens to C. C. Rumpf, 25 May 1673. R.A. Leg. 640.
15. *Het Staatsche Leger,* vi, 8–9.
16. Klopp, i, 336–8.
17. *Mignet,* iv, 142–4.
18. Klopp, *loc. cit.*; *Weensche Gezantschapsberichten,* i, 68.
19. William III to G. Fagel, 2 June 1673. *Correspondentie,* II, i, 236.
20. *Het Staatsche Leger,* vi, 15.
21. In English accounts it is called the battle of the Texel.
22. *Lettres de Pierre de Groot à Abraham de Wicquefort,* 159–60. Letter of 29 August 1673
23. Letter quoted in Rousset, *Historie de Louvois,* i, 467.
24. Queen-Regent to de Lira, *Correspondance de la Cour d'Espagne,* v, No. 458. Louvois to Le Tellier, in Rousset, *Histoire de Louvois,* i, 473.
25. A copy is in R.A. Familie-Archief Fagel 426.
26. *Het Ontroerde Nederlandt,* ii, 607–20; *Het Staatsche Leger,* vi, 19; Rousset, *Histoire de Louvois,* i, 480–1.
27. De Ségur, *Le Maréchal de Luxembourg et le Prince d'Orange 1668–1678,* 259.
28. *Journaal van Constantijn Huygens, den zoon, gedurende de veldtochten der jaren 1673, 1675, 1676, 1677 en 1678.* Werken van het Historisch Genootschap, Nieuwe Serie No. 32, 4 and *passim.*
29. *Correspondentie,* II, i, 299.
30. William III to the Secret Committee, 15, 18 October 1673. *Correspondentie,* II, i, 303–05.

31. Huygens *Journaal*, 10–11.
32. *Ibid.*, 12. *Correspondentie*, II, i, 307.
33. Huygens *Journaal*, 14. *Correspondentie*, *loc. cit.*
34. Cf. Hubert van Houtte, *Les Occupations étrangères en Belgique sous l'ancien régime*, Gand 1930, i, 81.
35. The account in *Het Staatsche Leger*, vi, 19–20, should be corrected by that in Huygens *Journaal*, 16–20.
36. *Correspondentie*, II, i, 309–10.
37. Rousset, *Histoire de Louvois*, i, 500.
38. *Correspondentie*, II, i, 314–16.
39. *Ibid.*, 320.
40. *Notulen*, 423–7.
41. *Wagenaar*, xiv, 327–9.
42. See on the authorship and the whole matter K. H. D. Haley, *William of Orange and the English Opposition 1672–1674*, Oxford, 1953.
43. Colbert de Croissy to Louis XIV, 20 November 1673. *Mignet*, iv, 235.
44. Same to same, 25 December 1673. *Ibid.*, 247–8.
45. Charles II to the States General, 10 February 1674. R.A. St. Gen. 4291, ff. 179–80.
46. R.A. Nass. Dom. 783.

Chapter 10

1. On the disorders of the Dutch in 1674, see *Original Letters Written to the Earl of Arlington by Sir Richard Bulstrode*, London, 1712. Bulstrode was a hostile and malicious witness, and his evidence should be treated with caution.
2. The main narrative sources for this period are L. Sylvius, *Historien Onses Tyds*, Amsterdam, 1684, which is an inferior continuation of Aitzema; and *Tweejaerige Geschiedenissen, Voorgevallen in de Jaeren 1674 en 1675*, Amsterdam, 1678, which is vol. iii of *Het Ontroerde Nederlandt* or at least serves as such. Wagenaar is less useful than before. For military history, beyond the standard French sources which are often exaggerated, there is W. J. Knoop, *Krijgs- en Geschiedkundige Beschouwingen over Willem den Derde*, ii, Schiedam, 1895. Knoop is too favourable to William and is also based exclusively on materials published in his day. Much has come to light since. *Het Staatsche Leger*, vi, is better but too succinct. The best sources, not always truthful, are the letters of the Prince. Heemskerk's dispatches in *Weensche Gezantschapsberichten*, i, are also essential.
3. William III to the Committee for Secret Affairs, 21 May 1674. *Correspondentie*, II, i, 363–4.
4. *Weensche Gezantschapsberichten*, i, 132.
5. William III to C. van Heemskerk, 6 July 1674. *Correspondentie*, II, i, 412–13.
6. *Weensche Gezantschapsberichten*, i, 128.
7. *Original Letters*, 38.
8. *Mignet*, iv, 304–05.
9. In addition to the sources cited above, the main source used for the battle was the letters of the Prince. *Correspondentie*, II, i, 457, 460–71. Pierre du Moulin made up a

Relation succincte de ce qui s'est passé de plus considérable sous le commandement de S.A. Mgr. le Prince d'Orange dans le campagne de 1674, which probably circulated in manuscript. It was not published until 1747. It is useful for the entire campaign.

10. William III to G. Fagel, 9 September 1674. *Correspondentie,* II, i, 487. Same to C. van Heemskerk, *eodem die, ibid.,* 488–90.
11. *Correspondentie,* II, i, 500–06.
12. *Weensche Gezantschapsberichten,* i, 135. It seems likely that the *Relation succincte* of du Moulin, referred to above, was prepared in the first instance as a threat to force the Habsburgs to agree to the change in command, and that their acceptance of the arrangement made publication unnecessary.
13. *Correspondentie,* II, i, 512.
14. *Weensche Gezantschapsberichten,* i, 155.
15. Sir William Temple to Arlington, 26 February 1675. Temple, *Works,* ii, 325.
16. See de Lira to Carlos II, 16 March 1677. *Correspondence de la Cour d'Espagne,* v, No. 636.
17. On William's imprudence and 'great imbecility', see 'A Relation of the present state of affaires in ye United Provinces written about the last of April of ye yeare 1675'. P.R.O.S.P. 84/198, ff. 285–96, esp. f. 288. Temple's suspicion of Fagel is expressed in his *Works,* ii, 326.

Chapter 11

1. *Mignet,* iv, 306–08; Temple, *Works,* ii, 315–16.
2. E. Coleman to the Abbé Rissini, 12/22 April 1674. Campana de Cavelli, Emilia marquise, *Les Dernières Stuarts à Saint-Germain en Laye,* Paris, 1871, i, Document, p. 143.
3. Huygens, *Journaal,* iii, 8, *sub* 16 October 1673. *Correspondentie,* II, i, 334–5. Kramprich dispatch of 9 March 1674, quoted by Klopp, *op. cit.,* ii, 4–5.
4. The account given in Thomas Carte, *The Life of James Duke of Ormond,* Oxford, 1851, iv, 493 ff. is better than that given by Burnet, ii, 60 ff. See also Dalrymple, Appendix, 109, and 119.
5. Temple to Charles II, 22 and 29 January 1675. *Works,* ii, 321–3.
6. *Refutatie, of Wederlegginge van de Brief Geschreven van de Prins van Orange, op den 18 Maert 1675, aen de Staaten van Zeelant,* Knuttel No. 11333.
7. *Eenige sware beschuldinge rechtmatigh tegen de Prins van Orange ingebracht.* Knuttel No. 11407.
8. Temple to Williamson, 4 October 1675, N.S., P.R.O.S.P. 84/199, ff. 160–1.
9. E. Bodemann, ed., *Briefwechsel der Herzogin Sophie von Hannover,* 213, 247, 308.
10. The figures are from R.A. Nass. Dom. 784, 785, 786, 787 and have been rounded off to the nearest thousand. The 1676 gross figure was fl.441,000 but this included fl.125,000 from Spain and fl.52,000 from the East India Company which I excluded from ordinary income, as also the fl.2,000,000 from Holland in 1674. All seventeenth and eighteenth century incomes fluctuated from year to year to a degree which we would find very uncomfortable.
11. Temple to (Williamson), 10 September 1675. P.R.O.S.P. 84/199, f. 130. The figures on Amalia's estate come from K.H.A. Inventaris 14, XIII, 12a and 13.

12. Charles Davenant to Williamson, 18 January 1676. P.R.O.S.P. 84/200, f. 20.

13. *Correspondance de la Cour d'Espagne*, v, No. 502.

14. There is a long correspondence on this topic. See *Correspondance de la Cour d'Espagne*, v, Nos. 524, 525, 536, 537, 538, 603, 614, 631 and also R.A. St. Gen. 7153 for a letter from Heemskerk dated 29 May 1675, describing a pleasant conversation with Villa Hermosa.

15. *Correspondance de la Cour d'Espagne*, v, No. 584, 600.

16. *Ibid.*, No. 602, 609, 614, 631, 636.

17. Huygens, *Journaal*, iii, *passim*.

18. Sir William Temple to Charles II, 30 November 1674. *Works*, ii, 315.

19. Sir William Temple to Danby, 26 March 1677. *Works*, ii, 453.

20. E.g. *Mémoires du Maréchal de Villars*, Paris, 1884, i, 18: '. . . les malheurs dans la guerre lui sont venus, en partie, de n'avoir jamais eu dans ce métier d'assez bon maîtres pour cultiver les dispositions que beaucoup d'esprit et une très grande valeur naturelle avoient mis en lui, et lequel, malgré ces avantages, n'a peut être jamais rien fait qui ait pu lui donner la réputation de général.'

21. 11 May 1676. *Correspondentie*, II, ii, 98.

22. Ernst August of Brunswick Luneburg, from 1689 Duke, from 1692 Elector, of Hanover. Father of George I.

23. In addition to the sources cited for earlier campaigns, see the letters of the Prince and Waldeck in *Wilhelm III von Oranien und Georg Friedrich von Waldeck*, ii, ed. P. L. Müller, Hague 1880, 272–312. There is also a pamphlet in English 'A Particular Account of This Last Siege of Maastricht', Knuttel No. 11375. Dijkvelt, acting as a field deputy, wrote reports on the progress of the siege to the States of Holland, some of which are preserved in K.H.A. Prins Willem III, xi b, 56. An interesting letter of J. Ellis to Sir Joseph Williamson, dated 29 July O.S., is at P.R.O.S.P. 84/202, ff. 124–6.

24. Müller, *op. cit.*, ii, 272.

25. See the reproaches in Waldeck's letter to William of 13 September. Müller, *op. cit.*, ii, 313–14.

26. William III to Waldeck, 27 September 1676, *ibid.*, 323.

27. Sir L. Jenkins to Sir J. Williamson, 26 December 1675/5 January 1676. P.R.O.S.P. 84/199, f. 301. Sir J. Williamson to Sir W. Temple, 27 April 1676 O.S., P.R.O.S.P. 84/201, f. 95.

28. H. Courtin to Louis XIV, 12 October 1676. *Mignet, op. cit.*, iv, 406.

29. *Receuil des Instructions données aux ambassadeurs et ministres de France* . . ., xxv, Angleterre, ed. J. J. Jusserand, ii, 194.

30. Sir W. Temple to Charles II, 15 January 1677. P.R.O.S.P. 84/204, ff. 21–2.

31. *Mignet, op. cit.*, iv, 408–16. The most important of d'Estrades' dispatches was that of 4 November 1676: Archives du ministère des affaires étrangères, Paris, *Correspondance de Hollande*, xciv, No. 4. There are MS. copies of some of these dispatches in K.H.A. Prins Willem III, xIII, 2, and it is these that I have used.

32. Temple, *Works*, ii, 448, 452–3.

Chapter 12

1. Sir W. Temple to Sir J. Williamson, Soestdijk, 26 February 1677 O.S., P.R.O.S.P. 84/204, f. 151.
2. Huygens, *Journaal*, iii, 151–3.
3. On the battle, see Huygens, *Journaal, loc. cit.*; Knoop, *op. cit.*, ii, 253–7; *Het Staatsche Leger*, vi, 65–6; Rousset, *op. cit.*, ii, 296–300; and William's own account, Knuttel, No. 11488.
4. *Correspondentie*, I, i, 4–5.
5. *Ibid.*
6. Huygens, *Journaal*, iii, 184.
7. *Correspondentie*, II, ii, 184–9.
8. William III to the Secret Committee, 24 July 1677. *Correspondentie*, II, ii, 189.
9. Huygens, *Journaal*, iii, 207; William III to G. Fagel, 29 August 1677, *Correspondentie*, II, ii, 199–204. See also same to the Secret Committee 15 August, *ibid.*, 192–4.
10. The account of Charleroi given in Rousset, *op. cit.*, ii, 334–41, is defective because the French commanders thought the siege to have been undertaken in earnest and were contemptuous of the Prince's poor dispositions. They did not realize that the siege began as a feint and never developed into anything else.
11. *Correspondentie*, II, ii, 199–204.
12. Huygens, *Journaal*, iii, 204. Colyear was the father of David, first Earl of Portmore, who accompanied the Prince in 1688.
13. This habit was noted, among others, by Halifax. H. C. Foxcroft, *Life and Works of the First Marquis of Halifax*, London, 1898, ii, 202.
14. Meredith to Williamson, 26 October 1677. P.R.O.S.P. 84/205, f. 152 b.
15. Diary of Dr Edward Lake, *sub* 21 October 1677 O.S. *Camden Miscellany*, i, 5.
16. The Danish resident at The Hague wrote to his opposite number at Dantzig on 13 November that the joy at the news of William's marriage was neither complete nor widespread, and that the acclamations were for the most part false. His letter was intercepted, K.H.A. Prins Willem III, XIII, 2, from the original in *Correspondance de Hollande*, xcix, No. 99.
17. Diary of Dr Edward Lake *sub* 4 November 1677. *Camden Miscellany*, i, 6.
18. The baby died within a month.
19. Sophie princess of Osnabrück to the Elector Palatine, Osnabrück, 5 January 1678. E. Bodemann, ed., *Briefwechsel der Herzogin Sophie von Hannover*, Leipzig, 1885, 309.
20. Sir Winston Churchill, perhaps relying on an erroneous statement in the biography of Marlborough by Lord Wolseley, thought that at this time William and Churchill were the best of friends and that the Prince would prefer Churchill to anyone else. The relevant portion of Barillon's letter to Louis XIV of May 1678 referring to Churchill is as follows: 'Ce n'est pas un homme qu'ait aucune experience d'affaire. On dit aussi que Monsieur le Prince d'Orange s'est declare quil ne faut point d'autre Ambassadeur d'Angleterre en Hollande que luy et quil est seulement necessaire d'y envoyer des gens dociles et qui se laissent conduire.'

P.R.O. 31/3/145, f. 160 b. The word 'luy' quite clearly refers to William rather than to Churchill.

21. This whole matter had been discussed at length by Clyde Leclare Grose, 'The Anglo-Dutch Treaty of 1678', *English Historical Review*, xxxix, (1924), 349–72 and 526–51. Despite a number of minor errors arising from an almost exclusive reliance on materials in English and Dutch, the chronology is sound. The chief sources to appear since 1924 are the *Correspondentie* and the letters printed in the second volume of A. Browning, *Thomas Osborne, Earl of Danby and Duke of Leeds* Glasgow, 3 vols., 1944–51.

22. G. Fagel to Waldeck, The Hague, 10 November 1677. *Bijdragen voor Vaderlandsche Geschiedenis en Oudheidkunde*, 2e Reeks, vii, 155; '... maer ick gelooff niet dat sijn Majt. de wapenen oyt tegens Vrankrijck opnemen sal. ...'

23. The treaty was signed 10 January, revised, and signed a second time on 26 January. See Grose, *op. cit.*, 349–55 and works noted.

24. D'Estrades dispatch of 14 June. *Correspondance de Hollande*, cii, No. 97.

25. *Correspondance de Hollande*, cii, No. 113; printed in *Mignet, op. cit.*, iv, 587–8.

26. H. van Beverningk to G. Fagel, Nijmegen, 10 July 1678. A.R.A. St. Hol. 2883. 'In 't opstaen spraken sij [the French plenipotentiaries] noch een woort van Mons ende seijden, indijen dije stadt in hare handen viel nae dat de tractaten met hare Hoog Mogenden souden geteeckent ende geratificeert sijn, dat sij dije dan souden restitueren, daer uijt men dan mocht besluijten, dat sij bij anderen toevallen het niet en souden doen.' Although van Beverningk thought the news important enough to send to Fagel by special courier rather than through the post, it seems to have escaped the attention of most later students of the period.

27. Huygens, *Journaal*, iii, 270–6; *Correspondentie*, II, ii, 270–3; *Het Staatsche Leger*, vi, 79–80; Rousset, *Histoire de Louvois*, ii, 514–32; Knoop, *op. cit.*, ii, 304–25, etc. Various papers on the topic given by Knoop and Fruin are conveniently gathered in R. Fruin and W. J. Knoop, *Willem III en de Slag van Saint-Denis*, Hague, 1881, which also contains a useful map. Even today the old story that William fought with the peace in his pocket is accepted by people who ought to know better and appears in secondary works, e.g. *The New Cambridge Modern History*, v (1961), 296. Every bit of evidence goes to show that he did not have the peace in his pocket. The real point, however, is that peace in the meaningful sense of the word would begin only on the ratification of the treaties.

Chapter 13

1. *Négociations de Monsieur le Comte d'Avaux*, Paris, 1754, i, 7–9.

2. *Ibid.*, 260–1.

3. The surviving accounts for these years are few. In 1678, a war year, the revenue was only fl.379,000 but there was a previous balance of fl.1,184,097 or a total of fl.1,563,097; the expenses were fl.71,616 for administration and interest and fl.1,122,630 for the Court, leaving a balance on 25 July 1678 of fl.368,851. A.R.A. Nass. Dom. 788. For 1680 the revenue came to fl.1,191,545 which, together with the previous balance of fl.239,803, gave a total of fl.1,431,349 odd.

The issues were only fl.406,867 and the new balance amounted to fl.1,024,482. A.R.A. Nass. Dom. 789. For 1682 the receipts were fl.1,109,951, the previous balance fl.1,115,929, and the total fl.2,225,880. The issues amounted to fl.443,838, and the new balance to fl.1,782,042. A.R.A. Nass. Dom. 790. From the balance figures it is obvious that the Prince reduced the level of his cash balances in 1679 and 1681 as well as in 1678, but he was probably paying off debt and he could not have known that the Spanish and the Dutch would be so slow to repay their debts to him. In 1682 the Dutch still owed him fl.430,437 of the fl.1,500,000 due by the Treaty of Westminster of 1674. A.R.A. Nass. Dom. 602, ff. 232-3. The Spanish, of course, paid nothing. It was a further inconvenience that the account for 1682 was only declared on 22 December 1687.

4. Hamel Bruynincx to Griffier Fagel, 5 February 1682. R.G.P. 67, 337-40. It was finally conferred on 11 December 1683. Klopp, *op. cit.*, iii, 153. The Prince was often and inaccurately given the style of Serene or Royal Highness throughout his early life.

5. York to Col. George Legge, 14 April 1679. Hist. MSS. Comm. 11th Report, Appendix Part 5, 30. Cf. the comment of Legge's son on the letter, printed in Burnet, *op. cit.*, ii, 198 n. B. Bathurst, *Letters of Two Queens* (1925), 91-2.

6. Sophie, Princess of Osnabrück to the Elector Palatine, 22 June 1679. *Briefwechsel der Herzogin Sophie von Hannover*, 363.

7. D'Avaux to Louis XIV, 21 September 1679. *Correspondance de Hollande*, cxii, No. 84, from a copy in K.H.A. Prins Willem III, XIII, 2.

8. William III to Danby, 13 January 1679. *Correspondentie*, II, ii, 289; to Ossory, mid-February 1679, *ibid.*, 291.

9. Ossory to Ormonde, 15 March 1678/9. Hist. MSS. Comm. *Ormonde* N.S., iv, 358. York to Col. George Legge, 28 March 1679. Hist. MSS. Comm. 11th Report, Appendix Part 5, 30.

10. James Macpherson, ed., *Original Papers*, London, 1775, i, 92 n. York to William III, 14 May 1679. Hist. MSS. Comm. 15th Report, Appendix Part 5, 129-30. Same to Col. Legge, 28 May 1679. *Campana da Cavelli, op. cit.*, i, Document No. 250.

11. Barillon to Louis XIV, 30 September 1680. P.R.O. 31/3/146, f. 305.

12. York to William III, 17 October 1679. Hist. MSS. Comm. 15th Report, Appendix Part 5, 140.

13. D'Avaux to Louis XIV, 7 September 1679. *Correspondance de Hollande*, cxii, No. 73, from a copy in K.H.A. Prins Willem III, XIII, 2.

14. Same to same, 21 September 1679. *Ibid.*, No. 84.

15. Same to same, 5 October 1679. *Ibid.*, cxiii, No. 4.

16. J. P. Kenyon, *Robert Spencer, Earl of Sunderland*, 1958, 36.

17. E.g. Barillon to Louis XIV, 7 December 1679: 'Beaucoup de gens tournent les yeux presentement vers Mr le Prince d'Orange, il a de grands menagemens pour le peuple et cherche a s'appuyer de ceux qui ont le plus de credit et qui sont les plus opposés a la cour ... Le Roy d'Angleterre est informé des desseins de Mr le Prince d'Orange et tesmoigne en estre fort aigri, ...' P.R.O. 31/3/143, ff. 102-03.

18. Sir Robert Southwell to the Duke of Ormond, 13 December 1679. Hist. MSS.

Comm. *Ormonde* N.S., iv, 567. Barillon to Louis XIV, 14 and 18 December 1679. P.R.O. 31/3/143, f. 118 and 121.

19. William III to Ossory, early February 1680. *Correspondentie*, II, ii, 317.

20. Barillon to Louis XIV, 25 January 1680. P.R.O. 31/3/144, ff. 44–5.

21. Klopp, *op. cit.*, ii, 237–8. Barillon thought that the money at any rate might be provided by the States General rather than Parliament. Barillon to Louis XIV, 19 February 1680. P.R.O. 31/3/144 f.

22. D'Avaux to Louis XIV, 19 October 1679. *Correspondance de Hollande*, cxiii, No. 16, quoting an interview of the Prince with Fitzpatrick.

23. Fuenmayor to Carlos II, 23 April and 7 May 1680. *Correspondance de la Cour d'Espagne*, v, No. 841 and 842.

24. For instance Clarke, *James II*, i, 661.

25. Barillon to Louis XIV, 28 October 1680. P.R.O. 31/3/146, ff. 338–9. Cf. James's attitude in June as reported by same to same, 20 June 1680, P.R.O. 31/3/145, f. 199.

26. For example Sidney Godolphin to William III, 1 November 1680. *Archives*, II, v, 436–7; Sir William Temple to same, 30 November, *ibid.*, 445–9.

27. Barillon to Louis XIV, 5 December 1680. P.R.O. 31/3/147, f. 405.

28. William III to Sir Leoline Jenkins, 10 December 1680. Dalrymple, *Memoirs*, Appendix p. 306. Van Leyden van Leeuwen to William III, 7/17 December, *Archives*, II, v, 451–6.

29. *Archives, loc. cit.*

30. York to Hyde, 14 December 1680. *Clarendon Correspondence*, i, 49.

31. J. S. Clarke, *James II*, i, 659.

32. J. S. Clarke, *James II*, i, 714.

33. Henry Sydney to William III, 28 June 1681. Dalrymple, *Memoirs*, Appendix Part 1, 9–13.

34. William III to Lord Hyde, undated but 1 April 1681. *Archives*, II, v, 493–4.

35. Barillon to Louis XIV, 25 August 1681. P.R.O. 31/3/149, f. 231.

36. Sir L. Jenkins to Henry Savile, 12/22 August 1681. *Savile Correspondence*, 217–18. (Camden Society, vol. 71.) Barillon to Louis XIV, 14 August. P.R.O. 31/3/149, f. 217.

37. Barillon to Louis XIV, 28 July 1681. Campana da Cavelli, *op. cit.*, i, Document No. 348.

38. Barillon to Louis XIV, 4 August 1681. P.R.O. 31/3/149, ff. 205 ss.

39. Hist. Mss. Comm. *Ormonde*, N.S., vi, 113–15.

40. Barillon to Louis XIV, 11 August. P.R.O. 31/3/149, ff. 213–16.

41. *Hatton Correspondence*, ii, 4. Barillon to Louis XIV, 14 August. P.R.O. 31/3/149, ff. 218–19. *Savile Correspondence*, 217–18.

42. Barillon to Louis XIV, 7 and 25 August. P.R.O. 31/3/149, ff. 211 and 230–1.

43. *Correspondentie*, II, ii, 338; see also 313–14 and the dependent notes.

44. *Ibid.*, 364–5.

Chapter 14

1. D'Avaux to Louis XIV, 12 January 1679. *Correspondance de Hollande*, cxi.

2. In his dispatch of 16 February 1679 d'Avaux reported that he saw many people

of good intentions but very few of capacity. Only Valkenier and Paets are abl€ men. *Correspondance de Hollande*, cxi. Paets, like Valkenier, did not have long t< live.

3. Sir W. Temple to L. Hyde, 27 December 1678. *Clarendon Correspondence*, i, 37

4. *Correspondentie*, II, ii, 301–03.

5. Or perhaps a parcel of the Empire. Hamel Bruynincx to the Griffier Fagel, 1§ March 1679. R.G.P., lxvii, 238.

6. D'Avaux, *Négociations en Hollande*, i, 18–19.

7. *Vervolgh van Saken van Staat en Oorlogh*, xvii, 35.

8. *Ibid.*, 65.

9. D'Avaux to Louis XIV, 3 August 1679. *Correspondance de Hollande*, cxii, No 46.

10. Same to same, 10 August, *ibid.*, No. 52. D'Avaux, of course, forgot to mentior quite a few of William's advisers.

11. See d'Avaux, *Négociations*, i, 18ff.

12. *Correspondentie*, II, ii, 336–7.

13. *Correspondentie*, II, ii, 358–73; see also the account of Constantijn Huygens of the 'Voyage de Cell' in *Werken van het Historisch Genootschap*, N.S., xlvi, Utrecht, 1888.

14. Barillon to Louis XIV, 17, 24 November and 1 December 1681. P.R.O. 31/3/150, ff. 323–42.

15. *Savile Correspondence*, 244.

16. A.R.A. St. Gen. 7315. A bowdlerized summary is given in *Négociations*, i, 196.

17. Note that the English did define a term which many scholars have accused then of purposely leaving vague. *Correspondentie*, II, ii, 416.

18. *Ibid.*, 422.

19. Barillon to Louis XIV, 26 February 1682. P.R.O. 31/3/151, f. 91.

20. P.R.O. 31/3/151, f. 4; there were conditions attached, which the Spanish refused to accept at this time.

21. *Archives*, II, v, 543–4.

22. D'Avaux, *Négociations*, i, 221.

23. *Ibid.*, 217. P.R.O. 31/3/151, f. 98.

24. J. G. von Rauchbar, *Leben und Thaten des Fürsten Georg Friedrich von Waldeck*, Arolsen, 1870–72, ii, 144–5.

25. *Wagenaar*, *op. cit.*, xv, 92.

26. On 20 August. The Resolution of the States General was printed. Knuttel No. 11816.

27. The *dragonnade* is described in *Verbalen Van't gepasserde in de Stadt, Ende het Prinsdom van Orange 1682*, Knuttel No. 11805.

28. *Journaal van Constantijn Huygens, den zoon*, sub Sunday, 11 October, 1682. *Werken van het Historisch Genootschap*, N.S., xlvi, 70.

29. G. Fagel to C. van Beuninghen, 23 October 1682. K.H.A. Prins Willem III, XI C, 115.

30. C. van Beuninghen to the Griffier Fagel, 5 January 1683 N.S. A.R.A. St. Gen. 7335.

31. Barillon to Louis XIV, 18 March and 8 April 1683. P.R.O. 31/3/154, ff. 310, 325. The Hanoverian match proposed in 1680 had fallen through.

32. Same to same, 10 May 1683. P.R.O. 31/3/155, f. 357: Le Sieur Lente [The Danish Ambassador to London] m'a fait plusieurs propositions en forme de discours sur lesquels je ne doute pas qu'il n'ayt eu ordre de faire une tentative. L'une estoit qu'on voulust icy prendre des mesures pour faire tomber la succession de la couronne d'Angleterre a Mr le Prince Georges a l'exclusion de Mr le Prince d'Orange.

33. Same to same, 10 June 1683, *ibid.*, f. 371.

34. *Correspondentie*, I, i, 16–17.

35. D'Avaux, *Négociations*, i, 249ff.

36. G. H. Kurtz, *Willem III en Amsterdam 1683–1685*, Utrecht, 1928, 67.

37. Kurtz, *op. cit.*, 77–8.

38. See, however, Kurtz, *op. cit.*, 121–3; Miss Kurtz appears to take van Banckem fairly seriously.

39. D'Avaux, ii, 202; Kurtz, *op. cit.*, 110.

Chapter 15

1. 'Il parle du traitté que viennent de signer les Estats comme d'une infamie qui n'a point d'exemple.' Barillon to Louis XIV, 6 July 1684. P.R.O. 31/3/158, f. 265. It was solely the conduct of the States General which the Prince was calling infamous, as Charles II and James realized. Cf. his letter to van Citters of 13 July 1684, *Correspondentie*, II, ii, 645.

2. See d'Avaux, iv, 4–6.

3. See on the attempts at reconciliation Gebhard, *Witsen*, i, 272–8; *Correspondentie*, I, i, 17; Müller, i, 293; and Kurtz, G. H. *Willem III en Amsterdam 1683–1685*, Utrecht, 1928, ff. 141.

4. See Strick's defence, *Correspondentie*, II, ii, 689–93.

5. See on this Wagenaar, xv, 259–79, which is largely based on d'Avaux, iv, 62–139; and also Gebhard, *Witsen*, i, 285–92, and Kurtz, *op. cit.* 155–63.

6. Barillon to Louis XIV, 12 June 1684. P.R.O. 31/3/158, f. 274 b.

7. William III to A. van Citters, 27 July 1684. *Correspondentie*, II, ii, 650.

8. Barillon to Louis XIV, 31 July 1684. P.R.O. 31/3/158, f. 281.

9. H. F. Thynne. The other was Dudley North.

10. A. van Citters to William III, 19/29 August 1684. *Correspondentie* II, ii, 656–60.

11. Barillon to Louis XIV, 10 September 1684. P.R.O. 31/3/159, f. 319.

12. Same to same, 19 October 1684. *Ibid.*, f. 344.

13. Same to same, 26 October 1684. *Ibid.*, f. 348.

14. William III to A. van Citters, 2 October 1684. *Correspondentie* II, ii, 665–6. Same to Charles II, *eo. die*, *ibid.*, 666–7.

15. A. van Citters to William III, 3/13 October 1684. *Ibid.*, 671.

16. *Ibid.*, 676.

17. A. van Citters to William III, 16/26 December 1684. *Ibid.*, 681.

18. Barillon to Louis XIV, 1 January 1685. P.R.O. 31/3/160, f. 2.

19. Dalrymple, *op. cit.*, Appendix, Part 1, 65–6.
20. Barillon to Louis XIV, August 1684. P.R.O. 31/3/159, f. 297.
21. Lord Preston to Sunderland, Paris, 23 August 1684 N.S. and 13 September N.S. Hist. Mss. Comm. 7th Report, Appendix, pp. 311–13. Preston, however, felt that the proposed league was purely defensive. In his *Négociations*, iv, 41–5, d'Avaux passed his trip off as, for the most part, a mere spectacle.
22. *Négociations*, iv, 86 and *passim*. It is to be noted that the dispatches of Barillon slight the work of Silvius and of van Citters and make the breach seem irreparable. D'Avaux is far more pessimistic.
23. William III to A. van Citters, 9 January 1685. *Correspondentie*, II, ii, 694.
24. A. van Citters to William III, 16/26 December 1684. *Correspondentie*, II, ii, 685.
25. P.R.O. 31/3/160, f. 30.
26. D'Avaux, *Négociations*, v, 106.
27. Barillon to Louis XIV, 26 February 1685. P.R.O. 31/3/160, f. 56.
28. *Mémoires de Monsieur de B*, 87.
29. Barillon to Louis XIV, 26 February 1685. P.R.O. 31/3/160, f. 56.
30. Same to same, 5 March 1685. *Ibid.*, ff. 73–4.
31. Sir C. Wyche reported to Ormonde on 3/13 March that the reconciliation had already taken place, and two days later Sir R. Southwell wrote: 'In Holland the Prince of Orange gets ground apace since the reconciliation, and that his Majesty has declared in his favour . . .' Hist. Mss. Comm. *Ormonde* N.S. vii, 334–5.
32. Sir C. Lyttelton to Viscount Hatton, 6/16 March. *Hatton Correspondence*, ii, 54. (Camden Society N.S. vol. 23.) Barillon to Louis XIV, 19 March. P.R.O. 31/3/160, ff. 84 *et seq*.
33. Dalrymple, Appendix, Part I, 117. As is well known, James's closing formula indicated his humour. If he ended 'as kind to you as you can desire' he was in a good mood; if he was displeased, he wrote 'as kind to you as you can expect'.
34. William's intermediary was the minister van der Waeyen. See William III to the Prince of Nassau, 30 March 1685: *Archives*, 2ieme Serie, v, 589–90. The loan story explains the Prince's order to raise f. 120,000, which was carried out in May and June. R. A. Nass. Dom. 603, ff. 16–17.
35. *Urkunden und Actenstücke*, iii, 778.
36. Burnet, *Own Times*, iii, 19 n.
37. Barillon to Louis XIV, 26 March 1685. Campana da Cavelli, ii, 28, Document No. 420.
38. Same to same, *eo. die*, P.R.O. 31/3/160, f. 194.
39. Bentinck's instructions, dated 4 July 1685, are at *Correspondentie* I, i, 20–21.
40. D'Avaux reported that this claim was grounded on the fact that the rebels used French coin. *Négociations*, v. 38–9. The source of their money is a fascinating speculation. On the whole it seems likely (1) that such operations cost relatively little in the seventeenth century and (2) that at least part of Monmouth's support came from the Prince's enemies in Amsterdam, men whom William would indeed call French. For the despair of Amsterdam at Monmouth's defeat, see *Négociations*, v, 87, 98. The Spanish and, of course, William himself were also accused of paying for the rebellions. The Prince's surviving accounts show no such expenditures,

and as I have indicated in the text William's policy at that time was the precise reverse of support of Monmouth.

41. Barillon to Louis XIV, 29 March 1685. P.R.O. 31/3/160, f. 100.

42. Same to same, 17 and 20 December 1685. P.R.O. 31/3/162, ff. 215, 218 b.

43. William asked for an establishment through Henry Sydney. Rochester to William III, 25 September 1685, O.S. *Correspondentie* II, ii, 717.

44. Barillon, in describing James's jealousy of William, wrote to Louis XIV on 26 March 1685: 'Cela le détermine à le jeter pour ainsy dire entre les bras de Votre Majesté et à chercher une seureté qu'il ne sçauroit trouver ailleurs. Je ne doute pas mesme que cet attachement aux intérets de Votre Majesté ne le rende dans la suite entiérement irréconciliable avec le prince d'Orange, et ne luy fasse prendre toutes les mesures possibles pour l'éloigner de la succession et donner sur cela des esperances à la Princesse Anne, parce que c'est une opinion establie icy qu'il n'aura point d'enfans qui vivent, et qu'on regarde encore comme une chose assurée que la princesse d'Orange n'aura point d'enfans.

'Je sçais bien que ce dessein paroistra d'abord chimérique et impraticable . . . Cependant je suis informé que non seulement les Catholiques, mais aussy tous ceux qui s'attachent fortement au Roy d'Angleterre, et qui le soustiennent dans ses desseins le pousserent à prendre des mesures qui aillent au delà de sa vie et qui les empeschent d'estre perdus et entiérement ruinez comme ils seroient, si le prince d'Orange venoit à la Couronne par la princesse sa femme.' P.R.O. 31/3/160, f. 94. The strong supporters of James undoubtedly included Sunderland, and also the Danish ambassador; the latter had proposed Mary's exclusion in 1683 and again almost immediately after Charles's death.

45. Barillon to Louis XIV, 19 November 1685. P.R.O. 31/3/162, f. 180.

46. *Clarendon Correspondence*, i, 165.

Chapter 16

1. These traditional figures have recently been challenged with some success by Warren C. Scoville, *The Persecution of Huguenots and French Economic Development 1680–1720*, 1960. Dr. Scoville puts the number of refugees as low as 200,000.

2. This was one of the most celebrated of the atrocity stories. The French government denied that the consul had ever been formally recognized as such.

3. Barillon to Louis XIV, 7 February 1686. P.R.O. 31/3/164, f. 260.

4. A. Heinsius to G. Fagel, Westminster, 15/25 January 1686. A. R. A. Holland 2910. Heinsius was in England to try to find a solution to the thorny problem of Bantam.

5. G. Fagel to A. Heinsius, 28 December 1685. Van der Heim, *Het Archief van Antonie Heinsius*, i, xciv-xcv.

6. Same to same, 1 February 1686, *ibid.*, xcvii–xcviii.

7. Same to same, 4 February 1686, *ibid.*, xcviii.

8. Same to same, 29 February 1686, *ibid.*, ciii.

9. Barillon to Louis XIV, 13 June and 1 July 1686. P.R.O. 31/3/166, f. 325, f. 1 (*sic*).

10. A. van Citters to William III, 23 July/2 August 1686. *Correspondentie* II, ii, 737.

11. Barillon to Louis XIV, 23 September 1686. P.R.O. 31/3/167, f. 53.

12. D'Avaux, *Négociations*, v, 309–10.
13. G. Burnet, *History of His Own Times*, iii, 274–5.
14. Barillon to Louis XIV, 29 July 1686. P.R.O. 31/3/166, f. 17.
15. Son of James II by Arabella Churchill. A. van Citters to William III, 8/18 October 1686. *Correspondentie* II, ii, 742.
16. For French fears of his possible success, see Barillon to Louis XIV, 20 February 1687. P.R.O. 31/3/168, f. 135.
17. Same to same, 30 January 1687. P.R.O. 31/3/168, f. 123.
18. William III to Gaspar Fagel, 30 March 1687. *Correspondentie* II, ii, 747–8. Although Dijkvelt's instructions have apparently been lost, the five letters from the Prince to Fagel on this subject give a satisfactory description of what occurred. *Ibid.*, 746–51.
19. Dated 7 March O.S. Printed in Dalrymple, *op. cit.*, Appendix Part 1, 187–9.
20. Barillon to Louis XIV, 14 August 1687. P.R.O. 31/3/172, f. 266 b. See J. P. Kenyon, 'The Earl of Sunderland and the Revolution of 1688', *Cambridge Historical Journal*, xi, 1955, 272–96.
21. William III to G. Fagel, 27 April 1687. *Correspondentie* II, ii, 751.
22. Barillon to Louis XIV, 24 March 1687. P.R.O. 31/3/168, f. 157 b.
23. Same to same, 3 April 1687. *Ibid.*, f. 165; same to same, 15 May. P.R.O. 31/3/169, f. 208; and same to same, 23 September. P.R.O. 31/3/172, f. 290.
24. Printed in Dalrymple, *op. cit.* Appendix Part 1, 190.
25. Klopp, *op. cit.*, iii, 329, 382.
26. 'Memorial Upon the Edict in Scotland of 12 February 1687', printed in *Correspondentie* I, ii, 20–1 and probably written by Patrick Hume.
27. Barillon to Louis XIV, 13 October 1687. P.R.O. 31/3/173, f. 298.

Chapter 17

1. Lucile Pinkham, *William III and the Respectable Revolution*, 19–20 and *passim*.
2. G. Burnet, *History of His Own Times*, iii, 276.
3. William III to Bentinck, 29 April 1688, *Correspondentie* I, i, 36: 'Mr Herbert et les deus Russels ont este icy; je ne vous dires pas ce qu'ils m'ont dit, puis que cela se peut mieus faire de bouche, espérant de vous voir bientost icy ou à La Haye; . . .'
4. William III to Danby 'A Loo ce 30 d'Avril 1688. . . . Je receu hier les deus lettres qu'il vous a pleu m'escrire du 27 et 29 de Mars, . . .' K.H.A. Prins Willem III, xi D, 10 n.
5. G. Burnet, *op. cit.*, iii, 241.
6. See his reports to the Prince, *Correspondentie* II, iii, 14–31.
7. Both printed at *Correspondentie* II, iii, 14, and one of them dated from The Hague.
8. Cramprich's dispatch of 20 May, quoted by Klopp, *op. cit.*, iv, 28–9.
9. Albeville to James II, Hague, 2 April 1688. B. M. Add. Ms. 32095, ff. 261–2.
10. Anne to Mary 14 March (1688), printed in *Lettres et Mémoires de Marie Reine d'Angleterre*, ed. Mechtild, comtesse Bentinck, Hague 1880, 31.
11. *Ibid.*, 62.
12. *Ibid.*, 71. Mary's dates in her *Mémoir* covering the year 1688 are in O.S.

13. *Ibid.*, 76. Of course the Princess wrote up her *Mémoir* at the end of the year, and it may therefore be argued that her descriptions are anachronistic. She did, however, have notes; the time involved was small; and the text certainly does not appear to be anachronistic. Since it is corroborated by so much other evidence, the *Mémoir* deserves perhaps more attention than it has been given.

14. Barillon dispatch of 17 May 1688. P.R.O. 31/3/177, f. 454.

15. Burnet, *op. cit.*, iii, 181.

16. H. C. Foxcroft, ed., *A Supplement to Burnet's History of My Own Time*, Oxford, 1902, 261–3.

17. Klopp, *op. cit.*, iii, 429; Gebhard, *Witsen*, i, 317–18.

18. P. von Fuchs to Frederick III of Brandenburg, 27 July 1688. Printed in Ranke, *History of England*, vi, 94.

19. Louvois to the Maréchal d'Humières, 25 August 1688. Dépôt général de la guerre, A¹ 822. Same to M. Dumetz, *eo. die, loc. cit.*, concerning Gravelines.

20. Seignelay to Bonrepos, 8 September 1688. Campana da Cavelli, *op. cit.*, ii, 255.

21. Louvois to the Maréchal d'Humières, 27 September 1688. Dépôt général de la guerre, A¹ 822.

22. Same to same, 4 October 1688. *Loc. cit.*

23. D'Avaux, *Négociations*, vi, 134, 137.

24. The account in the Register of the Resolutions of the States General is conveniently found in *Kronijk van het Historisch Genootschap*, Veertiende Jaargang (1858), 135–42.

25. John Evelyn, *Diary*, ed. E. S. de Beer, iv, 600.

26. Norfolk to Middleton, Norwich, 2 November 1688. B. M. Add. Ms. 41805, ff. 109–10.

27. Beaufort to Middleton, Bristol, 7 November. *Ibid.*, ff. 156–7.

28. Diary of Lord Clarendon *sub* 16 October. *Clarendon Correspondence*, ed. Singer, ii, 194.

29. B. M. Add. Ms. 41805, f. 281.

30. James II to Dartmouth, Whitehall, 10 December 1688. Hist. Mss. Comm. 11th Report, Appendix, Part 5, p. 226.

31. 'An Account of wt happen'd to King James upon his being taken at Feversham, Dec. 12 1688,' B. M. Add. Ms. 32095 ff. 302 ss.

32. I Maccabees, 11:10.

33. B. M. Add. Ms. 32095, f. 306.

34. Matt. 12:13.

Chapter 18

1. Lord Bath to Middleton, Plymouth, 6/16 November 1688: 'Yet the Common people are so prejudiced with the late Regulations, and so much Corrupted that there can be no dependence at present on the Militia, but only upon his Majesties standing Forces.' B. M. Add. Ms. 41805, f. 129.

2. Whitehall, 17 December 1688. Hist. Mss. Comm. 11th Report, Appendix Part 5, 236.

3. The famous Spencer House Journals. H. C. Foxcroft, *Halifax*, ii, 201–52.

4. Hearth Money or Chimney Money was a tax of 2s. annually on every fireplace imposed from 1663 to 1689.

5. J. Hop to William III, Vienna, 6 January 1689. Rijks Geschiedkundige Publicatien lxvii, 403.

6. N. Witsen to the States of Holland, 15/25 January 1689. *Secreet*. A. R. A. Heinsius 146.

7. J. Hop to William III, 20 and 21 February. R. G. P. 67, 408–12.

8. Legrelle, *op. cit.*, i, 357–60.

9. *Ibid.*, i, 349–54.

10. They accepted it at the Banqueting House exactly one month later.

11. Huygens, *Journaal*, i, 193.

12. E.g. Sir John Banks, father-in-law of Nottingham's brother Heneage Finch. Banks voted against the Prince and Princess on 5 February, but in the course of the year he is said to have lent them more than £5,000. D. C. Coleman, *Sir John Banks*, Oxford, 1963, 153.

Chapter 19

1. William III had hoped that Heinsius would succeed Fagel and was delighted when he was finally selected three months later. He persuaded the reluctant man to accept the office which he was to hold with distinction for thirty-one years.

2. On the day of the King's death, Heinsius made precisely one change in his appointments. Van Wassenaar Obdam, a restless and ambitious member of the Holland nobility, was promoted in the Dutch army.

3. Waldeck to William III, 14/24 December 1688. P. L. Müller, *op. cit.*, ii, 121.

4. Waldeck to William III, 16/26 June 1689, *ibid.*, 162; and *passim*.

5. William III to Waldeck, 25 February 1689, *ibid.*, 138.

6. Waldeck to William III, dated only 1689, *ibid.*, 197.

7. According to the testimony of Jan Hol, arrested in February 1689, which he later retracted.

8. William III to Portland, 16–17 January 1690. *Correspondentie*, I, i, 67.

9. Portland to William III, 25 January 1690, *Correspondentie*, I, i, 79.

10. Same to same, 28 January 1690, *ibid.*, 84.

11. Portland to William III, 2 March 1690, *ibid.*, 127–9.

12. In addition to the William–Portland correspondence on this affair, *Correspondentie*, I, i, 64–158, which is the best source, see *Archives*, III, i, 50, 52, 57, and the comprehensive account (not quite accurate) in Wagenaar, *op. cit.*, xvi, 51–96. (There is also supporting material in *Correspondentie*, II, iii, 141–60.)

13. William III to Portland, 7 February 1690, *Correspondentie*, I, i, 95; *Lettres et Mémoires de Marie Reine d'Angleterre*, 95–6.

14. William III to Portland, 24 January 1690. *Correspondentie*, I, i, 74.

15. Same to same, 14 February 1690, *ibid.*, 105.

16. 'I desire you will forthwith make a settlement of the Revenue; and I cannot doubt but you will therein have as much regard for the honour and dignity of the Monarchy in my hands, as hath been lately showed to others. . . .' A. Grey, *Debates of the House of Commons*, x, 2.

17. *Lettres et Mémoires, loc. cit.*

18. J. Hop to Antonie Heinsius, 30 May 1690, van der Heim, *op. cit.*, i, 33.

19. Klopp, O., *op. cit.*, v, 339. Hist. Mss. Comm. *Allen George Finch*, ii, 290–91. Huygens, *Journaal*, i, 282–3.

20. Lt-Gen. James Douglas to Sir Robert Southwell, 16 June. B. M. Add. Ms. 9708, ff. 1–2.

21. William III to A. Heinsius, 16/26 June. *Archives*, III, i, 68–9.

22. Comte de Lauzun to the Marquis de Louvois, 26 June 1690. Printed in L. von Ranke, *Englische Geschichte*, ix, 7. *Sämmtliche Werke*, xxii.

23. Huygens, *Journaal*, i, 292.

24. *Ibid.*

25. The battleground is well preserved. It is an easy drive from Dublin.

26. Sir R. Southwell to Nottingham, 1 July 1690, Hist. Mss. Comm. *Allen George Finch*, ii, 326–7; 'Autobiography of Dr George Clarke', in Hist. Mss. Comm. *Leybourne-Popham Mss.*, 272; *A Journal of The Three Months Royal Campaign of His Majesty in Ireland* by Samuel Mullenaux, M.D., 1690, 9. The latter account is so close to Southwell's letters as to indicate a common source. Cf. Huygens, *Journaal*, i, 295.

27. There are many and varying accounts of Boyne Fight. In addition to the works cited in the previous note, see the diary of the Jacobite Sir Thomas Phillipps quoted in Ranke, *op. cit.*, ix, 37; and the *Verhael* written by J. Hop and sent by William III to the States General the next day. It was published as a pamphlet, Knuttel No. 13387. C. Walton, *History of the British Standing Army*, London, 1894, is to be used with caution. His account of the Irish campaigns is vivid and fuller than some of the rest of the book.

28. Huisarchief Amerongen, Portefeuille X, 219.

Chapter 20

1. Spencer House Journals, 17 June 1689. H. C. Foxcroft, *Halifax*, ii, 221. The Marquis commented on this outburst, 'No untrue thing said'.

2. Nottingham to William III, 5 May 1691. Hist. Mss. Comm. *Finch Mss.*, iii, 48.

3. Mary to William III, 24 July/3 August 1690. Dalrymple, *Memoirs*, Appendix Part 2, 147.

4. Spencer House Journals, 27 May 1689. H. C. Foxcroft, *Halifax*, ii, 218.

5. See S. B. Baxter, *The Development of the Treasury 1660–1702*, 31–2.

6. William III to Heinsius, 12/22 July 1689. *Archives*, III, i, 30.

7. Huygens, *Journaal*, i, 225. Since Huygens was present and the Jacobite spy was not, I take Huygens's version as the correct one. He was by no means squeamish as a reporter.

8. *Ibid.*, i, 336.

9. *Correspondentie*, II, iii, 207.

10. Sydney and T. Coningsby to Portland, Dublin, 27 September 1690. Portland Mss., University of Nottingham.

11. J. Hampden to (Sir Edw. Harley), November 1690. Hist. Mss. Comm. 14th Report, Appendix Part 2, 451. (*Portland Mss.*, iii.).

12. On all these military developments see F. J. G. ten Raa, *Het Staatsche Leger*, vii (Hague, 1950). The work of Sir Jonn Fortescue on the British Army is, at least for this period, almost wholly valueless. Clifford Walton's *History of the British Standing Army 1660–1700*, London, 1894, has some interesting material on the Irish campaign of 1690 but that is all. The French works on the subject are better than the English, and equal them in the highly partisan nature of their approach.

13. Churchill, Sir Winston Spencer, *Marlborough, His Life and Times*, i, 288.

14. Walton, *op. cit.*, 61.

15. Whose records are in the P.R.O.: P.C. 6/2.

16. Shales was suspected of being a Jacobite, Harbord of being a 'republican'. Both men had originally served in the Treasury system.

17. Huygens, *Journaal . . . van 21 October 1688 tot 2 September 1696*, ii, 264. *Werken uitgegeven door het Historisch Genootschap*, N.R., No. 25.

Chapter 21

1. William III to Heinsius, 20/30 August 1689. *Archives* III, i, 33.

2. Same to same, 30 July/9 August 1689. K. H. A. Prins Willem III, XI C, 636, suppressed portion of *Archives* III, i, No. 26, 31.

3. One does not lightly disagree with Sir George Clark, who reached an opposite conclusion in his admirable book *The Dutch Alliance and the War Against French Trade 1689–1697*, Manchester, 1923. Sir George argued, pp. 139–40, that the war on French trade must have been a failure because it was not repeated in 1702. But by 1702 two changes had taken place: William was dead and Spain had changed sides. The first deprived the alliance of its disciplinarian and the second involved fundamental changes in strategy, especially in the field of economic warfare. A monograph of similar quality on the economics of War of the Spanish Succession is badly needed.

4. *Le Veritable Portrait de Guillaume Henry de Nassau*, 1689, Knuttel No. 13253.

5. Heinsius to William III, 31 October 1690. *Archives*, III, i, 103–05.

6. *Ibid.*, 102,

7. William III to Heinsius, 28 October/7 November 1690. *Archives* III, i, 115–16.

8. *Waar-agtig Relaas, Van de Overkomst van zyn Majesteyt William de Derde . . .*, Knuttel No. 13610. The awkward title happens to be accurate. Whatever may appear in printed versions of his letters, William as king always signed his name with the English spelling 'William'.

9. Huygens, *Journaal*, i, 396. See also the handsome work of Romeyn de Hooge, *Komste van Zyne Majesteit Willem III, koning van Groot-Britanje, in Holland*. The Hague, 1691.

10. Gastañaga to William III, 15 March 1691, *Correspondentie* II, iii, 213.

11. William III to Heinsius, 18 March 1691. *Archives* III, i, 167.

12. Huygens, *Journaal*, i, 416. William III to Heinsius, 7 April 1691. *Archives* III, i, 169.

13. Van der Heim, *Het Archief van Antonie Heinsius*, ii, 34.

14. P. de Ségur, *Le Tapissier de Notre-Dame*, 225.

15. William III to Heinsius, 7 April 1691. *Archives* III, i, 169–70.

16. Max Emmanuel to William III, 29 March 1691. *Correspondentie* II, iii, 222–4.
17. *Correspondance de la Cour d'Espagne*, v, No. 1386; Legrelle, *op. cit.*, i, 361–9.
18. Huygens, *Journaal*, i, 401.
19. *Ibid.*, 428.
20. The so-called 'Readmission' was achieved in 1708.
21. A copy of the treaty of 30 June 1692 is to be found at B. M. Add. Ms. 40798, ff. 36–8. Under its provisions the Electoral Prince George Lewis, later George I, commanded the men and had the right to attend all Councils of War. By a secret article William III and the States promised to do their best to turn the bishopric of Osnabrück into a hereditary possession of the House of Brunswick. The financial terms of the arrangement were so favourable that they constituted a hidden subsidy to the Emperor as well as to the Hanoverians.
22. Robert Harley to Sir Edward Harley, 26 January 1691–92. Hist. Mss. Comm. 14th Report, Appendix Part 2, 488. (*Portland Mss.*, iii.) Cf. J. Hop to Heinsius, 22 January/1 February, A. R. A. Heinsius 239; the Bonnet dispatch of 26 January/5 February printed in Ranke, *Englische Geschichte*, ix, 71; and the account of the same day sent to Dijkvelt, calendared in Hist. Mss. Comm. 7th Report, Appendix, 220.
23. William III to Portland, 19 May 1692. *Correspondentie* I, i, 168–9.
24. Huygens, *Journaal*, ii, 72–5. *Het Staatsche Leger*, vii, 57; Dijkvelt to Heinsius, 9 June, printed in van der Heim, *op. cit.*, ii, 54–5; Blathwayt to Nottingham, 9 June, B. M. Add. Ms. 37991, f. 88. Cf. C., Walton, *History of the British Standing Army*, 210.
25. The official Dutch account of Steenkerk, written by Dijkvelt on 4 August, was published as a pamphlet: Knuttel No. 13770. Blathwayt's official English account is preserved in B. M. Add. Ms. 9724, f. 27; a copy, addressed from James Vernon to Sir William Dutton Colt, is in B. M. 34096, ff. 76–7. An informal letter from Blathwayt to Nottingham, B. M. Add. Ms. 37991, f. 128, has some fresh detail. See also the criticism of Macaulay's account of the battle by W. J. Knoop in his *Krijgs en Geschiedkundige Beschouwingen over Willem den Derde*, iii, esp. the defence of Solms, 191. Fortescue makes many errors and more than doubles the accepted casualty figures. J. W. Fortescue, *History of the British Army*, i, 367.
26. Blathwayt to Nottingham, 4 August 1692. B. M. Add. Ms. 37991, f. 128.

Chapter 22

1. A. Francke to Heinsius, 23 September/3 October 1692. A. R. A. Heinsius, 229.
2. A. Francke to Heinsius, 9/19 September 1692. A. R. A. Heinsius 229.
3. Nottingham to Blathwayt, 27 August 1692. B. M. Add. Ms. 37991, f. 152.
4. *Supra*, 132.
5. Nottingham to Blathwayt, 9 September 1692. B. M. Add. Ms. 37991, f. 169.
6. Cf. John Ehrman, *The Navy in the War of William III 1689–1697*, Cambridge 1953, 607–8. Mr Ehrman's picture of William III is unsympathetic, or at least ungenerous, in reference to the early years of the reign. His book would have been even better than it is had it made use of the King's letters or of J. C. de Jonge, *Geschiedenis van het Nederlandsche Zeewezen*, Haarlem 1858–62, the standard work.

7. Paul Foley to Robert Harley, 17 September 1692. B. M. Loan 29/135; L'Hermitage to Heinsius, 4/14 October 1692, A. R. A. Heinsius 247.
8. Sydney to Portland, 26 July 1692. Portland Mss., University of Nottingham; L'Hermitage to Heinsius, 4/14 October 1692, A. R. A. Heinsius 247.
9. *A Dialogue Betwixt Whig and Tory, Alias Williamite and Jacobite*, 1693. Knuttel No. 13909.
10. L'Hermitage to Heinsius, 21/31 October 1692, A. R. A. Heinsius 247; same to same, 1/11 November and 8/18 November, *ibid.*; Bonnet dispatch, 28 October/7 November, printed in Ranke, *Englische Geschichte*, ix, 75; same of 4/14 November, *ibid.* 75–6; Huygens, *Journaal*, ii, 144.
11. William to Heinsius, 18/28 November 1692. *Archives* III, i, 299–300.
12. Apparently his failure to give thanks caused much comment. A. Francke to Heinsius, 24 January 1693 O.S., A. R. A. Heinsius 280; for the King's attitude about the supplies, see William to Heinsius, 14/24 February 1693, *Archives* III, i, 313.
13. L'Hermitage to Heinsius, ?9 January 1693 N. S., A. R. A. Heinsius 297. An undated fragment which probably belongs to the letter of this date.
14. See the letters of Heinsius to Dijkvelt for February 1693 in A. R. A. Heinsius 103 B.
15. Huygens, *Journaal*, ii, 196. The attack on Solms can be followed in Grey's *Debates*, x, 254–9, or in Macaulay. It was a curious affair, since there is no evidence that Solms was even involved at Steenkerk except from the English officers, who were of course interested parties. Knoop, *op. cit.*, iii, 191. My own impression is that the charges were not complete fabrications but relate to an incident which took place during the siege of Maastricht in 1676, when three English regiments were not supported and suffered heavy casualties on 30 July. This incident was then warmed over for use in 1692. It is a curious coincidence that the English colonel of these regiments at Maastricht was Sir John Fenwick, the later Jacobite and conspirator. My impression cannot be documented, but it is certain that the charges against Solms were substantially false as regards Steenkerk. Half of the supposedly English casualties were in fact Danish, and it was Ouwerkerck rather than Solms who would seem to have been responsible. Although it is possible that the charges against Solms contain an element of current truth it is likely to be a small element.
16. R. Doebner, ed., *Memoirs of Mary, Queen of England*, 59.
17. L'Hermitage to Heinsius, 27 March/7 April 1693, A. R. A. Heinsius 297.
18. Same to same, 30 March/10 April 1693, *ibid.*
19. William III to Heinsius, 30 May 1693. *Archives* III, i, 321.
20. Simultaneous negotiations were conducted at Brussels and Stockholm, at Brussels by Dijkvelt and at Stockholm by W. van Heeckeren. They can most easily be followed in van der Heim, *Het Archief ven den Raadpensionaris Antonie Heinsius*, iii, 6–51, though the version of the letters of the King and Heinsius in *Archives* III, i, 307–41 is of course more complete. Van der Heim's selection of these letters is thin. The best secondary account is by Mark Thomson, 'Louis XIV and William III, 1689–1697', *English Historical Review* lxxvi (1961), 37–58.
21. Neither Blathwayt's letters in B. M. Add. Ms. 37992, Huygens's *Journaal*, ii, 214–18, nor the letters of William himself show any of the allied panic before 8 June so

glowingly described by P. de Ségur, *Le Tapissier de Notre-Dame*. The more moderate comments of C. Rousset, *Histoire de Louvois*, iv, 518–19, are much nearer the truth.

22. Godolphin to William III, 14 July 1693. K.H.A. Prins Willem III, XI G, 171.

23. William III to Godolphin, 27 August 1693. *Correspondentie* II, iii, 325.

24. Blathwayt to Heinsius, 20/30 July 1693, in van der Heim, *op. cit.*, ii, 74. On the battle, see the accounts in Knuttel Nos. 13927, 13928, 13929; an account by Michael Fleming calendared in Hist. Mss. Comm. 12th Report, Appendix Part 7, 333 (*Le Fleming Mss.*); and, among secondary accounts, that of P. de Ségur in *Le Tapissier de Notre-Dame*, 380 ff. That of J. W. Fortescue in *History of the British Army*, i, 375–6 is typically inaccurate and typically hostile to the King. Those who cannot use the pamphlets catalogued by Knuttel will find most of the battle accounts and other official documents in L. Sylvius, *Historien onses tijds* (1685–99), which is a continuation of L. van Aitzema, *Saken van Staat en Oorlog* (1669–72) for the years down to 1697. Wagenaar's *Vaderlandsche Historie* is not nearly so useful except for the inner history of the Revolution, where he had access to material then in Ms. It seems hopeless even to attempt an estimate of the casualties since the authorities put them as low as 5,000 and as high as 22,000 men on either side. Blathwayt's letters in B. M. Add. Ms. 37992, ff. 21, 22, and 40 put the French losses at between 16,000 and 20,000, 'Ours not much exceeding a Third'.

25. William III to Heinsius, 3/13 November 1693. *Archives* III, i, 332: 'I see well that I shall have to do things that I do not care for, without knowing whether they will be successful or not.' Cf. J. P. Kenyon, *Robert Spencer, Earl of Sunderland, 1641–1702*, London 1958, 261-2. Dr Kenyon argues that the King made up his mind and was known to have done so before the Althorp conference at the end of August, while William's letter of 3 November is still in the future tense. With the exception of this one small point Dr Kenyon's book is virtually faultless.

26. Extracts are printed in van der Heim, *op. cit.*, iii, 53–60.

27. L'Hermitage to Heinsius, undated but late April or early May 1694. A. R. A. Heinsius 348.

Chapter 23

1. L'Hermitage to Heinsius, 13/23 November 1694. A. R. A. Heinsius 348. Cf. the Bonnet dispatch of the same date in Ranke, *Englische Geschichte*, ix, 135. *Sämmtliche Werke*, xxii.

2. L'Hermitage to Heinsius, 20/30 November 1694. A. R. A. Heinsius 348; Blathwayt to same, 20 and 23 November O.S., A. R. A. Heinsius 320; William III to same, K.H.A. Prins Willem III, xi C, 899. (Suppressed portion of *Archives* III, i, Lettre 207, 368.)

3. Huygens, *Journaal*, 437, 440.

4. L'Hermitage to Heinsius, 7/17 December 1694. A. R. A. Heinsius 348.

5. The most circumstantial sources are the dispatches of L'Hermitage of 25 December/4 January and 28 December/7 January in A. R. A. Heinsius 402, together with an undated sheet in A. R. A. Heinsius 348 which belongs with the letter of 25 December. See also the Bonnet dispatches of the same dates in Ranke, *Englische Geschichte*,

ix, 148–9; the King's own letters to Heinsius are at *Archives*, III, i, 377–8. The account of Huygens, *Journaal*, 441–2, is not accurate; that of Burnet, *History of His Own Times*, iv, 249–50, is much better.

6. J. Vernon to Lexington, 1 January 1694/5. B. M. Add. Ms. 46527.
7. Same to same, 4 January. *Ibid.*
8. L'Hermitage to Heinsius, 1/11 January 1695. A. R. A. Heinsius 402.
9. L'Hermitage to Heinsius, 15/25 January 1695. A. R. A. Heinsius 402.
10. Sarah, Duchess of Marlborough, *Conduct of the Duchess*, 111–12.
11. L'Hermitage to Heinsius, 15/25 January 1695, *loc. cit.*
12. Same to same, undated second page, *loc. cit.*
13. In accordance with custom, Mary's entrails were interred in the Henry VII Chapel of Westminster Abbey almost immediately after her death, while the remainder of the cadaver was embalmed and preserved for the state funeral.
14. In addition to the undated L'Hermitage fragment cited above, see Huygens, *Journaal*, 447.
15. L'Hermitage to Heinsius, 29 January/8 February 1695. A. R. A. Heinsius 402.
16. Huygens, *Journaal*, 452.
17. And, indeed, this consoling thought was offered over the Dutch radio network to the survivors of the 1951 floods.
18. Huygens, *Journaal*, ii, 456.
19. William III to Heinsius 22 January/1 February 1695. *Archives* III, i, 378.
20. Even in June he said that this was his last campaign. Huygens, *Journaal*, *sub* 13 June 1695.
21. William III to Vaudemont, 15/25 February. *Correspondentie* II, iii, 348–9.
22. A secret agent to Heinsius, ? February 1695. *Archief*, ii, 96–7.
23. William III to Vaudemont, 15/25 February 1695. *Correspondentie* II, iii, 348.
24. Bonnet, 25 January/4 February 1695, printed in Ranke, *Englische Geschichte*, ix, 154. See also Huygens, *Journaal*, *sub* 5 February N.S.
25. L'Hermitage, ?1/11 February 1695. A. R. A. Heinsius 402. The second pages of these dispatches are in some disorder and it is not always possible to be sure where they belong; only the first pages are dated.
26. Although, apparently, the move from Berkeley House to St James's was not completed at this time.
27. L'Hermitage, 5/15 February 1695. A. R. A. Heinsius 402.
28. Ralph is thus in error in saying that Anne had no access to confidential information after 1694; the Trumbull Cabinet Memoranda now at Reading (Berkshire County Record Office) show that George attended cabinet council meetings on and after 1 December 1695.
29. Trumbull Cabinet Memoranda, 16 and 24 October 1695, Reading.
30. L'Hermitage, 14/24 March 1695. A. R. A. Heinsius 402.
31. Guy to Portland, 31 May 1695 O.S. Portland Mss., University of Nottingham. Underlined portions in cipher.
32. Charles Montagu to Portland, 17 May 1695. Portland Mss., University of Nottingham.

33. Guy to Portland, 25 June 1695. Portland Mss., University of Nottingham, suppressed portion of *Correspondentie* I, ii, 60.
34. L'Hermitage, 26 February/8 March. A. R. A. Heinsius 402.
35. Respectively Archbishop of Canterbury, Lord Keeper, Lord Privy Seal, Lord Steward, Secretary of State, Lord Chamberlain, and First Lord of the Treasury.
36. William III to Heinsius, 9 June 1695. K.H.A. Prins Willem III, XI C, 929. Huygens, *Journaal, eo die.*
37. William III to Shrewsbury 17/27 June. Coxe, *Private and Original Correspondence*, 90. *Archives* III, i, 296.
38. Huygens, *Journaal, sub* 10 July.
39. William III to Vaudemont, 3 August 1695. 'A midy'. *Correspondentie* II, iii, 359–60.
40. Same to same, *eo. die* 'A 9 eures du soir', *ibid.*, 360.
41. 'Campagne de Flandres, commandée par Mr le Maréchal de Villeroy en 1695', printed in *Archief*, ii, lvii.
42. J. van Vredenburch van Adrichem to Heinsius, 31 August 1695. *Archief*, ii, 103.
43. L'Hermitage, 6/16 September. A. R. A. Heinsius 402.
44. The chief sources for the campaign of 1695 are: *Correspondentie* II, iii, 348 and 353–65; *Archief* ii, lii–lvii and 97–107; *Archives* III, i, 395–98; Coxe, *Private and Original Correspondence*, 91 ff.; *Het Staatsche Leger*, vii, 94–111; Huygens, *Journaal 1688–1696*, ii, 488–531; and Knoop, iii.

Chapter 24

1. A curious choice: his sister, on her conversion to Rome, had for some time been a pensioner of France. This was supposed to have affected her brother's conduct as ambassador to Louis XIV in 1679.
2. 18 October 1695. K.H.A. Prins Willem III, IV, 3. The States General were to be the executors, and the King reserved both the right to name guardians for the Prince and that of making such particular legacies as he pleased. Under the latter stipulation, the Lordship of Bredevoort and fl. 200,000 in cash were bequeathed to Albemarle by a codicil of 28 December 1695/7 January 1696.
3. William III to Shrewsbury, 8 October 1695. Coxe, *Private and Original Correspondence*, 107.
4. Shrewsbury to Somers, 31 October/10 November 1695. Coxe, *op. cit.*, 399.
5. L'Hermitage, 12/22 November 1695. A. R. A. Heinsius 402.
6. William III to Heinsius, *eo. die. Archives* III, i, 412.
7. The allegation that the child presented as James II's son was a changeling conveyed to the bedroom in a warming-pan, the royal child having (it was said) been stillborn.
8. Always, be it remembered, in the sense that Poland was a republic; the idea that a republic could survive without a 'great person' was not accepted until after the American Revolution.
9. For the Dutch attitude on the English failure to use torture, see Keppel to Heinsius, 23 February/4 March 1696. A. R. A. Heinsius 452: '... des officiers des gardes du Roy et des petites patrouilles ... ont pris cette nuit, jusques au nombre de quatorze

lesquels ont tient à present en toute seureté, mais comme selon les loix du pais, on ne sauroit mettre ses gens a la torture, il est a croire quil sera tres difficile, pour leur faire advouer, au moins quon ne trouve des temoins contre eux.'

10. Huygens, *Journaal, sub* 21 January 1696.

11. L'Hermitage, 14/24 February 1696. A. R. A. Heinsius 465.

12. The shares were not fully paid up, only 60 per cent of the par value having actually been subscribed. L'Hermitage 14/24 January 1696. A. R. A. Heinsius 465.

13. Trumbull Cabinet Memoranda, Reading.

14. Trumbull Cabinet Memoranda, Reading. A committee, as Dr J. H. Plumb pointed out in his important article 'The Organization of the Cabinet in the Reign of Queen Anne,' *Trans. R. Hist. Soc.*, 5th Series, vii (1957), 137–57, was a meeting in the King's absence of the same people who formed a cabinet council when he was there. This particular meeting, a large one of eleven persons, included the junior Treasury Lords because of the subject matter.

15. *Parliamentary History*, v, 977–8.

16. William III to Heinsius, 31 January/10 February 1696. K.H.A. Prins Willem III, XI C, 965. Suppressed portion of *Archives* III, i, 422–4.

17. William III to Vaudemont, 11/21 February. *Correspondentie* II, iii, 376.

18. William III to Vaudemont, 3 March 1696. *Correspondentie* II, iii, 378; cf. same to Heinsius, 4 March, *Archives* III, i, 428.

19. Beyond the well-known materials in print on the Assassination Plot, I have used the unprinted portions of William's own letters in K.H.A. Prins Willem III, XI C, in which there is a bare mention of the fact that he is too busy to discuss the plot; the extremely circumstantial account of Keppel to Heinsius, 24 February/4 March, A. R. A. Heinsius 452; L'Hermitage, 25 February/6 March, A. R. A. Heinsius 465; and Bonnet, 13/23 March, B. M. Add. Ms. 30,000 A f. 39.

20. *Patriarcha, or the Natural Power of Kings asserted*, by Sir Robert Filmer (c 1590–1653), published posthumously, 1680.

21. A. R. A. Heinsius 431.

22. L'Hermitage, 24 March/3 April. A. R. A. Heinsius 465.

23. L'Hermitage, 21 April/1 May. A. R. A. Heinsius 465.

24. Blathwayt to Heinsius, 17/27 April: 'Les remises pour la Flandre nous deviennent quasy impossibles par la manque des emprunts en Hollande …' A. R. A. Heinsius 431. William III to Heinsius, 21 April/1 May: 'I must to my disappointment inform your Excellency that the business of the money is still so confused here, that it has been impossible for me to send over any bills of exchange up to now.' *Archives* III, i, 438.

25. Bonnet, 12/22 May. B. M. Add. Ms. 30,000 A f. 138. The King paid 25s rather than the legal 22s for gold equivalent to a guinea to get as many ingots as he did.

26. William III to Vaudemont, 18 May. *Correspondentie* II, iii, 389.

27. William III to Shrewsbury, 4 June 1696. Coxe, *Private and Original Correspondence*, 118.

28. Vaudemont to Heinsius, 13 June. A. R. A. Heinsius 472. Richard Hill to Shrewsbury, 4/14 June. Hist. Mss. Comm. *Buccleuch and Queensberry*, ii, 344.

29. Blathwayt to Godolphin, 9/19 July. B. M. Adff. 160–1. d. Ms. 37992,

30. Richard Hill to Blathwayt, 12/22 July. B. M. Add. Ms. 9730, f. 64.
31. Bonnet 28 July/7 August. B. M. Add. Ms. 30,000 A ff. 192 ss.
32. *Correspondentie* I, ii, 671.
33. *Archief*, ii, 132 n.
34. Coxe, *op. cit.*, 127.
35. Chiefly by Klopp, *Der Fall des Hauses Stuart*, viii and ix.
36. William III to Heinsius, 20/30 October 1696. K.H.A. Prins Willem III, xi C, 1009.
37. William III to Shrewsbury, 6 August 1696. Coxe, *op. cit.*, 132.
38. K.H.A. Prins Willem III, xi A, 213a.
39. M. Prior to James Vernon, sr., 31 August O.S. P.R.O. S.P. 84/223, f. 196.
40. E. Southwell to Halifax (the second Marquis), 9 September. Halifax Letters, Althorp.
41. L'Hermitage, 9/19 October. A. R. A. Heinsius 465.
42. Heinsius to William III, 17 July 1696. *Archives* III, i, 463–4. William III to Heinsius, 23 July, *ibid.*, 468–9.
43. Heinsius to William III, 10 August, *ibid.*, 475.
44. William III to Heinsius, 13/23 November 1696, *Archives* III, i, 488–90. The French had promised to declare to the Swedish mediator at the beginning of the official negotiations that they would recognize William on the conclusion of the treaty. What they were now doing was to refuse to make the declaration, on the stated grounds that it would drive the Jacobites to despair.
45. William III to Heinsius, 27 May 1697, *Archives* III, i, 558.
46. The term is used of the years 1702–46, in which William III had no successor.
47. *Archives* III, i, 499–503.

Chapter 25

1. Huygens, *Journaal*, part II, 4, 140, 565, 581.
2. *Correspondentie* I, i, 198–9.
3. As he continued to do until June 1699. See the letters of Johnstone and Teviot to the Earl of Annandale calendared in Hist. Mss. Comm. 15th Report, Appendix Part 9, 108–9.
4. Huygens, *Journaal*, part II, *passim*.
5. Methuen to the Irish Lords Justices, 23 April 1698. Blenheim Palace Archives, Sunderland Letter Book 3, no folio numbers. For some reason this arrangement did not immediately take effect.
6. Which survive in A. R. A. Heinsius 611.
7. Villiers made the proposal to Richard Hill for relay to Rochester. See the correspondence in the Middlesex County Record Office, Accession 510. Eventually Albemarle married a Dutchwoman.
8. There is almost no evidence concerning any portion of the King's sexual life. He had grown up with a passion for privacy. On the basis of what very little evidence there is, one may conjecture that he was probably sterile, though not impotent, and that what had always been a very slight sexual drive withered away early. An invalid at twenty-five, the King was physically an old man by the autumn of 1694.

15*

9. William III to Heinsius, 5/15 February 1697. K.H.A. Prins Willem III, XI C, 1038; suppressed portion of the letter printed in *Archives* III, i, 526–7.

10. Blathwayt's 'Journall 1697', B. M. Add. Ms. 22, 031, f. 1. The Journal corresponds closely but not literally to the many letters Blathwayt wrote to agents abroad and at home.

11. William III to Vaudemont, 17 May, *Correspondentie* II, iii, 440.

12. *Ibid*; and Wassenaer-Obdam to Heinsius 26 May, van der Heim, *op. cit.*, ii, 146–7.

13. Williamson to Shrewsbury, 2/12 July 1697. Coxe, *Private and Original Correspondence*, 342.

14. Vaudemont to Heinsius, 19 August 1697, A. R. A. Heinsius 534. See also *Correspondance de la Cour d'Espagne*, v, 1734, 1736, and 1748.

15. William III to Heinsius, 11 July 1697, K.H.A. Prins Willem III, XI C, 1064.

16. See the copies in the Mackintosh Collections VI, B. M. Add. Ms. 34492.

17. *Ibid.*, ff. 11, ss.

18. Portland to Shrewsbury, 2/12 August 1697. Coxe, *Private and Original Correspondence*, 359.

19. B. M. Add. Ms. 34492, f. 28.

20. Matthew Prior to Lord Pembroke, 20 October 1698. Hist. Mss. Comm. *Marquis of Bath*, iii, 278.

21. Same to Lord Dorset, 26 December 1698. *Ibid.*, 305.

22. L'Hermitage to Heinsius, 1/11 October and 16/26 November, A. R. A. Heinsius 528; Burnet, *op. cit.*, iv, 373–4; William III to Heinsius, 16/26 November, *Archives* III, ii, 3; Bonnet dispatch, 19/29 November, B. M. Add. Ms. 30,000 A f. 378.

23. 17 March 1697. Hist. Mss. Comm. 14th Report, Appendix Part 3, 132.

24. William III to Heinsius, 19/29 November. K.H.A. Prins Willem III, XI C, 1080.

25. Heinsius to William III, 6 December 1697. K.H.A. Prins Willem III, XI C, 329.

26. J. P. van den Brande van Cleverskercke to Heinsius, 14/24 December 1697. A. R. A. Heinsius 500; Bonnet dispatch of the same date, B. M. Add. Ms. 30,000 A f. 398.

27. Coxe, *Private and Original Correspondence*, 560.

28. Jo. Methuen to (Lord Galway), 14 April 1698. Blenheim Palace Archives, Sunderland Letter Book 3, unfoliated. When I visited Blenheim this work was to be found in the Long Library.

29. Same to same, 3 May 1698. *Ibid.*

30. Bonnet dispatch of 14/24 January. B. M. Add. Ms. 30,000 B, f. 14.

31. Bonnet dispatches of 18/28 January and 1/11 February. *Ibid.*, ff. 13, 29–30.

32. Vernon to Shrewsbury, 8 February 1697/8. G. P. R. James, *Letters Illustrative of the Reign of William III*, ii, 2.

33. Shrewsbury to Vernon, 8 March 1697/8. B. M. Add. Ms. 40771, f. 153.

34. William III to Heinsius, 22 February/4 March 1698. K.H.A. Prins Willem III, XI C, 1102.

35. Tallard to Louis XIV, 3 April 1698. P.R.O. 31/3/180 f. 48 b.

36. Same to same, 9 May. *Ibid.*, f. 83.

Chapter 26

1. In addition to the first Partition Treaty, of 1668 with Leopold, Louis XIV had also negotiated this issue with the Austrains at Steckborn during the Nine Years War and with the Bavarians at Versailles in the autumn of 1697. One must view his attempt to negotiate with the maritime powers not only as a clever move to divide the alliance but also as an attempt to keep the peace.

2. The formal signature for England took place at het Loo on 24 September and for the Dutch at The Hague on 13 October, but the Treaty bears the date 11 October. A. Legrelle, *La Diplomatie Française et la Succession d'Espagne*, 4 vols. Gand 1888–92, ii, 493–6.

3. For the documents, one should begin with Legrelle, *op. cit.*, vols. ii and iii and the William–Heinsius letters in *Archives* iii, ii and iii. Legrelle, who seems to have approved of the Revocation of the Edict of Nantes, is consistently unfair to the English and Dutch positions. As a scholar he was markedly inferior to Klopp, his fellow Catholic. M. A. Thomson provided a useful bibliographical essay in *Trans. R. Hist. Soc.* 5th Series, iv, 1954, which indicates the lesser sources but does not come to much of a conclusion.

4. *Archives* iii, ii, 53, 57.

5. *Ibid.*, 88, 96.

6. Legrelle, *op. cit.*, ii, 299–300.

7. *Ibid.*, 320, 325.

8. *Ibid.*, 459–64.

9. Naples, Sicily, the coast towns of Tuscany, Final, and in Spain itself Guipuscoa.

10. *Archives*, iii, ii, 71.

11. William III to Heinsius, 28 April/8 May 1699. *Archives* iii, ii, 410.

12. Robert Jennens to Thomas Coke, 6/16 and 11/21 July 1699. Hist. Mss. Comm. 12th Report, Appendix Part 2, 389–90.

13. Henry Ireton to Viscount Irwin, 30 August 1699. Hist. Mss. Comm. *Various Collections*, viii, 83–4.

14. Both dates N.S. Legrelle, *op. cit.*, iii, 250.

15. B. M. Loan 29/335, ff. 26–7, *sub* November 1700.

16. Bonnet Dispatch, 16/27 July 1700. B. M. Add. Ms. 30,000 D, ff. 230–1; see also the Tallard dispatches in P.R.O. 31/3/186.

17. Bonnet dispatch of 25 July/4 August 1699. B. M. Add. Ms. 30,000 C, ff. 146–7.

18. Albemarle to Heinsius, 3 November 1699, A. R. A. Heinsius 611. The King's comments were in the same vein but more cautious. William III to Heinsius, 20/30 October 1699, *Archives* iii, ii, 487–8.

19. L'Hermitage to Heinsius, 4, 8 and 11 December 1699 N. S., A. R. A. Heinsius 623.

20. William III to Heinsius, 28 November/8 December 1699. *Archives* iii, ii, 543–4.

21. James Vernon to Shrewsbury, 22 June 1700. *Letters Illustrative of the Reign of William III*, ed. G. P. R. James, iii, 90–1.

22. James Vernon to Shrewsbury, 16 December 1699. *Ibid.*, ii, 394.

23. See the remark attributed to the King by Lord Dartmouth in Burnet, *History of His Own Time*, i, 512.

24. Charles Hatton to Lord Hatton, 20 January 1699/1700. *Hatton Correspondence*, ii, 246.
25. James Vernon to Shrewsbury, 18 January 1700. G. P. R. James, *op. cit.*, ii, 411–13.
26. James Vernon to Shrewsbury, 25 May 1700. G. P. R. James, *op. cit.*, iii, 63.

Chapter 27

 1. William III to Heinsius, 12 November 1700, *Archives* III, iii, 226.
 2. A. van Borssele van Geldermalsen to Heinsius, 12/23 November 1700 (misdated 1699). A. R. A. Heinsius 595.
 3. William III to Heinsius, 5/16 November 1700. *Archives* III, iii, 235–8.
 4. William III to Heinsius, 18/29 November 1700. *Archives* III, iii, 263.
 5. *Ibid.*, 264.
 6. Same to same, 20/31 December 1700. *Ibid.*, 337.
 7. Heinsius to William III, 4 January 1701, *Archives* III, iii, 344–5; Robéthon to Heinsius, 12 January, A. R. A. Heinsius 730, both N. S. Robéthon was simply forwarding an advice from the Swedish ambassador Palmquist at Paris; unlike Lilienroth, Palmquist was an agent of William III.
 8. Tallard to Louis XIV, 2 January 1701. P.R.O. 31/3/187, f. 281.
 9. Same to same, 13 January. *Ibid.*, f. 289.
10. Same to same, 17 January. *Ibid.*, f. 293 b.
11. L'Hermitage dispatch, 7 January 1701 N. S., A. R. A. Heinsius 733; A. van Borssele van Geldermalsen to Heinsius, *eo. die*, A. R. A. Heinsius 644.
12. Tallard to Louis XIV, 13 January. P.R.O. 31/3/187, f. 289. L'Hermitage dispatch, 21 January, A. R. A. Heinsius 733.
13. The most detailed accounts of the King's health are in the dispatches of L'Hermitage, A. R. A. Heinsius 733; but Tallard (P.R.O. 31/3/187), Bonnet (B. M. Add. Ms. 30,000 E), and van Borssele van Geldermalsen (A. R. A. Heinsius 700) also make comments from time to time.
14. L'Hermitage dispatch, 5 February 1701. A. R. A. Heinsius 733. Robéthon and Tallard also reported that the 'war party' seemed to have won the election, though Tallard prudently refused to commit himself until the 'West Saxons' arrived and Parliament actually sat. Tallard to Louis XIV, 31 January. P.R.O. 31/3/187, f. 300. Robéthon to Heinsius, 1 February. A. R. A. Heinsius 730.
15. See R. Walcot, 'The East India Interest in the general election of 1700–1701', *English Historical Review* lxxi, 1956, 223–39.
16. Later George II.
17. William III to Heinsius, 11/22 February 1701. *Archives* III, iii, 425.
18. William III to Heinsius, 9/20 February 1701. *Archives* III, iii, 423.
19. Heinsius to William III, 22 February, *Archives* III, iii, 426.
20. William III to Heinsius, 1 March 1701, *ibid.*, 436.
21. Tallard to Louis XIV, 3 March 1701. P.R.O. 31/3/187, f. 333.
22. Tallard to Louis XIV, 7 March. P.R.O. 31/3/187, f. 336. Bonnet dispatch, B. M. Add. Ms. 30,000 E, f. 55.
23. Katherine, Countess of Rutland to the Earl of Rutland, April 1701. Hist. Mss. Comm. 12th Report, Appendix Part 5, 166–7.

24. L'Hermitage dispatch, 8 March 1701. A. R. A. Heinsius 733.
25. Cf. L'Hermitage dispatch, 30 November 1700, A. R. A. Heinsius 676.
26. C. van Heemskerck to the Griffier Fagel, 25 March 1701. A. R. A. St. Gen. 7315.
27. L'Hermitage dispatch, 22 March 1701. A. R. A. Heinsius 733.
28. L'Hermitage dispatches of 8 March and 19 April, *loc. cit.*
29. Bonnet dispatch, 7/18 March. B. M. Add. Ms. 30,000 E, f. 67.
30. L'Hermitage dispatch, 18/29 March. A. R. A. Heinsius 733.
31. Le dechainement que le Comte de Rochester et le Lord Godolfin on paru contre le traité de partage . . . est pris par bien des gens comme un dessein formé d'oter au Roi le credit que Sa Majesté pourroit avoir dans les pays estrangers apres luy avoir osté celuy du pays; afin que Sa Majesté ne pust pas se servir utilement du pouvoir qui luy a esté donné de faire des Alliances, et tout ce qui sest dit, contre les Ministres qui ont eu part au traité; rejaillit si fort contre la personne du Roi que bien des gens ouvront les yeux sur la conduite quon tenu le Comte de Rochester et le Lord Godolfin; lesquels se sont distingues sur les iniures qu'ils ont dites. *Ibid.*
32. *Ibid.*, dispatch of 19 April.
33. L'Hermitage, 8 April, A. R. A. Heinsius 733; A. van Borssele van Geldermalsen to Heinsius, 26 and 29 April, A. R. A. Heinsius 700.
34. L'Hermitage, 13 May, A. R. A. Heinsius 733; and A. van Borssele van Geldermalsen, *eo. die*, A. R. A. Heinsius 700.
35. Albemarle to Heinsius, 18 May 1701, A. R. A. Heinsius 716. William III to Heinsius, 20 May, *Archives* III, iii, 524: 'Things could not have worked out better, and the people of the Lower House now begin to be so hearty, that today most of them have spoken of the necessity of a war.'
36. L'Hermitage, 10 June. A. R. A. Heinsius 733.
37. L'Hermitage, 6/17 June. A. R. A. Heinsius 733.
38. L'Hermitage, 24 June. A. R. A. Heinsius 733.
39. Bonnet dispatch, 17/28 June. B. M. 30,000 E, f. 269.
40. William III to Heinsius, 8 February 1701. *Archives* III, iii, 407.
41. Same to same, 18 February 1701, *ibid.*, 416.
42. Heinsius to William III, 18 March 1701. K.H.A. Prins Willem III, XI C, 561. Unprinted portion of *Archives* III, iii, 458–9.
43. William III to Heinsius, 22 March 1701, *Archives* III, iii, 465–6.
44. Heinsius to William III, 22 March 1701, *Archives* III, iii, 465.
45. Albemarle to Heinsius, 22 July 1701. A. R. A. Heinsius 716.
46. Klopp, *op. cit.*, ix, 296–7.
47. Many of the letters have disappeared, but the dates of those which survive indicate that William kept up his habit of writing to Heinsius twice a week by the ordinary post, as well as sending expresses when necessary. He also corresponded regularly with Marlborough. *Archives* III, iii, 546–61.
48. Marlborough to Godolphin, 3 October 1701. Quoted in W. S. Churchill, *Marlborough, His Life and Times*, ii, 245.
49. Bonnet dispatch, 28 January/8 February 1701, B. M. Add. Ms. 30,000 E, f. 22.
50. Followed by seven pages of bile against the Whigs. Godolphin to Marlborough, 9 September 1701 O. S. Blenheim Palace Archives F 31.

51. Sunderland memorial of 11 September 1701, printed in Hardwicke State Papers, ii, 445–7.

52. Robéthon to Heinsius, 23 September, from Dieren. A. R. A. Heinsius 730: 'La recognition du Prince de Galles pour Roy d'Angleterre est à mon sens la chose la plus heureuse qui nous pust arriver par rapport à l'angleterre ...'

53. Blathwayt to J. Vernon, 16/27 September, from het Loo. B. M. Add. Ms. 40775, ff. 171–2.

54. B. M. Add. Ms. 40775, ff. 109–10.

55. *Clarendon Correspondence*, ii, 410–13.

56. *Ibid.*, 419.

57. Robéthon to Heinsius, 11/22 November. A. R. A. Heinsius 730. de Vaudoncourt (to Torcy), 27 December. P.R.O. 31/3/189, f. 545 b.

58. Bonnet dispatch, 14/25 November. B. M. 30,000 E, f. 398.

59. Robéthon to Heinsius, 11/22 November. A. R. A. Heinsius 730.

60. Albemarle to Heinsius, 22 November 1701. A. R. A. Heinsius 716.

61. *Ibid.*

62. Albemarle to Heinsius, 29 November, *loc. cit.*

63. Robéthon to Heinsius, 2 December 1701. A. R. A. Heinsius 730.

64. Same to same, 13 December, *loc. cit.*

65. Same to same, 27 December, *loc. cit.*

66. Roos to Rutland, 13 November 1701. Hist. Mss. Comm. 12th Report, Appendix Part 5, 167.

67. Marinus Dibbout van Vrijbergen to Heinsius, 3 January 1702. A. R. A. Heinsius 800.

68. Robéthon to Heinsius, 24 January 1702. A. R. A. Heinsius 790.

69. The attempt, under Admiral Benbow, was not successful.

70. William III to Heinsius, 14 December 1701. *Archives* III, iii, 584.

71. Heinsius to William III, 30 December 1701. *Archives* III, iii, 602.

72. Same to same, 4 February 1702, *ibid.*, 651.

73. William III to Heinsius, 16 February 1702, *ibid.*, 661–2.

74. M. D. van Vrijbergen to Heinsius, 2/13 January 1702. A. R. A. Heinsius 800; A. T. d'Alonne to same, *eo. die*, A. R. A. Heinsius 806.

75. Dispatches of C. van Heemskerk, the Dutch ambassador in Paris, to Heinsius of 23 and 27 January, 3 and 10 February 1702. A. R. A. Heinsius 766.

76. Robéthon dispatches, 7 and 10 March. A. R. A. Heinsius 790.

77. Robert Molesworth to the Hon. Mrs Molesworth, 5 March 1701/2. Hist. Mss. Comm. Various, viii, 226.

78. Dr Bidloo published a book on the final illness of the King which includes a copy of the findings at the body's dissection, which took place on 10 March. The cause of death was apparently an inflammation of the lungs, which were found filled with 'frothy serum'. There are circumstantial accounts of the King's fall, convalescence, and final illness in the reports of the Dutch ambassador van Vrijbergen, both in A. R. A. Heinsius 800 and A. R. A. St. Gen. 7344, as well as those of L'Hermitage and Robéthon.

79. 'The Mock Mourners A Satyr, By Way of Elegy on King William,' 1702.
80. King William's Affection to the Church of England Examin'd, 1703, 8.
81. G. Burnet, History of His Own Times, iv, 567.
82. Charles Hatton to Lord Hatton, 9 March 1703/4. Hatton Correspondence, ii, 251.

INDEX

Cavendish, William, fourth Earl and first Duke of Devonshire, 230, 253, 306, 323, 327, 333, 335, 386

Chamilly, Marquis de, 121, 122

Chapuiseau, Samuel, 23–4

Charleroi, attack on, 1672, 96–7; siege of 1677, 145–7, 154; capture, 1693, 315

Charles I, King of England, 4, 5, 402, and see Henrietta Maria

Charles II, King of England, 22, 51, 69, 80, 128–9, 144, 186, 402; in Scotland, 1, 2; and the guardianship of W, 17, 49; at The Hague, 1660, 25–6; and W's visit to England in 1670, 54–6; and the War of 1672–1674, 86–7, 90, 101, 109, 110, 143; views of James, 139; and W's marriage, 144, 147–9; diplomacy of, 1677–1678, 151–3; and the Exclusion Crisis, 163–74; policy, 1681–1685, 183–4, 188, 197; death of, 200, and see Catherine

Charles II of Spain, see Carlos II

Charles XI, King of Sweden, 145, 162, 163, 169, 213, 292

Charles, Archduke of Austria, the Emperor Charles VI, 365–6, 372, 403

Chiny, county of, 173–4, 183

Chudleigh, Thomas, 197, 198, 202

Churchill, John, Lord Churchill, first Earl and Duke of Marlborough, 281, 284, 315, 359, 400; early dislike of, by W, 150; servant of James, 150, 172; servant of Anne, 219, 324, 385; joins W, 240, 243; takes Cork and Kinsale, 266, 376; drunk, 276; dismissal of, 298–300; suspicions against, 307; use of, 1701, 386–7, 390–2

Churchill, Sarah, see Jennings, S.

Citters, Arnout (or Aernout) van, 174–5, 197–8, 216–17

Clarendon, Lord, see Hyde, H.

Clarke, George, 285

Clarges, Sir Thomas, 277–8, 298, 301

Claude, Isaac, 209

Coehoorn, Menno Baron van, 136, 282–3, 303

Colbert, Charles, Marquis de Croissy, 45

Colchester, Lord, see Savage, R.

Cologne, truce negotiations at, 1673, 102–3, 127–8

Cologne, Elector of, see Bavaria, Joseph Clement of and Bavaria, Maximilian Henry of

Colyear, Alexander, 147

Colyear, Jacob, 297

Compton, Henry, Bishop of London, 224, 230, 243, 275

Condé, capture of, 1676, 134, 136

Condé, Louis II de Bourbon Prince de, 45, 52, 68, 70–1, 103, 108, 115–19, 209, 282

Coningsby, Thomas, Lord Coningsby and Earl of Coningsby, 277, 376

Conti, François-Louis de Bourbon Prince de, 358

Conway, Edward, third Viscount Conway and Earl of Conway, 171, 172, 174

Cooper, Anthony Ashley, Lord Ashley and Earl of Shaftesbury, 164, 165

Coote, Richard, Lord Coote of Coloony, first Earl of Bellomont, 309

Copenhagen, demonstration at, 378

Cornbury, Lord, see Hyde, E.

Courtin, Honoré, 139

Covell, Dr John, 205

Crew, Nathaniel, third Baron Crew, Bishop of Durham, 275

Cutts, John, Lord Cutts, 298, 310, 387

Dalrymple, John, second Viscount and first Earl of Stair, styled Master of Stair, 1690–1695, 273

Danby, Lord, see Osborne, T.

Dartmouth, Lord, see, Legge, G.

Davenant, Dr Charles, 132, 335, 393–4

Defoe, Daniel, 387, 395

Delamere, Lord, see Booth, H.

Devonshire, Lord, see Cavendish, W.

Digby, John, third Earl of Bristol, 241

Dijkvelt, see Weede, E. van

Dinant, capture of, 1675, 134

Dohna, Frederick Freiherr and Graf von, 8–9, 18, 33–6

Dordrecht, struggle with W, 1684, 195–6

Dorset, Lord, see Sackville, C.

Douglas, Charles, Earl of Selkirk, 276, 328

Douglas, James, fourth Duke of Hamilton, 216

Douglas, William, third Duke of Hamilton, 216

Date Due

Demco 293-5